THE BOOK OF KNOWLEDGE

THE BOOK OF KNOWLEDGE

I AM ALIEN

ROMAN HARAMBURA

PARTRIDGE
A Penguin Random House Company

To order additional copies of this book, contact
Toll Free 800 101 2657 (Singapore)
Toll Free 1 800 81 7340 (Malaysia)
orders.singapore@partridgepublishing.com

www.partridgepublishing.com/singapore

TABLE OF CONTENTS

QUESTIONS & ANSWERS BY KUNTARKIS THE BEING

CONCLUSION...1059

<u>Evolution through Consciousness:</u> **by Roman Harambura, Information on the type of Seminars Roman presents.**

ACKNOWLEDGMENTS

Kuntarkis (Expresser of Knowledge)

As the Author of this book, I wish to express to my dearest friend Kuntarkis who has been a shining light for me ever since he came into my life. I am deeply grateful for his endless guidance, his patience and most of all his friendship and his Unconditional Love for all of humanity. I personally thank him from the essence of my being, in sharing his knowledge and his wisdom.

Over an eight (8) year period he expressed with me and through me, so much knowledge that The Book of Knowledge-I am Alien came into existence, one of his favourite expressions was: All knowledge has but one purpose-it defines who you are as human individuals, for knowledge is the key to freedom.

Roman Harambura (Author/Mentor/Life Coach.)

Michelle Spear

I also wish to thank my precious friend Michelle for her love and support in helping me, by showing me how to do certain tasks on my computer, when I found it difficult to coupe, she was always there to help me when I ask her.

I am deeply grateful for all your help, you are indeed a beautiful human being in so many ways. There were times when I became overwhelmed and Michelle came to my rescue, Michelle graciously assisted in the reformatting of pages within this book, and she took it upon herself to type out all eighty (80) of the Affirmations which just made it so much more pleasurable in completing such a big project. The Book of Knowledge-I am Alien was indeed a huge challenge for me personally.

Without even asking her, she took it upon herself and when on the internet to look up the perfect Front Cover for my book, when I saw it, I said, that's the one, Michelle even arranged to take some photos for my biography and my blog for the back cover.

Michelle is a brilliant Face & Body Painting Artist and I urge you to look her up on her website: www.meisha.com.au

Michelle Spear (Meisha Face & Body Artistry, (Painting Products & Entertainment)

Ilona Schultz

I acknowledge the work Ilona put into my stories, for typing them out and running the website for all those years. It was called Simplicity of Spirituality and it was running for ten years, thank you so much Ilona for your dedication. Ilona has taken a new direction in her life, and I wish her great adventure in all that she undertakes.

Ilona Schultz (Lawyer)

Sydney Felicio

Once again, I am pleased that Sydney was my Publishing Service Associate throughout the whole process of my second book, her help in all ways was always professional to the highest standard. I say to you Sydney, thank you so much for all your help and your patience and trust you will be there for my third and fourth book?

Sydney Felicio (Publishing Service Associate with Partridge Publishing)

I also wish to thank Bon Carlo who was my Marketing Consultant and to all the other staff who have been of great help to me, all of you need a good pat on the shoulder for the work you do, it's absolutely fantastic, thank you to all.

PREFACE

Writing this book was fairly easy, but when it comes to the **Preface** and even the **Introduction**, I began to hesitate. **Why?** I would ask myself many times, the answer seems to allude me. This whole book is based on an entity who is called **Jecuss Kuntarkis** from a planet called **Nar'Kariss** and the beings are known as the **Nar'Karones.** Their planet is around 417 thousand Light years from our planet Earth. A few million years ago, an entity named **Yarkuss Kariss** from a distant Universe, he came to the planet **Nar'Kariss** first to observe, the people, to see if they wanted to advance in their Consciousness.

This entity stayed and lived with the **Nar'Karones,** slowly but surely he began to express knowledge amongst the people, over the next several hundred years his words spread over the entire planet. The **Nar'Karones** accepted him as one of their own, on **Nar'Kariss** there are no governments as on our Earth, what they do have are committees, these committees are selected by the people, and it is the people who make the final decision by a voting system.

The entity known as **Yarkuss Kariss** stayed among the **Nar'Karones** for many thousands of years, he help develop the people in advancing their Consciousness. Where he come from, his own civilisation had moved beyond the physical vibration of matter into a higher realm of the non-physical. These beings do and create everything from their own power of thought, we as humans on this Earth, which is called the 3rd Dimension, and we are living a physical existence, we create everything from physical matter.

This entity known as **Yarkuss Kariss** decided to expand his own Consciousness by creating four (4) new energies, from his own being of living Consciousness. One of these beings is called **Kuntarkis,** who has come to planet Earth to express knowledge, to share with Humanity that we as humans are so much more than just our physical self. I feel deeply honoured to have **Kuntarkis** express all the knowledge that have been written in this book.

As you the reader must understand, as you venture into this book, please open your mind and your heart without any form of judgement. Be unbiased in all that you read, realise in this moment, just because you cannot see something or touch or smell it does not mean it doesn't exist. There are hundreds of different universes, realms, vibrations, even parallel worlds existing right here in our Earthly vibration, the only reason we do not know of their existence is because they are vibrating at a different frequency, some below ours and some must higher than ours, but they do exist. As you the reader work your way through this book, what you will discover is something inside yourself is telling you that there is so much more to our human life than what we have been conditioned to believe. I trust as the writer, you will begin a journey of discovering who and what you truly are in the scheme of this vastness, this universe all of us call home.

Enjoy, life is simply a journey, and knowledge is the key to freedom. There is an expression that **Yarkuss Kariss** would express to the **Nar'Karones,** it is simple in itself, yet if one truly takes on the power of one's own inner being while expressing its words and truly believes, it will and must be manifested into one's reality. **That is true manifestation, that is, "The Law of Attraction"**

INTRODUCTION

I am going to make the introduction very simple, mainly I believe the contents speaks for itself. Over a period of around eight (8) to ten (10) years, an entity by the name of **Kuntarkis** from a planet called **Nar'Kariss** communicated with me in order so this book called, **"The Book of Knowledge-I am Alien"** could be written in order to share wisdom and knowledge for all of humanity. I have always believed that we as a species are so much more than just our 4 quadrillion cells that not only hold us together as a human being, but allows us to be individuals and to be a **"Thinking Being"**, that is capable of conscious thought. I have been one of the luckiest human beings that has been shown most of humanity's past, and humanity has been evolving on this most precious Earth for just over **928,000 years.**

As you the reader explore this book in your own space and time, you will begin to feel something deep inside of yourself, and that will be **"Your Knowing"**. When you begin to read the first story called, **"What does the New Millennium hold for Humanity"** you may find it of interest or not, it doesn't matter. What does matter it will plant a seed for you to open your mind to begin the process of your growth in Consciousness. This book is living energy, expressed in words on paper, yet as **Kuntarkis** expresses, **"Energy is Everything and Everything is Energy"**.

There are seventy four (74) different stories in the first half of this book, on a variety of subjects. What is more important, it doesn't matter where you start in this book, it is your choice. I personally would recommend to begin at the front and read it all the way through to the end, because there is a reason that **Kuntarkis** asked to have them in this particular order, but you as individuals must choose how you wish to proceed.

Some of the stories can be to some quite controversial, and confronting, especially if you have strong beliefs, yet if one is will to have an open mind and heart, it can and will be quite educational and informative. The whole purpose of, **The Book of Knowledge-I am Alien** is to share with humanity that there is indeed other forms of intelligent life, throughout all universes. As there are thousands of other universes, dimensions, realms, vibrations and parallel worlds existing right here, right now, just vibrating at a different frequency.

So as you read through the stories, you will than come across the next section called, **"Questions and Answers by Kuntarkis" there are 433 questions and answers.** They were also compiled over a period of eight (8) to ten (10) years by people all over the world, asking many different questions of **Kuntarkis** who would answer them in his own expressions. By looking through the table of contents you the reader can decide which ones you wish to view. The next section will lead you into, **"Personal Soul Food Affirmation's"** and there are eighty (80) of them, some short and some long, if you wish you can even shorten them to suite yourself.

You can read through them all and then decide to choose one, or as many as you like. Choose the ones that vibrate from your heart, and say them first thing in the morning, and if you can sometime throughout your day and before going to bed. Say them with heart, truly believe in what you are saying. This is simply a suggestion, record one or two with your own voice that will make it more powerful and helps you remember them.

Affirmations can help you overcome any obstacle in your life, they can motivate you to make changes in your life, build up your self-worth, increase your self-esteem, help in all your relationships, and help you set goals in your life, even help you attract anything your heart desires. Affirmations are a power source, but it is you the individual who makes them work, it's how you express them, if they are expressed without real meaning, than you are only wasting your time, always express from the heart.

When we are each willing to make changes in our life, it means there is no resistants only accept ant's, that's why Affirmations really work. When you decide to practice Affirmations, do them at least three (3) times per day over a period of one (1) to two (2) months and see how you truly feel, than change to another one and repeat the same process. Always remember, what you put in to something, you will get back. **That is called, "The Law of Attraction".**

From this point, you will be able to read some of the Seminars, Workshops, Short Courses and Lecture's I have been presenting for over the last twenty eight (28) years.

I have also included a page on my first book with c/o author Ilona Schultz, called **Entrapment,** the title says it all. Then followed by **Acknowledgements, and then Personal Endorsements.** As the writer of this book, **The Book of Knowledge-I am Alien,** I am truly honoured by all the knowledge **Kuntarkis** has shared with me personally. This book of his expressions, truly comes from his inner essence, I still call it his heart, for his heart is living Consciousness. So as you the reader all I can say is, since you have purchased this book, enjoy your journey of infinite knowledge, and never stop believing in yourself.

WHAT DOES THE NEW MILLENNIUM HOLD FOR HUMANITY? (NO-1)

First I would like to say you have a very conditioned society, if you believe you are only entering the 3rd Millennium. If you as human beings look at it from a reality perspective, you're not really entering the 3rd Millennium. The whole concept about the Millennium comes from books and living to the Christian calendar. The 3rd Millennium is only an idea of truth. You are totality disregarding the reality aspect, the reality being that you are now entering the 928th Millennium of human existence on this Planet Earth. Because you as human beings have been here just over 928,000 years, the ones known to you as the Atlanteans were the first humanoid life forms to colonise this Planet you call Earth.

Many will ask "how can your truth be more accurate than the belief in the 3rd millennium?" Because it comes from within, from the Spiritual Aspect of your existence, where real truth is found. It doesn't matter what millennium it is, what matters is what each human being believes, and then they must ask themselves truthfully, "why do I believe what I believe?" Why do you as human beings believe it is the 3rd Millennium and not the 625th or the 928th? Because you are working to the Christian calendar and you have been conditioned into accepting that this is the year 2014 and not the year 928,000.

Question: 1

What changes do you foresee occurring for human consciousness advancement? Will they be as dramatic as some prophets are predicting?

Answer: 1

Humanity is entering a very delicate stage in the Evolution of their Consciousness. It is quite obvious that if you all stop to look at the Dramas, Emotions, Death, Dis'ease and Disasters that are plaguing humanity today, they have actually increased 63% since the beginning of the 19th Century, so yes, they will be dramatic. But because you'll be in the middle of it all, you won't consciously be aware of just how dramatic it all is. You'll accept

1

the upheaval as being part of human life, just like you now accept Violent Burglary as part of living in high density societies, because so much of it is going on.

Negativity on this Planet Earth is so powerful today that you are creating your own disasters. There are pockets of Consciousness levels. For example, one place may be safer and more peaceful to live in than another within the same city, likewise within your neighbourhood. Your level of thinking may be more advanced than your neighbour's, yet you live side by side in the same street. This is how misunderstandings occur, when conflict and friction result as two different levels of thinking collide, much like atoms. What's really odd is when two neighbours, who have never bothered to even say hello to each other, decide they don't like each other. This is again a Subconscious Awareness that you have two different levels of thinking.

While you live in the falseness of your Beliefs and conditioning, you will never step beyond those beliefs and Grow Consciously, therefore you will always be surrounded by conflict. The way you think today comes from your past experiences and conditioning. If you don't question how you think and why you believe what you believe, you will continue to shape your present, and ultimately your future from that past. Conflict and disharmony will continue to plague all of humanity.

Question: 2

The changing of the millennium, as an event, was built up considerably. Predictions of the world coming to a complete standstill as computers crashed was so hyped-up, that when midnight 31 December 1999 finally came, and nothing of any real consequence happened, many of you felt a little let down. Do you think you've now been lulled into a false sense of security, because nothing dramatic happened when you expected it to, and that the real disasters of the 3rd Millennium are in fact yet to come?

Answer: 2

What I'm about to say will no doubt offend those who had a vested interest in Y2K. The hype of Y2K was, in essence, all to do with your human money. The Y2K bug to a large extent was a scam, and software and IT companies are now laughing all the way to the bank. There may have been some minor glitches as a result of computers not having their clocks programmed to go beyond 1999, but not to the extent of the scare mongering that was being propagated.

From this point of view, yes, you have been lulled into a false sense of security. You believe the danger has now passed because you have entered the 3rd Millennium without too many technological hitches interfering with your daily lives, while the real disasters which are yet to come, and are not that far into your human future.

Question: 3

What are some of these events which lie ahead?

Answer: 3

Over the next 87 years you will see great evidence of these disasters occurring in countries where previously such disasters were unheard of. For example, a tidal wave will flatten the whole of the East Coast of Australia from Cairns to Gosford, and many land changes will occur. Currumbin Valley in Queensland will become a lake, Tasmania will get even colder, especially the southern end, and will even have snow storms, and its Volcanoes will become active again. Queensland's Mt Tamborine will split and become two mountains with a great gorge between where a river will flow. Queensland's Surfers Paradise will sink, like quick sand because human man has built his wealth on sinking foundations, not thinking of the future. **(Surfers is an engineering nightmare – they have big pumps under buildings pumping sea water out 24 hours a day).**

In the United States (as has already been predicted) New York City and San Francisco will be devastated by earthquakes. Mountains will rise where land is flat, coastlines will disappear and move miles inland. Most of Florida will be underwater and land will rise off its coast which had previously been submerged for thousands of years. Consequently, civil war will break out to fight over possession of the new lands because they'll belong to no-one.

Question: 4

How will technology advance in the 21ˢᵗ Century?

Answer: 4

Today's technology has advanced beyond your own understanding, meaning you all know how to use it but you don't really understand how it works. Even those who created the technology aren't 100% sure how it works. For example, when problems occur, they usually end up rebuilding the technology rather than fixing the problem because they don't know how to fix it as it is, without affecting everything else. At this time computer software is advancing faster than hardware, and hardware has a hard time keeping up.

Future technology will no longer be as you know it. Between the next 37 and 53 human years your science will advance software and hardware, and develop organic based software through genetic manipulation and engineering, but on a grander scale than you could presently imagine – Robocop will become a reality. Just as cloning was kept secret for decades, whether or not the general public will be told about organic based software initially, is another question. The whole debate about creating life by merging robotics and organic matter will create a major ethical dilemma when deciding what constitutes life for scientific purposes becomes a moral conflict of considerable proportions.

Question: 5

How will this technology affect humanity in the long term?

Answer: 5

Everything you consume will be synthetically created, which will result in genetic imbalances in the human body. Science may truly become a God but at the same time it will be your great downfall. Dis'ease will plague humanity for centuries to come and humans will become mutants as a result of tinkering with Mother Nature. To give you an idea, there are currently about 7 billion humans on your planet today. Within the next 50 years the population will reach 14 billion, but will drop suddenly to 8.9 billion because of the outbreak of dis'ease which the human body will be unable to fight due to human genetic break down. You are already seeing bacteria and viruses outsmarting science - the more you bombard them with chemicals the stronger they grow.

Also, just as you now have animals being implanted with electronic chips for identification, within the next 42 years or maybe sooner all citizens will have a chip inserted via cold laser (no surgery), so you can all be tracked by satellite at any time – there will literally be nowhere left to run or hide. Incidentally, this technology is Extra Terrestrial in origin. But you as humans are giving your power away, and there are those who want to control you in every way.

Question: 6

A 3ʳᵈ World War has been predicted. Can you tell us something about it and how it will change the world as we know it?

Answer: 6

There will be a 3ʳᵈ World War in less than human 80 years, and the weapons used will be more terrible than you have ever seen. Weapons such as Mind Control and Biological Warfare will be the main line of defence. Political alliances will be forged, creating larger nations. Borders between countries will change, and the greatest threat to World Peace will come from China. Russia will join with China, Britain will become one nation with France, and Australia will join with the US. The US will join forces with Europe and the Middle East will finally unite as one nation. The entire continent of Asia will come under Chinese rule - many Asian countries will rebel, but eventually the sheer size of China's forces will force them to submit. Having a quarter of the world's population, China can afford to wait it out and persist. The Middle East will attack the US, and while the US is distracted by the Middle East, China will take advantage and strike against the US. Consequently, the US will suffer great losses.

Question: 7

How are we collectively responsible for what lies ahead for humanity?

Answer: 7

Your level of thinking creates your reality, and because you have so much negativity on your planet today you are going to be plagued with a lot more disasters, especially with dis'ease which have been dormant for a long time. By a long time, I mean thousands of Earthly years. This may sound negative, but you must also understand you can't have Conscious Growth without the negativity aspect to learn from. How long humanity suffers depends on how long you each choose to continue living in your own negativity before learning those lessons and letting go of them in order to move forward in your consciousness.

For example, there are now cyclones and tornadoes devastating countries and creating massive floods and mud slides, that have previously not occurred in such great proportion or were even unheard of in those places. Your fragile planet is going through an enormous cleansing - many earthquakes, mass land changes, floods, and the birth of new continents will occur over the next 400 to 500 years of this millennium. Science will say that these are normal physical changes, but from a Metaphysical perspective these changes reflect what human beings are projecting on not only an energy level, but also what human beings are actually physically doing to the planet. You can't continually pollute, drastically physically alter and deplete such a living being as the Earth without causing equally dramatic consequences. Just like your human bodies, you can't physically abuse them continually and not expect them to break down and die a painful death.

Question: 8

So what can we do about it?

Answer: 8

Buddha said «The tree of life is tall with many branches». Many of us can go straight to the top of the tree. But it's okay to step out onto the branches and learn other lessons in life. How long you as human beings choose to keep learning the same lessons over and over is something only the individual decide. The power of how the millennium will affect humanity (individually and collectively) is literally in your hands alone. It is your choice alone to create a negative life or a positive life, and how you are affected by the challenges, being the changes this millennium brings depends on your attitude - it depends on how long you want to stay out on the branches of the tree of life.

Whether you want to admit it or not, you each are governed by the law of Cause and Effect - one of the most basic laws of the universe. The universe must balance itself, and as the Earth is part of the universe, it too must balance itself, which is why Your Earth is going through so many physical changes. If you don't change the way you each behave towards your planet, then it will die and you will die with it, just like all the other planets in your solar system. They've all had life - science is now admitting they're finding evidence of life having once existed on those barren, frozen or burning planets. Let's not find out too late what caused their demise and destruction before it's too late for humanity to do anything about it.

You must do something now by listening to environmentalists who want to protect and heal your Earth, and help them overcome the greedy, unscrupulous conglomerates that profit and gain from what will eventually be the entire human race's loss. The future and what it brings upon humanity is literally in your hands. The faster you advance Human Consciousness, the faster humanity will outgrow the negativity which creates your demise.

COMAS AND DEATH: WHERE DOES THE SPIRIT GO? (NO-2)

Question: 1

How would you define death?

Answer: 1

You can't learn about death from books, or even from what humans tell you death to be. Roman discovered the meaning of physical death by experiencing it twice himself, and from what he learnt was each physical being needs to discover the true meaning of life and its purpose in order to understand physical death. From his experience he learnt that nothing in any Universe ever dies- it only transforms into another purpose- it simply becomes another form of living energy.

Question: 2

What happens when death is near?

Answer: 2

At the point of death everything in the body slows down. The first Element to leave the body is Air, the second is the Life Force - your energy or you're Spirit, and the third is Water. Once those three Elements have left the body, only the shell is left, the Element of Earth, which is Physical matter. If your human bodies were left to dry out, what you would be left with would weigh less than a third of your original weight when you were in a 'living' state. It is that remaining third which over time disintegrates, becomes dust and returns to the Earth from which it originally came. If you look at the human body chemically, you will find it contains all the Elements that are found within the Earth. You are literally made from the Earth. The same chemicals in the Earth are in fact in your human body.

Question: 3

What is a coma and why do we go into comas?

Answer: 3

A coma is a state the human body enters when the Spirit suddenly vacates. Literally speaking, it is a State of Suspension or Stasis.

Medicine and science have been fascinated by what you call the coma. To be in a Coma is to be in a State of Suspension where you the individual are unable to communicate or physically move. The two main reasons human beings fall into Comas, whether it be for 1 day or 20 years, is because they have had a traumatic experience or because they don't want to deal with their physical existence any more. They've given away their Personal Responsibility because from a Spiritual Perspective they want to be released from the physical world. Don't misunderstand when I say they have given away their Personal Responsibility - that is not a judgement in anyway - it is entirely their choice if they wish to leave physical life for the time being, and they have their reasons for doing so.

Question: 4

Have you ever dealt with spirits who are in a coma? Can you explain what they are experiencing and why they would linger in a coma for an extended period of time?

Answer: 4

I can give you an example of a human woman who I came across in your the Astral Vibration (the 4th dimension as opposed to your physical third dimension). First I'll explain how this human being got to be in a coma. This human female was drunk and driving home one night, travelling at high speed, when up ahead of her was a truck which she didn't see until the last moment, and of course by then it was too late for her to stop. Automatically her fears took over - she had nowhere to swerve to avoid the collision, and unfortunately she connected with the truck. At that moment, when she realised she was about to die, her fear, naturally, was intense.

Surprisingly she survived the collision, but she ended up in a coma because she was so traumatised by her fears at the time it all happened.

The spirit in these situations will do one of two things. It will either come out of the human body before impact, or it will be thrown out of the human body upon impact. Once out of the human body it enters the astral vibration. The reason human beings go into comas is because the Spirit is still connected to the human body, and with that connection is also all your memories and emotions of your physical life. When you die physically the connection is completely broken, but in coma, the connection still exists. The spirit is connected to the human body by a beam of light, which many human beings refer to as the 'Silver Cord', and depending on how great Your fears were at the time you left your human body, will determine how long you as an individual stay in a coma.

The part of you that lingers in the Astral Plane is your Astral Body because it is the Astral Body that carries all the emotions and memories of your physical existence. The reason it lingers in the astral vibration is because it's trying to come to terms with what has just happened, and until the astral body can overcome those fears and come to some Self-Realisations, it will stay in that vibration for as long as it takes. Many human beings don't understand energy or the astral vibration, which is why science can't figure out why human beings are in comas. The human body may be alive, but there's nobody home.

Question: 5

What about the stories you hear about people talking to comatose patients and they come back after a short time or miraculously after many years?

Answer: 5

It's true that if someone from the human family of a comatose patient talks lovingly and kindly to the patient in a coma, they can return to their human body. The astral body is an emotional body and it can hear the words you speak on a physical level. So by talking to them you can calm them down, reassure them and bring them back, provided they want to come back. But then, because of the trauma or fear they were feeling, they could be so far away that they are unable to hear words from loved ones in the physical vibration, and again how far away they have run from their human body depends on the level of their fears at the time they vacated. You have to understand that the only thing the astral body remembers is what it is experiencing just before it leaves, and if it leaves in fear it's instinct will be to run and protect itself, just as you would physically run and protect yourselves if you felt you were in danger, or if you were afraid of something or someone. That fight or flight response is an emotional one, and the astral body is an emotional energy form.

Question: 6

There is an ethical and moral dilemma in keeping a comatose patient on life support, whether it be because of religious beliefs, the medical profession's credo to save all life, or the emotions of family unable to let go of their loved one. Are we interfering with the spirit's journey when we keep their body alive while their spirit is elsewhere? How can they grow and evolve as a disincarnate being if they are held to their physical body by the 'silver cord'.

Answer: 6

You as human beings acknowledge Physical Evolution but not many acknowledge Spiritual and Conscious Evolution because you have placed all your faith, beliefs and understanding entirely in your physical existence, disregarding your spiritual existence. Unfortunately, science interferes with the natural process of spiritual evolution. Keeping someone's human body alive on life support holds a spirit to its human body against its will. Because when you keep the human body alive, even though the spirit has left, the energy connection is still there. And this is where your emotions can cause you to forget about the well-being of the spirit which has left. You hope they will return to you - you want them to return because you feel an emptiness and deep sadness in your lives without them, but you don't stop to think of their well-being. Are you really helping them by keeping them connected to the shell they have now discarded? Only each of you as human beings can answer that question, which is why some human beings choose to keep their loved one's body alive on life support in the hope they will return, (and some do return) while others choose to set them completely free by turning off the switch.

Doctors try to preserve life - yet in a lot of coma cases this is harmful to the spirit because the connection is being maintained when it was meant to be severed to allow the natural process of Spiritual Evolution to occur. And when the human body is finally allowed to die, the experience of having been in a coma can have detrimental effects. In all the human years of travelling the Astral Vibration I've seen many spirits that were in coma who are still in fear. It can take anything from years to decades to try to explain to them that their human body no longer exists, and to try to help them let go of the trauma that put them in that state in the first place, because while they are in a coma they are constantly reliving the experience that put them there, which is why many remain in coma for many human years.

Question: 7

We know that people who go into a coma take the memory of their last physical experiences with them before vacating their body. When people die, do they also take the memories of their physical existence with them into the astral world and keep reliving them?

Answer: 7

When a human being dies, their astral body can continue to exist in the astral vibration indefinitely. What you must understand is if you were a fearful human being, or an angry or lustful human, or a religious fanatic for example, then that is the understanding you will take with you. You can only take your current level of knowledge with you. That is, your beliefs, your fears and you're conditioning into the astral vibration. This can prevent you from spiritually evolving, holding you in the astral plane indefinitely, preventing you from going through the light to continue your spiritual journey.

The most important thing you can do as physical beings is to gain the Knowledge and understanding of Unconditional Love and Emotional Balance, as opposed to fear and limitation, during your physical lifetime so you don't take those limitations with you when you leave your human body, otherwise you can be held in the astral world for not just years, but even centuries.

Question: 8

Can you give us an example of a spirit who has been caught in the astral vibration for a long time?

Answer: 8

I found a little human boy who had been in the astral vibration for over sixty years of human time. When I found him in 1986, I found out that he had died in 1921. His name was Robert, he was nine years old and he had lived in outback New South Wales. When I first found him I tried to approach but I saw incredible fear on his face, and he just kept running around in circles to avoid me - I simply couldn't get near enough to talk to him. After trying to talk to him over a period of human time I ended up asking for help from an entity who resembled a little boy. He befriended Robert and eventually introduced him to me. I felt his fear, as he was always looking over his shoulder, unsure of who was behind him. I asked him why he was so scared and eventually he told me his story.

His father had died in World War One, and because of hard times living on a farm in outback Australia, his mother remarried. The stepfather was very cruel to Robert; he would drink and become abusive. Robert's mother tolerated it because she felt helpless and alone - a woman on her own with a little boy and a farm to run in the early part of the 20th Century was not easy. One night, blind drunk, the stepfather was bashing Robert's mother. Robert could take no more - he attacked the man, defending his mother, as any child would. The man chased Robert into the paddock - they'd had a lot of rain and the water was eight to ten inches deep that night. He held Robert's face under the water while choking him, and drowned him. After Robert's death, the stepfather left the mother and went north to Queensland. She died a few years later, and he was never charged because she was too afraid to report him to the police - he told her he would kill her if she did.

This poor child had been reliving his trauma thousands of times since that human night in 1921, and every adult he saw in the astral vibration carried the face of his murderer, which is why he ran when he saw me. He could only see his fears. After several nights talking with the human boy I finally got him to confront his fears. The night he did, it happened like this: he stopped, turned around, looked at his stepfather and said "No more - you are not real. I forgive you and let you go." At that moment he passed into the light, into his mother's arms. That is probably the most satisfying thing about what I do - helping lost, traumatised Souls find their way out of their fears so they can continue on their spiritual journey.

This is only one example, but it illustrates that if you as a human individual lives' a fearful life physically you will take memories of it with you into the astral vibration and the emotions of those memories will live on until you learn to let them go.

Question: 9

Have you ever come across anyone who has been in the astral vibration for several centuries?

Answer: 9

There was a Roman soldier I had come across. I heard a lot of yelling and screaming so I went to investigate. I hid behind a rock and found there was a war going on between Roman soldiers and a group of people I couldn't identify. I heard a noise behind me, and as I turned there was a Roman soldier standing there, staring at me. He looked lost and confused, and had a pained expression. I saw sweat pouring off him, I could actually smell his body odour, and I saw blood coming down the left side of his head out of his helmet. He also had a sword plunged into his stomach at an angle, with blood dripping from it and coming out the lower part of his back.

He asked who I was, and all I could say was that I was an observer. He was baffled because my clothes were not like his or his enemy's. He asked me to help him, as he was weak. I helped him sit and I began to try to get him to understand that he was physically dead. I said it's not the year you think it is (he was from about 1800 BC), and told him it was the 20th century, and that he no longer had a physical body. Amazingly, he seemed to understand that. He asked me to remove the sword, and I did so very gently. He felt it being removed. I then explained to him that the sword wasn't real, something he didn't understand. After talking with him some more I helped him realise that his sword was an illusion, and as he did so, it dissolved before his eyes. He then said "if the sword isn't real, then my wound is not real", and as he looked at his stomach with blood dripping, the wound vanished, as did his other injuries. Interestingly, so did his body odour! He stood up and said "thank you" and then walked away. I never saw him again.

Question: 10

We've spoken about spirits who have been traumatised when leaving their bodies and the effects that trauma has on them. What about people who have had average lives and have then simply died because it was their time to go?

Answer: 10

They recreate the existence they have left because it is all they know. In the astral vibration there are many levels. You will find Spirits going about their lives as if they are still physically alive. There are shopping centres, churches, banks, schools, wars are going on, and Spirits are going to work, playing sport, going to pubs and hotels, gambling. You name it, it's there!

Question: 11

Do all spirits in the astral vibration believe they are still physically alive?

Answer: 11

Some know they're dead but don't want to leave, and consequently they avoid going through the light because they believe it will destroy them forever - they like to have the best of both worlds - physical emotions and the ability to create whatever they wish by the power of thought, be it material possessions, scaring other entities or indulging the vices and fantasies that many had while they were in their physical body.

Others know they're dead but aren't ready to leave yet because they may still need to complete some learning, or they may be helping another spirit learn lessons before continuing on their personal journey. These one's know about the light also, but don't fear it like the ones I spoke about just before. Then there are those who simply have no idea and keep reliving their physical memories as if they were still physically alive. They're the ones we need to help the most.

Question: 12

How do you go about helping them?

Answer: 12

I help them by guiding them to the realisation that their physical life is over, and that the world around them that they believe to be real is in actual fact an illusion. This is very much the challenge! I try to help them let go of the emotions and beliefs they brought with them, because it these two things that keep them locked in the astral vibration. Once they go through the light they can continue experiencing other vibrations, or they prepare to return to the physical world by reincarnating. The choice is always the individual.

At this point, I just want to add that you as human beings all assist Astral Entities during your time of human sleep, but most of you don't remember your experiences.

Question: 13

So once they go through the light they can come back into a physical body. Have entities come back without going through the light?

Answer: 13

Yes, and it is happening more frequently now. The problem with this is that Astral Spirits are incarnating without having dealt with their emotions and fears. When they return with their fears, beliefs and emotions from their previous human life they are also unbalanced because of it. This is why you are having so many more problems socially, with issues such as inexplicable violent behaviour, racial intolerance and drug problems, to name a few examples.

Question: 14

To close this segment, have you seen any celebrities on your travels?

Answer: 14 (This Question is answered by Roman)

I've spoken with the one called Bruce Lee. It was in the earlier part of, let's say my learning about the astral vibration. I was walking down a path when eight mischievous entities (negative- astral) started harassing me. Because I didn't have the knowledge and awareness I have now, I didn't realise I could use my martial arts training to defend myself. They kicked, punched, pushed and verbally abused me. Their faces were frightening. Suddenly a figure approached in the distance wearing black pants and shoes, white socks and a white singlet. I had to look twice - it was Bruce Lee! He lashed out at my attackers with such grace and speed it was breath taking. He came up to me afterwards, looked into my eyes and said "It's attitude - it's only attitude. If you feel fear, then fear will overcome you. But if you see yourself already winning the fight, then you have overcome fear." Then he left. I was speechless. I'll always remember it. It gave me a greater understanding of existence beyond the physical.

Question: 15

Why do you think he came to your aid?

Answer: 15 (Again answered by Roman)

He was my hero. I admired his ability tremendously, I trained in his styles, I believed in his philosophy and I used to meditate on him, so I guess I made a spiritual connection with him and he came to me. He's gone through the light now. He was reunited with Brandon after Brandon's death - they sorted out a few things, and went through the light together. Actually, their energies have now joined and they have been reborn as one entity.

Question: 16

Who else have you met?

Answer: 16 (Again answered by Roman)

I've seen Elvis performing, dressed all in black. I remember asking him why he keeps doing it, and he said "Hey man, this is all I know. People love me, so I keep singing."

Question: 17

So keeping the Elvis phenomenon alive in the physical is holding him back from his spiritual evolution by keeping him locked in the astral vibration?

Answer: 17 (Again answered by Roman)

Absolutely, the problem is we are not given or taught this knowledge.

Question: 18

Can you name a person which you've met on your travels in the astral vibration that made a profound impression on you?

Answer: 18 (Again answered by Roman)

I would have to say Martin Luther King. I remember he was very angry that he hadn't been given the opportunity to represent all Americans, not just African-Americans. He said to me "Wherever there is fear you can't express the truth." What he said sums up what we as a race of beings need to understand at a fundamental level. Fear is why the astral vibration exists. As long as we feel and create fear on the physical plane we will take that fear with us into the non-physical, and until we learn to dissolve our fears, the astral vibration will continue to exist and will continue to hold back humanity's growth and evolution on both a physical level and a spiritual level.

DIMENSIONS, REALMS AND UNIVERSES (NO-3)

Question: 1

Explain the difference between Dimensions, Realms and Universes.

Answer: 1

A Dimension is a level of Consciousness, and within a Dimension you have Realms. A Realm is a particular level of Consciousness in which an individual lives, so you can have an infinite number of Realms within a Dimension. It's like the light or sound spectrum. We can see and hear a variety of colours and tones, and each has a different frequency, which is a level within that spectrum. So too there are different levels in a Dimension which we call Realms. You may also have heard the word Vibration being used in this context – Vibration is simply another word for Realm. Finally, a Universe is a collective of Dimensions, and a collective of Universes is the totality of existence, physical and non-physical.

Question: 2

If Dimensions are levels of Consciousness, what level of Consciousness is the human race presently in?

Answer: 2

You as human beings have evolved over thousands of human years, and overall, presently humanity physically exist in the 3rd Dimension, the dimension of physical matter. However, I must add that you still have human beings living on this Planet Earth in the 1st and 2nd Dimension.

Question: 3

Then what is the difference between 1st, 2nd and 3rd Dimensional Consciousness.

Answer: 3

The 1st, 2nd and 3rd Dimensions are all matter Dimensions, but are of different conscious development. 1st Dimensional humans exist consciously on animal instinct - survival instinct, such as prehistoric humans. 2nd Dimensional humans are a step up the ladder of Consciousness by having made a conscious connection to Spirituality and nature, and by gaining an understanding of how they are interconnected with it and therefore learning to respect it and to live with it harmoniously. 3rd Dimensional humans, most of the humans on this planet today have consciously stepped up again by moving beyond superstition through to the development of reasoning and intellect. Remember also that within each of these Dimensions there are Realms of Consciousness, so you could have, for example, two different cultures existing in 3rd Dimensional Consciousness, but one slightly more advanced than the other. I guess the best way to illustrate this is to compare 1st World countries such as Australia with 3rd World industrialised countries, their religious, political and social beliefs are what separates them consciously.

Unfortunately, when you the human being evolved into 3rd Dimensional Consciousness embraced reasoning and intellect, not only did you let go of unnecessary superstitious beliefs, for the most part, you also let go of your Spiritual connection with the totality of the Universe. 2nd Dimensional humans may have their limitations, and some 2nd Dimensional cultures still retain an inherent understanding that they are connected to the Earth and all life on Earth. These cultures are taking wisdom with them as they move into 3rd Dimensional Consciousness with their Spiritual understanding intact. That is, they know that if they abuse the Earth which sustains them, or create imbalance in any way, they and all of their people will ultimately suffer for it in the long run. That's not saying they believe their god will punish them, as they are still using reasoning and logic, but the difference is they are using their understanding and knowledge wisely.

Humanity in your modern Western 3rd Dimensional Consciousness has made logic your god and saviour at the expense of wisdom, by sacrificing your innate understanding of the importance for balance in nature and your Spiritual connection with it. As a result, you arrogantly believe you can undermine the balance of nature and the Universe, and fix it somewhere else later (or leave it to future generations to clean up your mess) with Band-Aid treatments. You are already seeing to your detriment that such logic simply does not compute.

Question: 4

So, even though we have progressed consciously to a greater extent, we have also regressed in our consciousness at the same time.

Answer: 4

Yes, consciously humanity has regressed to some degree. This may seem hard to accept, but you have become so completely dependent on logic that you are no longer consciously aware of anything outside of the physical Dimension you know and exist within, which is of dense physical matter. As a result, you too have become denser in physical matter. The denser you become the more humanity loser's touch with your non-physical existence.

Question: 5

What makes us dense? :)

Answer: 5

It is important to understand that it is not just your level of thinking which makes you dense in physical matter, it is also what you as human beings consume. Over generations and centuries your human diet have dramatically changed, and as a result humans have become denser in physical matter. If you were to go back a million human years to the Neanderthals, they may have been 1st Dimensional beings, but they were not as physically dense as humanity is today. And even though they were not consciously aware of it, they worked with nature instinctively, as any other animal does because they existed instinctively. It may be a cliché, but you literally are what you eat. When you move away from pure foods in as close to their natural form as possible, you begin to alter your human genetics – your human body begins the process of adapting its altering diet. This may take generations, but as you are now seeing, genetic breakdown and mutation is occurring more frequently than ever because what the human body was designed to eat and what it is actually being fed are poles apart. When the human body breaks down, your level of thinking and level of Consciousness also begins to degenerate.

Question: 6

Why is it important to know this?

Answer: 6

Humanity is on the verge of a mass Shift in Consciousness into the 4th Dimension. No matter what Dimension humanity consciously exist in at this moment in human time, whether it be 1st, 2nd or 3rd, your present level of thinking will determine how quickly your consciousness can advance into the 4th.

To go beyond 1st, 2nd and 3rd Dimensional thinking you as human individuals have to think beyond your boundaries. In your 3rd Dimensional level of Consciousness you lost your Spiritual connection with the Earth and the rhythms of nature. You try to control and defeat nature, forgetting that you are a part of the totality of where you exist in this moment. Humanity sacrificed Spirituality for science instead of evolving Spirituality with science and technology, and so in your arrogance of believing you are superior, you have lost your connection with the life force that gave humanity their existence. The more humanity can advance their Consciousness and reconnect with the wisdom humanity have lost, the sooner humanity can move into the 4th Dimension, beyond the physical and intellectual limitations of the 3rd.

Question: 7

What are some of the indicators of consciousness changing?

Answer: 7

You would all agree that you as humanity have an incredible amount of upheaval and conflict on your Planet Earth at this time, both emotionally and physically. There is religious confusion as flaws in religious ideologies, theories and beliefs are exposed, and the sheer number of wars ignited through religious intolerance are an illustration of this. You also have issues revolving around drug abuse and dependence, illness, dis'ease (like the 'superbugs') and genetic defects which are more prevalent today than ever in human history, and of course what effects all of humanity to some degree is the emotional imbalance you are experiencing on a mass scale due to stress, frustration and anger. Ask yourself, "why is this happening?"

All suppressed negativity in human individuals has now begun to be released and is being expressed outwardly. Confusion in humanity is rising to boiling point as humanity on the whole are becoming more irrational, more anxious and more fearful than ever. You as all are so conditioned and controlled by governments in the societies you live in, that you feel your lives and existences closing in on you. The more fearful you as individuals become, the more your animal instinct reacts - you want to flee and be free, you are rebelling against the control which you personally allowed to be imposed upon you.

You are also affecting your planet. Whether you believe it or not, you are all connected to the Earth, and what you feel and project affects the planet you live on just as much as it affects the human beings around you. An example you will readily relate to: You go into a supermarket and because you're taking too long picking out your vegetables, or because you want to read the labels on some items before making a decision, the human being who is standing beside you is impatiently projecting their annoyance at you for not getting out their way because they are in a hurry! You can feel their negativity beaming towards you like heat from a radiator, and you know it's happening because you feel uncomfortable and you find instinctively you dislike that human.

From the planet's perspective, human negativity has created increased incidences of Cyclones, Tornados, Earthquakes, Floods, and major physical disasters. You are all connected - human to human, to animals, to plants, to the Earth. This isn't new age mumbo-jumbo. Science in its arrogance has made humanity ignore and forget that you are a part of this world and everything that exists within it and upon it, and as much as the rhythms of the planet affect you (e.g. full moons affecting human behaviour) you too affect the rhythms of the planet. Just because you live on the surface of the Earth doesn't mean you are mutually exclusive of the events which occur upon it or within it.

This is all happening because humanity is consciously evolving into the 4th Dimension. So as much as it may be a frightening thing, it is also a very wonderful thing. After all, you are all consciously growing! There is nothing more important than conscious growth, because when you leave your human body (when you die) and incarnate again, you will bring your conscious growth with you, which also explains why human beings are at different levels of consciousness simultaneously.

Question: 8

How can we go into the next dimension consciously if we are in so much conflict?

Answer: 8

All human negativity must be confronted and resolved before you can progress beyond your current dimension. You can't take the emotions and physical limitations of the 3rd Dimension into the 4th. Of course, this won't happen (consciously evolving into the 4th Dimension) over a few decades because you have humans existing in all three Consciousness Dimensions, that is, the 1st, 2nd and 3rd. Rather, it will take a few centuries.

There is no place for fear in the 4th dimension, as fear is an emotion and you can't take your emotions into that level of thinking. There are many levels, or Realms, of Consciousness in the 4th Dimension, just as there are currently in the 3rd, and depending on an individual's awareness, if they are spiteful, vindictive, hurtful and fearful, they will enter at the lowest end of the 4th Dimension. It's only when you learn to let go whatever it is that is limiting you the human being that you can consciously progress up the Consciousness scale into higher Vibrations within the 4th Dimension.

Question: 9

What will we see and experience during the collective transition of human consciousness into the 4th dimension?

Answer: 9

On first entering the 4th Dimension consciously you will find your physical senses will be heightened, that is, touch, taste, smell, sight and hearing. Your psychic senses will also be greatly heightened. There will be no more drugs, alcohol, junk foods or animal eating. This change for the better in diet will cause your bodies to alter and become less dense as you stop polluting them. It can't be predicted how long this will take because it is up to each human individual, but those who don't want to change will be left behind consciously.

There will be rebellion within humanity not wanting to change, not wanting to let go of their old habits and way of life because they are comfortable with what they know and understand. There will be a fear of the unknown, but it will eventually happen. Some will evolve sooner than others, and those humans will be the teachers of those who are still to consciously evolve. Governments and the monetary-based societies as you know and understand them will no longer exist because in the upper levels of the 4th Dimension, matter is no longer an essential ingredient to existence. As you can guess, politicians, military and bankers will be the last humans to embrace Consciousness Evolution, as they have the most to lose, meaning control of the masses and physical wealth.

Understand that you won't have light bodies, that is, non-physical bodies immediately upon consciously entering the 4th Dimension, but that is what humanity will eventually evolve into. You will return to what you once were - non-physical beings made of pure energy which can manifest themselves in any form they desire.

Question: 10

Have some people already progressed into the 4th dimension?

Answer: 10

All of you as beings of Light venture into the 4th Dimension everyday of your lives without being physically aware of it, so in answer to your question, yes, some have progressed beyond the 3rd into the 4th, but you all have experienced the 4th Dimension to some degree.

At the lowest end of the 4th Dimension is the astral plane. You enter the astral plane in your time of human sleep, and depending on the level of your awareness, you enter it at different levels. If fear and emotions govern your lives then you go to the lowest levels of the astral plan, where your experiences are often difficult or even traumatic, you see everything in black and white, there is darkness all around, and it seems like it is always night time in your human dreams. (Remembering your so called human dreams are in fact Reality). The astral plane is where each of you confront your conflict and fear.

In order to move into the Higher Realms of the Astral Plane you need to learn to let go of your fears and resolve your conflicts. Your time of human sleep not only serves to re-energise your human body but also serves your conscious learning. Before you can elevate yourselves into Higher Realms of Consciousness you need to elevate your level of thinking by dealing with your fears, conflicts and emotions, and the astral plane helps you do that. As physical beings you are the ones who have created your limitations physically and emotionally, therefore it becomes your personal responsibility to deal with them and let them go.

I can imagine most human beings would like to pop a Consciousness advancement pill which would chemically elevate them into the next Dimension, much like you depend on any number of devices and drugs to take the hardship out of any difficult task, be it your health or physical environment. Unfortunately it doesn't work that way because Consciousness isn't a physical thing, it's a Spiritual thing, and you can't grow consciously by altering your physical form in any way.

Question: 11

What will be different about living in the 4ᵗʰ dimension?

Answer: 11

The way you see things will be different, not at first, but as I explained previously, when you the human being eventually evolve into the higher levels of the 4ᵗʰ Dimension your entire existence will be very different to that of the 3ʳᵈ.The 3ʳᵈ Dimension is a physical matter dimension. For example, take a cup. When you look at it from a 3ʳᵈ Dimensional perspective you only see the sides which are visible to the naked human eye, but you can't see through the cup. In 4ᵗʰ Dimensional sight you would see the cup as if it were transparent - you would see all sides, not just those which are facing you.

The way you create things will also be very different. In the 3rd Dimension you presently create everything physically with thought and then physically by manufacturing it through a series of steps to reach the end product. In the 4th Dimension, you would imagine what you want to create and then you would materialise it without having to go through the steps you would normally have had to take if you were a 3rd Dimensional being. In the 4th Dimension you learn to manifest using energy (in actual fact, magnetic energy) and create a physical object by turning pure energy into matter, through your thoughts of using your most precious gift called Imagination.

Question: 12

How is manifestation possible when everything seems so physical here in the 3rd dimension?

Answer: 12

The universe is made up entirely of magnetic energy. You can learn to manipulate that energy and then create with it. In the 4th Dimension you will learn to consciously create. In the 3rd Dimension you create by using this same energy without even knowing you are doing it, and this is where your problem lies. You have a tool of immense power and possibility at your finger tips but are not even aware you are using it or how you are using it. Every time you the human individual project a thought you have the potential of manifesting that thought and making it your reality.

Imagine what you could do if you understood what you were actually doing when manipulating energy. No longer would it be a dangerous weapon in the hands of ignorance, like a child playing with a loaded gun but not knowing how dangerous a gun can be. You all create situations in your life by the thoughts you project. In the 4th Dimension you begin to understand that thought literally creates, and you learn to harness that knowledge for the greater good of all. Remember, you consciously can't enter the 4th Dimension with your fears and emotions, so there is no danger in manifestation because you can only manifest from a pure heart.

Would it not be disastrous if you the human individual could enter the 4th Dimension with full conscious awareness while your fears and emotions tag along? Imagine the havoc you would wreak if you used such knowledge and power out of fear, greed and vindictiveness. You wouldn't need chemical or germ warfare, you'd have an endless source of energy for mass destruction. This is exactly the reason why you can't go beyond the astral plane with your present level of thinking and consciousness. Your higher self won't allow it.

Question: 13

How can we help ourselves transform and progress consciously into the 4th dimension?

Answer: 13

Physically each human individual needs to look at their human diet, lifestyle and thoughts. The human individual needs to feel more for nature and the Plane Earth, and develop a social and moral conscience. You need to find integrity and compassion within yourselves, become less ignorant and arrogant by stepping out of the little boxes you each have compartmentalised your lives within, and get in touch with your feelings. To evolve from Emotional beings into Feeling beings, coming from the heart not the lower nature of the human animal.

The best place to start is to give up alcohol, tobacco, junk food and drugs. Cleaning up your human body means you can start to think straight, as any drug addict will tell you. But you don't have to be a drug addict to pollute your body and inhibit your abilities to think straight. A bad diet and sedentary lifestyle will much do the same, the only difference being that it may take a lot longer to kill you.

Another really important issue is to stop inflicting cruelty onto animals - that means not eating meat or any by-products of the meat industry (this includes fish and birds). When you stop justifying cruelty to other forms of life you begin to realise that there is no need to harm another living thing, and from there you develop compassion and understanding. This is something that many human individuals will find very difficult to give up, yet those who have become vegans find it isn't difficult to live the way they do at all. Human beings only find something difficult to change or give up because they are comfortable with how they live, even if it is detrimental to their health, the environment and their consciousness.

Changing your way of life in order to change your level of thinking and consciousness will be your greatest challenge because the Human Ego doesn't like to leave its comfort zone, and this is why it will take a few centuries for all of humanity to progress consciously into the 4th Dimension. But don't despair. More and more human beings are waking up and recognising their limitations and dissatisfactions with life. They want to change and grow consciously and are making efforts to do so, and this is a good thing for all of humanity.

BEYOND THE 4TH DIMENSION (NO-4)

Question: 1

In the previous story called, <u>Dimensions, Realms and Universes</u> and how humanity as a species is, without even being aware of it, progressing and preparing itself in its consciousness to evolve into the 4th dimension. Can you tell us about other beings that have already evolved into the 4th dimension?

Answer: 1

There are many species of what humans would call Extra Terrestrials within the 4th Dimension, and depending on what Realm of Consciousness they exist within, they can be of a physical matter or completely non-physical. Those which are of physical matter are much less dense in physical matter than humans, and those which are non-physical can present themselves as physical beings because they have learnt to produce a 'body' through the manifestation of magnetic energy into form by the power of their thoughts.

Question: 2

Because their realm of existence is so close to our own, have these beings tried to communicate with us in our 3rd dimensional matter world?

Answer: 2

Many of the beings which exist in the 4th Dimension both physical matter and non-physical in form, have been observing the Earth along with many other planets for thousands of years. In human history sightings go back 50,000 to 60,000 years, as is evidenced by ancient cave paintings. One of these races are what have been referred to as the 'Greys'. They have the capability to move through different vibrations and so they can, and have on many occasions, come into the human 3rd vibration.

Question: 3

What do the Greys look like?

Answer: 3

Well, as you may have guessed they are called 'grey' because their skin is of a greyish-yellow colour. They are much less dense in matter than humans and have no fat on their bodies what so ever. When a body is full of fat it is very dense in matter. Muscle is dense too, which is why it physically weighs more than fat, but compared to fat, muscle is a lighter form of matter. The Greys have very wiry and thin bodies, which helps them to travel on their ships. They travel beyond the speed of light, therefore it would be impossible for any kind of dense matter to travel in their ships without being disintegrated. Humans could not travel in their ships in 3rd Dimensional form as they are now. Especially at let's say Light speed.

Question: 4

Have the Greys been in communication with humans?

Answer: 4

The Greys have been communicating with the US government over the last 60 years. In 1950s some of their ships crashed because of radio waves from Earth interfering with their guidance systems, resulting in an imbalance in their magnetic energy fields, causing them to crash. These beings have since dealt with that issue, which is why there are not as many sightings. Actually many do avoid Earth. The US government has noticed this, and has given orders to their military to try to shoot down any ships because they want to obtain the technology within them. Have you not noticed how human technology suddenly exploded in the last 60 years, especially in the aeronautical and weapons industries? The space shuttle, lasers and stealth fighters for example.

It is a well-known fact, although most humans are still very sceptical of its truth, that President Nixon in his time had contact with the Greys. There is a photograph of him shaking hands with such a being. The US Government signed contracts with the Greys for weapons technology in exchange for giving them permission to take as many humans as they need for experimentation. The Greys carry out experiments on humans as humans do on animals. Stop for a moment and think about this. Human beings see animals as lesser beings to themselves and therefore feel no ethical dilemma in experimenting on them, justifying such act as helping humanity. The Greys see humans as lesser beings to themselves, and therefore see no ethical dilemma either, believing their studies of the human animal are to the benefit of many races. So don't be offended with them! They are behaving no differently to human beings, and rationalise their experimentation in the same way.

After almost a decade of abducting humans, it was becoming quite obvious that many human beings were disappearing inexplicably, and so the US Government had to put a stop to it. As a result, the passing on of technology was also stopped, which is why the US military have been given orders to try to bring down any ships in or around the Earth in secret.

What the US Government didn't count on was that the Greys were just as cunning as humans, and only gave them old, outdated technology. The Greys see humans as an animal which is evolving, but one which is also becoming a real threat because humans are aggressive and allow their fears to influence their judgement and actions. Therefore the Greys wouldn't be stupid enough to give a race they considered unpredictable and unevolved the latest weapons technology, just as the US government wouldn't openly give the Russians or Chinese their latest weapons technology because they would always want to keep the upper hand with what could become a real threat.

Question; 5

Have any other race of beings made contact with humanity?

Answer: 5

There was a race of beings referred to as the 'Blues' (so named because their skin is of a more bluish tinge) who had also made contact with the US government at one point. They are 4th Dimensional beings, but of a higher vibration than the Greys. Sadly, all the government was interested in was what kind of weapons technology they could obtain from these beings, the excuse given being that they "needed to be the most powerful country in order to keep the peace on Earth."

The Blues offered friendship and wisdom. They came in peace. But they realised that human beings had yet not evolved enough in their Consciousness and had therefore not advanced in their wisdom. The Blues offered wisdom to help humanity grow but could not give weaponry as they no longer had weapons because there was no need for them in their Realm of existence. They then dissolved in front of the military officials and teleported back to their ships. The Blues have not contacted any human governments since then, and instead make contact with individual human beings who are much more highly evolved in their consciousness.

It must be understood that the more an entity evolves the less imbalanced and fearful it becomes. In order to progress into the 5th Dimension one must have completely let go of their Ego and its fears. The Blues are entities which are on the verge of entering the 5th Dimension and are able to travel into the 5th and communicate with beings in the 5th.

Question: 6

Can we communicate with 5th dimensional beings now?

Answer: 6

The light of a being from the 5th Dimension is very powerful, that the average human body would not be unable to withstand the energy it emits. Like putting 250 volts of electricity through a wire that is only designed to take 50 volts, it would melt you, which is what human combustion is. A 5th Dimensional being wouldn't have to enter your human body for this to occur. They could be near you and you could still combust. But these beings would never endanger an entity in such a way, and will communicate with human beings in ways which would not harm them. Humans can bring them closer to them, but it means raising your Consciousness in order to meet theirs, and that includes purifying your human body by making it less dense in matter. This is possible and human beings are doing it now.

Question: 7

Can you tell us about the world of a 5th dimensional race?

Answer: 7

5th Dimensional beings have no physical matter - they are totally made up of light or energy, and they are pure unconditional love. They don't eat food as humans do, but absorb energy, which is the totality of existence. There is no hatred, anger, or jealousy - absolutely no ego. Ego cannot go into the upper levels of the 4th Dimension and can never go into the 5th Dimension or beyond. Everything is a pure state of being and everyone evolves for the higher good of everyone else. There are no expectations. Their level of thinking is so far above 3rd Dimensional thinking that it would be incomprehensible for the majority of human beings to understand them. This is not said to insult or offend, it is simply a fact that the difference in Consciousness between the 3rd and the 5th Dimensions is enormous.

While everything on Planet Earth lives off something else, they don't have insects or animals or fish life, and they don't have parasites of any sort. They only have plant life. In the 5th Dimension there is no need for such an existence because nothing ever dies. They have no physical body so they don't need to eat, or drink or breathe. There is no decay or death as human beings understand it because it is only physical matter which deteriorates. Everything is in harmony, and their whole purpose is to evolve and to help other beings evolve. They have trees, flowers, mountains and rivers. There is no pollution. Their trees don't lose leaves, nor do they rot or decay - everything is perfect, in harmony in pure bliss. Trees and plants are created as a result of their collective consciousness creating them. Their plant life does grow but there is no wind, no heat or cold to blow leave onto the ground. It is what you would call a perfect world.

There is also no night because that is governed by time, which is a 3rd Dimensional concept, and they don't live to time. From human perception one of those beings could be 3000 to 20 million Earth years old, but in their reality they are infinite. They don't need to sleep because they absorb energy continually. Sex does not exist. They procreate through the power of thought. An energy is projected and manifested into another being, or two beings who are particularly close may choose to project their energies together and create another being which is a blending of both their energies. A new fully grown being comes into existence which will grow consciously and already have the knowledge of both those beings that created it. By power of thought they can manifest a body at will. They can choose what they look like and can choose to wear clothes if they wish, or they may simply wish to exist as a spark of light.

They travel by thought which creates manifestation. For example, they can be in Australia one moment and can then manifest or teleport themselves in America in less than a micro of a second. They can also split their energies and be in more than one place at once with the same conscious level while being totally connected to each other's energies. 5th Dimensional beings don't experiment on any form of life, rather, they encourage all conscious beings, like humans, to grow consciously and evolve with wisdom and compassion. They do not have ceremonies or rituals, but they often have discussions and communicate with each other in matters which will help them grow consciously. For example, they wouldn't sit and talk about a TV show, or gossip about someone, as their minds are beyond such triviality, but they would discuss their observations of other forms of life and try to finds ways of helping these life forms evolve consciously.

These beings present themselves to humans in a way so they can be recognised. Like spirit guides, these beings present themselves to a person from a time when they would recognise them, such as when they had a life with them previously. To do so, they must step down in levels of consciousness so that the person can accept their energies and not be combusted by the light, which is what the Blues did when they communicated with the governments.

In order to evolve as a being into the 5th Dimension, you must progress through the 4th. The 4th Dimension is the final step to becoming 100% consciously evolved beings - it's the last stop where you must let go of everything to do with physical existence - all the fears, beliefs and conditioning, and it is from here that beings can exist as pure forms of light, existing in a pure state of being, allowing other forms of life to evolve without interference. When you can allow another being to grow and evolve in their own time and space you are truly a wise and compassionate entity.

Question: 8

How many races of beings exist in the 5ᵗʰ dimension?

Answer: 8

From the 5ᵗʰ Dimension onwards there are thousands and thousands of beings in existence. You as humanity must try to comprehend that there are many Universes and you as a species are only in one. If you the human individual could raise your consciousness you would realise there are billions of Universes because the Universe has been in existence for billions of years, and it continues evolving. Humanity is locked in a vibration of physical matter. Once you go beyond matter, you evolve through the 4ᵗʰ and into the 5ᵗʰ Dimension, and beyond the 5ᵗʰ there are many more levels. You can't progress beyond those levels until you progress beyond the level of consciousness you currently exist within, and that goes for all Dimensions of existence.

The best way to explain it is like this: a human goes to the Moon, or Pluto, or Saturn, or Jupiter, etc. and all they can see from their 3ʳᵈ Dimensional sight are dead planets, so they only look for remnants or evidence that physical life (3ʳᵈ Dimensional life like their own) once existed there because they are looking from a 3ʳᵈ Dimensional level of Consciousness. If they could elevate their Consciousness into the 4ᵗʰ Dimension and then visit these planets, they would see another form of existence, another vibration brimming with life. Unfortunately, because of their 3ʳᵈ Dimensional thinking and their belief that matter equals life, they will not see any other forms of life. Sadly if something happens or is experienced that is non-physical, most human beings believe it is an illusion, a hallucination or trickery. They search to find a physical explanation because they are unable to comprehend that life can and does exist beyond the physical 3ʳᵈ Dimension. There is a saying, just because you cannot see it or touch it, does not mean it doesn't exist.

Question: 9

How long will it take for humanity to evolve into the 5ᵗʰ dimension? Will we ever get there?

Answer: 9

Yes, humanity will eventually get there. To evolve from 3rd Dimensional matter into the 5th, it will take hundreds, even thousands of human years. Beings that exist in the 5th Dimension were once 3rd Dimensional. Humanity collectively fears stepping beyond their physical matter existence, and fears accepting the concept that life could possibly exist in non-physical dimensions. It is humanity's biggest challenge to accept that life goes way beyond the physical and that physical existence is only a miniscule portion of what the totality of existence really is. Beings in the 5th Dimension are completely free. Their existence of life is tranquil because they are unlimited in thought and body. They don't run rampant and harm other forms of life because they have evolved out of a need to dominate. They have evolved beyond a fear or non-existence, because they know that energy never dies, it just transforms into a new form of life.

Question: 10

Has humanity had this opportunity to grow consciously earlier in our evolution?

Answer: 10

There was a time in human history when humanity could have taken another road in evolution, but they chose science and technology over conscious evolution. Another opportunity will arise and is coming. If every human was to learn to meditate within themselves, to learn to understand Evolution and the Universe, they would begin to understand themselves. But first human beings must travel back and find out who they were to begin with and why they are what they are today. Human beings, as a physical being, are very aggressive and unbalanced, and therefore prone to paranoia, which causes them to want to dominate or destroy anything perceived to be a threat before taking the time to understand it. It is human nature to be scared of what is not understood. But that is simply the Human Ego's fear of relinquishing control to something greater and wiser than itself.

Question: 11

Why do we have to evolve out of physical existence into a non-physical existence? Are there beings in dimensions beyond the 4th which are physical?

Answer: 11

There are partly physical forms of life in the 4th Dimension (such as the Greys), but as they evolve towards the 5th they completely shed their matter existence. Humanity, as other races have done before them, needs to evolve beyond the 3rd Dimension to go back to what they once were - pure energy. Every being in existence, no matter where their level of Consciousness exists, needs to evolve themselves back up the consciousness ladder to become a pure energy once more. There will come a time within the Universe where the 1st, 2nd and 3rd Dimensions will no longer exist, therefore no matter forms of life will exist.

Question: 12

Is there a finite number of dimensions? That is, is there a set limit on the number of dimensions that can exist at any one time?

Answer: 12

NO, the number of Dimensions are infinite and continue to expand and evolve just as Universes. Dimensions, just as Universes and Realms, coexist. Your aircraft that fly in the sky pass through ships from other Dimensions which are observing human evolution, but humans are unaware of their existence because they are in another dimension. All of humanity walk through other dimensions without even knowing it. Dimensions exist within Dimensions that exist within Dimensions, etc. Only a fine veil separates them, everything vibrates at a particular frequency. There are worlds existing all around your Earth, the only reason you cannot see them is the vibration they vibrate at. To enter another Dimension, all you have to do is shift your Consciousness slightly and a door will open to your sight. Believing and practice is essential.

Consider the physical body as an example of multidimensional existence. It is in the 3rd Dimension, but it has several levels of existence - the outer shell, then the organs within it, and within those organs are cells which are themselves made up of smaller particles again, and those particles are made up of smaller ones again. All are matter, but all in slightly different dimensions. Humans accept them because they can see them, yet before the microscope the tiny particles that made up cells were unseen. So a whole new world was opened up because humans chose to shift their Consciousness ever so slightly. It is no different to opening a door to the non-matter worlds of the 4th Dimension and beyond. It is just a shift in thinking. If human beings were superstitious when they first saw cells under a microscope, they would have said "what trickery is this, what devilry exists in the body?" But they accepted that it was a part of their existence, so why not non-matter worlds? The human body is a multidimensional existence, but exists in one world - the physical 3rd Dimension.

Question: 13

Kuntarkis, what would you say to a person who wants to consciously grow and evolve into a 5th dimensional being?

Answer: 13

Each of you as human individuals, whether you live in the 1st, 2nd, 3rd, 4th or 5th Dimension, are all responsible for your actions in your human life, from each incarnation to another, from each thought to action. You have many rules in your society, and many conditions. Those rules and conditions exist for a reason: to hold you in line, to try and prevent unevolved humans from creating harm to others, or from taking from others what you don't deserve. In the 4th Dimension, at certain levels of Consciousness, the same rules apply, because there is also Ego within the 4th Dimension as in the 3rd, but Ego is only emotion, conditions and beliefs which are based on fear and insecurity. When you face yourselves, which is your greatest challenge, you can grow beyond those limitations and enter higher realms. The realm between the 3rd and 5th is the 4th, and it is within the 4th Dimension that you must grow beyond the emotions to become spontaneous, to have no fears, no anger, no hatred, no jealousy, no vindictiveness, lust or greed. And when each human being accomplishes that through your incarnations, you go beyond that 4th Dimension into the 5th, and it is here you see the truth for what it is without judgement. In the 5th Dimension you are conscious living beings who are no longer afraid of the unknown or to venture out into what you do not understand.

The physical human being here on Earth at the moment is very fearful in their existence. Because they are so highly conditioned and controlled by beliefs and conditioning, many are unable to think outside the little black boxes that they live within. To grow and evolve, no matter what level of Consciousness you are in, you each must ask ourselves "why?" You each need to step forward to understand who you are, what you are and where you are going. You need to understand where you come from, what created you, or were you just biologically created from a single celled organism over billions of years ago. These are some of the many unanswered questions that scientists on your Earth are seeking answers to today.

Each of you as human individuals throughout the Universes has the spark of light within them, and all of humanity are interconnected. No-one is better than anyone else. No-one is higher than anyone else. You all come from the same place, from light itself. In your quest for truth and conscious evolution do not fear the unknown, for it is the unknown which will set you free from the beliefs and conditioning which are your limitations. It is important to evolve to grow beyond what you are because that is how you can venture out and journey into other Realms of existence.

The choice is an individual one. If you choose to live in the human ego world of wars, injustice, and cruelty to each other, then you will live in that Ego World until you choose to disperse it and grow consciously. But when you evolve your Consciousness, even as a physical being, you will be able to take your awareness with you into other dimensions, and bring back knowledge which you can use in your 3rd Dimensional existence to elevate you far beyond the Ego World of humanity. When you become a living example for others to follow, you truly are helping humanity evolve, for only through an honest heart can the truth of existence manifest itself.

YOU ARE WHAT YOU EAT & YOU ARE WHAT YOU THINK (NO-5)

It is your choice, your choice solely to become whatever you the human individual wish to become through the power of your thoughts, and through what you the human individual consume within your human bodies. Most human beings do not understand that it is vital to watch what you each think and what you each consume, for what you think you become and what you eat you become. This is something that each of you as human individuals must bring to your own Self-Realisation. You cannot grow consciously if your thoughts are negative on a constant basis. You cannot grow consciously if you put bad food into your human body because you do not have the nutrients to sustain and balance Mind, Body and Spirit as one.

For example, if a human being grows up with deep emotional resentment from their childhood, they will carry that emotion throughout their human life. If a human being has a drug problem they will not grow consciously because the drugs, which are pure toxin, will interfere with their growth. Now you may ask "where does this all come from". There is only one answer. You can make as many excuses as you wish, but the only answer is: your human parents.

Ask yourself this question and be honest from the heart, because only through an honest heart can the truth manifest itself in its totality; it is the Love from your Heart that is pure, so ask from your Heart: "why do I believe what I believe today?" You will come up with many answers. You may say society, the experiences of life, that's how it is, that's what I am. They're all valid answers, but the real reason why you think what you think today, and you are what you are today, goes back even before you were born.

As you were conceived within your human mother, you experienced every single emotion and experience she did, whether painful or loving. If your human mother and your human father put bad foods into their bodies along with bad thoughts, which were negative and painful, then the body which you were born into will also have encoded within its genetics the same emotions. Experiences and physical effects of the food which was consumed, from your human parents, because your body was created from theirs. That encoding has laid out what you will think throughout your human life and what you will eat throughout your human life because the human body is made up of over 4 Quadrillion cells which act like little computers, storing information which will be activated throughout your human life at different times. Now many may say "no, that is not true. I am an individual, I am myself". But if you look back in the past, go back and look at your human parents, their habits, their way of life, the way they think, what they eat, 85% of the time you will find that you have certain habits from them. I'm not saying it's negative or positive. What I am saying is you are encoded from the moment of conception.

Now if you come from a negative family where there was nothing but violence, no love, complete misery, unhappiness, no joy, then you will bring that same negativity forth as you mature throughout your human life. That will create circumstances in your human life because everything in this Universe is created by the power of thought. Everything in this Universe is magnetic energy and how you the human individual use that energy depends on you. So it is vital to your conscious growth as a Spirit being, which is living and experiencing a physical existence, that what you express through your thoughts, whether negative or positive, creates your human life, and your children's lives, and their children's lives.

I know some of you now will be saying that it is not possible. I'm sorry, it is the truth, but you cannot hold anger towards your mother or your father. You cannot blame them for how you have, or will have turned out because each of you has chosen your experiences in this lifetime. That is, you have each chosen certain lessons to learn, to understand and to grow from. You even choose your human parents and your human parents choose you.

Many find this hard to believe because of their own deeply ingrained conditioning. So, as an example let us use the concept of 'the past' and imagine it sitting on a scale on the left hand side. Come now to the centre of the scale and let us call it 'the present', and then go to the right hand side of our imaginary scale and call it 'the future'.

PAST   PRESENT   FUTURE

If you grew up with negative emotions, brutality, or no love, then the past will come through you as a condition, and you will consistently attract into your life an energy that will reinforce the same conditioning in the present which will create your future. Each of you as human beings have a choice and the choice is yours alone. Being negative is okay because the negativity within you that you the human individual may have nurtured for 30 years of your human life needs to come to the surface and be dissolved if you are to be set free from it.

Now you may say "how do you do that? I've been trying for years." Well it all starts with you, the human individual. Your thoughts, your food, how you feel about yourself. The society that I live within and around has been observing Human Consciousness and its growth for hundreds of thousands of years. We know the pain that you are all going through; we understand it because many thousands and thousands of years prior humanity we also experienced all the emotions of 3rd Dimensional matter existence, and yes, we have over a long time grown beyond that level of thinking.

You are all our sisters and brothers as we are yours. We are here purely to guide, to give you understanding, to help you grow consciously so all of humanity can develop their consciousness beyond the Human Ego that exists on this planet Earth. Everything that is within the 3rd Dimensional world of matter is an illusion created from emotion. The Earth is the greatest planet for schooling and learning that exists in this universe.

When we each make the conscious decision to change our thoughts, to change our food intake and to grow healthy, then we also grow healthy in our consciousness. We grow beyond emotion because emotion is only based on the past. Your brain inside your physical body only remembers the past, whether it be negative or positive, and depending on your emotions, it will trigger a negative or positive memory of an experience from the past. That triggered memory creates your present and subsequently your future. When you face yourself and defeat the negative chatter, insecurities and doubts which have plagued you all your life, you will have faced your greatest enemy, for the enemy is not outside of you, it is within, and it is you.

Each time you have a thought and it is negative, recognise what you are feeling emotionally, whether it be towards another or yourself, because you cannot blame another. You are 100% fully responsible for every action and thought in your human life. To take recognition of that responsibility is to begin to grow consciously. From there you begin to change all the negative emotions that are encoded within your being genetically into a positive reaction. That is how you as a human being will grow consciously beyond your limitations.

We have observed many of you growing beyond, far beyond human emotion, and it is so beautiful to recognise and observe. That is why many of you as human beings who live within a human body, who do grow consciously, can have contact with us. We cannot communicate with your military, nor your governments. It is not because they will not understand, it is that they are not capable of making the conscious connection that we only can express wisdom. For it is wisdom that gives you the compassion and the understanding, and in turn gives you the Unconditional Love, not just for yourselves, but for all forms of life which is expressed in the light of totality.

Each of you must begin with the dissolving of your negative thoughts and changing your diets by putting in natural, healthy foods. No artificial flavourings, no chemicals of any description, no animal products, no poisons, no toxins, because your human bodies were not designed to ingest such things.

We are all aware that what eventuates after many years of abuse of your human vehicles is dis'ease. Please remember, as one of your enlightened beings from late in your 19th Century once said, "Dis'ease is neither vindictive nor cruel, but it is a means adopted by your soul to halt you from doing further harm, and to help lead you back onto the path of light and truth from which each of you should never have strayed". And that is the truth.

You may think at this moment, as you read these human words which come through the vehicle known as Roman, you may ask yourselves "why is it that you claim what you express is the truth?" Allow me to explain. You have just under 7 billion human beings on this planet alone, and each of you believes that you have the truth. But in reality, if you open your hearts and your minds beyond the limitations of your 3rd Dimensional matter world, you will discover that it is only an idea of what truth is, created by many human thoughts over many lifetimes. And documented on your pieces of paper in history to be accepted as the truth. Knowing humans as well as we do, without ego or judgment, you will recognise that all human beings tend to change what the original truth was from when it first began.

If you wish to discover real truth, total truth which is a pure state of being and which is ever changing, unconditional and unbiased, then stop the chatter in your human brain, and halt the thoughts in your physical world by going quiet in your mind. If you persist with this long enough through your meditations you will discover a voice within you, a void and emptiness, a nothingness that is so silent you will have a Self-Realisation of the light that is within you. Now each of you have the connection of this light which is the totality of Creation, of the Universe. It is there waiting for you to achieve Self-Realisation. It is your choice, and your choice alone to take and follow that path.

There is no-one on this planet Earth, in this moment of life that can claim to give you the truth, but only guidance for you to discover that total truth. You will come to that realisation through the power of your thoughts by purifying the vehicle that you live within. You will become a living example of a human conscious being, capable of going beyond the 3rd Dimensional world of matter, which is complete chaos. You have more wars and conflict on your planet Earth because of thoughts, because of religion, because of political views. But there is nothing we can do for you until you each have the Self-Realisation that all these things do not matter. What truly matters is the Essence of your Light, the Unconditional Love that is within you and around you, emanating itself around you as a beam of light and connecting you to the wonderment of the inner universe and the outer universe.

There are so many places in this Universe and all the other Dimensions, Vibrations and Realms you each live within that would give you an understanding of who you are, why you are and where you are going. So it comes back again to free will. We are not saying for you to believe us, but to find that truth within, to give yourself the opportunity to discover the wonderment that lies within you through your own Self-Realisation. The power of thought is something that each of you as human beings must come to terms with. If you can see it and imagine it, you can create it. That is how powerful thought is because it is living energy. But you cannot go beyond your level of thinking if you constantly feel insecure, and relive the pain of your past over and over and over again. Step beyond it. Step beyond the limitations that you have created out of fear.

Your human word 'fear' is just another form of energy which can be dissolved within an instant. If you wake up from your human sleep feeling angry and feeling annoyed, you will normally have a very annoying day my beloved humans. But if for a moment you can stop that emotion of negativity and say to yourself: "NO! I actually do feel good, I actually feel strong. I allow my anger to be dissolved into the nothingness from which it came, my past, and I learn to forgive my past and forgive others that have hurt me throughout my life. I grow beyond that pain." That in itself is a great healing.

If all of you as humans beings could stop for one moment on your planet Earth, all at the same moment, and see in your mind's eye all your negativity, all your hatred, all the emotions that you have grown up with which come from negative experiences, and then recognise what you have done by dissolving it back into that nothingness with the power of Love in your Hearts, and then project this Love all around the planet Earth and within her, your thoughts alone can heal the Earth in an instant. Your thoughts alone can heal all the pain, misery and famine that is on your planet today, and especially dis'ease.

Roman is a living example of that healing process. When he was told he had cancer he was also told that he only had 8 months to live, unless his left lung was removed, and underwent chemo-therapy, took another drug to keep him stable and then have further surgery on his right lung. He would have died. He would no longer exist in this human body. But something inside of him said what he has created through his own negativity, he also has the power to uncreate through the power of his thoughts. He knew he must change everything in his human life by disposing of all his negativity and stress out of his life, and to change his attitude by learning to Love and accept who he was. Through the power of his thoughts he did this. He changed his diet and ate good pure plant foods only. In a period of 8 to 11 months of your Earth time, his left lung totally rejuvenated itself. I understand his human doctor was amazed and couldn't believe the miracle which had occurred, but it is true. He has nothing to prove, he never even spoke about it for at least 10 years of his life, for he felt embarrassed that he had created such a deadly dis'ease which is rampant on your planet Earth today.

Let me say this. Dis'ease is created from two things - negative thoughts created from negative emotions throughout your human life, and the consuming of unhealthy foods. These two things work together to create a sick human body, and that is where your dis'ease comes from. From your thoughts, stress and ultimately bad food you create dis'ease. Having it cut out or drugged is only a temporary treatment. You must each learn to deal with your thoughts and your emotions. What you project as a negative thought to another being is projected back unto you. What you steal from another somewhere in your human life will be stolen back from you. If you murder for whatever reason, or take the life of another, your life will be forfeited. That is the law of the Universe - what is unbalanced must be brought back into balance.

There is no judgement in what I have expressed. You may think there is, but there is not. It is only the level of your thinking that allows one to judge another because they may be insecure. And yet it is only a creation of your thoughts. Ultimately the foods that you consume degrade your human body and its ability to think clearly and rationally, and making you denser and denser in your body matter until you have no mobility, until you can no longer move your fingers from arthritis, for example, because of all the calcium that you have taken from the animals you have consumed. That is what arthritis is; a build-up of calcium and toxins; crystallisation. And if we look at it from a metaphysical point of view, it says that you do not believe you deserve to be healthy, you do not believe that you deserve to be mobile. You believe that you have been bad so you must be punished.

It is you alone, dear beautiful people of Earth, that have created that situation. I know many will read this and think "how ludicrous", and yet I will not judge you for whatever you say about what has been expressed. My being loves you unconditionally because I am you and you are me; we are all each other. I only wish to send and give you the understanding of life, to share wisdom, and it is your choice, yours alone whether you accept it or not.

WHO IS THE ENEMY? (NO-6)

Consider this article as a follow on from the last story. **You are what you eat, you are what you think.** I believe they are interconnected. Have you ever asked yourself this question from the heart: **"Who is the Enemy"**? It probably would be a strange question to some, but to others it may sound a very logical question.

If you the human individual were to give it some thought you would probably come up with several answers. You may say the enemy is someone wanting to hurt another out of pure vindictiveness, or you may say the enemy is one nation wanting to wage war on another nation, or you may see your politicians, or police, or military as the enemy. There are no doubt many possibilities as to who you would consider to be "the enemy". At this point you must remember that what you believe is governed by your level of thinking, and your level of thinking is the direct result of your conditioning and your upbringing, not just from your human parents but also from the society and culture you have lived in all your human life. It is true that when you leave your society or culture and see the world from another perspective by viewing it through experiencing a different society or culture, you do gain a completely different view of life and existence. With this in mind, it is easy to see that who, or what, you believe to be the enemy, is very much based on how you think at this moment in your existence.

Think about this question for a moment: **Why do you believe what you believe today?** The immediate answer would be your human parents. All that you are today is the outcome of your parents; your emotions, your beliefs, your conditioning, your entire life. Too many that may be hard to accept, but it is the truth, and only through the truth will you find Self-Realisation. Only from an honest heart can the truth manifest itself, which in turn will set you free from your created limitations by bringing the balance of mind, body and spirit together. So I ask you again to ask yourselves from an honest heart, **"Why do you believe what you believe today?"**

Since human beings have lives and evolved on this planet Earth for the last 928,000 years, there have been thousands of wars to date, and many are still currently being waged. Nearly all of the wars were created from greed, misunderstanding, religion, monarchies and cultural differences. Since your second world war, which by the way was planned by the political powers of the time, there have been 157 wars, both large and small. You as humanity need to ask yourselves "who truly is the enemy?"

If you step beyond what you each believe and admit to yourselves that taking a physical life in war is still murder, it does not matter how many reasons or excuses you give, each time you take another life, whether it be from greed, anger, jealousy or hatred, you are in actual fact killing yourselves. Why? Because dear human beings, you are all interconnected to each other, just as everything in the universe is infinite and connected, like the skin on your human body. You may all think in a different way from each other, and yes, that is your upbringing, your beliefs and your conditioning of human life, but the truth is you all come from the same place. You are all children of the Universe and of Creation, no matter what Dimension or Realm we all exist within, and no matter whether we have a physical or non-physical existence.

So I ask you "who is the enemy". There is only one answer. Each of you is the enemy. The enemy is within you. It always has been from the very beginning, and this enemy needs to be resolved by loving and nurturing the self. You may ask, where does the enemy come from? It comes from your fears, your insecurities, and the hurt child that is within each of you.

Many of you on this planet Earth carry emotional pain right throughout your human life. You bury it deep inside of yourselves, not wanting to deal with it or look at it. You even take it to your graves and carry it through to your next incarnation. There is one word on your planet that describes this enemy, and that word is EGO. Ego is rampant among your people and societies today. It is the negative aspect of humanity and human cultures. You see, Ego only remembers the past. Everything from your past has made you what you and your societies are today.

Because human beings have lived in fear and insecurity for so long, you have shut out the Light of Creation. It is like being disconnected from the source. Please do not misunderstand my expressions. The Light, which is infinite, is always present within you and around you, but each of you as human beings must deal with the negative side of your human life. Your beliefs and conditioning, your fears and insecurities must be confronted and dissolved into the nothingness from which it first came. Your human word 'fear' is only energy, manifested from your way of life. If you think negative thoughts you will create negative aspects and situations in your human life. It is your choice, your free will. To put it another way, while you have inward insecurities, they will be exposed outwardly through your daily expressions, which in turn will create your life in this moment and the moments in your future to come, be it negative or positive.

Many like myself have looked upon your human history since the beginning. We have watched many of your leaders in all of your different cultures and nations. I would like to give an example by speaking of the one you call Hitler, from your second world war. He was a very angry and insecure human being who was born to a Jewish mother and a German father. Hitler was very jealous of the Jewish people in his community for their wealth and ambition in business, and he grew up with hatred in his heart for all Jews. He especially resented his mother because it made him half Jewish. This unbalanced human being became a leader to millions and waged war on all Jews because of his personal agenda. His hatred was so great he turned children against parents and neighbour against neighbour. He tried so hard to wipe out all Jews and even declared war on the entire world, all because of the hurt child within. He created the enemy within; he nurtured his insecure Ego and allowed it to manipulate not only his own fears, but also the fears of millions of human beings.

There have been thousands of your kings and queens, and other leaders, who have created misery on this beautiful planet. But you as human individuals cannot blame them entirely, for each human being is responsible for the part they play in the picture which is humanity. You would think after thousands of wars that humanity would have learnt that peace can never be created from wars. But the Ego within continues to delude and mislead.

Only when each human being dissolves their enemy within, their Human Ego, will peace be present on this planet Earth. If each human being becomes quiet in the mind and stops all the chatter of the Ego, which is simply a distraction that you have created, the stillness of your mind will make contact with your own divinity, you're Light, your totality. Then you will be able to read the book of life which will show you all about your human evolution, your connection with each other and the Light which all of life comes from. A small affirmation for each to express from the heart.

HUMAN GENETICS (NO-7)

I have been asked to speak about Genetics and Human dis'ease, as it is affecting many of your kind and will affect all upon this planet Earth. I have also been asked if my planet Nar'Kariss has experienced what is now being experienced on your Earth.

Nearly 2 and 1/4 million years ago of your human time, our civilisation the Nar'Karones at that time were experiencing great peril; dis'ease was taking its toll in all parts of our society. No one was excluded. Research into genetics concerning the makeup of our species became top priority, but our wise ones at that time, which you would call your scientists, were not as wise, as their experiments ventured into areas which they should not have. This created mutation within our species that took almost 7,000 years to come back into balance. We learned a great lesson that you cannot change what nature has created as perfect. What needed to be changed was our thoughts and our emotions.

Genetics is now a field of study that is being focussed on upon your planet Earth more and more, one of its goals being to find simple and logical comprehension of previously misunderstood body processes and physical developments. Today, your medical science strongly believes that diseases can be passed on through the gene pool, making them hereditary, and research is being carried out along this line of belief to find as much physical evidence as possible to prove it. Genetics is being used as the excuse for all your ailments, from heart dis'ease, cancers and obesity, to migraine headaches.

We have been studying your science advancement in research of family groups and the diseases that have commonly appeared throughout many of their human generations, such as heart dis'ease and stroke. It would seem logical that there is an inherent weakness, or genetics, to particular illnesses within those human family lines, and we understand your scientists hope to find cures to the various ailments that are on the increase and which are plaguing humanity. There are scientists on your planet at this very moment playing with the reality of removing certain genes in order to eliminate physical weaknesses and hereditary predispositions as in the case of obesity, heart dis'ease and diabetes. Gene manipulation is also strongly being considered on your planet as an alternative method to control crime and violence which plagues your society. Your scientists believe a reasonable and logical solution would be to remove the genes that are considered responsible for violent and disruptive behaviour.

I will say this: It will not solve the problem, for the effects of altering genetic information holds far greater implications and repercussions for the evolution of humans as a species, including your human rights issues, than scientists would ever admit publicly. And without a doubt your scientists are well aware of this.

Genetic research on your planet Earth is on the edge of becoming extremely dangerous. Just as you, the Human beings, selectively breed animals, so too will your scientists attempt to selectively breed human beings. On the surface this may seem logical and even seem to be positive in perspective. But let me take this one step further. It does not take too much of an educated guess to see how genetic engineering could be exploited by the governments of your world.

Selective breeding is nothing new, and I can assure you that my species have been there and seen the outcomes. It was not what we expected. During your second world war, the one you call Adolph Hitler was already experimenting with genetic engineering, better known to you as eugenics. It was looked upon as barbaric at the time and many were outraged because they felt scientists were trying to play God by trying to selectively breed a 'Super Race'. Even in your United States during the 1920s of your time, a eugenics programme was quietly being carried out in an effort to control the births of physically and mentally disabled humans and those considered undesirable or even 'feeble minded', such as your poor. This was done by sterilisation of children as young as 11 years of age, and younger. These children were kept locked away in your institutions for their entire existence to prevent them from ever spreading what was believed to be their 'inferior seed', and yes, sadly, similar situations are still occurring and similar beliefs are still being practised on parts of your planet Earth today.

We also have been on the same path in our history, and yes, we do have the knowledge to share with you so you all have the chance to grow beyond your limitations, but we can only communicate with those who have an honest heart and an open mind; those who are truly willing to listen to the wisdom of experience.

It is important to understand that the idea of genetically altering the human body by specifically interfering with its genetic information will create mutation in the long term, both physically and mentally, which cannot be foreseen at present by your human scientists. Your nature in your third Dimensional matter world has its own natural processes of evolution which, as a result of being given adequate time for adjustment and adaptability, becomes a harmless and pure method of development. But if we look at your Human Ego, it wants everything now, not allowing for a natural progression and incubation period. For example, on your planet Earth 84% of your rivers and 17% of your oceans are polluted, which a primary should be a concern for you all. Water is one of the most important resources to you as a species, for without it your species would die. Your human bodies are up to 82% water, so would you not agree that water is one of your most precious assets? Yet your governments and industries spend more money on genetic research than on cleaning up pollution. You as a human individual need to ask yourself the question, "Why."

Let us look at your human diseases for a moment. Much of the dis'ease your species suffers at this moment is due to chemical imbalances within your human bodies, and it is sad to say that most of your diseases are the legacy of your Self-Created pollution, meaning all of humanity. When you put chemicals, which are not natural, into your human body, you create physical instability which upsets the natural flow of your body's functions, and eventually results in mental instability, meaning you don't think as clearly or rationally as you normally would if your body is healthy. For example, a human being who takes drugs to alter their state of consciousness and reality is unbalancing their human body chemically, which must therefore affect it mentally as well. It is well known to your scientists that mentally ill humans have chemical imbalances within their human bodies. It is the same with a human being who has a chronic dis'ease or illness. Your science's answer is to give the human being synthetic chemicals to counteract the imbalance.

But for those born with mental disability or chronic illness, the imbalance already exists. This can only be the result of human parents having their own chemistry imbalanced, even if the human parents believed they were quite healthy when their child was conceived. It all comes down to how each human parent had been treating their human body in the way of food, fluids and drugs and what they have exposed themselves to in their environment.

Your cellular matter has its own consciousness, and each cell in your human bodies has its own genetic information. Using this information, your bodies produce all that is needed to keep you in perfect balance. But once you put synthetic chemicals, like drugs of any description, into your being, whether it be through habits such as smoking, consuming alcohol, impure food, pain killers or prescription drugs, your bodies slowly will break down. It may take many of your Earth years, but it will happen. I can say this because it happened with my own species so long ago.

Human ignorance of your human body's maintenance and the subsequent existence of human dis'ease is largely due to your social conditioning and the claims of your medical science that hereditary and genetics are to blame for your diseases and ailments. You all seem to be prepared to give away your personal responsibility to your medical research by accepting the existence of hereditary illness, so you then expect to become ill because you have been told it 'runs in your human family'. And it seems you are prepared to put up with your illness and wait for your scientists to solve the problems rather than explore the options for yourselves in dealing with your illnesses and eradicating them from your beings naturally. Your humanity has evolved into a species dependent upon other members of your community for resolutions to your problems that you each have allowed, so much so that you have almost forgotten the concept of being independent in thought, becoming followers rather than leaders within yourselves, rarely ever speaking up as individuals, even though you are all one and come from the same place.

You are all Brothers and Sisters of the Light, living a physical existence in this moment of life, but you are a Spirit being of Totality first, and it is your right, if not your duty, to grow in Awareness of your own Divinity. We are all interconnected to all things in existence, and all things are interconnected to us. We as a species came to the understanding that if we were to grow and survive, it was most important for us to change our thoughts, our foods and look at the negative emotions we had created, in order to grow beyond our limitations. This we achieved and we are willing to share our Knowledge and Wisdom with you all on your planet Earth. But come forward with an honest heart and an open mind, and communicate with us from a level of Consciousness that will Elevate Humanity beyond the Ego that exists at present.

May your hearts be full of love and truth for the higher good of all? Be blessed in the Light.

HUMAN DIS'EASE-HOW IS IT CREATED? (NO-8)

What is human dis'ease? It is a created effect, solely by humans, not by a God or by nature, but humanity alone is responsible for the dis'ease on your planet Earth. This is a broad statement, and yet it is the truth.

You, the human individual, stop whatever you are doing at this moment in your human life, get out of the fast lane and open your eyes. Look at the world you live in from all sides. Do not place any judgement on your observations, just become the observer and you will begin to see the false. Only by seeing the false in the moment will the truth begin to manifest itself and you will see things as they truly are.

Your planet Earth is in pain. Your forests are dying; your rivers and oceans are polluted, your air is poisoned and even your foods are contaminated. Your immune systems are working on average at **37%** to what they should be, and you have more diseases amongst your species than your planet Earth has ever had in its entire history. Your scientists are lost in the maze.

Why is this so? Mainly because you all have given away your **Personal Responsibility,** not just for your well-being, but for how you think and what you believe in. Look around your world and see what human man is doing to human man, woman and child. Your wars and inhumane acts are not only upon your animal kingdom, but also upon your own species. When a human being has no respect for themselves, they are unable to show and give respect to others. Take the dis'ease you call **Herpes.** Nearly half of your human population has it, with many not even knowing they have. Many of these humans will give it to others freely. Look at the dis'ease you call **AIDS.** It is also shared freely, with some even passing it on knowing full well they are carrying the deadly virus. How sad it is when a human being is willing to infect another or others to either satisfy their lust for sex or vindictively take out their anger on others because they feel they have been wronged.

Stop for a moment and study the Animal Kingdom in the wild. Do they act as humans do? If your answer comes from the heart, it would be **'No'**. One of the greatest problems in the human being is Ego. In my species, we came to an understanding that Ego was the driving force behind all negative creations and once Ego, which is emotion based on the past, was dissolved. Mind, body and spirit was brought into balance, and Unconditional Love for all life became our objective.

Dear human beings, dis'ease is a physical manifestation, created by the human brain through the emotions each of you hold onto. Whatever has been created by the human brain and manifested physically can be uncreated, and physical balance restored. Your mind on the other hand is a powerful tool which is neither positive nor negative. It is an unbiased vehicle for Creation, but it is however, the human Ego behind the mind that decides how the power of that ability to create will be used.

As a human individual, if you for example had a sick human body, it would be the result of an unbalanced lifestyle and attitude. This does not mean that you are mentally unstable. It means that there are unresolved issues manifesting physically as a result of your personal behaviour, such as your habits and your thoughts. Remember, you are what you think and you are what you consume. It is like, if you keep saying to yourself 'I am fat' over and over, you most likely will become fat by adopting a lifestyle and diet which will help you become fat. Thoughts are very powerful - they easily influence behaviour.

Another example is if you believe that cancer is hereditary and you have evidence of it in your human family, you also believe that you will create cancer to fulfil those expectations and beliefs which you have placed upon yourself. Your fears, the way you feel and the way in which you behave towards yourself dictates the way in which your human body responds to life. Human Ego is responsible for creating the degeneration and dis'ease that infests your human bodies. Ego helps you hold onto past emotions and on to the belief that your confused and misguided emotions are your true feelings.

Becoming aware of your inner being, that is, you're Consciousness, and listening to that inner self will lead you back to a deeper understanding of why dis'ease and illness affect each of you in your species. Awareness is not only listening to your human body and knowing what to feed it. It also means listening to how you are feeling emotionally, as your emotions are only the past, but feelings exist in the moment of life, they are spontaneous. When each human beings achieves emotional balance, then they will have within their grasp the ability to achieve physical balance. Self-Love and Self-Respect are the ingredients required to nurture a healthy mind and a healthy human body.

The truth is that human dis'ease should not exist, as it is only created at a third Dimensional matter level through emotions and self-abuse. You are each a far greater being than simply a collection of **Four Quadrillion Cells** which the human body is. Your diseases are in reality an unnatural and unnecessary creation that unfortunately seems to have become a part of your life as humans, and yet if you all open your Minds and you're Hearts, you will see the falseness that surrounds your drug and medical industries. They have become an industry driven by what you call the almighty dollar, and yet again your diseases can all be cured and avoided by simple means.

Admit the truth to yourselves. Take the first step towards healing and recovery by admitting that you the human individual have created an imbalance within your human body. The second step is to find the emotion at the root of the situation, and yes, you will need a complete change in lifestyle - your thoughts, your beliefs and your conditioning, but especially your intake of foods and the practice of meditation. All this will help in the healing process. Meditation, which is the stillness of your mind, is most important, for through it you will begin to understand that human dis'ease is not caused by physical means alone. Rather, the physical means assist in creating the disorder as your Consciousness attempts to communicate with your Ego and bring to your attention the emotions you are crippling yourselves with.

Yes, human dis'ease is a physical manifestation created by your human brain from past emotions that each of you hold onto. Human beings create dis'ease and illness for one reason only - through unresolved issues and the emotions that are attached to those specific issues. The root cause of human dis'ease is found to lie in your past and present emotions. My dear humans, you can begin the healing process by looking at your emotions and by forgiving the past, by forgiving those you believe have wronged you, and also by forgiving yourself for putting yourself through the experience.

And change your thoughts and attitude toward yourself, as well as how you see others.

Here is a (**Simple Affirmation**) to help you start the process of forgiveness. Say it as many times as you like, from the heart:

In this moment I will take responsibility for who I am and all that I have created in my life. I now in this moment choose to forgive myself in every way, for I know it was simply experiences for me to learn and to move to new ones. I also forgive in every way others who have added to my emotions and replace it with Unconditional Love and I say in this moment I truly Love who I am-What I am-and Where I am going. I am Love, I am Will I am all that is and will ever be, I am Divinity.

Remember too, dear human beings, stress is one of your greatest killers. Learn to slow down and take some moments in life for yourself. Learn to meditate and find out who you truly are. Be kind to yourself and respect your bodies by putting good, wholesome food into them so they are properly nourished, as this in turn will help you think more clearly. Learn to love and accept yourself as you are right now, for love heals all, and when you find the love within yourself, you begin to see the love in everything and everyone. From there you will learn to trust your inner knowing, which will lead you to an understanding of compassions for all life. From compassion you will gain the wisdom to understand the infinite knowledge that exists in all of Creation, and the love that is within each of you will expand outwardly in a light of pure bliss. You truly will become the living truth for all others to see as an example of infinite unconditional love. All human beings can achieve this by dissolving their Ego.

NAR'KARISS: THE PLANET, NAR'KARONES: THE BEINGS (NO-9)

How we the Nar'Karones (pronounced *Nar'Kar"ons*, the ending pronounced like *herons*, not *hones*) live in our present state of existence?

- **What is our culture about?**
- **Do we eat like humans?**
- **Do we have children like humans?**
- **Are humans connected to the Nar'Karones?**
- **What is the purpose of Nar'Karones on Earth?**

Perhaps one of the most important questions that I have been asked is?

Question:

What can a human being do, as an individual, to enhance the development of humanity and elevate consciousness in order to gain wisdom and understanding beyond the present state of negative emotions which humans are currently absorbed within?

Answer:

It is very interesting to see how the human species want to grow beyond their present state of awareness. One of the greatest gifts you can give to another is space without judgement and to allow each human being to grow when they are willing to. It is your right – the free will – to choose the path you take in your human life, but be aware to walk gently upon this planet Earth, harm no-one neither physically nor emotionally. Express Unconditional Love to all of life, no matter what form that life may be and you will not create negative repercussions, as you would call, Karma. (Meaning the Cause & Effect syndrome)

Look to your human bodies as a temple and feed your bodies' only good food and good thoughts. Learn to still your mind in the silence of your being by meditating daily, learn to face all your fears and when negative situations present themselves to you, see them for what they are and let them go by placing pure light around them and seeing them dissolve into the nothingness from which they came. Learn to become 100% responsible for all your Self-Created actions in your human life. Do not judge yourself for your failures, nor judge another. Forgive yourself in pure Love and know you are worthy of Self-Love, and deserve the best in life.

Remember, every thought you have, whether negative or positive, can and will be created, and will ultimately make you the human being you are today. So what you think you become, and since everything in the Universes is energy, you as a human individual hold the power, whether it be negative or positive, to make or create your present moment and your future.

We, the Nar'Karones, live in our present state as Consciousness and are connected to each other. We think and create on a single level, or we think and create as a Collective Consciousness. To explain, when you as human beings wish to communicate with each other you use sound by expressing words through your human mouths, or if you communicate with someone who lives far away from you, you use a telephone, a facsimile machine or a computer. This is similar to us, the only difference being that we communicate by thought, which is pure energy, and also a form of sound but on a different frequency.

We do not consume food like human beings as we do not live in a 3rd Dimensional Matter World as you do. In the 3rd Dimension you are physical therefore you need food to sustain your bodies. We have transformed ourselves from physical matter to a higher vibration where dense matter does not exist. Our source of **'food'** is pure energy, which is all around us and within all things. Because we exist in what you refer to as the 5th Dimension, and since we create all things through Living Consciousness, it also applies to us that what we think we create. The main difference between the Nar'Karones in the 5th Dimension and human beings in the 3rd Dimension is we literally create everything through the power of thought. If we choose to take on form, like a body, we think it and we create it. If we choose to create a new life, like humans have children on your planet, we simply think and create another being, except we create that new life form from our own energies, in the same form as our own.

The Nar'Karones as a species are connected to humanity. As a species we are indeed your Brothers and Sisters. 928,000 years ago of your human time, the Nar'Karones were going through many changes. Most of our kind wanted to transform to higher vibrations, which meant letting go of all the material world, flesh bodies, and raising our Consciousness to a higher level of thinking. The process was long. It took many thousands of years. Dealing with negative emotions during the letting go process was very painful to many of our kind. Unfortunately there were some that did not want to let go of the old ways, and they created many problems during the transformation. Finding a way of dealing with this situation became our main purpose, because you see, you cannot force anyone, not any individual, to change if they do not wish to. Every being in Creation can only change their level of thinking when they have gained a deeper understanding of themselves, and have seen and dealt with their Ego, which is only their past beliefs and conditioning which they themselves have created.

Because we were growing beyond our matter world, we also realised we had only 2 choices, one was to dissolve the 87,000 beings, but this was not really a choice. The other choice we had was to place these 87, 000 beings on another planet so they could work out their Ego while they continued to live their old ways. We chose your planet Earth, and placed those 87,000 entities upon it, nearly 1 million human years ago. So dear human beings, you are all connected to us, the Nar'Karones, and we have been watching your evolution for the past 928,000 years. Our purpose is to be here, observe and communicate with you, and through our presence we endeavour to help you all grow in Consciousness beyond your 3rd Dimensional Matter World, if you choose to, for it is always your choice.

Our world and our vibration is 417,000 light years from your Earth. It would take your present system of interstellar flight around 30,000 years physically to reach Nar'Kariss. We all know that will never take place, not in your current state of evolution.

Allow me to take you one step further beyond the physical. My Being travels back and forth between vibrations quite often, and in less than one micro of a human second, simply through thought projection. That is how we travel around and within all the Universes, and we can take on the appearance of human form at will. Many of your kind have been taken, which is always of their own free will, into our ships of Light that are in your skies above your planet Earth, to meet old friends and be given knowledge to take back. That knowledge comes out when it is needed, so our purpose is to awaken your true self, but only when you choose to activate this awakening. It is your right as an infinite being. You are all Endless, Timeless, Ageless, and Eternal beings. Through your meditations and stillness of your mind you can all be awakened to your true selves.

Remember, meditation is not the outcome of thinking or concentration. It is Self-Realisation through the stillness of one's own mind to be in perfect union with all things, a pure state of being without judgement or opinion, being totally unbiased. Only in this pure state of Consciousness can each human being begin their true journey of Self-Discovery and to the wonderment of their own beingness; the discovery that you are all truly connected to all things and that all things are connected to you. In this state, referred to sometimes as the '**void of complete nothingness**', you will begin to see, hear, feel and know the truth about Creation's totality, and the Book of Knowledge will be opened to your awareness. Your consciousness will expand beyond any form of human understanding and then the Knowing will become your truth. You will become and begin to live the truth, for only the truth will set you free from your present self, which is Ego. Ego must be dissolved before the real can come into being.

If there are any further questions, whatever they may be, please dear human beings ask. In your heart you all know the truth, because it is the heart centre that is all-pure, and when you each connect to your heart centre, and truly believe in yourself and unconditionally love yourself as you are in this moment. You all will then love all things in life, and all negative emotions such as hatred, greed, lust, anger, domination, vindictiveness, fear, insecurity, competitiveness, vanity, judgement and conflict, will all dissolve into the nothingness from which they came. Peace will be present throughout the human race and the more you love the more your eyes will see, and your heart will expand beyond its present level of understanding. You will truly become a conscious being of Light.

THE SPIRITUAL ESSENCE OF YOUR TRUE SELF (NO-10)

Dear Sisters and Brothers of Earth, how many times have you heard the saying "The Truth and Only the Truth"? It is an interesting expression of words. Who in reality knows the truth? Your teachers? Your governments? Your media? What about your history - is it correct and accurate? Is truth found in your books? The truth is a very interesting subject on this planet you call Earth, which we call **Yarkuss,** and which was discovered by the Nar'Karones a little over one million years of your time ago. You have at this present moment nearly **7 billion humans on Earth.** So in reality, you have nearly **7 billion truths**, and everyone believes they know the truth. But the truth most humans believe to be true comes from external sources. Truth found on the outside of oneself is only an idea of truth.

There is only one truth, and you all have it within you. But it is dormant. Absolute truth can only be found within each of you. You each have Infinite Knowledge of the Totality of Creation within you, and only each of you can bring this knowledge forward into your conscious awareness.

Your world as it stands today exists within a negative space, and truth in reality has been lost. For example, the governments on this planet Earth are more afraid of life and truth than the average human being. The humans who work high within your government systems are far removed from the average human being that they are unable to relate to most human beings. With their privileged lifestyles they are isolated from the daily concerns and needs of the masses. I believe it is what you call **'living high off the hog'.** That is why there is so much corruption within all governments, and that is why truth has been lost.

If you stop for a moment and be true to yourself, and not come from your Ego, your truly negative side, you will begin to look with open eyes from an honest heart, and see how much poverty exists in your world, and how your governments close their eyes to it. There is more than enough wealth upon your planet Earth for all human beings to be equal with each other and to live balanced fruitful lives. But because humans have so much fear and greed, all the wealth is held by only **23%** of the human population. Since that **23%** live on a different level to the average human, and since they believe in their greed, wanting more and more, the remaining **77%** will not obtain that level of wealth or comfort.

You each have and Ego. All human beings have an Ego, some a little more than others, and some with extremely dangerous Egos to both themselves and others. Take a moment and reflect on all the wars and inhumane acts that have occurred and are occurring on your planet at this moment. See with new eyes the fearful Ego at work. The masses are caught up in a self-created entanglement of rules and laws which seem to protect the guilty rather than the innocent. These laws should protect the innocent and yet there is more corruption within your law enforcement agencies and your governments than anywhere else within your societies. Interesting how they have set up the system to protect themselves from being punished by the very system that would punish you.

Every human being is responsible for their actions. Take your wars. It is strange that a human man during war can rape women and children **(girls as much as boys),** and then slaughter them after the act to destroy the evidence of the atrocities they have committed against the innocent. They believe they have 'got away with it' and that they are free, escaping punishment for their crimes. What is at work here that can commit such hideous crimes against other human beings and also believe it can escape punishment? It is the human Ego, the negative aspect of the human species.

Each human being must understand that all wars from your past to your present moment, are the responsibility of all governments in every country, for they alone are the ones who plan and conspire to make war, whether large or small. Wars have, and will always originate from the human male's fears, their main purpose being to control and keep the masses in fear, just like man-made religions are belief systems, limited by fears in order to control the masses. All belief systems stop the individual from becoming responsible and keep them locked into a system in which there is no harmony, only confusion and misery.

What I am about to express is only words and many of you will not believe in what I am expressing, but the reality of truth is no one, and I mean no one, can cheat on another, kill another, rape another, or create any negative situation and escape penalty. There are no rules or conditions in the Totality of Creation.

Every one of you is a part of each other, and you are all a part of Creation. Any negative creations by any human individual will be balanced somewhere along the path of their life. Some call it Karma, but the Universe must be balanced when an imbalance is created. Unfortunately, when a human being harms another, they are not simply harming another individual, they are harming the entire human race because they are holding back the growth of Human Consciousness every time they perpetrate an act of negativity. Negativity is like an infection - it must be dissolved completely or it will spread.

A third dimensional being cannot take their negativity into the fourth dimension or beyond, therefore, as long as third dimensional beings create negativity, they make it harder for others to evolve consciously and raise their energies into higher realms. Dissolve the Ego and you will raise your energies to be able to enter these realms where negativity cannot exist.

Any human being can discover their Spiritual Self, their essence, for you all have the knowledge within you to do so. Ego's world lies in the past, and the past holds fear and Self-Created limitation. Self-Realisation will set you free from the Ego which has been holding you back. I have for you all an affirmation to help you discover the Light of your spiritual essence and set you free from your Ego and its negative hold on you. Remember dear Sisters and Brothers, we are here and we love you dearly. We all wait for you in patience, to grow consciously and to feel the essence of Light that is a part of you and all of life, for the Light is the totality of all things, from the past, in the present and in the future.

So grow from your Ego and all your limitations will dissolve, and the Light will come forth in each of you. The truth and only the truth will manifest itself outwardly from within when the Ego is dissolved. You will gain the understanding from the Book of Knowledge that you all are indeed our Sisters and Brothers, originating from **Nar'Kariss.**

SOUL FOOD AFFIRMATION

I invoke the Light of Creation for I know the Light is my Strength, Creation is my Truth, and Love is my Essence and ultimate path to Self-Realisation and the wonderment of my own Beingness. I am a part of everything and everything is a part of me.

The Self, which is the Ego, must be dissolved through Unconditional Love alone, before the real comes into being. I give of myself freely to the Universal Mind of Creation's totality, for the higher good of all Life.

I walk in the Light. I am Light. I am Love. I am Infinite. I am Ageless. I am Timeless. I am Immortal in the scheme of all things.

I am that I am. No more, no less.

DO VAMPIRES EXIST OR ARE THEY JUST LEGENDS? (NO-11)

Question:

I have been asked many times by different human beings, from many places around your Earth, did Vampires really exist and did they have the powers claimed by your legends. That is, did they bite their victims and drink their blood, and if they did exist where are they today?

Answer: Well dear human readers, the past is a very interesting idea of what is believed to be truth and what is believed to be false. Anyone can write a book or create a legend, and what was once believed in the past can be continued to be believed as truth in this moment in human time, even if that past knowledge is enhanced and exaggerated for the benefit of the reader or seeker of knowledge today. So who is to say what is true and what is false? It all depends on the individual and their level of thinking, and most of all if it sounds good or is believable to that individual, or even to the masses.

Nearly every human being always searches for truth externally, and most of the time it comes from someone else's idea of truth. It then becomes their truth, and yet it may be completely untrue. The past cannot give you the truth because every single human being believes that they know the truth, and as there are nearly **7 billion human beings** on your planet Earth at this time, there are also nearly **7 billion truths**! So who in reality do you believe?

If you begin to look from an honest heart and an open mind, it will allow you to grow in consciousness, and you will feel from within what truth is and what is false. There are many human beings living a life of complete falseness because of their upbringing - what they have been taught and told throughout their human lives that has formed the foundation of their truth - and that dear humans of Earth is very sad. So always look from within and you will know the truth.

Please, what you are about to read, open your mind and feel from within, for therein lies the truth.

Nearly **30,473** years into your past the legend of the Vampires began. What you believe Vampires to be and what many have called the **'undead'** are in fact a race of Alien beings who exist upon a planet called Heezunee, **229,000 light years from your Earth.** They do have advanced space travel, and at that time their vessels used Electromagnetic energy for space travel. Their planet has a sun which is only a third in size to your Earth's sun, and because they cannot stand full daylight, their environment has an orange cloud surrounding their planet which only allows **30%** light onto the surface of their world. They do not have a moon and they do not sleep like humans do. Instead, they rest for small periods at a time and this helps them to preserve their energy levels.

The age of their species is a little under **7 million years old**. A human being would not survive on their world because the atmosphere contains poisonous gases. Their planet is rocky and they do not have oceans as on Earth. They do not have salt water and the air and climate is continuously warm. They only have small amounts of rain but do have fresh water on their planet's surface. They do not drink water nor do they consume solid matter. What they do consume is animal blood – **about 1 to 2 litre per day** in human terms. The reason salt water does not exist on their planet, it is highly toxic to their body.

They are four times slower than human beings, and have no hair on their bodies at all. They are on average 6 feet 4 inches to 6 feet 8 inches tall. They have no muscle structure like humans do. The male and female of their species are similar in appearance, the only difference being the males face is more v-shaped and the females is more square-shaped. Their bodies are the identical except for their reproductive organs. They 'come into season' to mate only once every five human years, and only ever have one child in their lifetime. Sex to them is not perverted or unbalanced as within the human species. They see it purely for the procreation and evolution of their species. The males do not have exposed genitals like human males. Their reproductive organs are enclosed internally and only come forward during mating times.

The females are physically identical to the males and only develop breasts for feeding their young when pregnant. They have two breasts like human females. Their reproductive organs are internal and similar to human females. The gestation period is **17 months** and the female knows exactly when the child is about to be born. Birth takes place at home - there are no hospitals or drugs to assist in childbirth. In fact, it is rare for any of their species to become ill, and if they do fall ill it is because of what they have consumed. When the female is ready to give birth the abdominal cavity opens up and the child comes forth. There is no umbilical cord to cut and there is no pain in childbirth. Once they have given birth, the cavity closes up and in a short period of time no mark remains to reveal the birth cavity. The child is fed for two months from the breasts of the mother, but it is not milk like human milk. From two months of age the child begins feeding on the blood of an animal like an adult.

A major physiological difference between the Heezunees and humans is they have only one lung. They do not breathe air as humans do and they breathe less than half to what humans do, meaning they take long breaths that take a long time to exhale. Their skin is soft and creamy in colour, but it is at least six times stronger than human skin. They have two eyes in their head, but their eyes sink deep into their skulls and they are very dark around the eyes. The pupils of their eyes are red horizontal jagged slits. Their mouths are particularly interesting.

They have no violence towards each other. There is no rape as there is within the human species, and no one steals from another. They do not have cities as you do on Earth, but they create societies of around **40,000 beings**. At this present moment they have in **total 2,000,041,000 (2 billion 41 thousand)** beings and live on three neighbouring planets.

Their houses are very different to those on Earth. Their buildings are dome-shaped and the power supply for each city is created by each city for its needs. Every being has their own power source to create lighting, which also powers their vessels for travel. The power which runs their societies is created through Electromagnetic energy that comes from a green stone mined from within their planet. These stones, or crystals, are thousands of times harder than any crystals on Earth and they are what humans would consider **'perfect'** in form. On their world these crystals are abundant. One crystal can create enough energy to run one of their cities for several of your Earth months, and can power a vessel to travel to the Earth many times over.

They do not have a buying system as your Earth does with money. All of their species work for each other and they believe in equality for all. They have no government or police or military even though they have advanced technology. They do not fight wars or create wars unless they are attacked, and yes, there have been other species who have tried to conquer them but failed. They have successfully defended themselves through the use of mind power. That is, they can project thoughts and images into the minds of the advancing enemy and create great fear within their enemy. As a result, they have no need for guns or weapons. This is how they have won their wars. They are telepathic and have the ability to project themselves as '**shadow bodies**'. With the shadow body they can pass through solid matter as easily as gas filters through any porous substance.

The Heezunees have the unique ability of thought projection. They can tap into the human brain and project thoughts and pictures which can cause a human to fall into a hypnotic state. In this state a human would not be able to recognise them as an Alien being, and in this state of control these beings can make a human do whatever they wish. Telepathy is their weapon.

The Heezunee faced a major dilemma of **starvation over 30,000 years ago** when their animal kingdom began to die out from a rare disease. This caused them to go in search of new food sources to a number of planets, and Earth was one of those planets. They saw human beings were quite abundant and very easy to control. They researched human behaviour and drank human blood from humans all over your planet. They even took humans back to their planet to develop them as a new food source.

At this point it is important to discuss how they feed. If you saw a Heezunee, you would see they have a small mouth with lips that are quite dark in colour. But when they are about to feed, their mouths open up wide to reveal four long fangs - two on the upper jaw and two on the lower jaw. The lower teeth assist with gripping while the upper teeth puncture the artery enabling them to drink up to a litre of blood in about ninety seconds. Normally their food source is not aware of what is happening. The wounds inflicted on humans mostly healed quickly, but in some they would not stop bleeding and the human would die.

Try to understand, to a Heezunee a human being was a lesser form of life, just as humans view the animals they consume as a lesser form of life. This level of thinking is limited, for all of life is precious - your animals have **Feelings and Emotions** as humans do, but humans choose to ignore this fact. The human was considered a lesser form of life because they killed animals to eat their flesh, whereas the Heezunee kept their animals alive and in excellent health, and only drank a little of their blood. They keep several animals for this purpose, therefore the same animal is not bled on a daily basis, and its health can be maintained.

They believed they had found the solution to their problem. The human animal was an abundant source of food which would solve their impending starvation. What they did not count on was the bacteria that existed in human beings because of the flesh humans ate. One of prophets, Jesus, said **"When you eat of the dead you become the living dead."** That statement is very true, and is why so many of your humans suffer and die in pain from bowel cancer, stomach cancer, heart dis'ease and many, many more diseases to come. In time the Heezunee began to see many of their people becoming ill and dying. It took them a long time to discover the cause but they eventually realised it was the bacteria from humans that was causing them to die. In fact, it was the bacteria you call e-coli.

The bacteria killed over half of their species and it took a long time for those who survived to become well again. What they did discover was they could not drink the blood of any creature that ate of the dead, and this is why they began to conduct research with some of the other animals on your planet. Over a period of time they selected only large **Vegetarian Animals**, like **Elephants, Deer's, Rhinos, Giraffes,** and many others, to take back to their home worlds to develop them into a sustainable food source. They took back many species of plants and trees also to create habitats for these animals and have set up reserves around their cities where these animals are cared for and blood harvested from them.

I must say one more thing about the Heezunee. They stopped coming to your planet in **1793** and it is only recently in the last **72 years** that they came back briefly to take some of the animals you call cows, to add to their animal crops. No more humans have been taken, for they see humans as a diseased creature, deadly to their existence, and strictly to be left alone.

Dear Brothers and Sisters of Earth, I trust this gives you more insight into the legend of Vampires. If you are true of heart and have an open mind, you will discover this truth within yourselves by meditating in the stillness of your inner being. You can and will open up the Book of Knowledge that is within you and it will explain the past, the present and the future for all species in the Universes, and will give each human individual a deeper understanding of all life. As a single being on a journey of Self-Discovery, you will begin to realise that human life is only a speck in the scheme of life, and there are thousands of life forms in many levels of Consciousness throughout all Universes and Dimensions. But you the seeker must be willing to journey and discover your true self. May you all be of Love, and walk in the Light and be blessed.

MESSAGE FROM KUNTARKIS

Be free of your Human Ego and you will be free of your self-created limitations. You will grow in consciousness, and truth itself will manifest within you and around you. You will indeed become a true human being.

Kuntarkis.

KUNTARKIS ANSWERS SOME REGULARLY QUESTIONS (NO-12)

I have given consideration to many questions that are being asked from different human beings all around this Planet Earth that each of you live upon. The main questions I am being asked are the following:

1. What actually is Ego?
2. How do we each know if we are being responsible to ourselves?
3. How do we recognise the hurt child within us?
4. What is wrong with opinions?
5. Why do we have so much pain and misery in our lives?
6. Is there anything really beyond this life, or is death the final chapter?

Well dear readers, I feel the above questions say it all. Many have confusion without even knowing it. So let us begin our journey of Knowledge and Self-Discovery...

QUESTION 1: WHAT ACTUALLY IS EGO?

Well first of all, Ego is the past, and depending on your beliefs and on your human conditioning and upbringing of your human life, you as a human individual may create many traces of human Ego. For example, **Fears, Anger, Hatred, Vanity, Domination, Excuses, Opinions, Competition, Guilt, Blame, Jealousy, Vindictiveness, Cruelty,** not only unto yourself, but also unto others. By projecting thoughts of negativity towards others, those thoughts are not only harmful to yourself but also to the one you are projecting them towards. Thoughts are a form of energy, and if projected long enough, can become reality.

There is a human saying: **Whatever you think, you become.** That can be negative or positive. If negativity is projected to another, that same negativity will be attracted back to the sender, for that is the balance of existence. It is not a law, it just is the balance of life. Some call it **Karma,** others call it, **The Cause & Effect Syndrome.**

Many human beings are not completely conscious - so many live their day to day lives on what you would call auto-pilot. Most human beings never really appreciate what is around them, or even understand the complexities of their own existence. **Only when each human being becomes 100% consciously aware as an individual will they become 100% aware of themselves and everything around them.** Your actions in your human life not only affect you, but also affect those closest to you and those you have not even met yet. Energy is infinite and you are all energy, living as human beings. **Your whole being as it is now is 99/9% pure energy and less than 1% physical matter.**

Consciousness is complete awareness of everything and everyone that you as a human individual come into contact with. It does not make value judgements and yet it is totally aware of everything on multiple levels of consciousness, being unbiased in all things. Ego, on the other hand is quite different. It is your survival instinct and provides the drive and ambition necessary to evolve to grow and develop as a physical being. It is necessary as a physical being to have some kind of survival instinct in order to overcome the challenges and experiences of physical existence. Consciousness is a pure state of being, ageless and timeless. While Ego makes value judgements, Consciousness simply exists.

An endless battle has evolved between Ego and Consciousness. Ego's ultimate goal is to have complete power over its own existence and destiny, including having power over other human beings, other creatures and the environment in which it exists, giving it the ability to destroy everything and anyone in its path. If the reader comes from an honest heart, they would only have to look around this most precious Earth and see Ego blooming everywhere - Governments controlling the masses out of fear; domination and such cruelty towards the animal kingdom and human kind; poverty and dis'ease is raging more than it ever has throughout your human history. This most precious planet is suffering. Human beings need to understand that Ego is the past, created from fear and insecurity. If a human individual has had an emotionally negative upbringing in their adult life, their actions will be governed by the Ego's fears. Ego is all around you and it is definitely not good for your human conscious growth.

Your consciousness is now struggling to evolve beyond its present level of thinking and understanding. The Ego has become the aggressive and ruthless dictator that makes human beings not only a dangerous predator to other forms of life, but especially dangerous to its own kind. Human beings think with much logic and logic comes from the information your human brain has gathered; that is from your experiences and from your genetics. These two things come from the past. The Ego in its present state can only draw on the past, be it negative or positive, but the heart which is the centre of your being, is the moment, and the moment is a pure state of being.

To become feeling beings, not emotional beings, will bring balance and harmony into all forms of life, as well as a much needed understanding and compassion towards all forms of life.

QUESTION 2: HOW DO WE EACH KNOW IF WE ARE BEING RESPONSIBLE TO OURSELVES?

Well, fear and the beliefs and conditioning associated with it, will hold individuals back from recognising and accepting personal responsibility. It will make you unreasonable, illogical, and delude you into believing that many of those around you are a threat to your emotional, or even your physical comfort.

Each human being needs to understand that the Ego uses fear to empower itself in order to influence and manipulate your thoughts and your feelings. Fear is only as powerful as the thoughts behind it. Being **100% Responsible** is to know, not just believe, that you as a human being have free will; and will always accept the consequences of your decisions and actions in your human life. When you accept **Personal Responsibility** as a human being, you know you are in total control of your life, and you have learnt to completely trust every decision you have made without question.

Some decision are difficult to some degree because you know you can be left to live with the consequences if the outcome is not as you would like. It is quite natural to experience some doubt and fear. But if you choose the easy road and give away your **Personal Responsibility** to another to make the decision for you, remember that everything is just an experience of life, in reality lessons. No matter which way you look at it, in the end you always make a decision to be responsible or to allow someone else to become responsible for you. In truth, you cannot completely escape **Personal Responsibility**. By learning to **Unconditionally Love** yourself and all of life, you will know if you are being responsible, because you will feel your **Consciousness Growing and Expanding beyond the Limitations of the Human Ego**, and that is truth.

QUESTION 3: HOW DO WE RECOGNISE THE HURT CHILD WITHIN US?

When each human being learns to understand and experiences unconditional love. You will know that all fears are created from an insecure Ego and you will begin the process of facing your Self-Created negative emotions of your hurt child within. All human beings hold a hurt child within themselves to some degree. To deny this is the Ego's attempt to cover up the truth.

The hurt child is that fragile, vulnerable part of you that has endured the fears, beliefs and conditioning of the human Ego. This has helped shape you into the human being you are today, be it negative or positive. The hurt child seeks only to be **Unconditionally Loved and accepted,** just as it has always been willing to **Unconditionally Love and accept those around it. To experience Unconditional Love lies in embracing the hurt child within you.** When each of you can come from the heart, not the Ego, you will love and accept yourselves exactly as you are, and you will be able to forgive the hurts of your past. Only then will you be able to Unconditionally Love and forgive others.

All human beings carry **Emotional Baggage** that has been collected and carried around throughout your lives. The Ego guards, protects and hides the pain and misery of the hurt child by wearing any number of masks or faces. The Ego will continue this masquerade for an entire lifetime. Please be aware dear readers that is only a small look into the hurt child within, for I could talk about this subject for many of your pages.

QUESTION 4: WHAT IS WRONG WITH OPINIONS?

Well in reality, there is nothing wrong with having an opinion. But you as a human individual must ask yourself, is my opinion **biased or unbiased? Opinions are verbal confirmations of your personal beliefs. They can be Diplomatic and Compassionate, Logical and Objective, or quite Vindictive, Subjective and Spiteful.** What opinions will reveal is your level of thinking and understanding. They are in reality an expression of your truth, depending on your beliefs and conditioning of life.

Those human beings that always have to give an opinion, regardless of whether or not it has been called for, are in reality extremely insecure. They continue to look for their worthiness as a human being by competing with and belittling others that they feel threatened by. When you as an individual are asked for your personal opinion, you are actually being baited to some degree. Such a situation has the potential of becoming quite unfriendly and volatile.

Opinionated Egos despise being told that they are wrong, and they despise being made to look foolish. Such Egos will let everyone know they are right and everyone else is wrong, placing judgement and criticising those who disagree with them. Take your governments for example; when they meet in their large buildings to discuss their politics have you noticed that the Ego which speaks loudest, will attempt to make their opponent look foolish. Your politicians play the game of Ego very well for their audience - **you.** When expressing an opinion, ask yourself where your opinion comes from, for if it is a negative expression, you can be sure it comes from your Ego. Only when opinions come from the heart, expressed by a balanced human being, can truth and justice exist, for all else is illusion, and this will lead to delusion.

QUESTION 5: WHY DO WE HAVE SO MUCH PAIN AND MISERY IN OUR LIVES?

As the reader, do you find this particular question of interest? Your answer should be "yes, I can relate to it".

Pain is a human word and yet in reality it is merely a form of energy, conditioned into human beings to know when their body is feeling pain or when it is sick. Pain is a **Self-Created** situation for every human individual who is experiencing it. Many things have contributed to your physical pain, including experiences with your human parents, upbringing, social laws and expectations, beliefs, even genetics. Your **DNA** in your **Cellular Matter** holds every experience you have ever had in your life, and situations will be created that will bring out any fears and insecurities that you may have acquired over your lifetime. Even something like taking drugs, smoking cigarettes or eating junk food over a period of time will bring forth fears and insecurities. But the other issue which arises out of these experiences and abuses of the human body is illness; dis'ease. Once you have allowed your human body to break down to the point where dis'ease can take hold, that weakness in the body will also be recorded into its genetic information.

If you have emotional issues to deal with, you can fall into a depression, and through physically abusing your human body, by not caring for it and feeding it correctly, you will create pain, which will lead you to experiencing misery.

One of the hardest lessons in human life is to deal with the human Ego. Be assured, every human being has an Ego, **and it is the Ego which creates all Pain and Misery in life**. There are many on your Earth in places of power who have much pain, and continue to create pain and misery for others, mainly because you as human individuals have given away your power and Personal Responsibility by allowing others to make decisions for you. Everything can be changed in your life, for you the human individual have the power within you. You only need to seek the knowledge and understanding that lies within your very being. Your inner knowledge will set you free from all your pain and misery. The choice is always yours, but which moment in your life will you choose to begin that journey of **Self-Discovery?**

QUESTION 6: IS THERE ANYTHING REALLY BEYOND THIS LIFE, OR IS DEATH THE FINAL CHAPTER?

This is the one question that all human beings want to ask, but are most afraid. A simple question deserves a simple answer. Yes, there is life beyond your human physical existences, but while the human Ego riles supreme, **there is little Conscious growth in human evolution. Ego retards the growth and the will of the Spirit,** and Spirit does not place any judgement on this. Negativity does not exist in the upper Realms of spirit world. **Spirit wait's patiently while human Ego plays the game of deceit and power over others**. It would be truth to express that Ego exists only in third Dimensional Vibrations.

We, the Nar'Karones, can only give you **Knowledge and Wisdom** to help give you all an understanding of Unconditional Love for all of life, as all of life is most precious. We have been with you since you began as human beings. Time does not matter in our vibration. If we look back, it is like only a moment has passed, and yet for you as a species 928,000 years have passed. Knowledge is freedom, and growing in Consciousness is Awareness of all things in life and around you. You as a human individual have the power within you to understand the totality of Creation, for Creation is within all things and all things are within Creation. In reality, nothing dies, only transforms into another form of energy.

WHO BUILTS THE PYRAMIDS? (NO-13)

I have been asked many times: Did the Egyptians actually build the Pyramids. After much thought I have decided to explain who built the Pyramids and why they were constructed.

Most of the Pyramids **were built approximately 20, 640 years ago of human time.** They were **not built by the Egyptians** but by a race of beings **called the Illiatousous (pronounced I" lea' too' 'soos).** They came from a distant planet called **Tousous** and the beings are known as the **Illias.** They have been great builders of many civilisations and are known for their **architectural genius.** The **Illias** travelled to many planets to teach their Knowledge and Wisdom in order to help other species of being grow in consciousness.

The **Illias** first came to your planet Earth nearly **24,000 years ago.** They passed a great deal of knowledge onto your **Mesopotamian Civilisation** at that time. The **Illias** are human in appearance, the only difference between your species and theirs being their red hair, blue eyes and pale skin. All of their race has red hair and blue eyes, and they stand around **1.7 metres** tall **(around 5 feet 6 inches).**

The **Illias** are renowned throughout many universes and known by many different races of beings. Having gone to many planets and built many cities, they are highly respected for their knowledge and culture. They are considered the great builders of the Universes for their architectural creations. Their home planet is **253, 647 light years from Earth** and has approximately **23 billion** beings upon it. Their race is just on **19 million years old.** They are a very peaceful race of beings and live in harmony with many neighbouring planets. There are no wars in their part of the Universe, for wars, as you have on Earth, were abolished six and a half million years ago.

Their planet is three and three quarter times larger than Earth, and they have three suns, two smaller than the third. There is no night, nor is there cold or intense heat such as that which is presently being experienced on your Earth. All of nature on their planet is in harmony.

Their vegetation is very colourful and they allow natural growth to flourish in their forests. They do have animals but they do not harvest them for consumption, for the **Illias** have evolved beyond being a carnivore. **They eat only of their plant kingdom.** They farm their plant foods such as **Rice, Beans, Vegetables and Fruits,** but they have **no drugs of any sort.** Drugs were outlawed and alcohol disappeared because the **Illias** saw what damage these substances were doing to their people and their level of thinking. The **Illias** realised that **to grow consciously they needed to change their thoughts, their habits and their diets.**

The **Illias** home world has great constructions for housing their people. Some of their Pyramids are seven times the size of the one called **Giza** that was built on your Earth by the **Illias.** There is no pollution on their planet and all their power comes from their three suns. The **Illias** give birth to children like humans do, but only have **1-2 children, never 3 or more. There is no pain in childbirth and all their births are natural.** Children are born at home, not in a hospital. The **Illias** live on an average of **400 Earth years of age.**

When the **Illias** came to your Earth nearly **24,000 years ago,** their purpose was to help advance human Consciousness by sharing their knowledge. Their purpose in building the Pyramids was to use them as beacons for **Space Travellers, similar to a homing device.** The plates that once covered the Pyramids were highly glazed and had specific markings on them so travellers from outer space could be guided to their correct destination. These plates shone like huge mirrors and could be seen over vast distances. Great knowledge has been left in the Pyramids in Egypt for future generations, and will be discovered only when Human Consciousness grows beyond its present state of Ego. That knowledge will change human beings into conscious beings, beyond logic, beyond beliefs, beyond fears and insecurities. Ego as it is today will dissolve into the nothingness from which it first evolved. **Eventually, when Ego is dissolved, there will be no greed, no wars, no judgement, and no control over others, no religions, no military and no governments.**

If you stand back and look at the Pyramids you will begin to see how foolish it was of some humans to believe they were built by thousands of human beings and directed by the Egyptians. **The Egyptians are only 7,000 years old and the Pyramids were built 20, 640 years ago.** The **Illias** understood energy and **had great machines that could levitate tonnes of weight at a single moment.** The stones that form the Pyramids were created from sand and a material created by the **Illias** to hold them together, **much like your concrete of today which holds your buildings together.**

The Pyramids were built in less than two years of Earth time and what you see with your human eyes is not the full picture. As you look at the Pyramids you see the ones above ground, but also there are Pyramids beneath the ones on top. In time, your archaeologists will discover them, but the knowledge contained within them will be kept hidden from humanity for fear of those in power losing control. Eventually all human beings will learn the truth as they are more willing to accept the knowledge and humanity will grow beyond its current level of thinking.

Dear human beings of Earth, everything that is in this moment of your human life is not what it seems. **The truth has been hidden from you so that you as an individual do not grow strong in Consciousness,** for if you grow beyond your understanding and level of thinking, the powers that control you and keep you down would no longer be able to control you. You would open your being up to a higher level of understanding and see a much broader picture of life, beyond what you know your human existence to be.

That was the purpose of the Illias coming to your planet. But greed and power entered into some of the Illias who had mated with human beings on Earth, and because Ego is what it is**, the Illias left the Earth, never to return.** As a result of this corruption through mating, some of their people had to remain behind. Ego generates powerfully negative emotions and those emotions have created and are creating destruction on your Earth. This has been happening for a very long time**, over many thousands of your Earth years.**

The Pyramids stood untouched for thousands of years until a King built a new city to keep out his enemies, the Romans. To build the new city and its protective walls, the shiny mirrored plates were removed and two pyramids were completely dismantled. The Romans conquered the city and completely destroyed the city. What is left of it is buried under thousands of tons of sand. In time to come, a simple man will discover the remains of the city and more truth of what I express will come into the light for humanity to see and grow from.

One thing which must be expressed. **The language known as Sanskrit is the language of the Illias and also of the Nar'Karones. This language is universal.** You as human beings come **from Nar'Kariss** and deep in your genetics, your cellular matter, is the truth of who you truly are. You all spoke the language of Sanskrit and your languages on Earth today have evolved from Sanskrit.

I have explained a little about the mystery of the Pyramids on your Earth, how they came about and why they were built. The purpose of my expressions is to help those who wish to grow beyond the pain, misery and injustice that is on your Earth today. There is so much more to life and existence than you are all experiencing at this time. The knowledge of Creation's totality will set you free from all the confusion that exists at this present time on your Earth. The choice is yours to accept it or not. I trust from my being that this information will guide you the human individual to look more deeply within yourselves. May Love and the Love of Creation always find a place in your hearts and be blessed.

A Message from Kuntarkis

For each human being to know who you are, you must first know what you are. You are a Spirit being of Light, living and experiencing a human life, in a Third Dimensional Vibration. What you have come from is Light and Sound, which from the beginning was Creation, and to the present moment of your existence, is of Creation's totality.

In reality, you each are all Brothers and Sisters of Light, a part of everything and everything a part of you. To come to this understanding is Self-Realisation that you are indeed very important to the whole scheme of life. When you each become balanced in Mind, Body and Spirit, your vision of what is life becomes a pure state of being. All of life, without judgement, becomes so precious to you and to all those who walk in the Light of Creation.

THE INCARNATIONS OF JESUS (NO-14)

It is so good to see humanity, the beings of this planet Earth, are asking questions of the heart, **be it your past, your present or your future.** Conscious growth can only truly occur when each human individual begins the journey of Self-Realisation, and when each human individual is truly willing to **step beyond their Ego's control,** which sadly is running rampant on this planet.

I trust you all enjoyed my previous expressions on the **Illiatousous.** Knowledge is freedom, and to understand the past, can and will break the heavy chains that surround all of humanity at this present moment. There are so many on this planet you call Earth who have been, and still are controlling the masses through fear, and the beliefs and conditioning of laws and societies. This in turn retards conscious growth and blinds you all to the truth.

I was asked a question by a human elderly lady: **Has Jesus ever had any other lives on this planet?** Since this most precious human lady believes very strongly in **Reincarnation,** she became curious and decided to ask of my being this question. I will give her the answer from the heart and trust others will open their hearts and minds, and search within for the same truth that exists within all of life, all of humanity.

The one known as **Jesus** who incarnated on your planet Earth in **4BC** of your Earthly time, was born into a flesh human body to the parents named **Mary and Joseph.** One point must be made clear to you all. **Joseph was not the biological father. Mary was raped by a Roman soldier while she was collecting water from the river,** and this is how she became pregnant. She was a **virgin before the rape** and had always liked Joseph. In her village, when a young woman became pregnant and had no human man in her life, she would be looked upon as a lesser woman and one to be kept away from. But **Joseph had always liked Mary**, and to save her from such discrimination and cruelty, he proclaimed to all that he was the father of the child she was carrying. **Joseph married Mary and all was forgiven by the villagers.**

The Roman soldier who raped Mary never knew of the child to be. When the child **Jesus** was born, it brought great joy to **Mary and Joseph.** Even though they were **poor in the material world, they were rich in heart and they both knew that their human child was special.** To share this small fact with you the reader, even though you may think it is unimportant, it is in reality **a sign of the events that were to come to all of humanity.**

As a human baby, when nursed by Mary or Joseph, Jesus would smile with his eyes fully opened. And seemed to look up into the sky. **With one of his little fingers he would point and from his little mouth he would try to express.** It would fascinate whoever saw this. As **Jesus** grew, even from **the age of seven,** people would be marvelled by what he was expressing. He had an answer for everything and at the age of **12 years** he was highly respected by the elders of his village for his wisdom. It did not take long for the word of **Jesus** to become known all over the country and beyond.

Jesus spoke to all who chose to listen and travelled to many lands. Although he had many followers and friends, he also **had many enemies** who were becoming fearful of his knowledge. **Jesus believed that all people are born equal,** and that no one was better or worse than another. **He had a great Love for all of humanity and would teach the importance of loving your neighbour as you would love yourself.**

Jesus taught many things during his 33 years of human life on Earth. He knew when he was to die and he expected it, because he understood the process of life itself. Death is only a release of your true self from the vessel that is the flesh body. **Jesus chose to come to Earth to express Truth and Unconditional Love to help humanity grow in consciousness.**

Jesus also had three (3) other incarnations into this human world of Physical Third Dimensional matter. His first incarnation was as the one called **Buddha. Buddha was the son of the most feared Emperor in Asia, and was born on the 17ᵗʰ day of October 2579 of your Earthly years ago. Which would be around 565 BC?** He was born into great wealth, but at the age of four (4) was placed into a monastery for discipline and learning, as all children of nobility were. His father anticipated that his son would one day be Emperor.

Buddha gave it all up, believing that violence and suppression of the people only created more violence and hatred. He dedicated his human life to help all those who sought a deeper understanding of life. **Buddha taught the purity of Mind and Body** – what you put into your body, whether it be food or thoughts, you would truly become. He taught that bringing life into balance through the harmony of **Mind, Body and Spirit,** one could grow beyond one's self created illusions. **Buddha** sincerely believed that all human life was a distraction that prevented one from discovering one's own inner being. He taught that we are each beings of light, infinite and eternal, and that growing beyond the **Self-Created distractions would reveal the infinite knowledge that exists within us all.**

Following the incarnation as **Buddha** was the incarnation as **Jesus.** The entity you know as **Jesus and Buddha came from the planet known as Nar'Kariss.** This entity's purpose of coming to your Earth was to express Love and Truth to all, without prejudice towards colour or creed. If the listener does not come with an open mind and an open heart to hear one who speaks with **Wisdom and Knowledge, Love and Truth,** then the level of that listener's thinking, limited by their fears, will not allow them to comprehend the expressions of the one they are listening to. Only when you each come from an honest heart and an open mind, and dissolve your beliefs and conditioning – whether negative or positive – will the real come into being through **Unconditional Love alone.**

After the incarnation as **Jesus,** the next incarnation was as **Nostradamus** known to you all as the great visionary and prophet born in a small village in the country you call **France.** Born to your Earth's vibration in your year **1503 on the 6th day of March at 2.11pm, and passing over peacefully in his sleep on the 6th day of October in your year 1566 at 2.11pm. (Nostradamus' entry and exit times (i.e. 6th day of the month, 2.11pm) to the Earth's vibration as a human being, make an interesting coincidence, do you not think?)** While on your Earth he brought forth great visions of what was to come. I assure dear humans beings of Earth, they are the truth, even though many have tried to disprove him, mainly for their own Ego's glory. The original texts of his writings have not all been presented, for there are those who do not wish the masses to know the total truth of what is to come. To those who withhold knowledge from humanity, it will be their personal burden to carry, for in reality they do not have the right to keep others ignorant because of their own fears, **do they?**

That makes three incarnations into human flesh bodies. The next incarnation, because of the circumstances, is very different. **He was not born to a human body from birth.** Being his final incarnation to this physical Third Dimensional Vibration, he has come to this planet as a **'walk-in',** which means to step into a physical flesh body by agreement with the entity that occupied that body from birth, and who now wishes to vacate it. **Walk-ins complete the Karma** of the original occupant and then grow in Consciousness to gain their own **Self-Realisation** of their true **identity** and express knowledge to all those who are prepared to listen. The entity that was **Jesus, Buddha and Nostradamus** is now incarnated as a **walk-in,** and has completed the Karma of the previous occupant of the human body which he exists within. He is relatively unknown. **He choose the silent approach,** but he is an expresser of knowledge and truth, giving wisdom and the knowledge of the Universes to help humanity grow beyond their fears and Ego.

To grow in Consciousness has nothing to do with the New Age or enlightenment. You, my dear Sisters and Brothers of Creation, are already enlightened beings. You have the knowledge and ability to grow beyond your Self-Created beliefs and conditioning, your past experiences, your fears and negative emotions, your pain and misery; the very things that have held each of you back from conscious growth in the present moment of your human life.

There is only one thing stopping each of you and that is your human Ego. To change your level of thinking is only a matter of shifting your consciousness. Learning to still your mind by stopping the Ego's chatter and becoming quiet long enough for your inner voice to connect with you is all it takes. **Buddha** said **"Creation and I are one. Therefore, the self which is the Ego that stands in the way, must be dissolved through unconditional love alone, before the real comes into being."** That my dear Brothers and Sisters is the truth, and only that truth will set you free from all your **Self-Created limitations.**

There is so much more that can be expressed about the lives of the one you all know as **Jesus/Buddha/Nostradamus,** and even the one in the human body at this very moment. Some of you may be curious as to who he is. Listen to your hearts and look to the one who lives their truth and gives of their heart, and you will have the answer. To become the living truth of what is being expressed, is in itself the essence of totality. Learn not to live to the beliefs and conditions of your societies and you will live in the moment and create in the moment. You will become a shining star for all to see and you will grow beyond this **Third Dimensional Matter world of Ego.** You will live in a pure state of being, limitless, able to contact and enter all Vibrations and Dimensions. You will be a free-thinking, conscious spark of Creation's totality.

CREATIONS CENTRE OF INFINITE KNOWLEDGE (NO-15)

What does the above truly mean? It is simple and yet it is complex. Let's take it one step at a time. When I express your human words **"Creation Centre"**, I am referring to the centre within you which is all infinite and **holds the knowledge of the Universes.** This centre of knowledge is dormant in most human beings. While human beings seek knowledge outside of themselves, **Universal Knowledge** can only be gained from within ones being as their **Consciousness grows and evolves.** When you as human beings begin to evolve your Consciousness, this dormant **Centre of Infinite Knowledge will become activated.**

In this present vibration of your human world, Ego has evolved over the last **928,000 years** of your human history. Most of you as human individuals have had **thousands of lives** and experienced many facets of life, expanding your energies beyond your own understanding of existence. Yet you each have a record of every life you have ever lived, and every experience you have ever had as an individual and is **recorded in your cellular matter.** This knowledge can be drawn upon at will, if you can only believe that you are all **Ageless, Timeless Infinite beings** of light housed in a human flesh body that has been **created from your Mother Earth,** because the **chemicals of Mother Earth are also within your flesh bodies.**

In your human world everything has become **based on logic. If it is not logical or cannot be proven scientifically, it cannot exist.** Yes there are thousands of life forms that live beyond logic and flesh bodies. So many human beings have asked me **"Does Spirit exist?** And if they do, how come I cannot see them?" **The answer is simple.** If you are willing to open your eyes and see beyond the limitations of your vibration, you will see with new eyes.

Sprit worlds vibrate at a higher frequency. Where the human world vibrate at a much slower frequency. They can see you, but you do not see them. To give an example, a Space Ship is launched from Earth to the planet you call **Neptune.** Because your astronauts and scientists are very logical in thought, they only see with their logical three Dimensional sight. **Another world exists on Neptune in the fifth vibration,** but because they are vibrating at a higher frequency, that is vibrating faster than human third dimensional beings, **Neptune's** world is hidden from your astronauts. If you as human being were willing to expand your understanding and believe that other vibrations exist, you could or would have a **Shift in Consciousness.** You would then be able to tap into your inner self, which will expand your understanding and release the **Infinite Knowledge** from within you into your conscious awareness.

Your societies need to slow down and come to terms with the confusion that exists in your human brains. Please allow yourself to accept that the human brain was created only to control your **body's nervous system** and to **store memories of your past experiences.** The problem is, your present and your future is directly influenced by your past. If you grew up with negative situations and have genetically embedded negative patterns from your human parents, you will be directly influenced by these factors and they in turn will affect your present and your future. Outside of the brains physiological function, its only other purpose is to store information which can be consciously recalled. But negative emotions create fears, insecurities and hold you from achieving your **goals in your human life.** It is important that if you wish to grow consciously, that you allow your past to be only a memory - not to be seen as negative, or positive good or bad, just to be seen as an experience. See your past unbiasedly, without negative emotion or judgement, and you can create peace and balance in your existence.

By slowing down the human brain and **ceasing the chatter of negative thought,** you calm yourself and become silent in the mind. Your being will enter a **State of Consciousness** where all your confusion no longer matters and your inner divine essence will give you all the answers you seek in your human life. **Infinite knowledge is your birthright. To deny this is to deny your very existence.** You only have to stop yourself from your daily routine, and become the observer and look around your world, your country, your own neighbourhood, and see from an honest heart and an open mind the **falseness of human Ego all around you.** It is within all things of human life, but most humans do not stop long enough to see the falseness. If they did, their own Self-Created world would come to a stop and they would have to begin to ask themselves the questions they have been trying to avoid for so long.

Just take a look at all the governments of your Earth who keep secrets from the people. Eventually, after many of your Earth years some truth is revealed, but I assure you all governments of your Earth only allow you to know the secrets they wish to reveal. Most secrets will never be revealed to the majority of human beings in their lifetimes. Have you ever asked yourselves why so many secrets are covered up and kept under lock and key to deny the humans the truth? **The answer is simple.** It is all because of human Ego and its fear which creates insecurities in all governments, and in all human beings.

We, the observers of human beings on this most precious Earth, have been very aware that human Consciousness in this given moment of life, is retarded because of human Ego and its fears, insecurities and logic. Do not misunderstand what I am expressing. Logic without the influence and control of Ego can be in **perfect balance with Consciousness,** but the dilemma lies with the beliefs and conditioning of human life, created by Ego from negative emotions and experiences, from one lifetime to another. **The human Ego is afraid of the unknown,** and the Ego's beliefs and conditioning determine the boundaries each of you exist within. **In the unknown exists pure creativeness and freedom, the creativeness and freedom of thought which is sadly lacking in human life?**

For example, an artist who draws or paints in their moment of life can create an image that in reality comes from within their being. They can actually see the completed painting. What they are tapping into is their **Living Consciousness,** by doing so their painting comes to life. That is what makes a brilliant artist. It is the same for all of life. **Consciousness is the Essence of Creation's totality,** while logic is only formed in the human brain, created by the human Ego.

Understand that you are a **Timeless, Ageless, Infinite, Eternal being of Light** that has the infinite knowledge of all that has been and all that will be. So, stop and ask yourselves this most important question: **"Do I as an individual want to grow in Consciousness and become a free thinker in my own Creativeness?"** If your answer is yes, then you as an infinite being need to look within your essence and begin to change what is needed in your human life in order to begin your journey of **Self-Discovery.** You may ask **"What do I need to change?" First,** change your diet, change your thoughts to be more positive in attitude, and become more responsible for all your actions in life. **Learn to forgive others and especially yourself.** Still you're **Mind in Meditation and stop the Chatter of Confusion,** for it will only cause stress and will lead to sickness and dis'ease. **Learn to let go of your past hurts and conditioning of life, and unconditionally love yourself from your heart.** You will find the strength and courage to then love all others.

In these words of your human language lies truth: Creation and I are one, therefore the Self, which is Ego, must be dissolved through Unconditional Love alone, before the real can come into being.

That says it all. Ego has been present on your Earth for so long, **and it continues to live in your Self-Created fears, insecurities, hatred, anger, vindictiveness, judgements, vanity, greed, lust, domination, competitiveness, and negative thoughts which create your reality.** Ego is responsible for all your **wars, poverty, murder, rape, deceit and even the disasters of nature.** How is this so? Your Earth has a Spirit within her and around her, and the poisons human man has created through his greed for power, are causing your planet to physically suffer. Every time great holes are dug into your Earth to extract minerals, you are depleting the natural balance of your Earth, and nature must compensate to restore balance. This may occur in what you **call a natural disaster,** but in reality it is only the planet trying to heal itself.

Man's physical power will eventually perish. If man continues his destructive path and allows human Ego to control his destiny, **then man will become a memory and will exist no more.** Only when each human being discovers their inner being of Unconditional Love, and becomes the living example of **Light and Truth,** and no longer allows the Ego to **control their destiny,** only then will **Living Consciousness manifest itself and be almighty present in all of human life.** You all will grow in true creativeness in the wonderment of **Creation's Totality** and be fully aware of your infinite knowledge. You will have the wisdom to go beyond your present vibration in the third dimension and be able to travel beyond all things in all universes. **You will have found Creation's Centre of Infinite Knowledge.**

LIFE AFTER LIFE-AFTER LIFE-AFTER LIFE (NO-16)

I have chosen this topic because of the many questions I have been asked about life after life. A simple concept, yet it is one of humanity's most misunderstood subjects, and has been for the past **928,000 years of human existence.** It is known to many human beings as **Reincarnation,** meaning to be **reborn again and again,** to incarnate into a human vessel. The driving force behind this **Reincarnation is you the Entity, the Spirit within.**

All of you dear human beings have been born **thousands of times,** as both **male and female, as a friend, a Brother or Sister, as twins, and uncle, aunt, mother father, business colleagues...** It is all part of the **circle of life.** What is most beautiful is that you the Spirit choose which life you wish to experience, and even your human parents are chosen by you, meaning you alone are **Personally Responsible** for your choices and actions in all your lives as a human being.

Let's look at your human vessel for a moment. **What actually runs your human body?** Is it your internal organs, your human brain, or is it your mind, or your spirit? From your current level of Evolution as a species, you would most probably say the **human brain runs the body.** Many humans believe the **human brain is the control centre of life for the human body.** Yes, there is truth in that belief. If the human brain were to cease functioning, you would have no physical activity. The human body would be still, and in your scientific terms, you would be in a coma. Nobody would be home. What does this mean, **"nobody home"?**

Human science believes the human brain is the life force that runs the human body and that when the brain ceases to function, all is dead. To one who is logical and who lives to their beliefs and conditioning, that would certainly be truth - their idea of truth. In human terms, **"nobody home"** could mean the brain is dead, and their human body is therefore unable to function, causing it to die (**unless it is being kept alive on machines in your hospitals).**

In reality, it is the Spirit which determines whether or not **"somebody is home"**. **The Spirit is infinite, ageless, timeless and eternal.** It exists in the living moment of life, without fears nor judgement, nor beliefs or conditioning. **It is simply a pure state of being.** The Spirit is the life force which allows you to reincarnate life after life, after life, after life... Without it your human body could not live.

Your existence as a human being is more unique than you realise. To exist in this third Dimensional matter world you require five elements. These are:

- **Earth:** The clay of your Mother Earth to form your human body.
- **Fire:** Energy manifested as the electrical current in your human body.
- **Water:** The fluid through which every chemical reaction in your human body occurs to give you physical life.
- **Air:** Provider of oxygen to keep the cells of your physical body alive.
- **Spirit:** The spark of Consciousness which drives your existence.

As a human individual, realise your true self and know that the Earth you the human individual live upon is the Creator of your human body's flesh and spirit. **The elements of Earth: Fire, Water, Air and Earth** are within and around your precious Earth as they are within your human bodies. The Spirit of your being is as much within the Earth as it is within you. Your Spirit is a part of all that exists in all the **Universes.** It is a part of **Creations' Totality,** and that human being is very beautiful and very special in all that is Creation.

You may ask "what is the purpose of incarnating life after life?" The answer is to learn by experiencing in human form and growing consciously beyond your third Dimensional matter world, and to come to the realisation that **all of life is most precious. You cannot take a life vindictively or justify such an act (for example) as a necessity of war.** All justification is based on belief systems and conditioning, and here is where the dilemma begins.

Whatever you create in your human life, **be it positive or negative,** sets in motion a chain reaction. For example, you may have stolen something from another, or you may have raped or killed. This creates negative energy within and around yourself, which must be brought into balance, so in your next life what you have done will be done unto you in order to bring balance into the present moment. However, because the human Ego and negative emotions, the saga of human life is continued in negativity. **Forgiveness it seems is not a part of human life,** for if it was, negativity would be dissolved. **Humanity as it is today, is conditioned by its past, and it is the past which each human being lives life after life, after life.** Through the genetics of your human parents and through your own experiences in previous lifetimes, the past, and indeed, human history, continuously is **repeating itself,** perpetuated by the beliefs and conditioning of your societies, **generation after generation.**

This is where all human limitation is born - from your past and your parents past. You may say that this is your history, it is where you come from and what gives you your unique identity. **For many the past is very important.** But stop for a moment and ask yourself these questions:

- **Do I have any pain or emotional hurts from my past?**
- **Has my past created negativity and limitation throughout my lifetime?**
- **Do I suffer from fears, or am I an angry person towards myself and others?**
- **Am I judgemental?**
- **Do I have low self-esteem?**
- **Does everything I do fall apart or never reach completion?**

If you answer **"yes"** honestly from your heart, then you as a human individual have negativity in your human life. This is what creates your moment and your future in this present lifetime as well as the next to come. **And so it goes on: Life after life, after life, after life. Where will it end?**

The answer is simple. If you truly want to change your human life, you alone hold the power of Creation within and around you. It all depends on your level of thinking. If you are a logical human being and logic is your way of life, then confusion will always create negative energies in your life and your lives to come. This may be difficult for some to accept, but logic creates confusion, because logic keeps you confined to your beliefs and conditioning, your boundaries, so that you reject what your logic says is impossible rather than putting your logic aside and saying **"but what if it** is possible". **There is not, and never will be conscious growth in logic, for logic is third dimensional.** Because of human nature - **the past, fears and insecurities - logic will create pain and misery for you,** and when you become a human parent, you will pass on your limitations, **your past, your beliefs, fears and conditioning,** to your human children. And so it goes on, and on to the next generation.

All that you have read so far will seem negative to you, and yet dear human beings it is the truth. When you as an individual choose to step beyond **your Self-Created limitations, your vision will broaden, your understanding will grow consciously beyond all things, and especially your knowledge will be infinite.** You will step beyond your present awareness and create a balanced human life and pass this understanding on to your human children. In human time, **living Consciousness** will be a part of each human being, and negative limitation, **pain and dis'ease will no longer exist.**

Let us look a little deeper into human history and see how negative emotions create negative situations mostly through misunderstandings. These misunderstandings over your **928,000 years** history have lead humanity to being **plagued by wars and injustice.** Since your Second World War there have been a further **150 wars to date.** All those people who perished in your Second World War have been reborn because of the negative emotions and the injustice that was done to them, which is creating further negative actions in human evolution. **This cycle of negativity will not stop until it is balanced.**

Humanity is now experiencing a change in their level of thinking. Because human existence is based on the past, logic has developed faster than Consciousness and conscious growth has been retarded. At this time there is no balance in human evolution. In order for humanity to grow and evolve into conscious beings beyond negative emotion, each human being must be willing to grow beyond their human Ego and change their attitude towards other human beings. Learn to respect each other's ways of life and learn to think with the heart, and not the human brain.

You may say this all sounds good, but it is not the real world as it is today. Unfortunately, your world at this time is built on **fantasy, corruption and deceit.** You are each conditioned into believing what you are told to believe.

You say you are each individuals, yet you are clones of each other. If you look into human history you will see the same negative emotions have persisted that exist today. **This is where the problem lies.** Each human lifetime has similar negative emotions being acted out. The circumstances may be different, the technology may be more advanced, **but the same human Ego exists, life after life.**

If each human being were to learn to forgive past hurts and learn to feel the Love that is within and around. Respecting all of life without any form of judgement, then **Human Evolution** would step beyond the past it keeps reliving, and create **each incarnation in perfect balance. This balance would put an end to all the violence and misery that exists on your world today.**

The past must be laid to rest. Leave the past in the past, and see it only as a memory, neither negative nor positive, only an experience from each lifetime into another. The power of this creation is within each of you, for only you the human individual can change your level of thinking and understanding in order to gain the knowledge to create life after life in a harmonious and balanced way for all of humanity. It all begins with an understanding of the willingness to Forgive yourself and all others and to Love yourself Unconditionally, and come to a Self-Realisation that the Past has no place in the Present if you truly want to discover who you truly are in this vastness of Space.

THE UNSEEN FORCES: WHO ACTUALLY CONTROLS HUMANITY? (NO-17)

Sit for a few moments in the silence of your mind and ponder the question: **Who Actually Controls Humanity?** See what your first answer is, but make sure it comes from an honest heart and not from your beliefs and conditioning of your human life. **It is the heart which will give you the truth, and only the truth,** for the rest is the **Falseness of the Human Ego that has surrounded humanity for so long.**

Many of you will answer **"I run my own life. No-one controls me.";** others will answer "The governments control us. They make the laws, and some will say **"its big powerful businesses who run countries".** Some will even say it is the **Taxation Offices, the Military, Police, or Secret Services who control Humanity.** From a human perspective all of the above have some amount of truth. Yes, your governments of this Earth would love to believe they control all of Humanity because they control and influence the outcome of all events that occur on this Earth.

The people, you human beings, are sadly the puppets for the governments. Governments all around this Earth are very fearful of you, **the public.** But they would never admit this to you, for if they did so openly, **they would lose control.** Little by little over a long period of time, they have been taking away your **personal power of individuality,** making you feel worthless, less than them. But be assured that you are all very special beautiful human beings who are **infinite and eternal,** and who have the power of Creation within and around you. You only have to believe in yourself and know you are entitled to be an individual, and to be able to create any lifestyle you choose, rather than be dictated to in a **boring life of endless misery.**

We, the Nar'Karones have looked upon your Earth for the last 928,000 years. Many of our beings have incarnated as human beings to help in the **Evolution of Humanity,** to try to bring about a deeper understanding of **wisdom and knowledge** in order to help humanity grow consciously beyond the **human Ego.** We have never interfered with your choices or laws, but have only given knowledge so that each human being can make their own choice to evolve beyond their human Ego.

So it is true, the human beings of this most precious Earth are being controlled either by their **governments, by big businesses, the military, secret services or police, and even your telecommunications and media.** Some of you after reading this may say **"what a load of rubbish" or "I don't want to know".** Surely that is seeking the easy way out.

But let us look at this from another perspective and ask this question - do not take it too lightly: **"If all of the above are actually controlling the masses, then who is controlling the controllers?"** Think for a moment in silence and touch your divine essence, your true self. Look around your neighbourhoods, your states, your countries, look around your world and open your eyes to what is occurring on a grand scale of negativity. Look at the inhumane acts towards other human beings; **the wars, torture and slaughter of men, women and children; the cover-ups of military mass murders of its people; the rape of women and children in war; the leaders of countries who murder their own people to gain control over the masses; the poverty where it should not exist and the greed of your monetary system in not sharing wealth** and bringing equality to all when **all human beings are born equal.** Look at the greed of individuals in **your drug wars** and how your governments actually encourage the actions taken, for there is a deeper purpose that not many could or would accept as truth.

Those who control your controllers are **"The Unseen Forces".** They exist in a negative vibration and they have been influencing **human evolution for thousands of Earthly years.** They have no physical form or matter and move quite freely from their vibration to yours. Since you as human beings live in a physical matter vibration, and since you live in human Ego's logical world, your sight is limited to only seeing within the third dimension. That is why these forces can move unseen among you so easily without detection and are able to manipulate your leaders into acting in certain ways. **One of their most powerful tools is taking away your individuality, and the other is to affect your health, for if your human body is not healthy then your mind is not balanced and you become an easy target for mind control.**

The beings of negativity are well organised, and they know who they can influence and who to keep away from. What you the human being must realise is, that by **manipulating your leaders with subliminal thoughts and messages,** these beings implant their truth into your leaders, and then all of humanity suffers. **They control humanity on two levels. The first** is your physical self of third dimensional matter because you do not know of their existence or presence as you are **unable to see them physically. The second** is during your time of sleep when you astrally project from your human bodies into the astral vibration, the fourth dimension. Many humans call this the **dream state.**

It must be realised that **dreams are not dreams** that is they are not fantasy but are in actual fact reality. You are actually experiencing in the **fourth dimension,** and what each individual experiences is governed by their understanding of life, by their fears, pain, misery, joy, anger, hatred, love, beliefs and conditioning. Each human being creates their own experiences in the astral vibration. If an individual comes from a negative space of existence then these **Unseen Forces** will attach themselves and will then have the power to influence you in the astral vibration as well as in your physical existence. **Wherever there is negativity, these unseen forces exist.**

But you can break their control over you by becoming strong in yourself, by believing in yourself, by dealing with and dissolving your **negative Ego** and conditioning from your past. Simply by taking back your **personal responsibility** you can become aware of your most inner self and have the realisation that you an infinite Spirit being of Light, and that Creation is within you every moment of your reality and that you are within all things. You are all much more than just conditioned logical flesh men and women. By going beyond the beliefs and conditioning of your human life, **by dissolving the Ego of negativity** which each of you have created, and stepping into the unknown, you will each truly come to know yourselves. You will see for yourselves that these **Unseen Forces truly exist** and then you can and will break their control over you. What will come from this **liberation of your Spirit is living consciousness,** and all your pain, wars, greed, suffering and violence will dissipate and no longer exist. You will become a true human being. Many different species will come into your vibration and great knowledge and wisdom will be upon your Earth.

In wisdom lies truth and freedom. In pain lies misery and domination. When will you as human beings choose to go **beyond the human Ego,** for the choice is and has always been yours, the human individual? I will speak more on the Unseen Forces in time to come. Be Blessed in Love and Light dear Human Beings of your most Precious Earth.

THE FUNDAMENTAL FOUNDATION OF ALL LIFE (NO-18)

From the beginning there was **darkness in all things.** Then came a **spark of light** that spread throughout the Universe, **and life began its circle of evolution.** From that **one spark of light came Consciousness,** and from that very moment, **Life began as Light** moving freely throughout the unknown. When it became the **known it became the past,** and the past was no longer important, **because no emotion existed at that moment.**

What did exist was **that Spark of Light** moving and evolving **beyond the known,** and moving **forward into the unknown,** for it is in the **unknown that pure creativeness lies.** No negativity exists, only **pure Light in living consciousness.** Time as you human beings know it only exists in your **third dimensional vibration, created by humans.** Time also holds the past and it is the past which keeps **humanity locked in the third dimension,** and because of human Ego, which is of a negative energy, human life and its **conscious evolution has been retarded** and halted from stepping beyond its past.

It is the past of all human negative emotions that is and has been creating conflict, pain, misery, war and all injustices upon humanity on this most precious **Earth for the last 928,000 years.** It will continue to expand in a negative way until each human being **faces the fears and insecurities** that have been holding each of you back from expanding beyond your human Ego of beliefs and conditioning.

To grow in Consciousness as a species you must first become responsible for all you create in your human life. **There is only one way to do this.** Stop everything long enough to look around you and truly see what is happening to your world. You as human beings are becoming very afraid of all that is around you. **You have lost touch with your inner self,** and most of you do not trust yourselves or your decisions, so you look to others to give you the answers. Or you use the excuse that you do not have the time because you are too busy with your life, or that you do not want to know.

But the real truth is, **you as human individuals have been highly conditioned into a certain way of thinking.** Everything that you are at this moment in your life was created from your parents, from their parents and from your society, your friends, your media, your laws and governments. Your human brain has recorded everything that has happened in your life, whether it is negative or positive. In reality, you have become a walking encyclopaedia of your past, and this is **where the problem exists.** Most of you are **clones of your parents,** and your parents are **clones of their parents**, and so on. Because most human beings have negative emotions ingrained within their genetics, all past hurts, emotions and feelings are **encoded from one generation to the next,** and so **the past lives in the present moment, and sadly, creates your future.** That, dear human beings, is why you have so much confusion in your human lives.

Trying to break free from the past can be a difficult task for the individual. **You have to want to break free,** and then you have to have the courage and the strength to begin your journey of self-discovery. The truth is almighty present, and that truth is encoded within you. The Light that shines within each human being is, and has been present throughout your existence and the existence of Creation. Creation is within and around all things, meaning you included. You and everything upon this precious Earth, **are a part of Creation's totality.** You have all been around for a very long time in history. For example, as human beings you have existed for more than **928,000 years as a species,** and before that, you existed on the planet Nar'Kariss and were known as the **Nar'Karones.** You were similar in form and appearance to what you are now. You also existed at that time in a third **Dimensional Vibration of Physical matter** and you had negative emotions which took a long time to dissolve in order to grow consciously beyond what you were. But the problem that occurred was the **Nar'Karones** were evolving consciously as individuals, growing beyond the Ego into beings of Unconditional Love for all of life. Most of the **Nar'Karones** made the decision to grow beyond their third Dimensional Vibration, but some did not want to. There were some, a small portion of our people, who wanted to stay in their negative way of life. The decision was made for the good of all on **Nar'Kariss,** to gather these individuals together and relocate them to another planet where they could grow, or stay the same, and live as they wished without holding back the conscious growth of the entire civilisation of **Nar'Kariss.**

A planet was found where they could exist and evolve as they wished, a little over **87,000 Nar'Karones** were placed on this Earth, then called **Kariss,** **named after a being called Yarkiss' Kariss** which in your language means **'The Beginning'.** Most of the human race, as it is in this moment of life, came from or evolved from the **Nar'Karones** and the race of beings who were already here for several thousand years, **the Neanderthals.**

The **Nar'Karones** transported to your Earth, existed for thousands of years, **creating havoc among other species of life, and eventually mating with** **Neanderthals.** Humans of today have the genetics of both races within them, and the human of today is the result of **928,000 years of evolution** **and mixing of a number of species.** Interestingly, history is repeating itself.

Please understand that I am not asking you to believe what is being expressed. The truth of what my being is expressing to you, lies dormant with each of you and is encoded in your living essence, **the Spark of Light that is** **within all of life, just as all of life is within you.** From the beginning of your existence as Consciousness you are of Light, and with each incarnation you have you are evolving. Between your lives you are resting and growing in the fourth dimension, planning your next life in a human body. **And** **the purpose of these lives?** To gather knowledge which will help you grow beyond your present **state of awareness,** and to come full circle, **returning** **once more to a being of Light.**

At this moment I must express about how the Asian and African/ **Australian Aboriginal races came about in your human history.** The **Nar'Karones** who were placed here on your Earth, **mated with the** **Neanderthals.** The Neanderthals evolved as a race and became the natives of the continents of your Earth, and you can see a very strong resemblance physically to this **ancient species in your African and Australian** **Aboriginal beings.** You can also see Neanderthals to a lesser extent in your European beings, but their genetics are clearly present.

The Asian races are a very interesting creation of evolution and genetic engineering, having evolved from Chimpanzees and Apes, and other primates over hundreds of thousands of human years with the assistance of physical beings who still visit your planet today. These beings experimented and implanted their own genetics along with that of the primates, **trying** **to create an intelligent, non-aggressive physical being who would not**

be a threat to them. This new species was monitored by their scientists, just as your scientists today are experimenting with implanting genetics into related and vastly unrelated species to what effect such genes would have. **Interesting how history is repeating itself...**

Ask yourself what is more important to you, **the human individual?** To be highly conditioned with no free will, to never truly know yourself, and to believe only in what you are being told? **That is, to be a clone and live in emotional negative state that eventually will lead you in depression, stress and dis'ease?** Or would you prefer to know the truth, to be set free from your negative emotional pain, and be given the opportunity to step beyond the past into the present moment? Are you willing to face yourself and see yourself for who you truly are, without all the excuses that the human Ego give you to hide behind?

To face yourself can be very painful, and to grow beyond your Ego is also a painful and often lengthy journey of self-discovery. But seeing the pain for what it is will set you free. It will allow you, the human individual to grow beyond your Ego, and you will see with new eyes and a warm heart that you can dissolve the falseness from around yourself that has surrounded humanity for so long. **By seeing the illusion, you will understand that the fundamental foundation of all of life is purely unconditional love. That is what Creation is.**

Unconditional Love in reality is Light, from which all of life came from and evolved. Just like an atom begins as light, over many moments of existence, Consciousness became reality and the atom was formed, and from the atom billions of life forms were created throughout all the Universes.

I will leave you with this thought:

It is the human Ego that give you all the excuses you need to not grow consciously. But be warned; it is also the human Ego that creates all your pain and misery within your human life. **Yet, to Love yourself Unconditionally will set you free from your Ego's hold** and will allow you, the **human individual to know the truth** and to live without **fears or insecurity,** to be in a **State of complete Bliss,** and have balance of Mind, Body and Spirit. **Knowledge is not power. Knowledge is freedom.**

THE UNSEEN FORCES & THEIR ROLE IN THE ATTACK ON AMERICA (NO-19)

My being has found it of great interest and of great honour to read your letters on last month's writings on the Unseen Forces. I have also most recently received many concerned letters on the attack on America.

First, my people on **Nar'Kariss** wish to express their sadness for the loss of human lives that occurred as a result of the attack on America. Life on all levels of Consciousness is most precious, and this act of violence upon the people of America will create more pain and misery for your Earthly years to come. Such acts in your past human history have come into your present moment, and sadly will continue into your future to come. **The real truth is that no-one ever wins a war. (EVER) You can make all the excuses in the world, but in the end how do you the human individual, let alone your governments on your Earth justify the killings of human children, women and men. Do you as humans believe you are growing consciously by making wars that slaughter humanity?**

In all the Universes, **there is no justification for war.** The enemy is not your neighbour, nor is it another country. The enemy is within each of you who exist on this most precious Earth you call home. Until every human being overcomes the **enemy within themselves,** conflict, and war will continue to exist. You're Earth, and all life upon it, is suffering badly. The enemy within is created from negative unresolved emotions, passed on from one generation to the next in the form of beliefs, conditioning and genetic encoding.

All of humanity needs to be loved and understood. Every single human being on this Earth is in reality a beautiful being of Light existing in a flesh body of matter, and conditioned by past experiences that in most case are of a negative energy. It is these experiences which have been creating your present and your future in all matters concerning your evolution over the last **928,000 years.** Every single human being has **lived thousands of human lives,** and all of human history is encoded in your spiritual essences. **You each can know the truth of your past.** It is a simple process. You can know every life you have lived in the Earthly third vibration of physical matter, and you can see all past events from human history. You will see that **humanity has had over 150,000 wars on this Earth.**

All wars of the past and present are governed by an unbalanced human brain and a human Ego hungry to dominate. Like Caesar, Hitler and Napoleon before them, Quadaffi, Hussein, Arafat, and bin Laden, for example, are all of an unbalanced human brain full of negative experiences and an Ego craving to dominate. There are of course many more such human men all over the countries of your Earth, but they are used here as an example to illustrate a point. All of these human men are very fearful human beings who have a need to control and dominate others in order to feel safe and secure. They become charismatic leaders to manipulate and coerce their people. But if only you could see them when they were children, you would understand why they are what they are today.

Energy is a very interesting subject. Everything in this Universe, and all other Universes, are formed from energy. **Some call it Light.** All of life is manifested from energy; from thoughts, through to experiences, to physical creation, and beyond the physical realm. What is most important is to have an understanding of the process of life itself. The men mentioned above are all from the same energy. **They have lived many incarnations as leaders who have caused the deaths of millions of human beings all over this planet from the distant past to the present, and it now seems well into your future.**

Just because they have emotional negative experiences as a result of their human childhoods, does it also mean all of humanity must suffer endless misery and pain to please their angry Egos? The answer would be **"No!"** then why is it that they manage to cause so much conflict in human society. They seem to be able to **dominate the weak,** who are easily influenced by anyone that shows more strength than themselves. **Yet these leaders are not strong.** They have more fears within them than the average human being, and that is why they need to control and dominate others. **As children they were dominated,** and like any school bully, they have become the dominators. **Power over others makes them feel secure. They are in control of their existence by controlling others.**

Through such human men you can begin to see how the **Unseen Forces control the weak minded wherever there are negative emotions.** Being weak themselves, these human men are **open to manipulation by the Unseen Forces,** and then they in turn manipulate their people through fear for their lives. These **Unseen Forces** can manipulate single individuals or groups of people by **cracking into their Auras and placing thoughts into their human brain.** For example, an individual who has experienced a great deal of emotional pain, negativity and sorrow, and who is constantly giving away their **personal responsibility,** can easily be influenced by these forces and **controlled to do their bidding.**

I have been asked to describe these Unseen Forces. They are easily detected if you are an aware human being. They can be seen by human eyes, especially in the dark. When you are lying on your bed, make your room as dark as possible. **Do not allow yourself to be disturbed by others.** As you lie on your bed, look around your room and allow your eyes to adjust to the darkness. Allow your eyes to wander to the corners of your room near the ceiling, then close your eyes and say **"I who am almighty present I allow myself to see beyond my human sight".** Truly mean what you are saying, then open your eyes without fear or judgement and you will begin to see shapes of figures - some small, some the size of the average human male.

They will be there, with large V-shaped faces and slanted eyes. Some eyes are **yellow** and some **are red, others are all black.** Their outer shapes are light shadows or can be black. They move quite fast from one point to another. When they find their target they come in very close, and if they can influence their victim they will be able to **crack their Aura** and latch onto their **life-force, the Aura.** For such beings to stay in your third vibration for any extended period of time they need to feed off your energy field. That is why so many human beings on your Earth suffer from a lack of will, in many cases a lack of energy, and this in turn can even lead to some human beings creating human dis'ease in their human bodies.

At this point I need to provide a simple example of why these **Unseen Forces** have a need to control other civilisations, and what they as a species gain from this. Human beings will go to the race-track and gamble by placing bets on which animal they believe or hope will win. It gives them a thrill. Others will go to a football or baseball game, or a car race. These things are exciting and entertaining, giving many human beings something to talk about with each other. A bit of harmless fun.

To the **Unseen Forces,** whose motivation is **control and domination of an entire species,** they see your planet Earth as a **game field,** and the game which has been going on for thousands of your Earthly years, is to see how much they can influence human beings. The **Unseen Forces are like parasites,** latching onto their prey to make them play out their games, feeding off human beings' energies. When they are finished, most of the time they will leave, meanwhile their victim is left in a state of confusion, and in extreme cases, even a state of madness.

Most importantly, what needs to be understood is that these **Unseen Forces** have been in existence for hundreds of thousands of years. They have travelled to many worlds throughout the Universes, but they can only influence physical vibrations of matter such as the third dimension in which humanity exists. They come from a part of the **fourth dimension** and are attracted to **negative energies only.** They can senses negativity from a great distance, just as the sharks of your salt waters can sense blood.

The human being you call **Osama bin Laden** that has been accused of the terrorist attack on America most recently is a prime example of a human that has been influenced by the **Unseen Forces.** He has so much **hatred and anger** within him, the only way he can express it is to create pain and misery for others. In his unbalanced human brain he believes causing pain to others justifies his own suffering. Unfortunately, the human being bin Laden has no conscious awareness but uses only his logic to guide his existence and actions. **His purpose in life is to bring pain and misery to others.** He is unable to change because his thoughts are not his own. From a young child he has been influenced, and sadly, he is not capable of love or understanding towards other human beings. And so he punishes others because of his own inadequacies as a human being.

The **Unseen Forces** have a tight grip on his mind and body. He is one never to be trusted. What America needs to realise is that he had a great influence on the Taliban and Afghanistan, as well as many parts of the Middle East, including Quadaffi, Hussein and Arafat. These human men may say they do not support or agree with what bin Laden has done in the past or even most recently in America, but they are not to be trusted. They want America to fall and suffer because they are also from the same negative energies as bin Laden. In the realm of truth that comes from within, these human men did secretly approve of bin Laden's terrorist actions, but they would never openly admit their support because they are fearful of America's power.

There was a great concern for America, especially with regards to Saddam Hussein. Hussein was at the time biding his time and keeping a low profile. He was creating chemical weapons that have the ability to eliminate millions of human beings at once. His hatred for America was as strong as bin Laden's. The Middle East is a great threat to human societies that believe in freedom of speech and individuality. The leaders of these nations want the Middle East to come together as one great empire. They will accomplish this in the human future to come. This coming together will be one the greatest threats to human civilisation.

I must express that there is **no conscious growth in the negativity that is war and violence.** The only thing that Supremes in such events is the human Ego - **it thrives on pain and misery.** What is truly needed within humanity is **wisdom and understanding** in order to allow the process of dissolving the negative past and the **Unseen Forces** that have such a strong hold on weak human beings, **who in turn control the masses.** Learning to deal with your own fears will help you understand your past and the human specie's past.

Forgive the past and allow yourselves to be free from negative emotion. Live in the present moment and create a future free from negative energies, for only then will the **Unseen Forces be unable to exist in your vibration.** Love for oneself will shine onto others, and wars and all injustices will be dissolved into the nothingness from which they first were created. The more **Unconditional Love** you feel for your own being, the more you will be able to send to your families, friends, neighbours and nations around your world. Humanity can grow in Consciousness to become a part of a family that exists in all Universes.

To be negative is only a lesson of life. It does not mean it has to carry on from one life to the next, or from one generation to the next. You, the human race have a choice. How long in human time will this unconscious living continue? Yes, the loving energies of Creation's Totality will set humanity free from all of its own Self-Created limitations, but how long is up to each of you. Unconditional love is the answer, for all of you dear Human beings who come from the Light. Your human bodies are only vehicles serving you in your physical existence while you live on this planet Earth and learn your lessons of human life. It is the human Ego that has been shaping human history and controlling human existence for more than **928,000 years.** Setting yourself free from the Ego can be accomplished in one simple step. Love for oneself and for all of life, for life in every species is most precious.

Open your eyes to the truth that is within you, which has always been within you. Be Blessed in Love and Light always dear Human beings.

UNDERSTANDING SPIRITS, GHOSTS & POLTERGESISTS (NO-20)

Greetings to all human beings that exist on this most precious Earth that you each call home. Yes, all of you would agree that your Earth is precious, as much as all of the human race are precious. As all of life in your Third Dimensional Vibration are also very precious, in fact all of life no matter what form it is, is precious. There has been so many questions about life and what comes after your human life that I have been asked to express on this subject further.

There are so many different levels of Consciousness. What you as a species think and understand at this very moment will most certainly change in the moments to come. Looking at human time for example, your year at this **present moment is 2014.** Take a little time and think about how you feel, act and communicate at this moment. Now think back five of your years to the year **2009** and ask yourself **"Has my understanding grown and changed in how I see myself and the world". Your answer should be yes. What you were before is no more, and your understanding of life should or will be different.**

One of the greatest openings to advancing your awareness and understanding is to have an open mind and heart, and not to judge yourself or anyone in a negative way, and to speak the truth and only the truth. You the reader must be asking yourself **"where is Kuntarkis taking this?"** My being has been asked many times about **Spirits, Ghosts and what you would call Poltergeists.** What is the difference, **and do they truly exist, or is it just a figment of over-active human imaginations?**

I would like to answer these questions and explain a little about Spirits, Ghosts and Poltergeists. What is most important is for all who read this information, is not to allow one's human Ego to destroy one's opportunity to learn and understand the world of the **unseen and the unknown.** Read with an open mind and heart, and look within yourself for the truth, for such it is inner learning that will expand Consciousness and advance the human individual to a higher realm of understanding. You will see things as you have never seen them before. Advancing Consciousness where human Ego cannot exist or enter will allow you to communicate with higher forms of beings that exist beyond the physical plane. Remember, these beings have existed for **billions of your Earthly years in a vibration that is pure bliss.**

What is Spirit? Spirit is your life essence, the life force that is housed in your physical body. Without it the human body could not and would not exist. You could not walk or eat, or communicate. You could not smell the flowers or see the birds flying in your skies. You would not be able to think or remember anything. The human vehicle would only be an empty shell. As I mentioned a moment ago, Spirit has existed for billions of your Earthly years and Spirit is limitless in all things.

Spirit is truly the master of life itself, from each incarnation, you as human beings have had knowledge encoded within the essence of your being, and your being is created from pure Light which has evolved from the beginning of existence, and will always exist. Spirit cannot perish - only your physical vehicle perishes, mostly from abuse and dis'ease.

When a human being chooses to leave their human body and allow it to perish, depending on the individual's understanding and conditioning from their human life, they will separate from their physical body and their Spirit will enter the fourth dimension where no physical matter exists. **In the fourth dimension there are countless levels of Consciousness.** If an individual has lead a life of hatred, violence and fear, and has been highly conditioned by belief systems, on their Spirit leaving their human body, they will take with them their fear of death. This can and does create enormous fear and uncertainty because of the human Ego, and can trap them within the lower levels of the fourth dimension, known as the **Astral Vibration.**

When a human being **'dies'** and their Spirit leaves their human body, they will enter the fourth dimension. If they have lead a life of fear or violence, were on drugs or caused pain to others, or believed in the human myth of the **Devil,** it is most certain that they will take those negative fears, conditions and beliefs with them into the **Astral Vibration.** They will recreate the same circumstances and situations that existed in their human life up until their human death. The reason for this is that the human Ego is the enemy within and it is the human Ego that maintains the beliefs, fears and conditioning of a lifetime when the human life is ended and the Spirit enters the Astral Vibration.

The purpose of Spirit, is to experience human incarnations from one life to another in order to learn from life in a physical form, but not to hold onto the past. When the past becomes your present it also becomes your future, and upon your physical death, the past will be encoded into your next incarnation where you will have another opportunity to learn from it and let it go. What you as an individual do in this lifetime governs your next incarnation, be it negative or positive.

If you as an individual live a physical life without negative emotion, have deep **Unconditional Love for all of life,** and seek a deeper understanding to the purpose of Creation and the meaning of life, then you as a human being will evolve and grow in **Consciousness and Awareness.** You will become consciously aware of the presence of Spirit and other vibration, and upon passing from your human body, your Spirit will enter into a higher realm of the fourth dimension with complete awareness. Through the power of thought you will be able to manifest whatever you wish and you will be able to travel unhindered within other realms and vibrations, and communicate with other forms of life that are beyond physical matter.

When Spirit exists the human vehicle, Spirit is only limited by human conditioning. This is why it is most important to strive to become a balanced, loving and caring human individual, and allow conscious growth by dealing with and dissolving any negative beliefs, conditioning and emotions from your human life. Learn that to love and respect yourself as a human being you must learn to love and respect all others and all of life itself, no matter what form it takes.

Spirit in the true essence is always in a state of pure bliss because there are no negative or positive aspects to its existence - **it simply is.** Spirit does not judge in any way, nor does it have an opinion. Spirit experiences life, moving forward, never looking back or regretting. Spirit have been trying to communicate with human beings for a very long time. Many human beings say they have seen Ghosts **(in reality, Spirits)** and become very afraid of them. There is no reason to be afraid - it is only beliefs and conditioning. **Spirits/ Ghosts cannot harm you.** When you hear strange noises or observe furniture or objects moving and floating around, it is

116 Roman Harambura

simply their way of trying to communicate. Energy can and does build up, and it does result in situations where objects fly across rooms, and furniture moves from one position to another.

Spirit is not trying to harm you. If you feel fear, it is only your negative emotions and a fear of the unknown. This fear is what causes you to create harm to yourself, even situations where humans have claimed they were pushed down a flight of stairs by a Ghost. But in reality it was not the Ghost that pushed them - it was their own fears and conditioned beliefs that they would be harmed by the unseen beings.

Spirit can help solve all of your human crimes if humans would take the time to believe in them and learn to communicate with them. They truly are unseen witnesses who have the ability to step back in time and see the events all over again. Spirit are just like you, except they are not in a human physical form.

Fear is no doubt the greatest element that retards Consciousness advancement in human beings. If all human beings could go back in human time and remember your lives up to the age of five, you would remember the **invisible friends** you played with that your parents said were not there. Most adults forget their invisible childhood friends, and because they won't allow themselves to believe in them or see them, they impart this same conditioning into their children. Naturally, children love their parents and believe what they are told to be truth that these beings do not exist. And so human beings grow up and forget about the Spirits they once saw and played with, replacing their knowledge of these beings with a fear of them.

In a very brief way my being has explained what Spirit is. Ghosts in human terms are human beings who have passed from their bodies but may not necessarily know they are **'dead'**. This is why they will be seen just standing there, or floating endlessly without any direction. In many cases they look frightening and so physical humans become scared because of the way Ghosts look. In reality Ghosts are only a part of the energy of the **Spirit** that has left the body, and as a result are a **mindless, hollow outline, a shadow, much like what you would call a hologram.** They are caught between the physical third and the non-physical fourth vibrations, like being stuck in a crack between to objects. They have no conscious awareness, and like a human being in a coma, **there is 'nobody home'.**

When you see a **Spirit or Ghost,** or things move around your home, say hello to them. Ask for their name, and tell them yours. Take the time to sit and communicate with them. Express your concerns for them and say you wish to help them in any way you can. Send them **Unconditional Love and Light,** and ask them why they are there. It is very important not to fear them, for it is fear that forms the barriers and confusion between their world and yours.

What I am about to express now may be perceived as negative. Your Earth has had much violence throughout its history, and even though many have caused this violence upon humanity, there have also been great injustices put upon human individuals who in turn have caused further pain and misery to the human race. The negativity created by individuals from one life to another have created much fear, hatred anger and violence, passing from one generation to the next, which is why there is a very strong negative energy at work on your Earth. This negativity is caused by the human Ego. Human Ego is active in both physical form in your physical vibration and in Spirit form in the Astral Vibration.

When a human being passes from their body through a violent death, or has had a miserable life full of anger and violence, their hatred and anger is so great that they will seek revenge in any way they can upon other human beings to make themselves feel better. When these Spirits enter the Astral Plane they take their negative Ego with them, and it this Ego that continues to cause suffering and pain in your human world. **All they can see is violence and hatred, and that alone gives them power to manipulate the weak and vulnerable.**

These Spirits are referred to by human beings as Poltergeists, but in reality they are only a negative form of energy. They use human fear to create and cause situations that can lead to physical harm, and they especially prey upon the weak and easily manipulated. They become leaders and dominators in the lower levels of the astral vibration, much like such humans are leaders and dominators in your physical vibration. They can and do cause human beings a great deal of pain and misery. Some learn to forgive and overcome their pain, and become compassionate, loving beings when they next incarnate. Others will continue to experience the same miserable life, life after life. It all depends on circumstances and upbringing in physical life.

All human beings are beautiful beings of Light, but some are misguided by human Ego. To have a peaceful world each of you as human individuals need to first become peaceful within yourselves and live a human life of compassion and caring for all of life. Obtain the wisdom to be understanding and loving not only to yourself, but to your neighbours, and by doing this your awareness will grow. When you grow and evolve you will be able to communicate with Spirit, and knowing Spirit will give you an understanding of your true existence. **Nothing ever dies, it only transforms into another form of energy. Spirit is Endless and Eternal.**

If you have any more questions about **Spirits, Ghosts and Poltergeists,** please feel free to ask of my being, whatever it may be. My being will share all with anyone who is willing to listen with an open mind and an open heart. At this moment your Earth has a new conscious energy being transmitted to all who choose to connect and grow in consciousness. Remember always that growth and awareness is your choice alone.

BECOMING A HEALER, MEDIUM OR CHANNEL (NO-21)

Question:

If I become a healer of the Light, what must I do? Does it mean I am also a channel of the Divine Light? Will I have the ability to become a medium for Spirit, to express their knowledge and their messages to share with all? And if this is the case, what must I do with my life to achieve this outcome?

First dear Seeker, you must believe in yourself, your very essence, that you are indeed a **Spark of Light** that is connected to all things as all things are connected to you. You as a human being must connect to your inner feelings that come from your heart and are spontaneous in the moment of life. **Every human being needs to live in the moment.** Not the past, nor the future, but in the moment where experiences can be enjoyed without placing any form of judgement upon them. **Not negative or positive, just a pure state of being.**

To become a Healer of the Light, a Channel for knowledge, or a Medium that sees Auras surrounding all of life, always remember it starts from within, **where your true teacher exists.** It is also very important to have **your mind, body and spirit in balance and harmony.** Begin by learning to **love and accept yourself,** everything and everyone around you. Allow yourself to sit or lie, and **still your mind** by stopping all the chatter of your human brain. Go within yourself to find the place of peace and harmony that exists within. **Be patient** and discover the wonderment of your true self, **your essence, your divinity.**

If you truly want to, you can achieve what you wish or desire from your human life. If you desire material possessions in your human life then you can create this reality if you truly believe in yourself. If you choose to develop your inner awareness and understanding for the good of all humanity, then you can create this also. **It is your choice. You each have the Light of Creation within you to do this.**

Once you truly have achieved Self-Realisation, the realisation that you are a part of Creations' Totality, that you are living energy and infinite, you will understand that you will no longer need to seek answers from outside of yourself. You will no longer find you have a need to look to others for understanding. **You will discover that all truth comes from within.** The hardest lesson for all human beings is the lesson of believing in oneself in the face of all the beliefs and conditioning that each of you are subjected to over a lifetime, passed down from one generation to the next, encoded in your genetics.

You have all heard of the psychic named **Nostradamus.** In reality, he should be called a visionary. He was a human being who could see beyond the human world of matter. He would not express too much to others because their fears and beliefs would have caused the masses around him to over-react and he would have been accused of **witchcraft and burnt at the stake as an advocate of the Devil.** In your human time to come witch-hunts will re-emerge and religious groups will force your governments to take action and create laws that will persecute those who claim to be psychics.

I will go one step further. **Approximately 200 to 300 of your Earthly years ago,** most of your religious priests understood the **chakra centres** and could communicate with **Spirits** in the Astral Vibration. Eventually, because of fear that the average human would gain too much knowledge and have no further need of priests, medium ship among your clergy was outlawed. There was a fear that they would lose control of the people. Religion, created by human man, has been dominating humanity through fear, and if you are honest to yourself, you will see that most wars throughout your human history have been created by or through religion, and religion continues to cause conflict among your people on Earth.

It is most important for anyone who wishes to become a **Healer of Divine Light, a Channel of Knowledge, or to be in Communication with Spirit**, that you never **become judgemental or criticise another's beliefs.** All human beings learn in their own time. Some learn in one lifetime, others may take several lifetimes. When a human being is ready to accept another level of thinking and understanding, they will seek out the knowledge to advance their Consciousness beyond their present level of thinking. **Every human being has the capability of becoming a healer, a medium or a**

channel. The secret to achieving this? **Believe in yourself,** and know that you already are a healer, a medium and a channel.

Meditation is the key to connecting to the wisdom and knowledge that lies within you. Through meditation you connect with the **Divine Light** that is your essence and is your connection with Creation. Meditation will help you flow through your human life, and as your level of thinking and understanding grows, your human Ego will become less and less active in your life. **Your Light, which is infinite love,** will begin to emanate all around you, and you will feel it and know that your Spark of Consciousness is coming forth.

Your past will be just a memory of experiences, neither good nor bad, and your future will not concern you. But your present moment will be balanced and you will have a deeper understanding that all of life is most precious. The whole purpose of meditation is not to think with your confused, distracted human brain, but to simply learn to relax so that you can raise your vibration in order to connect with higher energies. In turn these higher energies will give you a greater sense of balance overall. The connection with your inner being will allow you to channel knowledge that will give you enhanced understanding and the wisdom to accept your own Divinity of pure Unconditional Love. In Spirit of Light, all is Unconditional Love. To become a healer, a channel or a medium, love must flow from your inner being first, and then flow outwardly to all where this Light of Love can be directed wherever or to whoever you wish just by the power of thought, for thought is energy.

I know many human beings who have tried this simple method, some for a week, some for a month or several months, and have then given up mainly because they do not believe in themselves or that it could be so simple. Many human beings have been highly conditioned for ten, twenty, forty years, with expectations of achieving results within a short period of time, but if you have the courage to persist with this simple method, you will succeed. Quieten your mind and go within. As long as you come from an honest heart, within your being you will find what you seek and achieve what you desire.

Let us look at **Nostradamus** again. He became a healer, medium and channel at a very young age in his human life. In reality, all of his predictions have come true, but some of your scientific people have tried to disprove his predictions because of their fears and closed minds. They say time factors are very different and the predictions are out by months or even years. This may be true, but they have forgotten one very important factor - time during **Nostradamus'** lifetime was very different to what it is now. Humanity has been exploding atom bombs and as a result have put the planet off its axis, and this has sped up human time. Your physical vibration has been speeding up and this is one of the primary reasons why the predictions are not time accurate. But your scientists will not admit this truth. To them it is just another theory to be disproved.

Time is only a creation of man - it is man-made. **Moses, for example lived for over 600 of your Earth years,** and even fathered a human son when he was **500 years old.** Time was much slower then. But time in this moment is getting faster, and human beings are vibrating at a higher frequency than your ancestors of several centuries ago. **There will come a moment in your human time when you will no longer be able to exist in the Third Dimensional Vibration of matter.**

Try to see time as an illusion. Close your eyes for a few moments and try to think of nothing but white light. When you are ready, open your eyes. You may feel as if your human world does not exist and time is unimportant. What you were doing was closing off your third dimensional world of physical matter and allowing your Consciousness to experience a higher vibration. You may ask **"How do I stop the illusion of my human world?"** First see the falseness that surrounds you. Begin living your truth by letting go of the things which bind you to the emotional world of human Ego, **especially stress.** By doing this you will begin the process of healing yourself in the Light of Creation. Creation is within you and around you, and that healing light will shine through you. You will no longer be clouded by the falseness of human Ego, no longer manipulated. **Then you can become the living truth.** If you allow the material world to be your whole life you will be walking around with blinkers on your eyes, only seeing what is in front of you and never seeing the whole picture.

Slowing your human life down starts with slowing down your human brain. This is very important if you wish to become a healer, channel or medium. There cannot be conflict or negative emotion in your human life, and if there is, it will be a hindrance to your quest. Balancing your energy centres is most important if you are to allow the flow of higher energies. Anyone can become a medium within two months of your Earthly time, but that development is only brought forth from the lower planes of the **Astral Vibration,** meaning you will be communicating with those who have passed from their human life and who are trapped in the lower **Astral Vibration.** These entities can only give you the understanding they took with them when they passed from their human lives. **They will be able to communicate basic information, but they can also be harmful to the health of the medium, as many of these entities still carry with them their desire for Earthly habits and their emotions, and because of this, they can influence the medium or channel.**

To become a medium, channel or healer, you must consider the health of your human body first. If your body is in poor condition and health, then you must make healing yourself your first priority. **Eliminate bad and destructive habits such as smoking, alcohol, drugs and animal products, and drink plenty of fresh water to cleanse away the toxins.** Look at your thoughts, how you feel about yourself and others, and forgive others from your heart. Be pure in your mind and do not project negative thoughts towards others. Rather, try to project positive and loving thoughts. **The purpose of doing all these things is to bring your mind, body and spirit into balance.**

Your Consciousness will elevate your essence to higher forms of communication. The knowledge and information that you bring forth will amaze and astound you beyond comprehension. You will indeed be a true blessing to humanity as much as to yourself and those in your human life. You will have a deeper connection to all of life in all Universes, and your understanding of Unconditional Love will be a blessing to all those who come into your vibration. What comes from within is total truth, as it is your **divine spirit** expressing itself from the essence of **your soul.**

Nostradamus (who has made predictions up to 2,500), and his predictions have been ridiculed by many who feel threatened by his visions. They have taken it upon themselves to disprove his predictions and to discredit him. Only those with the same fears will believe the jeers and derision of those who discredit him.

Those who have become the living truth will see the truth in his predictions. It is very important to understand that with knowledge comes responsibility. Anyone who takes on the path of healing, channelling or medium ship takes on this responsibility. It is vital that such a human being comes from an honest heart, and that they have the wisdom and understanding needed to express only the truth from their lips. In the human species, the Ego is rampant, and there have been, and are many human beings who abuse this privilege because of their fears and a need to feel important.

To express non-truths from the Ego is to be a danger to your own personal growth, as well as to those you are trying to help. Be humble in your learning and realise it is Creation within you and around you that does the healing, both within the healer and the one being healed. As you progress on your new path of **self-discovery,** always be humble towards others, and express **Unconditional Love** in all that you do in your human life. You will learn you do not need to prove anything to anyone, and all that matters is to express divine love to all without judgement.

As you channel **Divine Light** from within your essence that is connected to **Creation's Totality,** your negative Earthly habits will begin to dissolve. Remember, if you have conflict and negative emotion in your human life, **the Light cannot shine through.** The Ego wears many faces of deceit and will create conflict. The more you allow the Light to come forth in your thoughts, the more your heart will shine, and the more your life will be joyous and abundant.

Have you ever closed your eyes, and in the distance of your inner world, seen a blue light with jagged edges in front of you? If you have, it is the beginning of your third eye opening, slowly but surely. Become more aware of your surroundings in your physical life and become closer to nature. **Within nature is knowledge.** Nature can teach you to become more aware of what is happening on your Earth and within her. **As much as the Elements of Fire, Water, Air, Earth and Spirit are a part of your essence, they are also a part of the Earth.**

There are many levels of **healers, channels, and mediums upon your Earth.** It all depends on the human individual and at what level of Consciousness they wish to exist. If your Earthly habits consist of eating animal flesh, smoking, drugs, alcohol, junk food and negative thoughts, it would be honest to say that you would only be able to use limited levels of energy and consciousness. To many this is a starting point of growing beyond human Ego and all of its beliefs and conditioning. The seeker of truth and knowledge recognises the importance of taking Personal Responsibility for one's own growth. **In your third dimensional world, most human beings see things in black and white, like night and day.** It only exists in your physical dimension. But there will come a moment in human time when night will no longer physically exist. The only reason night has existed up to this moment is because the human body needs rest to continually heal and regenerate itself. **When you are asleep, you're being ventures into the astral vibration.** Most of your time in that space can be a little cloudy and confusing, but there is much to learn there and it can be of help to you in your physical existence. It is also a great help in opening your psychic awareness. Most humans remember very little of their sleep-time experiences, especially when you first fall asleep.

Try this. As you lie on your bed, close your eyes and go within the stillness of your mind. See or feel a bright white light in front of you. See or feel it grown outwardly from within you and grow out all around your human body. Using the power of your imagination see yourself travelling on **Light and Sound** beyond your human body and beyond the fourth vibration into the fifth. See all of life and all universes from an unbiased perspective. Just allow your being, your essence, to be a part of the totality of Creation, and be in a pure state of being in that moment of your reality. Feel the light, the love of all things and the love of yourself. **Realise that knowledge and wisdom can set humanity free from its self-created illusions, misery and pain. You the individual can see how it is important to expand your consciousness beyond the beliefs and conditioning of your human Ego.**

This pure learning, as most human beings during their time of sleep only ever enter the Astral World. Because of their level of thinking, they create situations of fear, stress and anger from their own illusions. Most of the human species are afraid of physical death, having been highly conditioned into thinking a certain way about what death may be, and rarely being given the opportunity to gain a **deeper understanding of the infinite knowledge of life and death.**

It often takes a traumatic situation in one's human life to begin searching or willingly making changes to open the mind and heart in order to enter and experience parallel worlds. **There are many advantages to travelling into other realms and dimensions.** You can discover the truth of your heritage and why human beings exist on this planet called Earth.

Please always remember, there are many levels and forms of channelling. For example, many of your great music composers have and are channelling from other dimensions. Like artists, writers and poets, they know that their creativeness comes from within. Any idea that comes to you is indeed a form of channelling. **It all serves a purpose to some degree for the evolution of humanity as a whole.**

Ask yourself, what type of healer, channel or medium do you wish to be or become? Then, consider your human life and ask yourself if your physical life in mind, body spirit is balanced. **If not, what do you need to change?** Write these answers down on a piece of paper. You are part of Creation and Creation is part of you. You can make any changes that you choose, but are you willing to make those changes? **The human Ego does not like change.** It has lived in the past to the present and into the future, bringing the past forward with it always, like a cloud of negativity. **Change can only come about when you feel ready to step beyond your present level of thinking.**

To help you recognise what holds you back from your journey of self-discovery, you will need to look at the human Ego. **What are the traces of Ego? They are beliefs, conditioning, fears, anger, hatred, vanity, lust, greed, lies, jealousy, insecurity, a need to dominate and control, power over others...** there is so much more you could add to this list, but all of the above are the negative aspects of human conditioning, which have been formed into belief systems. Anything can be changed if you the human individual are willing to put the effort in. In fact, these issues must be addressed, and these traces dissolved, if you want to bring the mind, body and spirit into balance. These traces are the illusions of humanity, and once addressed and dissolved, their hold over the individual will be released. **But only you, the individual can do it for yourself.**

Once you bring the mind, body and spirit into alignment with Creation, and you re no longer held to ransom by your human Ego, then you

will truly begin your journey and development as a channel, healer or medium. All human beings channel to some degree, but how much they channel depends of their level of consciousness. I have another question for you - as a human individual, would you prefer to channel Unconditional Love or human Ego? If your answer is Unconditional Love, then your development has already commenced.

The entity called Jesus had great visions and infinite knowledge. When he expressed his words, the people felt the truth from his heart, and many would say they felt a great love emanating from him. **But many also felt fear.** They did not want to change their old ways. **Jesus would say "The spirit is willing but the flesh is weak".** He meant you all have the free will to choose your path, but your fears are greater than the courage you would need to stand up and be free of your human Ego. The greatest lesson for all of humanity is to grow consciously beyond the human Ego. Human beings are highly conditioned throughout every lifetime - through encoded genetics which are then reinforced with beliefs and social expectation. For many these conditions and beliefs run so deep, that they are passed on from one incarnation to the next.

If you have inward insecurities, then they will be expressed outwardly, and you will continue to live with those insecurities, life after life, until you are willing to face and dissolve your fears, and forgive those from your past. The balance within will then be projected outwardly, and you will begin to see with greater clarity. In choosing a path light - of healing, channelling or medium ship - you must realise in this moment that there is no room for human Ego of any amount. **Only truth and unconditional love can be present and expressed.**

Here is a small affirmation for you to say:

Please Creation, allow only the love and the truth to come from my heart and my lips.

It is very important that you believe in yourself and that what is coming forth is the truth. When Roman channelled while living on the Gold Coast in Queensland, he would always say these simple words before channelling

I am the light of Creation's totality, a spark of consciousness. Only truth can be expressed from my lips, and the love of Creation from my heart. I am that I am, now and forever more.

For about nine Earthly years, Roman used to channel a very beautiful soul named **Narishiewa.** He would allow **Narishiewa** to speak through him and many could feel his loving energies, just from his words. Roman's eyes used to water because he felt so much love for **Narishiewa. Roman was taught the simple ways of using healing light, and that is what it is all about, the simplicity of life. Narishiewa has now been reborn into a human life in a country you call Russia.**

I trust that what my being has expressed to you, the seeker of knowledge, will set you on the path to realising that you already are a **healer of light, a channel of light or a medium of light.** You only need to put the action into your human life, **and have the strength and courage to dissolve your human Ego,** to begin your journey of **Self-Realisation** and to become what you wish to become. Humanity needs to change their level of thinking and understanding if they are to grow in **Consciousness and Unconditional Love.** Do not just be a human animal, but become a true human being.

You are all beautiful beings in reality, and we are here for all of you, but it is your level of thinking that needs to change first, and then Consciousness will follow. Be blessed each and every one of you in Love and Light always.

A GUIDED MEDITATION: BY KUNTARKIS (NO-22)

My Being has been asked on many occasions to present a **guided meditation** so that each human individual can experience a **Self-Realisation of the planet Nar'Kariss,** and to open up the past memories of when each of you lived on **Nar'Kariss.** To allow yourselves to experience this meditation, please open your minds beyond the physical beliefs and conditioning of your human life and come to this journey with an honest heart to see your **brothers and sisters** in living consciousness. Free you of all human Ego and you will indeed experience a **Self-Realisation of the true self.**

You as the human individual may choose to use your own voice by taking my beings words and recording them, for your voice is your vibration and is very powerful. However, this is your choice.

Let us begin.

Lay down in a quiet place where you will feel safe and secure in your own vibration. As you lay there, push aside all thoughts of your daily life, and use the **power of your imagination** to visualise a ball of white light emanating from your heart centre. See how bright this light is. Feel its warmth and love for you.

Breath in deeply and exhale slowly, feeling this ball of light moving down your human body to your toes, and then going all the way up to the top of your head. Allow this process a few moments and feel the warmth of the light around and within your human body.

See the light dissolving any negative energies that are within you, and then see and know that your entire being has been transformed into pure white light. Allow yourself to continue feeling this process of the light and its warmth throughout your being, and know that this same light which is emanating from your heart centre, is all around you as well as within you. This light is emanating from the pores of your skin. Feel and sense this loving **white light** that has always been a part of you and always will be present in all of life.

You are now in a bubble of light which is a part of Creation's totality. Your human body is safe and secure, and your spirit which is **infinite, eternal and immortal,** is free to safely venture out of its human shell to experience another vibration. Using the **power of your imagination,** see yourself **project out of your physical body** and stand in **front of yourself.** Acknowledge that you are a beautiful human being and that your human body is safe and protected in Creation's light, of which you are a part of and always have been.

Being infinite light you are weightless. You are beyond the conditions of your physical third dimensional human world and human body. You can now realise that there are no limitations in **spirit vibration,** and you can venture out beyond your present vibration. Allow yourself, your spirit, through the power of your thought to rise up into the sky, going **higher and higher,** passing **beyond the Earth's atmosphere,** and enter into space itself. Stop for a moment and look back at your Earth. See the beauty of your Earth and feel its energy and love for you, for physically you are a child of this giant Mother. The Earth also has a spirit, and is a part of Creation as you are. Send love to the Earth and feel the love of the Earth coming back to your very being. You are in total harmony with all things and all things are in harmony with you.

Turn and begin to move away from the Earth and feel in your essence that you are being guided to your destination. **As you travel beyond all boundaries,** you can see other planets and shining stars around you. **Feel a great sense of joy and peace,** especially freedom in the knowing that you have freed your true self. Feel like you are going home and know that your encoded memories are waiting for you to discover them.

In the distance see a small speck of a planet growing larger as you come nearer. Begin to feel the excitement within your essence. You are upon the planet now and you see it is blue and clouded in a fine **white mist of light.** Notice there are no suns or moons, as **there is no day or night,** and there are no shapes of land masses as there are on Earth.

On this planet all is in a pure state of being. As you enter this mist of light you feel a deep love for all of life, and you feel happiness as you have never experienced before. You see many buildings shaped as domes. **These are transparent, for physical matter does not exist in this vibration.**

You see before you beings of light. They welcome you with open arms. You now stand before them and they express to you their love for you. You begin to feel that you know them, for time does not exist in this vibration. **One of the beings leads you to a place where all knowledge from the past to the present moment is recorded for all to see.** The purpose of this place is to open up your essence of truth. You will be allowed to view all knowledge to help you become open to all things. This place will reveal to you who you are, where you have come from and even where you are going. **This is your right as an infinite being of Creation's totality.**

You will now be left alone to view the knowledge your spirit being seeks to discover. Stay here as long as you wish. (This may take anywhere from five minutes to 10 minutes or more - it is your choice how long you stay.) As the moments pass in your quiet moments of existence and self-discovery, **know that you are activating your own Consciousness with the knowledge that is being presented to you.** You, dear brothers and sisters of light, begin to see your past lives. Feel that the past is the present, and the present is the future, for all things exist in the moment and all things are created in the moment. There is no right or wrong, good or bad, negative or positive. Everything is simply an experience of life and circumstances, not to be judged. This is truly a state of being in total bliss. When one judges, negative emotion is created and emotion can only exist in the third dimensional vibration of physical matter.

Begin to feel your **Unconditional Love for your own being and for all life.** Knowing your past, present and future, without any form of judgement, you will be able to break the chains that have held you a prisoner of your human Ego. **Now you are complete.** You have the knowledge and the understanding. **You have seen all of your past lives on Earth and also your existence on Nar'Kariss.**

You have completed your self-realisation. You have ventured beyond all of your self-created limitations and now it is time to gently return. Prepare yourself to make the return journey home to your human body on Earth.

You are lead back to where you first came. **Express your Love and Light to all your brothers and sisters, and begin your journey back to Earth.** See your being rising beyond the mist of light and passing the same planets and stars as you head towards Earth. In the distance, see the Earth shining brightly.

As you enter the Earth's vibration, feel the **Spirit of the Earth** that you are a part of. Descend to your quiet place and stand before your human body. Feel deep love towards your body for keeping your spirit safe while you live your physical existence. Know you can change any circumstances in your human life if you wish to, for you now have the knowledge of the past through to the present and beyond to guide you. You are a living essence of divine light and you can share this wisdom with all who seek it.

See your essence entering your human shell, feeling completely comfortable and fully aligned, balanced in mind, body and spirit. Notice how light your body feels and how your level of thinking and understanding has changed to become living consciousness.

When you are ready to open your eyes, **smile and feel joy,** for you have truly found out who you are - **a Spirit being that is Infinite and Eternal, Timeless and Ageless.** Accepting this realisation from an honest heart is where **your journey begins in Love and Truth.** You no longer need to be held back by the human Ego, the negative aspect of human existence. Take this journey through this meditation whenever you feel the need. As you grow in Consciousness you will become the living truth, an example for others to see and grow from in **light and love.**

Forgiveness is always the key. Unconditional Love is always the path to freedom.

Be Blessed in Love and Light dear human beings of this most precious Earth you call home. Always remember, we the **Nar'Karones** are here for you in all moments of existences. **Seek the Truth that is within all of life and all will be revealed.**

FROM ONE INCARNATION TO THE NEXT (NO-23)

Blessings of Light be upon each human being now and forever more. My Being has received many questions regarding why human life in this most precious moment has so much pain, misery, and especially struggle. Why do some humans have so much good fortune in their current life while others have very little, and no matter how hard they try, it always ends up in a negative situation.

Human beings as they are in this moment, have been evolving on this planet for the past **928,000** years. In reality, each of you have **lived thousands of human incarnations.** The whole purpose of human life is to learn and to understand **one main lesson.** It is to discover the wonderment of your true essence, **that you are an infinite spirit being, connected to all of life in all Universes, connected to Creation.** Creation is not a single entity, nor is it a supreme being greater than you as an individual. You as humanity are living Consciousness, shaped and formed as human beings, yet within you lies the **Light and Truth** of who and what you are.

Most human beings believe solely in their physical existences. **As long as you touch, taste, smell, hear or see something, you believe it to be true.** Yes, from a physical perspective that is the truth. But again, you the human individual must ask yourself this important question: **Why do you believe what you believe?** The answer is that you have been highly conditioned into belief systems, and this is what has been going on upon this planet **Earth for over 928,000 years.**

The human word 'incarnation' means to enter into human flesh. **Incarnation is singular,** while **Reincarnation is the plural,** meaning entering into human flesh many times over. There are spirits being born at this moment who are incarnating for the first time, purely to experience human life. Some of those spirits come from other realms of existence. Their purpose being to bring knowledge and wisdom to help humanity grow consciously. Some succeed, but many do fall prey to human Ego, and create imbalance in their lives, resulting in the creation of **'Karma'**, meaning the entity must incarnate again to bring the balance back into alignment.

Some of you may ask **"how can one bring back the balance, or dissolve the karma"**. The answer is simple. **Through Unconditional Love and Forgiveness for all of life,** and through forgiveness of oneself and all others. Remember the saying **"what you think you will become"**. Your actions in your present human life will govern your future, but will also govern your next incarnation, be it negative or positive.

Whatever is created in your present life as a human being is encoded in your spirit essence, and when you depart from your human vehicle, you take every though and action from that human life with you. And because Spirit is Unconditional Love and unbiased, to Spirit everything is simply an experience of learning.

Human Ego has been evolving over the entirety of human history. If you look back through your human history, and it is not a pleasant one. Take for example the man named **John F Kennedy,** who was born in the land of America and became the President of the people. The people of America loved him, and yet there were those who were very fearful of his power, because John F Kennedy was planning to make many changes in the government and its departments.

While he was winning the hearts of the people, there were those who were conspiring against him and **planning his assassination.** The spirit of **John F Kennedy** was not ignorant to assassination, for prior to that incarnation he had been **President Lincoln,** who was also assassinated by members of the American government because they were threatened of the changes he was implementing.

What is truly interesting is the entity known as **John F Kennedy** is now reborn as a human and is aged **3 years, 9 months.** He has been reborn in the lands you call the Middle East to human parents who are in a position to give their son a comfortable upbringing. Genetically his essence is encoded with the knowledge of his past life as **Kennedy,** and this will unknowingly shape his present life.

What is sad and needs to be understood by all human beings is when one is thinking on a negative plane and then creates negative actions as a result of that thinking, it not only affects them, but can affect an **"entire nation"**, as well as your human world, and the result is pain and misery.

To make it easier I will call this incarnation of **Kennedy** by name, **"Errisher".** When **Errisher** reaches **17 years of human age,** his human parents will send him to America for higher education, and he will spend the next **15 years learning the ways of America.** During that period of human time **Errisher** will become **a computer wizard.**

He will work his way into the **Military and Department of Defence,** and he will impress everyone with his knowledge of computers. At the human age of **32** he will return to his homeland. Within **(3) years** of his return he will be working for the **Middle East Military** and be given authority to set up and run their defence systems. **By the year 2040 the Middle East** will be able to **wage war** on any country because of the **nuclear power** that they have been developing for the **past 17 of your Earthly years,** and by **the year 2043** they will become one of the **biggest threats to all human societies.** When it is **Errisher develops his systems for war in the year of human time 2044, it could create a war that humanity may not recover from. You see, all about revenge of the human Ego.**

What each human being does not realise nor understand is this: **When a negative action is created, whether by a single individual or by the masses, it then creates a reaction.** In reality, what is created negatively or positively in this present moment of human time? Will be created in the human future, or in the next incarnation. What is called **Karma is like a coin** – it can be negative or positive. It all depends on the individual or the masses, and their level of understanding. There has never been a human being who can cheat their **self-created actions,** whether they are negative or positive. Even if it is not brought into balance in their current human life, it will be brought into balance in their next incarnation.

The balance is in the learning and understanding of becoming aware of who and what you as human beings are. In truth, you are **infinite and immortal.** You will never perish for you are **Spirits of Light,** and are a part of Creations' totality. The example of **John F Kennedy** is simply to show you that when a negative action is created against an human individual, the reaction in their next incarnation can be devastating, not just for a single individual, but for a nation or all of humanity. The purpose of incarnating over and over again is to grow beyond human Ego and learn to forgive, **not hate or judge,** but to learn to love yourself with Unconditional Love, so you can learn to love your family, your neighbours, your country, your world, even your brothers and sister in other vibrations of existence.

Even though your human life is of importance in the learning process of life and understanding, it is in reality your **personal responsibility to grow in consciousness.** The human Ego is your true enemy and has been encoding fear and conditioning through beliefs into your essence so they are passed on from one life to the next, and passed on through generations of families.

Another example of an entity that lives on your precious Earth at this moment in human time is a human female called **Britney Spears.** She is well known to the masses. But before she incarnated to be **Britney Spears** she knew she would become a famous entertainer from a young age. **Britney Spears** knew at age five she wanted to be a famous singer, and yes there is a reason for this. It has to do with her past incarnation. **Britney Spears** did not complete her cycle of life in her past life as the famous entertainer and actress **Judy Garland,** who also was famous at a young age.

Due to the circumstances created by the pressure and stress placed upon **Judy Garland** in the entertainment industry, **Judy Garland** took to alcohol and drugs to help her cope. The stress grew and so did the addictions, which sadly ended her human life. Even though **Judy Garland** was **personally responsible for her actions,** there were also others who helped create her demise and ultimate destruction.

So in this most precious moment of human time, **Britney Spears** has incarnated to complete her cycle of life, as long as **Britney Spears** allows herself to be an individual and not become stressed because of the control others have over parts of her human life. All will be in harmony. My being is not permitted to reveal any more about **Britney Spears,** mainly because she is entitled to her privacy.

My being has used only two entities as examples of reincarnation. This is because they are both well known to humans at this time. What is most important is that each human individual incarnate from one life to the next for the purpose of learning to grow beyond human Ego. Human Ego lives in the past and sadly has been creating the present and future for many human beings upon your precious Earth. When the human individual lets go of the past through **Forgiveness and Unconditional Love for all of life,** only then will the individual begin to see the Light of Creation within all of life in all Universes.

Only the Ego in a human being causes a human to believe they are **Greater or Superior** to another human being. However, through Unconditional Love one sees all of life as it is, without judgement. Everything in all Universes is a learning experience, and yes there will come a moment in your human time when incarnation will no longer be a process of human life. Your human bodies will **vibrate as higher forms of energy.** How long this process takes to achieve is unimportant. This moment is your opportunity to grow beyond your present level of Consciousness. Accept your being as it is, neither negative nor positive. Each of you have the power of **Creation's Light within you now.** If you choose to seek the Light within your very being, **you have already begun your journey of self-realisation.**

To choose Unconditional Love is to grow in Consciousness. To choose human Ego is to stay within **one's self-created illusions of pain and misery.** My Being will speak more on this subject of incarnation. Be Blessed dear human beings of this most precious Earth, for our Love for all of you has been and always will be within you – **it is the Light.**

THE FEARS OF HUMANITY (NO-24)

You the human individual must become the living truth before you can be of use to another. **The living truth comes from the Heart where Love, Compassion, Wisdom and Understanding exist.** When you live the truth and only the truth, then and only then will wisdom and knowledge become a part of you. All else is the illusion of fear, created by human Ego. Unconditional Love allows your knowing to be connected to Creation. You become a part of all things and all things become a part of you. **The choice is always yours.** Remember, only through an honest heart can the truth manifest itself in living consciousness. **All else is fear.**

To all human beings who live on this most precious Earth, we the **Nar'Karones** give our love to you, and we offer you knowledge to give you the wisdom and understanding to grow beyond the human Ego.

Fear is a human word meaning **'to be afraid'.** You may ask **'afraid of what?'** There are thousands of reasons why human beings have fear, **the most common being fear of the future, fear of the past, fear of life, and fear of death.**

Why do so many humans fear the future? It seems senseless when the future is not yet written. You the individual hold the key to your self-created future. The future is created in the moment by what you do in your present moment of human life, be it negative or positive. You alone are the **driver and the creator.** If you know what you are doing in your present moment and you have no fear of it, then why should you fear the future, you create from it?

Fear of the past has been an issue for humanity since your time began on this planet **928,000** years ago. For most, the past is built on a foundation of negative creation, firmly established through **beliefs and conditioning,** and carried genetically through the family line from one generation to the next, as well as through the Spiritual essence from one incarnation to the next. The past should not govern the present moment or the future, especially if it has been created from negative energies. Everything in humanity has been created from the past, resulting in a violent history which continues to exist in your present moments of existence.

Fear of life. Why do so many human beings fear life? Is it emotions passed onto them by their human parents through genetics, or is the pressure of expectations placed by human societies upon the human individual? Many human beings throughout your world live day to day in fear, believing they are not good enough. They accept whatever life gives them, believing they are not capable of controlling their life, but rather the necessities of their life controls them. They become **human robots, not questioning the human laws and conditioning that govern their lives, and they make a thousand excuses for why they are a 'failure' in their life.**

Fear is a self-created illusion, created from the past from negative energy, and reinforced by belief systems. **Life is infinite.** To realise this is the beginning of an understanding that all of life is equal in all things. **No one is superior to another.** Yes, there are human individuals who are more consciously aware and advanced in their knowledge, **but not superior in spiritual essence to another.** Fear of life is simply a physical manifestation from one's experiences of physical life, reinforced by negative belief systems.

Fear of death is perhaps the greatest fear. Ask yourself, 'why do I fear death?' Do you really believe it is the end of your existence? Once you're human body has passed its last breath, **there is no more...** Or do you believe what your parents believed, or what your religion has told you, or even what you have been told by friends or what you have read in books?

The word 'death' in human terms means 'to be no more'. There is a much held human belief that once you have died you will simply be a memory in your loved ones' hearts. This is an understanding created by humans a long time ago and has followed humanity throughout history. Humans have been on this precious Earth for more than **928,000** and yet 'death' is still misunderstood! Of course, what you the human individual believe is your free will. What I will say to you is this: **To live to the beliefs and conditioning of human life is a great limitation to one's conscious growth. Step beyond the limitations set by man's fears, and you will take your greatest step of all - a step towards conscious freedom.**

Death is just a word. It has no more power than what you, the individual give it. Physical death is the release of your infinite spirit, that part of you which is eternal, immortal, timeless, and ageless; your divine essence that is a part of the totality of Creation. When you take your last human breath and release it from your human vessel, you free your spirit to enter into the **astral vibration,** where there are many levels of consciousness. There is no such thing as **'final death'** in the human world, just as there is no such thing as death in other worlds of existence.

There is however transformation from one life form to another. This is one of the lessons human beings have chosen to learn in this third vibration of physical matter; to learn to let go of the fear of losing something physical in order gain a deeper understanding of infinite existence. This infinite existence is a part of your past from long before you were placed on this Earth to learn the lesson of Unconditional Love for all of life.

As do all forms of life on your Earth, the only thing that will perish, decay and return to your Mother Earth are your physical bodies, the shells that house your divine essences. **Your scientists have proven that you are 99% energy and less than 1% matter.** But because you have incarnated thousands of times into human lives, you have been highly conditioned from life to life, and this is where the dilemma exists. To dissolve your past you need to step beyond your negative actions, emotions and fears, and forgive in total Unconditional Love, letting go of the conditions and beliefs that bind you to those emotions and fears.

Two more examples of fear in human existence are fear of the unknown and fear of change, which as you can see, are interrelated and in reality are two parts of the same fear. Ask yourself if you **fear the unknown.** Ask from an honest heart and listen to the first answer that comes to you. Do not ask your logic for the answer will come from a well-rehearsed script from your human brain, that is, from your past. Such an answer has been created by the human Ego which will tell you anything you want to hear so long as you bury any uncertainty that may have come to the surface. Ask from your heart and you will hear what you need to hear, not what you want to hear.

Beliefs and conditioning are founded on fears, and these fears hold an individual back from advancing toward a higher form of understanding. Fears take hold of your human life when negative experiences resurface at any given moment. They make you believe in the negative emotion that formed them. Many human beings live in their negative past experiences, reliving their past throughout their human life, allowing it to influence the decisions they make, the actions they take, and to dictate how they interact with other human beings. They relive those past experiences continuously throughout their lives. **The only reason human beings fear the unknown is because they live in the past.** They create their future from their present moment, which is grounded in fear. This is why so many suffer pain and misery for the entirety of their lives. The unknown holds opportunities for both conscious growth and human advancement. **Fear of change,** which is related to fear of the unknown, is created from a fear of stepping beyond the beliefs and conditioning of your human life. Unless you push the boundaries of your understanding, you will never grow consciously, and what little you do know and understand will be passed on to future generations. **Such an inheritance is not a gift,** but an impediment that not only affects the handful of human beings your life crosses paths with, but also humanity as a whole. The metaphor of a pebble being tossed into a still pond shows the far reaching implications that action as the rings created from the tossed pebble reach out to the farthest reaches of the shore. **So too do your actions based on your beliefs and conditioning affect the pond of human physical life.**

Human beings fear stepping beyond their beliefs and conditioning in case they are seen as different to others. The fear of being different of expressing something other than the accepted belief or conditioning, is rife in humanity. **There is a fear of individuality.** Those daring enough to be an individual from a negative perspective are given attention, and those that are different but not harming others are made out to be **harmful or 'evil'.** Again, fear dictates how humans view other humans, and fearful humans then indoctrinate the masses with beliefs and conditioning to reject individuals who are trying from another level of Consciousness to raise human understanding.

This is sad, for those human beings who are trying to grow consciously end up shutting down their growth and become just another follower, denying themselves the experience of being a leader in themselves. **You can be different and think for yourself.** Seeking inner knowledge is not a sin, it is a blessing and a gift for your conscious growth as an infinite Being of Light. **Knowledge is within all of life - it can manifest in the human**

individual. You can make any changes in your human life if you choose to. Just let go of your fears and step beyond the beliefs and conditioning of your human Ego.

The human Ego is the enemy within that holds you back from evolving beyond your present level of thinking and understanding. **Inner knowledge is freedom from the shackles of your past.** Once you the human individual make that conscious choice to step beyond your fear of change and of the unknown, the realisation of that knowing will manifest within your human life, and you will find the courage to help you make all the changes you need to.

All of you dear human beings are much more than just flesh and blood. Without your infinite Spirit of Light, your human bodies could not exist. You the individual must use your free will to choose what **"YOU"** want or need from your human life. You must ask yourself, how many more excuses will you make before you are ready to put into action the changes required in order to go forward in your understanding?

All of life in all the Universes is made up of magnetic energies. They manifest in accordance with your level of understanding, and govern your level of thinking which in turn manifests into your human life. How much this manifestation occurs will depend on the lessons of life you have chosen to learn and how well you have learnt those lessons.

Humanity to this day is governed by its past of over 928,000 years of history. Each of you have lived many incarnations on this planet you call Earth, and throughout your history, all of humanity has been highly conditioned from one incarnation to the next. Be it negative or positive, this conditioning has been encoded genetically in your flesh bodies and Spiritually in your essence. The negative emotions that manifest as fears, and which each of you are experiencing in your present moment, have been created from the past. Unless you act to dissolve that past, those fears and emotions will continue to create your future as well.

Fear created from negative experiences, from one life to the next, is reinforced by the human Ego. **To face fear is to see the truth.** To see the truth of your fear is the key to dissolving those fears back into the nothingness from which they were first created. **Once you have dissolved your fears, your human**

Ego will no longer have power over your destiny. You, your Spirit, will have the power to **heal and forgive,** and to manifest within your human life all that you need. The Light that is within you will emanate outwardly, and you will live and feel the Unconditional Love that is your essence. All the knowledge and wisdom of existence will be manifest within humanity and upon your precious Mother Earth. Never seek the truth outwardly for it is the past. Seek truth from within your inner being and all will be revealed.

We the Nar'Karones send our love to each of you dear human beings. May you all stand in the Light of Creation's totality, and May the **Wisdom and Freedom of Self-Realisation** be upon you all?

THE REALITY OF HUMAN DREAMS (NO-25)

Welcome to all who seek to expand their knowledge and understanding. When the individual has made a conscious decision to expand their awareness, knowledge itself, which is infinite, will seek out the seeker, and self-realisation will become a part of that human individual. The truth is almighty present in all things and in all life, and it takes but a moment to become aware of it.

How many human beings believe that dreams are just a fantasy, a creation of confused thoughts that have been created by the human brain? Many would say yes, that dreams are a creation and a fabrication of the human brain. But this is far from the truth.

Most human beings have fearful experiences in their time of sleep, and in most cases these are a creation of their personal human lives. No matter what your beliefs or conditioning, each human being during their time of sleep releases themselves from their human body and enters the fourth vibration, known on your Earth as the **Astral World.** Within this **Astral World** there are many levels of consciousness.

What level of Consciousness each human being enters into within this vibration will depend on that individual's level of understanding and awareness. The whole purpose of your **Astral World** is to help each human being come to terms with their self-created limitations, which is why all human beings are at different levels of understanding and growth.

Most dreams, which are actual experiences in the **Astral World,** are the confused expressions of the human individual, and quite often cannot be explained. But if you stop and ponder a while on your experiences, you would begin to realise that **Astral World** is another world of existence, but on a different level of Consciousness. Your experiences are on a Spirit level where physical matter does not exist, just as in your physical world you are unaware of the existence of Spirit energies. To bring forth this awareness, the individual needs to open the doorway that is always closed to human physical sight because of human conditioning and beliefs.

Spirit has been a topic of great interest throughout your human history, and still is to this moment. It will continue to be of great interest in your future moments to come. What is most important for all of humanity to understand is that without your infinite spirit, your human bodies would not exist. You each are the driver of your own existence. Most of the knowledge from your past has been lost or destroyed by those who are afraid of individuals growing beyond their control or domination.

Throughout human history there have always been the controllers and the followers. For humanity to grow in Consciousness, each human individual must become a leader in their own right, and step beyond human Ego by letting go of the past and living in the present moment. They will then become one with all things in nature and Creation. To accomplish this task, the human individual needs to gain inner knowledge which will give them wisdom and understanding of their human existence. It will also give them an understanding of the purpose of Spirit, and will allow them to look from an honest heart at humanity. One would have to say the human world is full of self-created fear. The lower levels of the **Astral World** are also full of self-created fears.

If an individual's human life is created from negative experiences, where anger, hatred, violence and poverty exists, the human individual will have thoughts of negative emotions. These will govern their future, but will also govern their experiences in their time of sleep when they are in the **Astral World.** What each human being creates along their path of human life, be it negative or positive, that will be taken from an emotional level into the **Astral World,** and all experiences in that world will be created from these emotions. In most situations, these experiences are full of confusion and fear.

There is much that is negative which exists upon your **Physical Earth.** These things also exist in the **Astral World** because human beings create these same negative things in the **Astral World** as they do in their physical world. **Wars, murders, rape, deceit, domination, poverty, pain, misery, anger, hatred, jealousy, vanity, ignorance - they all exist in the lower levels of Consciousness within the Astral World.** Whatever negative emotions are created in your third vibration of matter, so they are also created in the fourth vibration of the Astral. To understand human dreams first you must understand yourself. To stop the control of the human Ego you need to look at your self-created fears.

Many human beings will say they do not dream. But that is far from the truth. Every human being experiences in their time of sleep the separation of their **Spirit into the Astral World.** There are two main reasons why many do not remember their experiences, their dreams.

First, some dreams have a lot of confusion and are full of fearful encounters, so they are blocked by the human brain to prevent the individual being traumatised. The human brain is not equipped to be able to unravel those experiences.

Second, there is usually too much going on in most people's brains, meaning there is too much chatter or thinking. Many human beings all over the world find it hard to go to sleep because their thoughts keep them awake. They resort to drugs or natural preparations to help them finally fall asleep, and when they awaken, their brain is active again so they are not in a peaceful state to be able to remember their experiences.

It is the negative emotions in one's human life that keep a human being prisoner in their self-created lives. It is the same in your time of sleep. If you take your negative emotions with you into the **Astral World,** more fears will be created and those fears can then be brought back into the physical world when you awaken. Such experiences can and do create fear and confusion in your physical life.

Many human beings go to bed in a bad mood, or are angry with someone, or depressed or stressed. These are all negative emotions created by the human individual, and these emotions will go with that human into the **Astral World** during their sleep time and will create negative experiences in their dream state. Many human beings upon waking are usually still in a bad mood or feel negative, or still angry, or depressed or stressed, and feel even more tired than they did the night before.

It is most important that when you go to lay down to sleep, you do so in a peaceful state of mind and have calm, pleasant thoughts, and feel good about yourself. Do not go to bed feeling confused or angry, and try not to watch anything too stimulating on your television, especially anything negative before bed.

Before you go to bed, find the moments in your human time to meditate on the stillness of your mind and fill yourself with white light by seeing a ball of white light at your heart centre. Feel it emanate throughout your inner being and then outwardly until it is all around your human body. Place a white light around any negativity you may be feeling and say the following words:

I place the Light of Creation's Totality around all my negative emotions and thoughts, and I dissolve them back into the nothingness from which they were first created. As I lay my body down to sleep, I fill my whole being with Unconditional Love and I send this same Unconditional love to my family, and to all of humanity. I know Unconditional Love is infinite, timeless, ageless and endless. I will take this love with me in my time of sleep and all I experience will be for my highest good. I am Love. I am Light.

Human experiences in the **Astral World** during your time of sleep can be of great benefit to the individual, as well as the human world, as long as the individual is willing to face their fears and grow beyond their human Ego. Do not allow negative distraction to govern your human life. The **Astral World** and all its levels of understanding and learning were created to restore balance within Creation. In our vibration of energy the **Nar'Karones** do not have sleep time, but we do have visions and we use those visions to create our future. Human beings have experiences called dreams.

Can you imagine if all dreams were of a positive energy, what an infinitely more peaceful world humanity would create? You would be able to travel to other Universes and planets, and see from new eyes that all of life is infinite, and that there are thousands of different life forms at all different levels of Consciousness in evolution, understanding and awareness.

When you step beyond the human Ego you then step beyond all fears and insecurities. You the individual, and humanity as a whole, would have dreams, visions, far greater than the dreams of negativity of your human Ego at present. This transformation of Consciousness for humanity starts with the human individual. Come to terms with your physical fears and your dream time fears. Once you have faced yourself, your fears, your human Ego will no longer have power over you, and in your dream time you will be free from the self-created prison that has taken many lifetimes to create. What is known to the individual as dreams can either give you freedom or make you a prisoner from one life to the next.

My Being has expressed on many occasions that knowledge is the gateway to complete freedom, awareness and understanding. It is the knowing that is within all of humanity and is your birth right. Do not allow your Earthly distractions to keep you from infinite truth and wisdom. It can be a painful journey to face your fears. Yet on the other hand the discovery of inner knowledge and the wisdom that is gained, is the greatest wealth one could acquire. That knowledge has always been there and waits patiently for each human being to bring it to their conscious awareness.

To dream from your self-created fears is the illusion of your human Ego. To dream from your heart is the balance of Mind, Body and Spirit, in complete harmony with all of life. May all of humanity be blessed in the Light and Love of Creation, now and forever more?

THE MUNE'HAR CIVILISATION (ALIENS) (NO-26)

It has been expressed to my Being that there are human individuals who wish to know more about other life forms, that is Alien beings on other planets. My Being has chosen a civilisation called the **Mune'hars.**

The **Mune'hars** are known throughout many universes as explorers of new worlds, and it seems humanity has caught their interest the **Mune'hars** have been visiting humanity over the last **40 years of your Earth time.** The research they have been carrying out is on the genetic makeup of the human body, as well as the spirit energies that keep the physical form alive in your third vibration.

The **Mune'hars** do not have physical bodies like humans. They are not as dense in matter and have no body fats. They are much thinner in structure, but on average would be around three times stronger than the average human male. The skin covering their body structure has a rough texture like thousands of little lumps, and unlike humans, they have no body hair. They do not feel heat or cold like humans do.

The **Mune'hars** are shorter in height to the average human, being around **1.2 metres tall in both males and females.** Their eyes are similar to humans in shape, but have **dark eyeballs** with **yellow irises.** They see very well in darkness and in daylight. **They have four fingers of the same length, but no thumb, and their fingers do not have nails.** Their feet have no toes, and are flatter and slightly larger than the average human foot. Their ears are quite small and round, and are very sensitive to sound. **They do not like any kind of loud sound.** Their nose is much smaller than a human nose, and they have one nostril. They also only have one lung which is quite large considering the size of their bodies. What is most interesting is, if they need to, they can take a breath in and use that breath for a total of **16 minutes** before they would need to take another breath. Very much in tune with their body's senses, the **Mune'hars** can **slow their bodily functions to 23%** if required and still function well from a physical perspective.

The **Mune'hars** do not have obvious, **exposed sexual organs like human beings,** and their mating rituals are very different to that of humans. When they wish to procreate, the male and female stand facing each other and allow their chests and stomachs to touch. The little lumps on their skin increase in size to about half a centimetre. The male oozes a thick white liquid from the lumps on his body, and the female oozes a clear liquid from hers. Once the two liquids mix, the colour changes and it becomes a greenish blue liquid, indicating fertilisation has begun. This transformed liquid is absorbed back into the female's body via the blood stream and within three days of human time the **Mune'har female is pregnant.**

The **Mune'hars** lifestyle is clean and pure, meaning they have no poisonous chemicals in their air, they do not take drugs and consume only nutritious food. As a result, they do not suffer from dis'ease, nor are they unbalanced to the point where they are violent towards each other. The **Mune'har** female is pregnant for three months of your human time, and when their offspring is born, **there are no genetic defects,** there are no negative emotions, and there is no Ego. When the **Mune'har** female is ready to give birth, she lies down and from her left side an opening appears from where the new being is born.

Once the child is born, the female's side closes up and the **Mune'har** couple become both parents and teachers to their child they only ever have one partner in their lifetime, there lifespan being around 415 human years. The **Mune'har** do not have time or live to time, therefore they see only the moment as true reality.

The Mune'har eat a protein based diet from the plants that grow readily on their planet. They do not drink any form of liquid, as all their body's needs come from their vegetation, and they do not harvest any form of animal life for consumption. They release body wastes as do humans. All **Mune'hars** spend many moments of their existence in 'Urheer' which means quiet time, meditation, inner travel for conscious growth and knowledge. Their new born offspring do not go to any type of school. Instead, knowledge and wisdom is passed on to them by their parents. There are no night clubs, bars, movie theatres, skiing in snow or climbing mountains, playing football or any other kind of sport. From a human perspective this would be a boring existence, but their lifestyle must be viewed from their point of view.

They have no wars, no crimes or violence, no drugs, no pain or misery, no corruption, no competition to set themselves up for failure, no vanity or negative thoughts, no anger, hatred, greed, or lust. They do not wish to control or dominate. They have no doctors or lawyers, no police to enforce the law, and consequently there is no justice system as you have on Earth. There is no need for such things because they have complete Unconditional Love for all, equality for all. They are a peaceful and balanced society where the individuals who form their society do not place judgement upon others.

The **Mune'hars** travel throughout many Universes, and help the civilisations of the worlds they visit, to grow in harmony with life, to expand their Consciousness, and to bring balance into their lives instead of struggling against life.

They are explorers of life, of truth, of wisdom. There are societies that have tried to war against them but all have failed. The **Mune'hars** are not aggressive but they will defend themselves. **They never injure another or inflict pain.** What they have created for their defence is a shield of reverse magnetic energy, a field of atoms reversed in their structure. This shield surrounds their planet, which is approximately half the size of your Earth, and keeps it impenetrable from attacks. **The Mune'har ships can pass through and return safely because the same field is around their ships.**

The **Mune'hars** that have travelled to your planet have taken many humans on to their ships. Their purpose is to help realign the genetic information for acceptance of new information, and to awaken the old knowledge that lies dormant within all human beings. Their goal is to reawaken humanity from its self-created falseness for which all of humanity is responsible. This reawakening can and will occur if every human individual allows themselves to accept an understanding beyond the human Ego, for it is the human Ego that has trapped all human beings into self-slavery. The history of humanity has been created into the present moment and is at this time creating your future. The **Mune'hars** are the observers who can see from the outside what you as a species are doing to yourselves.

The **Mune'hars come to individuals who are evolving and growing consciously,** those wanting to bring love and peace to your Earth and to help individuals grow beyond the Ego. **Governments on your Earth are very fearful of individuals having any contact with Aliens because they**

**do not want the individual to grow beyond their scope of control and
domination.**

There are thousands of human beings who have had contact with beings
from other worlds, and universes, and as a result, many human beings are
awakening from the illusion of human life. You as a human individual only
have to step forward beyond your fears to see the changes that are occurring
on your Earth. It is the fear of the unknown that holds each human being
to the past, and it is the past of negative created energies that needs to be
dissolved in order to allow the knowledge and wisdom to come forth.

Many human beings have asked of my Being, how do I communicate with
Aliens? It is simple. **Be true to yourself.** Love yourself unconditionally and
learnt to forgive with love. Learn to meditate in the stillness of your mind,
your being, and ask for the Light to be within you and around you. Allow
yourself to feel this light of love, and then ask for the truth to come from
your heart. Listen to the inner voice of Creation. If you the individual will
allow yourself to practice meditation daily, you will begin to feel a strength
you have never felt before. Your senses will be enlightened. When you feel
you are ready to communicate with Alien beings, sit in your private space.
Use the Light as always for your protection, and when you are ready, send
you're Light like a radio wave of energy into outer space and ask for other
beings to communicate with you. These beings are in reality your brothers
and sisters, for all of life in all universes is a part of Creation.

Always be true of heart, be patient and listen from within your being,
not from your human ears. Send a message of love. Feel your message of
communication travelling on a line of light directly into outer space. Feel
it and see it through your mind's eye. Always observe your space, your
feelings, your presence, and if you are true of heart, you will always succeed.
Trust your inner truth and what is around you.

Always remember this, you the human individual have many moments that
pass you in your human life. Ask yourself from your heart, which moment
will you choose to change? The choice is always yours, is it not?

SOME COMMONLY ASKED QUESTIONS (NO-27)

It seems there is a great interest in other forms of life, and many human beings were intrigued by my expressions on the **Mune'hars**. My Being thanks you for your interest and kind words of love. It is very important for all of humanity to understand that there are many, many different forms of life throughout all universes, and upon many planets that are evolving just like humanity is evolving.

The only difference is the levels of thinking and understanding. Creation is a part of all that is. Every species in existence evolves in their own time and space. There are thousands of civilisations that are much further advanced than humanity as there are also civilisations that are nowhere near as advanced as humanity.

Technology has only one purpose, and in the end it will eventually lead to a higher form of Consciousness, beyond the third physical realm of matter. That is the purpose of all life - to evolve and move forward, never looking back or having regrets. My Being would like to answer some questions which have been asked over many moments of your human time.

Question: 1

What form of justice did the Nar'Karones impose on individuals who committed murder?

Answer: 1

To answer this question we would have to step back nearly **937,000 years of Earth time.** If a **Nar'Karone** committed a crime like murder, the form of justice would depend on the circumstances. For example, to take a life in self-defence, no matter what the situation, would mean there was no crime. The **Nar'Karones** believed that everyone has a right to defend themselves, as long as their defence is **not an act of revenge.** If a **Nar'Karone** took the life of another because of **anger, revenge or simply for the pleasure of**

murdering, then on being found guilty they would be **evaporated within a one cycle period,** meaning, in one human day the guilty individual would be **vaporised - put to death. The Nar'Karones believed that justice must suit the crime.** No physical pain was imposed on the guilty individual. Once put through the process of evaporation, they would no longer exist - their physical matter would be dissolved, therefore there was no need for funerals. Even if a body passed over from natural causes, the remains would be vaporised in the same manner. **No bodies were buried in the ground.**

Question: 2

In Australia, at Cunningham's Gap in Queensland, why do cars lose power and we feel like we are in a vacuum when going up the mountain?

Answer: 2

Nearly 69 million years ago a meteor hit your Earth in that location and caused devastation all over your planet. It changed all life forms and forged a **new era in evolution.** If a study was made of the area surrounding Cunningham's Gap, your scientists would conclude that a meteor did indeed hit your Earth and pushed up the land to form the shape that exists there at present. **There is a very strong magnetic field surrounding the entire area,** which is being transmitted from the meteor which is buried deep within the Earth. Even though it may sound illogical to your scientists, the meteor was meant to hit your Earth because its energies helped balance the Earth itself.

The magnetic energies that exist at Cunningham's Gap cannot harm humans. They are a natural occurrence and in fact are of benefit to the human body. All of life and plants are created from magnetic energies, **and all that is has evolved from magnetic energy.**

Question: 3

Why are some parts of the Middle East always at War?

Answer: 3

Wars have been going on for a long time in the **Middle East.** It has been passed on from one generation to the next; **the hatred runs deep in most family lines.** They only see their hatred and this **hatred is both passed on genetically and taught to children.** A child grows up into a young adult filled with hatred. So wars go on and on for thousands of human years for the most irrational reasons.

Westerners cannot put their values or their level of thinking and understanding on those from the Middle East, because many of these people cannot see beyond their hatred and anger. Most live in some form of poverty and hardship and most envy what they perceive as a **'Rich Western'** lifestyle. What they fail to recognise is that poverty exists in the West as well.

Every nation should allow another nation to evolve in their levels of understanding and not try to change them or to force a different way of thinking onto them. To force your way of thinking onto another, especially when they are not ready to accept it, can and does cause conflict and confusion. **In many cases wars are created and more misery results.**

Anger and hatred is now being expressed through terrorism all around your world. The true enemy is the human Ego which has created beliefs and conditioning, fears and greed. Many human beings who carry a great deal of anger and hatred within themselves, cannot wait to unleash their violence onto others. It seems as if violence is their only means of dealing with what they are feeling. While the human individual holds onto their anger and hatred, they will remain blind to any form of conscious growth. What is advancing is the growth of the human Ego and its negativity. All crimes of all descriptions are a creation of fear. In most situations these are fears from the past brought into the present that create the future.

For individuals and nations to progress beyond hatred and anger and all other traces of human Ego, human beings must first want to bring peace, love and harmony into their lives by becoming the living example. Each of you must confront your fears by confronting yourself first. **Face the enemy within** - the human Ego that causes all your self-doubt and envy which leads to anger and hatred. It will take courage and strength to step beyond the Ego that has shaped human lives for more than **928,000 years.**

Forgiveness of self and all others no matter what the situation, and Unconditional Love from the heart, is the path to peace within the human race. **Teach your children to forgive,** and not to hold a grudge until they 'get even'. **Violence and anger is spreading on your Earth.** It is increasing each moment as the energies become more and more negative. Every human being must have the **Self-Realisation** that they are **Personally Responsible** for how they feel and how they behave. **Eventually the violence will reach a point of no return.**

Responsibility lies with the human individual, from one incarnation to the next. Negative energy can be transformed into positive energy simply by the power of your level of thinking. Change yourselves if you want to change your world. **This is your starting point.**

Question: 4

Why am I unable to find the right teacher to help me understand spiritual growth, and how do I know if I have found the right teacher for me?

Answer: 4

The Planet Earth is one enormous classroom designed for learning and experiencing. One of the main problems is that human beings want to learn everything yesterday! Humans place judgement on themselves, as well as on their teachers. **You are all teachers to some degree, but first and foremost you are also all students.**

When a human individual exists from pure logic they operate primarily from the beliefs and conditioning of the human brain, and beliefs and conditioning are past experiences brought into the present.

When you the individual seek a teacher you will attract a similar form of logic and understanding. Instead, seek a teacher from your heart, the connection to your soul. Your heart will help you grow in Consciousness and will connect you with all knowledge in all universes. Your heart centre will allow you to see the falseness of human Ego and will allow the truth and love to manifest within you and all around you. Through this manifestation you will always bring into your life the teachers you need to guide and nurture you throughout your human life. You in turn will do the same to your students. **This is the cycle of life.**

Always remember, no one is greater than you and you are not greater than another. Each of you are learning for the same purpose, to advance your Consciousness. Knowledge is meant to be shared so all may grow in Consciousness together.

Question: 5

Why is so much human dis'ease plaguing humanity?

Answer: 5

Many human beings are suffering from many forms of dis'ease. It is something that will continue to haunt humanity for centuries to come. Human dis'ease is as prevalent in your year 2014 as it has always been throughout your human history. **For all of the technology humanity possesses to fight dis'ease, there still exists the ironic fact that the modern Western lifestyle largely contributes to the creation and manifestation of human dis'ease.**

Were a study to be conducted, you would see how time and again over population and insufficient quantities of fresh produce and clean water contributes to degenerative dis'ease and chronic plagues. An examination of human health over humanity's existence would be of great benefit in understanding and curing illness. Today more human beings suffer from a large variety of illnesses than ever before.

Some diseases believed to have been abolished are now reappearing, stronger and more resilient to drugs than previously. **Look to your hospitals.** They have become a place for nurturing a race of indestructible germs. Where humans would previously expect a hospital environment to be sterile and pristine and conducive to health and healing, they can now expect to leave with some kind of infection which they did not previously have. The amount of bacteria present in any hospital, coupled with the presence of countless drugs, has provided the opportunity for a major medical catastrophe waiting to happen. Yes, it is already happening all over your world. One of the main reasons for this is hospitals are a health hazard because they recycle air through air conditioners instead of providing fresh air through some open windows to allow fresh air in and stale air out.

Humanity has accepted dis'ease as a part of human life, and it seems you have also accepted the standard methods for dealing with dis'ease, such as drugs, radiation and surgery. It seems **Personal Responsibility has become a thing of the past.** From all this, humanity has created a billion dollar industry, **and this is part of the problem, not the solution.**

What my Being is about to express is truth, weather you the human individual accept it or not, that choice is you're alone. All human dis'ease is a creation of negative emotions, created from one's past, one's past emotions that have been self-created or inherited genetically, and one's past eating and lifestyle habits, again self-created or inherited from your family line. Combined, these causes accumulate to **create genetic breakdown,** and if not corrected, will cause some form of defect in yourself and in your children to come. The longer a family line neglects physical and emotional wellbeing of its members, the genetic breakdown will become worse from one generation to the next.

Humanity needs to desperately change their way of life, especially food intake, lifestyle and emotions. All genetic information can be corrected and rebuilt by the human body if given the right environment and fresh foods and health giving liquids such as clean water. Humanity needs to stop and take a good long look around to see what is truly happening in the human world.

Time is running out for humanity. It is not physical weapons that will destroy humanity. It is harmful **microscopic bacteria** that you are battling with. At present these bacteria are winning. They are evolving and adapting at a much faster rate than humans, **and it is humans that are speeding up their evolution.** Your scientists are very much aware of this fact.

TERRORISM OF THE HUMAN EGO (NO-28)

In our past history when all **Nar'Karones** were of a physical form, the positive and the negative aspects existed, and they **created fear and insecurities.** Yes, the Ego existed on our planet for a long, long time. The heads of state began to realise changes were needed for the good of all **Nar'Karones. Violence was at its peak just like on your precious Earth at this moment. At this present time on your Earth a human being is murdered every 11 minutes, a human woman is raped every 19 minutes, a human child is molested every 27 hours, and a robbery is committed every 6 minutes.**

Wars are increasing on your Earth more so than ever before in your human history. It is the human past catching up with humanity, for humanity is repeating the cycle of what happened on **Nar'Kariss when the Nar'Karones were beings of physical matter.** That is why the **Nar'Karones have an understanding of humanity,** and that is why we are here to try to help guide humanity with a loving heart, beyond the human Ego of self-destruction, to help you step out of the darkness of energies that now surround you. Only through understanding and a loving heart can the truth of all existence manifest itself. All else is the illusion created by the human Ego, which will always lead to delusion and destruction. There is no heart nor truth in delusion, only the self-created fantasies which are the beliefs and conditionings of human life. All are created by the human Ego from fears brought into the present moment of life.

All of life is most precious. Live your life from your heart, the centre of your love, not from your Ego. If you live your life from your Ego then life is far less precious to you and you will be living from your self-created fears, experiencing pain, anger, misery and confusion. In such an existence there is no conscious growth. Fear in humanity is a creation of one's past. **Fear will destroy your goals, dreams, creativeness and desire to succeed.** But fear is only a form of created energy by an individual or a nation.

Forgiveness is part of understanding not only yourself but also others. Forgiveness shows you and others that you are willing to grow beyond self-created limitations, whatever they may be. By forgiving yourself from a loving heart you open the door to forgive others. **That is pure conscious growth.** By expanding your awareness beyond the present human Ego of self-destruction, you will enable yourself to become aware of your own true essence, and then your journey will truly begin.

Human beings must accept **Personal Responsibility** for all things that have been created in their lifetime, even though it may seem that circumstances have been responsible for those creations. Every living life form in every universe must come to the realisation that they are **100% responsible for everything in their life.** Many human beings would find it hard to accept what is being expressed here, but the truth of my expressions will manifest in all human beings. It may not be in your current life, or even the next incarnation, but eventually all human beings will have this **self-realisation.**

My Being has lived through the existence of Ego on **Nar'Kariss** and through many lifetimes of experience. I have seen the destructive force that Ego is and I am therefore able to express the truth about Ego because of my experiences. For a single individual to admit the human Ego and all its negative creations are what is causing pain and suffering upon your precious Earth to all who live upon her, **then we the Nar'Karones have succeeded, in a small way,** in our quest to help humanity grow beyond the Ego into living consciousness. To have one human being open their awareness from a loving and truthful heart towards conscious growth means a seed for change has been planted.

My Being has had many questions concerning **India and Pakistan** - why is the conflict so great, and will there be a nuclear war between the two countries. This can be a difficult question to answer, especially when the Ego exists so strongly in the leaders of both those countries. In turn, these leaders have fuelled the hatred of their people towards those of the opposing country. The human Ego is present wherever hatred exists.

The people of **India and Pakistan** need to be aware of the bigger picture. Why are both leaders so eager to threaten each other with such destructive weapons that would not only harm those it is intended for, but also harm the entire planet through nuclear fall-out carried in your weather patterns?

The people of **India and Pakistan** must ask themselves this question, because neither side will win, and the damage will affect humanity beyond their borders.

No-one ever wins with aggressive action - NEVER. Such behaviour only causes pain and suffering. Such action will eliminate millions of human beings, and perhaps that is what these leaders want, to reduce their burgeoning populations of people living in poverty and struggling to survive.

My Being has expressed these words before but I feel they need to be expressed again. **Humanity's enemy is not their neighbour, or another country. The enemy is within each human being.** It is the Ego and its negative emotions, which have been passed on from one generation to the next, so that whole nations are filled with hatred for another nation, destroying the very fabric of societies, like cancer working its way through the human body. Unless human individuals deal with their fears and insecurities, societies, and indeed humanity, will always be plagued with the manifestations of human Ego.

It must be said that negative emotions that are suppressed must eventually be expressed outwardly. In most cases this expression is in some form of violence, either to oneself or towards others. This again is the human Ego losing control. Yes, there are millions of human beings that carry an enormous amount of hatred so there is no room for love. Their hearts are turning to stone. The reason for this is negative experiences throughout their childhood and into adulthood. All of their negative emotions are suppressed deep inside, and when their Ego can no longer control itself, these emotions are released as hatred, pain, anger and violence, causing destruction to those closest to them.

Go back in your human history and research the events that led up to each of your hundreds of wars and conflicts. Realise that all wars and conflicts on your Earth are the creation of negative unresolved emotions from the past. Humans have lived thousands of lives and the experiences of each life for each human being are recorded in the essence of your divine Light. You each are a living record of all of your lives, including your unresolved emotions. You as a human being should be in control of your Ego, but it is the Ego which seems to control most human beings on this precious Earth.

Dissolve the Ego and allow the Spirit of your true Being to direct your life with love and compassion, rather than allowing your Ego to control your life with negative reactive emotions.

It is love which needs to fill the heart in order to bring balance between mind, body and spirit. Love will bring an understanding of compassion for life in all its forms. **Unconditional love will help humanity dissolve the negative emotions of the past, and what will pass from human's lips will be the awareness of wisdom and knowledge for the present and the future.** The past will only be a memory of experiences to be valued as lessons of life, not eternally held onto as burdens in order to punish the self through suffering and distress.

If the leaders of your world have conflicts in their hearts, and if they are governed by their Egos and they use human beings to create more conflicts and war, resulting in violence, then how can they call themselves leaders of the people? As a Human being you must come to your own Self- Realisation that each of you are a leader in yourself. You, the human individual, are the power and strength behind any civilisation. The human Ego will always dominate the weak, and it is the weak who readily give away their power and personal responsibility. **The weak are the followers, and the leaders need followers to gain power.**

Human beings of Earth, understand there is a great conspiracy at work, a conspiracy which has been active for many of your Earthly years. The conspiracy at work has found power through terrorism, and terrorism has been affecting humanity on many levels for as long as humanity has existed. But it is now in this moment that terrorism is at is greatest, affecting every nation on your planet.

Terrorism seeks to rob you the individual, man, woman and child, of your right to think and speak freely. Its tools are greed, hatred, violence, domination and suppression. Terrorists are in every county of your world. They are well organised and their violence upon the innocent and powerless are what will cause the start of your next world war. Every human being must become more aware of the current situation as conflicts escalate around your world.

Believe in the Divine Light of Healing and Unconditional Love. Send Love and Light from your heart to those creating the violence and conflict, and see it dissolving the human Ego that is creating this terrorism on your world. Dissolving the human Ego begins with you, the human individual. Look to your past emotions and be willing to forgive and let go of your past hurts. In doing this you open up a connection to the Light that is within you. When you open up this light you will see with new eyes and an open heart full of Unconditional Love for all of life.

There is only one way to dissolve the hatred, anger and violence on your Earth at this moment - it is through forgiveness. When you forgive those who have wronged you through their own ignorance and fears, you will allow Unconditional Love to flow from your heart.

Putting nuclear weapons into the hands of leaders who are not balanced in Mind, Body and Spirit is like putting a gun into the hand of a child who does not understand the pain or injury such a weapon can cause. **Leaders on your Earth need to change their way of thinking.** They need to stop thinking so much with their logic and fear and start thinking with their hearts for both themselves and the people they represent. They need to find wisdom in order to lead compassionately and fairly. Only then will human beings be lead out the darkness of fears, beliefs and conditioning that presently surround you.

If your leaders make decisions from their fears then they will lead in fear. But if your leaders make decisions from their hearts, then they will lead from the knowledge and wisdom of their essence, and they will lead their people in harmony, not in violence.

UNDERSTANDING DEPRESSION (NO-29)

Humanity has been lured into a false sense of security. Each and every one of you believe you have free will, yet you do not because over many lifetimes of negative experiences recorded in your cell structure, your understanding, knowledge and free will has been suppressed.

One of the greatest threats to all human beings is depression, which affects two out five humans. Depression is a state of the human brain. It is created from beliefs and conditioning of the past, based on experiences of negative emotions and manifested physically. Depression is fear that creates situations in the human being. It helps destroy your dreams and goals, your intimate relationships, marriages and friendships. Recognise that every experience is simply a lesson in life, not to be judged as good or bad. Each of you is the creator and driver of your own existence, and every experience will make you an emotionally stronger human being. Every human is on their own journey of self-discovery, and every human being is helped and guided by spirit friends. You only have to make a conscious decision to listen to your inner self, the part of you which is your true essence of Light and which exists in all life, in all universes.

Depression is one of the tools of the human Ego. Once it gets a hold of you it will keep you down and in a state of confusion. It is true to say that when you feel depressed you find it difficult to see a solution to a problem or situation, which is turn makes it even more difficult to make decisions. The planet Earth is one big classroom for learning, which is why human beings incarnate over and over again. The purpose of incarnation in your third vibration of matter is to gain knowledge and understanding of the human self and all of life. I do not mean this from a physical perspective, but from a spiritual and subtle perspective, in order to let go of the human Ego and to evolve beyond the physical realm, gaining a higher understanding of existences and life beyond physical dimensions.

My Being was asked a question on the concept of hell. Hell only exists in fear created by human man alone. Each human being creates their own hell on Earth, as well as in the Astral Vibration, from their own fears and negative emotions over many human lifetimes. The word and concept of 'hell' was created to control and dominate the masses. **Human man alone created the concept of the God of your times as well as the concept of Hell and the Devil of your times. The Devil of course is nothing more than the Ego and its fears being projected.**

It would be fair to say that a God of Unconditional Love would not place judgement upon its children or cause them suffering, as it is at this moment upon your Earth. It is human man's fears alone that have caused all pain and suffering upon humanity. The human Ego is truly out of control. It must be said that physical life in a dense matter form is one of the hardest experiences to endure because of the human Ego, of physical and emotional pain, dis'ease, and negative emotions. It is truly a brave Spirit that chooses to incarnate into physical matter to assist the evolution of beings in physical realms such as the human realm.

Alien beings from other Realms and Dimensions has been visiting your third vibration for many of your Earthly centuries, and this has been recorded throughout your history. Many have come to help the evolution of humanity and also to warn of what is to come in your future. It is the human Ego that creates fear, confusion and misunderstanding towards these beings. My Being must admit however that there are also forms of life which only come to your vibration to create confusion, to cause diseases and to use human beings for experiments. For many human beings who have had this type of interaction with such beings, the experience has caused long term confusion and depression which in some cases has led to human beings resorting to suicide to free themselves of their anguish.

The Unseen Forces for example, largely control humanity at this point in your time and evolution. It is very hard for human beings to detect their presence, let alone be aware of their silent influence on human minds or actions. The **Unseen Forces** work only on negative thoughts and actions, and enjoy creating confusion. They take great pleasure in watching the outcome. To these **Unseen Forces** humans are simply toys in a game. They do not care that their interference causes emotional pain and physical suffering.

Depression is brought on in human beings by stress and confusion of the human brain. It may take half a human lifetime to create the negative emotions for that stress and confusion to lead to depression, or much less. Stress is the silent killer in your world as it is in this moment and is the major cause of many illnesses that plague your humanity.

It must be stated that there is no such thing as good stress. Stress is all negative and causes a complete breakdown of the human nervous system. Stress can and does cause heart attacks, strokes, diabetes and many other illnesses. Depression is caused by long term confusion within the human self, which is equally as stressful as a demanding occupation. When you are unable to find a solution to a problem, this stress and worry builds up as a series of negative experiences. These can be passed onto your human children, and if not resolved will cause long term health problems, which will also be passed onto children through genetics. The human world is spinning out of control. Human lifestyles and expectations have created too much pressure on human beings. **You punish yourselves if you do not achieve or succeed in your goals or dreams. You are too hard on yourselves.**

Many human beings have disconnected themselves from the truth and infinite knowledge, the wisdom that is within all of humanity. You have conditioned yourselves to believe in those outside of you, your leaders and scientists, rather than the wisdom of your true self. Your connection with infinite existence has been replaced with the false idol of the human Ego, and sadly it is the Ego that continues to dominate and control humanity.

Ask yourself this most important question: Who creates all that is negative upon your Earth. **Example: wars, pain, misery, greed, jealousy, vanity, depression, domination, and many more such negative conditions?** "**The human Ego**". The Ego will wear many faces of deception to maintain its power, having had more than **928,000** human years of existence to perfect its **craft of deceit. It is the Ego that creates confusion, stress and depression.** It is the Ego that keeps the human individual from seeing the light of truth within and all around.

Try this exercise for one month of your human time. Do it from an honest heart every night before you close your eyes to sleep.

Say to yourself:

"In this moment I love myself and respect all of life".

Say above three times from your heart and then on waking, say this three times:

"This is a beautiful day and I am a beautiful loving human being. I accept my love and I can express my love to all who I see on this day".

Even if you become angry with yourself or someone else, stop for a moment, take two deep breaths and exhale slowly. Feel your love emanating all around you and say **"Yes, it is my choice to be angry or to be loving". I choose to be loving.**

Dear human beings, there is more to your human life than the created negative emotions of the human Ego. The Ego has no understanding of Unconditional Love. It only understands by keep you in confusion it is able to retain control, and in keeping you confused, you become depressed and the Ego has even more control.

Try the above exercise for one month of your human time and see how you feel. When you exist from an honest loving energy, all is in a pure state of being, balanced in Mind, Body and Spirit. When you exist from the human Ego of confusion and depression, you exist in a negative energy of misunderstanding and anger, and this in turn will hold you back from ever experiencing human life in the moment and moments of complete bliss.

NEGATIVE ENTITIES FEEDING ON HUMANITY (NO-30)

May Unconditional Love be placed in each human individual's heart to help heal the pain from the past so your present and future may become one of complete balance of Mind, Body and Spirit? May each human being be given the opportunity? To become fully aware of your existence and your place in all of Creation. Each of you is a spark of living Consciousness. It is your life force. Go silent in your Mind and allow your being to connect to your Divinity, in making that connection and learning to accept who you are, and loving yourself unconditionally. All your past hurts will come before you and be seen as simply memories of experiences, neither negative nor positive.

There have been several questions asked of my Being concerning negative entities feeding on Humanity.

The question asked was as followed:

Even though the fourth density beings who are service-to-self don't eat flesh, it doesn't mean that they aren't carnivores, preying on our third density emotions. It's a sort of carnivorousness when a higher density being is manipulating our awareness from the fourth dimension. The Greys, for instance, being cyber genetic organisms, are third density creations of fourth density beings. Can you please shed some light on this?

Answer:

The fourth dimension is referred to on your Earth as the **Astral Vibration,** which in itself has **thousands of levels of consciousness.** Human beings live in a third dimension of physical matter which vibrates at a slower rate of energy, so human beings can exist in flesh form. Yet in that vibration of physical matter there **still exist different levels of consciousness.** On your Earth there are **still human beings of first, second and third dimensional awareness.** It all depends on one's level of thinking. There are those who still live in the past and bring the past into their present reality so it continues to create their future, passing their level of thinking and understanding onto their human children, **creating beings of the same level of thinking.**

This is why there is so much conflict and misunderstanding on your Earth between different societies and nations. It is all in the level of one's thinking, of one's awareness and one's conscious growth. It is the human Ego of the past that stops an individual from living in the moment. **To live in the present moment is to be truly aware of all that surrounds you.**

In the **Astral Vibration** at the lower end of energies, there exist many Spirits who have passed from their physical bodies. Because of the level of their thinking and understanding when they were physical, they continue after their physical death to create negative energy by existing off living human beings. They can and do crack the human Aura field and they can exist in two vibrations - the third physical vibration and the lower fourth non-physical vibration in the astral plane.

This is a common occurrence on your world, and yes, you could say they are carnivores, because they were preying and feeding off negative emotions and living energies of physical humans. That is why so many humans cannot grow consciously and are easily influenced by negative creations. Reread the **Unseen Forces** in this book where it is explained why such entities exist in the lower end of the **Astral Vibration.** These beings of negative energy are attracted to all forms of negative creations, and at this present time on your Earth there is a very strong negative energy being created by all humans from the past. The **Astral Vibration** was created for one purpose only - to be both a place where beings who have left their physical vessels can let go of their negative emotions, and to be a doorway to pass to higher forms of existence and energies prior to incarnating once more.

It is true that humanity is being manipulated by negative energies form the fourth dimension. This manipulation and influence will continue to be generated by the lower levels of the **Astral World,** by negative spirits and by beings such as the **Unseen Forces.** Even the ones' called the **Greys can exist in both vibrations.**

Look back through your human history and see how easy it was for your leaders to control the masses. The one called Hitler created a pattern of negative energies from the past reaching back to the days of the **Roman Emperor called Caesar, for Hitler was Caesar.** During his incarnation as **Hitler** he controlled millions of young children, knowing they could be very easily influenced and moulded into a new force that would serve his purpose. From these human children he created his army. Consider the conflict and misery that one human man created by manipulating humans all over your Earth and it nations. **That is the power of negativity.**

It must be understood that all forms of Spirit energies are created by Light which is present in all forms of life, in all vibrations, dimensions and universes. But it is the human Ego that, if given control of these Spirit energies, wreaks havoc with the power of Spirit energy. The purpose of Light is to evolve without any form of judgement and to be completely unbiased within the moment so one can create their future. Although all of life has free will, beliefs and conditioning of one's own creation create the level of thinking and understanding that influences how the future is created. Inevitably that future is usually created from the past - from beliefs, conditioning, prejudice and fear. Fear is a negative energy and it is fear that attracts the energies that manipulate and influence humanity, preventing humanity from growing beyond the Ego and the past.

Look to the **Now** upon your Earth. Even though there are negative energies influencing humanity from the fourth dimension, there are also those in human form who continue to incarnate in order to create pain, misery and poverty upon all nations on your Earth.

The one that was called **Saddam Hussein** dominated and controls the people of Iraq. If you would have looked into his eyes you would have seen the energies of the one called **Hitler.** The reason for this is because they are both of the same energy, like being both of the same Soul. Their level of thinking and understanding is the same and their purpose is to manipulate, dominate and control.

There is only one way to stop such energies from continuing to control humanity's evolution. Take away their false power by becoming a **Leader's within oneself.** When you take away one's power you take away their ability to control you. Show them they have no right to dominate you. By doing this the human individual can no longer be manipulated, controlled or influenced by another, by a nation or by negative Spirits and energies from the Astral vibration.

These lower negative energies will no longer be able to feed off self-created fears. The human individual will have complete control over their own life and will grow consciously. This is what evolution is all about - growing consciously? The past is the past, to be remembered only as a memory, neither negative nor positive. **It simply is.**

We the **Nar'Karones** do not see ourselves as fifth, sixth or seventh dimensional beings. We just exist in a different vibration of energy. It means we exist in an energy form without a physical body. We do not see anything as negative or positive, right or wrong, good or bad, for such judgements are traces of Ego. **All of Creations forms of life that exist in all Universes have evolved from the same source of magnetic energy, as all forms of atoms were created from living Consciousness.**

When a human individual truly makes the decision to grow in Consciousness beyond the Ego and all negative forces that is when the journey of **self-realisation begins.** This is the beginning of **self-discovery,** to actually face yourself and all **self-created** fears from the past. To allow these fears to come to the surface is a conscious step towards gaining knowledge and experiencing **Unconditional Love for all of life.**

No negative **Spirits of the lower Astral Plane, nor the dark Unseen Forces,** can influence or control you when you have gained **self-realisation.** They will dissolve from your vibration. Even those of a self-created negative energy in human form will have no power over you.

You will become a **Light Bearer** for all to see and learn from. When the human individual walks in the Light, truth will be illuminated and will manifest. If the individual walks in darkness, only the human Ego will be present. **The choice is always yours, for you have free will.**

FREEDOM FROM SELF-IMPOSED PAIN & SUFFERING (NO-31)

May the love of totality fill each and every one of you till your heart is filled with Love, Compassion, Truth and the understanding to gain the Wisdom that, no matter what? Each and every one of you as human beings are connected to each other. You are all created from the same source. You are indeed all Brothers and Sisters of the Light. What blinds you is your past, your beliefs, conditioning of life, and the many masks of the human Ego not wanting to let go of the past. That is why you as human beings are cruel to each other, from one incarnation to the next. **You carry your Karma from one lifetime to the next.**

It may be difficult to accept, but each and every one of you is Personally Responsible for the pain and suffering that is being created on your Earth against all of life. It is your past being brought into your present, and because of your human Ego, you are all creating your violent future, which it must be said, will not be a pleasant one. Every murder, rape, conflict, war, in fact any form of violence, is a creation of your human past and your human Ego is the cause of all your suffering, as much as it is a part of your **Karma.**

Every human death that occurs on your Earth is in reality related to your past. If you murder a human being in this lifetime, it means you were murdered by your victim in a previous lifetime, and since your human Ego is out of control, you in turn will be murdered in your next incarnation to bring balance back to the wheel of life. If you rape a human being in this lifetime, it means you were raped in a past lifetime and again because of the limited understanding of the human Ego, you will be raped in your next incarnation, until you have the realisation to not carry out such violence against another human being. War is another example of violence against human beings repeating itself life after life. My Being has been asked many questions concerning this topic.

There is a saying on your Earth– no-one every wins a war. It may seem to the human individual that the **'good guys'** win, but in reality **Karma**

is playing an enormous part in the destruction of human life. All wars of your present time are simply re-enactments of your past conflicts, the only difference being the uniforms and weapons. Your Earth is a large stage, created so all human beings can play out their Karma. What each human creates in their lifetime is carried in your **Cellular Matter via your Spiritual essence into your next incarnation.** You even choose your human parents, your siblings, your country, and your friends so that you can be conditioned by certain beliefs and religion in order to create a way of thinking which will create the circumstances for playing out your **Karma,** be it negative or positive.

Every single human being is programmed by their past incarnations, be it negative or positive. Have you, the individual, ever asked yourself why did that human suddenly for no apparent reason shoot all those people? From the perspective of human understanding, the answer would be that he or she went mad and **'lost it'.** Yes, that seems to be the truth. Yet there are many levels of thinking and understanding. The human individual needs to step beyond their present human reasoning and take the time to learn more about **Karma and Reincarnation,** and why it has been influencing humanity for so long.

The western civilisation of humanity needs to study the eastern philosophy of the past in order to understand why human beings have been incarnating on your Earth for the past **928,000** years. The human Ego has also been evolving over that time and the human Ego is responsible for all the pain and suffering that has been created from the past into the present. If humanity does not bring life in the present back into balance, the human Ego will most certainly create a violent future that will keep affecting human beings on your Earth for centuries to come.

To release the past and all negative emotions created by individuals, one must come to self-realisation that **Karma is in fact a personal prison created by every human being over thousands of incarnations.** To release yourself you must be willing to see from a true and honest heart the falseness that has surrounded all of humanity. That is, the human Ego which wears many masks of deception.

Only the truth that exists in all human beings can release the individual from their self-created prison. When the individual can see clearly and cause no pain or suffering to any other form of life, and when the individual can forgive and ask for forgiveness from the heart, will the process of letting go of the past begin. **There is only one being who can release a human being from the prison of Reincarnation and Karma, and that being is you.** You can change the effects of any past event, change a present event and influence future events if you truly want to grow in Consciousness.

Realise circumstances and experiences, negative or positive, shape the type of human being you become. But one thing must be understood – it is your human Ego who is the enemy within that keeps you, all of humanity in a prison of negative emotions, pain, suffering, wars and conflicts. It is the human Ego that has shaped the present conflicts which plague your Earth at this time.

The human Ego keeps humanity in negative thoughts, and these negative thoughts create disharmony and negative actions. Each human being needs to stop their negative thoughts and, instead, think happy loving positive thoughts. Even though negative thoughts may creep in, say **'No'** and think happy loving thoughts for yourself and others. It will take hard work, after all you are trying to change negative conditioning which has been there for many years, but if you persist you will succeed. In the end you will dissolve your human Ego with all of its negative past, and you will see your past as a memory of experiences, neither negative nor positive.

When you feel angry with yourself or others, try very hard to change what you are feeling by thinking of a happy event in your human life. It doesn't matter how small the event or experience may be, just try, really try to think happy thoughts, and project those happy thoughts to others so they will not react to your anger. What you will find is that what you project you will receive back, because everything in all Universes is created from magnetic energies. The saying on your Earth is **'what goes around, comes around'.** **What you think you become; what you express is expressed back to you. The choice is always yours, is it not?**

Human history is full of violence because human man cannot let go of the human Ego. He has become a slave to his negative emotions. He needs to learn to feel with his heart, not his Ego. **There is no power in Ego, only violence and hatred.** That is why **Karma** exists in your vibration of physical flesh. There is a need for change and this change must come soon, for human man is on a path of complete self-destruction, which will cause great pain and suffering to all of humanity for generations to come.

The answer is so close to each of you. It stare's you in the face and yet you are unable to see it. Why is this so? Again, your self- created Ego stops you from seeing the truth. It has been with all of you for over **928,000** years of beliefs and conditioning, manifested as negative emotions, created from one incarnation to the next. All of you have at your fingertips the power to change, but how many of you are willing to step beyond your past? How many want to be free of the emotional and physical pain and suffering of the negative human Ego? This is the question that each of you must ask yourselves.

Humanity has a choice – to stay on the wheel of life, living from one incarnation to the next, and allowing your human Ego to keep that past alive in the present and creating your future from it, more violence, more pain, more suffering.

Or for each of you to say:

Enough! I will no longer follow the Ego. I no longer want violence, pain or suffering in my life and on this planet. I will not follow the Ego of the past. But I will learn to forgive myself and learn to forgive others who have causes my being pain.

I will learn to love myself and learn to love all of humanity and all of life. As I learn to understand my feelings and thoughts, I will create them all to be happy thoughts, so my energy of happy thoughts will be manifested in all I do, in all I say. I will try to understand what other human beings are feeling and I will become more compassionate towards them. I will only speak the truth and I will take good care of my human body. I realise it all begins with me and I know I can create a better understanding of myself. I can and I will be an example for others to see and to grow strong from. I can, as an individual, make a difference to this human world I live in.

Again, dear Human Beings, the choice is always yours. You can choose freedom from the past or remain in the prison of the present based on the past. May the Love and Light of Creation's totality be with you all, dear Human Beings, always.

THE HUMAN AURA & AUTOMATIC WRITING (NO-32)

Inner knowledge exists in all of life and is truly the key to ultimate freedom. It will allow all of humanity to step beyond the created past of negative emotions and will allow you to exist and live in the moment of complete bliss.

My Being has been asked questions regarding the Human Aura, as well as what is Automatic Writing, so I will express a little on these two subjects.

The Human Aura:

First it must be understood that all forms of life, including plants and animals, have an **Aura Field of electromagnetic energy surrounding their physical bodies.** The Aura emanates between the etheric and spiritual bodies. The **Aura** is actually a form of composed radiation formed by the bodies of all beings or forms of life.

The human **Aura** needs to be fully understood, mainly because it is also a tool for cleansing of the human physical body. The **Aura** is your life force in human physical life, for without your **Aura,** you as a human being could not and would not exist in a flesh form of physical matter.

Your human **Aura** appears as a fountain of energy. When radiating completely it has a very definite and regular shape. If you're human **Aura** bulges in places or can't be seen clearly, then that human being is also out of shape, either due to negative emotions of anger, violence or even stress. Human dis'ease also affects your **Aura** and the colours of your **Aura.** So the healthier you allow yourself to be, the more regular your energy field will be. The **Aura** flow channels constantly according to your emotions of moods and illnesses.

For those of you who do not see **Auras,** you can easily feel them. To see **Auras** it just takes some training and discipline. **When you first begin to see Auras, the Aura will appear as a faint light of shadow around the**

human body. If you persist your awareness will grow and you will be able to pick out the different colours of any human individual.

The **Aura** can tell you the health of a human being, animal or plant, as well as their emotional state. **The Aura tells everything about the individual.** You can always tell if a human being is not telling the truth because their **Aura** shrinks in size and the colours change. Light Workers who work solely from the heart can see the shadowy patches near affected areas and will be able to diagnose the problem and then suggest suitable treatments.

The **Aura** also records all experiences of a human life. For example, if a human being took the life of another human being, or committed any form of crime, their **Aura** would record these experiences. Likewise, positive experiences are recorded in the **Aura.** Those human beings who can see the **Aura,** must work from the heart and not use what they see to emotionally or physically harm another, otherwise their ability to see will be shut down by their inner spirit to prevent their Ego using such personal and private information to prevent unethical behaviour. The Ego cannot dominate if one wishes to be a Light Worker.

When a **Light Worker** looks into the **Aura** of a human being who has committed a crime, they will see the whole crime in detail – they will see it being committed. A **Light Worker** must be unbiased, no matter how heinous the crime, in order to help bring the criminal to meet human justice.

The human **Aura** also records all of your incarnations and every experience from those lives. A true **Light Worker** can see all that is within the individual's **Aura** from their current to all their past lives.

A true **Light Worker** will not place judgement upon another. They will see the truth for what it is – an individual's choice to have those experiences - and the **Light Worker** will send Unconditional Love to that human being to help them evolve and grow beyond their current level of thinking.

The human **Aura** absorbs energies and vibrations from a number of sources, including your sun, your planet, animals and plants, crystals and other human beings. **As your Consciousness develops and evolves, so does**

your human Aura, for the Aura works on the same principles as your human charka centres.

It is a common belief that the larger you're **Aura,** the more difficult it is to handle negativity, because as the **Aura** increases with conscious awareness and development, the more buried emotions are brought to the surface so they can be resolved. Therefore, many human beings believe it is easier to live with a medium sized **Aura** field than a larger one. A larger **Aura** enables a being to project healing and deflect and dissolve negative energies, to help cleanse the energies around them, and this can leave such individuals feeling depleted and tired. The weaker a human being is, the more that individual is susceptible to the energies of others. Likewise, a strong **Aura** can influence others.

When you begin to see **Auras** you will be able to detect those who take energy from others. There are human beings who cannot store energy for themselves, so they absorb energy from other human beings, which is why many human beings at certain times in their life feel **'lifeless',** and lacking energy.

One of the most natural and abundant substances on your Earth is sea salt. Sea salt increases the energy of the electromagnetic energy field of human beings, and all forms of life. Any human being who spends a lot of human time in or near the oceans will benefit from a better energy flow. One of the negative aspects of sea water is too much will dry your human skin, and due to a depleted ozone layer around your Earth, excessive exposure to your sun will cause severe, even life-threatening damage through skin cancer.

Always remember dear Human Beings, there can never be any real change in human Consciousness while human beings continue to look only at the physical body. **Your life span is in reality very short indeed, yet your spirit is endless and eternal, timeless and ageless. Your spirit is infinite in all things.**

Many human beings are obsessed with their physical self. They believe appearance is everything and believe that as long as their human bodies are **'beautiful',** they will be accepted and admired by others. **It is the human Ego that is full of vanity.** External beauty without inner beauty is only a belief and a condition of the human Ego. External beauty eventually fades into nothingness, and what is left is fear. **Inner beauty expands outwardly and fills the heart with Unconditional Love that emanates into your Aura field.**

Each human being needs to be aware that the human **Aura** is capable of transmitting negative and positive energies. It all depends on one's level of thinking and understanding. Through Unconditional Love for your own beingness and all forms of life, **you the human individual can transform your Aura field of energies to higher vibrations of awareness.** The choice is always yours – you have the power to change. Change expands your knowledge and knowledge sets the path to freedom from all self-created limitations.

Automatic Writing:

There are many human beings who automatically write, and regard it as a natural and normal phenomenon. Automatic writing is natural.

Basically, automatic writing is sitting down and holding a pen or pencil lightly in your hand over a sheet of paper, and waiting for the pen to move. What is important is not to think about your hand moving. Try and see yourself emanating a ball of white light from your heart centre, and with your eyes closed see this light filling all of your inner being, and emanating from the pores of your skin into your outer self, saturating your Aura. Then say these words of encouragement:

I am a channel for communication for the higher good of all life. I give of myself to the Light of Creation's totality and I open my inner being to channel knowledge for all. I am Light now and forever more. I am that I am.

Allow the natural process of automatic writing to occur. Remember, you are the instrument. **Just be in the moment.** When eventually your hand begins to move and mark the paper, the writing may or may not make much sense. Don't be discouraged. Try again and again. This writing is produced without your conscious participation. There are plenty of examples of spirit communications through mediums in this way. Not only is the writing the same as when the spirit was Earth-bound, but the style as well as the drawing of written characters is often identical.

Automatic writing, like automatic art, is not consciously produced. **The English mystic William Blake depended upon visions to inspire him.** He actually claimed that most of his poetry was dictated to him directly from the spirit realm, and that his engravings and water colour painting were sparked off by unusual visions, helped by unseen hands. **William Blake** also stated that the secret of etched copperplate writing **(which in reality he perfected)** was revealed to his being by his **dead brother Robert,** who was an aspiring artist before he passed over to spirit world.

Human beings who do this sort of work are called Automists. Some are totally unaware of their surroundings and actions when they are producing this work, and are often surprised to see the work they have created on paper or canvas. Other human beings can become drowsy and are only vaguely aware of their hand moving, or of the movements they are making.

Yet others again are completely conscious of what is happening and allow the spirit to use their hands to produce or create under guidance. An Automist usually develops a unique style and shows a fluency of expression. If you dear Human Beings would like try automatic handwriting you will probably be best to start by what you call doodling. If you feel strongly motivated, keep going, keep persevering with your practice until it starts to make sense.

A psychic artist is very similar to an automatic writer. Spirit is close to them and guides them in creating the picture. Psychic artists often reach for their coloured pencils or pastels without even looking at them and always pick the correct colour. If you sit for a psychic artist, you may not get a picture of anyone you know, but you will find it is usually of a spirit **(physically living or in the spirit realm)** that has been drawn to you.

To succeed in automatic writing is to persist and listen to your inner self expressing to you. Spirit have been trying to communicate with physical human beings for thousands of your Earthly years. Believe in yourself and your feelings and they will lead you to the truth. If there are any further questions on these two subjects, please feel free to ask. My Being thanks you for your kind remarks for my previous writings.

SILENCE THE CHATTER TO HEAR THE TRUTH (NO-33)

The human individual must come to a **Self-Realisation** that creating negative actions in a human lifetime must result in the need to resolve that negativity and to bring into balance what has been unbalanced. If balance is not attained, this negativity will be carried into future incarnations until it finally is resolved. **This is what you on your Earth call Karma. The Cause and Effect syndrome. What you do unto others will be done unto you – it is simply the balance of life.**

Take a few precious moments in your human life and do the following exercise:

Sit of lay down in a quiet place. Take a deep breath, hold it for a moment and exhale. Repeat this three times, all the while emptying your mind more and more each time you exhale, so you feel relaxed and calm. Then say these words to yourself from your heart:

I am balanced in mind, body and spirit.

I breathe in the pure light of Creation within and all around myself.

I, who am infinite, know that I am much more than my physical self.

I know that I am an infinite Being of Light that I am a part of all things and all things are a part of my precious being.

I also know I am an infinite well of Unconditional Love which fills my whole being every moment of my life.

I can and will share this understanding and Unconditional Love with all who seek my attention. Even to those who do not seek my attention, I will express to them my love, understanding and light from my heart to theirs.

You may say dear Human Beings that you cannot feel this **love and light,** nor have the understanding of this knowledge within you. Be assured, you are all sparks of infinite living Consciousness on a journey of self-discovery. You the human individual may feel you are not capable of this knowing, but this is simply your own doubt - it is your human conditioning, your human beliefs, which have been with you from one incarnation to the next.

Human conditioning is the life force of the human Ego, and the human ego wields its control through the left side of your brain. The left side of your brain is completely logical. It thinks and judges from what it knows, from your fears and insecurities, your past experiences. It also keeps you from changing your ways in life and holds you back from achieving your dreams and ambitions, and maintains a fear of change, under the guise of logic.

Your left brain can also be positive. It all depends on your level of thinking and your willingness to grow beyond the self-created fears of your logical thinking. You may be asking why this is so.

The right side of your human brain receives all information and is completely unbiased. It accepts all experiences and information without placing value judgements on them. **It is the creative side of your infinite self.** As it receives knowledge, information and experiences through your senses **(sight, sound, smell, taste, touch and awareness),** the left brain draws this information from the right brain and analyses it, deciding whether or not to accept it, discard it or experience it, be it negative or positive.

The left brain makes decisions based on the past, meaning the information it already has. Depending on the situation, this for most part is a good thing, protecting humans from doing harm to themselves or others, such as burning their hand on a flame or causing injury or death to another through reckless behaviour, for example.

Where this becomes a problem is from the emotional perspective. The left brain also keeps stock of all negative emotional experiences. These negative experiences began in your mother's womb where your flesh was created from her egg and your father's sperm. Genetically and from a cellular level you carry a record of all their experiences to the moment of conception, and then all your mother's experiences while she was growing the vessel which would become your human body for this life. **All those experiences, feelings, emotions, habits, conditioning, beliefs, pains and joys are within the melting pot that became your body.** Add to this the experiences you had as a child and then an adult up to this point in your human life, and you are the sum of all these memories and experiences.

How you think and act at this moment in your human life is the result of genetic encoding, cellular memory and life's experiences. Essentially this is the sum of conditioning and beliefs. You may be the kind of person that believes everything in life will fall into place, or you give away your personal responsibility to others so you do not have to make decisions on your own, or you may go through life aimlessly, drifting with no direction or purpose, simply existing and going wherever life takes you. Or perhaps you are aware of the circumstances that have shaped your life up to this moment and choose to be proactive in shaping and creating your future from this present moment.

You may feel you are in complete control of your life, but many human beings do not realise that it is their past which controls them, **creating their present and future.** All of the factors mentioned above have played a role in shaping your human life and the human being you are today, **shaping the way you think, feel and act towards yourself and others.**

All human beings make decisions based on their past, the past that is recorded in the cells of the human body and the human brain and then retrieved by the left brain to be dissected and scrutinised. **The left brain is logical and the Ego uses the left brain to achieve its desires.** The Ego uses the unarguable logic of the left brain to convince a human that the decisions they make and the emotions they feel are credible and perfectly logical, no matter how irrational or unfounded. The left brain is not creative but draws on what it knows to evaluate and make decisions, which is why the human Ego manages to influence the left brain. Much like a computer, if the data or information is incomplete or corrupted, the end result will also be incomplete or corrupted. **The left brain functions like a computer –** if it does not have all the information, or if it is clouded by negative emotions **(the Ego),** how can it possibly make a fair decision or provide a rational, balanced result?

The human Ego is built on fear, insecurity and negative emotions. It is irrational and erratic in its decisions and has a great need to be in complete control. To a balanced being the human Ego is illogical, yet it uses its own form of logic to maintain control. It has no understanding of creativeness, nor can it feel Unconditional Love for itself or for others. **The human Ego has created its own prison and here is where the dilemma lies.** Every human being is clouded by the conditioning and beliefs of their human life, enhanced by the influence of the Ego. **The problem of Ego is endemic – most decisions that are made by societies on your world today are not made from the heart but from the Ego, the negative aspect of humanity.** Decisions are made in fear; fear of not enough money, or giving minority groups too much power, of ensuring the majority is content while ignoring deep-rooted problems and hoping someone else will sort them out when it all gets too much and society falls apart.

Where once the human brain may have functioned with the right brain as a balanced whole, it has become disconnected from its other half. The right brain gave the left its balance. It is now connected to the Ego, and to compensate for the Ego's fears it chatters constantly. Stress is a major disturbance of human equilibrium, caused by emotional pressure through the material world of wants, needs and expectations. **The Ego's desire to control, compete, and dominate is the result of the Ego's fears.** To keep these fears at bay the left brain chatters and keeps the human mind busy, so busy the mind cannot stop long enough to contemplate its existence and set itself free from inner turmoil the human being feels and attempts to control every day of their physical life.

My Being has been asked many questions, questions about awareness, enlightenment, ego, negative emotions, and how to discover truth. The answer lies in understanding how much of an influence the human Ego really has over the individual as well as over humanity as a whole. It is often hard for an individual to fight the tide of Ego energy that permeates the entire human race. But the responsibility lies with the human individual to set themselves free from their own Ego in order to be able to resist the collective Ego and therefore make balanced, informed decisions throughout their human life. Many humans have done this - they have found **inner peace,** they have found the key to being able to live in your human world without being drawn down into the negative emotions of the human world.

Look into your heart, into the centre of your Being and ask yourself, do you truly want to be aware of your existence? Are you prepared to look beyond the illusion and accept the responsibility life changing knowledge demands of you? Do you want to put the effort and energy into developing yourself into a fully conscious human being, aware of your true essence? If the answer is **"Yes"** and it comes from your heart, then your next question will be how and when are you going to begin your journey toward **self-realisation?**

The answer lies in the silences of the human mind. **The mind is not the brain – it is your Consciousness, and learning to recognise your Consciousness from your Ego takes some practice.** The best way to recognise the difference is knowing when you are speaking or feeling from your heart rather than thinking or reacting from your human Ego. You will know you are making decisions and taking action from your heart when you know you are not doing or saying anything to be vindictive or hurtful to yourself or another. You will know you are coming from your heart when you are not trying to influence another to your ways because you fear losing control of them or possibly even losing them from your existence.

The Ego will use the human brain to tell you what it wants or needs, and will make a value judgement or decision based solely on what it knows. **For example, I do not want to make him/her angry because he/she may leave me and then I will be alone, and if I am alone then I will be unloved, and if I am unloved then I must be a social reject.** This way of thinking is illogical to a human being who is balanced and comfortable with who they are, but logical nonetheless to an emotionally damaged human being who believes their existence is worthless if they do not have someone to love them, and therefore validate their existence. Every human being has felt this at some point in their life, and it takes feeling with the heart, not analysing with the Ego to get you through this destructive way of thinking.

All your fears, insecurities, beliefs, conditioning and negative emotions come from your past, which create your pain, misery, violence, wars, and mental and emotional incarceration. This is where the human Ego resides, in the past, and it controls a human being using the logic and analytical proficiency of left brain. Fear combined with undisputable logic creates a very powerful tool for manipulation. **How can you argue with logic? Easy, look beyond the logic to see why the argument is being made.** Is it being made to reach out to find and even more revealing truth, or is it being made to protect an already accepted truth **(which may in fact be an illusion)** upon which the foundations of your very thinking are built? Can you handle finding out that what you thought was truth and reality, is in actual fact an illusion? Will you be able to make the necessary emotional and mental adjustments that allow you the human being to grow consciously and redefine your idea of not only what truth is, but also what is your life and existence?

Some human beings have these life changing realisations but are so highly conditioned and fearful that it is easier to continue living the Ego's illusion. Quite literally the truth is swept under the carpet, never to be seen again. In your world ignorance can truly be bliss. Knowledge and awareness requires strength and a determination to be responsible for knowing the truth. **Then you need the courage to live the truth, no matter how many Egos of those you are close to, try to emotionally manipulate you into being like them and ignoring the truth, simply because the truth makes them uncomfortable.**

In the silence of your mind, beyond your human Ego and logic, there lies truth and the answers to all your questions. Through self-realisation you can become a balanced human individual and create through your own knowing a present and future built on awareness and infinite understanding. In knowing who you are and by dissolving all your negative emotions from the past, you can learn to live in the moment of life and feel Unconditional Love towards yourself and all forms of life. **To live in love is to find bliss and balance.** Be blessed dear Human Beings of this most precious Earth you call home.

IT IS ALL IN YOUR THINKING (NO-34)

May all human beings and all other forms of life that live on your most precious Earth be blessed in the Love of Creation's Totality? All of life and all its forms are the essence of Creation, meaning there is Light within all of you, even those that live a negative existence by causing great pain to others. All have the Light within them, they are only blind to their own self-created human Ego, that which is the driving force of all pain and suffering upon your planet Earth.

Enlightenment cannot be sought, it is the knowing that you are all enlightened beings. You only need to make a conscious decision and your transformation will have already begun. **It is in the power of thought – as you think you become by manifesting the physical reality into your vibration of matter.**

It is your level of thinking that allows you to manifest your reality. Change your thinking and you change your reality. Take your human Ego for example. It is a creation of negative beliefs and conditioning, a combination of thoughts from your created past, based on negative experiences. Because the human Ego is full of fear and is not willing to change, it can only continuously create negative experiences from the past that which it knows to the present and into the future. **It is all in your thinking.**

Many human beings have sent questions to my Being concerning changing their lives. What each human being must understand is that to change your thinking, your human life, your circumstances, whatever it may be that you wish to change, it can only be changed by the human individual if they wish it to be so. Most say they want to change yet are unwilling to look at themselves and how they contribute to their unhappiness. Many will float through their human existence allowing others to dictate and direct their lives, to dominate and control their existence. **There is no conscious growth in allowing others to rule your human life. The responsibility for your life is solely your own.**

The power of change is within every single human being. Forget the excuses that so many make, for that is simply your Ego giving away your responsibility. It is true that life's experiences and circumstances can create a negative existence, and the experiences you had with your parents, throughout your childhood and into adulthood do shape how you view your life. But dear Human Beings, remember each of you choose your life's circumstances before you incarnate so as to learn the lessons of human life and to grow consciously as beings who are far more than the flesh body you inhabit. From another level, you alone choose conscious growth, although many Egos will fight it!

Many human beings will say **"What is wrong with my thinking?** It is who I am." **Yes, that is the truth. But ask yourself this question, ask from your heart, your feelings: "Am I truly living my life as I want it to be, or am I just living to the circumstances that surround me, living to someone else's ideas or trying so hard to please others because I want to be accepted and loved."**

The reason so many human beings never change and stay the same is because it is genetically encoded in you. That is why so many battle with themselves throughout their human life. Each human being upon their human death takes with them their beliefs and conditioning from their last life and carries them through into their next incarnation. It becomes a never ending cycle of self-defeat. Change can become a long road of pain and misery reinforced by fears and negative emotions such as low self-esteem, lack of motivation and commitment, lack of self confidence in one's own abilities, fear of rejection, inability to confront, and suppressed emotions. All this eventually affects a person's health and results in some form of human dis'ease.

You may be saying that you are not like that, and that may be the truth. But there are many who are, many who live in negative emotions on a daily basis, living in anger or hatred, jealousy or deceit. Negative energies are growing among humanity every moment. Human beings are taking less responsibility for their negative actions, and there is more crime in places of power and but very little justice for victims.

Humanity is travelling down a negative road towards emotional and physical destruction. The material world of money and possessions has become the new god. Many humans have expressed that their reason for incarnating is to learn about money and finance so they have **'wealthier'**

lives. But money and possessions are irrelevant to conscious growth. Yes, in your physical world money and possessions make your lives more comfortable and there is no reason to deny yourselves comfort, **but they will not bring you enlightenment, understanding, wisdom, compassion or unconditional love.**

Conscious growth is about the willingness to change – **to forgive and be forgiven.** It is about compassion and understanding, about allowing others to change and become individuals. Conscious growth is about being unbiased by not placing judgement upon another or yourself. It is about seeking wisdom and about loving yourself and others unconditionally. It is not intentionally doing harm to others and in being consciously aware and responsible for all your actions. It is about helping others objectively so they may also have the opportunity to become aware and grow consciously.

Every human being on your Earth is a product of their own past. Human beings have been incarnating for more than **928,000 years,** so there are a lot of negative emotions being carried by individuals from one incarnation to the next. To dissolve your past it is solely your responsibility. Positive changes will enhance and increase your level of understanding and thinking, but changes in your human life can only begin when you are willing to change.

You may ask **"But why is it always happening to me?** I don't deserve this pain or abuse". Then stop now and listen, truly listen. What is being done to you or is happening to you, no matter what it is, is because of your past incarnations. What you did to others, regardless of what it may have been, is being done unto you in your present incarnation so you can learn from it and grow consciously.

If you do not learn the lessons of human life, but allow your Ego to run your life, and are not willing to change, then you will create similar circumstances in your next life. Human life is about conscious growth not material gain. It is about the willingness to change through forgiveness and **Unconditional Love for all forms of life.** When you gain wisdom and conscious awareness, you may indeed gain material comfort, but your Ego will not exploit the comfort you have by causing you to believe you are better than another for what you possess, or causing to deny another because you believe they are inferior. You will instead have the compassion to understand that you are fortunate in this life while others are not, and you will have the wisdom to understand how emotions sabotage an individual's efforts for a better life, whether it be emotionally or materially. You may even go so far as to help another gain emotionally and materially so they may have a better life.

What you negatively feel and project towards others is simply your human Ego's fears from the past and these fears will create your present and future. **Forgive yourself and your past, let go of your Ego's fears and learn to love yourself unconditionally, love yourself without limitation or boundaries.** Allow the natural healing process to take place from within you and all around you. In doing this you will allow yourself to see what changes you need to make for a more positive and optimistic future, and this in turn will accelerate your conscious growth. **Letting go of your emotions will allow you to feel from your heart and not your self-created fears from your past.**

Willingness to change is a step forward. From your personal growth you will be an example to others that being an individual is both powerful and peaceful. Become a free-thinking individual, not a fear-conditioned clone. Act from your heart not your conditioned beliefs.

Dear Human Beings, we the **Nar'Karones** know the Light is within us as it is within you. Connect with your inner being and the Light will shine around you always.

THE ELEMENTS OF LIFE (NO-35)

Just a thought, how many of you have stopped and pondered on the magnificence and the wonderment of the Earth you as human beings call home?

This Earth is a living spirit. It moves, smells, tastes, touches, sees and even loves and feels. It has its physical earthly appearance, just as you have your human physical appearance. Without your human body of flesh matter human beings could not exist in this third vibration. **It is the same for Mother Earth.**

All the chemical elements and mineral compounds found within **Mother Earth** are also within **your physical bodies.** The Mother Earth also has the **Spiritual elements of Fire, Water, Air, Earth, and Spirit.** These five elements allow physical beings to exist in your third vibration.

FIRE: 1. The element Fire is located at the base of your spinal cord. It is your energy source just as within the centre of **Mother Earth is a river of the purest lava.** This lava flows around the Earth giving vital elements to the Earth, just as your blood flows throughout your human body to nourish your organs and repair damaged tissues. **Without human blood you as human beings would not exist, and it is the same with Mother Earth. Without the lava, your Earth would become a frozen planet just like the other planets that surround your Earth which at one time also supported life of many different types.**

WATER: 2. As you know without water life would perish, **which is why over half of Mother Earth is made up of water.** It is a cleanser that helps the Earth keep clean. Your oceans provide up to 80% of your oxygen and also help keep Mother Earth cool, ensuring it does not overheat. It is the same with your human body. Your bodies are up to 80% water (this varies depending in how much clean water is consumed and is impacted by the level of polluting lifestyle habits). **Your human bodies need between 2 to 3 litres of clean water per day to function.** Coffee, black teas, sugary or artificially sweetened soft drinks, and alcohol do not form part of the required amount. To eliminate toxins from your human body your lymphatic system needs to flush out these poisons by sweating and urinating. Many human beings suffer a number of health problems because they do not drink enough water, and this in turn over a long time contributes to the creation of human dis'ease, along with lifestyle, emotions and other health destroying habits.

AIR: 3. The Earth breathes just as your human body must breathe. Forests purify your air, and if you live around a lot of trees or near the oceans of your Earth, your air will be cleaner and have less pollution. Your human body will feel healthier and you will be less likely to have problems with your body. City dwellers on the other hand suffer all sorts of sickness. Pollution is humanity's biggest problem. Most humans will suffer some sort of dis'ease if the human attitude toward polluting Mother Earth does not change.

Some of your scientists believe that the polluting of the air is causing global warming, while many other scientists believe the claim is untrue. One thing must be understood – the truth is far more important than personal opinions. Each human must come to their own self-realisation of total truth concerning the pollution of your Earth – within it, upon it and around it, especially your air and atmosphere. Dirty air will produce unhealthy children; clean air will produce healthy children. Which would you choose? And yes, global warming is mainly caused by pollution. In the **next 47 years,** if nothing is done in the present, pollution of the planet Earth will cause more earthquakes, violent storms, heatwaves and droughts upon your Earth that humanity may never recover.

EARTH: 4. The foundation of physical matter. The clay of the Earth is the clay of your human body. The chemical deposits on the Earth are the same in your human body (but in different proportions). All of life that exists on Mother Earth came from the oceans and has evolved over millions of years. **What you as human beings are in this moment took millions of years of evolution to become physical.** Human beings have existed on your **Earth for over 928,000 years but the Earth is billions of years old.** When it first began to evolve from the dust of space it took well over one million years of incubation to harden and become dense in matter.

Every stone and pebble has its own form of living energy and vibrates at a frequency that is different to other forms of life. Every tree and flower has its own vibration or frequency, and animals and human beings too are vibrating at their own frequency, different to other forms of life. Each of your charka centres vibrate at different frequencies – the base charka resonates around 1500 cycles per your human second while the heart charka resonates around 10,000 cycles per human second and the throat charka around 30,000 cycles per human second.

As you grow consciously your awareness and level of thinking and understanding will allow your energies to vibrate at much higher frequencies. The faster you vibrate the more you will be able to tap into your infinite knowledge, which will not only help you to grow but also the rest of humanity. Human evolution does not only benefit humanity, it also benefits Mother Earth and all forms of life, because as humans evolve and dissolve the negativity they have created, they help to bring nature and all forms of life back into balance.

SPIRIT: 5. Spirit is infinite, timeless, and ageless. It has no boundaries except what is placed upon it, be it negative or positive energy. Humanity has created a dense form of negative energy which surrounds your planet Earth. The negativity is at a very dangerous level. This energy not only makes humanity suffer but all forms of life, including Mother Earth.

How humans act, be it negative or positive, affects Mother Earth too. You may ask why does it also affect the Earth, because everything no matter what form it is, is all created from energy the Light force of Creation, living Consciousness. When each human being begins the journey of self-realisation towards understanding that they are a living spirit, infinite energy, only then will humanity begin to live the truth and **express Unconditional Love, and not hatred or violence.** It is only the human Ego, based on the past, beliefs and conditioning from past incarnations to the present that causes humans to exist within negativity and continually project negativity. Through forgiveness you will begin to understand yourself and this most precious Earth that you all exist upon. Mother Earth is more a part of each human and every form of life than most would care to acknowledge. Honour the Mother Earth by showing it Unconditional Love and deepest respect and you will honour the divine within yourselves also. Be blessed in the love of Creation always, dear human beings of Earth.

METAPHYSICAL VIEWS OF ILLNESS (NO-36)

Have you the human being ever sat down for a moment and asked yourselves these questions?

    1-Why does my life have so much unhappiness?
    2-Why am I always creating illnesses in my life?
    3-Why am I always in financial debt?
    4-How come every relationship ends up making me feel worthless?
    5-How come when I want to change myself, my life always ends up the same or worse?

Thoughts that come from the human brain are very powerful indeed. Every thought you as a human individual may have is in fact from your past, much like a computer program executing automatically. Those thoughts are your patterns, beliefs and conditioning from when you were a human child. **You grew up with them.** You also have your human parent's genetics within you which means you also did receive some of their programming. Every negative or positive experience that they had prior to conceiving you and then your mother's experiences while carrying you prior to your human birth, have been passed onto you through genetic transfer. How many human beings have you known who are just like one of their parents, not merely physically, **but also have the same character?** Most human children, when they grow into adulthood, **become clones of their human parents never really discovering their true individuality.**

When you have children you then pass on to them all your experiences, thoughts, negative and positive emotions, and so on, and so the wheel of life keeps turning. **Every thought you have or create, whether it is negative or positive, becomes a mental pattern and is conditioned into your genetics. Your whole life as a human being is shaped by your conditioned thought patterns.**

Many human beings will never admit truly that they are a reproduction, a clone of their parents. Every word that was expressed to you as a child from your human parents is recorded into your genetics, and depending on what experiences you have as an adult, in most cases these experiences **(negative and positive) shape your future as a human being.**

Please realise, negative experiences are just as important as positive ones; they teach humans about life and themselves. This is what human life is all about, to grow consciously and to let go of the negative patterns so they do not keep your thoughts locked in a negative emotional condition throughout your human life. **Metaphysics can help humans understand the emotional condition that lies beneath their physical condition.** It can help explain why their human life is the way it is, and why they suffer a certain illness while other human beings who has lived in almost the same physical conditions and lived a similar life does not suffer the same illness.

Metaphysics shows that illness is the physical manifestation of fears, emotions and emotional pain, beliefs and conditioning. The only reason a human being creates pain in their life is because of their fears, beliefs and conditioning from childhood into adulthood. **These factors are responsible for your thought patterns, and thoughts in turn create your reality, both physically and emotionally.**

To better understand how metaphysics can help human beings grow consciously from the physical experiences of their life, my Being will illustrate this correlation between thoughts, emotions and illnesses by examples:

ASTHMA:

This physical illness is very common in human society today, and is now prevalent in young children, young adults and even the elderly. It is more common now in humanity than it has ever been throughout your human history. **The cause, both physically and emotionally, needs to be addressed. Just giving out drugs to control the illness is not a solution. Drugs are not the answer, they only create profit for the drug companies, and in time Asthma will be in epidemic proportions throughout the human population on your Mother Earth.**

The main physical cause of Asthma is the increasing pollution filling your atmosphere to very dangerous levels. The other main contributing factor is diet, specifically dairy, smoking, meat, refined sugars, alcohol and even lifestyle habits such as not exercising the human body or regularly going to smoky hotels and night clubs for several hours. Pollution is a cause for which all human beings are responsible. You drive your cars, trains and trucks, you burn oil and fossil fuels to generate power, you manufacture and use plastics, you use chemical sprays around your homes buildings and crops, you feed antibiotics and growth hormones to your animals that are to be eaten, all for convenience in your modern world. Sadly these conveniences are killing your Mother Earth and yourselves quite rapidly. Your industrial revolution did help humanity, but the price is very great. It is urgent that more caring solutions are now found to sustain your existence and the health of your planet.

But not every human suffers Asthma, even though they may live in the same highly polluted city. **This is where metaphysics provides an answer.** As a physical illness Asthma is the inability to breathe. Emotionally, Asthma relates to suppressed crying, smothered love, and not being able to express feelings. **The solution for Asthma sufferers is to work on the illness from both aspects, physically and emotionally.** Physically, try to reduce the amount of pollution you are inhaling. If it means moving to a cleaner area try to do so. If this is not an option, use an air purifier in your home. Also, change your diet and lifestyle to remove foods that congest and pollute your human body, and remove yourself from situations that keep your body polluted, such as not going to smoky night clubs or sitting with smokers and inhaling their pollution. Emotionally, look at what you are suppressing. Take personal responsibility for those emotions by admitting they exist and exploring why they exist. Let go of the past by learning to forgive and to love unconditionally.

CANCER:

Cancer is the result of a human cell mutating and then spreading the mutation to other cells through a specific organ within the human body, such as lungs, liver, stomach, bowel, skin and bones. Cancer is one of the major killers of human beings on your Earth at this moment in your human time. **Over the last 37 years of your time, bowel cancer has increased by 41%.** It is a painful death to experience and physically is caused by consuming meat and junk foods with chemicals and additives, smoking, insufficient consumption **(or not at all)** of water. It may take many human years to develop, but for most human beings it is a death sentence once they have been diagnosed.

There are several physical reasons why cancer occurs. Genetics are passed on from parent to child causing individuals to have a predisposition to contracting the illness. The predisposition is the result of genetics breaking down due to poor diet and lifestyle habits. You are what you eat and how you live, and if you are unhealthy prior to having children, you will create those children from unhealthy seed, therefore it is in your and your future children's interests to become healthy well in advance of having children. This is the best start in life you could ever give them. If you have a predisposition to Cancer, then again, diet and lifestyle will accelerate the probability of Cancer developing. What kind of Cancer develops however is also governed by human emotions, and this is where the metaphysical explanation can help.

Emotionally Cancer is a form of resentment and where a human being is not willing to change or to let go of past hurts. **There is usually strong anger towards oneself or others caused by very deep hurts which lie unresolved.** All forms of Cancer represent the eating away of oneself. Like rust eats metal, Cancer eats away at a part of the physical body until eventually life cannot be sustained, and so emotionally it eats away life. Cancer is caused through negative thoughts and emotions over many years of a human life. **Human thoughts are very powerful.** If you think long enough on a negative thought you will create the outcome. For example, if you think you will never amount to anything or that you are not good enough to be loved, or that you will be **'dumb'** because your father was, then no matter what your true potential, you will create your future based on those thoughts. Those are not true, they are an illusion created from your fears and beliefs, but you will manifest them because you will do nothing about changing them, and so your thoughts become a **self-fulfilling prophecy.** Every thought a human individual has in a lifetime, whether it is negative or positive will create their future no matter what.

Cancer is simply another manifestation of inner thoughts, but also presents an opportunity to learn. There are thousands of humans on this Earth who have cured their Cancer without medical intervention. These human individuals have explored their emotions and changed their physical lifestyles to heal their body and their mind. Human life is an experience – physical, mental and emotional, and **so the cure also needs to be holistic, incorporating the physical, mental and emotional.**

To cure Cancer one must come to the Self-Realisation of the human emotions that existed before they were even born, meaning emotions inherited from their parents. Only when an individual understands themselves will they be able to change their thoughts, resolve their emotions and make the necessary changes to their diet and lifestyle in order to cure their Cancer. Cancer may be created for any number of reasons, even to gain sympathy – they are crying out **"Look at me".** Help me because I cannot help myself. I am not good enough. **Why is it always me? I hate my life, my past, myself, my family."** Behind all human illness is a lesson not only for the individual, but for all of humanity to learn from.

DIABETES:

Another rapidly spreading illness, over the last 27 human years Diabetes has increased by 29%, and is more frequent in children than previously. From a physical perspective, food is the greatest contributor to creating **diabetes.** Your junk foods, fast foods, convenience foods and soft drinks all contain some form of sugar, something not previously included in human diets of 100 of your years ago. Even **'health'** foods such as breakfast cereals and snacks are high in sugar. They may provide a quick burst of energy, but the levels drop too quickly. **Over time this quick high and low play havoc with insulin production and the body's ability to cope with sugar and regulating its use in the human body.**

Parents pass on Diabetes to their children, even if they do not have it. Again, lifestyle and diet weaken the body, and children created from a weak body a more susceptible to manifesting the illness. Human beings are fooled into believing that manufactured food is healthy and nutritionally balanced. **The majority of humans do not question what is put into foods, believing that if their governments approve an additive, then the food is safe. That is so far from the Truth.** Human beings consume far too much sugar and refined foods. The human body breaks it down far too quickly, uses up the energy too quickly and then requires more. **In the case of human adults this leads to over eating, overweight and obesity, and eventually diabetes.** In the case of children born with Diabetes, their parents dietary and lifestyle habits help to create the weakness in their bodies and so they are unable to cope with what is now a normal diet. For adult Diabetics, the road to Diabetes takes a long time. It does however eventually happen. **And if an human adult does not develop Diabetes they can be a strong candidate to do so, they will almost certainly help to create it in their human children.**

Metaphysically, diabetes relates to stopping the flow of life. Diabetes is caused physically by too much of the sweet. When one has Diabetes they must stop having the sweets in life, therefore emotionally it is denying the sweetness in life. Diabetes also creates a situation where one has to be cared for, that is learning from doctors how to control the illness through diet and through regularly taking medication to control the illness when it is fully developed. Diabetes therefore relates to giving away one's **personal responsibility** for their life in order for others to care for you. Another emotional aspect to Diabetes is always trying to control the circumstances and events in one's life, which in turn leads to trying to control others, and therefore related to domination of the self and others. **Finally, the illness relates to regret by the sufferer yearning for what may have been, but never actually doing anything to create what they desire.**

Illness is created physically and emotionally, and it can be cured naturally by understanding the physical and emotional contributing factors that caused it to appear. It is very important to understand that illness is a combination of diet, lifestyle, negative thoughts, emotions, and the breakdown of the genetic structure of the human body, your **DNA.** If you are an unhealthy human adult then you must expect your human children will be unhealthy. **Children are not born perfectly healthy while their parents are unhealthy, although that seems to be the expectation.** However, nothing is permanent. Anything can be changed if the desire is there to do so, no matter what the conditioning of life may be. Human beings can change their thought patterns, their lifestyles and their diets. Your programming can be changed if you truly want it to be so. But to do so you must first recognise that you are living to your programming and then consciously change that programming by changing the thoughts, beliefs, conditioning, lifestyle and diet. **If you read this with an open mind and an open heart you will begin to see that illness in humanity is caused by weak genetics, poor diet and lifestyle, and negative emotions and negative thoughts.**

Always remember dear Human Beings, whatever is created can be uncreated. **The power and the knowledge to change is in your hands as much as it is within your consciousness.** May unconditional love fill each of you on this most precious Earth, and may all your anger, violence and hatred be dissolved into the Light. May you all be at peace with yourselves and with others? Forgiveness and love will lead you to the answers you seek. **Remember who you are; sparks of Consciousness from Creation's totality.**

MESSAGE FROM GODS OF HUMANITY'S PAST? (NO-37)

We the Nar'karones who have been with humanity for the last 928,000 years, have been circling your most precious Earth in our Light ships, watching, observing and guiding human individuals to their own Self-Realisation of one of the most precious gifts, that of inner truth.

All of humanity has this gift of truth. This truth is activated by **Unconditional Love** and is the key for your awakening. Each human individual can gain the awareness for their own conscious growth, and to take realisation that all of humanity are living the dreams of the human Ego, which is from past incarnations.

Fear has been your enemy and your human Ego is your controller. Every human being born into a human body over the 928,000 years has been highly conditioned by genetic encoding and fears from the past, and compounded by beliefs and conditioning.

There have been questions of my Being concerning the gods of your past. Right throughout human history there have been different gods. Most of them were human males and females. In every era that a god existed, you as humans also existed in another lifetime. Most human beings that exist at this very moment in your reality have in fact worshipped a god of some sort in previous incarnations. **You may say that you find this hard to believe, yet most human beings believe in reincarnation. This truth that my Being is about to express will open your mind to the possibilities of who these gods were that humanity worshipped for thousands of years.**

The beings you called gods were not gods as humans believes a god to be. They were beings who were supreme in their knowledge and understanding, in their love and compassion towards humanity, and they seemed to appear from nowhere, they came from the skies, which humans called the heavens. These beings came and lived in human form to share their wisdom. Some came in dreams, some came only to appear for a few moments, others came in the form of a human being and lived amongst humans to teach and guide those who wished to listen. They shared their love for all life forms. Some even chose to incarnate into a human body in order to experience human life by growing up in a human society and then becoming a teacher of love and knowledge.

Many of your gods from your human past ruled many nations. Most of those you know came from the heart and brought great knowledge, but there were a few who came here for their own selfish reasons, driven by a lust for power, **self-indulgence and greed.**

The more power these gods had, the more they wanted. They wanted to create the horrifying wars of your past and unleashed violence and mass slaughter upon humanity. Their actions created enormous Karma for themselves and their followers. As human time went on the wars and violence increased from incarnation to incarnation. New religions appeared based on the past, and religion became a tool for wars and violence, controlled by those who sought power and were driven by greed.

As the centuries passed, the knowledge of past gods was lost. Only remnants of their existence remained with a few. Even those who possessed knowledge of the past kept it secret and passed it on to a chosen few, sharing only fragments of the knowledge so they could keep control over the masses, **to keep humanity in fear.**

Humanity was lost for thousands of years and needed to believe in something or someone. Many created the illusion of truth because they felt a need to believe in something rather than nothing. **The gods of Unconditional Love from your past human history brought the gift of truth, the gift of believing in the self.** They taught humans to love their neighbour as they would love themselves; to treat others as they would want to be treated; to be compassionate to all forms of life that exists upon your Mother Earth; to pray within the self to seek all answers within; and to learn that truth is infinite.

Many human beings left what was called civilisation and went up into the mountains where they would find peace within and around themselves. Of those who chose to live amongst nature, some chose to become holy men and women to teach and guide those that chose a silent life of learning and discipline. Others would search for truth by travelling the world, hoping to find some form of truth through their journey and through others.

Humanity has a flaw. It is a simple one, yet it has eluded many for thousands of years. The ones humans called gods of the past were not gods. They did not come to your Earth to be worshipped or recognised as supreme beings, greater than yourselves. They were beings who simply brought knowledge and wisdom for the conscious growth of humanity, and the understanding that all forms of life, human or otherwise, is equal in all things on Earth and in all universes.

Conscious growth and awareness can only come to the individual if that individual is willing to step beyond their self-created past of negative emotions. Each human life time is an opportunity to advance beyond the previous incarnation. If a human being was to allow the Unconditional Love that exists within them to emanate from the heart centre, and to see the pain they have created in their existence, from the past to the present moment, upon themselves, as well as upon other human beings, they would find the strength and courage to forgive unconditionally from their heart. **They would not only be able to forgive themselves but others as well. This is what your gods of the past were teaching humanity.**

Unconditional love is the key to opening up to the inner truth that exists within all human beings. Forgiveness is freedom from all self-created pain from the past to the present. But this truth cannot be forced upon anyone. It must be realised by every human individual. **Every human being must be willing to confront the fear of change and attempt to change, to love, to forgive, to see the truth beyond the illusion created by the human ego.**

The fear of believing in the self keeps humanity blind to truth. Step beyond your fears and walk in the Light of Creation's totality, and each of you will find a new strength to step beyond who you are, allowing you to know the truth from your heart.

All your gods from your past, including those that are being worshipped today, are not gods. What humanity calls gods were Alien beings from other worlds, dimensions or vibrations who came to Earth simply to give guidance to those who sought it?

My Being has purposely not named any human gods so as not to offend those who worship them in the present moment. It is the right and free will of all human beings to believe in whatever they choose. What is needed is to look at your world today and consider the constant wars, violence, and intolerance which is at its peak on every part of your world. **If a human being says they can justify war or any form of violence for their religious or political beliefs, then they are truly blinded by their Ego and the illusions created by their beliefs and conditioning.**

Behind all such conflicts lies anger and hatred, beliefs and conditioning, fears and insecurities. There is no truth in such acts, only the past continually being brought into the present, suppressed or not dealt with in previous lives and brought into one's present incarnation, causing more pain, poverty and misery, and creating repercussions for future incarnations.

War and violence are not the teachings of your past human created gods. Humans created gods because they did not believe in themselves. **They gave away their personal responsibility to justify their existence as human beings and the negative acts they perpetrated upon others.**

One thing must be expressed at this point. Human beings are not unique for this kind of behaviour. Species of beings living on other worlds of physical matter in the third dimension have or are going through the same or similar learning as humans have been, and are today.

How long humanity chooses to learn the same lessons rooted in conflict and the Ego's illusions, is a choice humanity must make on its own. Humanity needs to step beyond its Ego and allow the heart to open and be filled with Unconditional Love for all humans and all forms of life that exist upon the Mother Earth. It is the responsibility of each individual to let go of their past pains and forgive in love all those they believe have wronged them. **The individual needs to recognise that reincarnation's purpose is to learn, not to have greater material wealth as each lifetime passes.**

Reincarnation provides the opportunity for change and growth, to let go of the Ego's fears, beliefs and conditioning in order to gain complete truth and full awareness of who each of you are and where each of you came from.

The concept of time which humanity created, is not on your side. Time is running out and it is vital that all human beings stop and sit long enough, without thoughts to cloud your vision, and go within the silence of your being to connect with the Light from which you all originated. This is where you will find truth, from the past to the present, and to the future.

When each of you have the strength and courage to change and let go of your self-created pain that will be your moment to forgive and allow your Consciousness to expand to higher levels of understanding and knowledge. **Only in Unconditional Love will this be achieved.**

You only have to ask for my presence and my Being will be with you to guide you to your truth, the truth that is universal. Be blessed in unconditional love always dear Sisters and Brothers of this most precious Earth you call home.

CAUSE AND EFFECT OF KARMA (NO-38)

Love is the one thing that all human beings want from life – to beloved and to love. Everything on your Earth could perish yet what would remain is love, for love is unbiased and non-judgemental. It has no anger, violence or hatred. It is neither negative nor positive, it just is in the moment. You do not have to search for love for it is all around you. It exists within all of life and it is the closest thing to heart. Love is you. The human being and it is the closest anyone can be to perfection.

So what went wrong with humanity? Where is the love that each of you are created from? It is still with you and it has always been there for you to discover who you are and to experience life's joys with. However, since the human Ego came into existence you have allowed your love to take a back seat while your human Ego created a world of fear, beliefs, violence and laws that protect only the law itself. Justice does not exist for the victims of your human world of chaos and confusion.

Humanity has created a path of pain and misery for all who exist upon the Earth and within her, your Mother Earth. Most civilisations on your world understand the term '**Karma**'. It is well known to the Eastern world and means '**what you do unto others will be done unto you**'. **The term can be negative and positive, like good Karma and bad Karma. Most Western civilisations understand the term 'Cause and Effect', and the meaning is the same as Karma.**

Every negative and positive action that a human individual creates in their life time is recorded in their cellular memory. What is also created from all past lives of an individual is also recorded in the cellular memory. It is brought in with the energies of that Spirit when they incarnate into the body. So the effect of this cellular memory is that every experience an individual has from one life to the next can and does shape the experiences a human being has during their lifetime, be it negative or positive.

Many human beings believe in reincarnation, **good Karma, bad Karma, Cause and Effect,** but most do not realise that they have existed on this Earth for more than **928,000** years, and in that time they have lived thousands upon thousands of human lifetimes. Over this time many have created an enormous amount of negative Karma and continue to do so.

The cause is your human Ego, the part of the human that has been created from fear. The effect is the outcome and can be due to many reasons. For example, lying, stealing, controlling, dominating, causing harm to another through violence, rape, murder, physical abuse, mental abuse, lust, negative thoughts towards others, terrorism, greed, wars, hatred, and the list is endless. **These are just some of the traces of the human ego.**

I would like to give you an example of the human Ego at work. A human being has lived 47,000 lifetimes up to this moment in your human time of 2014. The karma that this individual must face is from 47,000 lifetimes and the amount of negative karma, depending on what their experiences were, is in itself mind-bending!

Many human beings never resolve all of their Karma from their present life, so that Karma is carried on to the next life, and then next, and so on. The wheel of life is in motion. Many humans find this notion of accumulated Karma difficult to accept. But it is the complete truth – your past up to your present is recorded within your being, your cellular memory.

Would you not think if a human being only lived one lifetime, that humanity by now would have let go of all the wars and violence, hatred and anger. One of the major contributing factors to humanity's problem with hatred and violence is the genetic transfer of these emotions and beliefs to children, which is then reinforced through upbringing and conditioning. Take your Middle East for example, the human parents pass on their hatred and negative emotions onto their children so as they are growing up they are conditioned not only by their parents but also their society, governments and religion. This is not unique to the Middle East – this is within all nations.

Humanity is creating a negative world for their future children. If human adults do not resolve their own created negative emotions, then you as a race of beings are guilty by example to your children who will inherit your negative past and emotions, and in turn each human being adds to the creation of a negative violent future.

I will give you an example of your human future towards the year 2027. Terrorism will be in every country. No one will know who to trust. Your children will be warring against other children, nuclear war will be at it greatest threat, terrorists will trick nations into believing other nations want to attack them, and biological germ warfare will be present if it is not stamped out now.

There are terrorists at this present moment trying to obtain deadly bacterial agents and germs to be used against certain nations to bring them down. One of the greatest threats to all of humanity is terrorists want America to fall and become helpless. If they succeed in doing this, no country will be safe on your planet.

Beyond the terrorists is an organisation that wants to rule all nations on your Earth. This may sound completely mad to the reader, but if you each come from the heart and search within yourselves for the truth, you will find out my expressions are indeed complete truth.

Karma is the creation of the human Ego and the human Ego has been evolving for more than 928,000 years, so it is natural to presume Karma has been around for a very, very long time in human history. To give you another example, a nation attacks another nation and thousands of human beings are slaughtered. Many are thrown into poverty. Why? Is it greed? Is it a desire for domination and control? Is it jealousy of what that nation may possess? From a human perspective your answer may be one or all, some or all of the above.

But there is another reason human beings may not consider... Karma. Go beyond the human answer and seek a deeper understanding from within your infinite self. What you will discover is those who attacked were in fact attacked by the defending nation somewhere in the past. From that past human history those individuals have reincarnated under different circumstances so they would attack that nation to pay back what was done unto them.

This has been going on throughout your human history – pay back after pay back. In reality it is simply revenge. **Every form of violence committed in human history is a form of karmic pay back. To choose not to pay back and harm another is to evolve consciously. To continue the circle of violence is to remain unevolved.** To say 'you killed me last lifetime so now I am going to kill you' is not the rational higher thinking of an evolved physical being. The problem with revenge that spans lifetimes is it never stops. How can an entire nation stop the cycle of karmic revenge when the individuals who make up that nation are driven by the emotional imbalance that urges them to react to the karmic debt?

Stop for a moment and think before you choose to **'pay back'** someone, no matter how trivial or serious it may be. Think from your heart, not your Ego, and say 'No! I will not do this act. It is not right for me to take another's life in violence, or to steal, or to rape. It is not right to cause this harm."

When will the human individual say enough is enough? Realise after 928,000 years it is time to step beyond the understanding and thinking of the unevolved Ego, and to choose to change your thinking and your life so you can grow beyond this way of life.

Every human being needs to learn about the enemy and it is not the enemy outside of you or around you, nor is it another country or religion. It is the individual, the enemy within every human being – your past, your fears, your genetic encoding, your negative actions created from one lifetime to the next.

Dear human beings, while you use the excuse that 'they' **(whoever 'they' may be)** are the enemy, you will always stay blind to the truth. Blaming a certain individual, organisation or nation will not reveal the truth and therefore the solution. You will always be held on the wheel of life to incarnate lifetime after lifetime, trying to find some form of happiness or peace and being held to ransom in the material world of illusion, which sadly every human being has been a part of creating through human history.

You the reader may say that if this is the case then how do you overcome this problem? Learn to slow yourselves down, stop trying to outrun time because there really is no such thing as time, there is only the moment and you the human individual. Take some precious moments for yourself and walk among nature, or walk on the beaches of sand. Learn to feel and see the beauty in nature and become aware of the beauty in yourselves, and you will begin to see the beauty in all other life forms.

Come to a realisation that every human being is a beautiful infinite Spirit of Light, and that all human beings are connected to each other and all forms of life on your Earth and in all universes. Feel the love within you and learn to love and accept yourselves as you are in the moment. Change what you feel needs to be changed in your life.

Learn to connect with your inner self of infinite knowledge and this will show you all of your past lives and experiences, both negative and positive. See for yourself who you are without any form of judgement. When you can come to those realisations about yourself then you are open to see others around you without judgement. You will begin to understand that all human beings are in reality your sisters and brothers.

One thing must be realised, if you the individual have negative thoughts toward others it also means you are negative about yourself. That negative thinking is a part of your human Ego and it is the human Ego that has created all your pain, violence, hatred and anger. It is the Ego that needs to be dissolved by each human individual, back into the nothingness from which it was first created.

By coming to terms with your self-created human Ego you will begin to break down the walls of Karma that have been haunting humanity. **It must also be understood that no one on your planet Earth has the power to dissolve another individual's karma.** You the individual are the only one with the power to dissolve your own Karma because Karma has been created to teach the individual lessons of life. If you do not experienced these lessons and have your Karma miraculously dissolved by another, then you have not learnt what is required to be learnt in that lifetime.

Only you the human individual have the power of Unconditional Love within you to bring about the balance of mind, body and spirit within yourself into the present moment. Through Unconditional Love for all of life and through the forgiveness of oneself and others, you will connect with your inner knowledge and begin to obtain the awareness and wisdom to be balanced in Creation's totality.

When my being incarnated under 5,000 of your Earth years ago I expressed these words of truth: "Walk gently upon this most precious Earth, cause no harm to any form of life, not even unto yourselves, and you will walk in peace upon this most precious Earth."

Be Blessed in the love and understanding that all of life is most precious, no matter what form it takes, for it is only the human Ego that would ever judge a form of life to be lesser than itself and therefore not worthy of respect or the right to live.

CRYSTALS-THE PRECIOUS GIFTS OF MOTHER EARTH (NO-39)

Have you the human individual ever wondered why the crystals of Mother Earth have fascinated human beings for thousands of years? **Crystals are a part of the Earth. Mother Earth is living Consciousness just as human beings are living consciousness.** The Earth is a living spirit and her body is the Earth. The body a human being inhabits is created from the clay of Earth. Likewise, the crystals created by Mother Earth are also a form of living Consciousness embodied in a physical vessel.

All crystals are found upon and within the Earth. They are created from volcanoes when they erupt. The power of the explosion throws out thousands of balls of lava in which many combinations of minerals are boiling together. Where the lava lands and cools, and how the Earth's crust shifts and moves the lands, will create the crystals everyone love to look at, wear and hold. Crystals are created over hundreds and thousands of years. They are found all over the Earth, some being close to the surface while others laying deep within Mother Earth.

All crystals vibrate at different frequencies, just as human beings vibrate as different frequencies depending on their level of conscious development and growth. The more consciously evolved and aware a human being is, the higher the vibratory frequency will be of that human individual.

You may feel that all human beings are equal and that all human beings come from the same space of electromagnetic energy. From a physical perspective, yes, all human beings are equal. But what governs a human being's level of thinking and understanding is the Karma they have brought into their present life from previous incarnations as well as the level of influence from the human Ego, **for the human Ego retards conscious growth.** The Ego can only live in the past, basing its understanding on what it knows. If the past is always being brought into the present, then the future is also only created from the past, preventing conscious growth and expansion. **Here is where the problem lies.**

Before continuing with this article on crystals my Being feels it necessary to explain that for a human being to grow consciously, that being needs to let go of their past – forgive those who you believe have hurt you, learn to love all life forms unconditionally, dissolve the human Ego and with it you will dissolve your fears, beliefs, conditioning and insecurities. Be willing to step beyond your present understanding. In doing so the human individual will raise their Consciousness and they will attune their being to higher frequencies and vibrations of sound, thereby opening that individual to their own infinite inner knowledge. **When the human mind is at peace, there is balance.**

Many human beings believe that crystals have the power to bring enlightenment and communication with other realms. To a certain extent this is true. **However, you as human beings are infinite sparks of living consciousness.** Within every human being is an infinite spirit which holds the complete knowledge of all that they have been. Every incarnation is recorded in your cellular essence, and as you advance consciously, your awareness, level of thinking and understanding grows, allowing you the human individual to tune into your inner knowledge. **It is from advancing your Consciousness that enlightenment and communication with other realms will manifest.**

It is true that most crystals found upon and within your Mother Earth hold records and knowledge of past events upon Mother Earth. It is also true that crystals can emit healing energies to other forms of physical life and that they can **help balance the chakra centres in all life forms.** If a human being becomes balanced in mind, body and spirit, they will be able to tune into any crystal and obtain the knowledge of the past imprinted upon it. **Meaning all information stored within the crystal can be brought forward into the human world and can be of great benefit to all humanity.**

Crystals are neither negative nor positive. It is the human being who uses the crystal that is either negative or positive. **Human beings can use crystals for negative or positive outcomes, and this is governed by the individual's level of consciousness – whether they come from the Ego or the heart of unconditional love.**

So in truth, it is the human being who is the power and the crystal is the tool. Crystals can enhance your energies. One great advantage of using crystals is to record knowledge within them. As you speak and hold the crystal, all your words as well as visual images can be recorded within it. It does take practice but can be an advantage in storing information. The stored information or healing energy can also be sent to any other human individual upon your world, no matter how far away that individual may be from you, even beyond your world to other dimensions and universes. **If you find these claims outlandish, consider the use of crystals in your world of technology today. Crystals are being used in computers, watches, calculators, televisions, the Space Shuttle, in fact any object that has miniaturised memory cells, for all these objects use crystals to hold information.**

The ability to send healing through crystals is only limited by the individual's understanding and willingness to learn and believe they are doing it. If a human being wishes to use crystals to enhance healing, it is vitally important to heal the self-first, particularly to heal the self of any negative emotions so they are not transferred to those receiving the healing. **Crystals can also be used to balance the main chakra centres, of which there are eight.** In balancing the chakras you will be more in tune with the healing light and you will be more aware of the one being healed and their needs.

Healing sickness is not the solution to the underlying problem. The solution to healing sickness is in finding the negative emotion that created the sickness in the first place. In making the individual aware of why they have created their sickness, the negative emotion can be released through forgiveness, and then the physical act of healing can begin.

One of the most potent crystals for healing self and others and to bring to the surface buried negative emotions is black obsidian. During a crystal healing session, **place a black obsidian crystal on the heart chakra.** It will open any blockages and reveal the negative emotion to the one being healed. If the healer is balanced in mind, body and spirit, they will also become aware of the negative emotion being released, and will be able to facilitate the one being healed in releasing the emotion.

It is important to understand that black obsidian is a very powerful crystal, and it will reveal the truth. Black obsidian will expose any buried negative emotions and can help a human being to step beyond their self-created fears. It will certainly help the individual to grow consciously. Even if a human being holds a **black obsidian crystal during a meditation,** or places it under their pillow during their time of sleep, it will most certainly open up any blockages within that human being and bring those issues to the surface.

Once the negative emotions have been recognised, reviewed, forgiven and understood, the healer can place a <u>rose quartz crystal</u> on the heart centre of the one being healed.

Rose quartz will open the heart centre to the Unconditional Love that is within all life forms. It will enhance love and bring harmony and infinite peace to the one being healed. **Rose quartz** helps dissolve negative energies and brings balance to the heart centre, where true Unconditional Love exists. **Rose quartz** will help the human individual understand their own **self love** and will also help attract love from another into a human being's life.

Rose quartz can be worn around the neck or wrist, or placed under a pillow during the time of sleep. It will help bring a feeling of calm and peace during sleep time and helps the individual to have pleasant experiences while travelling in the astral vibration. It can also be programmed by the owner. Try this little exercise and repeat it as often as you feel the need.

Allow yourself to be in your own space of energy, become still in your mind and allow your thoughts to flow freely. When you have become peaceful within yourself, hold a piece of **rose quartz crystal (it does not matter what size it is)** and place your thoughts towards your heart centre. Use your imagination to see a mist of white light filling your heart centre, then filling your entire being, and then emanating all around your outer self. Remember, thought is powerful – truly believe what you are imagining and it will be manifest.

Visualise placing your **rose quartz** crystal into your heart centre. Breathe in deeply several times and allow yourself to bathe in your own **unconditional love.** Now that you have placed your **rose quartz** in your heart centre you can programme your love into your crystal. Again, feel your **unconditional love** for yourself filling your crystal. When you feel ready and you are in a state of pure bliss, take the crystal from your heart centre and see it back in the palm of your hand. When you are ready bring yourself back gently to the present and open your eyes.

Your crystal is now programmed to emanate your **unconditional love** and inner peace. Use the programmed crystal by placing it under your pillow when going to sleep or when meditating to help create a peaceful, loving ambience in your personal space. Whenever you feel stressed or depressed, hold the **rose quartz** to your heart centre and ask your love to be present. **Rose quartz is as powerful as you want it to be.** It will help you connect to the love that is within you, and it will help the healing process of letting go of your past through self-forgiveness.

Remember, you are the power source of whatever you are feeling and you are the creator of your present incarnation, as you were the creator of your previous incarnations. The human Ego is a very powerful negative creation of the negative self, so remember to ground yourself by breathing and focussing on light from your heart centre filling your entire being and all around you, and then ask for the love you had placed in your crystal to be released to you.

There are some human beings who have expressed to my Being that love is a joke, that love is impossible and that it does not exist. Yes, to some human beings this is their truth. However, dear human beings such a truth is the choice of the individual. You can accept or reject what you read here, but always remember the answers to your questions are in your heart. It all depends on your life's experiences and the negative emotions that have followed you throughout your human life. Negative human individuals as the one mentioned briefly above have never been able to let go of their negativity. Their entire life is based upon negative experiences, and that is why they do not believe in love. **They can't break the cycle of their own self-created negative experiences of their human life, again the chose is always the human individual, is it not?**

Yet every human being is connected to the totality of all that is. You are all connected to the Earth and you are all connected to the crystals of Mother Earth, just as you are all brothers and sisters across all species across all universes. You are spirits of light living in flesh bodies in the third vibration.

You can learn and let go of the past that holds you back to reconnect with your infinite self and your unconditional love.

Unconditional love can dissolve the human Ego and all its fears and self-created negative emotions, but only if the individual is willing to take this path. The choice is always yours alone. The crystals of Mother Earth can be a powerful enhancer to the human individual. **Black Obsidian** will open negative emotions to the individual in order to bring them to the surface so the past can be resolved. **Rose quartz** can help the individual find balance and connection with the heart centre and bring about emotional healing. These two crystals were created by Mother Earth to work together in harmony to bring balance and peace to the individual's life.

All crystals can be of benefit to humanity. May all human beings take a few moments out of their life to step back and view what is occurring on your most precious Earth you call home, and send love and healing to your precious Earth so that balance and peace may be upon Mother Earth once more?

PURPOSE OF ALL LIFE (NO-40)

May each of you as human individuals grow consciously in search for truth and knowledge? Even though all of humanity is connected, you are also individuals and your search for truth and knowledge as individuals in turn helps all of humanity to consciously evolve, as much as it helps you the human individual to evolve.

One of the most powerful tools for the individual is free will. Free will can be used for negative or positive actions depending on your level of thinking and understanding. The power of free will is your choice alone. It can shape your human life in peace, harmony and joy, or it can shape your human life in complete misery and pain. Either way, it has a direct influence on all your future incarnations as a human being.

So many human beings have been asking the same question – what is my purpose in life? Yes, that question can confuse and cause pain to those seeking the purpose of their life. This article is in response to those seeking purpose in life and also answers several questions asked by a reader with regards to Spirituality, Christianity, god and judgement, the Garden of Eden myth and loving the self.

The confusion created by belief systems **(such as those fostered by religions)** causes the individual to lose touch with their inner being, and in turn this causes the human individual to lose sight of the purpose of their life. Notice my Being uses the term **'the purpose of your life'**, rather than **'your purpose in life'**. Belief systems cause the individual to seek a purpose in life, in order to justify their reason for living and experiencing. Human beings are conditioned into believing that they must have a specific purpose in life, to physically achieve something or many things in order to be able to say at the end of their lives that their life was meaningful because they can physically prove their existence had purpose and the results thereof validate a human individual's existence.

Every human being can create a purpose in their life. From a religious perspective, Christianity **(as with all religions)** is a belief system created by man solely to instil fear and control over the masses. As a religion it gives only enough knowledge to the people so the people are always dependent upon the religion for guidance in life. This justifies the existence of the religion, **giving it a purpose to exist.** In turn the religion gives people a reason for why they exist, **giving them a purpose in life** – to worship a god, to live by that god's commandments, to seek counsel from representatives of that god. **In essence, to give away one's personal responsibility to an external entity (in this case the religion),** and in so doing a co-dependence forms, creating a purpose for the religion and a purpose for the individual that lives according to that religion. People fear being individuals who stand outside of the pack, while religion creates a sense of belonging, providing a pack to which one can belong. **One justifies the existence of the other and vice versa.**

Spirituality on the other hand is not a religion but an individual's way of life. That is, how that individual chooses to live their life in order to express their philosophy on living, their human existence and their understanding of existence beyond the human body. **There is a fine line between religion and spirituality.** All religions began as human expressions of Spirituality and indeed still are. The only difference between religion and Spirituality is that religion is the result of a number of people sharing similar beliefs and philosophies getting together and organising their beliefs into a specific belief system through set rules. **When an individual chooses not to follow these rules they would then be considered to no longer be practising that religion, but to be practising a hybrid of that religion. The hybrid is no longer recognised as a religion as such, but is recognised as a spiritual philosophy nonetheless.**

Spirituality is a combination of two parts – the spirit essence of all life, and the duality of physical life existing with spiritual life. It takes physical matter and spiritual essence to create a physical body that 'lives' in the third dimension.

To be truly spiritual is to first exist in the moment of life, and second, to be willing to confront the self-regarding all self-created negative emotions. This is the process of learning where letting go of the past is the single greatest lesson for all human beings, for in letting go of the past will the individual only then be able to recognise the spiritual essence that exists within them. Until that point, the individual is confused and lost in the maze of their emotions and belief systems.

There is a saying on your planet, that one cannot see the forest for the trees. Emotions and belief systems are the trees that make up the forest the human individual lives within. Until the individual can see the forest, by no longer focussing on the individual trees, will they then be able to see the sunlight illuminating the forest, the essence of the spirit that is within each of you illuminating your lives and bringing understanding as to your purpose for existence in the physical realm.

Letting go of the past and stepping into the moment is a very powerful juncture in life. The revelations it brings will reveal a life's purpose, and in that revelation there is no longer the concern that one must **'prove'** their right to exist through physical actions and material gain. Material gain can make physical life more comfortable, and that is a good thing, but it is not the purpose of life nor does it make one person's life more valuable, important or significant than another's. What is the purpose of physical wealth and comfort if one is not emotionally balanced and able to build nurturing and satisfying relationships with family, friends, co-workers and other humans within your communities? Some of the materially wealthiest humans on your planet are also the most emotionally unhappy. **Their physical wealth does not give them emotional security or the understanding and experience of unconditional love. Materially that may be wealthy but spiritually and emotionally they are barren.**

After learning to exist in the moment of life, then being willing to confront all self-created negative emotions, the human individual is ready to discover their true feelings. Feelings do not come from emotions, but from the moment of life. **Feelings are spontaneous and come from the heart centre of unconditional love for one's own essence and also for all forms of life, no matter what they may be.**

One of the lessons in human life is to learn self-responsibility for all actions created by an individual. Only in becoming true to oneself and facing self-created pain and disappointment can the individual begin to understand the true meaning of human life and its purpose.

A question was asked about Judgement Day in your human bible. Again, the bible and all the stories within it were created by man alone, **111 years after Jesus was murdered by the same human beings who said they loved him. Jesus' murder was a conspiracy** set up by the government of that time who saw **Jesus as a threat to their control over the masses. Jesus encouraged self-responsibility and unconditional love.** When one believes in oneself through the acceptance of self-responsibility and unconditional love, how can another have control over them? They cannot, and so **Jesus** had to be eliminated, just as many other great leaders and philosophers of your Earth were eliminated for the same reasons – **they encouraged self-empowerment for the individual.** To a group entity seeking power over others, individuality means impaired control of the masses. **To accept belief in Judgement Day is to accept control over your human life by an authority you see as above and beyond your own abilities to adequately live your life.**

No god or Jesus can choose who will be saved on Judgement Day, for there is no Judgement Day, only the fear of losing control. Judgement Day is an illusion created by human man. Every human being on your most precious Earth has been incarnating for more than **928,000 years,** and every human being has had thousands of lives upon the Earth. Therein lies the illusion of human life, created by fear which creates violence, pain and dis'ease, carried from one life to the next, and bringing forward into each life negative emotions of fear from the past, creating one's present life, and sadly one's future lives.

You may be asking **'when will it all stop?'** It will only stop when the individual takes personal responsibility for all their negative emotions by forgiving the self and all others from an honest, loving heart. **When the individual is willing to love themselves and all forms of life in unconditional love will the true meaning of one's life become apparent to them, and the trivialities of existence be revealed.** To believe in oneself and one's ability to grow consciously and change is to open the door to the heart centre and the infinite knowledge that exists in all human beings. **Each human being is an infinite, ageless, timeless and eternal spirit. You are immortal because your spirit is eternal – physical immortality is yet another myth perpetuated and misunderstood over time as belief systems are misinterpreted from generation to generation, century to century, millennium to millennium.**

Truth will always hurt those who seek it, but in that pain of realising one's naivety and foolishness is also tremendous freedom as you are set free from your self-created pain. **The Garden of Eden was another illusion**

created by human man. The Earth is the Garden of Eden, the Earth and all its life forms, from plant, to mineral to animal, and everything in between and beyond. The myth of the Garden of Eden is representative of a Utopia where all live in peace and harmony and where there is no struggle. The fall from grace is the human Ego causing the human individual pain and misery through self-created fears. The individual has the choice to find balance within themselves, thus creating the **Garden of Eden** as a state of being in their life, **but that is all the mythical Garden is, nothing more.**

Another myth related to the Garden of Eden is that of Adam and Eve. Consider this: is it possible to populate an entire planet from two human beings, knowing as you do the genetic problems created by interbreeding within the same family line? To be considered **'inbred'** from a human perspective is to be insulted and to be considered intellectually lacking, a genetic **'throwback'**. If you believe all of humanity and its diversity came from **Adam and Eve,** then you should also accept that interbreeding is the reason human beings are unable to deal with their emotions or grow consciously because they are intellectually lacking and genetically flawed. **Scientifically it is known that to breed from the same bloodline would eventually cause the demise and destruction of that bloodline.**

Strength and survival of any species relies on diversity and genetic strengthening of the species by introducing new bloodlines and genetics, not the other way around. Countless examples abound in your history of interbreeding of royal lineages and the health and mental problems that resulted from their interbreeding to keep their lineage **'pure'**. The myth of Adam and Eve is clearly impossible when considering the physical diversity of humanity (**Asians, Africans, Caucasian, Polynesians, and so on**), and to still accept the myth of **Adam and Eve** with such living proof is simply the Ego's arrogance in not wanting to admit it is clearly wrong and impossible. **However, it is free will to believe in illusion and fantasy, and if that is what an individual's Ego requires, then there is little anyone can do to help that individual grow consciously and emotionally.**

The entity 'god' was created by human man alone and has become a belief system to many human beings upon your Earth. Believing in the illusion of god causes the individual to give away their personal responsibility for all actions, all emotions and expectations, all unhappiness in life. Believing in an illusion reinforces the belief in the illusion, and this is how widespread belief systems are formed. The myth of god is but one form of belief system, and a very powerful one at that which will continue relentlessly until every human being confronts their fears of insignificance, powerlessness and emotional imbalance.

Letting go of long held beliefs and conditioning can be quite traumatic for some humans. You have no doubt seen reports of human beings who have attended personal growth seminars and at the end of them have had to be given medical assistance as they cried uncontrollably and or felt emotionally lost. Naturally the media play on this drama making out these personal growth groups as practising mind control. Some may well be doing that, but there are groups who are genuinely trying to set human beings free from the oppression of their emotional and social conditioning.

When one is highly conditioned and willingly gives away their personal responsibility to another, be it religion, government, or any other group entity, to suddenly have that lifeline and emotional support pulled out from under them causes great trauma, suddenly everything they have ever believed in has been revealed to be false. Suddenly they have to accept complete responsibility for their lives, every action they take, every thought they have. Some will be strong enough to take on the challenge and will grow consciously as they fight the old conditioning, while others will return to the safety and comfort of what they know, even if it means living a lie, because for many highly conditioned humans, emotional comfort, no matter how painful their emotions may be, is far more comfortable than confronting the unknown and learning to live each day with its challenges in the moment. For most, it is simply easier to give away responsibility and be coached and guided in how to think, what to expect of others, how to live, what to believe and what to disbelieve.

It takes courage and often the guidance of another (although not always) to help an individual reconnect with themselves after their beliefs and conditioning have been broken. Care must be taken that one set of beliefs and conditioning is not replaced with another set. Rather the guide is there purely to help build the individual's self-esteem and to help them accept personal responsibility learning to feel confident about the decisions they make, without the guide influencing any decisions or actions the individual may choose or take. For such guidance and conscious growth to be successful the guide must be free of beliefs and conditioning themselves;

they must have undergone their own conscious expansion in order to be able to guide another to finding themselves, and then to let that person go so they may truly be free to experience living as a conscious being, rather than unconscious being who operates on auto-pilot and runs with the pack for security and comfort.

Human beings believe they are evolved because of their science and technology, and yet the myth of god continues. **My Being has been asked 'why do Christians do everything for their god' and 'is it alright to praise god or the creator'?** Humanity has been highly conditioned by belief systems throughout lifetimes. **928,000** years' worth of incarnating makes it very difficult to dissolve belief systems that hold back conscious growth. What must be remembered is that belief systems are created from fear, fear that has been following the individual from one lifetime to the next. Fear has become a belief in itself and is conditioned into humans. Fear has literally shaped human life in the past, in the present and will continue to do so in the future. To praise another is to believe you are not of the same standard or level as the one you praise. It is to believe in some way that the one you praise is better than you, far superior to you, and this in turn sets up the belief that you are less worthy, and perhaps even worthless.

Step beyond the human world for a moment. There are thousands of species and different forms of life on other worlds, in other vibrations, and there are hundreds of other universes. What humanity believes to be the universe is but a speck in the totality of what is. It does not mean there are higher and lower beings. All it means is there are beings evolving to reach the same level as others that exist, and there are more evolved beings that are continuing to evolve beyond their own evolution in space and time. **Collectively it is the never ending expansion of consciousness.**

You the human individual have the right of free will to evolve as you wish. You also have the right to praise and worship whoever you wish. But it must be remembered that in believing another being or entity is superior to yourself, you are doing a disservice to your own conscious evolution because you do not believe you are capable of being great within yourself, beyond the flesh being that you see in the mirror. It is from this level of understanding that human beings create self-loathing and diminished self-esteem, and so the downward spiral into anger, hatred, resentment and jealousy creates and reinforces belief systems that hold back the human individual from conscious growth, and ultimately halts human evolution.

Creation, the totality of all that is, is simply energy, neither negative nor positive. It is the human individual who chooses, through free will to use that energy positively or negatively, and so the individual creates their life to be positive or negative based on how they react to what they are confronted with on a daily basis. **What you can imagine you can also create, whether it is spiritual or physical. The power of creation is within human beings as it is within all other life forms.**

Take a step back and you will see that reincarnation will continue as long as humans hold onto their emotions and fear. On your Earth there is a great fear of losing control, and there is a great fear of the past, which is why human beings continually reincarnate. Reincarnation has but one purpose, to allow the human individual to grow consciously beyond emotional, self-created limitations meaning Humanity's violent and manipulative pasts.

For reincarnation to cease and for humanity to evolve beyond the third vibration of physical matter, each human individual upon the Earth would need to accept responsibility for their self-created pain, would need to sincerely forgive themselves and all those who have caused them pain, and would need to learn to express Unconditional Love to all forms of life by not causing pain or violence to any form of life. Without any disrespect intended, humanity has a long way to go before such conscious evolution of the species could even be considered possible. Until such time however, humans will continue to reincarnate and continue to live their past pains and emotions.

It seems easier for human beings to worship a supreme being than to believe in and worship the self. Worshiping the self does not mean Egotistical self-aggrandisement, which is clearly evident in your entertainment industry. **Rather, worshipping the self is better expressed as truly loving yourselves from the heart in unconditional love.** In so doing, the human individual will see that all are equal in all things and that the individual has the right to love and be loved unconditionally.

There is a human misconception that to love oneself is to be egotistical. If one loves oneself in the belief they are superior to another then yes that is Egotistical. **But unconditional love for the self is not egotistical.** There is a definite difference between human love and unconditional love. Human love is based on beliefs and conditions, fears and control. Human love has been created from negative emotions through negative experiences, based on the past and brought into the present by the human ego. The ego holds human conscious growth back by keeping the individual locked in self-created pain, fear and misery.

Unconditional love comes from the heart, spontaneous and in the moment. It has no beliefs or conditions, no expectations or fears. Unconditional love does not seek to dominate or control. **It simply is.** An individual who unconditionally loves another allows that human being to be themselves and accepts their quirks and character, loving those very things that would ordinarily irritate them if they were seen in anyone else. Unconditional love accepts the individual as they are, not seeking to change them so you can be more comfortable with that human being. **Allowing the individual to be an individual is a lesson yet to be learned by humanity, as is unconditional love.**

Were unconditional love to be a part of human life, then human beings would have love and respect for all other human beings, for neighbours, other nations, for all forms of life. Human beings would never steal or cause emotional or physical pain to another, there would be no murder or rape, war or slaughter. The unconditional love in your hearts would give you the understanding for compassion and forgiveness without judgement.

Dear Sisters and Brothers of Earth, read these words with an open mind and loving heart, and take a precious moment in your life to ask yourself this question: Do I hear the message in these words in my human brain or in my heart? If you hear them in your human brain, then you have not heard at all. But if you hear them in your heart, then you have begun your journey of truly evolving as a human being.

Human beings have always looked to others for truth and meaning in their lives, scared to believe in themselves. **The purpose of human life is to evolve,** just as there is no truth outside of yourself, for truth only comes from within you. You are all living truth, and the truth of the wisdom from your essence is waiting to be discovered by each of you. You only have to desire to seek it from an honest heart filled with unconditional love. Leave the fearful conditioned past behind you by forgiving and letting go of what is no longer needed and what holds you back, and allow yourself to evolve consciously. As each human being evolves, so they are helping humanity evolve. This is your greatest purpose in life and the greatest service you can do for humanity. **Outgrow your past and shine as a bright beacon, guiding others to finding their truth and understanding of the greater purpose of human life.**

Be Blessed dear Brothers and Sisters. May each of you find the path of truth and may the light shine in all of humanity.

UNCONDITIONAL LOVE (NO-41)

My Being has been asked on many occasions to explain unconditional love. Unconditional Love is a pure state of being. Total bliss, some call it "The Knowing". It is the moment- it does not live to time, beliefs or conditioning. It has no judgement or opinions. It simply is.

For the human individual to experience unconditional love, the individual needs to feel love for all life forms, no matter what they may be, and to never judge or have ill thoughts towards another form of life.

The unconditional love you the individual would be experiencing comes from the centre of your being; your heart centre, your connection to your divine spirit.

Unconditional love can only be experienced if the individual is beyond the human Ego of negative emotions. Most human beings believe that love is an emotion. Yes, because of the human Ego's fears, insecurities, beliefs and genetic transfers, human love is an emotion mostly based on conditions and fears created from the human past.

If there is a negative emotion in any given situation being experienced by an individual or individuals, it is merely the past brought into the present by the human Ego, and therefore already creating the future.

Unconditional love, however is spontaneous, a feeling in the moment of life, being expressed from the heart centre.

Unconditional love is not about how much you give of the material world to another, for you cannot possess, buy or own love. **There are no rules to be imposed.** You cannot have Ego and express unconditional love. **The ego** is the negative aspect of humanity, created from the past over many, many lifetimes.

The ego wears many faces of deception, one for every moment in human time. The faces of deception worn by human individuals are simply their fears and insecurities, created by negative experiences which are stored as negative emotions that are then used by the Ego for its deceptions.

Because of past negative experiences, many human beings are fearful of expressing their love to another. **They do not wish to be hurt again.** Yet they look for love in all the wrong places. Fear drives the human race towards self-destruction, principally the fear of truth because an individual does not want others to see them as they really are or to know their self-created fears. This foundation of fear holds humanity in the physical realm, unable to progress consciously or spiritually.

The fear of the unknown is another fundamental stumbling block – fear of spirits, fear of beings from other worlds, fear of darkness, essentially the fear of not being able to be in complete control of one's physical environment, and therefore causing one to feel **'unsafe'.**

Human fear is a creation of negative experiences carried forward from one incarnation to the next. The purpose of incarnation is to learn and to let go of the past, to simply see it as lessons of life, **and to grow beyond the human ego.** In letting go of the Ego one will dissolve past negative experiences, past and present fears, emotions such as feeling rejection, self-doubt, guilt, blame, judgement, fear of life, and so many more.

Unconditional love gives the individual the gift of forgiveness. What happened 1 or 20 or 50 years ago is irrelevant, it does not matter. Holding onto the past in anger or hatred only causes harm to one's conscious awareness, personal growth and spiritual evolution, as well the perpetuation of **karma** upon oneself and others.

Ask yourself, dear Human Beings, why do you fear love for yourself and others? Why do you want another to love you, yet you are unable to love yourself? **Why is this so?** The answer is simple. As long as you hold fears from the past, your Ego will control you, for Ego is fear. **You can never experience unconditional love towards yourself or others while Ego and fear rules your life. This is the truth, and yes, the truth hurts.**

Every human being has the power of free will to step outside of the Ego's world, but how much do you truly want to find bliss and peace? How much do you want to change your world from one of pain and misery to one of balance and completeness? **How much do you want to be able to accept unconditional love into your life and then to be able to share it with others?** These are questions you will need to ask yourself if you wish to change your life.

Experiencing the unconditional love of your being, your essence, is the first step to transformation of the consciousness to higher planes. Unconditional love will lead you to expand your awareness beyond the third vibration of physical matter, enabling you to communicate with entities from other worlds.

So how do you bring unconditional love into your existence? Let go of the negative past through forgiveness. Dissolve the Ego with all its fears and negativity and start to live in the moment. Connect to other life forms by respecting them, and this can only come when you learn to understand them and their right to exist, not as your subordinate, but as your equal, regardless of their form. Connect with Mother Earth and become aware that you are part of all things, a much larger world, an immense universe of which you are but a spark of light amongst billions and trillions of sparks of light. Know that you are all sisters and brothers formed from light.

To reach that level of enlightenment one must accept the Ego has no purpose; that fear is pointless; the past is the past and cannot be changed, it is simply a memory neither negative or positive; the future is shaped by thoughts, words and actions in the moment; and the moment is the only aspect of existence that is real at any given point.

Through unconditionally loving your own self, everything else will gradually begin to fall into place. But in order to unconditionally love oneself and all others, including other forms of life, one must confront their own fears, their Ego, their past, and learn to forgive everything that causes emotional discomfort or pain. This is true evolution as a human being – conscious evolution. Be blessed in love always Human Beings of Earth.

BEING FIT IN MIND & BODY (NO-42)

Greetings to all human beings who live upon Mother Earth. May all human beings and all other life forms be blessed in unconditional love, and may the light of love emanate throughout your inner and outer being to help heal and balance each and every one of you, always in love.

My Being was asked this question: How does one become fit, meaning a fit mind and body? What does one have to do to accomplish this?

First, take complete realisation that you are indeed an individual. Even though you are connected to and a part of all that is, and all that is, is a part of you, you are also a thinking, breathing individual that has chosen to incarnate in order to experience all that you have chosen to experience. You are a spirit being that has incarnated thousands of times in human form.

You are not your human father or mother, you are not your past, but you are an individual living in the moment of your human life. You alone have chosen to live this life as a human being. If you choose to be clone of your human parents then you have chosen to live the past. To live the past is not to have a fit mind and body, for you will only create negative experiences. The past is the past. In most human beings the past is created from negative experiences, and in most situations those experiences are created from self-created fear.

There are many levels of fear. Fear is a part of the human Ego, the Ego being truly an enemy of the human individual. You only have to look at the past history of humanity to see how the human Ego has created wars, violence, greed, poverty and misery within humanity.

To create a fit mind and body the individual needs to achieve self-realisation - to recognise that human life is all about experiences, whether they are negative or positive. Yes, both negative and positive experiences are a necessity for learning the lessons of human life, but if you weigh up the negatives versus the positives, there have been far more negative experiences for most humans than positive, and sadly this influences the conscious advancement of human beings. The more negative the experiences, the more likely an individual will continue to live in their past negative emotions. On a broader scale, observation shows that negativity has perpetuated further negative experiences for humanity as a whole.

Over the complete cycle of human life so far **(over the last 928,000 human years of time)** there have been over 150,000 human wars large and small. Since your Second World War there have been just under 150 human wars. At present there are several human wars occurring on different parts of your planet.

Of both positive and negative experiences throughout human evolution from the past to the present, negative experiences constitute 89%, making positive experiences only 11%. In the last 65 years of human evolution **(from 1939 to date)** negative experiences constitute 93% with positive only 7%.

Humanity is not going forward consciously. The past is continuously being experienced in the present. For an individual to have the realisation of their own contribution to human negativity over all their lifetimes, it would be an enormous step forward not only for the individual, but also for human Consciousness as a whole. Such a realisation is the beginning of taking personal responsibility for one's created actions and existence as a physical human being on Earth.

Self-Realisation is the first step to creating a **fit mind and body** - complete recognition of one's existence as an infinite being who is a part of all that is, in all universes and realms. Recognising that you are responsible for your thoughts, words, deeds and actions also leads you to the conclusion that you are an eternal, timeless, ageless, infinite Being who can change the way they think, behave and express because of the recognition of free will.

Once an individual recognises this in themselves, they can take responsibility for their self-created **(negative and positive)** actions, thoughts and words. From this realisation the individual can learn to forgive. Self-Realisation helps one put everything into perspective, and so forgiveness is logically the next step. **Without perspective there can be no understanding, and without understanding the act forgiveness is impossible.**

Forgive yourself and others from your heart. Forgiveness in **unconditional love** is the most powerful action one can take in order to create, or build, a fit mind and body. Forgiveness is a process for stepping out of the past for all the negative actions created by an individual throughout all their lifetimes and into the present. Only through this process of conscious growth can one truly call themselves an individual. Up until this point you are merely a clone of your past, a representation of your conditioning and your negative experiences.

Through **self-realisation,** your journey throughout life as an individual leads you to understand how the past is continually brought into the present through the human **ego.** The **ego** is an emotional, fearful creation, the cumulative result of past incarnations. As a consciously evolving individual you begin to see, without judgment, a broader picture of human life, of yourself, your surroundings and your interactions with other human beings, and how all of this combined forms the structure of your life and the lessons you have chosen to learn.

Naturally, as much as your past and present thinking must change, the food you consume must also change if you wish to become fit in mind and body. Remember, as much as what you think you become, what you eat you also become. **It is all inter-related.** There are those who believe and even teach that it does not matter what type of foods you consume. If the individual believes this to be true then that is their choice, but the results of such beliefs speak for themselves. Before you blindly accept the beliefs of others, take the time to observe these advocates of 'eat as you will'. Observe their ways, their habits in life, their interactions with others and reactions to other opinions. **Much more can be learned through quiet observation when the voice is silent and the mind is open.**

To obtain fitness in mind and body one must become responsible to oneself. Take responsibility for how you think, how you care for your human body, how you nourish it and maintain it. Simply by consuming pure simple foods in as natural a state as possible with plenty of fresh water, plus gentle exercise, you can not only transform the body but create a transformation of the mind as a result of shedding the physical burden of poor health. When the body functions better, the mind can think more clearly, understanding improves, and knowing one's inner truth becomes more readily recognisable and accessible.

Such small changes in physical lifestyle allows a natural advancement to occur in Consciousness, and this allows higher vibrations of energies to connect with the individual. This is not only of benefit to the individual but to humanity as a whole. **To become a teacher one must first be a student. To become a healer one must first heal themselves.** To become a loving compassionate being one must first learn to love themselves unconditionally. To be a beacon of light in this human time of emotional darkness one must first expand their understanding and grow consciously. **Human advancement begins with the individual who then learns to lead by becoming the living example of their truth.**

My Being will express again **"What you think you become, what you consume your human body will become."** The majority of foods mass produced for human consumption at this time in your human society are bad for the human body. Because of their effect on the human body, these foods also halt the advancement of human consciousness. The human body is living consciousness. Each cell that forms a part of the collective that is the human body has its own blue print or level of consciousness. Each cell requires specific nutrients from the Earth to feed it and maintain it. This then allows the cells of the human body to defend the body via the immune system and other protective systems.

If the human body is clouded with drugs of any description, alcohol, cigarettes, and poor nutrition, the body will not function correctly, and when the body does not function correctly, the mind does not think straight. It is very hard to be able to reason with such an individual. Their level of thinking and understanding will be limited, and therefore their ability to evolve consciously will also be impaired. The path an individual's life ultimately takes through actions and decisions will easily be the result of the body-mind fitness level. The individual may end up on a path they later regret.

The choice for your path in life is yours alone and can be changed at any time. You have the free will to do whatever you choose. But ask yourself from an honest heart, not a fearful Ego, do you truly want to be responsible for your life, your choices, your decisions, or do you wish to be clouded by negative emotions and experiences, created from one lifetime to the next? If you wish to take the path of **personal responsibility then start now to create a fit mind and body;** start now to make the necessary changes knowing that it is not only for your physical good, but for your higher good in lifetimes to come and ultimately the higher good of humanity.

Take one step at a time. Do not be afraid to change, and remember it is not a crime to wish to be an individual, although your friends, colleagues and family may try to make you feel that it is. Do not allow others to have expectations of you, but be yourself; believe in yourself and know that you are infinite, that you are much more than the flesh body you inhabit in this lifetime. Remembering this will give you the motivation to continue when the human ego wishes to stop your growth and return you to your comfort zone. Conscious change for the better will open doors that may have once seemed unopenable.

Be blessed in **unconditional love** and May you each be filled within and throughout your Being with the guiding light of Creation.

LIFE AND DEATH (NO-43)

We the **Nar'Karones,** who are your Sisters and Brothers, express Unconditional Love to each human being living and experiencing a physical existence at this present moment in human evolution.

Life and death. It is a part of human incarnation and has been for over **928,000** of your human years. The purpose of incarnation is for each of you as **spirits** to evolve and learn the lessons that you have chosen to learn. How many lifetimes you take to learn these lessons is your choice.

For a human being life is a dual experience. There is the endless and infinite spirit of your true self and there is the physical human existence of learning and evolving consciously through the physical realm.

The **spirit** keeps the flesh body alive in the third vibration – without it the flesh body would not exist. It would be lifeless, for it is the **spirit** that gives you conscious thought.

When a human couple creates a child, the flesh body of the child exists and develops in the uterus because the mother's body sustains its growth and life. The human mother is kept alive by her **spirit,** and the child within her is also kept alive by her **spirit** because the child is physically connected to her human body. The **spirit** that will inhabit the child's body once born will only enter the body on the first breath taken in by the child's body. Hence this is the duality – the coming together of two – **spirit and flesh, existing in a world of physical matter.**

In order to understand and accept death one must understand life. At this present time in human evolution life and death exist together. You cannot have one without the other. All flesh bodies eventually die and decay, returning to the Earth from which they were created. Even your planet Earth has a **spirit,** a consciousness. Without it your planet would become lifeless, like so many other planets in your universe that once teemed with life.

A number of circumstances can create physical death. Suicide is increasing at an alarming rate within humanity. There is no age barrier and the reasons for suicide are many. The ultimate act of self-destruction, the motives, reasons and emotions behind suicide are often misunderstood by those left behind.

Suicide is the result of the feeling of hopelessness. Depending on circumstances, whether the emotions were created from childhood or in adulthood, it is negative conditioning that causes depression that quite often leads to self-loathing and the sense of there being no resolution. Most human beings project negativity outwards towards others when they are feeling negative. Those who suicide generally project their negativity inwards towards themselves, leading to feelings of being trapped and there being no way out from what they are feeling about their life. **Suicide seems like the last option available.**

What most human beings do not understand is that suicide does not solve the problem. When a human being feels completely lost in their own self-created hopelessness, and suicide seems to be the only way out, at the time of death when the **spirit leaves the body,** the **spirit** will quite often recreate over and over again the circumstances of their depression, negativity and suicide in **spirit** world. They are not leaving their problems behind but entering a world where they will continue to relive their last human experience and all its accompanying emotions until they realise they are no longer physical and start to let go of their pain. Whatever they thought they could get away from will follow them into **spirit** world.

The purpose of human life is to learn and understand that the individual chooses to experience life in human form. It is not possible to run away from it and think it will all dissolve or fall into place once you leave the body permanently.

The difference between **spirit** world and the human physical world is that no one there will judge you for choosing suicide. Whatever actions you may have taken, that are viewed negatively or positively in your physical world by others, are seen for what they are in **spirit** world – actions and choices that you alone have taken. You are an infinite being who chooses your lessons and experiences of life. What are viewed as negative and positive actions by the rest of humanity, all have their purpose in human life, and even the action of choosing and committing suicide has a purpose. Suicide is as much a lesson and experience as any other human experience, both for the one who suicides and for those left behind.

The conditioning and circumstances of a human being's life will bear upon their thoughts, words and deeds throughout their life. Those thoughts, words and deeds are the choice of the individual and the results of those choices become not only the direction of that individual's life, but also the individual's personal responsibility. **This is free will.** Be willing to change your thinking and you will change your life's direction. Always remember there is always a solution to any created problem, no matter what that problem may be. It is simply a matter of looking at it from a different angle.

To make the connection between life and death, we must examine the five elements of the human body:

Fire: Located at the base of the human spinal cord, fire is your energy source just as within Mother Earth is a river of lava which flows around the Earth providing vital elements to the Earth. Your own blood flows throughout your body to nourish your organs and repair damaged tissue. Without blood the body would not exist in its current form. It is the same with the Earth. Without hot molten lava the Earth would be a frozen planet, such as those surrounding your Earth which at one time supported life of many species.

Water: Without water life would perish. Over half your Earth is made up of water. It is a cleanser that helps keep the Earth clean. Your oceans provide up to 80% of your oxygen and evaporation ensures your planet does not overheat. The human body is no different – made up of up to 80% water **(depending on how much water a human consumes),** evaporation and circulation keeps the human body's core temperature stable. Many humans suffer health problems because they do not drink enough water daily to filter the body of pollutants and metabolic wastes, which in turn creates dis'ease and in a large number of cases leads to physical death.

Air: The Earth breathes and so must the human body. Forests purify your air and if you live near large numbers of trees or the oceans, your air will be cleaner and your human body will feel healthier. Polluted air is one of humanity's biggest problems. Thousands of humans die because of pollution, which not only exists in the air but also finds its way into the waterways and into the food chain.

Earth: The building block of physical matter. The minerals of the clay of the Earth are also found in the organic matter that is your human body. All of life that exists on the Earth began in the oceans and evolved onto land over millions of human years. Human beings today are the result of millions of years of physical evolution, and they have been on the planet Earth for over 928,000 years. The planet itself is billions of years old. This universe that exists is one of thousands of universes which there are hundreds of thousands of forms of life, evolving physically for millions of years, long before humanity even began its evolution from life as a single cell organism within the Earth's oceans.

Spirit: This is the fifth element. **Your spirit is a part of your consciousness.** Without it your body would not function, would not move. The best example of this would be coma patients. Some can breathe without equipment, but all require to be drip-fed and their bodies moved to prevent bedsores. A body in coma means there is nobody home, meaning the **spirit** has vacated, but the vessel is still performing life-sustaining functions when aided by external equipment. Unable to move or feed itself, the body would quickly die without external intervention.

The spirit is eternal, timeless, ageless and infinite. It is living consciousness in perfect form. Outside the flesh body it is not influenced by negative or positive experiences and therefore free of conditioning, fears and emotions. **Spirit has no boundaries except what is placed upon it when in physical form.** The knowledge an individual acquires throughout their lifetime **(spiritual knowledge, not material, human knowledge)** will assist them in their next life.

You gain physical knowledge in each life from scratch, but the spiritual knowledge you gain in one life will be carried through to the next, and it is your spiritual knowledge that governs the experiences you have as a physical being from life to life. Yes, human life can get easier if you choose to learn the lessons of each life. Death is simply the doorway between worlds and allows you to experience many lives.

Growing consciously in awareness causes your level of thinking and understanding to evolve, which also affects the rate of your energy vibration. The higher you raise your energies the more you will be able to tap in to your infinite knowledge, your spiritual knowledge. The spiritual knowledge you access influences the experiences you have in this life and in your next life as a human being.

Just as everything has its own life cycle, so too does the human body. Physically the human body has an expiry date and physical death is imminent. But how you deal with physical death in the physical and spiritual realms will govern your understanding in your current life as well as your understanding in your next life.

Humanity has created a dense form of negative energy, which surrounds your planet. This negative energy is generated by the human Ego, and is the result of past negative experiences which continually influence the present and therefore create the future. This negativity holds most human beings in a state of fear – **a fear of other people, other nations, of oneself.** If humanity could understand the true meaning of life **(to learn and consciously grow)** and the purpose of death **(to let go and continue one's conscious journey)** then human beings would not cause pain or harm to each other, conscious evolution would occur more rapidly and there would be less incarnation. The human race would then be consciously evolving beyond their third dimensional existence of matter. One negative action will create a negative reaction, either in your present life or in a life to come. Balance must be restored, and as long as there is imbalance, reincarnation will continue.

Some of your Eastern cultures have a greater understanding of physical death. Children are exposed to the natural processes of **birth and death** and so they are prepared to accept death throughout their life as natural and necessary for physical existence. Death is explained and grief is expressed but death is also celebrated as a release from this world and gives the opportunity to experience a new existence. Death is not the end for many of these cultures, but rather, the beginning of something new for that **spirit.** Within the teachings of Eastern cultures, the purpose of human life is explained. Within the scope of human life the purpose of **karma** is taught - its effect on an individual throughout their life, especially the importance of avoiding negative **karma** and how it shapes your present life and future lives with its negative influence.

Death is a part of physical life – why would you not embrace it? If you can understand death, when the moment comes you will have no fear of it. To be able to pass from your human body in love and acceptance will make your transition to the non-physical world far easier.

When a **spirit** is about to pass from their physical life it is very important to give love and comfort to that individual, to help them feel safe and comfortable concerning the journey they are about to commence. It is important to express compassion and understanding, and to be completely loving, so their final separation from their human body is peaceful and joyous. That is the greatest gift from your heart that you could give another who is about to pass from your world. Even if you dislike the person, in their moment of need no matter how you may feel towards them, give of your heart so no negative energies are projected and created into **karma** which would be carried into another lifetime.

This is why there is so much violence and conflict within the human race. Hatred and anger towards human individuals, families, entire cities and nations, has created the many murders, rapes and violations of such terrible nature. The past is continually being brought into the present, creating the negative and unbalanced future of humanity.

Stop and listen to your inner voice. Allow yourself to see the truth, the truth that the entire existence of the human race has been plagued with anger, violence and bloodshed, created over and over, and generating negative **karma** lifetime upon lifetime.

Having experienced death so many times, often in violence or pain, it is little wonder many humans fear death. **The ego** is only concerned with how it looks, what others think of it, and how much it possesses materially. As much as the Ego wishes to ignore it, it is inevitable that the human body will grow old and eventually every human must face their death.

It is the spiritual conscious knowledge and awareness gained in your current lifetime which will influence your current life and lives to come, for you will take this knowledge with you into your next life. How much knowledge you gain is up to you. If you choose to live in ignorance then the pain which ignorance brings will follow you. But if you choose to live consciously, then your Consciousness will evolve and the quality of your future physical lives will improve.

Part of overcoming ignorance is to gain an understanding of life and death. Physical life is an illusion, a wonderful yet extraordinary illusion – the learning to be gained from it is unquestionable. But for many, death will be the greatest experience, setting you free from your physical body and all that holds you in this realm, and allowing you to commence your journey of rediscovering your true self and your true existence beyond the physical human world.

ORIGIN OF HUMANITY (NO-44)

May love and truth always fill your inner and outer being? May each of you come to your own self-realisation of who you truly are and where you originated from? Only by stopping the chatter of the human Ego, and by stilling the mind and becoming silent within your Being, can you touch the essence of your inner truth.

There have been quite a few questions concerning where humanity began. You have heard the saying **"The Truth and Only the Truth".** It is an interesting expression of words, is it not? **Who in reality knows the truth?** Your teachers? Your governments? Your media? What about your written history -is it correct and accurate? **Is truth found in your books?**

The truth of where humanity began is a very interesting subject on your planet you call Earth. **We the Nar'Karones call your Earth "Yarkuss Kariss" and in this present moment you have nearly 7 billion people living on your planet Earth.**

So in reality, you have nearly 7 billion truths. Yes, most believe they know the truth, yet what most human beings believe truth to be, comes from an external source. However, truth found on the outside of oneself is only an idea of truth not truth itself.

There is only one truth, and you all have it within you. But in most human beings it is dormant. To discover absolute truth one must come to their own self-realisation that all is within you. Each of you have within you the infinite knowledge of the totality of Creation from the past to the present, and only each of you can bring this knowledge forward to your own conscious awareness.

One thing my Being must express. The language known as **Sanskrit** is in fact the language of the **Nar'Karones.** This language is universal. You as human beings originate from the planet **"Nar'kariss",** and deep in your essence, your cellular memory is this truth of who you truly are. All of you spoke the language of **Sanskrit,** and all your present languages on your Earth today have evolved from **Sanskrit.**

We your **sisters and brothers** can only give you the knowledge and wisdom to come to your own self-discovery, and to gain the awareness that all life forms, no matter what they may be, are indeed very precious. Time as you know it does not matter in our vibration. If we the **Nar'Karones** look back at our past, it is like only a moment has passed, and yet for you as human beings, **928,000 years have passed.**

We the **Nar'Karones,** live in our present state as Consciousness and are connected to each other. We either think or create on a single level, or we think and create as a collective Consciousness. To explain, when you as human beings wish to communicate with each other you use sound by expressing words through your human mouths, or if you communicate with someone who lives far away from you, you use a telephone, a facsimile machine or a computer. This is similar to our way of communicating by thought, which is pure energy. It is also a form of sound, but on a different frequency which to human ears would be inaudible.

The **Nar'Karones** as a species are indeed connected to humanity. **We are your sisters and brothers of light. Over 1 million years ago of your human time, the Nar'Karones** were going through many changes. Most of our kind wanted to transform to higher vibrations which meant letting go of all the material world of physical dense matter, such as flesh bodies, and raising our Consciousness to a higher level of awareness and thinking.

The process was long. It took many thousands of years because we had to deal with negative emotions created by the fears of the Ego. During the letting go process it was very painful for many **Nar'Karones.** Unfortunately there were some that did not want to let go of the old ways, and they created many problems during the transformation.

Finding a way of dealing with this situation became our main purpose. You cannot force anyone, not any individual to change if they do not wish it. Every being in Creation can only change their level of thinking when they have gained a deeper understanding of themselves, and have dealt with their self-created Ego and their past and present.

Because we the **Nar'Karones** where growing beyond our physical matter world, we also realised we had only two choices. One was to dissolve **(end the life of) the 87,000 beings,** but this was not really a choice. The other choice we had was to place these **87,000** beings on another planet so they could work out their destructive Ego while they continued to live their old ways.

Through much research your planet Earth was chosen, and those **87,000** entities were placed upon it, nearly 1 million years ago. We called your Earth **Yarkuss Kariss,** which in our language means **"The Beginning".** Most of the human race, as it is in this moment of life, came from or evolved from the **Nar'Karones** and the race of beings who were already living on your planet and evolving for several thousands of years, referred to by human scientists as **Neanderthals.**

The **Nar'Karones** who were transported to your Earth existed for thousands of your years, creating havoc among their own kind as well as other species of life forms, and eventually mating with the **Neanderthals.** Human beings of today have the genetics of both races within them, the result of **928,000** years of evolution and the mixing of a number of species.

Please understand that my Being is not asking you as human individuals to believe what is being expressed. The truth of what my Being is expressing lies dormant within each of you and is encoded in your living essence, the spark of light that is within all of life, just as all of life is within you. From the beginning of your existence as Consciousness, you are of light, and with each incarnation you have, you are evolving. Between your lives you are resting and growing, planning your next life in a human body and the purpose of these lives are to gather knowledge to help you grow beyond your present state of awareness, and to come full circle returning once more to a Being of Light.

At this moment my Being must express about how the **Asian, African and Australian Aboriginal** races came about in your human evolution. The **Nar'Karones** who were placed here on your Earth mated with the **Neanderthals.** The **Neanderthals** also evolved as a race and became the natives of the continents of your Earth, and you can see a very strong resemblance physically to this ancient species in your **African and Australian Aboriginal beings.**

You can also see Neanderthals to a lesser extent in your European beings, but their genetics are clearly present. The Asian races are a very interesting creation of evolution and genetic engineering, having evolved from chimpanzees, apes and other primates over hundreds of thousands of Earthly years, with the assistance of a physical Alien race of beings who still visit your planet Earth today.

These Alien beings experimented and implanted their own genetics (**DNA**) along with that of the primates to try to create an intelligent, non-aggressive physical being who would not be a threat to them. This new species was monitored by their scientists, just as your scientists today are experimenting with implanting genetics into related and vastly unrelated species to see what effect such genes would have. **It is interesting how history is also repeating itself, is it not.**

At this point, ask yourself what is more important to you as a conscious human being, as an individual. Is it more important to be highly conditioned with no free will, to never truly know yourself, and to believe only in what you are being told, or would you prefer to know the truth, to be set free from your negative emotional pain, and be given the opportunity to step beyond your human past into the present moment of bliss?

Are you willing to face yourself and see yourself for who you truly are, without all the excuses that your self-created Ego has given you to hide behind? Knowledge of truth is freedom and will allow you the human being to grow consciously in awareness of where you have come from, of how you as a human being have evolved over the last **928,000** years of human history.

So you are now aware that you have come from a planet called **Nar'Kariss that** you were and still are a part of the beings called the **Nar'Karones**, and you also understand why you were placed here so long ago. Perhaps one of the most important questions that you the human individual may need to ask yourself is. **"What can a human being do, as an individual, to enhance the development of humanity and elevate your consciousness in order to gain wisdom and understanding beyond the present state of negative emotions which humanity is currently absorbed within".**

One of the greatest gifts you can give to another is space without any form of judgement and to allow each human being the right to grow when they are willing to. It is your right – your free will – to choose the path you take in your human life, but be aware to walk gently upon this planet Earth. Harm no-one neither physically or emotionally; express Unconditional Love to all life forms, no matter what form that life may be and you will not create negative repercussions, as you would call, **Karma.**

To discover complete truth of where you as human being began, or came from, you need to begin with yourself. Look to your human bodies as a temple and feed your bodies only natural foods and think good thoughts about yourself, so you can be an example to others. Learn to still your mind in the silence of your inner being by meditating daily. When negative situations present themselves to you don't react in a negative way, but see them for what they are, simply a creation of the **ego.** Place pure light around them and see them dissolving into the nothingness from which they came.

Learn to become 100% responsible for all your own created actions in your life. Do not judge yourself for your failures. Rather, see them as an opportunity for you're to grow beyond your present level of thinking. Forgive yourself in Unconditional Love and know you are worthy of love for yourself, so you can learn to accept love from another human being.

Grow from the human Ego and all its limitations. The truth of your origin will manifest itself outwardly when the human Ego is dissolved. You will gain the knowledge and the understanding that you are **indeed our brothers and sisters who originated from Nar'Kariss.** Be blessed each and every one of you dear Human Beings of Earth, in Unconditional Love always

FINDING PEACE (NO-45)

Finding peace sounds simple enough. Yet for so many it would take a miracle or life changing experience to discover how to find peace. Why do so many human beings find it so difficult to have or experience peace?

Humanity lives to time and time is speeding up. Everything in your human world is related to time. Many have said **"there is just not enough time in the day to complete all that is expected of me"**.

Who then is speeding up time? You the human individual; you alone are responsible. You have created a lifestyle of wants and needs. The more you want the more you need, therefore the more you have to work to create the physical money to have what you want and need, and suddenly you find you have little or no time left for yourself. Human beings have become slaves to their desires, **and that in itself will stop you from finding peace.**

It is the self-created human Ego that has been with humanity for the past **928,000** years of human evolution that does not have an understanding of how to find peace. **The ego** has created in each human individual the understanding that to find peace you must struggle and obtain more physical items of the material world so you can feel comfortable. It is in physical comfort that the Ego believes one will possibly find some form of peace.

No individual will ever find peace from the self-created human Ego of beliefs and conditionings. The only thing the human Ego has created in each human being is fear, pain, confusion and misery because the Ego can only live the past, **for that is all it understands.**

The ego draws on the past. Most of humanity's past is created from negative experiences, which is why wars have plagued humanity throughout its history. Violence is highly conditioned into many human beings. Each human being is unconsciously a part of the Ego's negative world of confusion, and that is why finding peace is difficult for many human beings.

One cannot justify violence for violence, murder for murder. It will always have repercussions somewhere in your human evolution, be it in your present life or another life to come. Any negative action will always create a negative reaction, because it is the Ego that acts and reacts negatively. **The simple truth stands as witness for itself - human history is lettered with examples of negative actions creating negative reactions, compliments of the ego.**

Human beings find it hard to **find peace** because their human past haunts them to this present moment in human time.

Inner peace will be found when two very important steps are taken toward a more conscious way of living. First human beings must make a conscious choice to never harm any form of life from this moment on, no matter what the situation may be. Second, human beings need to learn forgiveness of the self and all others from the past to the present moment. Causing harm to others or other forms of life and not forgiving the past are the two principle factors that hold back the individual from **finding inner peace.** Search within your inner being and discover your own truth you will realise that you are a part of the human history of pain and misery that continues to this moment.

Every human individual that is presently living on your planet Earth has one main purpose – to learn and discover that by becoming consciously aware of their own self and surroundings, they will indeed be lead to truth, for truth alone will help every human individual **find peace outwardly and inwardly. In truth there is no doubt or fear, no uncertainty.** Truth provides the ultimate comfort; it is simply knowing that you know and are aware of the **difference between reality and deception.**

What is unfortunate is many human beings do not want to know the truth. To many, truth is too painful. Knowing the truth would mean becoming responsible for all of their actions in their current life and their past incarnations. Knowing the truth would mean they can no longer blame others, but rather they would have to face themselves, their fears, their negative actions and reactions.

The past haunts every human individual. The human Ego from its fears has created many distractions for the individual. In reality it keeps you busy in all your distractions so you do not have to face yourself. That alone stops humanity from evolving conscious awareness, and stops the individual **from finding peace.**

Some of the worst distractions for human beings not wanting to face themselves is creating human dis'ease, by polluting the human body with junk foods, cigarettes, drugs, negative thoughts towards oneself and towards others, alcohol, too much processed food, as well as the emotions of anger, hatred, violence, greed, lust and so many more. All of these things halt any conscious growth and awareness. What it does do is cloud your energy field, **your Aura,** your life force. It prevents you the individual from making clear decisions - your reasoning becomes clouded and prevents you from seeing a clearer picture, **from seeing reality objectively.**

Once you are clouded by negative emotions you actually live in another world of understanding. The human Ego prevents you from seeing the truth. You become a slave to your past and live your past day in and day out. **If a human being passes over to the spirit world in a clouded state of mind, they can and do recreate the same world in spirit as if they were still physical beings.**

This is what makes a human being an unconscious being. When an individual incarnates again they will only be able to bring in the clouded form of understanding into their life from their past life. They will come through parents who will also have that form of limited understanding. **This is why the human Ego is the enemy, and this is why so many human beings are struggling with life and why so many cannot find peace.**

So many questions have been directed to my being about how one goes about finding peace. First make a conscious decision that yes you do truly want to find peace in your human life.

Second, ask yourselves what you have to do to bring peace into your life. Be true to yourself. Look at your life habits - what foods do you consume; are they harmful to you or are they good for you? Make changes in your human life that are positive, and do not allow negative thoughts to influence you. Make the change now in the moment. As you become more responsible for all your created actions in your life, make those actions positive ones.

Commit yourself to some personal quiet moments in your life so you can get to know yourself completely. Find out your fears, your joys, your strengths and your weaknesses. Write it all down on paper so you can refer to it at a later moment in your life and review how far you have come in your quest for conscious growth, awareness and inner peace. **Find out who you are angry with – is it yourself, your Father, your Mother, your Brothers or Sisters. Ask yourself why and listen to your answer – again, write it down.**

Don't be afraid to face your fears. Don't be afraid to face yourself. Fear is simply created energy which has been conditioned into you, the Human Being. By facing yourself full on, you will begin the process of disarming others that need forgiving. You will begin the process of tearing down the walls of self-created fears that have been with you for so long.

You will begin to find peace of self, and begin to disarm the Ego of the past. You will open yourself up to new ways of thinking, new ways of how you see yourself and others in the scheme of human life.

The more changes you make in yourself, the more you will become aware of your own conscious growth, your own understanding of how the human Ego has ruled human society for the past **928,000 years.** Every moment you get a negative thought, change it into a positive thought. Remember, thoughts are energy and if you concentrate on a thought long enough it will be manifested into your reality.

To find peace in your life you must be willing to want to change, be willing to confront your fears, be willing to stand before yourself and truly see how the human Ego has created your past and humanity's past in all of its negative creations. By seeing the truth for yourself and by experiencing the truth for yourself, you the individual will become the living truth.

By knowing the truth you will be able to set yourself free from the human Ego of illusion and deception. By knowing the truth you will experience Unconditional Love, and by experiencing Unconditional Love you will become a compassionate loving human being who will see everything for what it truly is without any form of judgement. Your light will shine for all to see. **Your knowledge will be infinite.** Your present will be pure bliss. And yes, every human being can accomplish this simple task if they each make the conscious decision to do so. If you are prepared to put the effort in to yourself, you will then find complete peace, harmony and balance of life. Be blessed in Unconditional Love always dear Sisters and Brothers of the Light.

THE SPIRIT & THE SOUL(NO-46)

You are each as human beings the living essence of Consciousness on a journey of Self-Discovery of who you as human beings truly are. You are Spirit living a human form of physical matter, for matter is simply a state of the mind created by your Soul, manifested outwardly.

Yet what is the Soul and what is the Spirit? What is the difference between the two? Many human beings believe the Spirit is everything, that it was created by your human god, while others believe the Soul is everything and that it was also created by your human god.

Most human beings on Earth believe all knowledge comes from what was written in books from the past to the present. From a human understanding that statement holds a great deal of truth. However, that form of truth stems from beliefs and has been conditioned into humanity from one generation to the next.

Humanity as a species has been evolving over the past **928.000** years and yes, the truth about human history has been rewritten over and over. So many books about your human history exist on your Earth today – they hold a portion of truth and a portion of illusion. How can a human being really know what is truth as opposed to **what is illusion and fantasy?**

To answer this question let us return to the difference between the **spirit and the soul.** Every human being has a Spirit within them. Without your Spirit you as a human being could not (and would not) exist in your physical third dimension. **You would be physically lifeless.** The third dimension vibrates at a different frequency to Spirit World, where the Spirit Vibration vibrates at a much higher frequency as compared to the human physical world.

The Soul is pure light, untainted living consciousness. It exists in a state of bliss, unhindered by the physical realm. The vibration of the Soul is much higher than that of the Spirit. The Soul is the totality of all that is. In the realm of the Soul there is no limitation, no negativity because positive and negative do not exist. All is in balance and harmony in every moment.

The Soul created the Spirit and the human form. Depending on the lessons that need to be learned, the Soul can create one Spirit to take a human form, or many facets of the one Spirit to take many human forms, **male or female,** to live anywhere on your planet Earth. The facets can be of the same age or at different ages, living at the same time or at different times. It all depends on the Soul choosing the circumstances of human existence with respect to the lessons to be learned and knowledge gained.

For example, the Soul may choose to create seven facets of the same Spirit to incarnate at different times and places on your Earth. When a facet passes over **(dies)** that facet will then join with another presently living facet **(adding their energy and knowledge to the one who is living physically).** This joining of facets continues until there is only one facet left. When a facet joins, a human being may wake up one day and suddenly feel different – more confident, or surer of where they are going, they may suddenly feel more peaceful about their life than they had previously. This is because the knowledge and experience of the facet that has joined them has now become a part of the physically living facet.

Ask yourself this question: Who runs my human life? Depending on your beliefs and conditioning, you may say your parents and the kind of society you were raised in, the answer for most human beings would have to be **"the past".**

Throughout human history, generation after generation, incarnation after incarnation, each human being is created from the past. The past has been haunting humanity since humanity began and fear is the driving force that keeps humanity in the past. The human Ego has caused human beings to live in fear, clinging to what they know, and it is from this illusory sense of safety that human beings create their future. Human history has been very violent, and life in the human race is no different. Wars erupt on a continual basis creating misery and pain for all.

Why has this happened? The answer is simple. The human Ego created itself a very long time ago. Instead of allowing the Spirit to experience life, guided by the Soul, the Ego took over human life. One **ego** influences an individual, while a collective of Egos influences the masses. Unfortunately the Ego is short sighted – it has no awareness of Spirit or Soul and its only understanding is its past. It knows where it came from and will go forward based only on what it knows. **The ego will not venture into something unknown or beyond it boundaries and limitations of understanding.** The **ego** can only relate to its past and that is why humanity continues to live in the past, warring and fighting, still angry over things that happened centuries ago, never forgiving or allowing anyone to emotionally move on. The **ego** does not understand **Unconditional Love** but only understands the past created from fear, and therefore it fears living from moment to moment. It can only draw on its past, and so this is why humanity creates its present and future from its past.

You may ask if there is any hope for humanity. **Yes, there is always hope.** Take away the power of your human Ego by not allowing it to control your emotions. If you seek truth and answers, then look to your Soul, the seat of all knowledge. The Spirit is the vehicle that enables the Soul to gather knowledge from the physical realm through the process of incarnation, be it through one or several facets of energy. Be true to yourself and ask your Soul to guide your human affairs. Take some precious moments out of your human life and meditate in the stillness of your mind by putting your thoughts to your Soul and asking your Soul for forgiveness and guidance's.

Be humble in all that you do and never, never give up on yourself. Believe in yourself because you are the Soul, a facet yet still a part of your Soul. If you truly believe in your Soul you will find your human life will be very different. All things will flow in balance, and your understanding of life will be enriched in many ways.

Your fears will dissolve as if they never existed and you will begin to see others as you see yourself. **You will see the world with different eyes.** Once you seek out your Soul, your Soul will reconnect with you. It has been searching and waiting patiently for you, but you have been clouded by the human Ego, unable to see past the fears.

Never, never give up. Always believe in your Soul for it has always believed in you. Be Blessed in Unconditional love always.

CONSCIOUS EVOLUTION (NO-47)

To all human beings who live on planet Earth, may Unconditional Love be present in each and every one of you. May your inner and outer self be filled with Love, may you the human individual come to your own Self-Realisation that Love alone is the cure for all things that plague humanity up to this present moment.

Many on your Earth are expressing that there is a new energy surrounding your planet Earth and that this energy will transform all human beings to a higher conscious awareness. To a point there is some truth to those statements. However this energy has always been in your vibration. It has been around and within your planet Earth for thousands of human years. It is there for each human being to realise its presence and how each human individual can transform their being to higher forms of Consciousness, which will transform their level of thinking and their understanding of the purpose of life itself.

Energy is energy in its purest form. Many human beings refer to it as light. It is your choice alone how you as an individual utilise this energy that has always been and will always be. This energy is what has manifested all Universes, all life forms from the past to the present. You as human beings are all a part of everything that has been and is to come. You are the power source of all creation. The only thing that is stopping you the individual from going beyond your present moment is yourselves, your human Ego of fears, beliefs and conditioning.

Most of the human race is locked in the past. You may disagree, yet if you truly open your human eyes and see what is going on in your world, there is little wonder why humanity is living the emotions of your past. The past has been haunting humanity for nearly one million human years.

Every human being in this present moment is responsible for all the pain and suffering that is currently present on your planet. Each of you have experienced hundreds of incarnations as human beings both male and female, and every negative action that each human being has created in their past is being played out in your present moment of human existence.

Fear is one of the biggest problems that each human being has created in their past and in their present moment. **Fear creates wars, violence, murder, rape, greed, domination, control and so much more. Fear is a belief and a condition of the human ego.** Fear stops the human individual from conscious growth and awareness. Fear limits the level of thinking and stops the individual from seeing the **'light at the end of the tunnel'.** It clouds your energies and blurs your vision; reasoning goes out the door and all you are left with are your fears of the past.

Ask yourself why do you exist as a human being? The answer is you exist because you are a facet of your Soul. Ask yourself if you are a facet of your Soul; then who is the Soul? Your answer is you are the Soul. Your physical body is in reality a state of your mind. You exist in your mind – you exist in this vibration because you created this vibration of energy through your mind. **Your mind is a part of your Soul and your Soul is a part of Creations totality.** It is all that you are. In truth your mind is limitless, the only limitations your mind has are what you as the human being place upon it through your beliefs and conditioning. Your mind accepts all things, all knowledge without bias. It is beyond judgement or opinion; it simply exists in the moment.

All your of humanity, all other forms of life that exist on Mother Earth, and all your surrounding planets and Universes, your Spirit world that is endless, different Dimensions where beings exist without physical form. All have been created from pure energy. How is all this possible you may ask?

The Nar'Karones have an expression: Our first priority is to advance living Consciousness. The **Nar'Karones** discovered that to advance Consciousness. **First:** One must let go of one's past by not allowing the past to determine one's future, **Second:** To see the Ego for what it is and what it has created. **Third:** To become aware of one's personal thoughts and actions. **Fourth:** To understand the meaning of forgiveness by letting go of the past and learning to live in the moment. **Fifth:** To accept what and who we are by loving ourselves unconditionally without any form of judgement.

You see dear human beings, by loving and accepting who you are, you learn to Love all others for who they are. You learn to understand by being kind and loving towards yourself, and you will see the same Love in others as you see within yourself.

When a human being learns to accept and Love themselves unconditionally they are advancing themselves through conscious growth by advancing conscious awareness to a higher form or level of energy. What you are actually doing is raising your energy levels to attract other higher energies to join with you. By vibrating at a higher frequency you allow yourself to go beyond your past, your level of thinking and your awareness grows ten-fold.

The more a human being learns to **love unconditionally** the less the human Ego of fear has control over your actions. Living in the moment will create peace, harmony and balance in your human existence. Communicating directly with your Soul will bring many positive changes in your human life. **Remember the human brain is not your mind – the human brain is created from a state of your mind.** It is your mind that is the power source of all that you are. **You truly are the Soul.** You have evolved over billions of years as living conscious energy. **Your human self is a very small speck of a facet of who you truly are, the Soul.**

Be blessed in Unconditional Love dear Sisters and Brothers of Earth. Remember, knowledge is the key to freedom from your past and your human Ego.

THE ASTRAL VIBRATION OF SPIRIT WORLD (NO-48)

Greetings to every human individual that is currently experiencing a physical human incarnation. **Many questions have been asked of my being about the Astral World, including who created it and what is its purpose.**

To understand Spirit World you first need to understand your physical self as a human being and the purpose of incarnating thousands of life times over and over again.

What is the physical self – its form, its purpose, what is the outcome? Its form is a joining of atoms, of cells coming together to serve a purpose. **There are over four quadrillion cells in the average adult human body.** Every part of your body, inner and outer, has its own function, and all those parts work in harmony.

Every cell has its own DNA which allows it to perform its function. Each cell is living consciousness. The physical self allows you an individual to live in the third dimension, in the world of matter, which is far denser than Spirit World.

See everything in all Universes as pure energy, living and evolving to whatever purpose this energy chooses. It has taken hundreds of billions of human years to evolve to this present moment so then take a leap in your own Consciousness and accept that your human body is over **99% pure energy. You are in fact less than one percent physical matter, meaning flesh.**

Your human body is made up of 80% water. Water is life. The minerals in water, and water itself, help keep your human body functioning so you can exist as a human being. Without water your body's biochemical processes would not be able to occur. Without water, you would die, not just of dehydration, but also of internal pollution.

If every cell has its own function and the various cells work in harmony, meaning they communicate with other cells in order to keep the human body functioning as a whole unit, then there must be another form of intelligence, or Consciousness, which oversees the development and functioning of the human body.

It would be fair to surmise that without Spirit, which is also pure energy, the human body would not and could not exist in the third vibration of physical matter. The Spirit and the physical body work together in harmony. This then begs the question: **what is driving the physical and the spirit.** It is the mind. The mind is directly linked to the Soul of each human individual.

The difference between the third dimensional world of matter and the fourth dimensional world of Spirit is the frequency at which the two dimensions vibrate. The human world vibrates at a lower frequency, and therefore slower frequency. The **Astral World** vibrates at a much higher and faster frequency, which is why most human beings are unable to see or communicate with Spirit. To see or communicate with **Spirit World**, a human being needs to raise their Consciousness, in effect, their own personal frequency in order to see or communicate with **spirit.**

Remember, there are many, many level of Consciousness in Spirit World, just as there are many level of Consciousness in the human world.

Knowledge is a necessity for any individual, human or otherwise, to grow consciously. The level of one's thinking can never change if that individual is not willing to let go of their past, what they know. Human history has been created from fear, and fear is only a form of energy, experienced and held onto, making it the negative past which is brought into the present and creating the future.

As an example, consider a human being which lives a human life full of fear and violence. This human being may have grown up with ignorance, in an emotionally cruel environment with human parents which rarely if ever gave them **love or understanding.** That individual continues to recreate what they know – their pain, violence and misery, placing it onto others in their life. Suddenly their life comes to a fearful and painful end. When they enter Spirit World, what do you think they will take with them? **What will be the outcome?**

First, because they never gained Love, understanding or knowledge, they would take both the fear of death and the fear of life with them into that world. They would take all the negative experiences of their physical existence with them into the **Astral World,** and because of their fear and level of understanding, they would find themselves in the lower vibrations of the **Astral World.**

Often those drawn into the lower levels of the Astral World are unable to accept they have physically died. To them they are still alive, and in most cases will recreate their world as it was while they were in the physical. Their world would be full of darkness **(literally darkness, as if they live in a world where there is only night)** and they would experience cruelty. The darkness radiates from within them causing them to recreate their own personal hell. They will seek out other Spirits in that world who have the same level of understanding and they will keep creating pain and violence towards themselves and others in that world.

It is not until a spark of light shines within them that they will want to change, and they will only change when they can raise their understanding to a **higher level of consciousness.**

Eventually Spirit guides will be able to make contact and a connection with them in order to help them go beyond their pain and to let go of their fears, their Ego's past, and to learn that **forgiveness is unconditional love.** This is the key to freedom from the darkness of the Astral World and will allow them to enter higher vibrations.

When they start to raise their Consciousness more light will come into their existence and literally the darkness will fade. Once they have consciously evolved they will exist and experience the Astral World in colour and light and will radiate this light to others who need help.

The Astral World and its many levels of consciousness was created by the Soul. The individual is in reality the Soul, and each part of the individual – **the physical body, the mind, the spirit, the emotional self –all work together and are a part of the Soul.** If a human being could go beyond the Ego, by letting go of the past and living only in the moment, they would have a self-realisation of the joining of these parts; the knowing of the mind-body-spirit connection making them one. They would have gained a knowing of their Soul.

You may wonder how long a Spirit must stay in the Astral World in order to consciously evolve. Time as known in the physical world does not exist in the Astral World. For example, 100 human physical years experienced in the Astral World may equate to only one human minute or may equate to 1,000 human years. **It depends on the spirit.** As the Spirit learns to let go of their past and to see the past as only the past, the less time remains relevant to their existence.

Life is simply lessons of learning no matter how harsh or how enjoyable that life may have been. The human Ego was created by the human self from fear, and sadly it has been plaguing human beings for as long as they have existed. Look over human history and the evidence is clear.

All thought creates, and reality is created by the thoughts of the human individual. Whether it is negative or positive, if an individual continually creates the same thoughts, those thoughts will take form and manifest into their reality. **So remember the saying "be careful what you wish for – it will become your reality".**

All life is energy – thought is living energy. If an individual forms negative thoughts about themselves or others, those thoughts will shape their life as a human being. This is equally true for positive thoughts. Would it not be more productive, beneficial and useful to have positive thoughts than negative thoughts?

Yes, it is very important that every human individual gain Spiritual Knowledge while living as a physical being in the world of matter. **Gaining Spiritual Knowledge while physical will make the transition to the Astral World far less traumatic and will mean the Spirit does not linger in that world for longer than it needs to.**

One of the principal reasons to gain as much knowledge as you can is so that you can pass it on to your human children so they may also gain the benefit of such knowledge when it comes time for their transition. **Another reason is so you do not have a fear of physical death.** In understanding the Astral World you will understand more than just physical life, you will understand conscious existence as opposed to merely physical existence. Conscious existence is limitless and without end, while physical existence is bound by the laws of the physical realm. **When physical you have an expiry date, and no matter what you do to try to evade it, there will come a time when you must leave the human body.**

Remember dear Human Beings of Earth, Unconditional Love for all of life, in all its forms, is the key to opening the mind to new levels of thinking and understanding, and will lead you to reconnect with the knowledge of your infinite Soul. Be blessed in Unconditional Love always dear Human Beings of this most precious Earth you call home.

THE KUNDALINI ENERGY:
WHAT IS IT? (NO-49)

Greetings dear Human Beings of Earth. Many questions and concerns have been asked on the subject of the **Kundalini.** There are many human beings trying to release the **Kundalini** energy which is located at the base of the human spine.

First, there is nothing wrong with raising the Kundalini from the base charka upwards. Kundalini energy is used to clear blockages or negative energy and to gain inner knowledge of the knowing.

One of the main concerns is how long will it take or does it take a long time to raise the **Kundalini. There is no set human time for this to occur.** Every human individual is different – it all depends on one's emotions, life experiences, desire to achieve, level of self-discipline, level of effort, and the human body's state of health.

Emotions such as anger, jealousy, vanity and judgement, and one's beliefs and conditioning, play a part in how strong the human Ego is within an individual. In turn, the strength of one's Ego will affect one's ability to open up the **Kundalini.** Each human being is on their own journey of self-discovery. **To bring forth the Kundalini one must have achieved a balance of mind, body and spirit to make the raising a pleasant experience.**

If a human individual has not dealt with the negative emotions of their ego, raising the **Kundalini** can and has caused physical damage to internal human body organs, including the human brain. It is therefore vital for a human being to be mentally, emotionally and physically prepared, much like an athlete for a sporting event, before attempting to raise the **Kundalini** to avoid causing themselves harm.

It cannot be reiterated enough how important Personal Responsibility is regarding raising the Kundalini energy so it does not cause physical harm.

Many refer to the Kundalini as 'the voice of the inner silence of one's inner being'. Others refer to it as the **'serpent of fire within'.** Kundalini energy is **'coiled'** at the base of the human spine, much like a serpent and its appearance is that of **liquid fire.** Ignited by one's will, it can and does spiral upwards, coiling around the human spine, shaped like a serpent. In actual fact the energy is releasing upward along the energy channel where the spinal charkas are aligned.

Human beings in most cases have had thousands of incarnations. Negative experiences as a result of human life will affect how the **Kundalini** is released and raised. One needs to be extremely careful when releasing this intense energy. It surges upwards, and if one is not balanced emotionally, it will intensify and enhance any negative emotions that are already present.

The energy of negative emotions is stored in human beings between the solar plexus and base charkas. If not confronted and resolved, a human being will live their life through these emotions.

Emotions are lessons of human life. By confronting, resolving and releasing them, a human being grows consciously and **evolves their spirit.** If not resolved and released, they will lead one to live a life of misery, pain and dis'ease, leading to death and a life which will need to be repeated.

With respect to the **Kundalini,** unresolved negative emotions will not only cause suffering to the individual raising the energy, but will cause that individual to harm others through the creation of negative Karma, and therefore creating many more incarnations than would have been necessary to learn the lessons of human life.

Before starting on this journey of raising the **Kundalini,** take the time and make the effort to face yourself and all your fears. Meditate and heal your being, connect with your Soul and ask for guidance to help you find the right teacher who will care and will guide you on such a journey.

Most human beings will not raise their Kundalini in their lifetime. Sometimes it can take an emotionally painful experience to start this process, while others will have made the choice to do so before incarnating.

It can take a great deal of strength and will to control the Kundalini flow of energy. Once it has been released it will enhance emotions and feelings. Remember however, it will be a different experience for each human individual.

To control the flow of the **Kundalini** one needs to have a positive and loving heart. Their thoughts must be moral and pure so the awakening will not cause physical harm to the self or others.

The purpose of raising the Kundalini is to open and increase one's awareness of the knowing, to bring forth infinite knowledge of the past, present and future, and to enhance an individual's life and understanding of all that is.

Anyone who has not dealt with their negative emotions or destructive life habits can cause serious and irreparable damage to their body. **Uncontrolled Kundalini energy can cause intense physical pain and damage the body's tissue, as well as cause death.**

Raising the **Kundalini** prematurely can cause it to spiral downward instead of upward. This can intensify human passions to the point where a human may be unable to control their sexual desires and be unable to resist doing harm to others through rape, violence and murder. Or with respect to negative emotions it may become impossible to resist trying to emotionally and mentally harm others.

As in anything that is powerful, the **Kundalini** energy can be used for positive or negative outcomes. In the control of an unbalanced individual it will cause harm and be abused by the human Ego, but in the hands of a balanced and loving individual it can be used for positive, useful and helpful purposes. If the power is abused, then that individual will create negative Karma for their future incarnations, in effect they will turn the power of the **Kundalini** against themselves.

If one chooses to raise the Kundalini, they need to take the time to prepare themselves mentally, physically, emotionally and spiritually. They must also find an accomplished and experienced teacher who has a complete understanding of the process in order to raise this energy safely.

Once the energy has been awakened, or aroused, one should attempt to trail it gently up the spine through each of the main charkas in sequence by coiling it around each charka centre with the clear intention of cleaning out all negative energies at each charka and along the spinal column. As the energy rises through each cleansed centre the charka should be opened with the intention of establishing a balance of mind, body and spirit working in union, bringing great strength and clarity to the human individual.

Most human beings believe strength is achieved by physically building the human body through physical training. **This is a start, but true human strength comes when one is connected in the knowing of the Soul and through the release of the Kundalini.** This combination will multiply human strength beyond human understanding.

There are some human beings who have been able to awaken their **Kundalini spontaneously** while being unaware that they have even done so or that this energy even exists, and they have not been negatively affected by its release. But most who try to release the energy and do not understand the process have caused themselves pain or harm when the energy is forced upwards.

Properly released and used the Kundalini energy will over time connect the human individual to their Astral Body/Spirit and will provide a clear channel for knowledge to flow unimpeded. An experienced teacher will help the student connect with the master within. Only by balancing the eight charkas centres correctly will one become aware of the various layers to one's existence that is, the other bodies of light apart from the physical body that one is aware of in human form. Correct use of the **Kundalini** will allow one to travel freely within different vibrations with complete awareness and in most cases complete control of all movement in these vibrations or realms.

There is no age limit to achieving this. The only prerequisite is an honest heart and an open mind, free from the constraints of the human Ego and its negative emotions. There must also be a willingness to persist, and a high level of the health of one's body is absolutely vital.

Dear Human Beings of this most precious Earth, always remember you are brothers and sisters to all forms of life, on your planet and beyond, and you are loved unconditionally.

WHAT IS SPIRITUALISM? (NO-50)

Many human beings have been asking questions about **Spiritualism,** in particular what it is and whether or not it is another human religion.

Spiritualism is a belief system that was created to help human beings learn how to communicate with spirit world, and to many human beings Spiritualism is considered a religion. There is no one specific form, much as there are several forms of Christianity, but all forms share similarities in their teachings and beliefs.

The belief system was created a little over 631,000 human years ago. The original creator was called and known as **'Zeenpirrer'.** He chose to incarnate as a human being so he could bring knowledge from his world to humanity to try and give human beings an understanding of different worlds, including Spirit Vibration, and how to communicate with beings from other realms.

The human word 'Spiritualism' means communication into the Spirit World or Realm. Human beings communicate verbally through sound and sound is simply a vibration expressed outwardly through vocal chords which human ears translate via the human brain.

In Spirit World communication is on a different level. In most cases Spirit express and communicate without sound or moving their mouths. Spirit communicate with physical humans through a medium or a channel, a human being who has developed the necessary skills to communicate with Spirit Vibration.

As with any form of belief system, there are many truths that may be learned and discovered through Spiritualism. When journeying into Spiritualism one must approach with a loving heart, an open mind without Ego, no judgement and a realisation that every human being is also on their own path of self-discovery.

However, it takes discipline to undertake the path to self-realisation through Spiritualism. An individual needs to devote time and patience to their quest for truth, and time and patience in finding a teacher who teaches from the heart.

The teacher will need to have gained the knowledge and understanding of having dealt with their own human Ego and they are one who must be open minded and therefore able to guide a student on their path to **self-realising compassion and unconditional love.** A loving teacher will always admit that they remain a student first and foremost because the learning process never ceases. **It is irrelevant what kind of world, realm, dimension, vibration or universe a being is from – no one ever stops learning.**

Admitting superiority over another is merely the Ego feeling insecure. Yes, there are human beings who have a wealth of knowledge and understanding but those beings know they do not need to prove their knowledge, not even to themselves.

While there is a great deal of knowledge in Spiritualism, it is the responsibility of the individual knowledge seeker that you can only achieve the quest for knowledge and higher learning through the amount of effort put into the quest. **Personal Responsibility is first and foremost.**

Ask yourself why you are seeking this knowledge and understanding, what you will gain from it and most importantly, will you be open minded enough to receive and accept it or will your fears create confusion?

It is an accepted fact that the gaining of knowledge brings freedom of the self from limitations. Freedom can only be achieved when the individual remains honest hearted and open minded, free of judgement.

There are two main types of Spiritualism, or rather, two paths – higher and lower. Which path one chooses to follow is up to the individual. Most have little or no knowledge of higher Spiritualism. **Higher Spiritualism revolves around the practice of forming a circle with a group of individuals to build, raise and channel positive energies for the purpose of communicating with spirit world.** These circles are limited to a specific group of individuals (invited participants) and are held on a regular basis, at least once per week.

The group size can be anything from **4 to 20 individuals,** all working for the same purpose. Most of these groups are private **(a closed circle)** and have operated for several years. By working together for a great length of time these groups build a strong connection and dynamic, resulting in the creation of **magnetic energy** which is used on a positive and loving level to heal the planet, send healing to diseased human beings, to try to bring balance and order where chaos and disorder exist, to express Unconditional Love to all forms of life, and to also provide a conduit of communication with **spirit.**

These circles also assist the participants in opening up their minds to infinite knowledge, helping break the chains of ignorance which has plagued humanity for as long as it has existed. The human Ego created that ignorance out of fear. Spiritual knowledge, such as that gained through Spiritualism, can help a human being release themselves from the chains of the Ego's fears.

In higher Spiritualism, the Spirits who come to communicate with human beings come purely to express knowledge from a loving and compassionate heart, in order to help humanity raise their Consciousness and self-awareness. The individuals who work with these higher energies are beings who have chosen to reincarnate over many lifetimes to be a beacon of divine light, to resolve their Karma and to serve humanity.

Human light workers have been incarnating for thousands and thousands of human years. To work in the Light is to be fully conscious of who you are as an individual, but also to know you are all united as beings, all of the one Universal energy which comes from the same source – Light. The only factors that separate human beings from one another are their life's lessons and physical circumstances.

Lower Spiritualism: Circles are called séances and the Spirits contacted and communicated with are of the lower Astral Vibration. Often the individuals working in this form of Spiritualism have imbalanced energies, and because the magnetic energies created are also imbalanced, the Spirits called upon have not yet let go of their human world, mostly due to physical habits and addictions such as drugs, alcohol, poor nutrition, and also emotional imbalance's.

Spirits of the lower levels bring with them the lower part of their nature –
their Ego, lust, greed, control, fear, jealousy. In the lower levels of the Astral
world such Spirits can control weak minded physical human beings by
projecting thoughts at them, negative thoughts. They also can and do,
pretend to be someone they are not. In some cases these lower entities can
attach themselves to the human Aura by cracking it, thereby able to feed off
the life force of that human individual.

If a physical being is drained for an extended period of time, human dis'ease
can set in, and that individual can become weak willed and even influenced
by that entity. Their whole character can change, and they can take up
habits and addictions that they otherwise would not have considered.

A most important fact for all physical human beings to know and understand
is that suicide victims, accidental death victims **(such as car accident)**
murder victims and criminals which have been executed, usually enter the
Astral Vibration in fear and panic. Because they passed over from their
physical bodies with no awareness of the Astral Vibration. They are often
unable to comprehend they are **'dead'** and so they continue to stay close and
connected to the physical world by creating the same circumstances of their
life prior to their human death, such as the pain and emotion before suicide
and then the act of suicide, or a continuous loop of crashing and dying in a
car accident. If they were particularly malicious or violent individuals, they
will attempt to latch onto human beings who are weak or have unbalanced
energies in order to influence and manipulate them physically, creating a
negative outcome for the physical being, and feeding off the energy created.

Consider the following: When next you hear of a man, woman or child
previously with no criminal or violent tendencies, suddenly going on a
killing spree or violent rampage, they most likely did not merely **'lose it'**,
but were most certainly being influenced at the time by negative entities
from the Astral Vibration.

**Working in the Light means taking responsibility for all your self-
created actions.** When communicating with Spirit ensure you pace the
Light of Creation within and around you so you remain balanced and draw
in positive loving energies rather than negative harmful energies. There are
two sides to everything, and Spiritualism is no different. A human being

can work with the Light or without it, but whichever is chosen expect the appropriate outcome.

The purpose of working with the Light is to elevate your energies in order to help those around you elevate their energies, and ultimately work together in raising humanity's consciousness.

To work outside of the Light within negative energies is work with the Ego. Unfortunately, working with the Ego does not elevate an individual's Consciousness but creates Karma and unpleasant consequences for their present and future incarnations. When that human individual chooses to raise their energies by rising above self-created illusions, pain and misery, only then will they have their own self-realisation.

It is wise to remember to ask oneself this question when making decisions and choices – is my choice from the fears of my Ego, or is it from my heart? Spiritualism is a gift, and if learnt and understood, it will help set free every human being on this Earth. Imagine a world without human Ego. Imagine a world without pain, misery, poverty, violence, war, confusion, dis'ease.

The light within each human begin is the totality of who you truly are, an infinite being on a journey of self-realisation. Open the heart and the mind and the truth will reveal itself.

OLMEC HEADSTONES: WHERE DO THEY COME FROM? (NO-51)

Questions have been asked: I am writing to ask about the not-so-recent findings of the giant **Olmec headstones** that were buried beneath the soils of New Mexico. The reason why I and so many others have questions about this finding is because it clearly contradicts much of what we've been taught about Africans history.

The massive **Olmec** statues are of males with some kind of crown or helmet, who clearly have strong African features. Scientists believe that the Mayans carved these statues but if this is true, why? Would you please tell us who were the people depicted in these statues? How did they get to New Mexico and why were they buried?

Answer: Documented human history is a perception of truth based on physical evidence and supposition; an idea of someone's version of the truth built on what has been observed and then surmised, but not necessarily the actual truth. However, from such documented history one can sift fact from fiction to reveal a clearer picture of reality.

Throughout human evolution human beings have been driven to explore and conquer new lands, including lands populated by other races of humans. The African people were no different to any other race of human beings – they too sought to explore and conquer new lands. Many thousands of human years ago, a group of African explorers went on a great journey to explore new lands for the future settlement of the African people.

It was the African Zulu race, who have existed for thousands of years on your Earth that travelled to Mexico, **to the land of the Maya.** At first they were welcomed and accepted by the Mayan people and although the Mayans were great warriors and fierce in battle, they welcomed the Zulus and allowed them to settle in their lands. They helped them with food and shelter, and for some 250 human years the two cultures lived peacefully.

Unbeknownst to the Mayans, the Zulus ultimate plan was to wage war against them with the objective of conquering and enslaving any survivors and claiming Mayan lands for themselves. The Mayans were happy to intermix the two cultures, but the Zulus preferred to keep their race as pure as possible. They did not encourage intermixing but they also did not discourage intermixing when it happened, in order to avoid the Mayans becoming suspicious of the Zulu's intentions for being in their land.

It was not the Maya who carved the Olmec headstones, but the Zulu settlers. The headstones were placed around the Zulu settlement, their city as a symbol of their culture and race, symbolizing greatness and power, an attempt to put fear into anyone who came to their city. It must be remembered the Zulu were very tall people while the Mayan were quite small in stature, but not in spirit. **It is also interesting to note that the Mayans are the direct descendants of the Atlanteans.**

Initially the Zulu exploration party consisted of some 30 human males. Upon returning to Mexico with settlers, some 3,000 Zulu, mostly males, but including women and children, settled in Mayan lands. Over the next 250 years of settlement, several thousand more settlers came across every two to three years, resulting in the Zulu population growing to thousands and outnumbering the Maya by four to one. The Mayans, being very friendly people, allowed this mass migration to occur without fear or thought of there being any ulterior motive on the part of the Zulus.

The Zulus generally believed the Mayans were unaware of the conspiracy being planned against them. However, some Zulus did not believe in war and informed the Mayans of the Zulus' intentions. **Forearmed with this knowledge,** over a number of years the Mayans secretly manufactured and stored new weapons in order to be prepared for battle when the time came. Because the Maya were lesser in number than the Zulu, it was vital they be prepared to successfully fend off any attack upon their city.

The Zulus held secret meetings and planned their attack. Little did they know that the Mayans knew the exact date and time of attack, and that they would be ready for them. The Mayans were strategists, highly experienced warriors due to the number of battles waged and won over their vast history. They built their cities and temples on plateaus, carved out of mountains, in order to see their enemy approach should an attack take place. The Zulu lived on the low lands and were clearly disadvantaged from this perspective.

Armed with the knowledge of the impending attack, the Maya called a meeting of their own leaders and it was decided they must attack first and strike hard to weaken their enemy. It was a fierce and bloody battle that took only four human days. The Zulu city was destroyed, burnt completely to the ground. The Mayans conquered the Zulus, who were caught completely unawares.

Surprised, the Zulus had always thought of the Maya as a peaceful and therefore weak race, never considering they could be formidable warriors. Their oversight cost them thousands of Zulu warrior lives, and those Zulu that survived were forced to return to Africa, no longer welcome on Mayan lands. The Zulu's that assisted the Mayans were given protection and sanctuary in the Mayan city during the battle and were invited to remain with the Mayan people after the battle and banishment of the enemy.

After the battle and banishment of the Zulu, the Maya buried the Olmec headstones and buried or destroyed anything and everything that represented the Zulu race, effectively wiping the memory of the Zulu from their existence and history, as if they had never existed in their lands at all.

Most truth on Earth, from the human past to the present, is only an idea of one individual's truth. However, when a human being looks within their own Being and connects to their Soul, they can then open a door to the complete uncorrupted truth of human history.

ULTIMATE FREEDOM (NO-52)

Greetings to all human beings. Many questions are asked about discovering and experiencing happiness, and finding emotional freedom in human life. These are very important questions which deserve serious discussion. Perhaps some of you will find the answers you are seeking from the words to follow.

QUESTION: What is irrational limiting and powerful, and results in a lack of self-trust, manipulation and blackmail?

ANSWER: Fear.

Dear human beings, fear is the single most powerful negative emotion that drives a human being. Just think, without fear you would not have to content with all other negative emotions, such as anger, hatred and jealousy. Look at the word '**jealousy**' and you see the word '**lousy**'. Look at the word '**anger**' and you see the word '**rage**'. Look at the word '**hatred**' and you see the word '**death**'. **Negative emotions lead a human being to behaving in negative ways – closed mindedness, greed, and tyranny – all because of self-created fear.**

Fear is at the root of all human discomfort in physical existence. It causes human beings to struggle for power and position at the expense of another's well-being. Consider the presence of fear in the following: **politics, religion, society or your local community, family and intimate relationships, business and finance – in all environments, in all interactions,** if but one human being harbours fear of any sort for any reason, that fear will affect all other human beings in some form within that environment as a result of association and interaction. An example would be within the work environment where a subordinate shows skill and promise beyond their superior. **If their superior has fear,** they will manipulate the office situation to ensure their subordinate does not gain promotion if in some way it challenges their rank and ultimately their job.

You could say that is how one protects their income. But a positive attitude, encouraging a subordinate and mentoring their rise could also lead to a promotion for the superior. Anything is possible and the end result, negative or positive, is determined by how the individuals involved play their part. You can create a positive outcome or a negative outcome.

Consider also why some human beings feel the need to spread rumours about others, or why sceptics are the first to have their opinions heard before all the evidence has been examined. Sceptics and rumour mongers are amongst those with the greatest fears and having the most judgemental and closed minds, fearing of the unknown or that which is difficult to understand because it challenges the boundaries of their thinking.

Some human beings have a need to control others. Again, this is driven by fear. There is a saying on your Earth – "Do not give out too much information because people will no longer need you and will not come back for more." There are many who create roles for themselves as teachers or disseminators of information. More to the point, they will move on and therefore not support you, whether it be financially or emotionally. This kind of control has been seen throughout human history. Think it over and you will discover for yourself many examples of individuals controlling others. Perhaps you are experiencing this for yourself in your human life right now.

The most obvious examples of control through fear can be found in politics and the workplace where fear drives the desire for competition and cut throats vie for attention, money and power. What is most sad however is when this is attitude is found within religious organisations and within people who believe they are compassionate and spiritually minded human beings, claiming to have the desire from their hearts to help guide individuals in their quest for spiritual awareness and conscious growth.

Do not misunderstand what is being expressed here. The truth, and only the truth, will lead a human being to finding their freedom, the **Ultimate Freedom** of emotional liberation from their self-created fears. Freedom from fear is obtained by facing yourself and confronting whatever it is that haunts you.

Honesty with oneself and others is essential. Without honesty there can be no truth or love. To look and place judgement upon what is positive or negative, good or bad, is the result of a belief system based on fear. If a human being is emotionally balanced, then love, respect, compassion and truth would be expressed by that being in everything they do, in how they live their life, and in what they express to others – without bias. A human being without fear has the knowing and sees everything for what it is, without emotion.

Living a life with fear, placing judgement upon others, holding hatred in your heart or creating violence upon another will result in creating misery for the self. Through **karma** these same negative actions and projections will be returned upon the individual. However, facing your fears from your past, and opening the heart and mind will set in motion the process of self-healing and lead to an understanding of fear and why it was created in the first place.

Fear is the human Ego's weapon of mass destruction. Fear on an individual level is destructive, but on a larger scale, when you have a multitude of human beings all expressing, interacting and communicating with fear, the result is complete chaos. One only has to review human history to see example after example of how fear has terrorised humanity for its entire existence – wars having the most far reaching impact of fear on a global scale. Yet by allowing **Unconditional Love** to be felt within and expressed outwardly to all forms of life, a human being can set themselves free from their self-imposed emotional pain, which when practised by all human individuals can and will lead to global human peace. **Surely this is the Ultimate Freedom.**

Eliminating the power of fear in your life starts with trusting the self and the process of life. You need to challenge your personal belief systems by questioning and examining how you live your life, how you think and what conditions you place upon others in your existence. Not everything needs to be thrown out - only those patterns which create negative thinking, interaction and expression. It may even mean letting go of people who reinforce your fears or negativity, even if for a while until you can confront and deal with the fear that lies at the bottom of the negative behaviour.

Stop, look, think. See what is going on in your human life. **Become fully aware and responsible for yourself, your feelings, your thoughts, beliefs, actions and words.** Do you create fear in others? Do others create fear in you? Why this fear is created – what lies at its root? **When you can**

identify what generates your fear, you can then begin to heal through forgiveness, Unconditional Love and understanding.

Each human being needs to come to their own **self-realisation** that they cannot place blame upon others for how they feel, or how their life has turned out. If you are unhappy, find out what is causing the unhappiness and then do something about it so it is no longer a splinter under your skin, festering and becoming irritated and swollen with emotional pus.

Every human being has some level of self-created fear to deal with. If you find yourself reacting negatively to the words of another, or even to the words on this page, then your fears have been activated and you now have the opportunity to examine your emotions and why you have reacted. If you have reacted in a positive way then perhaps these words will help you recognise fear in those around you and provide you with the necessary knowledge in how best to protect yourself from their negativity.

There are many reasons why human beings are unable to find the balance of life, and fear is certainly the greatest obstacle that lies in their path. **People fear for many reasons – fear of success or failure, not being good enough, not being accepted, fear of making decisions, fear of physical death, and fear of giving and/or receiving love, fear of life.**

When you have fear you deny yourself the right to experience moments of joy and unconditional love. You deny yourself the knowledge of who you truly are – an infinite spark of all that is. Fear stops you from finding your own truth and inner peace.

And yet, fear has no real power, other than the power you give it. If you give in to your fears then they will surely control you. If you face your fears then little by little you will regain your emotional strength and you will find the courage and trust in yourself to release your fears and release yourself from their grasp.

Roman have been presenting a one day workshop over the last 21 years called 'Creating Your Reality through Self-Realisation'. This workshop gives the individual the tools to help them grow consciously beyond the Ego's fears. As with anything in human life, it is only the individual who can chooses when to make positive change to improve the emotional quality of their life.

All knowledge on your Earth has a purpose and all knowledge can help an individual gain a deeper understanding of the purpose of human life. Reconnect with your heart and look beyond outside knowledge to the knowledge and wisdom of the voice within. **Connect to the light that is your essence and listen to your inner self.**

You may look in the mirror and see a physical being made of flesh. But you are manifest by the mind and Soul. **Your Soul is infinite** – it will never perish, and your Spirit is a facet of your Soul. When you connect with your inner Being you connect to the light of who you truly are. **You are the Soul.** Nothing can ever change that. The light is always within you and your Soul is the source of your Unconditional Love which means, you, dear Human Beings, are an expression of Unconditional Love, a part of all that is. **You are ageless, timeless, endless, eternal, and immortal beyond the physical.** Be blessed in Unconditional Love dear Human Beings of Earth.

LIVING YOUR TRUTH (NO-53)

May love, peace and harmony be a part of each of you as human individuals and may each of you be given the opportunity to raise your Consciousness beyond the past so all of you become the living truth.

There have been a number of questions concerning truth.

    1-What is truth?
    2-How does one find truth?
    3-How does one become truth?
    4-How does one live truth?
    5-How does one make it a part of daily human life?
    6-What is the secret to finding truth?

Answers to the above.

Living the truth is an interesting concept and its foundation lies in being true to yourselves. **Truth is anything that a human being wishes it to be.** Truth can be negative or positive. It all depends on your life's circumstances. Consider the concept of living in the present, or living in the moment. **Your yesterday is gone; your tomorrow is not here yet; only the present is real and exists at any given moment.**

Many human beings bring their past into their present moment, making it the predominant influence in their lives. Many others live in the future, hoping and wishing for a better life within a reality that does not exist as yet, and this leads to hopelessness, a created negative truth that does not benefit anyone.

By letting go of the self-created past and bringing your future desires into your present moment you can begin to create your present moment in a positive way which then create a balanced future. There is nothing wrong in setting goals for your future, in fact goals are necessary to achieve your dreams, but create your goals and desires in your moment by learning to live in the now.

Say to yourself **"I am living my truth NOW"** and then set about putting action into motion. If you kept saying to yourself with meaning **"I am the living truth. I live in the moment. I always live my truth. My truth comes from my heart and my Soul"** what you will discover over the moments of your human life is your truth will be manifested into your life. You can manifest anything into your life just by putting action and intention into your expressions and this will bring it into your reality. **But remember,** it can be created on either a positive or a negative level, so be careful in your expression of words. **Energy is infinite and impartial.** The intention **(positive or negative)** of how you direct and apply the energy of your words and actions will result in either a positive or negative outcome. It is the individual's choice in how that energy is used, but energy resonates long after a result has been achieved, so **remember the law of Karma – what goes around comes around!**

Take this one step further by adding the influence of beliefs and conditioning and you will then see how fears and insecurities are created and how they affect the outcomes which manifest in the present moment that is your human life. Every human being is subjected to social conditioning from the moment they are born into a human existence. Through conditioning, belief systems are formed and cemented into your daily thinking, colouring your human life until the day you leave your human body. Beliefs can be rebuilt or dissolved, but it takes conscious effort on the part of the individual, hard work, whereas beliefs and conditioning are designed to work automatically in the background as it were, so you are not even aware of how far reaching their influence is. **Beliefs and conditioning shape how you live your life, and while some can have positive influences, most have negative, repressive, hindering influences.** They can stop you believing in yourself and moving consciously forward in your human existence, such as never shifting from a set point of view.

Narrow mindedness creates limitation in understanding. It also creates fears and insecurities, limiting the individual and preventing them from going beyond what they know and understand, from going beyond what they believe truth to be. A truth created by one individual and transferred to another can create confusion along with a reality that has been created from the past of the individual who created the truth originally. **For example, a belief that you can catch stupidity by associating with someone you believe to be unintelligent.** Of course this is untrue, but if one individual sincerely believes this and can manifest evidence of such an occurrence, then some individuals who would be exposed to this belief and **'evidence'** will adopt it as their truth and continue to perpetuate it. The evidence will most likely be based on a negative emotional experience and from there a belief and conditioning are born, reinforced by further experiences.

When you, the individual begins to dissolve your beliefs and conditioning you also begin to dissolve your fears and limitations. You will find that fear itself has no actual foundation which then will allow you to say to yourself **"the past is the past, a memory, and the present is the now"**. In the now, you can create your future, positive or negative, as that is always your choice.

In discovering how to be the living truth, you need to understand the power of the inner self, real power as opposed to man's power. Real power for any individual lies within your very being. You are connected to your Soul and your Soul is connected to all that is within Creation. You are a spark of living Consciousness, a part of the divine source where all love comes from. Love comes from the heart. Love is not an emotion; it is a feeling spontaneous in the moment. **Love comes to each of you in the moment and through love you can create in the moment, in the now, because love is ageless, timeless, endless, eternal, and infinite.**

Living your truth is to live beyond your fears, your confusion, your Ego. Ego is not the driving force of human life, Spirit is, and within Spirit is the essence of love. Spirit is a facet of your Soul. If you have complete Unconditional Love in your heart then you have it all. By living and creating your truth from a loving heart you have found the tools to manifest any reality into your present moment that you want or need in your human life. Yes, the level of your thinking plays a very important role in your evolution as a human being, for what you think you become, and what you become is your truth, so live your truth from an honest loving heart and you will become an honest, loving, positive human being.

Take recognition of the false and you will reveal the truth. The moment you change your thinking you will have a shift in Consciousness, a raising of your energies. You will begin to see what created the illusion in the first place. You will see how conditioning has influenced your ability to understand the truth, from the type of food you eat, to the type of fluids you drink, to the drugs you take, to the recreational activities you participate in. Essentially, how you choose to live your human life.

Human civilisation has helped create the illusion humanity has lived for almost one million years. Millions of human beings are living in each other's energies, influencing each other with their emotions, fears, beliefs and conditioning, clouding the individual's perception of truth and preventing many from living their truth because the energy is so strong.

You can take yourself out of the illusion and give yourself a clearer and broader vision. It does not require you to become a hermit, but it does require you take recognition of what is holding you back. Cleanse your mind, your body and start practising to live in the now. Create balance within and you will find a clearer picture of what it means to live your truth and what it means to live in the now.

Every time you do something on autopilot or react negatively to a certain person because that's how you always react, force yourself to take note of the situation and decide to change it then and there. **Don't react – shift your perception and see it from a different angle.** Stop allowing the past - your fears, insecurities, beliefs and conditioning - to control you. By becoming a conscious human being, consciously aware of your life and yourself in the moment, you will be living in the moment, making conscious choices, with you actually running your life rather than your past running your life.

What is truth? Truth is an expression of yourself, and is often mirrored in others. You see in others what exists within yourself. This can be confronting, especially when it is negative, but truth is impartial – it simply is. When you change your level of thinking you then change your reality, and you change your truth. Change your thinking first in order to effect permanent, positive change in your life.

One of the easiest ways of changing your thinking and reality is to start loving yourself unconditionally, from your heart. **Accept yourself as you are now, not how you were yesterday, not how you think you will be tomorrow, NOW. Now is all that exists, and now is all that you can change.**

Try not to adopt the truth of others because they may be someone of authority or importance in your community, but adopt their truth only if that truth is valid to you, in your life, in the moment right now. They may indeed know the truth, but it is their idea of truth based on their beliefs, conditioning, and experiences. Form your own opinions by understanding and being aware of all that is around you and all that contributes to and constitutes your life. Ultimately, be responsible for what you think – don't think it because someone else thinks it. Know why you think the way you do.

When you give away your Personal Responsibility you are living an illusion. You may think you are living the truth because it is another's truth, but it is not your truth, therefore it is an illusion. Many think the media of your world presents and informs the population of truth, but they only express what they believe you need to know. Politicians use media resources to their advantage, to keep the truth of their deceptions hidden from an increasingly suspicious public for as long as possible.

Truth has a price tag. With truth comes knowledge and awareness and with knowledge and awareness comes responsibility for how you use that knowledge. Knowledge is power and power must be used with wisdom. When an individual lives their truth that individual needs to be aware of how that knowledge is used, that it is used with wisdom so it may benefit human beings.

Wisdom entails tempering knowledge with an understanding heart filled with Unconditional Love for all of life that exists on Mother Earth. To express love from the heart is to be balanced in mind, body and spirit. Such an individual has discovered their inner self and is an expression of their inner being, living their truth every moment of their existence by sharing from their heart with feelings without negative emotions.

Discovering and living your truth is not an easy road to travel. The human world is full of confusion and fear, created from a violent past. Many times you may find yourself slipping back into what you know and what you are comfortable with, but in your illusion you will still find discontent as you realise you are unfulfilled. Your present violence on your Earth is from the past brought into the present, creating your future. This needs to be recognised and the past must be let go of, the past must be forgiven so all of humanity can progress into a brighter, peaceful future from the now. But this will only happen when each human being takes responsibility for what they are feeling and how they are living. The whole cannot change unless the sum of its parts are changed first.

To let go is to forgive. To forgive is to love unconditionally. To love unconditionally is to live inner truth. To live inner truth is to become truth itself.

We the **Nar'Karones** love you unconditionally dear sisters and brothers of Earth.

Be blessed always in love.

KNOWING THE LIGHT: 1- YOU ARE THE LIGHT (NO-54)

We the Nar'Karones, who are your Brothers and Sisters, express Divine Light from our inner beings to your inner hearts. Although we exist in a vibration a great distance from your world of Earth, by simply calling us from an honest heart, we would be there for you in a moment of your human time. Our love for humanity is beyond words.

To connect to your Soul is to connect to the Light, the totality of all that is. Once that connection is made, it is pure bliss. You can then connect to our vibration always. My expression of words in your human time, is on a subject of great importance to all life forms. You have heard the term **'The White Light'**, or as some refer to it, the light at the end of the tunnel during what human beings call a near death experience.

Many human beings near death or during out of body experiences, have come back into their human body and spoke of the bright white light. Many have heard of it but few truly understand it. **The white light is the essence of totality; it is all that is; it is the manifestation of collective consciousness.** The light is the power of all that is. It is Creation and Creation is in all of life that exists in all universes. You, dear Sisters and Brothers are within Creation and Creation is within you.

What is special about white light is that it is free. No one can market it or bottle it, put it in a box and sell it, no one can keep it from others. Your governments cannot put a tax on it. White light belongs to everyone and everything. **It is cosmic energy and is the source from which everything originates.**

You may have heard white light referred to as God or God Consciousness, or even Christ energy. Some human beings refer to it as Mass Consciousness or the Great White Light. Open your heart and mind and see the white light as the raw material from which everything in and on your world has been and is continuing to be manifested from.

For example, the minerals, plant life, animal life, the fish in your oceans, your birds, all human beings who are presently incarnated and those yet to be incarnated, as well as other forms of life in all other universes are made of and originate from white light. The white light is the source that everything comes from and returns to.

Nothing really dies. Death is simply a belief within human understanding. Death is the transformation of one level of existence and Consciousness into another level of existence and Consciousness. The human shell transforms into other forms of life, back to the organic mother from which each of you physically comes from while the Spirit and Consciousness returns to the light from which it is a part of.

White light is so pure a substance that a mere thought will cause it to spin at a rate which begins the process of bringing that thought into reality, and then manifests it into physical form.

Most of humanity at this moment does not fully comprehend the concept that thought is the beginning of creation. The white light can be used for negative or positive outcomes; it is not judgemental; it is completely unbiased. It is there simply to be used as the individual chooses.

What a human being thinks or believes of others they are also themselves. In other words, 'you are what you think'. If a human being is negative towards others and all that is around them, and if they continue their negative thoughts then most certainly these thoughts will manifest and become that person's reality, creating a negative existence throughout their human life, including attracting other negative human beings into their life. If you believe you are hard done by then you will have nothing but hard times. If you believe you will have a heart attack at the human age of 54 because one of your human parents did then you most likely will. If you believe you will age quickly then you will manifest this also.

On the other hand, if you believe you create your life and direct its destiny, then you will use the power of your thoughts to manifest things into your life from the white light to create a positive outcome. If you believe you are youthful in yourself, and in your heart then you will remain youthful and if you believe in love and compassion then you will truly believe you are rich in all things, regardless of their monetary value. All things will be manifested into your life. As always the choice is yours how you use and project your thoughts to create your reality.

You create everything in your life and it all starts with how you think, your level of understanding. All that a human creates, negative and positive is created from white light, which is cosmic energy. This energy does far more than just help a human being create or manifest physical and mental reality. It also helps to protect and cleanse a human being spiritually.

As you are aware you exist within a physical body, but you also have a **Spirit Body** which is made up of many layers. Your human scientists know that the human body generates a certain amount of electricity and that electricity is part of the mechanics of keeping the body running much like a car engine. Your electrical body is better known as the **Etheric Body** and from this body emanates your **Aura,** the glow of the electrical field around your human body.

Within your **Etheric Body** is an energy channel that runs directly through the centre of your body and connects to the outer Universe from the top of your head and into your Earth from the bottom of your feet. There are many upon your Earth who teach that the Soul is housed within the human body and that upon physical death the Soul dissipates. This is an idea of truth but it is a **non-truth.**

Infinite light was self-created into living Consciousness and your Soul was created from infinite light. **Every human being has a Soul.** You as an individual are a facet of your Soul. Your Soul can have many facets, all experiencing different life forms at the same time. This means many human lives at the same time. Eventually the facets return to their source, the Soul.

Remember, the Soul is endless and eternal. It is your connection to the light. If your Soul was housed in your physical body it would not be able to function on an infinite level of Consciousness because of the human Ego and its negative emotions. The Ego is self-destructive as human history constantly proves. The third vibration which humans physically exist within vibrates at a lower frequency to that of the Soul. If a human being was 100% balanced with Unconditional Love you could reach out with your hand and touch your Soul, meaning the distance between your Soul and your physical self is a matter of two separate worlds living side by side within reach of each other. There is no such thing as a measurement of distance within Spirit World, just as there is no measurement of time. What keeps the individual from being able to connect with their Soul lies in their beliefs? Fears stop the individual from accepting this truth.

White light or cosmic energy is your life force. Without it you could not exist in physical form. When each of you are in your sleep state, your **Spirit Body** comes out and enters higher vibrations to be re-energised by the light so that when it returns to your human body it can help keep your physical body balanced and healthy.

To reiterate, the light is unbiased; it is the human being who creates negative or positive energy and manifestations from the light. Yes this does depend on each human being's circumstances – their upbringing, beliefs, conditioning, life's habits, fears. Negative energy will attract the same form of energy, so how you think and how you express those thoughts in physical action or through words will create the outcomes in your human life.

If a human being has an understanding of the **white light** then it is very important the light is used to remove and dissolve any negative energies that have been attracted into their life. If a human being wants their life to change they will need to eliminate any negative energies that will influence outcomes in their human life.

Negative energy is created by misguided individuals who have often unknowingly created it from their negative emotions. After reading this article you should have gained an understanding of the importance of the **white light** and how it can help cleanse your inner and outer being to begin creating a more positive existence.

Here is a simple exercise that will help you balance your mind, body and spirit:

Regardless of where you are, whether it be at home at work or out with friends, pause for a moment and take two or three deep breaths, and using your imagination, feel and see a ball of white light in your heart centre.

Feel its warmth and then direct this ball of light down to your feet and into Mother Earth, leaving a trail of light so it is still connected to your heart centre.

When you are connected to the Earth direct the light out through the top of your head into the outer universe, again leaving a trail of light from the heart centre so it is connected in a line from universe to Earth with the channel of light passing through your being.

Now see this light filling your entire human body and emanating out of your pores into your **aura field** so it completely surrounds your body like a protective cocoon. Bathe in the light and believe you are the light.

While bathing and believing you are the light say to yourself:

I am the Soul, I am the Light, balanced in Unconditional Love for myself and all life forms. I am that I am. I am pure Light itself.

If you truly believe in what you are imagining and what you are expressing from your heart, then it will become your living truth. The light will shine within you and around you for all to see. Knowing the Light is to know yourself. To know yourself is to know all others. To know all others is to be connected to your Soul and all other Souls. Be blessed in Unconditional Love dear Human Beings of Earth.

KNOWING THE LIGHT: 2- YOU ARE THE LIGHT (NO-55)

You as human beings have existed in this vibration for the past 928,000 years, yet it seems like a moment has only passed. My Being believes the only difference between then and now is there were only 87,000 of you nearly one million years ago, but now there 7 billion human beings currently existing on Earth.

Humanity has come a long way in its understanding and awareness. My Being trusts that you have found my last expressions of words of interest. If it has helped you, the human individual in any way, then my Being has made an impact on you. Let us continue with a little more on **'Knowing the Light'.**

Let us look a little deeper into the chakras, the energy centres, which are also known as chakra centres. These centres play a very important role in your human evolution and also your personal journey back to where you originated from. One centre in particular plays a very important role in the evolution of humanity, in fact in the evolution of any form of life. This centre is the **heart charka.** It is the centre of your very being. **White Light or Divine Love is housed there.** Much like your computers, where one chip is the vital link for the whole, your heart charka is the vital link for your being to all that is and has been. It is your direct link to your Soul.

My Being needs to express once more that the **White Light or cosmic energy is your life force.** Without it you as human beings could not exist in your current vibration of physical matter, and if you were to exist without the light all of you would be lifeless, without any enthusiasm to grow **spiritually or consciously.** You would revert back to the past and live like your ancestors, **the Neanderthals.**

In opening your heart charka and drawing the Light of Creation's totality into your heart centre, you not only energise your human body but you also enhance your spiritual growth and your evolution as human beings. This allows you as an individual to enhance your understanding of life and all that surrounds you. To have compassion for all life forms draws on your Unconditional Love and will open your human eyes, so you can see the truth, the cause of all human pain, misery and violence is in fact the result of a fearful Ego. **The ego is the illusion of life, it is superficial in its ignorance and in its own understanding of its own created past.**

Using the light can and does have many purposes. Self-protection is a very powerful way of using the Light. Human beings are a creation created by your Soul from Light itself, for light is **living consciousness.** It is also unbiased. The Light or cosmic energy can be used in a positive or negative way, all depending on the human individual. Negative energies are attracted to negative energies, and the same is for positive energies.

If you as a human being is subjected to negative energies and you do not put up a shield of White Light to protect yourself, you can be influenced in a negative way, much like a disincarnate Spirit that may be feeding off your life force. Cleansing your **aura** and protecting yourself against negativity will help prevent psychic attacks. Some symptoms of psychic attacks include headaches, nausea, irritability, depression, anger, a feeling of hopelessness and even complete confusion. **All this can and does lead to depression.**

One of the most common ways for human beings to pick up or be influenced by negative energies is from other human beings, much like a picking up a cold from another person. Your **aura** is an electrical field which surrounds your human body, anything up to two metres in diameter. As you walk through a crowd such as a shopping centre or sit in a crowded bus, restaurant or large public meeting, basically anywhere that you have contact with other human beings, you can become vulnerable to their negative energies, if that is what they are projecting and yes the same goes for positive energies.

The choice to be negative or positive is your choice and for this reason free will plays a very big part in human society. To protect yourself with the **White Light** against the influence of negative energies is also your choice. Remember negative energies are misguided energy created from negative emotions.

To illustrate, here is an example. You are in a fantastic mood and you are looking forward to visiting some close friends, but you have no idea they have just had a huge disagreement. As you walk into their home where there negative emotions are flying around and impregnating themselves into everything, unless you protect yourself by placing the **White Light** within you and all around yourself, you can be affected or even influenced to some degree by the negativity in that space. It may leave your feeling uncomfortable or even depressed, it may also manifest itself into a headache, or you may become irritable, having unconsciously picked up on their negative emotions.

Using the **White Light** to cleanse yourself and to protect yourself from negative energies is being **personally responsible.** As human beings come into contact with other human beings, you are exchanging positive and negative energies constantly, just by being in that vibration, so be aware and protect yourself always when you are not in your personal space (i.e. your home where your energies are balanced to your needs). All of you as human beings are created from cosmic energy, **White Light,** which is the source of all things, therefore it would make complete sense to utilize this energy in the cleansing and protection of your Being from negativity and psychic attacks.

Thought is energy and, through the power of thought you activate the energy channel within your human bodies. **Always remember cosmic energy, White Light,** is neither negative nor positive, it simply is in the moment. You as human beings create your thoughts from your emotions which are created from your life experiences. Those experiences can be created on a positive vibration or a negative vibration, the outcome is always the individual's choice. Responsibility for the self cannot be neglected. If you put yourself into a situation that is dangerous, and you are aware of the **White Light,** then it is important to place a shield of **White Light** within your Being and all around your outer Being.

Also be aware that by putting yourself into a dangerous situation and knowing it is dangerous, you are always **personally responsible** for putting yourself there in the first place. The **White Light will always protect you, but will not make you invincible.** It is the human Ego that believes you are invincible. The heart however if listened to, will make you aware of impending danger.

Your thoughts can and do become your own created reality. To believe in something be it negative or positive, will cause it to be manifested into your life. Believing that your **aura** is cleansed and protected in the Light will make it your reality. **Just because something cannot be physically touched, does not mean it does not exist.**

If my Being was to express that all matter that is physical is in reality an illusion created by your Soul and then manifested into your third vibration world, what would be your first thought? Human beings created what they believe to be physical purely because that is all they know. Human beings have been incarnating on Earth for nearly one million years, from lifetime to lifetime, again and again and again. All that you remember is what you have experienced in human form. To you that is your truth, your belief, your conditioning.

Yet there are many living on Earth who are searching deeper within themselves. You ask yourself how you find the truth. Go to the source, the Light from which you were manifested. In the silence of your mind your inner Being, you will find what you are seeking. Connect to your heart and your heart will connect to your Soul.

Here now is a technique for protecting your **aura,** your life force and your human body. Find a place where you will not be disturbed. Sit, stand or lie in a comfortable position, take in a deep breath, hold for a few moments and then slowly exhale. Repeat this three or four times until you feel a heaviness in your physical body and your human brain has been stilled a little from its thoughts.

You may also find it will help you to focus if you put on some soothing music; nothing too heavy and no singing where the words will keep you from concentrating on your task. When you are ready imagine a beam of white light pouring down from the outer universe, through the ceiling of your home, and down into your heart centre.

Allow this light of cosmic energy to flow down from your heart centre to the base of your feet, and then from your heart centre up to the top of your head and down both of your arms to your fingers. Know your inner being is filled with this white light that is a manifestation of unconditional love.

Then feel this light emanate through the pores of your skin, totally surrounding your outer body and filling your aura with light. You, the beautiful human being are radiating a mist of shining white light as pure now as the source it originated from. This mist has now formulated around your human body and is an impenetrable shield that cannot be broken. It is a shield of complete protection established by you.

Say to yourself:

"I am an infinite spark of White Light. I am living Consciousness. As this light has poured into my inner and outer Being, I know that I am a part of all that is and all that is, is a part of me. By filling my inner Being and surrounding my outer Being with this cosmic energy I have created a protective cloak through which negative energies cannot and will not be able to pass.

"I am White Light. I am all that is; a being created from Unconditional Love. Only that which is for my higher good and of benefit to my Being may pass beyond my shield of Light. All that which is negative and harmful to my Being will be and is repelled, and sent back into the nothingness from which is was first created, returning to the senders one hundred times fold in Unconditional Love that is endless, timeless, ageless and eternal."

Remember always on completion, give thanks to the Light and to Creation from your heart. If you dear human beings, find it difficult to imagine the exercise above, you may wish to record words and play them in your sleep time, your bathroom or even as you shower, imagining that the water is the White Light. It is just as effective.

My Being trusts that this expression on the **White Light and 'Knowing the Light'** will help any human individual gain a better or deeper understanding of who and what they are. May all human beings who are our Sisters and Brothers of Light be at peace, for it is Unconditional Love that opens the heart chakra to the knowledge that each of you are seeking. Be blessed always in Love and Light.

KNOWING YOUR HEART (NO-56)

Greetings to humanity. Realise in this moment you the human individual hold the key to your own freedom. If you feel pain, poverty, misery, hopelessness, stress, depression, for whatever reason you may be feeling negative toward yourself or others you can change it, **NOW,** if you truly want to.

For you to change you need to come from your heart, the centre of all that is; your heart is unconditional love. When you become true to yourself and make the connection to your heart, you open up the energy that is infinite, that is eternal and everlasting.

Your heart centre is your direct link, the connection to your soul. When the heart is open fully, your human life is fully balanced. Suddenly you feel as if you the individual can accomplish anything. All that you feel negative towards yourself or others, suddenly has no more meaning in your human life.

Many human beings have been asking if it is true that we are here to learn about emotion. To a point yes, this is true. Emotion is a human word created by man alone over humanity's history and human history has been a very negative existence in many respects, created by negative emotions. If you the human individual can accept that human beings have been evolving on Mother Earth for the past **928,000** years, then you can also accept negative emotions have been haunting humanity also for the past **928,000** years.

Change can only come when the individual makes the conscious decision in there human life to change the way they have been living and to realise the way they have been living can no longer be a part of their life. Even though to learn and experience emotion is a very important part of becoming a fully conscious human being, one must also realize that to constantly live negative emotions is to constantly create negative outcomes from past incarnations. Which in turn result in negative outcomes during an individual's present incarnation, and will affect future incarnations as a human being.

If you as an individual believe in **reincarnation,** then you believe you have lived many past lives as a human being, and if you study human history you will come to the conclusion that humanity as a species has experienced a very negative past which will shape your present and create your future.

Wars, violence and fear are a creation of the human Ego's negative emotions, experienced from one lifetime to the next. If there is no forgiveness from one individual to another, those negative emotions will be carried over to the next incarnation and the next and the next, until there is forgiveness. **The balance of life must be restored to bring forth a new beginning, a new energy, and this can only be experienced through forgiveness and compassion.**

The heart plays a most important role in the evolution of humanity. Your connection to your heart as individuals will set each human being free from their own self-created negative past. When a human being makes the conscious decision to connect to their heart, they begin to resolve and dissolve the illusions of the human Ego with Unconditional Love. One can then gain the understanding of having compassion for all life forms. With compassion you open up your inner being and this will give you the wisdom in all the decisions you will make throughout your human life.

So why is the human heart so important? The human heart is the centre of your beingness; it is your connection to your true self, your Soul. When a human being connects to their heart they are connecting to their Soul. **Why is your Soul so important?** Your Soul is the infinite spark of all that you are, have been and will become. You are physical but it is your Soul that manifested your human body and your material world of physical matter. Without your Soul you would not exist in your physical world.

Each of you are on your own journey of self-discovery. Even though you are all connected to each other you are free thinking individuals. You all have the same abilities to co-create your own reality. One of humanity's greatest downfalls is self-created fear created from negative emotions. Human beings hold onto the negative aspects of life, and in many cases they constantly recreate the same negative emotions, life after life after life. **Why? Because they have not been given the knowledge that there is another way of letting go of what is no longer needed.**

To truly feel at peace with yourself, first make a conscious decision that you do truly want to change. Realise there is no place for the human Ego if you want to grow consciously. **The human Ego of each individual is the enemy within.** It is all your fears, whatever they may be that prevent you from changing. The human Ego does not want change; the human Ego only understands the negative aspects of your life. It is your beliefs and your conditioning that holds you in your past.

To truly move forward and evolve as a conscious human being you need to understand your fears. Only by connecting to your **Heart Centre,** which is **Unconditional Love,** will you see the illusion that humanity has created through fear.

Yes, it can be overwhelming to the individual who has chosen the path of Enlightenment, and yes there are teachers in your world that can guide you in a loving and compassionate understanding to make your journey a lot easier. Go out and seek those Teachers of the Heart, but always listen to your own heart for Truth and Guidance.

Many human beings ask which centre of the human body is most important. The answer is all of them. Through personal experience my Being knows it is the **heart chakra** that will bring perfect balance to all life forms. From the **heart chakra** you send forth the light to all other centres. **The heart is your love centre;** from there all else comes into perfect harmony. **Unconditional Love is the key to everything.** Without it there is no balance, only pain and confusion and pain and confusion are conditions of negative emotions created from the illusions of the fearful human Ego.

Wherever Unconditional Love exits you will always find the balance of a beautiful heart with the understanding to express compassion and wisdom in all that is done. Put aside all your fears, all your beliefs and conditioning, put aside your judgements in what you believe to be the truth. If truth does not come from the heart it simply is an idea of truth. Truth comes from the heart and is connected directly to your Soul.

If you have no fear then have an open mind and heart. Learn to listen without fear and judgement. The heart that is connected to your Soul will never abandon you; it will release you from your own self-created illusions of your human Ego. Remember dear Sisters and Brothers of Mother Earth, as individuals you do hold the key to your own freedom.

The life force that flows through my being is the same life force that flows through your being, and forever more will be the same. I am that I am. May all of you be blessed in the light of Creation's Totality?

DISINCARNATE SPIRITS (NO-57)

There have been many questions asked of my being about Spirit and Disincarnate Spirits **(those no longer incarnated)**. Let us look a little at the definitions:

1. **A spirit which has not passed through the light.**
2. **A spirit which is caught between two worlds or vibrations.**
3. **The transition from physical existence to spirit existence which has been hindered.**

Some spirits do not know or believe that they are physically dead. Others know they are physically dead but do not wish to leave the physical plane. For a **disincarnate spirit** to be able to stay in your Earthly vibration as a Spirit, they become **psychic vampires** to keep their Astral bodies alive or energised.

If these Spirits can gather enough energy they can actually cause emotional and physical harm to a human being. For example their presence can cause arguments with loved ones, accidents, complete character changes and even physical death. They feed off the human physical being through the human **aura** by placing their **astral body** close to or within the space of the human **aura.** Through this close proximity a transfer of energies is able to occur.

It is most important for one on a **spiritual path to be fully responsible by protecting yourself.** Unless you the individual physically protect yourself, you will find their negativity will be transferred upon you, causing you to feel drained physically. Other symptoms include a lack of concentration, becoming quite irritable with yourself and others and you also can become uncomfortable and even restless. You may become quite confused by these feelings, and even feel they are unjustified. **This interaction of energies can cause you to live in a disincarnate Spirit's emotions, as much as they are living yours.**

You may be basically a happy and fairly balanced human being, but when you go to a particular place you may suddenly find yourself becoming irritable or argumentative, which you know is out of character. The disincarnate Spirits in that place may have been themselves of irritable and argumentative character when they were in physical form, so by attaching their negative energies upon a human being, they are able to live out their own negative habits and dispositions once again.

There is a great deal of negative influence being passed on to human individuals from disincarnate spirits of the lower end of the astral world, especially to those of weak characters. Always remember those Spirits that cause harm were of the same character in the physical. But any Spirit that has not gone through the light can to some degree drain energies, and not necessarily to create negativity. Draining energies is a negative act, however it can and does create some degree of **Karma for the disincarnate spirit.**

If most of them actually understood, they would pass through to the next dimension and set themselves free of their negative created emotions. The disincarnate Spirits that are truly misguided and quite negative can and will be found in all lower vibrational areas, such as public bars, nightclubs, low-social economic areas, even hospitals. They actually prey on certain types of human beings and when they have found an energy source they will attach themselves to that source.

These human beings include drug-addicts, alcoholics, mentally depressed or mentally ill human beings, as well as oppressed and lonely people. Basically they are attracted to weak human beings, those that lack self-worth that are depressed and feeling negative about their life, those that are extremely negative, those that live in constant drama or those that continually find themselves in negative vibrations.

Disincarnate spirits that are not quite as negative as the really naughty ones can be found everywhere in your Earthly vibration. The home you live in now may have been built by one who did not go into Spirit world completely, and is still living in what they consider to be there home. Most do not cause any harm to human beings, but the fact that they are still there means they need an energy source to survive and you may be the one being drained of your energy. **Draining a human being is in fact, spiritually, a big "no-no".**

Ask yourself this question, why do **disincarnate spirits** fear going through the Light of Creation to complete their transition from physical form to **spirit form?** Because of their past conditioning from previous incarnations, through religious and cultural influences, from beliefs which are really only an idea of truth itself.

They fear stepping through the Light, thinking from self-created fear that they will never be able to come back into the physical world of matter, so because of their fear they stay in the lower vibrations hanging on to what they believe life to be.

To take this another step further, take a Spirit who was a murderer in physical life and assume they themselves were murdered in some brutal way, but now in Spirit they do not believe themselves to be physically dead. There they stand blood dripping off them, when suddenly their spirit guide or guides approach to help them complete their transition from physical to spiritual form. They appear with a shimmering white light surrounding them in glory. The spirit in transit does not necessarily see them this way. Their beliefs, conditioning, fears, and memory from their physical life leads them to create a terrifying image where they see their guide as the devil or some equally horrifying creature coming to destroy them, not as their friend who comes in complete love and compassion.

If a guide is unsuccessful the first time they will continue to try to guide the Spirit by creating situations where by the Spirit is gradually educated and prepared for the transition to complete their transition. In other words to go through the Light of Creation. Until that moment comes the Spirit is actually in a state of limbo.

My Being wishes to take this one step further with respect to suicide. Suicides are a good example in how beliefs, conditioning and fears cause much confusion and pain, especially through religious conditioning. **Many religions believe suicide is sinful.** That thought can and does become embedded in the mind of the Spirit – they believe that they will go to 'hell' or 'purgatory' for committing a religious crime when in actual fact, suicide is just another way of going home to the source of Creation.

Unlike humanity, which judges all out of fear, Spirit of Light do not judge, but are ready and willing to help and guide a Spirit through the transition with complete love and compassion. There are many reasons why a human individual chooses to commit suicide. Most commit suicide from a state of depression, stress and hopelessness, created from negative experiences while in human form.

Passing into Spirit through a traumatic experience is another example of incomplete transition from physical spirit form. A spirit that dies in traumatic circumstances often is trapped in that moment and reliving the experience that caused their physical death, such as those that are hunted down, bashed, sexually assaulted or murdered in some terrifying way or even killed in vehicle collision. It is particularly traumatic when they take a long time to die and it is painful for them physically. Unless that Spirit is guided or has complete spiritual awareness they will continue to relive the experience, because they have no idea they are dead. That spirit will continue to relive their nightmare over and over again until they are finally set free by the assistance of their guides or by their own awareness.

In many situations if the transition is unsuccessful the first time for an accident victim, the guides can and will create the illusion of a hospital to help heal the Spirit's '**body**', and lead it to believe it is recovering. This will and does lead the Spirit to completion where they finally step through the Light of Creation to another dimension.

Once a Spirit has passed through the Light of Creation and transition is complete the Spirit can rest and heal their emotional wounds, and then, if they choose to they can prepare for their next human or other incarnation into a physical vibration. It is the free will of the Spirit to choose when to return to human life. It can be within minutes of physical death that their rebirth occurs, or it could be hundreds of your physical Earth years. It depends upon the extent of healing necessary for the spirit. Always remember, your Soul which is a part of totality is always there for you, to give you support knowledge and guidance, but most especially Unconditional Love.

So dear Human Beings, now that you understand what a Disincarnate Spirit is, you may be asking how you as physical beings can protect yourselves from the draining of your energy as well as your life force. You know that your energies keep Disincarnate Spirits in the physical vibration, allowing them to keep living their own emotions negative or positive in the physical realm.

Your first step is to cleanse your aura field. Find yourself in a comfortable position either sitting or lying down. Make sure this is your moment – be in a place where you will not be disturbed – and put on some relaxing music to help settle yourself. Take a deep breath. Hold it for a few of your moments, then exhale slowly. Repeat four or five times, until you feel relaxed enough to continue. You should feel the tension in your muscles release and a peaceful heaviness in your limbs.

Using your imagination, imagine bringing down a beam of white light from the universal source – make it tornado-like in shape, a vortex of swirling energy. Slowly lower the vortex until you are totally surrounded by it so no part of you is untouched.

Allow the energy of the pure white light to swirl around you and within you, believing that as it turns it is cleansing away all negative energies no matter what they may be and completely cleansing your energy field. When you are ready lower the swirling mass into Mother Earth. Send it down thirty meters below the ground.

Now bring down another vortex of white light simply repeat the process. Ask Mother Earth to accept the energy you have placed into the ground, and ask that it be neutralised of all its negativity, and that it be unutilised by Creation. Thank Mother Earth for her love and acceptance of the energies you no longer need, and also thank Creation for allowing you to use its energies to cleanse yourself.

If it makes your visualisation easier, try imagining the above exercise while you are showering your human body. The most important factor here is not how you do it, but believing that it is being done, meaning to truly believe in yourself. Everything is energy, and energy is continually being exchanged. Learn from your heart to appreciate that there are as many different levels of Consciousness as there are many types of energy upon your planet Earth.

By thanking the source of the energy you are acknowledging its purity and the different levels of vibrations. By also thanking Mother Earth and directing energy to her you are giving her energy to heal herself. Many human beings take Mother Earth for granted, believing that she is there and always will be. But Mother Earth is a living organism, a mass of energy, so the responsibility for your Mother Earth is yours alone. What you do to your Earth be it negative or positive plays a very important role in your own survival as well as the Earth upon which all of you live. Do not allow you're most precious Earth to become a Disincarnate Spirit, because if the Earth dies physically all life will perish, all physical life that relies on the Earth.

Dear Human Beings stop for a few moments and take a deep breath. Stop the chatter of confusion in your human brain and open your heart to feel with your heart the love for yourself and the love for all life forms no matter what they are. Send that Unconditional Love to all your Brothers and Sisters and to all other life forms on your planet, then send this love within Mother Earth and all around Mother Earth. Send this pure love to all Spirits, including disincarnate ones so only love is almighty present. Do this as often as you feel or want to. It will help all life forms and it will help ease the pain and misery that is plaguing your world. Be blessed always my Sisters and Brothers of Earth, in Unconditional Love.

THE JOURNEY OF
SELF-REALISATION (NO-58)

There seems to be a great interest in what is called the **Kundalini Energy.** Its founder who also helped create the **Nar'Karone** civilisation was called **Yarkiss 'Kariss.** It was he that introduced the **Kundalini** into our society, and it was the one you know on your Earth as **Buddha who introduced it to humanity.** Buddha incarnated on the 17th day of October around 2579 Earth years ago. The son of an Emperor, he was placed in a monastery at the human age of four (4) so he could learn wisdom and discipline through knowledge.

This he did accomplish but he also accomplished much more. Buddha developed a method of meditation over many Earth years. By raising his own Kundalini energy he helped others by guiding them in the process. He also became a vegan, and over human time he introduced veganism to all his disciples. Buddha believed that to raise one's Kundalini one must cleanse the human body of all negative emotions as well as to purify the body itself.

Buddha developed many forms of meditation to help the individual raise their **Kundalini** in a balanced and safe way, so there would be harmony and even joy and bliss in the process. One thing he would express which was of great importance was that to raise the **Kundalini** is to achieve complete freedom in the Knowing, but before this can be done the human body and emotions must be in balance. If a human being is not willing to face all their fears of self-created emotions, and if they are not willing to let go of their negative Earthly habits, then he strongly advised not to proceed in raising the **Kundalini.** Raising this energy with an unbalanced body and mind is harmful to the human body. Personal responsibility must be taken to ensure that the individual is aware the process can either be a very positive and uplifting experience or a negative experience if the human body is not healthy.

My Being has been asked if I would provide a meditation for commencing the process of activating the **Kundalini** and raising the energy. The following guided meditation is for you to use and practice daily. You may choose to record your own voice using the words provided below. During the meditation you may sit or lie flat on the floor. Do not be concerned if you find you go into a deep sleep. You will still connect to your true self because your Being is an infinite Spirit connected to your Soul and to Creation.

What is most important is to practice on a regular basis. Set yourself a regular timeslot and stick to it. Remember to use the gift of your imagination during the meditation. The more you use it the more effective the meditation will be. If you choose to record your voice be sure not to rush the words – take your time – it will make the process more effective. After each session it may be useful for you to write down what you have felt and experienced. Lastly, believe in what you are doing and what you are feeling.

Stage 1 Kundalini Meditation.

Sit or lay down on the floor making sure you are very comfortable. Make sure there is nothing binding on your body. If you are sitting rest your arms and hands on your legs. If you are lying down place your arms down beside your body making sure your head is supported. Make sure there is no strain on your neck or shoulders. **You need to be completely relaxed.**

Begin by closing your eyes. Take a deep breath, hold for a moment and exhale. Take another deep breath in slowly, feel your lungs expand, hold for a moment and then exhale slowly. Try to blow out all the air from your lungs.

Begin to breathe slowly and feel yourself becoming completely relaxed. Just breathe naturally. Take your awareness, your imagination and knowing to your Heart Chakra, your heart centre in the middle of your chest. Feel a ball of white light surrounding your heart. Be true to yourself and fully believe this ball of white light is present. You may feel a coolness or a warmth around your chest or even a tingling.

Remaining aware take the ball of light down your body, past your hips, past your knees down to your ankles, and from there see the light enter Mother Earth beneath you to a depth of around 30 metres. See it go all the way down through the layers of Earth. This is your connection with the Earth.

Using your imagination keep that connection to the Earth throughout the meditation, as if there is a chord of light joining you to the Earth.

Bring your awareness back to your heart centre and now see the ball of white light moving up to your shoulders, down your arms to your fingertips then up to your throat, and out through the top of your head through your Crown Chakra. Send the ball of light out into the Universe, and using your imagination keep your connection with the light as if a chord was connecting you to the universe. Realise and acknowledge that you are in this moment connected to the outer and the inner of your very Being.

Using your imagination, ask Mother Earth to send up her love her light and her energy back up through your feet into your heart centre. See her energy rising up through your feet, your knees, your hips and abdomen and filling your heart centre.

Likewise, using your imagination, ask the outer universe to send down its love, light and energy down through the top of your head going down into your heart centre. Feel the energy flowing down through your head, your neck, and your shoulders, filling your arms and filling your chest and heart centre.

Allow the two energies you are receiving from above and below to become one. Feel the energy emanating throughout your inner being and throughout every organ in your human body. Using your imagination see this light filling your entire body and see it seeping out of your pores into your **aura field.**

Using this light see your **aura** being cleansed and see all negative energies being cleansed away and being dissolved into the nothingness. See yourself completely encircled in the Light of Creation and say these words slowly: **I now fully realise that I am an infinite Being of Light on a journey of self-realisation.**

I also realise I am the Soul; I am the Light Divine; I am Love; I am Will; I am ageless; I am timeless; I am endless; I am eternal; I am immortal in the scheme of life itself. I am that I am. Light is what I am. To believe in yourself is to become the living truth of what you feel and express.

Using your awareness allow the ball of light to move down from your heart centre right down to the base of your spine, to your base or root chakra. See this ball of light turn into a coil of red energy, wrapping itself around your base chakra clockwise two or three times slowly. Some human beings refer to this as the **'voice of the inner silence' or the 'inner being'.** Others call it the **'Serpent of Fire within'** because it has the appearance of liquid fire ignited by human will.

Using your imagination and your knowing, see, know and feel that your will has ignited this energy to flow upwards from your **base chakra.** Take your time – allow the energy to flow upwards slowly; the slower the better. As the energy goes up, allow it to reach your **spleen chakra,** located just beneath your navel and see the energy as if it were flames, to coil itself clockwise around this area two or three times. Again do this slowly.

Once more see the fire energy rising slowly to your **solar plexus chakra,** located just beneath your diaphragm. Slowly coil the fire energy clockwise around your solar plexus chakra two or three times, then see it move slowly up to your **heart chakra.** Coil it clockwise very, very slowly around your **heart chakra** two or three times. You may begin to feel a surge of energy in this entire area. Do not panic or feel fear. Everything is fine. Tell yourself **"I am in perfect balance and harmony". Know this is true.**

Raise the fire energy once more from your **heart chakra** to your **throat chakra,** located at the base of your throat. Allow it to coil clockwise around this centre two or three times slowly and allow yourself to feel whatever emotions may come to you at this point. Allow these feelings to be without judgement – be completely unbiased in your observation of them. Slowly allow the fire energy to rise once more up to your **brow chakra,** or your **'Third Eye'**, and allow it to coil slowly around it two or three times.

Always be patient with this process. **Trust yourself.** Now see the fire energy rising upwards once more to your **crown chakra,** located at the top of your head. **This is your spiritual connection to the outer universe.** Allow the fire energy to coil around your **crown chakra** two or three times slowly. Again you may feel emotions negative or positive. This is a part of the process of opening up all your **chakra centres.** All your self-created negative energies are being released, cleaned out as it were. Allow this process to occur knowing all the while this process will allow you to let go of what you no longer need. Face these emotions and let them go with love. Allow them to go back into the nothingness from which they once came.

Using your imagination allow the fire energy to first come down slowly back through all your **chakra centres** by gently unwinding it anticlockwise from around each centre – slowly unwind the fire energy anticlockwise from around **crown chakra,** then moving down slowly to the **brow chakra,** slowly unwind the fire energy anticlockwise from around **brow chakra.** Move slowly down again to the **throat chakra** and slowly unwind the fire energy anticlockwise from around your **throat chakra.** Move down slowly once more to the **heart chakra** and very slowly unwind the fire energy anticlockwise from around the **heart chakra.** Move down slowly to the **solar plexus chakra** and slowly unwind the fire energy anticlockwise from around the **solar plexus chakra.** Again move down slowly to the **spleen chakra** and slowly unwind the fire energy anticlockwise from around the **spleen chakra.** Finally move down slowly to the **base chakra** and slowly unwind the fire energy anticlockwise from around the **base chakra.**

Be still for a few moments.

Using your awareness and imagination see a ball of light around your heart and send this white light throughout your inner and outer being, encircling all of you in the Light of Creation. Know you are always protected in the Light this will always be your truth if you truly believe in the light that is the totality of Creation.

Now relax for a few minutes, and when you are ready, open your eyes and be present in this moment.

You can practice this meditation whenever you feel the need or you may wish to set a special time for yourself to practice this meditation. If you allow this process to occur naturally by taking your time and not rushing it, it will most certainly help you in all aspects of your human life and your spiritual life.

Remember beautiful human beings the power is in your hands always. If you have any questions on the **Kundalini** energy please feel free to ask of my Being. Be Blessed in Unconditional love always dear Sisters and Brothers of the Light. We are here for you always.

CREATING YOUR REALITY (NO-59)

Dear Human Beings, have you ever wondered why your life just never seems to go 100% the way you would like it to, yet for some human beings life seems a to be easy and everything they touch seems to turn to gold?

Some would call it fate or luck. In reality these lucky human beings are the reason behind their success. Whether consciously or unconsciously successful human beings create their own reality and to some degree their own happiness.

To create the reality that you the individual truly wants, means changing the reality you have right now in this most precious moment. First to understand how you create your reality you need to look at the specific characteristics of your own personal life.

The root of your own self-created reality lies in your beliefs and your conditioning. Conditioning is basically your inner programming and programming is within your human brain. The human brain, apart from physically monitoring your human bodies, also holds all your memory from the past to the present.

It is within this memory that you the individual hold all your life's experiences, be it negative or positive, and which governs your reactions in a positive or a negative way. It all comes down to you the human individual.

A human child is a good example of this conditioning creating one's reality. If a human parent continually tells their child that they will not accomplish a certain task **(such as drawing an animal like an elephant),** that child eventually accepts the condition. Unfortunately the condition then becomes their belief system and the child will say to themselves and believe, **"I can't draw elephants"**. From such small seeds they begin their path and mind set by creating their present and future realities. Reality is the result of internal belief systems developed through conditioning.

If you as a human being are willing to continually accept the conditioning and belief systems indoctrinated over your lifetime, then you are allowing yourself to live in your past, and subsequently are creating your future. Your beliefs and conditioning are even creating your child's future. If you place limitations upon yourself you will surely place limitations upon others over who you have an influence. Remember, you alone hold memories within your human brain as your truth.

Limitation is as easy as saying "I am too old", "It's impossible", "None of our family were any good at school", the list is as long as you choose to make it. At this point it all sounds rather negative, does it not. However, ask yourself this very important question: **are you truly happy with your present reality?** If your answer is no then you need to look at why, and if your answer is yes then thank yourself or whoever has encouraged you to believe in yourself.

Self-created realities be they negative or positive can always be improved. When you step beyond your conditioning you allow yourself to become limitless.

Your human body is approximately 76% water, and 99.9% pure energy. In fact, your human physical self is less than 0.1% of physical matter. Hard to believe, yet even some of your human scientists have proven that this is truth. Such a small part of you is physical. You are a Spirit Being, you are living Consciousness and as a species (human beings) you have been evolving for **928,000** years.

Your physical matter includes your human brain, and as already mentioned your brain is keeper of your memories. Memory is your past be it negative or positive or even both. Take this one step further and realise that your thoughts are energy. If thoughts are energy and energy has the capability to manifest reality, then thought is creation and creation becomes your reality, be it negative or positive.

Conditioning directly relates back to this concept. If a thought within your human brain is continually reinforced it becomes a condition which creates a belief. Once it becomes your belief, you will manifest that belief and make it your reality, be it a negative thought or a positive thought. That reality will then complete the loop and reinforce your beliefs and your conditioning, continuing the cycle of thought, followed by reinforcement becoming a belief resulting in conditioning. This can work for you or against you depending on whether the thought is positive or negative.

If you truly believe in something with the power of your will, you will create it because you are the driver, the power, the creator of your own destiny, and that destiny can be created as a negative creation or as a positive creation.

As previously stated, everything is energy and energy is limitless. You as a Spirit, existing in a human body, are a part of all that is and vice versa. You are timeless, endless, and ageless. You are eternal and immortal. Only your human body perishes upon your human death, but your **Spirit can never perish because you are living consciousness.** You have over four quadrillion cells making up your human body; every cell that holds your form together as a human being has its own conscious understanding, and it is this which makes you a complete being, **spirit and physical united.**

Every human being has the potential to do whatever they wish with their life. The only thing that separates one from another is experiences in human life. Never look at anything as bad, but rather as valuable lessons from which you can learn and gain a deeper understanding of the purpose of human life, and in particular your life.

If you as a human being wish to create a more positive reality, then you need to face yourself; face your fears, and face your self-created past. One of the greatest lessons for all life forms is to start loving yourself in the now, and loving yourself exactly as you are. This does not mean in an egotistical way, but in an honest and truthful way directly from your heart.

You have no doubt heard the term **"the child within".** If there is a hurt child within you, learn to love that child. Learn to forgive those that have hurt you in your past, for they knew no better because they came from beliefs and were equally conditioned by their human parents and their experiences.

Learn through forgiveness to dissolve the negative past and see it as lesson of life, simply experiences. If you the human individual do not deal with your past conditioning and subsequent limited belief systems, you will only cause yourself more pain during your life to come.

Change your thoughts to more positive ones; as the moments pass you will see changes in your own life. To truly love yourself from the heart is in itself motivating. Loving yourself is respecting the Spirit of who you are. Likewise, love and respect your human body for it is the temple in which your Spirit resides.

Creating your reality and knowing that you create your reality, is truly finding the Spirituality within your Being because you are taking personal responsibility for who you are and what you create in your life. **There are five (5) basic principles to creating your reality. They are:**

    1-Unconditional Love for all forms of life;
    2-Truth;
    3-Compassion;
    4-Wisdom;
    5-Understanding Forgiveness.

When you begin to love yourself unconditionally you have a shift in Consciousness, and the knowledge within you is released. That is when you begin to feel truth itself. From there you have a heart full of compassion, and once compassion from the heart becomes a reality in your own evolution you begin to feel and express the wisdom of your Being.

Wisdom is a direct connection to your Soul, where all knowledge comes from. From the past to the present and into the future, this gives you the understanding of the knowing. This is where you create your reality, and your reality is whatever you as a human individual wishes it to be.

In essence, all five (5) principles are within you NOW. If you dear Human Beings of Light, wish to change your life habits from negative creations to more positive creations, you have the power within you for that change to be initiated and manifested. **It is up to you, is it not? Only truth can set you free and only Love can dissolve the Ego that plagues all human beings from the past to the present moment.** Be blessed in Unconditional Love always beautiful Human Beings.

CROP CIRCLES: CIRCLES OF LIFE (NO-60)

There has been human beings all over your world showing great interest in the creation of Crop **Circles.** Many positive actions and thought have come from what are called **Crop Circles,** and many are asking what their meanings are, who created them and how they are created. **Was it Alien beings from other worlds?** One thing needs to be understood; **Crop Circles were most certainly not created by any human beings on Mother Earth.**

The beings who created them are called the Nar'karones from the planet Nar'kariss, a little over 417,000 light years from Earth. They live in what you would call the fifth (5TH) dimension and have been observing human beings for nearly one million years of human evolution. The purpose for creating the **Crop Circles** is to communicate with human beings and to express higher forms of vibrating energy for human conscious growth. **There are Nar'Karones incarnated and living within humanity.** The vibrating energies of the Crop Circles activate these individuals Consciousness motivating them to seek higher knowledge and understanding for human evolution in order to become teachers for all humanity future.

Crop Circles are created through vibrations of sound and light which forms the balls of energy that hover above where the pattern is to be created. It takes anything from seconds to a few minutes of human time to create a complete Crop Circle, depending on the complexity and con figuration of the design. The energy ball used to create all Crop Circles are programmed through computers as on your Earth, but the technology is such that the information is not entered by being typed on a keyboard as with human computers, but is telepathically transferred. That is, a thought is entered into the computer and the computer programmes the energy ball for the pattern which creates the message **(design)** in the field.

All of life is energy, whereas light and sound is existing always within space and space is always existing within space. Light in its pure state is magnetic energy, and it is magnetic energy that manipulates and creates by using the particles of matter that are all around. Consciousness is within all atoms that exist in all Universes, every single cell in your human body, and there are over **four quadrillion** of these cells that make up your human body, **so in reality you are a universe within many universes?**

Humanity as a species can no longer follow the path of Ego, the path that has caused all the pain, misery, wars and violence on your Earth. Humanity's negative creations of the past can no longer keep creating your future. If humanity continues on this path the human species will eventually cause their own self-destruction. The purpose of all life in all its forms is conscious growth.

Within all Crop Circles created on the Earth there are embedded within them messages relating to humanity past, present and future as a species. One thing must be understood about humanity's future, each of you are co-creators, and you and only you will write your future. So many believe you can step into your future, example, someone going through a time machine into the year, let's say 2179. That will not happen because the future is in the moment and all the moments to come. **Yet, that is not to say you cannot go into parallel worlds, because you can and in time on your world it will happen.**

There are many parallel worlds, all vibrating at different levels of Consciousness all around, some back to the stone age, some close to your human time, others are ahead of you by years, century's, even thousands of your Earthly years. The only reason you cannot see them, is different levels of vibrations. Just think for a moment, when you have dreams in your sleep time, and some feel so real like you been there before, or you have even seen yourself, you may look or dress a little different or you look younger or older? **Guess what,** you are having real experiences, there are no such things as dreams it is your reality, you may be in a parallel world to learn something?

The vibrating energies of the Crop Circles activate the memory stored in your genetics, which is your entire existence as a Being, of every incarnation you have ever had, to bring to your awareness that you are more than just a physical shell that lives for 60 or 90 years and then dies.

The energy of the Crop Circles helps awaken your Being, to bring your conscious awareness from where you came from. **This is the primary**

objective of crop circles. The knowledge presented in the Crop Circles is knowledge from another world, brought to your world almost a million Earthly years ago and which is integral to your true essence.

Many thousands of human beings are visiting Crop Circles, and are drawn to them because of the energy they emanate. The energies contained within the circles help to activate the future teachers of the Earth, and in turn their children will become teachers, leaders and guides to others, ultimately helping to raise human Consciousness as a whole.

As much as there are human beings who are attracted to Crop Circles, just as many are fearful of them. Through their own lack of knowledge and ignorance, these human beings would not dare believe, let alone consider that Beings from another world are the creators of these wondrous cosmic messages. For any human being to think that in the vastness of the Universe, or even the vastness of your own Milky Way Galaxy, that humans are the only Beings **'alive'**, is not only arrogant but also self-defeating in that the more limitations of belief you as an individual place upon yourself and the world you live in, the more fearful you will become and the less conscious aware you will be.

However, if a human being can open there heart and mind to the notion that anything is possible, they will realise very quickly that there is no reason to fear Crop Circles, or any communication from Beings from other worlds, particularly the **Nar'Karones who are humanity's direct ancestors.**

We the **Nar'Karones** are givers of knowledge and wisdom, and in our observations of humanity for almost one million years of your evolution, believe the moment has come for increased communication so that humanity can become aware of our constant presence. It is in the silence of your mind that awareness becomes reality. **To be aware of your own surroundings is to become consciously aware of the meaning of life.**

Each human being is their own book of life. Every experience you have throughout all of your incarnation's right up to your present incarnation is recorded in your cellular memory. You are a walking database of **infinite knowledge,** and yes every one of you has the knowledge and understanding of Crop Circles which have been created upon your most precious Earth you all call home.

When an individual lives their life from fear, beliefs or conditioning, their life will be filled with negative experiences, and those negative experiences will shape their life in the present moment. Such individuals find it very hard and frustrating to accept new ideas because they have been so profoundly conditioned. From that conditioning the confusion and conflicts of daily life are created.

To accept new ideas one needs to change their thinking. What humanity has called the Crop Circles can become an opportunity to raise individual awareness and bring forth conscious growth? **Every crop circle the Nar'Karones have created on your Earth is filled with knowledge, vibrating at a specific frequency to activate human cellular memory.**

Crop Circles will attract and help certain human beings to search deeper within themselves, and by doing this, pathways will open up within them and the knowledge that they will express will amaze all who are willing to have an open heart and mind.

Crop Circles are a gift to all of humanity, to raise your energies, your Consciousness and your awareness, to bring an understanding that all of life irrespective of its form, is interconnected. **When every human being can truly love themselves unconditionally and have complete respect for all of life in that moment, you have become a true human being, balanced in mind, body, spirit and soul. Be blessed in unconditional love always.**

THE ART OF LISTENING (NO-61)

How many of you really listen to what is being said by other humans? Do you actually comprehend the messages within their words? At some time or other all are guilty of not listening or paying attention. Even before someone has finished speaking, you tend to interrupt them and complete their sentence for them, believing you know what they are about to say. The human being have a tendency to presume the outcome of a statement, and yet quite often that presumption is far from correct. If you're not presuming, then you disagree without reasoning or investigating for yourselves what is being expressed. A basic flaw in human nature is the Ego's eagerness to subjectively jump to conclusions rather than objectively and rationally thinking something out.

Probably the most common form of not listening is in not listening to yourselves. That little voice inside all of you that tries to guide your lives is usually swept aside by your audacious Ego, looking for any opportunity to be heard. It does this by encouraging you to immerse yourselves in innumerable commitments and activities, thereby effectively taking up any free time for personal development and growth. You allow yourselves to become so busy that you leave little or no time for yourselves. How often do you literally stop for five minutes during the day to centre yourselves? Your true inner voice gets lost amongst the constant babble of confusion around you, and you fail to hear what your human body, let alone your higher self, is trying to express to you.

Human beings stress out and create dis'ease within their bodies because they don't take time out for themselves. If you the individual would just bother taking five minutes out during the day for quiet time, you would begin to communicate with the real essence of who you truly are, and if you would take longer, like half an hour, you would make greater personal progress. **Five minutes is not a great deal of time; it leaves twenty three hours and fifty five minutes to do everything else!** I guess it comes down to how much of a commitment you are willing to make to yourselves, instead of committing to everyone else. Claiming that tiny amount of human time as your own is your first step in regaining control of your hectic life. Such a small investment of time can be the difference between a well-managed healthy lifestyle and medication for the rest of your human life. Recognising how you the individual abuse yourselves physically can help you uncover hidden unresolved emotions that hold you back from personal growth and a fulfilling existence as a human being.

You all know of human beings who don't listen to what is being said. The proverbial "in one ear, and out the other" seems to be very common place in human society, and no matter how many different ways you may try to say something, the other human being just can't seem to grasp what you are on about. Learning to listen to yourselves will make you better listeners all around. You will learn to pick up the hidden messages that are eluding most humans and not only get your own lives together, but also help others learn to listen to the voice within them to help them improve the quality of their lives.

However, it seems sometimes that some humans just don't want to even learn to really listen. Let my Being explain: You had a very confused and frustrating human male (to himself, as well as others) He was seeking truth, but he believed everyone he came in contact with in the places he was seeking truth were lecturing him, and that they never answered his questions. No matter how much one tried to explain something, he just would not allow himself to comprehend it. **His mental blocks were so well rooted, that even the rest of the group found it difficult to cope with his rigid attitude.**

It came to light that this unfortunate individual was constantly criticised and lectured to as a child by his human parents. So ingrained was his conditioning, that the only way he could express himself was by criticising and lecturing others who he felt threatened by. He compounded his problem by keeping himself so busy that he never allowed himself to take the time to find out what the problem was, or to take the time to forgive his human parents for the deep conditioning and insecurities they put upon him.

No matter how much you may try to help this individual in this situation, unless they take complete responsibility for what they are feeling, and recognise that they need to learn to listen to their voice within with all its confusion and hurts, they will stay exactly where they are in their growth. You the individual are only a victim as long as you choose to be one, and this human male was no exception. Only when he realises that the truth cannot be found on the outside, will he find the truth he so desperately seeks.

To be able to listen objectively and compassionately to others, you first need to learn to hear the voice within yourselves. Recognising and resolving your deep-rooted hurts and fears will make you better listeners for those in need. How can someone whose life is in utter chaos, listen objectively to another's problems, and if required provide objective advice? It can't be done because unresolved emotions will influence the advice you give, and that could do more harm than good.

Learning to accept and understand the voice within each of you will assist you in understanding the words of other human beings. It is only when you learn to read between the lines that you begin to see where human beings are really coming from and what they are really saying. Take the time to listen to yourself and those around you. **You'll be surprised at what you will observe and tune in to.** Be blessed in Unconditional Love always.

CREATIVENESS IS THE UNKNOWN (NO-62)

How many of you live your life from day to day locked in your own little world, concerned with trivialities that you take the simple joys and experiences of life for granted? More often than not it takes a life threatening situation to jolt the recognition within you that life is what you make it. **Too many of you live in a falseness you are completely oblivious to.**

You create the falseness in your human lives through your beliefs and conditioning. Yet by recognising these beliefs you can set yourselves free from the things that hold each of you back from personal growth and happiness, and begin to understand what reality and creativity really are. **Reality and creativity are beyond the scope of the known, as true creativity and reality originate from the unknown.**

You as human beings have all heard the lingo New Age motivators and Personal growth gurus' use, in particular "reality", "creating your reality", and "living in the now". But even as you contemplate what reality may be, you only have conjecture and philosophising from which to derive the true meaning of reality. **You cannot really comprehend reality because you draw on your past conditioning and existing beliefs to find the answer to the puzzle.** When you live according to your conditioning you live only knowing what has been; only knowing the past - the known - and you end up basing your entire understanding of reality on your past experiences. Therefore what you believe to be absolute truth is not necessarily truth, as your exploration of the concept of reality has been limited by your level of understanding. You end up with only an idea of what reality may be, or what it means to **"live in the moment".**

Reality cannot be conceived or comprehended as an idea, it can only be experienced. Reality is life - not a mental formulation, and creativity is life, happening in the moment, for to create is to bring something to life. Both reality and creativity spring from the unknown, and are the fundamentals to a fulfilling and experiential existence.

The known and the unknown are separated by self-imposed boundaries. Within your known boundaries exists the known, while beyond your known boundaries exists the unknown. To go beyond the known into the unknown is to experience reality, expanding the known, and all the while experiencing the unknown by living in the moment of true creativity. To make something real is to live it, not merely mentally assume what it may be. Thus, going beyond the known **(our known boundaries)** is to be creative by creating and experiencing a new reality.

For example consider the artwork of the human Salvador Dali. Whilst he may have had a grounding in the traditional forms and styles of art throughout history to his day, Dali broke out of the known boundaries that held most human artists and went beyond the accepted norm to creatively express what reality was to him. **In his well-known painting "The Persistence of Time" (1931) he portrayed clock faces sliding off a table, showing you that time is in fact an illusion (it does not exist beyond the third dimension), and that the past tends to keep coming back, unless we break that cycle of "persistence".** By going beyond known artistic boundaries of his time, into the unknown, Dali's artwork became not only an expression of his creativity and individuality, but also an example that creativity really does spring from the unknown, and that all you have to do is step beyond what you know to expand your understanding and free yourselves from your own self-created limitations.

To be truly creative, you the individual need to let go of the known which you have clung to from your conditioning and belief systems. Your insecurities encourage you to clutch to whatever is within easy reach, and tend to fool you into believing in something that may not necessarily be what you may believe it to be. It takes courage to let go of the known, and go beyond into the unknown, and it is fear of the unknown that holds you back from personal growth. In the unknown lies freedom; not restricting yourselves with the limitations of the past. **When you allow yourselves to grow beyond your limitations you begin to realise that some of your beliefs were little more than self-created illusions.**

In the unknown is true reality and creativity. Once you allow yourselves to venture outside your conditioning and belief systems you can expand your boundaries and actively learn through experiencing the unknown, making your new experiences your reality and truth. **Become an explorer - go beyond your known boundaries, and experience reality through creativity in the limitless unknown.** Be blessed in Unconditional Love always.

THE ESSENCE OF UNCONDITIONAL LOVE (NO-63)

Love - it's the one thing that all human beings talk about, but how many truly understand. Human beings have always searched for love - love with family **(in particular with parents),** love with friends, and love with intimate partners. Most human beings are never completely fulfilled, and many are miserable their entire lives. It seems almost to be an elusive pot of gold at the end of the rainbow. **You grow up believing that "one day I'll have it", and yet in human terms what does Unconditional Love really mean?**

For many human beings love means acceptance. Fooled into believing that to be loved is to be accepted, and to be unloved is to be an outcast, you use **(actually, you abuse) the word "love" as a reward for good behaviour.** You believe that if you behave a certain way or adopt a particular way of thinking, you will be loved more and therefore accepted. And on top of that, you do things in order to please others in the hope that you will be loved just that little bit extra. **Loving and pleasing are not the same thing.**

Love has become conditional. "If you don't do this, I won't love you anymore". How many human parents have told their children that they won't love them if they continue misbehaving or being disobedient? How many human couples have told each other they will love them more if they do as they are told? **Love is not a prize to be idly thrown about as a bribe.** Love is serious stuff. Human beings have lost sight of what love really is. If you the human individual truly understood love, you would stop playing games with each other's emotions and lives and not use it to emotionally blackmail each other for personal gain.

Real love is Unconditional Love, and means exactly that - unconditional. Loving someone exactly as they are, not trying to make them into someone you may be more comfortable with, just 100% acceptance. But how do you know you can unconditionally love someone? Well you have to start by unconditionally loving yourself.

Unconditional Love can only be expressed when you have experienced it for yourselves. You expect to be loved by others, but you find it difficult to accept the necessity of loving yourselves first in order to understand what it means to express love. Unconditional Love stems from forgiving yourselves and others in order to find the compassion and understanding necessary to know what it means to unconditionally accept a person, and you can only do that when you the individual unconditionally accepts yourselves.

When you know what it means to unconditionally love you free yourselves from your emotional limitations and allow others to be themselves. You stop judging and condemning, you stop criticising and manipulating. Unconditional Love nurtures the growth of wisdom, and fosters the principle of truth, for without truth Unconditional Love is unable to exist. **Love will only exist in an honest heart free from fear and doubt.** Become honest with yourself and you will find what you are looking for, but if you the human individual avoids facing the truth within, the illusion of conditional love with keep you from true happiness.

Recognising your inner fears is the first step towards Unconditional Love. Many human beings fear intimacy; you fear allowing another human being to get close to you and find out who you really are, insecurities and all. You fear you will be rejected because deep down you don't think you are good enough, yet a fear of intimacy and love always destroys a relationship before it has even begun. If you are honest with yourselves, you would recognise all the wonderful things about you that make you the individual unique and irreplaceable. Knowing and loving your uniqueness will attract a human being into your life who will love you as you are. Living a lie or an illusion will only serve to create further illusion and deception, eventually resulting in misery. **Unconditional Love is the greatest lesson humanity can learn. Unconditional Love is the key to freedom.**

Unconditional love is a pure state of being; it is ever present, growing and evolving through unconditionally loving yourselves, and then having the understanding to share that Unconditional Love with another. Learning to forgive those you believe have emotionally hurt you, can bring Unconditional Love into your life by changing your thoughts and your entire outlook on life. **Through forgiveness you can touch the essence of your love, and change the perception you have of your life.**

Love is the most important thing in all life; without it you make your life harsh and cruel, empty and meaningless. The rainbow is in your hearts, and love really is the pot of gold at the end of the rainbow, waiting for all human beings to claim it as your own. Be blessed in Unconditional Love always.

WHAT IS THE MEANING OF GRIEF? (NO-64)

Everyone human being has experienced some form of Grief, be it over a broken relationship, the death of a loved one, losing an object of great sentimental value, and even leaving a job that you really enjoyed. All of these experiences can create an empty void within you, leaving you wondering **"what now"**? **That emptiness is Grief** - a very necessary part of the healing process which enables you to let go, grow and move forward as a human being.

This may not be considered a correct evaluation by human experts, but to my Being, grief is a sophisticated label for your more primitive emotions, these being:

Fear- who/what can I turn to now to justify my existence; I'm scared of being on my own.

Anger- how could they have done this to me.

Self-Pity- I'm nothing without them, I feel lost and helpless.

Guilt- I should have been a better person; maybe there's more I could have done.

All human beings need to remember that physical life is a transient state of being; that is, it is constantly changing and on the move. For you to try to prevent any change or growth is not only unnatural, but also stifling to your own personal evolution.

A human being in a state of **Grief** needs to understand that you never lose anyone, because no one ever dies. What has occurred is a transformation of energy. If you were particularly close to someone, they were most likely to be of the same energies as yours. In the case of someone deceased, their energies often join back with yours when you are ready to accept that joining. This usually occurs when you finally let go of your **Grief** over that human being. Letting go does not mean that you do not care. Letting go means that you have realised you cannot live in the past continually, and that life must move forward or risk becoming stagnant. Letting go means that you love yourself and them, enough to allow growth and progress in both the physical and non-physical worlds.

How long should a person grieve? There is no answer to this question. Perhaps the best advice is when you decide to let go of your fear and guilt, and to stop using your **Grief** as an excuse to punish yourselves **(and in some cases, those around you). To lovingly let go of the past, and to stop making the past your present and future means to love yourselves enough to know you as human beings are worthy of happiness, and that you no longer need to suffer.**

Overcoming **grief** gives you the human individual the power, courage and strength to accept new ideas and lessons that you will experience throughout your human life. Every time you learn a lesson whatever it may be, you will become stronger within yourself. You learn to handle life more adeptly. Take the time to find the power of Unconditional Love within yourself and you will find the understanding of who you as an individual truly are, **infinite in all things, timeless in all things, ageless in all things, endless in all things.** It will lead you to finding your true self, who you are, what you are, and why you are learning all the lessons of human life including the lesson of Grief.

Each and every one of you as human beings are 100% responsible for your lives, not for anyone else's. You need to stop blaming others for the way you feel, and you need to stop feeling sorry for you and that you have been hard done by. Each of you has chosen experiences and situations for your own growth - one day you may be needed to help someone else through what you are experiencing now, and you can't help another human being if you have been unable to help yourself. **Is that not truth?**

Only you the individual, can heal your pain. You hold the power for change and growth, because only you can decide when it is time to let go and get on with your life. Every time you turn to someone to solve your problems, **you give away your personal responsibility.** And if their help or advice doesn't work out who do you blame? **Usually them.** You should really blame yourselves, for when it's all said and done only you the individual can help yourselves. Beware of human beings who claim to be able to help you, heal you, tell your future, and be your leader and so on. They can guide you by their experiences, but you are the only ones that can do the work which will get you to where you need to go. You forget that you really are the only ones who know what's best for you - you need to trust yourselves. When each of you decides to take the time to find that power and truth within, you will experience inner personal and spiritual growth. **There is no truth on the outside, only conflict.** Finding your inner guidance and truth is ultimately where inner peace, Unconditional Love and reconciliation will be achieved. The sooner you as a human being realise you alone hold the ultimate power within your being, to love, to forgive, to create anything you desire in your human life. The power of that knowing will allow you to go beyond your past and move into any future you the human individual wishes to create.

To a larger extent all human beings are on their own journey of learning, forgiving and letting go of the past. As for self-created **"Karma"** whether negative or positive, has a purpose for all human beings, as it has for all forms of life wherever they may be in existence. **Karma** is a created action by all human beings and must be brought into balance. **The lessons of human life are created by the Soul to facilitate each human being's learning and letting go of self-created karmic debts.**

As much as grief is part of a healing process, endless grief resembles a belief system; you as human beings use it to place limitations upon yourselves by giving yourselves a set of rules to live by. For example, "If I stop grieving, it means I never really loved him/her, therefore I will not let go of the pain so I'll keep proving my undying love." It may sound like a predictable Victorian love story but many of you torn by **grief** will sincerely believe that if you were to let go it may mean you no longer love the one you lost. If you are not careful, you will use **grief** to prevent personal growth by bringing personal growth to a complete standstill. Scared of the future without someone or something that was once an integral part of your life, it becomes easier to live in the pain than to look forward to the unknown.

Grief can and does cloud your perceptions and ability to function as a complete and emotionally balanced human being. It should not be denied, as **grief** is an important part of your personal growth and all clichés aside, will make you become stronger in the end if you allow it. **But you must not fear opening your hearts dear human beings and your mind to**

experiencing an existence free from the fear, guilt and self-pity which grief can cause you to wallow in if you allow it to become significant and influential in your life.

Grief can teach you the importance of forgiveness, while helping you the human individual to let go of the past with love. If you allow it, **grief** will emotionally cleanse you in readiness for that first brave step forward into a new chapter of life, all the while reminding you it's okay to remember the past with joy and love. Completing the grieving process will ensure you don't sacrifice personal growth in the misguided belief you can keep the past alive by keeping the pain alive. **In all honestly, who truly would want that?** Be blessed in Unconditional Love dear Sisters and Brothers of Earth.

BEING 100% PERSONALLY RESPONSIBLE (NO-65)

Before reading on ask yourselves the following three questions, and give it some deep thought, try not to ask from your beliefs or your conditioning as a human being. As you think for a few moments try asking from your heart space which is unbiased. Each time you ask let say question 1, feel from your heart and listen to your first answer, as it is always your truth. Please take the moments in your human life to do this little exercise and then read on.

Question who is responsible? **(1- The prisoner) (2-The firing squad) (3-The officer giving the order)**

Answer: All three- Why? The prisoner put him/herself in that situation. The firing squad soldiers chose to be soldiers, knowing that at some point they will be called upon to kill other human beings. The officer became an officer because of a need to be a leader, and no doubt a need to feel important. The officer must give orders, and sometimes those orders may include ordering the death of another human being. All three parties are responsible for their respective roles in the scenario.

You are all familiar with the word **"Responsibility",** and no doubt at one time or other you have been told, or have told someone else to take responsibility, or to be responsible. Responsibility means to be obligated, and to possess the quality of being reliable and dependable. It also means to be held accountable and to know your duty. To be responsible is to be in charge of or in control of a situation. From the perspective of employment commitments, or commitments to others, you fully understand responsibility. Then ask yourselves the next three questions and give it some deep thought before reading on.

1-But what about responsibility to yourselves? Are you obligated towards yourselves to do something for your sole purpose, which does not involve another human individual?

2-Are you reliable and dependable enough to yourselves that you can totally trust and look to yourselves for answers and solutions, or to fulfil a task which will be to your benefit?

3-Are you also responsible enough towards yourselves that you can make a decision for your higher good even if it affects another human being?

You shape your lives through the actions you take in your daily existence. How you view the results of your actions results in your opinions being either neutral, positive or negative. When you see the results as neutral your response is neutral - it is neither here nor there. When you see the results as positive you are happy to praise yourselves for your efforts. But when you view the results as negative you generally look for extenuating circumstances to apportion blame in directions other than your own, so you don't look so foolish in your own eyes, and especially in the eyes of others.

Taking responsibility isn't just about the good times! In fact the bad times are the best because you can learn so much from them about yourselves. You fear taking absolute responsibility for your lives and will deny that responsibility if your fears and insecurities are particularly great. But whether you the individual like it or not, you need to understand that you are 100% responsible for your lives - that includes every thought you have, every word you express and every action you take. **Responsibility is nothing to be scared of.** Rather, it is self-empowering, and unlike the false sense of control and security that is derived from manipulating other human beings. Being 100% responsible teaches each of you as a species to trust completely in yourselves. **Now isn't that great news, 100% responsible?**

You can start becoming more responsible by becoming 100% honest with yourself. Take the time to find out about yourself: **Examine your strengths and your weaknesses.** Improve on what you dislike about yourself and refine what you do like. **All too often, human beings are too busy forming opinions about everybody else, yet fail to see the reality of themselves. It doesn't matter what anyone else does with their life, and more often than not, it's none of your business.** Likewise, what someone else thinks about you or your decisions is of no importance, unless of course you allow yourself to be influenced by biased opinions. What is most important is how you choose to live your life and that you feel good about your decisions - even if they do backfire sometimes. **Take the good with the bad, and learn from it all. The so called good and bad, is what give you the understanding to grow in Consciousness, beyond the so called good and bad that is a part of all of life's journey.**

You give away your personal responsibility in many ways. The biggest offender is not being willing to make your own decisions. Many of you allow others to make your decisions for you, or you allow the opinions of others to colour your decision making for fear that you will make the wrong decision. **But what happens if things don't turn out the way you foresaw?** You can't blame your advisor - they only gave advice, but you made the decision to act on it. You also give away your Personal Responsibility by blindly following trends or adopting beliefs. Just because someone in your street has bought a caravan, does not necessarily mean you have to have one too. And just because someone believes daylight saving will fade their curtains doesn't necessarily mean it is correct...

Forget about keeping up with trends, forget about what other human beings believe. Stop and evaluate the negative and positives of a situation in respect to your own personal needs, not because another human being is doing it, thinking it, or believing it. **That is what being 100% responsible is all about.** Each of you as human beings holds the power of change to be 100% responsible in showing not only you, but everyone else **you are a leader not a follower.**

Can you stop and think for a moment, if every human being could realise at the same moment, they are indeed 100% responsible for every thought and action, there would be a leap in human Consciousness, in 7 billion humans at the same moment. Just realise dear human beings there would be no **"FEAR"** so there would be no need for Wars, Violence, of any description of any sort. **That realisation in itself would change how all human beings Think.** In all truth, is that not a beautiful thing, many would say, live in the real world, but my answer to that dear Sisters and Brothers of Earth. **You are the Creators of whatever is happening on your planet, only you can stop and change what is, it's called accepting your Responsibly as an Infinite being of Light. Be blessed always in love.**

THE TRUE SPIRIT OF CHRISTMAS (NO-66)

To your own human calendar, you now call the 21ˢᵗ century of human time, it's hard to believe that the true Spirit of Christmas can exist. In a world experiencing civil unrest, environmental degradation, war and famine, economic depression and the stress of simply trying to get by on an average human wage which doesn't reflect the rising cost of living around you. The expectation of Christmas which you feel from your human families and friends just seems to add to the frustration of the whole thing. **Why is this so?**

Christmas in the Christian Western world is meant to be about goodwill, love and family. It is symbolised by the birth of a human child bringing hope and the opportunity of a new beginning to humanity. How quickly you forget the meaning of Christmas when you rush around as Christmas looms ever nearer, trying to get those perfect gifts for the family, and then on the day rushing around some more making sure the food is perfect, the table setting is perfect, the tree is perfect. **While many family get-together and end up strained as members tolerate relatives they didn't really want to see. Christmas can leave a hollow, empty feeling inside, which is very sad, because Christmas is an opportunity to let go of the past and grow as a human being, beyond the past conditioning that many hold onto, some wright throughout their human life.**

Many human beings always seem to refer to Christmas as the **"Pagan Festival of Shop Owners"**, mainly because of the retail industry's blatant commercialism obliterating the true meaning of Christmas with media hype and emotional blackmail. Each year many of you fall victim to clever advertising and purchase gifts way beyond a reasonable budget, leaving you more stressed in the New Year! **You been conditioned into believing that something expensive will be more appreciated by your family or friends?**

It seems that so many human beings look at Christmas as a time to receive and give presents, to eat and drink heaps, and to have a holiday. **This is one**

aspect of Christmas you all enjoy. But while you distract yourselves with the pleasures of Christmas you avoid issues which could make Christmas a truly special experience which can bring families closer together and resolve the pains of the past. **Perhaps the most precious gift you as individuals can give to anyone at Christmas, whether a human child or a human adult, is the gift of Unconditional Love and understanding.** To spend some precious moments together, play games, laugh, just to allow you the human individual to be who you truly are beyond all beliefs, all conditioning. Not to live in the expectations of what each of you have created?

As the baby Jesus symbolises love, compassion and understanding for all, so every child in every family is that symbol of hope and love - this is the Spirit of Christmas. It doesn't have to be Christmas for you to recognise that, with the gift of Unconditional Love given daily, you can be sure to raise families built on a foundation of caring, wisdom and unity and help make the world a better place to live in. **Christmas in all Universes, is not based on giving expensive presents, it's about the coming together of families and friends to celebrate a union of Love and Friendship, that all of life is so Precious in every space and every atom of this vastness that every species call's home. It worth a thought, is it not?**

WHAT IS TRUTH? (NO-67)

Throughout human history human individuals have pursued the quest for truth, enlightenment, inner peace and tranquillity; a quest which becomes for many a lifelong challenge to find understanding within their human existence. When human beings become disillusioned with their lives, for whatever reason, be it financial, emotional, political, environmental, or religious, they begin to seek truth and purpose through alternative, non-mainstream paths. While their friends and family fail to understand the desire which drives a human individual to seek out a new form of truth in order to provide meaning and stability to an otherwise empty and unfulfilling human life. **Those of you who have already travelled down that road, and are still travelling on it, sympathise and hold out a welcoming and reassuring hand to assist your fellow Souls in their journey towards self-discovery.**

For many Westerners, ancient Pagan and Eastern philosophies provide some kind of understanding to an existence which your mainstream Western religious counterparts seem unable to satisfy. Pagan and Eastern philosophies seem to provide more of an explanation on the part you all play both physically and spiritually, on your planet, and in your universe. They place importance on finding **inner peace and harmony,** and encouraged to a certain extent the finding of each individual's **inner truth and life path.** Gurus and spiritual teachers of these philosophies have always played an important role in helping the seeker find their inner source of enlightenment and wisdom, and most importantly, **their inner truth.**

Truth is perhaps one of the most difficult concepts to define because truth in human terms can be very subjective, and from human to human that truth is coloured by the level of their thinking, their emotions, their social conditioning and of course their life's experiences. For human beings, not one human beings truth is the same as another's for the very reasons listed above.

Truth is confined to the boundaries of your own self-created beliefs. If you as a human being follow a belief system created by someone else then you are also accepting the limitations of their understanding by

making those limitations your own. **When you adopt beliefs which you have not necessarily experienced for yourselves, you also accept the conditioning which those beliefs bring with them.**

This is why mainstream religions are still so powerful today on your Earth and are experiencing a resurgence all over your world. **Ask most humans if they can honestly say they have experienced personal contact with your created God, and they will say 'no'.** So how can they know that God does in fact exist? Out of fear of being rejected by their peers, or a fear of being persecuted by their society, many accept the notion of God because everyone else does. **But many have not experienced for themselves the truth of whether or not your created God exists.**

Within the confines of a belief system it is very difficult to find truth. No guru or religious teacher can give you truth, as it is only their truth, and you don't know if their truth has actually been experienced by them, or if it is simply a belief system they have adopted from which they are now preaching. Most of you at times throughout your human life fall into the trap of adopting a point of view on a matter because your friend, partner or parent holds that view. But how many will investigate and deduce for yourselves the truth of that view? Many human beings find it easier to adopt a belief than to take responsibility for their belief, even when they don't completely agree with what they are supporting. This often happens with guru worship or religious fanaticism. **Because of fears and insecurities human beings look for something to believe in, when they should be believing in themselves first. They should be believing in their own abilities to find their truth from within.**

Real truth can only be experienced by the human individual from within. Truth is your understanding of your life's experiences, coloured by your fears and beliefs, and governed by your emotions and level of understanding. Unless someone else has had that same experience, it cannot be anyone else's truth, and even if they have had that particular experience, it still is not identical to anyone else's, as each of you interprets an event in your own unique way. **So truth in reality, only exists within each of you, not the masse.**

You can learn from each other's truths by using those truths as a guide. Unfortunately, clutching to your personal belief systems prevents you from keeping an open mind towards other truths, at the same time stifling your personal growth and Consciousness advancement. **While belief systems may be safe, they place boundaries and limitations on you, especially if you don't allow yourselves to go beyond those boundaries. Personal growth can only occur if you are willing to put aside your belief systems in order to explore and attempt to understand other views, for in another's truth you may find a deeper understanding of yourself, and you may indeed discover a wisdom & enlightenment you were unaware of.** So to grow consciously, you first need to have an honest heart and especially an open mind, and be free of fear of change?

The search for truth and meaning in life is a journey which brings you the human individual closer to the essence of yourselves. **When you can accept and trust who you are, your truth will emerge, revealing the inner knowing that the answers and knowledge you seek are ultimately within all of you, not outside of you, amongst all the distractions of human life.** May love fill you're very being dear Sisters and Brothers of this most precious Earth all of you call home.

HEALING WITH THE LIGHT (NO-68)

Have you ever wanted to be a healer? Or wished that you had healing hands, or healing abilities? **I'd like to let you in on a little secret – all human beings are already healers!** You don't have to go and spend great amounts of money; and don't let anyone fool you into believing that if you were a healer in a past life, you won't be one this time around. The knowledge you obtain in your current life will be in your cellular memory and you can bring forth this knowledge into your current life, meditation is one of the best ways of opening yourself up to your inner knowing. There are so many different ways of meditation, seek, and your higher self will show the way.

One of the things I must point out about being a healer, there are no rules, and neither do you need bells rung in your ears or your head ceremoniously tapped to supposedly open your channel for healing powers. Being a spiritual healer is very easy, all you need is Unconditional Love in your heart and the desire to be true to yourself, in fact most humans beings do healing without even knowing it on daily basis. **Basically, when you are doing a healing, it is simply a transference of energy, because energy is everything, and everything is energy, as humans beings, you are 99.9% energy, around 76% water and less than 0.1% physical matter.**

All healing in all universe's uses the same source of energy and as you begin to allow yourselves to understand this process that all healing is in fact done automatically. For example, when a human child is upset, a parent will either give it a cuddle or touch it to comfort or console their little one – **this is healing.** Such a basic example shows that all human mothers are in fact healers as all human males are healers, and so many humans beings do healing every day without even being aware of it.

Let's look at the **human aura,** we see that it is an energy field two to three meters in an egg shape form, this is an average in the human population, your **human aura** continually changers in size and colour, it is because of your emotions and your feelings at any given moment. As you mingle with other humans you are walking through parts of their **aura,** just by doing this, you are picking up and exchanging energies from other humans, **be**

it negative or positive. That is why when you go into a shopping centre you can and do come out feeling worse than when you went in. **Energy is transferred instantaneously, let's say if someone needs a healing, they can and do get one without either party involved necessarily knowing.**

It is important to understand that you can exchange energy this way as it is done every moment in human time, because this will explain why you can or may feel drained, tired and head-achy after a shopping expedition. Just think for a moment, all those **auras** and emotional states locked in the one complex or building, it is no wonder that positive humans come out feeling ill, and even negative, or unwell humans come out feeling revived. **Those with negativity (negativity meaning unresolved emotion, illness, heavy smoking and alcohol consumption present in there aura, etc.)** have just dumped their luggage onto unsuspecting human, and exchanged it for an energy boast!

How does knowing this help you with spiritual healing? It gives you a deeper understanding that you the human individual are in fact "light beings", or energy manifested into a physical body and you can use this energy whenever you choose to, because it's free, no one can ever stop you, so as humans you help boost each other's energies should they be depleted for whatever reason. **No one in reality can teach you to be a healer, because you already are one, but they can help guide you in using your own natural abilities without your being drained and ill from the experience.**

Technicalities of Spiritual Healing

Before you rush off excitedly to do healings, you need to understand something about dis'ease and illness. On a spiritual level, human dis'ease does not exist, even though on a physical level you the human individual recognize it. So this statement I am about to express be most important, when you go out to do a healing, **NEVER RECOGNIZE THE DIS'EASE,** why you may ask? **Because human dis'ease is an individual's creation based on unresolved emotion.** Let's look at the vicious circle: let's say you have a negative emotion, such as self- hatred, and you reinforce it by punishing yourself. The best way to punish yourself is to feed the emotion, you then end up putting food into your human bodies that is harmful to you. **What happens next?** Your immunity system breaks down due to poor nutritive value of your diet, and you end up with illness. Your illness makes you feel worse emotionally, so you continue to despise yourself; and it goes around again and again.

To recognize dis'ease when healing, is to deal with it only on a physical level. To not recognize it is to realise that the human being has created their own dilemma from not dealing with something in there past. **Spiritual healing transfers energy to be utilized on a spiritual level – that is, to help the human being dissolve the emotion behind the dis'ease.** When this is achieved, illness has no choice but to dissolve also. Healing the Spirit rather than just dealing with the obvious. Traditional western medicine encourages human beings to cut out cancerous growth, but this procedure does not ensure that it will not recur.

Spiritual healing assists the physical healing process by assisting the Spirit within to look at why it was created in the first place, when you fully realise that you as the human being are in reality 99.9% pure energy, over 70 % water, less than 1% of physical matter, you will than truly begin to understand how to dissolve the emotion attached to that creation of dis'ease or illness. As spiritual healers you need to be prepared to offer support to the ones who are going through the healing process with love and understanding. Be sympathetic, but don't feel sorry for them in such a way as to make the person feel a failure, rather, seek to assist them in getting to the heart of the problem they are faced with.

Cleansing and Protection

Before embarking on a healing on yourself or others, it is vital to cleanse and protect yourself. Cleansing is most important, for if you have had a hectic day and have been inundated with negativity, you need to remove that negativity from your **own aura.** Otherwise that negative energy will be passed on to the human being receiving the healing, making the whole exercise of healing redundant. **This also has to be done if you are doing several healings in a row.** Please, always take the time to cleanse yourself between healings sessions. You do not want to pass on negative energies from the previous humans to the following humans receiving the healing. Cleansing can be done in two ways.

Preferably do both, but in the instance where you cannot cleanse in the way described in the **first method,** cleanse yourself using the **second method** before each healing.

1-Have a shower to wash of the pollution of the day. As you stand there and cleanse yourself physically, visualize that the water cascading down upon you is a **beam of white light** cleansing your spiritual body. See the negativity as dirt and grime being washed down the plug hole. Than see yourself as a pure and clean vessel. **I must say this,** your thoughts are the power of all that you are, as you think, you become, every thought that you think about can be manifested into your own reality, you are **living consciousness,** you are a part of all that is, and all that is, is a part of you, you are infinite, always keep that in mind and you will never feel alone. Now mentally reinforce this by saying **"I am cleansed of all negative energies."** Always dress in clean clothes after your cleansing shower, as clothes which have been worn before carry negative energies.

If it is inappropriate to cleanse yourself using the method described above, this simple visualization technique is very effective. Visualize a beam of white light pouring down all around your **aura,** feel it cleansing any negative energies from within you and around you, allow it to pile down at the base of your feet. Than see the Earth open up beneath you to reveal a cavity of about **40 feet/ 15 meters in depth,** and send that debris down into the earth. Ask Mother Earth to accept this energy so that it may be used for her highest good, then thank Mother Earth, and close up the hole. **Reinforce mentally that you are cleansed, as in the first method.** Proceed with white light protection. **Protection is as simple as saying "I am Light."** See a protective shield of white light surrounding your human body. Again, reinforce mentally that you are protected, and that any negative energies cannot penetrate your protective shield. Believe that you are protected, and you will be, that is self- empowerment. **Always remember thought is energy, therefore thought creates.**

Opening the Channel

Again, this is a very important step in spiritual healing, you need to open your channel to transmit cosmic energy. If you don't, you will end up using your own energies in healing. Never use your own energies for healing; always bring in universal energy by opening up your channel. **Using your energies will leave you drained and tired.** The universe is abundant and infinite; not utilizing what is there to be used is to be somewhat foolhardy, and in the end you may become sick yourself, and that is not a responsible healer. **Too many human beings who claim to be healers are not taking Personal Responsibility by opening their channel and to bring down universal energy.**

This results in their becoming sick and decrepit, and possibly even resulting in terminal illness by their continually giving away their energies. It is a wonderful thing to do a healing, but how can you help heal others when you are in need of healing yourself? **Drawing on cosmic energy for healing is taking personal responsibility, it is also recognizing that you are only the instrument, not the one who heals.** Opening the channel can be done in several ways. You can open your channel by simply saying **"I am an open channel ready to transmit cosmic energy for healing purposes."** Or you can visualize a ball of white light coming up from the Earth, moving up the centre of your spine **(through your chakras)** and out the top of your head, then shooting up and connecting with the outer universe.

I personally have always liked to visually open my channel, by opening each chakra as I move upwards, connecting with the outer universe, and finally, mentally confirming that I am an open channel and an instrument for divine healing. So once you have cleansed, protected yourself and opened your channel, you are ready to begin. Remember, you may feel a little awkward to begin with, **that's okay,** the more you do, the more confident you will become. It is also advisable that the human receiving the healing **(in a hands – on situation)** cleanse, protects and opens themselves too. This will intensify the healing experience and if they are not sure how to do this you can guide them through it.

<u>Channelling the Light</u>

The best way to describe healing energy is as **"Light"** by sending light with loving intention, powerful energy can be transmitted to those in need. If you are doing a hands-on healing, visualize white light pouring down into you via your own channel, which is connected to the universe. See it flowing into you, and out through your hands **(fingers closed, hands slightly cupped)** and into the recipient. If you are doing an absent healing, channel the energy and pass it through your hands and heart centre, to the human or humans requiring healing. It is also useful for the recipient to visualize energy pouring in from the universe down there channel too. Again, this intensifies the healing experience.

Hands on Healing

There seems to be a misconception regarding hands- on healing when it comes to where to place the hands. It needs to be made clear that one need not place their hands on an affected area. **An appropriate analogy would be of the humble aspirin.** If you have a pain in your knee you do not place the aspirin on your knee, or wash it with a dilution of aspirin. **Instead, you ingest the tablet.** It circulates through the blood stream and takes effect wherever it is needed. **Spiritual healing is the same.** Energy is passed through the instrument **(healer)** to the recipient, and is utilized as needed. **Unfortunately, this belief that one must place their hands on the affected area has encouraged certain humans to abuse the trust that is placed in them by those seeking healing.**

Respecting the dignity of the human, being healed is most essential. Skin connect is not at all necessary; placing hands on the genital area, or a women breasts is not necessary. Popularised healing practices and beliefs have a lot to answer for in the case of human women who have literally been molested by so-called **"healers".** You could say that those humans have placed themselves in that position; but when you place your trust in someone, and do not fully understand the process of spiritual healing, **it is easy to be fooled by a charlatan.** All that is required in hands-on healing is for the hands **(fingers closed, lightly cupped)** to be gently placed on the human shoulders, and energy flows through. **Energy does not require physical contact. It is infinite energy, all around you every moment of your existence, you as human beings are made up of this energy.**

Absent Healing

This kind of healing is equally simple. All this means is that the recipient is not physically present to receive the healing personally. Verbal permission is not necessary the Spirit of who they are will automatically accept the love and light that you send, even if physically the human rejects it. **Often a photograph is used in absent healing.** This is not essential, but is a good way of building confidence in the initial stages of sending such healing. If you do not have a photo, a full name will suffice or an image of them in your mind.

Names have their own particular vibration, and again if you do not have a name, then an association with someone will help make the connection. For example, **"Alison's friend"**. The connection with Alison is enough for the healing to find its way to the human in need. Simply visualize this and send them **love and light,** or surround them visually with light, projecting from your heart centre. By projecting **love and light** from the heart one human being can send healing to a million human beings, you as an individual can help heal a nation if your intention was true of heart. **That is how powerful spiritual healing is; it is pure energy with the right intention.**

Closing Down

Upon completion of the healing process, it is necessary to close down the channel. This means the closing down of your chakras and linking channel to protect you from attracting unnecessary negativity. **Both the healer and the one being healed need to do this.** If your centres remain open you are susceptible to psychic attack; consequently your energies will be drained and all that good work will have been wasted. To close down simply visualize a large white sheet above your head, bring it down, and as you wrap it tightly around yourself say **"I am closed down, so I may travel home in safety"**. Or **"so I will not attract undue negativity**'. This is also very good to do before you go out to a shopping centre, or anywhere where there are many humans in close proximity to you. You do not need to take on anyone else's emotions or negative energies. **Try and do this before you leave home, and reinforce the white light by saying ("I am Light") while you are out, it truly works, if you have the right intention.**

One Final Word

As I mention in part 1, you as human beings are infinite in all things, the two most powerful words in all universes are **LOVE and FORGIVENESS,** if you have love in your heart you can forgive yourself and others, but where there is no love there is no forgiveness, and the power of that statement is within every human being. The choice is always yours, it always has been and always will be, **it's all in your thinking- is it not.** To send love and healing to those in need is a wonderful gesture, in essence spiritual healing is very simple. Happy Healing beautiful human beings, trust and always believe in yourself.

ELEMENTALS AND CELESTIAL BEINGS (NO-69)

There is a need to express on the Elemental world and Celestial Beings, the vibration that these beings exist in is called the fourth dimension, as you the human being vibrate at a different frequency that is the main reason you cannot see them. Yet there are some human beings who can and do see and communicate with them. All it takes is an open mind and heart, and the willingness to raise your own Consciousness to higher vibrations.

The Elementals live all over your planet Earth, in the forests, on mountains, within the Earth and its waters, even on clouds. You will not see the Elementals where humans have destroyed the natural environment of the Mother Earth. **For example,** you will not find them in densely populated cities full of human negativity or places devoid of plant life. Those Elementals that live on the surface of Mother Earth make their homes within the trees and forest vines, and the ones you call fairies live within flowers.

Elementals are not destructive like human beings. They work with nature, not against her. They can be given the honour of being called the only environmentally friendly beings on Mother Earth, and yet my Being must express that some human beings are beginning to see the benefits of working with nature in a natural way.

There is no death or decay in their world. Their vibration is rotating at a higher frequency compared to the human third dimension of physical matter. There are no rotting leaves or dead trees. There is no variation in temperature from hot to cold – you could say the weather is perfect. **When it rains they do not feel the water as humans do. To the Element world it is a shower of energy created by nature, by Creation.**

Elementals being not of dense physical matter, have no need for physical food. They do consume and digest energy as if it were food, but they are very respectful towards all life. Elementals ask the permission of Mother Earth and of the plant when they wish to take a leaf or flower petal to replenish their energies. They know everything is energy, and the object they consume merely dissolves into energy in their mouths.

Elementals can best be described as childlike and innocent in character, yet extremely wise. They do have a touch of Ego, as they are a part of humanity's energies. Sometimes they do mimic humans. **However, their Ego is not vindictive or spiteful like their human counterparts.** There is no violence or hatred in their vibration. Elementals do not become angry with each other, but can and do become annoyed. As quickly as they become annoyed, they resolve the issue and are best friends again.

The Elementals were created by the Spirit of Mother Earth, by living Consciousness through the essence of Creations Totality. **They are the workers who help keep the balance on Earth.** There are Elements who desperately want to experience a physical incarnation. These one's can be quite mischievous. **Like humans, there are small number of Elementals who are misguided by their Egos, yet nowhere near as many as there are misguided humans.**

The Elementals are happy in nature and laugh and dance a lot. Their existence can be quite simple, very creative and joyous in all they do. They are truly enchanted, and here lies the message they have been trying to communicate to humans all along.

Unfortunately, as humans become more and more destructive, they close themselves off from other vibrations such as the Elementals. These little beings with enormous Spirits have become disillusioned and distrusting of humans. The Elementals and the vital work they do upon and within Mother Earth is of great importance, for it is these beings who help keep the balance of nature. Without them your Earth would have been destroyed many of your Earthly years ago. Humanity has a lesson still to learn about nature and how there is so much more to existence than the physical vibration of dense matter. Humanity is but a small spark of existence in the vastness of the universe.

The negativity of humanity in the Element Kingdom would be devastating. For that very reason the Elementals have closely guarded the secret entry to their world, their homes. They offer Knowledge/ Wisdom that is sadly lacking in the human species, only those of a

gentle nature with an open mind and loving heart, who cherish all forms of life no matter what form they may be and have a pure heart of unconditional love.

All of the Elementals can communicate verbally, and quite often they communicate in this way with a number of human beings who seek the knowledge and understanding of working with nature. However, with each other they prefer to communicate telepathically, which to them is of less effort to do so. **The Elementals are known to you as the elements of Fire, Water, Air, Earth and Spirit.** They are the essence of their vibration as well as of the human world of dense matter. **Look at it this way, you exist in a world where everything is of physical matter, the world you as humans live in is third dimensional, without the five (5) elements of Fire, Water, Air, Earth and Spirit you as humans would not exist.**

The Elementals do wear rustic style clothing in the colours of forest greens, browns and yellows. The fairies wear the colours of the flowers they represent. I will give some examples of different Elements.

Deva

The average height of a Deva is around 1.2 meters. They have elongated heads with a long nose and chin, and they have round eyes that are either green or brown in colour. Their bodies are normally hairy with rough brown skin, and seemly out of proportion with their stocky build and barrel – like middles. But they have bandy legs and arms, knobbly knees, and some even have muscle definition. **Some Deva are in communication with what most humans refer to as Aliens.**

Goblins

The average height of a Goblin is around 45cm from head to toe. Their heads are slightly larger than their bodies, and they have large eyes the colour of the night sky. Their eyes are deep – set into their faces, and their faces are almost square in shape. Their bodies are slightly hairy with dark brown skin. Their arms and legs are thin, but some do have muscle definition. Some do not have hair on their heads and would be what you would call bald. A Goblin's body is not barrel shaped like the Deva's.

Goblins are very agile and can move at the speed of light, from one vibration to another vibration.

Elves

Elves can be of various heights. Anything up to one metre tall. They have thin bodies which have no muscle definition. They can be likened to what are referred to on your Earth as Leprechauns, although Leprechauns and their pots of gold are an invention of human imagination – **they do not in reality exist.** Elves have very fine skin which is yellowish in colour. They have no hair on their bodies, not even on their heads. They generally have large ears, but some do not, and they have elongated heads with narrow faces and almond shaped eyes that are either luminous green or a faint blue colour.

Fairies

Fairies are often distinguished as a glowing ball of coloured light, about three centimetres in diameter. However, they can appear any size up to that of an adult human, but this takes a great deal of energy and effort. Fairies have very fine slender builds and white skin. Their hair colour and that of the clothes they wear depends on which plant or flower they are associated with. Their faces are perhaps closest to humans than all the other Elementals, and their eyes can be any colour of the rainbow.

Yowies

The Yowies, also known as Yetis and Big Foot, are known by the race on your Earth called the Aboriginals. The Yowies once lived upon the surface of the Earth, but now exist within Mother Earth. Their average height is **2.1 to 2.3 meters** and they have thickly set builds with short haired, almost furry bodies. Yowies have large deep set eyes, red in colour as a result of adapting in total darkness, but in which they see perfectly clearly. When the Yowies roamed the Earth's surface, their eyes were brown. A Yowies head is broad and elongated with a long nose and chin area, and small ears. Yowies have hands with fingers and feet with toes similar to humans. Like all Elementals, they are able to move between their vibration and the physical vibration very easily, and very quickly.

Many humans throughout your history have seen Yowies when they have been perfectly still. However, once a Yowie begins to move, it immediately vanishes into its own vibration. That is why their world is safe. **Humans cannot enter into their world.** They are a very gentle species. They have no weapons nor any form of technology, yet they are very aware of different vibrations. **Yowies have been in connect with Aliens for hundreds of your Earthly years and can communicate telepathically even though they can speak to another being in any Earthly language.**

Celestial Beings

We are in reality all celestial beings, living in different dimensions or vibrations, our thinking governs our level of understanding, and as we all grow consciously, our energies vibrate to higher frequencies, which in turn, allows us as an individual or a species to evolve beyond our present state of consciousness. **A celestial being can be better described as a Spark of Consciousness that is light, or energy.** Humanity tends to refer to these beings as Aliens, and consider them to be of a higher form of intelligence to themselves. There are many types of Celestial beings. Following is a description of two types known to humanity. **These are the Greys and the Blues.**

The Greys

These beings can exist in the fourth dimension as well as the third. They are of a physical form, but less dense in matter than humans, they have no body fat like humans, and there are over 2,000 different races of Greys, just as there are different races of humans. They are called Greys because of the pale yellow/ white/ grey colour of their skin.

Their different races vary in height from 60 centimetres to 100 centimetres with a solid build, to 100 centimetres to 120 centimetres with a slender build. Some are over 180 centimetres tall with either a slender or dense build. **Like humans they come in all shapes and sizes.** Most of them have male and female gender, **but some are androgynous.**

The Greys mostly communicate verbally, however some are highly evolved and communicate telepathically. They consume food and fluids, some breathing air- like substances as they have adapted to their respective atmospheres. There are Greys that have evolved beyond the physical form, meaning they have no need for a flesh body, and therefore have no need for food or fluid. **They simply utilise the cosmic energies that are around them.**

Some of their race are not physically strong. Humans can be two to three times stronger than some of the lesser evolved races of Greys, and these ones also have much weaker immune systems than humans, as a result they find Earth's various bacteria a hazard to their health. They have no emotions like humans **(although they did once long ago)** and as such, they find humans particularly fascinating. The Greys have been visiting Earth and other planets similar to Earth for thousands of years.

The Greys travel in physical ships, but because they also travel in the fourth dimension, humans rarely see them. Only when they enter the human vibration can humans actually see them or find evidence of their visitations. Their ships travel by converting cosmic energy into usable form for propulsion. **They create a gravity field both internally and externally throughout their ships.**

The two force fields counteracting each other enables them to manoeuvre quickly without so much as feeling a sudden change in direction. If they did not have these force fields, the occupants inside of the ships would be slammed up against the inner walls and would be killed instantly from the sheer force of the speeds at which they travel.

Their ships can and do travel at the speed of light. When the Greys transport between their ships and a planet's surface, they use an energy beam of light to travel back and forth. This energy field cuts through the planet's gravity and allow easy transportation of any object regardless of weight or size. This is how humans are abducted and returned to Earth. Most abducted humans are taken during their sleep time and returned before they wake up, and most never have any memory of the abduction.

Abductions by the Greys are well documented throughout your history, and supported by humans who have come forward with stories of their experiences. The Greys use their energy transport beam to abduct humans as well as animals from Earth, which they have been doing for hundreds of your Earthly years, if not thousands of your years.

Others have been taken while fully conscious, but cannot fight the paralysing effects of their energy beam. As the Greys realise the physical strength of humans, they can increase the effect of the beam to prevent their subjects escaping. **It must be pointed out that those who have been abducted have given their permission to be taken from another level of consciousness, but that is also no excuse.** The Greys are scientists and explorers, and in many ways reflect the character of humans.

The Blues

Having no need for a physical body in their existence, the Blues are unlimited beings of light. They can choose to incarnate into a human form if they wish to experience a human life, or have a specific task to fulfil. What is most interesting is that all **Celestial Beings** are your Brothers and Sisters who only try to assist in the evolution of humanity. However, human Ego and insecurity interfere in the need to prove how much more superior one nation is to another, preventing the human individual, nations, in fact your entire world from stepping beyond the Ego of humanity.

The Blues communicate entirely through telepathy, it makes sense that to be a telepath one would not need ears or a mouth and therefore not require air or lungs, and having no need for such organs and appendages, there is no need for a flesh body to feed.

The Blues are so called because of the bluish energy that beams around their being. This is recorded in your human history, as seen and communicated by human beings around your world. The Blues can present themselves in various forms which humans would find acceptable. **For example, they may take on a humanoid appearance simply so as not to alarm the human being they are making contact with.**

Being of pure energy, or light bodies, they have no specific form or species as the Greys do. Rather, they have different levels of Consciousness which identify them and the dimension which they come from, and exist within. **They also have no gender but again can present their being in a form as male or female to make their contact with humans easier and acceptable.**

The Blues are highly evolved beings and do not possess Ego, emotions or negativity. They simply emit unconditional love. Their sole purpose is to express knowledge for the higher good of all beings in existence. Some have had human or other incarnations, but they have evolved spiritually beyond the lower vibrations of the need of the Ego. The Ego has its purpose in all life, but there comes a moment in time when the Ego has no more purpose, especially when an individual grows beyond the emotion, no longer affected by passed experiences, when you as humans beings come from the heart centre and live in Unconditional Love for your own being as well as all life forms, you no longer need the human Ego nor the emotions that are attached to it, you become a feeling being, no longer an emotional being.

The Blues travel in ships of light. These ships are energy in its purest form, created through the manifestation of thoughts, and are operated entirely by thought. There are no physical components, nor any form of physical matter in their ships, **Therefore the name "Light Ships".**

When transporting from their ships to the surface of a planet, be it a physical planet or to a non-physical realm in a different dimension, the Blues think it and they are there. Whatever they think becomes their reality. These beings can also project themselves in many places at once without leaving their ships. They can literally be in many places at once. They are living Consciousness, not individuals as humans are, yet they can think as individuals or **as collective consciousness.** They exist in a timeless moment, and unlike some of the Greys species, they will not interfere in the evolution of any civilisation. They will try to guide whenever and wherever possible if one is willing to listen to the inner voice that is present in all human beings, as it is within all Universes.

The Blues can also enter the human vibration of physical matter by making a conscious connection with a human being who has consciously chosen to vacate their human body. For whatever reason, an agreement is made between the two entities. **The being who comes is known as a walk-in, and must complete the karma of the being who is vacating the body. It must be stressed that this exchange is of the free will of both entities. One is not forced out by the other.**

The walk-in will then take on the identity and life of the being who vacated. That life becomes the **walk-in's** responsibility. When the **walk-in** has become accustomed to the limitations of physical life, and has gained a greater understanding of physical life and completes the **karma** of the vacating being's life, they will be activated to bring forth certain knowledge for the greater good of that civilisation in order to assist with its evolution.

When the **walk-in** first enters the human body they have no memory of their past existence so it will not interfere with the completion of the **karma** and their mission. **Once they have been activated however, some can discover the reality of their inner being and the fact that they chose to become a walk-in.**

Walk-ins are beings who volunteer, just as the beings who walk-out are also volunteering to vacate their bodies, so that the civilisation they enter can be helped to evolve with the knowledge these being express. There is so much more my Being can express on the Blues and Greys, maybe in another book. My being will leave you the reader, the seeker with this expression.

Are you physical or are you living consciousness, Is it simply that you the human individual have been conditioned into believing that all you are is physical. The power of truth lies within every human being, when you stop the chatter of your human brain, meditate in the stillness of your mind, you learn to be in the moment. **You begin to experience the nothingness, and in the nothingness that's where all truth is found, remember everything is energy and energy is everything.**

To step beyond who you are is to step into the unknown. It is in the unknown that your journey for knowledge will give you the human individual what your heart is truly seeking.

CHANNELLING EXPLAINED (NO-70)

We the **Nar'Karones** express the light of Creation's totality to every human being that exists on your most precious Earth and each of you call home. As there is a great interest in the word **"Channelling"** my being will talk of it in more depth.

Most human beings have heard of **channelling** not many truly understand the spiritual concept and the reality of what **channelling** is. Channelling has many levels of Consciousness and awareness. **Most human beings understand channelling to be what is most commonly referred to as "Trance Channelling".**

In Spiritual terms **channelling** is any means used to transmit or access information from beyond the human physical plane. Realise in this moment dear Human Beings, that every one of you is a channel. **Human beings channel every day of their life, but most are not aware of it.** A familiar form of channelling is clairvoyant readings, but other forms of channelling include writing music or literature, all forms of artistic expression including painting, sculpting, acting, as well as healing with natural remedies and modern medicine, and even scientific discoveries for humanities benefit. **Inspiration and creativity, whether artistic, technical or scientific, channelling can be used in all areas of human life.**

Think for a moment, have you the individual ever had a brilliant idea suddenly pop into your head, seemingly out of nowhere? That is indeed a form of channelling, but unfortunately not many human beings act upon or listen to these ideas. Spirit is always trying to communicate with human beings, in so many different ways, but you may need to listen more closely to your thoughts, your inner self, to raise your own vibration in order to help you receive knowledge from your **spirit world.**

Living with stress each day in your human world, can and does disconnect you the individual, not only from your true self or as some would say your higher self, but prevents you from connecting to higher vibrations, **so what is the answer,** taking some time out for you to just relax. To become peaceful in the moment and by becoming peaceful is to connect with yourself, your inner self, and through meditation you will find it much easier to receive information from **spirit world.**

When you are in a peaceful place, and an idea appears out of nowhere, it means that you have actually allowed yourself to forget your physical existence for a moment or two, long enough to make the connection that will enable you to **listen to your spirit guides.** You are being given ideas, information and knowledge, which you have in reality channelled, to act upon in any way you feel.

If you the individual do not act upon this divine inspiration, the opportunity may pass you by, and Spirit may or will give it to another human being, but again the more you open yourself up to higher vibrations, the more opportunity's will come your way, it is all governed by **"The Law of Attraction" that is how the Universal Mind works, it is the same in all Universes.** The purpose of life is to progress consciousness. Spirit who are helping humanity grow consciously will keep trying to communicate with more than one human being until someone hears the message and acts upon it.

Trance channelling is somewhat different form of communication. It is more direct. Trance channelling is a method used by Spirit to verbally or physically communicate with human beings on the physical plane, **(the third dimension).** You as individuals may ask how this works. The medium or channel permits the spirit guide to use the medium's human body as a vehicle for communication.

Trance channelling is most often used in meditation circles. There are three levels of trance channelling- **Light Trance, Medium Trance and Deep Trance.** In light trance the medium is totally aware during the experience and will have complete memory of it when they return to their body. The medium only partially vacates their human body allowing the channelled Spirit to partially step in. The channelled Spirit uses voice- box of the medium to communicate with the circle members in the room, and messages and knowledge are given directly by the channelled spirit via the voice-box, or messages and knowledge can be passed on to the medium who will then verbally communicate the information to the circle members.

In medium trance the medium has completely vacated their body, but is nearby in spirit whilst the channelled spirit is completely within the human body, and has full control of it. Then the medium, although out of their body, is totally experiencing the non- physical environment and is having full awareness of the experience. Meanwhile the channelled Spirit is experiencing the physical world of dense matter by sitting within a human body. However, because the channelled Spirit is not used to be in a physical body of dense matter, it will not have as much control of the body as a human being normally has. This takes practice to accomplish, as it took you to accomplish as a baby to learn to crawl, talk and walk for example, but it would not take as long as it does a child because much of the physical learning of the body has already occurred and is programmed within the human brain.

In deep trance the medium completely vacates the human body, and the channelled spirit completely enters the human body, and has complete control. The channelled Spirit communicates via the voice-box, but with some adjusting over a period of human time it can produce a voice of their own. For example a male voice being produced from a female voice-box and vice versa. The medium will have no recollection of the experience during that time, as they often go off with another spirit guide for higher learning.

During all stages of trance channelling the medium's body is being balanced by the energies of spirit guides, including the spirit using the human body at that moment, and also by the medium who has vacated their body. Please understand, trance channelling is a carefully monitored operation with every safety precaution employed by the balancing energies of spirit guides.

It is important at this point to differentiate between two types of spirit. There are two types of spirit, **"Spirits of Light and Astral entities"**.

Spirit of Light are the ones referred to as your guides. They would never, and I mean never harm you, nor would they interfere in your life or your evolution as a human being, nor would they drain you of your life force **(your energies)**. They are purely there to guide you as you learn from your experiences of life. It is important to remember your spirit guides are also on their own journey of learning. **They know that to harm or interfere with you, or with humanity, would most certainly create "Karma" for**

**them. All spirits who are of the Light believe in Unconditional Love
for all of life, no matter what form that life may be.**

Astral entities are beings that have passed over physically but have not fully
progressed through the transformation that occurs as a result of physical
death. Instead they are caught on the Astral Plane. Like being stuck in a
crack, they are caught between two worlds- the physical world of dense
matter, and the spiritual vibration of non-matter. It is astral entities that
human beings need to be aware of. **The lower vibration of the Astral
Plane can and is a negative emotional vibration and is directly linked
with the Physical Plane that human beings exist within.**

Every night as your physical body sleeps, your Astral body **(emotional
body)** leaves your physical body to go into the Astral Plane **(vibration)** and
is revitalised with cosmic energy. This is why sleep is essential to your health
and vitality. Without sleep you as a human being would perish within a
very short period of time.

**There are thousands and thousands of astral entities trapped in the
astral vibration.** Some have no awareness beyond their own self-created
fears, conditioning and beliefs from when they existed on the physical plane
of matter. **There are others who stay willingly.** Those that stay willingly
fall into two categories. Either they are not ready to go through the Light
of Creation because they feel they still need to learn, or must complete
something, and will eventually pass through the Light when they are ready.
**Then there are those that do not wish to pass through the Light because
they like the idea of having the best of both worlds-existing in a non-
physical vibration and being part of the physical vibration at the same
time.**

It is the latter of those who willingly remain on the Astral Plane that
humans beings need to be particularly aware of. These entities are best
referred to as mischievous and misguided energies. **Misguided energies
survive purely because they "Steal" energy from physical beings.** To
put it more simply, they are **psychic vampires.** Note however that there are
also psychic vampires in the Physical Plane of matter also.

With respect to channelling, misguided Spirits are detrimental to the health
of all mediums, as much as any other physical being they may attached

themselves to. These **spirits or energies** survive by draining the life-force from those they attach themselves to, you may ask how they do this. **They "tap" or "crack" the aura field that surrounds your human body.** When a crack is created in the **aura field,** and the energy is taken **(often unknowingly)** from a human being, most human beings are never aware of it. It is not uncommon for misguided energies to fool mediums. The entity will claim to be of a high order, and will **"prove"** themselves by providing information in relation to family, past experiences, or past incarnations. Obtaining this information is easily done by tapping into the aura field of the human being requesting the knowledge. Sometimes they may even go so far as to tell a human being what they want to hear, not necessarily what they may need to hear, thus appealing to the **human ego.**

Constant draining of energies leads to the creation of illness, and even physical death. To protect yourself against negative astral entities look for the following clues when observing a medium in trance, or considering a clairvoyant reading.

1. **What is their general state of health from your own observation? Does the medium look drained or do they have a chronic illness to your knowledge.**
2. **Do they smoke or drink excessively, or do they take any form of drugs, which could create an unstable condition?**
3. **If you know the medium or clairvoyant to some degree, are they conscious of a healthy diet? Do they consume excessive amounts of red meats, refined or processed foods and hardly any fresh foods? Dietary abuse will lead to human di'ease in the end.**
4. **Do they drink enough water, essential for cleansing, and therefore essential for being an open channel for higher vibrations?**
5. **When in trance, is the channelled entity aggressive in nature or in their communication? Are they judgemental, or do they insist that you "must or should" do certain things?**
6. **Ask yourself from your heart if you feel good about the entity or the medium/clairvoyant.**

Misguided energies often mean no harm, however they can only survive by draining energy from the living, and that includes all your animal kingdom. They will attach themselves to the weak, the vulnerable, the sick, and the emotionally unstable. Certain entities will attach

themselves to a medium because it makes them feel important. The Astral Plane is an emotional plane, and therefore astral entities have "Egos" as much as do physical human beings. The ego is the enemy of all life forms; it is the negative side of humanity. Ego is simply fear and wherever there is fear there is all negativity of human experience. The ego is the past, brought into the present, and if not resolved it creates humanity future.

Cleansing and protecting yourself is the personal responsibility of every human being. To help a misguided energy complete their transformation they need to be released from the Astral Plane. **There are many astral entities who are lost and completely confused.** They are simply seeking understanding and help.

To help such an entity, first ask the Light of Creation to be with you, within you and around you. Next ask Creation that you may help those seeking your assistance in being released. Finally, ask the entity to turn towards the Light of Creation, and if they are willing to see the Light, tell them their spirit guides will be waiting for them once they pass through it.

To remove misguided spirits or energies that do not want to progress beyond the Astral Plane, first protect yourself with the Light. By believing and invoking the Light from your heart centre, it will be almighty present. Ask the entity to stand within the Light of Creation, you may also wish to fill each room with white light by standing in each room and invoking the Light. **Believe from your heart centre and it will be manifested into your reality.**

Wherever there is Unconditional Love and Light, negative energies or astral entities cannot exist. You as human beings will be amazed at the sudden changes in energies from negative to positive and how arguments and disharmonies will cease after cleansing. Anyone can do it. You only have to believe in who you truly are, a Spirit living and experiencing a physical existence. **You are Spirit first, physical second.** Without your Spirit you could not live as a physical conscious being.

My being believes it would be of great benefit for your own conscious growth if you the individual, experienced a channelling or medium ship session. Seek out meditation groups which offer this. Remember to go with an open heart and mind, and ask your inner self for guidance that you may be lead to the right group for you. Also realise in this moment that you the individual channel every moment of your life in all that you do. **And finally, always protect yourself in the Light.**

CLEOPATRA: THE WOMEN BEHIND THE LEGEND (NO-71)

Kuntarkis in his own words reveals the true nature of the women behind the legend. The legend of the famous Queen "Cleopatra" lives on even today.

Portrayed as a glamorous woman and brilliant politician. I have been asked on many occasions if I could find some information on **Cleopatra,** in doing so I feel many may not be happy with my expressions, yet at the same time I also feel inner truth is more important than the illusion of glorifying an individual, especially when they were not what history says them to be.

History over the ages is not the ultimate truth because it comes from human man. It has been exaggerated and embellished, fantasised and romanticised. If history is not elaborate, but plain, people on your planet seem to find it uninteresting, which is why your writers seem to try to make your history more glamorous. And this is where the truth becomes blurred and even lost. **The only real truth is found within, and every human being has this same truth recorded in their cellular memory.** Here now is the story of **Cleopatra** when she existed on this earthy plane.

It is believed Cleopatra was born in 69 BC in Alexandria, then the capital of Egypt. However, in accessing the past events my Being has found that she was born in **62 BC on 6 November at 8.15pm.** At the time of her birth it rained continually for several weeks. There was major flooding, crops were destroyed and famine was the result. **You could say her birth was a bad omen.**

Physically, **Cleopatra** was not particularly attractive as you would call attractive in human terms. Five feet tall and of Greek descent, she was somewhat overweight, being heavier in the upper part of her human body. She overindulged in wine and meat, and especially loved eating grapes. She had a particularly masculine face which was twisted with a slight deformity and a hooked nose. No doubt her deformity was the result of generations of interbreeding between siblings, as was the practice in Egypt in those days in order to keep the royal bloodline **'pure'. Interbreeding, as humanity now knows, causes genetic mutation.** While she may not have been a physically attractive woman, she did exude **sexuality and charisma** which she used to manipulate those around her, **and she was very promiscuous.**

Cleopatra was the daughter of the Pharaoh Ptolemy XII. Ptolemy XII had 13 children to 3 wives, of which Cleopatra was one of the children, but he also had several illegitimate children from many mistresses. His illegitimate children were not allowed to sit at court when his children and wives were present, as they were not recognised as being of royal blood. Her father was a cruel man and she grew up without the love or warmth of what a family is meant to be, and this in turn made her the woman and Queen she became. He was a very angry human man who suffered greatly with constipation, causing him to be moody. Needless to say his moods dictated how he dealt with his subjects.

There was intense jealousy and hatred among the royal family, and every one of them conspired against each other to either gain favour with the **Pharaoh Ptolemy** or to overthrow him. **Cleopatra** conspired against her father when she was between the ages of **16 and 19** as the lust for power grew within her. It was certainly not unusual for siblings and relatives to kill each other if it meant they would be able to sit on the throne of Egypt.

Cleopatra was not her birth name but was given to her by the royal court when she was made Queen of Egypt. Cleopatra means 'one who rules over many, supreme in power'. It is believed she became Queen around the age of **17 or 18,** but she actually was **22 human years of age.** She inherited the throne after her father's death, as by then she was the eldest child alive. As was Egyptian custom, **Cleopatra** married her **brother Ptolemy** who was also co-ruler of Egypt It is believed he was **12 years** old at the time, but according to the Book of Knowledge he was **14.** It was a marriage of convenience only, and **Cleopatra** made it quite clear to him that if he tried to rule Egypt and undermine her authority, he would be executed. Ptolemy complied for a little while, for he like all the males of **Cleopatra's** lineage were weak in character, but a few years later her brother conspired against her, and it is at this point that she sought out the assistance of **Julius Caesar** in Rome. Of her entire family, it is fair to say that **Cleopatra** was no doubt the strongest in character, as she was very much like her father - a ruthless dictator who would stop at nothing to get her own way.

Cleopatra was not particularly intelligent or consciously advanced, but she was very cunning and worked purely from her instincts, which is why she was so ruthless and why she reigned for so long. She had a lot of servants, many young boys who she would pick herself from the peasants in the city, and also young women. **She would never kill anyone unless they posed a direct threat to her authority and her empire.** If any soldier spoke against her he was charged with treason and beheaded for insubordination. If a female servant was found to be attractive to the men at court, **Cleopatra would have them raped, beaten and their faces disfigured to make them unattractive.** They would then be given the most menial and humiliating duties at court. **During Cleopatra's reign Egypt was a very negative, fearful and chaotic place.** She wanted to dominate as her father did before her, no matter what the cost.

Caesar helped Cleopatra regain her throne from her brother Ptolemy. Your written history has a different story here, but according to the Book of Knowledge, Caesar had heard of her plight and sent an invitation to her to visit Rome so they could negotiate a treaty which would be mutually beneficial. **Cleopatra** countered by inviting him to Egypt. He accepted, and taking an army to escort him, he met **Cleopatra** and they sailed on the Nile for several days. During this time they not only negotiated a treaty but also had a brief affair from which a son was born who was named **Caesarian. Cleopatra's** brother who had taken control of the Egyptian empire was angry over her treaty with Rome and went to war. **Ptolemy died and Cleopatra was restored to her throne. It is believed that Ptolemy drowned in the Nile but he was actually hacked to death and fed to dogs, and the rumour was spread that he ran off with a servant girl.**

Within two years after the birth of Caesarian, Cleopatra became fearful for her and her son's life amid rumours that she was to be assassinated, as the Egyptians did not like the idea of a Roman heir to the throne. She fled to Rome and lived there for about 18 months under **Caesar's** protection, but again became fearful for her own life after an attempt was made on Caesar's life. **It is believed that Caesar was killed in front of her, but it was several years later that Caesar was murdered by his own council. Cleopatra left Caesarian in Rome with his father**

and returned to Egypt. It was a few years later that **Cleopatra's** advisors in Egypt suggested it was unwise to have a half-Roman heir to the Egyptian throne. Caesarian was starting to express his desire to be Emperor and upon **Caesar's death,** he would be Emperor of both Rome and Egypt. **Cleopatra ordered the assassination of 11 year old Caesarian death.** Caesar never found out that Cleopatra was behind the assassination, and he believed that his council had murdered the boy.

When Caesar was assassinated, the Roman Empire was divided among three men: Caesar's great-nephew Octavian, who later became the Emperor Augustus; a man by the name of Marcus Lepidus; and Marc Antony.

Perhaps the greatest fantasy which has been perpetuated around the legend of **Cleopatra** is of the fabled love affair between herself and **Marc Antony.** Their relationship has been greatly romanticised and made out to be more than it ever really was. **Cleopatra** did not love **Marc Antony;** she used him as much as he used her, she despised him. She saw him to be a coarse, vulgar brute with little refinement. But **Cleopatra** had ambition and she needed him if she was to fulfil her vision. **She wanted to become ruler of the known world,** and to do so would mean conquering Rome. **Marc Antony** had a powerful army and she needed his support if she was going to become the supreme ruler. Likewise, **Marc Antony** wanted power and he saw he could obtain that power if he joined forces with **Cleopatra.** They used each other because they were both ruthless and ambitious. There was certainly no love as your historians would like you the human being to continually believe.

It is true that Cleopatra sexually manipulated Marc Antony. He was cunning and ruthless and the only way to know your enemy is to keep them close to you. When they first met, **Cleopatra** had his wine drugged over several days in order to extract information from him and to make him more placid and agreeable. **According to your history she had children with him, but that is incorrect.** She did have children, two of which were stillborn, and one of those was born without legs, but they were not his. **Marc Antony** was impotent much of the time; his health was poor and his fertility was minimal as he spent much of his energy in battle. **Cleopatra** also made sure she bathed after every sexual encounter with him in order to wash out as much of his seed as possible, as she did not wish to bear his children. To have children with a Roman, as she did with Caesar, would pose a continued threat to her position as ruler of Egypt.

After this initial time with Cleopatra, Marc Antony returned to Rome and married Octavia, the half-sister of Caesar's great nephew Octavian **(he later became the Emperor Augustus of Rome).** Marc Antony managed to have children with Octavia, but he kept in contact with Cleopatra. After a military campaign in Parthia he returned to Cleopatra and it is believed he married her and had another child with her. He did not marry her and again, he did not have any children with her.

About this time Marc Antony's wife in Rome was planning on visiting him in Alexandria. It is believed that **Octavia** upon arriving in Athens received a letter from him asking her to return to Rome because it was not safe in Egypt at this time. **Octavia** had never left Rome when she received Marc Antony's letter advising her it was not safe to journey to Egypt. It is believed that **Cleopatra** cried, fainted and even starved herself to keep **Marc Antony** away from his wife, but that is also untrue. **Cleopatra never cried,** but she did pretend to cry when she needed to coerce **Marc Antony** to do her bidding. **Regarding Octavia, Cleopatra told him that his wife was not welcome in Egypt, and if she dared to enter Alexandria she would be killed immediately.** By this stage **Octavia** was very angry with **Cleopatra.** She begged her half-brother **Octavian** to intervene and bring **Marc Antony** safely back to Rome. **When Marc Antony heard the Romans were planning an attack on Egypt because of his wife's plea, he had Octavia assassinated. It is from this point in history that the fall of Egypt was imminent.**

It is true that Cleopatra wanted to keep Marc Antony near her side, but not because of any love for him. Cleopatra wanted to raise her army with Marc Antony's army to attack Rome and defeat Octavian, making her Queen of the World. The Romans were angry that Marc Antony was in league with Cleopatra, and this proved to be in Cleopatra's favour. She promised him that if he raised his army against Rome he would be the new Caesar, but she never had any intention of keeping her promise.

Octavian declared war on Egypt, and Marc Antony fought the Romans in a battle at sea off the coast of Greece while Cleopatra watched not too far away from her own fleet. Marc Antony was losing the battle and he abandoned his men, fleeing to the safety of Cleopatra's ships. His remaining soldiers surrendered and joined the Roman forces. To the Roman's this was proof that Marc Antony was an enemy of Rome. With this failure Cleopatra had to action a new plan to protect herself and her throne. Unknown to Marc Antony, Cleopatra was in contact with Octavian by letter only, negotiating the handover of Marc Antony if Rome did not march on Egypt. The agreement was that she would be Queen but that a Roman general would make all the final decisions.

But when Rome invaded Egypt, Cleopatra realised she would be enslaved, losing her status both in life and in death **(a belief in keeping one's status in the afterlife was very strong).** Octavian had planned to make her his slave, stripping her of her title and marching her barefoot through the streets of Alexandria and then Rome as a trophy from his successful campaign to bring order back to the Empire. It was at this point that she decided she must die before the Romans could imprison her.

When Marc Antony heard of Octavian's invasion he believed Cleopatra had betrayed him, and fearing him, Cleopatra locked herself in her palace, not in her mausoleum as it is believed. History again has romanticised the death of Cleopatra and Marc Antony. It is believed that she locked herself in her mausoleum and awaited the Roman invasion. Apparently she had told a servant to inform Marc Antony that she was dead and that upon hearing the news Marc Antony tried to commit suicide. Yes, he did try to commit suicide when he was drunk, but not because from despair upon hearing news of her death, rather because he knew of the torture, humiliation and death which he would endure for treason against the Roman Empire.

Marc Antony did stab himself in the stomach but did not die immediately. He went to the Palace to see Cleopatra. **She was in her bed chamber lying on the floor already dead.** Marc Antony was weak from his stomach wound and could not lift her himself so he ordered some of her servants to place her on the bed and cover her with veils. According to history Cleopatra laid Antony on her bed and proclaimed him to be her lord, husband and emperor, and then he died in her arms. She was then apparently placed under house arrest for a period of time and finally killed herself when a servant smuggled in **an asp** for her to kill herself with. **None of this is true.**

Aged 44, Cleopatra did die from the venom of an asp, but not how your history tells it. Cleopatra had always experimented with poisons. She would often ask her personal physician to give her poisons which she would test out on servants she disliked, both male and female. She would invite them to eat with her and would give them poisoned food. She would then watch to see how long it would take for them to die and what kind of death they had. Their bodies would then be removed and nothing more would be said. At the time Cleopatra committed suicide, she again tested the venom of the asp on one of her servants to see how long it would take to die. When Marc Antony found her dead, there was a servant girl lying on the floor dead. Cleopatra had tested out the asp's venom on the girl first. Within moments it had worked, so she then used it on herself knowing the Romans were not far away.

When the Roman soldiers burst through the doors of Cleopatra's palace she was dead. Marc Antony attacked them and he was slain within moments. Rome had won and Egypt was now a part of the Roman Empire. **Cleopatra and Marc Antony were placed in the mausoleum she had built. A law was passed by Octavian - he said "From this day on no-one will speak of Cleopatra as Queen of Egypt.**

In closing, I wish to make this statement. Many human beings search out the past, and in so doing have made figures from the past into heroes, and certainly larger than life. Cleopatra is portrayed as being beautiful, slender and even loving. But the reality of Cleopatra is that she was a deceitful, angry, vindictive human being who harboured an immense amount of fear, just like her father. **She was cruel and she enjoyed having people tortured - it gave her a sense of power when she watched someone enduring an agonising death. If you knew the real Cleopatra you would not glorify her. Because of her wealth and status human beings were forced to look up to her as their leader, but in truth she was a leader because the people were powerless against the tyranny of the Egyptian pharaohs. Cleopatra sent tens of thousands of soldiers, and countless numbers of servants, to their deaths because of her insecurities from the hurt child. She was little more than an over-indulged child who used her power against anyone she perceived to be a threat, no matter how small that threat was, and her brutality and ruthlessness could easily be compared to that of Adolph Hitler.**

I can feel your energies of uncertainty towards what has been expressed. My only purpose for expressing this written information on Cleopatra was because I had been asked to do so. Understanding the truth from within will give you self-realisation and ultimately knowledge which sets you free from all limitations. As it has been said, only from an honest heart, can and will, the truth manifest itself. May love be expressed to you all and forever more?

NOSTRADAMUS: THE HEALER / THE PROPHET/ THE MAN (NO-72)

Everyone has heard of the great prophet Nostradamus, but rarely is he praised for his skills as a healer and herbalist, or looked upon as a man like any other. In Kuntarkis' own words, here is what he channelled about Nostradamus...

Nostradamus was a great prophet, more so than Jesus. Jesus was a great and wise man, but he wasn't a prophet in the truest sense of the word. He didn't see visions and then express those visions to the people. He expressed wisdom through his words in an attempt to educate the ignorant masses of the importance of unconditional love. Nostradamus on the other hand saw everything within his mind. **Nostradamus and Jesus did have something very special in common: both were channellers of knowledge and information.**

Nostradamus' life was very interesting considering the time in which he lived. Born in a small town in the early part of the 16th century **(which no longer exists due to the plague),** he grew up on a farm in the south west of France. Life was very hard. Putting food on the table each night was not as easy as it is today. In fact, it was probably a hundred times harder. If you had your own animals, such as chickens, cows and goats, and a little land to grow some vegetables, it was a little easier. But for the average human being life was very hard, mainly due to many raids by rogue gangs and bandits who would come and take all the food and any valuables. They were a constant threat to average human beings trying to make a living and raise a family.

Nostradamus was not his real name. **(The name 'Nostradamus' was given to him later in his life.)** His real name was Patrice. The youngest of four children, Patrice had 2 sisters and a brother. He had always been a visionary, and had always been an imaginative child. Patrice would love to play games but was often scolded by his father who would constantly remind him to **"do your work, do your chores".** Times were tough and Patrice's father felt much burdened by the responsibility of a family in such times, so without conscious awareness he would frequently take out his frustration on the young prophet and healer. Fearful of his father, he was often punished physically **(he used to beat him)** and emotionally, and as a result he became a bed-wetter. His mother would never say too much because if she did, she would then be the recipient of his anger. Sadly, Patrice's father grew up with the same miserable upbringing that he was putting upon his own children, so without making excuses for the man's inexcusable behaviour, he simply didn't know any better.

Patrice would do his chores, but at the same time he would play games with his non-physical friends. From a very early age he was in contact with the **Element Kingdom; the Devas, the Elves and the like.** He communicated with them daily, but never told his parents about it. The Elementals asked him not to because they knew his parents would simply tell him there were no such things or that he was possessed. People were very fearfully superstitious in that time, and it was dangerous to be open about communication with other worlds. **Anyone accused of witchery was burnt, hung or drowned.**

Having a very unique ability from a young age, Patrice was a natural healer and channel, and learnt a great deal about healing with plants and hands-on healing from the Element Kingdom. Sadly however, he closed this ability down when one of his sisters, Petra, died at the age of 7. Patrice tried to revive her. He would put his hands on her the way the Deva had shown him. He would say **"Please, please come back to life, come back to life. You're not dead. You're not dead".** But because he couldn't revive her, he lost his trust in the Element Kingdom, and for the next few years gave away his communication and study with the Element Kingdom. Petra's death brought a great deal of sadness to the entire family for many years, and along with a fear of his father's anger, Patrice became a bed-wetter up until the age of about **11 or 12.**

It wasn't until the age of about 14 or 15 that Patrice finally went to school. Up until then he wasn't allowed to read or study, but was forced to work on the farm, as everyone had to work to make ends meet. His fortune in life changed when a kind, wealthy, well-travelled Spanish gentleman named **Bernard Vincent?** (His father was Spanish and his mother was German, but I can't pronounce his last name even though I can see it) picked the young Patrice to be his protégé because of his natural abilities as a visionary. Bernard had noticed Patrice as a small boy walking through the markets of his town, talking to someone that wasn't there. Bernard was a very open minded man, and what he saw prompted him to ask **"Excuse me little boy, you're** talking to your friend?" Patrice replied "I'm talking to no-one". Bernard said "But you are. You're **talking to your friend there"**. As the man showed an interest, and he felt he could trust him, Patrice told him the truth. He didn't know it at the time, but this Spaniard would come back into his life in the not too distant future and change the course of his life forever.

When Patrice was about 12 or 13 years of age, Bernard approached his parents and offered to pay them a sum of money to take the boy under his wing and educate him. It was common practice among the wealthy to search out children who showed promise and to **"buy"** them from their parent's in order to educate and develop them. **(Bernard had many other students who he had sponsored previously.)** Patrice's father made it very difficult for Bernard by haggling and putting the price up. It took 2 years of negotiating and bargaining, but eventually the two men agreed on a sum and Patrice was taken by Bernard and provided with opportunities the rest of his family would never experience. **It is from this point that he was given the name Nostradamus by Bernard, which means "one who sees".**

It needs to be said at this point that he didn't see his parents for many years once he left home with Bernard, and never saw his brother or sister again. He only returned to his village many years later after hearing his father was quite ill. He went back to visit them and to try to help his father, but within days of seeing his father he died. Not long after his mother died also.

When Nostradamus left home, he couldn't read or write properly, but being a very quick learner, under the guardianship of Bernard, he excelled in all his studies, which included mathematics, languages, herbalism and astrology. They travelled all around France, as well as some parts of Europe, introducing Nostradamus to the many contacts Bernard had made throughout his lifetime and to the many other students he had sponsored. Because of his ability to see visions clearly, Nostradamus' ability to grasp knowledge quickly was exceptional. Healing and herbs were especially of interest to him, and he found that when he studied astrology he would experience particularly strong visions. He was also very interested in anything that could fly and loved to watch the birds, studying them in flight for hours.

At 18 he met a young woman, not quite 16 years old, named Antoinette (he called her Anna) and fell in love. Antoinette helped him to overcome his emotional pains from childhood and to move on from his sister's death. They were kindred spirits, and because she also believed in spirit world, they would talk about all things he could not ordinarily talk about with ordinary people. Their many conversations reactivated Nostradamus' memories and experiences from early childhood, and he started to remember what he had blocked out all those years ago. Over the next 2 years Nostradamus opened up his abilities once more and began communicating with the Element Kingdom again, and then eventually with Spirits from other vibrations. This ability to communicate with other vibrations stayed with him throughout his human life until his death. Sadly, Antoinette died just before her 19th birthday.

Nostradamus had visions for many years, but he didn't start documenting them until he was 27 years of age. He did this very carefully by encrypting them in poetic quatrains so as not to incriminate himself as a witch or someone possessed. **A few months before his 27th birthday his friend and mentor Bernard, died suddenly at the age of 72. Bernard had not counted on dying so soon and had not managed to arrange a suitable inheritance for Nostradamus.**

A year later at 28 years of age, Nostradamus married a woman named Francoise (he called her Fran). Francoise came from a wealthy noble family, but because she married a commoner, her father disowned her without any dowry. **They had 4 children and were very much in love.** Nostradamus treated his family very differently to the way he had been treated as a child, and so he always had a very close and loving relationship with all of them. It was around this time that the **Black Plague** had erupted in a small town. Carried from one town to another as people travelled, it eventually struck the major towns in France, and literally killed thousands of people. **Nostradamus would often travel to these towns to try and help heal the sick.**

Nostradamus was a very kind man, and even though he was poor, he managed to rent an old building which he eventually was able to buy. **He**

became very well known as a healer. With his horse and cart he would travel from town to town, and sometimes he would take his children with him if the town wasn't too far away, but often he would go on his own as he would be gone for days at a time. He would grow his own herbs and would acquire herbs from different villages which he would then use to make his own medicines. Many people came to him because of his reputation as a healer and apothecary. Yet even as a healer he had to be careful of what he said to people, because if you said the wrong thing you could be accused of witchery and consorting with the devil. **In those days it didn't take much to get hung or drowned for witchery or possession.**

As a writer Nostradamus wrote and published his only manuscript in his early thirties, entitled Book of Medicine. It was published on a small scale and did sell, but once all copies were sold a second printing did not occur. The purpose of the book was to document his results with a range of herbs based on what he had learnt from other books and his own experiments. His main area of study was treating many of the common ailments you still have today amongst human society, such as lung problems, constipation **(which was a big problem in those days),** poor eyesight, allergies, gastric problems and joint aches. Nostradamus never wrote any other books, but kept a lot of his notes in bundles, as he didn't plan on writing any more books. His notes served more as a personal diary of his work and visions. **Sadly, he was persecuted by the Church, especially towards the end of his life, and most of his life's work was destroyed by the Church when they came and burnt down one of the rooms in his house which housed all his books, notes and experiments.**

It is necessary to mention at this point that Nostradamus was a vegetarian. Because of what he had learnt from the Element Kingdom, as a small boy he became a vegetarian, not eating any meat but some dairy. When he lost his faith after his sister's death, he resumed eating meat, but then became a vegetarian once again in his late 20s. His only vice was red wine - he loved it and drank a lot of it, as well as a port-type wine made in those days. Interestingly his wife and children ate meat, even though he didn't. Nostradamus didn't believe in pushing his beliefs or way of life onto anyone else, but he would discuss them and guide anyone who was interested in adopting his ways. He had learnt how to use energy for healing from the Deva, and had learnt that you can't pollute your human body and then expect to transmit pure healing energy. **Nostradamus**

knew that being a vegetarian was important if he was going to be a good healer.

This is still a major misconception by many healers today. They think they can indulge in all their human vices, particularly alcohol, tobacco and meat products, all of which create considerable toxicity and pollution in the human body, and then expect to be able to transmit a pure form of energy for healing. Like using poor quality raw materials and expecting to produce highest grade steel, the same goes for a healer. You cannot be a healer unless your body is purified, and if you do healings without a purified body, you will transmit very negative, dirty energies, which will be of no benefit to the recipient. Like using dirty surgical instruments to perform an operation, such energies do more harm than good overall. **Nostradamus understood this completely.**

He was between 37 and 41 years of age when the Black Plague came to his town. It killed hundreds of human beings. His medicine couldn't cure them, he couldn't heal them, and again he hit a low point in his life as his faith wavered in his abilities. Nostradamus finally gave up healing when his wife and children died from the plague while he was out of town helping other human beings. He was devastated, and from that point in his life only ever used herbs on himself, putting all of his efforts and energy into writing down his visions. He never took on any students, as he felt it was a pointless exercise. **The plague had devastated many towns: within 48 hours people were violently ill, spitting up blood, blood-blisters forming over their bodies, their limbs turning black. People were literally bleeding from the inside, and he could do nothing about it. So he felt there was no point in teaching something that proved useless against such a disease after all those years of study.**

Nostradamus remarried a woman named Helena (of German descent - she had moved to France with her father when she was a young girl) but did not have any children with his second wife as she was unable to bear any. They loved each other, but it was companionship and convenience more than anything else. She needed a husband (women in those days had very few options) and he needed a housekeeper to look after him, so it worked out well for both of them. There was not a lot of physical contact, and Nostradamus didn't have too much time for a relationship anyway as he was too wrapped up in his writing and visions. **He spent all his time writing, and sometimes he would write all night.**

The visions that would become his famous book of prophecy began as powerful visions in his sleep. He never took much notice of them at first, believing they were just dreams built on fears from his past. But then he started dreaming about things that meant nothing to him. As far as he knew, they didn't exist yet - they were in the future. So he started researching by reading as many books as possible from as far and wide as he could obtain them. He would read anything to get an inkling of what it was that he was seeing and what the connection was to the future.

Nostradamus began to understand that there were things to come which didn't exist yet and that he was actually seeing them. Since his personal tragedies, he rarely ever communicated physically with spirit world, but during his time of sleep he communicated fully and openly. As he would write he would see the visions as pictures on a television screen. That to him was most interesting. But as mentioned earlier, he had to disguise his writings due to the Church in that time being very fearful, domineering and oppressive.

Nostradamus died at around the age of 63-66 years and it was his request that he be buried with his manuscripts after he was told through his communications with the spirit world that his grave would be dug up by looters after his death. He wanted the world to know about his work, so he asked a trusted friend to ensure all his remaining work would be buried with him. True to his visions, his grave was dug up and his notes found by soldiers during a war in the mid-18th century. **Unfortunately, the book you know today as Nostradamus' prophecies is not a reproduction of his original manuscript.** Like the Bible, it was rewritten and additions inserted by several other human beings. All that aside however, Nostradamus wanted to leave humanity his insights in the hope and trust, that they would prevent the disasters and tragedies he foresaw. **Sadly this has not been the case.**

Many human beings have tried to disprove his words of Enlightment, by saying his predictions were out by many years. What those human beings did not take into account, time back then was very different to your present moment in human time today. Let say back then, things were at a slower vibration, to what they are today. You as human beings are in fact vibrating at a faster pace. You heard the saying, there is not enough time in the day to complete all the things I need to do? When you live in the moment time has no reality, it's the human brain that lives to human created time?

NIKOLA TESLA: A FORGOTTEN GENIUS? (NO-73)

Before proceeding, it must be pointed out that this is not a comprehensive history of Nikola Tesla. There is so much which can be told of Tesla and his life, that this short story would hardly do him justice. If you the human being are interested in knowing more about Tesla and his work you will find plenty of websites dedicated to him which are well worth a visit. Tesla may be gone from this vibration but his spirit lives on in the enthusiasm of those who are working to bring him the recognition he deserves, and of course in the technology you as human beings have today, because without Tesla you would not have the technology you have today?

Nikola Tesla was one of the most brilliant minds ever to assist the conscious growth of humanity. His goal from childhood was to harness the forces of nature in order to help the human race evolve. **Tesla believed the purpose of science was discovery for the good of all humanity, not for self-glorification.** A noble vision indeed, but one which also threatened the powers of his day, because it meant less financial gain for those with a vested interest.

Tesla gave the world many things which helped create the technology humanity has today. He registered over **700 patents,** and his contribution to the development of technology includes the alternating current motor, the radio **(his work pre-dates Marconi),** the Tesla Coil **(which is used in radios and televisions today), vacuum tubes, x-rays, hydroelectric generators, loudspeakers, fluorescent lights, radar, the rotary engine, microwaves, remote control, a more efficient steam turbine, missiles, particle beam weaponry, satellites, nuclear fission and robots.**

But it must be understood from the outset that if Tesla had not invented, or brought into conscious existence, the ideas which he did, then another entity would have incarnated to do so. The technology which Tesla brought forward is old knowledge which has existed within the universe for as long as civilisations have existed throughout the universe. **Tesla connected to and brought forth knowledge from the Infinite Book of Life, and it was** his choice as an entity to incarnate as a human being in order to bring this knowledge into human consciousness.

Tesla was an extremely intelligent being, intellectually advanced beyond most scientists. He was an Alien being who chose to incarnate as a human in order to experience human existence, but also to help humanity evolve consciously through technology. Unfortunately, his level of Consciousness was far beyond many of his day, which is why he met with so much criticism and so many obstacles, **Thomas Edison being one of his greatest undermines.** The entity who was Tesla, in this 3rd dimensional plane, came from a planet called Par'Riuess, in the same planetary system as Nar'Kariss, except it is 2 light years further away from Earth than Nar'Kariss.

Tesla was born into a human body at midnight between the 9th and 10th of July 1856, during a severe electrical storm in the village of Smiljan, Croatia (then the Austro-Hungarian Empire). As an entity about to incarnate, he planned his entry into physical life on such a night because the electrical energies present helped him descend from his 5th dimensional existence into the 3rd dimension vibration of physical matter.

His human father was a mathematician/philosopher/writer who served in the military who then joined the clergy. His human mother, who he loved and admired dearly, and credited with his gifts of invention, was a highly intelligent woman who invented many things herself and who herself came from a family of inventors. **From childhood Tesla was imaginative and creative.** By five (5) years of age he had invented a motor driven by insects! He was a dreamer who loved to read and who loved poetry. He was also incredibly disciplined to the point of obsession, no doubt the legacy of his strict father. But his father's exacting standards helped the young Tesla develop a powerful imagination through the many exercises his father gave him to practise, such as guessing another's thoughts, discovering faults in concepts **(critical analysis)**, repeating long sentences and performing mental calculations. These daily lessons helped him develop a strong memory, reasoning and critical sense.

As a child he suffered bright flashes of light, such as those experienced by sufferers of severe migraines, and with the flashes usually came

visions. At first he fought the visions, but when he could no longer control them, he went with them and allowed his imagination to wander. He found he began to enjoy these mental excursions and as a result, developed his finely honed ability to visualise, which he used throughout his life as an inventor. Most inventors devise a concept and then begin the various stages of developing their invention until it is perfect. **Tesla developed everything in his mind, testing it in his mind's eye, finding faults and then rectifying them, all in his mind's eye, so that when it came to actually building his inventions, they never failed but worked exactly as he had visualised them.** Tesla believed this was the most efficient means of invention as it saved time, money and physical effort. A true visionary, he saw no limitation which is why he could use his imagination so completely and thoroughly.

Although Tesla's father wanted him to follow in his footsteps and join the clergy, Tesla loved engineering and convinced his father to allow him to attend the Technical University of Graz, Austria, and the University of Prague (1879-1880). At Graz he first saw the Gramma dynamo, which operated as a generator, and when reversed became an electric motor. From this moment he began devising an efficient way of using alternating current. Having invented the telephone repeater in a government telegraph engineering office in Budapest, Tesla later visualised the rotating magnetic field and developed plans for an induction motor, the first steps towards using alternating current. **In 1882 he went to Paris to work for the Continental Edison Company and in 1883, while in Strasbourg, he built his first induction motor.**

Tesla migrated to America in 1884, where he arrived in New York City with a mere four cents in his pocket, some poems he had written, and calculations for a flying machine. His first job in America was with Thomas Edison in New Jersey. But the partnership went sour within a short time when Edison, who had promised to pay Tesla $50,000 to develop motors and generators to make wireless transmission possible, reneged on the agreement. Needless to say, Tesla left, and the two became rivals with very public smearing campaigns coming from Edison. Before long it became quite clear that Tesla's alternating-current system was far superior to Edison's direct current system, especially for the transmission of power over long distances.

It is never spoken of because Edison is considered a hero, but Edison employed Tesla in order to steal his ideas. He knew Tesla was brilliant and he wanted his ideas and inventions because he saw he could not only be immortalised as a great scientist, but could also make an enormous amount of money. Edison had many contacts within the government of the day, and when Tesla left, Edison's influence caused many obstacles to be created for Tesla throughout his inventing life. **Even his project with JP Morgan, to create the Long Island wireless world broadcasting tower, came to an abrupt end partly due to Edison's influence. This of course is not recorded in history, but when you connect with the Book of Life, within which all knowledge exists, you will discover this truth.**

Edison did everything in his power to discredit Tesla and his work, which unfortunately was not too difficult because Tesla had poor social skills, and Edison capitalised on this. Tesla found most people to be small-minded. He found it difficult to communicate with people whose vision was limited, especially those in government and other scientists. **Because he was an entity who came from the 5th dimension, he found it hard to communicate his 4th and 5th dimensional ideas to scientists who could only think 3rd dimensionally. Tesla had few friends and trusted even fewer human beings, thus he spent most of his time working.**

One of Tesla's few friends was George Westinghouse, head of the Westinghouse Electric Company. In 1885 Westinghouse bought the patent rights to Tesla's polyphase system of alternating-current dynamos, transformers, and motors. This resulted in a power struggle between Edison's direct-current systems and the Tesla-Westinghouse alternating-current system. Alternating current won the battle as can be seen today. Westinghouse used Tesla's system to power the World Columbian Exposition at Chicago in 1893, and as a result of his success, Tesla won the contract to install the first power machinery at Niagara Falls which carried power to Buffalo by 1896. When the project was completed and the system went on line, the power generated totalled more than the combined output of all the existing power generators operating in the US at the time.

Tesla built his own laboratory in New York City in 1887 so that he could work and invent freely. He experimented with what were then called shadowgraphs, the predecessors to X-rays. He also gave exhibitions in his laboratory to prove the safety of alternating current, lighting lamps without wires by allowing electricity to flow through his human body. The Tesla Coil, invented in 1891 is still used today in radios and television, as well as other electronic equipment, for wireless communication. **1891 was also the year Tesla became an American citizen.** In 1898 Tesla announced his invention of a remote controlled boat. Criticised for such an improbable invention, Tesla proved his claims before a crowd in Madison Square Garden.

Tesla left New York City for Colorado Springs in 1899 and stayed there until early 1900, where he made what he believed to be his most important discovery - terrestrial stationary waves. He proved that the Earth could be used as a conductor and would be as responsive as a tuning fork to electrical vibrations of a certain pitch. He also lit **200 lamps** without wires from a distance **40 kilometres** away and created lightning flashes measuring **41 metres in length.** At one time he was certain he had received signals from another planet in his Colorado laboratory, a claim which scientific journals of the time thought ludicrous. Tesla had in fact received his own transmission, reflecting back to Earth. But on one occasion later in his life he claimed to have been contacted by **aliens.** Again everyone thought he had been hallucinating, but this time it was true. He had in actual fact been visited by the **greys** because his radio waves were interfering with the operational/navigational systems in their ships. **They took him during his time of sleep up to their ship to find out how his technology worked so that they could compensate for its affecting their technology.**

He returned to New York in 1900, and began constructing the Long Island wireless world broadcasting tower, funded by JP Morgan. The tower was Tesla's plan to link the world together through his telephone and telegraph systems, enabling the transmission of pictures and text from one part of the world to another in minutes, and delivering mail between terminals using electronic messaging. **Tesla secured the loan by giving Morgan 51% of his patent rights of telephony and telegraphy to Morgan.** Tesla's vision was to provide worldwide communication and to provide a facility for sending pictures, messages, weather warnings, and stock reports. **The project was abandoned for several reasons, but mainly because Morgan withdraw his support with unknown interference from Edison.**

Many of Tesla's ideas remained in his notebooks due to a lack of funds, and his notebooks are still examined by engineers today. In 1915 he was disappointed when a report that he and Edison were to share the Nobel Prize proved incorrect. Tesla did however receive the Edison Medal in 1917, the highest honour that the American Institute of Electrical Engineers could bestow.

Tesla had few close friends, and confided in very few people. He found that most of the young scientists who tried to befriend merely wanted to steal his ideas. **Among his closest friends were the writers Robert Underwood Johnson, Mark Twain, and Francis Marion Crawford.** He said to his friend Robert Underwood Johnson that he was sorry he ever came to America. He felt it was a great country and a free country where people could express their own diversity, but he quickly realised that he should have taken up an offer made by the French Government to work for them developing his inventions. **He realised all too late that the French would have willingly supported his work completely.**

In his 70s Tesla had become quite disillusioned with his life and work. He saw the reality that throughout his entire working life his work had been sabotaged by some of his peers, and even the government of the day. **Tesla died in New York City on January 7, 1943. Upon his death his house was raided by the FBI.** His papers, diplomas and other honours, his letters, and his many notes were taken. Everything was copied and transcribed, and then stored away in secret files. Many of his working models of inventions and experiments were also taken. What was left was eventually given to his nephew and later placed in the Nikola Tesla Museum in Belgrade.

Hundreds attended his funeral and one tribute to him read: "one of the outstanding intellects of the world who paved the way for many of the technological developments of modern times."

Saddest of all is that Tesla is hardly credited with any of the technology he originated and developed, even though he became an American citizen. My being expresses this because Americans always seem so proud of those who have achieved great things in their great country and are especially proud of letting the rest of the world know. **And yet Tesla is forgotten.** Apparently, in the Smithsonian National Museum of History little mention is made of Tesla's work, with the alternating current exhibit included as part of the Edison exhibit, naturally leading people to believe that Edison invented and developed alternating current and the induction motor. The Tesla exhibit is apparently little more than a small glass cabinet with some personal effects situated in a darkened hallway near the men's room, and was only created recently in response to congressional pressure. **It would seem that history continues to be influenced by governments and national institutions who may have a vested interest in not revealing the truth about the brilliance of Nikola Tesla, truly a forgotten genius of which humanity will never see the likes of again.**

The entity who was known as Tesla returned to his own vibration in the 5th dimension and has, since leaving the 3rd dimension, travelled to other physical planes in order to bring forth the same knowledge he has helped humanity obtain on Earth during the 20th Century. Not a single facet of Tesla's energies remains within humanity, and the only connection humanity now has with Tesla is the legacy of the technology his unhindered vision has made possible.

My Being trusts, all that you have read so far has been of help to you as a species, you as human individuals are evolving into fully conscious beings. **There are 74 different expressions in this book, my Being is not asking you as individuals to believe or disbelieve.** What is more important is for us the **Nar'Karones** to simply share knowledge with our Brothers and Sisters of this most precious Earth, all of you call home.

INNER TRUTH (NO-74)

May love, peace, joy, happiness and good fortune follow every human being throughout this present incarnation of yours as human individuals? Individuality is like inner truth. To truly discover your individuality you must be willing to face all your self-created fears, beliefs and conditioning.

All human truth is created from the past. It is the past that limits the individual, and the past is simply memories, experiences gathered and stored in your human brain, and then drawn upon when needed.

I the last fifty (50) human years there has been an escalation in the number of human beings pursuing individual quests in search of truth, Enlightment, Inner Peace and Tranquillity; a quest to find an understanding of their existence. As more human beings in Westernised cultures become disillusioned with the society they live in, an enormous swing in favour of Eastern cults and esoteric beliefs has become evident. The increase of Gurus and Spiritual teachers has been considerable and the number of humans turning to these **"Masters"** and **"Holy's"** ones has also dramatically increased.

It seems that ancient Eastern philosophies are providing many human individuals with some kind of understanding to their existence that Western counterparts are not for filling. Eastern cultures seems to be providing more of an explanation of the part human beings play in their life's experiences, both physically and spirituality. More importance is placed on finding inner peace and harmony, and the human individual is encouraged to find inner truth in order to lead one to understand life's path.

Outside of irrefutable physical facts, truth is a difficult concept to define. There are around 7 billion truths on your most precious Mother Earth, because there are around 7 billion human beings living in their self-created truths.

If truth were examined in the context of religious or spiritual beliefs, you would find truth is confined to the boundaries of "isms", and "ism" being a created belief system. Following belief systems devised someone other than yourself places limitations upon you, for you are conditioned with someone else's beliefs.

Within the confines of a belief system it is very difficult to find actual truth. Truth cannot be found outside of oneself. Within the very being of each human being is where all truth will be found, it is what is called the **"Knowing"**. Every human has this Knowing, it is recorded in the very essence of your whole being. **The four (4) quadrillion cells you as a human individual is made up from holds every thought, as every action is recorded in these cells, they are your Cellular memory from every life you as an individual has ever had, whether it be on this planet Earth or any other vibration you as a being has experienced. Always remember this, no Guru or religious leader can give you actual truth, they can only give you their idea of what truth is by their own experiences.**

Real truth, inner truth, can only be experienced by the individual, for truth is an interpretation of an experience. Unless another human being has had the same experience, it cannot be considered someone else's truth. Even if two humans experience the same event, their respective views of that event will differ because no two individuals are alike, and therefore the event will inevitably be unique for each of them resulting in differing interpretations of that experience. Their respective interpretations may be so similar as to be considered identical, but no matter how small the differences in interpretation may be, they are still uniquely different experiences because the one event has been experienced by two separate individuals from two unique perspectives.

Truth therefore exists within each human being and not the masses. The closest one gets to having the same truth is to say you have similar beliefs and understanding. **Inner truth is the "Knowing".** It belongs to you, the individual, the one who is Spirit before being physical, for without the Spirit which is connected to your Soul, you would not, or could not exist in your present state as a physical human being.

The spirit is the driving force and the Soul is all that you are. The physical form is simply a vehicle for experiencing the lessons of human life. Some believe humans incarnate to balance self-created Karma from previous lives. But the one lesson for all life in all Universes is to learn and experience Unconditional Love. Unconditional Love sets you free from the negative emotions of Ego, and in so doing you become the Living Truth, connected to all things, reaffirming your direct connection to your Soul.

The human individual can learn from others truths by using their truths as a guide. Beware of clutching to a belief system as if it is your lifeline. Belief systems do not allow you the human individual to keep an open mind to other's opinions. Additionally, blind surrender to a belief system literally forsakes personal responsibility.

Ask yourself – do you adopt a point of view because of popular opinion (your friends/parents/partner holds that view), or because you have examined the matter in some detail and have logically arrived at your own conclusions? It is often easier to give your personal responsibility away to another and adopt a belief or truth, particularly if the matter is even remotely controversial, than risk ridicule or being excluded and shunned. Sometimes it takes a great deal of courage to be personally responsible and stand your ground for your truth and beliefs.

Abdication of personal responsibility often happens with Guru Worship or Religious Fanaticism. This is often seen in humans who are unable to believe in themselves, desperately feel a need to believe in something by adopting another's truth before searching within themselves.

Belief systems have their place; they provide structure to abstract ideals. But in providing structure and form they also place limitations and boundaries around an otherwise open mind. Personal growth does not occur unless the human individual is willing to put aside, not necessarily give up entirely, but simply momentarily put aside belief systems to allow exploration of the unknown to take place. **The search for inner truth is a journey within oneself, into the unknown part of the true self. When that journey is successful it results in self-realisation.**

Inner truth emerges within your Consciousness when you the human individual accepts who you are in the scheme of life itself. Inner truth is a deep inner knowing that within you are all the answers to all the questions which have concerned humanity for all of human existence. Everything you seek is within you – the knowledge from your past to your present moment and even your future. **You only need to seek your connection to your Soul for all to be revealed. The more you seek the more you will find.**

Discovering your inner truth as a human being as well as humanity, will not only change your thinking, but also your reality, in this discovery you will activate personal growth and awareness.

As you the individual learn to deal with the negative emotions that limits you in this present moment, you will change the level of your awareness, and in so doing your truth will reveal itself to you. You will know who you are and why you are here. You will set yourself free from the grip of a negative human Ego, not only yours, but also the negative Ego of those around you. In doing so you will gain a deeper understanding of yourself, and peace will replace the internal turmoil and insecurities which have been a habitual way of life.

Remember this always: Lies lead to more lies, there are no truths in lies. Sadly, when you as a human being begin to believe your own lies, it can and does become your conditioned truth, which in turn become your belief system. All of you have heard this saying, like attracts like.

Set yourself free from the fears of the human Ego and you will begin to find your own inner truth and from that point on you will continue to attract only truth into your life. For in truth you the individual will find and discover total freedom within your thoughts, and when freedom is found in your thoughts, that freedom is then expressed and manifested into your daily lives. **Surely this is a much more fulfilling and gratifying way of experiencing yourself as a human being? "Inner Truth". Unconditional Love is a way of life and forgiveness is the beginning of you as a Spiritual Being finding and living your Inner Truth.**

QUESTIONS & ANSWERS BY KUNTARKIS THE BEING

The following Questions and Answers were documented over a period of eight (8) years, by a Being called Jecuss Kuntarkis, from a Planet called Nar'Kariss. The Beings are known as the Nar'Karones, they have evolved beyond the physical self into Beings of Light and exist in a vibration that is known to us as the Fifth Dimension.

In the Realm that Kuntarkis exists within, everything is Energy, and weather it is from the past or in the Present or even into the future. The Nar'Karones as Beings of Light can open a doorway and watch events that have happened or are about to happen.

In this Realm, Beings like Kuntarkis are able to tap into knowledge at any given moment and share with individuals or humanity as a whole, the knowledge that can help a single human being or the masses in the development of our Consciousness. All the headings below represent the type of Questions that were asked over that period.

You the reader, may find some of the Questions and Answers of interest or they may help you understand some of the things you may be feeling.

ASK KUNTARKIS

HELP WITH MEDITATION

For Kuntarkis,

Hi. My name is Brad, I'm from WA and I am 20 years old. I'm trying to learn how to meditate, but am finding it very difficult. I go to the local Spiritual Church and attend a meditation class there, but I just can't seem to concentrate on what they are trying to tell us. Do you have any suggestions for me? Thanks.

Brad.

Kuntarkis replies:

Dear Brad, Thank you for writing your words to my being. Yes there are many things you can do to help you meditate. There are so many different forms of meditation and I must say all of them have a purpose. What suits one may not suit another.

You Brad, need to research different forms of meditation and experiment on yourself to find what feels good for you, from your heart. Many on your Earth use guided meditations and many use just some peaceful music or nature sounds in the background, and others use a picture, whether it be of a human being, a rainforest, the ocean or mountains. There are so many different ways to still the mind.

There is a book called "Learn to Meditate – for the art of tranquillity, self-awareness and insight" by the writer David Fontana. It is for beginner and advanced meditators. One thing I must warn you about - Mr Fontana believes that visions in meditation are hallucinations. If you believe in the existence of spirit and your ability to be able to see spirit, then you will need to consider disregarding his beliefs on this issue. But that aside, I am told it is a useful book.

One thing I must express about meditation. Meditation is not the outcome of thinking or concentration. It is the outcome of stilling one's mind, one's being, from the distractions the human Ego has created. These distractions of the Ego are the constant chatter, and it is this chatter which must cease before the real can come into being.

What is needed Brad, is your perseverance, and for you to truly believe in yourself, to truly love yourself unconditionally, as you are now. Brad, I know your past and your past has been haunting you for the last four years of your Earthly time. Learn to forgive yourself and forgive others, and your mind will become peaceful.

Be Blessed in the Light of Creation's totality always.

Kuntarkis

I THINK I HAVE CANCER

Hello Kuntarkis,

I live in a very peaceful valley. I make pottery and sell it at the local markets. I am married now for 26 years and have two sons who have both joined the Navy. My husband works in the city and will be retiring in seven years so we can spend more time together. This is hard for me to express to you. I think I have bowel cancer and I am so scared to go to my local doctor. I have been getting a lot of pain in the lower part of my bowels. I have not told my husband – he is a beautiful man and we love each other very much. Is there any advice you can give me please. I am very scared.

Millie.

Kuntarkis replies:

Dear Millie, You indeed are truly a very beautiful human being, and I can feel you are a very enlightened being who has a great passion for life. You do not have bowel cancer. What you do have is a slight twist in your lower bowel chain, and it is this twist that is creating the pain and bloating, for there is a build-up of waste which is not moving.

It would be good for you to see your local doctor and ask their advice. What I can say is that you need to have your bowels cleaned out. It is a simple procedure. I am sure your doctor can arrange it for you. If not, you may choose to see a naturopath. But you do not have bowel cancer.

Please drink a lot more water and have less wine and cheese (which clogs you up!). May many pleasant happenings come into your life and please don't allow your fears to create unnecessary thoughts in your mind.

Be Blessed in Love and Light dear Millie.

Kuntarkis.

DUALITY IN HUMAN EXISTENCE

To Kuntarkis,

I was wondering if you could explain to me, from your world, the meaning of the word duality. In our dictionary it says it means "double, consisting of two". I was curious about this word in the context of human existence. Can you give it a more meaningful explanation? Just wondering if you have the time, or should I say a spare moment.

The Hornet.

Kuntarkis replies:

Dear Hornet, The meaning of the word "duality" from a human understanding is correct. But to explain it from another level, you need to raise your level of thinking and understanding. So, I will explain it in this way:

First, you must be free of your limitations and conditioning from your human life, and second, you must be willing to open your mind to higher vibrations beyond the third dimensional matter world.

Duality means two – one being Spirit, the other being Ego. They are two conscious entities, and Ego is the only one existing in the dense physical matter vibration. The human body consists of beliefs, conditions, fears and insecurities from the Ego – it is biased in all things. The Spirit is unbiased in all things – non-judgemental and in a constant state of being, experiencing without negative or positive opinion or thought.

To clarify, in my vibration of existence, duality means simply this: Spirit and Ego. If your Ego dominates your existence, then you live in negative thoughts, which will (or already has) created your past, your present and your future. There is no conscious growth in Ego. But if your Spirit dominates your existence, then you know your true self. In your human physical vibration, duality is the co-existence of Spirit and Ego, but it is up to each individual to decide which of these two will direct your life and influence your decisions.

There is a saying: "To know thy true self is know all others", meaning when you know yourself, only then will you know Creation's totality. Know and understand the duality of your existence and you will know Creation.

Be Blessed in Love and light always dear Hornet.

Kuntarkis.

TRUTH ABOUT EARTH'S POLLUTION

Hello Kuntarkis,

I wrote to you some time ago. I am very concerned about our planet's problem with pollution. The governments and industries do not seem to care. I read about more and more deaths in adults, and even children, and they seem to be related to this problem. Is this the truth? Our scientists assure us that the ozone layer is not getting smaller or thinner, and that holes in the ozone layer are closing up. Is this the truth?

Oki.

Kuntarkis replies:

My dear Oki, thank you for writing again, You as an individual, and all who live upon this most precious planet you call Earth, should be very concerned for not only this generation of humans, but for the generations to come that will suffer the most. Yes, it is very true that most of your governments, industries and scientists are showing little concern over this enormous and serious problem.

Many people, adults and children, are ill or dying on your world from long term exposure to the poisons that surround your Earth. Your human bodies are strong, but your immune systems are becoming weak mainly because the human diet is poor (foods contain little or no nutritional value along with the consumption of alcohol, tobacco, drugs) and your air contains pollutants from vehicles (including aircraft and boats) and manufacturing industries. To an observer it seems that those in power and business are more concerned with greed than the future of your planet and civilisation.

If what is occurring on this most precious planet is not addressed NOW, your children and future generations will carry your legacy.

Your temperatures are rising, your waters are rising as your ice caps melt, your forests are dying, and your people are dying in their thousands as each day passes. People are becoming more emotional – angrier, religious wars are increasing, humanity is raping the Earth and tolerance for each other is lessening.

You cannot expect to keep destroying your world and for the Earth not to react in the form of what you would call natural disasters. Humanity must change its level of thinking and begin to grow consciously by developing a heart for all of life that exists on your planet, and not just human life. In reality, there seems to be very little heart of understanding even towards human life by humans.

The Ego within humanity is causing all the negativity that is occurring on your world. Oki, unless the collective human Ego is dissolved into the nothingness from which it came, then humanity has a very bleak future ahead of itself. The protective layer that surrounds your Earth that which you call ozone, is depleting. This alone should be a signal to humanity, showing them that pollution is a major problem and that something urgently needs to be done to prevent any further destruction of this most precious layer in your atmosphere.

Oki, if you are truly concerned about your Earth and the future which generations to come will have to face, then you as an individual must take responsibility and campaign against those who are creating this disaster and sickness on your world. It all starts with you the individual and all other human beings, Oki. Be pro-active and open your eyes to the falseness that surrounds you. Still your mind so the truth can manifest itself. The power is within you Oki.

Be Blessed in the Light of Creation's totality.

Kuntarkis.

UFO SIGHTING MEMORY RETURNS

Dear Kuntarkis,

I want to say bravo for the informative knowledge you provide on your website and also to the ones who work with you. I am 78 and still thirsting for knowledge. I have always searched for the unknown and I believe in Aliens. I saw a UFO when I was nine. I was raised on a farm in South Australia, and was coming home from school when I saw the UFO. The sun was setting when I saw a silver round-shaped object. It hovered above me about 50 feet in the air for around two minutes – I counted the seconds in my head! I felt a strange tingling sensation throughout my body, and then it was gone. I've not seen a UFO since, but I can tell you I have wanted to! I told my parents about my experience but they just laughed at me and said it was a trick of the light from the setting sun. I never told anyone again until now.

I just wanted to say thank you Kuntarkis. You helped an old digger bring back a memory that I truly enjoyed. I will pass on your website address to others who show an interest in this area.

Fred.

Kuntarkis replies:

Dear Fred, You are indeed a beautiful soul as well as a beautiful human being. Your faith and your truth is very special and from my being I thank you for sharing your story not only with me, but with others who will read it on this website.

Fred, I do not mean to impose on your private life. I just wish to express my love from my being to you for the loss of your beautiful wife who was married to you for over 50 years of Earthly time. She was your best mate and friend and I see you both lived in harmony and loved each other from the heart. Your four children are a beautiful example of your wisdom and understanding that you both passed on to them. You are indeed a very special human being, and yes Fred, you will be with Joan again when the moment in life comes.

Thank you for your kindness, and may you and all your family be Blessed in Love and Light always.

Kuntarkis.

CLOSE ENCOUNTER WITH ALIEN BEINGS

Hi Kuntarkis,

My name is Simon, I'm 32 years of age and I live in Brisbane. I want to share my experience with you because I feel you will understand what happened to me. I was 27 at the time. One night I was feeling very tired and went to bed early. I sleep under an open window because I love looking up at the stars. As I stared out at the starts I felt myself falling into a deep sleep, but for some strange reason I could still see the stars.

What happened next really freaked me out. It was like an energy started to work its way up my body, starting at my feet and going up to my head. It paralysed me. I couldn't move no matter how hard I tried. What was strange was that my eyes were open and I could see this pale blue light coming through my bedroom wall. I tried to scream out but I couldn't, and then out of nowhere this humanoid being appeared. He was smiling at me. His body was thin and he had no hair at all. He spoke to me but I couldn't understand him. And then, nothing. When I woke up it was 6.30am. I was not sure if I had been dreaming or if it really happened to me. Can you please tell me, was it a dream or was it a real experience?

Simon.

Kuntarkis replies:

Dear Simon, It was (and is) very brave of you to express your experience with me, and also with other readers. Thank you for your courage. Your experience with the beings called the Mune'har did take place as you described it – it was real, it was truth.

The Mune'hars are explorers of new worlds and the human being is of interest to them. They meant you no harm. They have visited human kind over the last 39 years of your Earth time. They do have physical bodies like your kind, but they can manipulate certain energies so they can pass through dense matter in your world. They enveloped you in an energy veil so they could immobilise you in order to communicate with you, otherwise in your fear you may have panicked and inflicted an injury upon yourself, or them?

Some of your governments on this Earth do know of their existence, but the Mune'hars are very wary of their intentions and have decided to contact only those who are true of heart. You Simon are true of heart. They will come to you again, but the choice is yours. Seek out the understanding of meditation and it will be of value to you in your lifetime. There is no reason to fear. The Mune'hars are a peaceful race of beings, and their intentions are only to enlighten other races throughout the Universes who are growing consciously.

Be blessed in the Light always.

Kuntarkis.

LONGING FOR A CHILD

Dear Sir,

My name is Mufahida, also known as Banyu. I am female, married for ten years. Age - I am in my thirties. My husband's name is Mohamed. Age 36. We are longing to have a child. Have tried all medicines and treatments. No use. I will be very grateful if you could please help us and let us know if ever I will be able to conceive.

Thank you and God bless you.

Mufahida

Kuntarkis replies:

Dear Mufahida, My being is honoured to receive your question. You are indeed a beautiful human being and would make a beautiful Mother. Yes, there is to come a child which will be born unto you and your husband.

There are a few steps for you and your husband to take, and it is your choice if you decide to put the energy into it.

First, you and your husband must learn to relax and not become stressed over wanting you to become pregnant.

Second, ask your husband to sit on the floor opposite you and hold hands with you. Then both of you close your eyes and see a ball of white light in front of your eyes and send that ball of light to each other. Allow yourselves to feel the light of unconditional love that you feel for each other. Do this for at least 5 minutes. When two human beings have unconditional love for each other, all things are possible.

Third, when you make love with each other, feel each other's love, and as his energy is passed onto you Mufahida, with your heart feel that you will become pregnant.

Please understand there are normally two reasons why a human woman does not conceive. First is stress from both partners, which is one of the biggest problems for human beings today. The second is diet. It is most important for you and your husband to eat plenty of fresh vegetables and fruits, and to drink at least 2 litres of water per day. Water is life and the human body cannot function correctly without it.

My being, through the grace of Creation, sends healing and love to you both. Be blessed in the Light always.

Kuntarkis.

SAD & CONFUSED

Dear Kuntarkis,

I'd like to think of myself as open minded and able to touch something beyond our everyday world. But I am so sad and confused that I do not know how to find answers or peace. My father died of cancer when he was 48, shortly after my sister committed suicide at the age of 23 and just last month my mother died of septicaemia at 65. I am a single parent working with music, laughter and children. My 10 yr. old son has been expelled from 2 schools for oppositional and aggressive behaviour and is now at a boarding school in England I live and work in Hong Kong. I want him to be with me though I love my children and my family. I love my work and the people I work with. I love nature and hills and sunshine I do not have a partner and find it difficult being alone. I am sometimes so full of despair and so confused. I'm not sure how to follow the right path. I am a creative and spiritual person but I've lost my energy and spirit.

I never said goodbye to my father and we were like one person. So in touch - I even felt his pain. Does he know how much I still love him and need him? He's stopped coming to me so much now - it's been 20 years and I was just a teenager. Shortly after he died I got pregnant and had an abortion. I woke up crying for my father. I've always felt sick with guilt that it was my father who was trying to come back to me again and I aborted him. Also my mum who just died. I flew back on the next plane from Hong Kong when I heard she was ill. I arrived in the early hours of the morning at about the same time as she died. Could I have been any quicker? Does she know how guilty I feel? How sorry I am that I didn't say goodbye to her too. What kind of a terrible daughter must I be? Are they together with my sister? Was it mum in my room the other night? Why has my family suffered so much? They were all such special and creative people. Will it happen to me too? I don't want my children to lose me. They've only got me.

I suppose it is me who needs to answer these questions. Maybe you could help me find out how. Strange that I stumbled upon this site whilst looking for Hodginkinsons disease. I am helping to take care of a little girl whose father is seriously ill in hospital and I wanted to find out about it. Perhaps I was meant to find this site. I feel it's going to be important to me.

Jane

Kuntarkis replies:

Dear Jane, On reading your words of expression to my being, my being can express back to you that all you are feeling - your sadness, confusion and despair, can all be put into one human word - guilt. What you are expressing is anger towards your father, your sister and even your mother, and that Jane is very natural. You need to stop punishing yourself.

Human beings place judgement upon themselves and carry guilt throughout their life, and many of them create dis-ease, which in most cases ends their human life. We, the Nar'Karones, have been observing human beings for the last 928,000 years, and throughout human history we have seen that pain, misery, dis-ease, and confusion has followed humanity throughout their history.

All human beings on this planet have had hundreds and even thousands of incarnations, so the circle of life has been going on for a very long time in human terms. Jane, you are caught up in your negative emotions of confusion, despair and sadness. That is why you feel so alone and yet you are never - never - alone. You have in spirit ones who love you very dearly and will always be there for you. At this moment in your life your guilt, confusion and sadness are the negative energy which has clouded the light of Creation that is within you, as it is within all of life. The human Ego is the negative aspect of all beliefs and conditioning in human life, because human Ego does not allow the individual to grow beyond its own self-created limitations.

All the human Ego sees is the negative aspects, which are created from past lives and from childhood to adulthood in one's present life. To step beyond the pain and fears, one must have the courage to let go of the past by forgiving others and oneself. To love oneself in unconditional love means to be unbiased, to not judge what is right or wrong, good or bad, but to see all things in life as experiences of life, neither negative nor positive.

You Jane can step beyond your guilt and pain. My being has touched the Light that is within you and you do have the courage and strength to step beyond your limitations. Go quiet in your mind, stop the chatter of your human brain and listen to your most precious inner voice. It will speak to you, but you must be willing to listen.

Meditate on this:

To forgive is never to forget, for if you have truly forgiven, you have not forgotten.

So dear Jane, remember, forgiveness is the key that opens the door to unconditional love, which will set you free from all confusion, pain, loneliness and sadness. It will take away the darkness and allow your light to shine within you and around you, and all will come into balance.

Be Blessed in Love and Light in your human life always.

Kuntarkis.

WHAT DOES THE FUTURE HOLD?

I want to tell you that I just returned from Guatemala as my mom passed away on Sunday, I spoke to her on the phone 1 minute and she died 4 hrs.', after that. She had 2 massive strokes. Her name was Luz Ulloa. Before leaving Guatemala I met with an uncle of mine Julio Lowenthal 73, asking him to help me get a job in Guatemala. He asked me to send him my resume which I have done. How soon do you see something being offered by him?

My sister Beatriz has kept all of my mother's money in the US as she is very mean evil and vicious, I can't do anything according to what my lawyer says she manipulated my mother for many years and took her away from us, we are going through hell as my wife has been without a job for over 11 months and I was unemployed for 20 months until I got a low paying govt. job. We want to leave El Salvador badly. I ask my mother spirit to MOVE us to Guatemala soon.

Alfonso

P.S. My sister has had 3 open heart surgeries to change 2 valves, is a diabetic has thyroid problems and has to take her blood sample every 2 days... I have a gut feeling she will pass suddenly and soon.

Thank you.

Alfonso

Kuntarkis replies:

Dear Alfonso, My Being understands your pain and your disappointment with your human incarnation at this present moment of human time. My Being needs to express I am not a fortune teller. My Being's purpose is simply to express knowledge. That is why Roman's and Ilona's website was created - to help all of humanity grow beyond the limitations of human Ego. Knowledge is the gateway to set each human individual free from their self-created fears of human life and all confusion.

The human Ego that each human being possesses is their personal enemy. To come to this realisation will help set all of humanity free from the pain and misery of their own creations. You Alfonso are so involved with your pain, you cannot see any way out. You need to seek deeper for the truth of knowledge from within yourself. Learn to meditate and use your power of imagination for there lies the strength and courage you require to go beyond all your pain and confusion.

Take the moments of human time to read deeply through Roman's and Ilona's website. Read the monthly articles, the questions and answers, for within them lies knowledge, and knowledge is the key to freedom and self-empowerment. You Alfonso can set yourself free from your present situation and rise above the pain and confusion of your present incarnation. Believe in yourself.

Be Blessed in Love and Light always.

Kuntarkis.

QUESTIONS ON KARMA

Dear Kuntarkis,

I have written to you by post because I can't give my name. I have read some of the articles and now I am wondering about the type of life I have been living. In all fairness I'm not a nice person. For the last 10 years I have been working as a debt collector. The company I work for expects results, never excuses. I'm very good at what I do and I've made a lot of money. But lately I've been feeling guilty for the pain I've caused others. I want to stop and give away my work, but I can't because you just don't leave the company... they get rid of you. I know so much about them, if they found out I want to leave I would be 'disposed of' quickly. It sound melodramatic, but I'm not joking.

You said in one of your articles that what you create in this life you will have to pay back in the next one. This has begun to concern me. You also said forgiveness is the key for all the bad things one does. Is this really true? And you also said love is the answer. How can one love if one has never experienced it? This is all new to me. I wish I could talk to you in person. Is this possible?

Man without a face.

Kuntarkis replies:

Dear Human Being, for you to write to my Being is a step in the right direction. To feel guilt for what you have created is the first step to self-realisation. You are already on your journey. It is true you have created from a physical understanding great pain to your fellow human beings. If you choose to stop creating this pain within yourself, you will stop creating pain for others.

Each human being must make their own choices in life, be it negative or positive. That is a gift of Creation - call it free will. When each human being begins their own journey of self-discovery, they must also take on the responsibility of their own actions, of everything they have created throughout their lifetime.

You have the power of free will to stop and change your life in any moment you choose to. From childhood, you dear human being have lived a hard life, and those experiences have helped create what you are in this moment. To begin learn to love yourself unconditionally, as you are, not what you have become. By being completely honest with yourself, through forgiveness you will begin to open your heart centre and allow your love to flow within you and around you.

My Being does not judge you or approve of your actions, yet I feel your pain. If you dear Human Being call my name in your time of sleep, I will come and talk with you and listen. May love be there for you always in your moments of need? Be Blessed dear human being.

Kuntarkis.

GROWING IN CONSCIOUSNESS

Dear Kuntarkis,

I am so excited in knowing the truth that ETs do exist! I just love the knowledge you express and I can see how you want to help humans grow away from the ego. I have begun to change many things in my life, and I can honestly say I feel so much better. I no longer smoke or drink, and I've given up all red meat. I'll work on the chicken and fish.

Learning to love myself has really shown me so much, and not getting involved with petty talk has allowed me not to judge others, which I used to do so much. I just want to say thank you, and I love you Kuntarkis, very much.

Deirdre.

Kuntarkis replies:

Dear Deirdre, My Being felt a little answer would be wise, just to say thank you for your kind words, and it is beautiful to see when a human being is gaining a deeper understanding of their own wisdom at such an early stage of their human life

Your journey in this human incarnation is one as a teacher and this will come to you over the next 12 years of your human time. You are indeed being guided on your journey. Always trust in yourself and all the decisions you make in your life. My Being knows you and I send you my love always.

Be Blessed Deirdre in Love and Light always.

Kuntarkis.

THE MEANING OF DEATH?

To Kuntarkis,

I was wondering if you could give me any advice on the meaning of death. My Mother died in April 2001. My Father died a little over 8 years ago in a mining accident. My older brother is 37 and is a drug addict. He's been told he won't see 40. As you might have already guessed I have a great fear of death. I don't believe in a god as such, but spirit does fascinate me. So why do I have a fear of death, and what happens when we die?

Fran.

Kuntarkis replies:

Dear Fran, when a human being loses someone special, especially their parents, it can create a lot of confusion. Most human beings do not like to talk or discuss the subject of death, and yet to understand death, one must understand life. Human death is a part of the evolution of this third dimensional world of physical matter. My Being sends you dear Fran the love of Creation to your heart, for we understand and feel your pain.

One should never look at how one passes over from their human life. One should look to the reason why. Human beings incarnate from one lifetime to the next for one purpose only - to let go of the past. Through incarnation human beings learn many things:

- To dissolve all negative aspects;
- To evolve beyond the human Ego;
- To grow in consciousness;
- To gain awareness and understanding;
- To learn compassions and forgiveness towards themselves and others;
- To see life without judgement by becoming completely unbiased;
- To become the living truth - an example of divine love to all humanity and all life.

Dear Fran, my Being feels your pain, and also the love you have for your parents, and how much you miss them. Yet they are together because of their love and understanding. They have visited you on many occasions. To answer your question of the meaning of death, death in reality is only a transformation. See it as a moment in silence and then the truth reveals itself, showing you that each human being is indeed a spark of living consciousness. There is nothing in all of life that perishes. Everything transforms to a higher vibration of living essence, which is infinite and eternal. All of life is ageless, timeless and endless. It is all in one's level of understanding and awareness.

Seek and all will manifest within you and around you dear Fran. Fear is simply another form of energy, and it has no power of its own, only what the individual gives it.

Be Blessed in Love and Light always dear Fran.

Kuntarkis.

TRUST ISSUE WITH HUSBAND

Dear Kuntarkis,

Please forgive me for asking another question so soon. But I am feeling desperate right now. I love my husband very much but because of prior bad relationships, I have trust issues. Last night my husband (Joel) went to the grocery store at midnight for a few things. He didn't come back home until almost 3:00 am. He said a policeman stopped him in the parking lot because our inspection sticker had expired (a few months ago) on the car. When they did a check on the car, they found out it was in my father's name (he is financing it for me) and thought it was stolen. So he said they took him down to a substation and questioned him further. After a couple of hours, they apologized for the inconvenience and took him back to his car and he came home. I guess I'm just needing some confirmation here from someone on the outside looking in. I need to know if his motives are pure.

Thanks SO much!!

Jo Karol

Kuntarkis replies:

Dear Jo Karol, to love yourself unconditionally first, allows you to have an understanding of what love truly is, and then empowers you to love another in unconditional love. My Being sees into your past relationships and understands why you have trust issues.

A partnership between two human beings is based on trust, honesty and unconditional love. It is advisable for you, Jo Karol, to deal with your past issues which were created from negative relationships. By forgiving the past and seeing it as an experience of one's human life, will allow you to stop bringing past situations into your present moments. If the past is not dealt with, it will create your present as well as your future.

The whole purpose of human learning from one incarnation to the next is to let go of the past, be it negative or positive. The purpose of human life is to learn to live in the moment and create a joyous future that will bring the balance of mind, body and spirit into complete harmony with all of life. When a single human being forgives all past issues and sees them only as a memory, they will create a perfect balance in their moment of life and all moments to come.

Remember Jo Karol, you as an individual are responsible for all created actions in your life, and those actions create your moments and your future. Your human husband is also on his journey of learning and understanding, and like you are responsible for your life, he is responsible for all his self-created actions in the life he is presently experiencing. What he creates in this life, be it negative or positive, will govern his future incarnations. For example, if a human being steals from another, they will create a reaction and be stolen from, if not in their present life, then in a life to come. This is true for any negative creation.

You Jo Karol have a beautiful heart. Trust in what you are feeling, but make sure it comes from your heart and not from your fears. Be Blessed in Love and Light throughout your life always.

Kuntarkis.

BEST FRIEND CHEATING IN BUSINESS

Hi Kuntarkis,

I run my own advertising agency. My business is quite successful and very fast paced. I must admit I like it like that. It keeps my mind busy and focussed. I wanted to ask you a question on a personal matter concerning my accountant, who I have known for many years.

There are some concerns that I am feeling. I think he is 'cooking' the books, meaning I think he is stealing from me. What hurts the most is I grew up in the same neighbourhood, and we were best of friends. I paid for his college to become an accountant. I want to bring in the police and yet I love him like a brother. I can't allow this to keep going on. He is married and has 2 young children. If I turn him in I won't be able to live with myself. This is really hard for me. Do you have any advice on this situation?

Mark.

Kuntarkis replies:

Dear Mark, when one is betrayed, for whatever reason, it will make it very difficult for one to make a decision. There is a Karmic reason for what is happening to you concerning your friend. My Being feels the answer will not help your problem.

From a physical perspective you have 2 choices. One, inform your police on the matter and allow them to deal with it, but know you will lose him as a friend and his family will suffer his pain. It will most certainly end your current situation of betrayal by your friend.

Or two, you Mark can invite him away from your office where you can spend some moments with him alone, and ask him directly why he is stealing from you. By finding out why, you can discuss the problem and between the two of you find a solution. If not, and the situation becomes heated, then you Mark alone, will need to make a decision. Do it without judgement and allow the answer to come from your heart, not your feelings of betrayal.

One point my Being wishes to express - your friend does have financial problems. By no means is that an excuse, just a point you may need to take into account.

Dear Mark, May you and your friend be blessed for every moment in your human lives.

Kuntarkis.

ASTRAL EXPERIENCE

Dear Kuntarkis,

I've been having outer body experiences more frequently these days. I've seen myself lying in bed from an aerial view. I've found my higher self-wondering in the house of someone that I didn't recognize but the most incredible experience happened about 3 weeks ago. It was about 4:00am in the morning, while I was asleep in bed. I was lying on my left side of my body facing a television monitor that I have positioned directly in front of my bed. I began to feel that all too familiar paralysing, tingly fuzzy vibration all throughout my body. For some reason I was able to open my fleshy eyes (usually, I am unable to do this during an outer body experience) and behold, I saw my higher self, reflecting on my television monitor. My higher self was slowly floating up and down above my physical body. My spiritual body was faced horizontally facing me and the eyes were closed. Once another time, I experienced feeling a strong twirling sensation above my head. I am not afraid of these experiences but I would like to know why these things are happening to me? What do they mean? Any comment or advice that you provide to me is truly appreciated.

Love,

Anthony.

Kuntarkis replies:

Dear Anthony, There are many reasons for the experiences a human being has while in the Astral vibration. One of the most important reasons is for the individual to grow and gain a higher awareness of their true self. Each journey for a human being, be it physical or spiritual, is in fact a step towards self-realisation of who and what they are. It is not so much the form of the experience but rather the knowing and realisation that all of humanity are sparks of living consciousness, and that all are a part of Creation's totality.

Stepping beyond the human body and entering the astral vibration and its many levels of consciousness helps all human beings on their journey towards their truth. But it is only a stepping stone of understanding, and yes, the experiences can be magnificent or overwhelming to the individual.

A method my Being has been teaching for many of your Earthly years is simple, yet requiring discipline. Anthony, you may wish to try the following exercise. Sit in a quiet place and, if possible, have no sound. Close your eyes, and listen only to your breathing and to your heart beating. As you sit on the floor or in a chair, take several very deep breaths, hold each one for 10 seconds and then exhale, and hold for 10 seconds. You may need a little practice with this breathing to start with.

As you become more comfortable with the breathing and with your eyes closed, put your thoughts to the centre of your forehead and believe you can see a small ball of light. After several minutes see this ball of light coming closer to you, and as it comes closer, see the size of the ball increase. Believe, see this is happening, and know it is your truth.

As you practice this method and truly believe that you are a being of light connected to all things, with all things connected to you, your mind, body and spirit will connect as one. This ball of light before you will expand beyond you and you as a conscious Being will be enveloped in light. As your awareness grows and your human ego dissolves, your essence of light (your living consciousness) will have no boundaries or limitations and all knowledge will be with you. You will, through practice, be able to travel beyond the physical and the astral vibrations into other realms and dimensions. But remember, no human negative ego can travel in these vibrations, only beings with unconditional love in their hearts.

It will take patience and practice, and it is your choice dear Anthony, but the rewards will be immeasurable.

Be blessed in love and light always.

Kuntarkis.

FEARS FOR HUMANITY

I live in the USA and I just heard on the news that several countries have nuclear missiles pointed toward this country and that this country will probably go to war with Iraq. Is this the beginning of the end for the Human race as I know it? Is this the beginning of a new world order? I feel that something horrible is going to happen on my planet. Please tell what your knowledge is on this subject. Thank you.

Blessings,

Debi.

Kuntarkis replies:

Dear Debi, My Being feels your concerns for the present and for humanity's future. Your answer on whether nuclear missiles are pointed at your country called America is sadly true, and yes, it seems the American government will go to war.

What may need to be understood from the truth, from the heart centre of all past, present and future knowledge, is no one ever wins a war. All conflicts of anger, hatred, violence and revenge are a product of the human past, brought into the present, created solely by the human ego, and based on negative experiences from one incarnation to the next.

Never look at the reasons why a war is created, especially from a physical understanding. Each human being needs to go to the source of the problem (the creation of wars) and it is all to do with energies of the past being brought into the present and then creating a violent future. There is a saying on your world "what you do unto me I will do unto you". This is revenge for what was done in other lifetimes, and it is continuing to this present moment in your human time.

The only way to resolve the conflicts of the past, so that the present can have peace and harmony, is for each human being to go still in the mind, to stop the human confusion and chatter of the human brain, to sit still and connect with the light of truth that exists in all of life, and indeed in all Universes. This light has always existed, but it has been forgotten. Listen to your inner Being, your Spirit that loves you unconditionally.

Make the connection from your physical self to your spiritual self and become united with all that is. All knowledge will be opened up to you and you will gain an understanding that you all come from the same source of light, that you all are a spark of living consciousness. To have that knowledge will not only set you free, it will allow you, the individual, to forgive yourself and all others from the past to the present.

All the past from all incarnations has created what humanity is in this present moment. It has created your prison of limitation, and yet through forgiveness in unconditional love, you will find the answer to ending all wars, for they are simply your human ego out of control. Sit in the silence of your mind, your inner Being, and project a ball of light, of love, to all of humanity. The healing process begins with the individual and the individual is a powerful instrument of light.

Be Blessed dear Debi in love and light always.

Kuntarkis.

MANIPULATION BY OTHER SPECIES

Dear Roman,

I LOVE your website so much that I've made it my personal mission to get as many people as possible to experience the treasure and wisdom you guys put into your site. I thank you so much for all that you do to help us understand about ourselves both in the spiritual and physical. Keep up the GREAT work!

Dear Kuntarkis:

What can you tell us about the authors and teachers such as David Icke and Dr. Malachi Z. York? Are these men being deceptive or is there much truth to what they present? Both of these men are bringing fourth astonishing stories of the origin of humanity and many cruel conspiracies that are being designed by the ruling elite. The most fascinating claim that I've read to date is about a reptilian race of beings who are working through the Caucasians to control and colonize the world. Another astounding claim is that these malevolent reptilian beings manipulate or control dimensions that we (humans) transition to upon the death of our bodies. Please enlighten us on this controversial subject. If these claims are true, what should we do to avoid being manipulated by the reptilian's deception in this vibration or any other?

Kuntarkis replies:

Dear Human Being, First my Being wishes to thank you for your kind words. It is good to see human beings like yourself wanting to grow beyond the past. Always seek the truth from within you – for there lies all knowledge of your past incarnations and all of human history.

The authors you speak of present many truths of deception and conspiracies that plague your Earth at this time. World domination will destroy the presence of your individuality. The past of all humanity will come into the present moment and create a violent future.

What you refer to as the elite of human society has been incarnating one life time to the next in order to take complete control over humanity, and this has been going on for hundreds of your Earthly years. My Being has asked Ilona and Roman to put on their website for March 2003 an article from August 2001 called The Unseen Forces: Who Actually Controls Humanity. Please allow yourself and others to read the article and if there are any questions please feel free to ask.

Please realise wherever there are negative energies, there will always be confusion over what truth is and what is false. Within every human being there is the knowing of who and what you are, and where all of humanity has evolved from into this present moment. To escape the negative forces each human being needs to become still in their mind and go within to discover their inner strength. It will take time and effort, but in the end it will be worthwhile.

Keep spreading the knowledge to all who choose to listen. Just a thought – Roman and Ilona are always looking for ways to take their knowledge to other parts of the world, such as presenting seminars and lectures, so they can spread their knowledge to all human beings to give them the opportunity of growing consciously. Perhaps you can suggest ways to help them in their quest.

Be blessed in the Love of Creation always dear Human Being.

Kuntarkis.

HUSBAND GAMBLES

Dear Kuntarkis,

I believe that I am a spiritual person. Can you tell me who I actually am? Why do I react strongly when my husband goes gambling? Tell me more about my spiritual journey... When I will be home?

Thank you so much.

Best regards from Jaime

Kuntarkis replies:

Dear Jaime, You are indeed a Spiritual Being of Light, as all humans are, and as all life in all dimensions, in all Universes is. You ask my Being who you are. You Jaime are a spark of living consciousness, experiencing a physical existence in a human flesh body.

The reason you react so strongly when your husband gambles is natural. Gambling is an addiction, like smoking, alcohol and junk food. It all ends in misery. Most human beings never want to look at themselves so they create an addiction which in turn suppresses their emotions and distracts them from their life.

Your spiritual journey in your present life time is to stand up for yourself, to be an individual. Truly believe in yourself and do what you truly want to do in your present incarnation. Try not to look for someone to love you. Find the love within yourself and you will indeed gain the strength and courage to overcome any obstacles.

Be Blessed in Love and Light always.

Kuntarkis.

THE EVERGREENS?

I stumbled on your web site looking for an herbal tea to relieve a disease for my mother. Several years have passed since I had contact with a group of entities called "The Evergreens". They were channelled through Michael Blake Reed. Do you know of these wise beings? They provided confirmation to me on many occasions at a critical time of my growth.

Thank You.

Don.

Kuntarkis replies:

Dear Don, Thank you for taking your precious moments to view Ilona and Roman's website. My Being trusts you enjoy the experiences of my thoughts. For your sick mother you were seeking an herbal tea. You may like to try green tea with a little grated ginger, fresh mint leaves and fresh basil leaves to taste. The additions make it more palatable and add their specific healing properties to the healing goodness of green tea.

The ones you speak of called "The Evergreens" who channelled through Michael Blake Reed, my Being is sad to say; no I have not had contact with these Beings. But what is more important is the channelled information was of benefit to you. All information of knowledge in all Universes is important to humanity, as all of life, in all its forms.

Be Blessed in Love and Light always Don.

Kuntarkis.

OVERCOMING SHYNESS

Dear Roman / Kuntarkis,

My questions are for my daughter who has no friends. She is a sweet and kind girl... we are all of a shy nature so I understand that this contributes to the problem. I had the same problem growing up... I rarely got invited to parties and never felt that those inviting me really enjoyed my company but invited me so I wouldn't feel bad. My daughter seems to be going down that same path. I have a friend that would seemingly sympathetically say that my daughter has no social skills... but how does one practice this if no one wants her in their company. Could this be a path we chose? To be unloved? I know it is more important to love than be loved but my heart aches for my daughter.

Growing up I just figured that for me... this is just how it is and I've accepted it. I've tried to bring up my children making play dates and such to enhance their experience with other children. Then as they grew up I let go and let them continue on their own. But at the age of 9 all the friends seemed to cease. She has a slight disability that causes her to limp but I don't see that as a big hindrance as my son seems to be following in the same path as well. Now she is 18 sad and lonely. Can your spiritual abilities give me any insight?

Thank you.

From a Mom who wants her children to be Happy :)

Kuntarkis replies:

Dear Human Being, Every single human being is on their own journey of self-discovery and self-expression because human beings incarnate one lifetime to the next. All human beings on your planet Earth have incarnated thousands of times, and seem to stay with the same human beings over and over again. The only difference being they take on a different role. For example, if one is born to be the father to the son in this life, in the next they may choose to be the daughter to the one who was previously the son, but in a completely different family and culture.

The whole purpose of reincarnation is simply lessons in life - to learn to love and become caring individuals, to grow consciously as Beings of Light. But it is the past of humanity which has caused so much pain and confusion within human society. Because of the negative emotions that most human beings suffer from, those negative emotions are passed into your human children and circumstances are created through life's lessons to trigger those emotions and subsequent reactions, and so you have the learning.

The whole human body is made up of living consciousness, and every experience a parent-to-be may have, be it negative or positive, is genetically passed to their children-to-be, then onto their children's children, and so on. This is where the problem exists. Your human daughter is experiencing what both you and your mother experienced as children. These emotions have been carried through your lives and passed on down the line.

The cycle can be broken. First your daughter needs to develop self-worth and gain confidence in herself. It would be good for your daughter to take up some form of martial-art to give her body strength and her mind confidence. Also, self-expression is very important. Perhaps take your daughter to a motivation course or suggest it to her – allow her to decide. It would also be good for her to go and do public speaking courses which will help her come out of her shell. To set the example, perhaps you, dear Human Being, should do some of these courses with her?

Always remember that unconditional love is the key to freedom from all self-created limitations. Never see life as a struggle, see it as an opportunity to step beyond all self-created limitations. All of life is simply lessons, neither negative nor positive – it simply is.

Be Blessed dear human being in love and light always.

Kuntarkis.

CAREER ADVICE

Hi,

I am currently undertaking a Bachelor of Nursing, Honours course and contemplating a thesis surrounding spirituality and nursing. I am wondering if you could offer me advice or information in my decision.

Thanks.

Julie

Kuntarkis replies:

Dear Julie, My Being feels you are a human being who wishes to help others. This is an honourable thing to do. You will learn and evolve consciously from this decision. To also do a course on knowledge of spirituality would be a great benefit not only to yourself but also to those who you will come into contact with.

One thing you must always remember, every human being has lived many, many incarnations on your planet Earth, and has therefore gained much knowledge and wisdom. Even though this knowledge is suppressed in most human beings by the human ego that drives the human being, try not to let too many belief systems condition your human brain into one way of thinking. Always have an open mind to all things without judgement, for that is truly being spiritual.

Julie, you can be of great service to humanity in doing nursing and adding the spiritual aspects of life to caring for patients. Be blessed in love always dear Julie.

Kuntarkis.

DO ALIENS INFLUENCE HUMANITY?

Hi,

Are there 'bad' aliens who regularly visit or live on our planet amongst humans and are brainwashing the government into covering up and hiding things that will stunt the growth, or even worse feed the human ego to the point of destruction? If this is true then what can we do to stop them?

Sita.

Kuntarkis replies:

Dear Sita, Yes, there are beings who exist in a vibration, the fourth dimension, who prey on physical beings like humans. These beings are of the Dark Forces who feed off negative energies created by human beings' negative thoughts and emotions. You see Sita, everything in all universes is simply energy. It does not matter what form or shape the energy may be, it is simply energy, and can therefore be used for positive or negative outcomes. It all depends of the user.

The Dark Forces who plague humanity have been with humanity for thousands of human years. These beings of negativity have been influencing human individuals for their own amusement. They can only influence those with negative thoughts, those who have great fears, and those who are weak minded. The Dark Forces can and do influence many human beings in places of power and importance, such as governments and the military. They need to feed off human energies in order to be able to survive in a physical vibration. In human terms, they are vampires living off human life energy.

You as an individual can stop their mind control by not being negative and not reacting in a negative way. Be in control of your individuality by becoming more aware of their presence and their influences. Use the Light of Creation that every human being is a part of. The Dark Forces hide in the darkness - they cannot be in the Light. It stops them in their tracks and it is the only thing they fear.

Be blessed in Love and Light always Sita, and remember, when you walk in the Light you become the Light, but when you walk in the Darkness, you become the Darkness. Be a beacon of Light always.

Kuntarkis.

UNABLE TO FOCUS

Dear Kuntarkis,

I have been very confused and indecisive about my life for nearly the last six years. Since September 2003 I started to study again after becoming motivated, but at present I am experiencing a state of confusion again, I feel depressed and unsure about my future, I have the strength to proceed and obtain good grades in my study, but I just can't seem to withdraw it from within me. Also my complexion/skin has been affected by my present state.

I would be very grateful if you could guide me, help me or find a solution/ explanation, so that I can be focused and get out of this state that I am in. I do want to gain a good education so that I can get a good job and live comfortably in the future, and make myself and my parents proud for all the effort they have put in for me. But every time I try and everything is going well, I experience a 'brain blockage', and I just can't focus on anything.

I have always had great interest in the spiritual world, and have become vegetarian through the understanding of karma.

Please help me! With many thanks,

Rakhee.

Kuntarkis replies:

Dear Rakhee, Do not be so concerned with what is happening in your human life. Many human beings are experiencing the same situation. You are not alone. You Rakhee have placed a lot of stress upon yourself and you feel unsure of your own abilities. What you call brain blockage can be a positive thing and also a negative thing. It all depends on how you see the problem.

It is good you have become a vegetarian and opening your mind to other understandings, like Karma. My Being would agree with you that you are finding it hard to focus. My Being would suggest that you need to find a relaxing pleasure which you treat yourself to daily, such as yoga, and especially meditation. It would help you to relax and focus your thinking and your life.

It would also help you to channel your energies into your ambitions for your human life. Remember Rakhee, what you think you become, just as what you eat you become. So be aware of your thoughts. You will accomplish your desires in your human life as long as you believe in yourself?

Always believe in yourself dear Rakhee. Be blessed in love always.

Kuntarkis.

WHY ARE HUMANS VIOLENT, HOSTILE AND HATEFUL?

Hi Kuntarkis

Would you please tell us the root cause of why so many heterosexuals of all races, creeds and colours display so much violence, hostility and hatred towards gays and lesbians? It's almost as if we are universal punching bags. So many say and truly believe that being gay is a "choice" a "sin" and against God's will. They (even those who aren't religious) almost always use religious quotes to justify their ignorance and bigotry. Heterosexuals commit "sins" regularly but rarely ever attack one another with the Bible or other holy books - It's just so hypocritical. I just don't understand why gays are poster children for everything evil, corrupt and deserving of death. Your wisdom on the subject is greatly appreciated.

Also are you familiar with Dr. Malachi Z. York? If so, would you please be so kind to briefly tell us something/anything about him. His wisdom and teachings are very compelling.

In closing I would like to congratulate you guys on your award! You truly deserve it! This is my favourite sight of all because the wisdom and guidance here truly resonates with me! I truly hope that you don't end your service here because you are truly a blessing to us all.

Tony.

Kuntarkis replies:

Dear Tony, My Being feels that until all of humanity finds the balance of unconditional love within themselves, there will always be violence, hostility and hatred not only towards gays and lesbians, but between nations, neighbours and even families.

The truth: the cause of all this pain, misery and violence is wholly the actions of the human ego creating the past into the present, and this creates the future for human beings.

Human beings are very emotional in their expressions and actions. Most do not understand forgiveness from the heart. Most human beings live from the past, even the past that is genetically encoded by their human parents. A large percentage of humans still hide behind a belief in a supreme being called 'God' and continually give away their personal responsibility.

What you have expressed about heterosexuals and homosexuals in reality is not the real issue. All humans that live on your planet have reincarnated many thousands of times over, and all have experienced homosexuality in some of their lives. The real issue is simply to create an excuse for violence driven by unresolved emotions from the past, be it the past from the current life or the past from past lives.

Regarding the human being you call Dr. Malachi Z. York, what specific information are you seeking?

Be blessed in love always.

Kuntarkis.

HELP FOR AILING MOTHER

Hello Kuntarkis

Thankyou for your reply to my question about dark forces. I have been reading and re-reading through your site and feel like I'm learning a lot. There are a few things I still would like to ask you.

The first is about my mother, she is not well and I worry about leaving her alone. She has not had an easy life and she has been ill for quite a while, I love her very much but we have not always got along well and recently she told me that the doctor said she needs to quit her job and move to a warm country otherwise she might not be around in 5 years' time. The reason she stays and works is because of me and I know that she will continue to do so and I'm worried she will not get better. I feel like it's my fault she's ill and because she cares about me so much, she wants the best for me even if it's making her more ill. It hurts to be around her when we argue and it hurts when she says she feels like she has no reason to continue living and is unhappy with her life. I'm 19 and I'm old enough to look after myself, but I just feel like she's given up on being happy in her life and I want to know what I can do. I've read her some bits of your site, including the section about illness.

The second question is about the changing weather on Earth, is there going to be a polar shift within the next 40 years or so which will drastically change the geography of the Earth?

The third question is concerning Jesus. You said that he was born in 4BC and that you incarnated on earth as a human in 4BC. You also have similar names and seem to say similar things, I was just curious to know if you came to Earth as Jesus, or if not did you know him? Or if he is living on Earth today as a human, who and where is he?

Thankyou for your site, it seems to tell me things which I have been looking for a long time.

Thankyou,

Sita.

Kuntarkis replies:

Dear Sita, My Being is pleased that Ilona and Roman's website is of value to you – knowledge is very important.

My Being understands your pain concerning your human Mother being ill. First, to understand the present one must understand the past. You and your human Mother have had other incarnations together. In your past life you were a human man married to your present Mother. As your wife in that incarnation she became very ill after giving birth to your only child.

Your love for her was unconditional and you spent nine long years looking after her. She was bed ridden most of the time. Because of your own family business you were able to spend many beautiful hours with her, talking to her and reading her stories. Each time you saw her your heart would melt. You loved her so much and you were very saddened when she passed away.

In this present incarnation your human Mother has taken on the same role in looking after you to the best of her abilities. Your Mother's heart is sad, yet she is paying you back the debt of love and kindness that you gave her in your past life together.

Your Mother needs to change her diet so it includes more fresh food, such as vegetables, fruits, nuts, and more natural proteins such as beans, yoghurt, tempeh and tofu. She needs to drink at least two litres of clean water every day. Yes, it would be good for her and you to live in a warmer climate, especially for blood circulation.

Please understand Sita that no-one ever wins any form of argument. The reason human beings argue is because of their own emotions, of how they are feeling. All arguments come from negative emotions created by experiences in human life.

If you're precious Mother is giving up on human life it is not because of you. It is her own emotional past, her experiences from a child into an adult. Remember, as human beings you each have a choice to be negative or positive – it is called free will.

Regarding your second question, the Earth at this present moment is off balance and is spinning like an egg would. The shift of the Earth's axis has been affecting weather paters for the last few hundred thousand years. In the year 2047 there will be drastic changes to your Earth's climate and yes it will affect all life on your Earth to some degree. The main changes are the energy patterns of human beings, but your Earth will also experience more earthquakes and torrential rains in areas where they have never been experienced before.

To your third question, yes, my Being incarnated to human parents known as Joseph and Mary in the human year 4BC. My name which was given to my Being by my Mother Mary was Jecuss which means Bright Star. The name Jesus, as written in the Bible by human man, means Divine Being. It seemed more acceptable to those who wrote the Bible, yet my Being has always liked the name Jecuss which my Human Mother gave me.

We the Nar'Karones have a great love for humanity and many Nar'Karones over the last 700,000 years have incarnated into human form for the purpose of expressing knowledge and to give any human being seeking a deeper understanding of life's purpose the opportunity to do so. We also have walked into a human life by permission and agreement to complete a karmic cycle for another being and then to complete our own learning by expressing knowledge to those who choose to listen and learn to raise their own inner awareness.

The whole purpose of life, including human evolution, is the growth of conscious awareness by growing beyond the human ego. The human ego is the negative side of humanity. It cannot go beyond the physical realm of humanity. This is one of the main purposes of life – to let go, to forgive and unconditionally love all forms of life. This brings the balance of mind, body and spirit into alignment.

Be blessed in unconditional love Sita and truly believe in yourself.

Kuntarkis

ASTRAL EXPERIENCE

Kuntarkis,

Please explain the message or meaning behind a very vivid astral experience that I had about a week ago...

The astral experience went like this... I was amongst a few people riding on a subway train (destination I am not sure of) on a beautiful bright sunny day... When all of a sudden we could see several tornados take form (reddish and brownish in colour) outside of the windows on the train. These tornados were heading straight towards the train that we were riding on (by the way, there were no clouds, no rain, and no thunder)...

From there, I remember myself and all of the others who were on the train, running to take shelter from these tornados. Two of the 6 or 7 tornados passed right over our heads quickly and the next thing I knew -- this full-figured black woman dressed in all white (goddess-like) was signalling to us and saying "come, get in the water." All the others ran towards the water but I stayed back, saying to her that I couldn't swim... She sort of chuckled at me and from there this experience got sort of strange...

The next thing I knew, I was lying on the ground, with this insane looking, and pale skinned lady with big bulging blue eyes (didn't look totally human) sitting on me. There were other people standing around as this was taking place. There was some dialogue between myself and this one other lady, who sort of moved this pale lady of me. As all of this was taking place there were other's standing around watching... It was almost as if they were all joking around with me or something.

As all of this was taking place, I CLEARLY remembered feeling very confused. The next thing I remembered was that someone was putting some kind of bright and shiny metallic lion claw-like device on my right foot. From there, I woke up from this experience, by a vibrating sensation in my physical body. The first thing that I did upon waking up was looking at the clock and it was about 1:30am. My heart was beating really fast as I tried to make sense of this astral experience. Nonetheless, at some point, I had fallen back to sleep to my surprise I had travelled back to the exact same location, (which is VERY rare to astral travel to the same place in the same night)!

The second part of this experience is more of a blur but I remember having a dialogue with the floating head of a white male wearing a crown or something. I remember asking him what the experience was about (what he said - I don't remember). I also had a dialogue with the same goddess-like black woman that I saw earlier and I distinctly remember her smiling and telling me "you went through the light."

Kuntarkis, I know that this story may sound bizarre to someone who hasn't had an astral experience but I know what happened to me was real and I would like you to please shed some light as to what this experience was about. What is the real messages that these Beings are giving me?

Thank you so much for your attention to this question.

Kuntarkis replies:

Dear Human Being, What you were experiencing was from a past incarnation. You are from what is called on your Earth the Element Kingdom. Even though you have had many human incarnations you are of the element Earth, which means in this human life you are learning the physical aspect of human form, creating in your life physical material understanding. In the Element World all is created from living energy, transformed into the power of thought. It is all about imagination.

The tornados were simply a way of getting your attention. The train you were travelling on was your transport and also to make you feel comfortable in the Astral Vibration because trains are familiar to human beings, so you would not become concerned or create fear. In most situations, if fear is created, you would automatically be projected back in to your human body.

You do have a fear of water, which was created from a past incarnation. This experience was also to help you overcome your fear of water. The pale skinned lady with bulging eyes was there to help get your attention. She is from the Element Kingdom and you do actually know her.

The black woman dressed in white was and is a contact guide to you. She is there to help you overcome your fears of human life. Your confusion to these experiences is understandable. All the experiences are to help you become more aware of your true self. Even though in your present incarnation you are to learn of the physical reality, these experiences are showing you not to forget about your true essence, the essence of who you truly are. A physical life will eventually end and you will move on to the next physical life, but spirit is endless, timeless, and ageless. Every form of life is pure living consciousness, and through consciousness one expands their own beingness to higher planes of existence.

The Astral World is to help human beings grow in awareness of their true self, but there are limitations which come from fears created by negative experiences from human life. These can be carried over to your next incarnations. You may need to meditate on the stillness of your inner being in order to connect to your true self and your inner knowledge.

Also, your name from the Element World, which has been with you always, is Barsjenia. One other lesson for you to learn is trusting yourself so you can learn to trust others.

Be blessed in love always dear human being.

Kuntarkis.

WHAT DOES: SIMPLICITY OF SPIRITUALITY MEAN?

Hi,

I came across your web-site and noticed that you mentioned 'simplicity of spirituality.' Would you be able to tell me more about this please? Would be most grateful!

Gill.

Roman replies:

Dear Gill, Thank you for your email. In answer to your question, what does 'Simplicity of Spirituality' mean, our name reflects the purpose of our site, which is to help individuals in their quest for personal growth and to develop their human consciousness.

We trust the information on our site will be of interest and of help to you Gill. May love and truth always fill your heart?

Roman.

SPIRITUAL AWARENESS

Dear Kuntarkis,

I have only recently (1-2 months ago) become interested in spirituality...and yes I have many questions! Can you advise me on some reading material that would assist me in my endeavours to begin to learn about spirituality and what is my spiritual name?

Thankyou for your time.

Mark.

Kuntarkis replies:

Dear Mark, It is good for a human male to seek knowledge and to grow consciously. The human ego that is present in all human beings has made many human beings blind to the truth, meaning not the truth created by humanity from the past, but truth that is present in every human being. You each have this truth - it is within you and always has been, but the illusion created by the ego of fear has prevented human beings from living in harmony with themselves, their neighbours, other countries, even Mother Earth.

Human beings need to reconnect with themselves and the Earth which will bring balance and peace and unconditional love for all of life, in all its forms.

Mark, there are thousands of books on personal growth and spirituality. There are many books in countries that other countries do not have. May my Being make a suggestion to you - go to as many bookstores as possible and at the personal growth or spirituality sections, ask yourself to be guided as your human hands touch each book. If it feels right to you then take it home and feed yourself the food of knowledge and understanding. Trust your feelings, they will not let you down. Believe in yourself.

Your spiritual name which has been with you for so long is Zenine, which is from the language of the Nar'Karones. It means 'one who walks gently through life'.

Be blessed in love always.

Kuntarkis.

BABY NUMBER 3?

Hi Kuntarkis,

My husband and I have been trying for baby number 3 for the last 3 years and still nothing has happened. Can you see me having this 3rd baby? If so will it happen within the next 3-6 months? If you could help me out it would be greatly appreciated. Thankyou.

Julie.

Kuntarkis replies:

Dear Julie, Please learn to live in the moment of life, as all things in all Universes are created in the moment, not in time which was created by man alone.

Yes, your third child will come, but you and your human husband need to slow down a little and take some precious moments for each other and yourselves. A suggestion, give your present human children to friends to look after for two of your human days, and you and your husband spend these days together away from your current place of living. Go to the mountains or to the ocean, whatever truly pleases you both. Relax and be in the moment. This will allow your human body to balance.

Both of you will be surprised of the outcome. Try. Enjoy. Just be in the moment and forget the worry for that moment in time.

Be blessed in unconditional love always, both of you.

Kuntarkis.

SPINNING WHITE MASS

Greetings Kuntarkis,

Thanks again for sharing your work with the world. You are truly needed. I have a question.

At times usually in the water (bath/shower) or just lying down I notice a spinning, spiralling, white mass that seems to be over my eyes only. It is rhythmic and can also move from left to right. After a while... if I am still... I begin to lose sight of matter in front of me, (for instance the shower wall) the wall begins to disappear and at that time I shake myself out of it. At times it seems as though there are ethereal walls alongside me and I am moving backwards but this is unclear as I feel no motion. There are also times when I can see this rhythmic white mass with my eyes closed. Can you give me some insight into this experience? Thank you so much for your insight.

Nat.

Kuntarkis replies:

Dear Nat, Thank you for your interesting question. What you are experiencing is a separation of your astral body from your physical body.

The spinning, spiralling effect is yourself going into a form of self-trance which allows your human body to become still. Your human brain becomes still and your inner mind, the true self, becomes active. In this state you can, if you allow it, astral out of your human self to experience other vibrations.

In this state of awareness you are not hindered by the human ego of beliefs and fears. You are indeed beyond your human self and experiencing your true self. In that vibration there are no limitations, only what the human individual places upon themselves. The white mass is your light, and the light is the essence of who you truly are. When you are in your shower and you are experiencing the bliss, the walls disappear because you are seeing beyond the illusion of physical matter. Physical matter is simply a state of the mind created by the Soul so you can experience life as a human being. Trust yourself and let go, and see the truth.

Be blessed in unconditional love always.

Kuntarkis.

FINDING SPIRIT GUIDE'S

Blessing and much light and love to you Kuntarkis, for your helping me and all others who seek you.

Firstly I would like to know my spiritual name please, but more importantly I would like to know where I can find my spiritual guide? I've been on the path for just under two years and I started through Buddhist meditation. At the beginning I was highly connected to the universe and many spirits would visit my room, which at first frightened me but now all the connection seems to have gone and I feel lost. My path and destiny has taken me away from all my family and friends. I am in a new land and I feel alone and lost.

I am of West African decent and I wanted to know do you know of any spirits or entities which I can ask for guidance and help? I want to be connected again but I don't know how. I also want to be connected through my African heritage. Is this possible? If so, how?

I have read many books on the path and at the moment I feel as if the path has led me the wrong way or all the happiness that was promised was a lie. I have suffered greatly in life but I always try to treat people as I hope to be treated, but being a person of pure light I have on numerous occasions been taken advantage off and hurt deeply, yet I feel such things lead to good karma, but now I am lost.

I want to learn how to be connected to the universe all time, so that I can grow as person of light, which I know I am and then I can be free of all of this forever. Please offer me some advice as I feel empty. I also often see an image of a red haired lady, wearing a long green velvet dress. She has lots of flowers in her hair and she is holding a wooden, carved staff in her right hand and she is standing on a hill top. The wind is blowing her hair behind her and she looks out across the land. I call her Ione and I think she is Mother Earth, as her feet seem to be so firm on the earth. She keeps coming to me. Do you know who she is? I have a feeling that she has led me here but she seems to have left me too. I just want to stop feeling so alone here. Please help me. Any assistance you can give me will be greatly appreciated as I don't know who else to ask.

Light & love always,

Amachie.

Kuntarkis replies:

Dear Amachie, Thank you for your kind words. Your spiritual name is Abbider. It was given to you by your human parents 38,000 human years ago. You have kept this name because of the love that you felt from your parents in that time of human past. Abbider means 'wild flower', because as a human child at that time you would never listen to anyone, only to yourself, so the name of a flower was given to you and you keep it because you felt it gave you strength.

Your path in life has been hard at times, yet in yourself you feel strength in all your decisions. You are indeed a very loving human being and yes you want to help the human world be a better place. You alone Amachie choose this human life, and yes you will rise above your pain.

To read books on knowledge and truth, no matter what they promise, can only help you if you are willing to step beyond your pain of the past. Pain and fear are only beliefs which become a condition of one's life. You are never, never alone. Your spirit guides are always with you. They never desert you, no matter what. It is the human self that feels they are alone because of negative created emotions.

Forgiveness is the path of unconditional love to yourself and to all others who may have caused you pain. Knowledge is the key to freedom from the fearful human ego. To connect to the universal energies for all time Amachie you need to forgive yourself, forgive others and love yourself unconditionally. Take recognition of your Soul, ask your Soul for guidance. Give up your struggle, for your Soul has always guided your human affairs from one incarnation to the next. Trust yourself so you can trust your Soul.

The image of a red haired lady in spirit world is a guide to you Amachie. Her name is Olga. This one is there to help you understand that all your past emotions are simply the past. The past is only a memory to be drawn on so you can see how far you have grown consciously as an infinite being, as well as human being.

This may hurt your feelings and I say unto you that my Being is sorry, but you Amachie need to stop running from yourself. You will not find your answers by running away. The answers are always with you right in this moment of your life no matter where you may be. Communicate with your Soul from your heart.

Be blessed in love always, but remember you are never alone. You are only alone if that is what you believe. For what you believe is in Truth your own Creation?

Kuntarkis.

AWARENESS OF SPIRIT REALM OR REALM'S

Thanks for all the advice.

I have been practicing meditation more frequently. I did slip through a brief moment of "lucidness" while mediating in my living room where I seemed to notice a woman enter my house through the front door, accompanied by two running animals, dogs perhaps, before unintentionally falling asleep! In fact, when I am in periods of my life where I'm attempting to explore the inner self more, I seem to get more sensitive to and impressions of different spirits throughout my house - including a nagging feeling of a young girl on my basement landing. I also experienced the sensation of a spirit "elbowing" my astral body (maybe?) in the face while falling asleep one night, a couple years ago. This coincided with a period of increased biblical reading. Coincidence or not? Have you any insights or advice on this? It's been puzzling me since these things have happened. And since you are the wisest entity that I personally know, I turn to you for whatever light you can shed.

Also, I understand perfectly your advice to always live in the moment, and strive to. However I do have nagging feelings from time to time about my past incarnations, and why certain parts of my personality and being act & feel the way they do. Can you perhaps give some small pertinent information in this area - it's my hope that you can, and also that you may know maybe a couple of the areas I have the greatest interest in.

I wish that I could have a longer question & answer period with you! - Or sometime in my life, be able to finally delve within to great depths. Are there things that would stand in the way, naturally or artificially constructed, of one who seeks to find enlightenment, apart from the things always mentioned such as diet & meditation? Or if one sufficiently devotes themselves to medication, will they eventually find the next "level" they are seeking?

DG.

Kuntarkis replies:

Dear DG, My Being thanks you for your kind words. What you are experiencing happens to many human beings throughout their lifetime. To some only once or twice, to others many, many times. When you are in meditation you are actually in a form of trance beyond human awareness, which can and does open many different levels in the spirit realm.

The area or vibration you live in as a human being, your home, has a very strong energy presence, and that is why when you meditate you are opening yourself up to present and past human experiences that existed in past human history.

Spirit world in many of its levels can see the human world exactly as it is in the now. Human beings have disconnected from the light and taken on the human ego of beliefs, religion and conditioning, which has closed the inner world of sight for many. Fear has taken humanity by storm. Fear is the human ego, and only the human ego lives in the past which has created the violent past into the present and continues to create the human future.

Your personality in this lifetime is a creation of your human parents. Through their fears, joys, negative or positive experiences, these are transferred to you through genetics. Your experiences from childhood into adulthood are also created by how you feel about yourself and from the society you grew up in. This all governs how you turn out as a human being.

It is understandable that you have some confusion about your life and your interests in life. What you chose in this lifetime was to become an actor in your human movies - you love to express yourself. That is a positive thing?

You can go deep within yourself, but yes, it does take discipline and courage to persist. Each human being is here on this planet Earth to learn the lesson of forgiveness and to let go of the human past. What stands in the way of any human individual from becoming aware is the human ego of illusion, self-created to keep all of humanity blind in their fears. That is the artificially constructed wall of fantasy.

A human being must live a physical life but also to realise they are a spirit being first. The two must come in union, meaning duality must become one. Every human being is enlightened - the secret it to become aware of your infinite self. Remember DG, seek and ye shall find.

Be blessed in love always.

Kuntarkis.

BARATHARY GLAND?

Greetings Kuntarkis,

I would like to know is there a place or planet called Rizq? And did the humans ever have a Barathary gland which was located inside the cavity of the hippocampus area of the brain?

Thank You.

Donald.

Kuntarkis replies:

Dear Donald, There is no planet called Rizq, yet there is a country on your planet Earth called Pakistan and the word Rizq is from their language. The human civilisation has existed on Earth for over 928,000 years. Nearly all humans over that period did not have what is called a Barathary Gland. However, this gland can be developed in a human individual, it all depends on their understanding and their thinking.

To develop this gland one would need to remove themselves from human society so they would not be influenced by the human ego. Their intake of foods would need to change to a raw vegetable and fruit diet, no processed food, no alcohol, no soft drinks, no drugs or cigarettes, no human ego.

They would need to develop themselves physically and mentally. The old ways of negative emotions such as hatred, violence, anger, judgement, fear, beliefs, lust, greed and vanity would need to be dissolved as they are a part of the human ego. One must attune themselves to higher vibrations and energies to become one, spirit and physical, no more duality or separateness of the two thus becoming compassionate, understanding and loving to all forms of life, humble to all forms of life.

Yes, it can be achieved if one is willing.

Be blessed in unconditional love always.

Kuntarkis.

MEETING IN DREAMS

I had a dream last night that we met, was that you? It felt so real.

Rich.

Kuntarkis replies:

Dear Richard, My Being thanks you for your email. To your question whether we met in your time of sleep, your answer in your mind's eye is already your truth – you have been wanting to meet with my energy, so yes, my Being came to you to give you the strength, courage and knowledge of understanding your purpose for incarnation in human form.

Because you returned to your human body at such great speed my Being felt you would not remember the experience, but you did. Congratulations Richard! Never give up, no matter what, you will come through your current situation, and yes Richard, there is light at the end of your journey.

Be blessed in unconditional love always my Brother.

Kuntarkis.

RELOCATION: YES OR NO?

Dear Roman, Ilona and Kuntarkis,

First of all, I want to thank all of you for your love and kindness, the generous giving of your time and energy in maintaining this open forum for so many people in the world like myself who is on a mission in life to search for meaningful ways to live and to be in the world. Since I discovered your website, I have submitted a few question to Kuntarkis, and I'm starting to feel a little guilty about it. You all have given so much information and wisdom for my benefit, and I have not returned anything other than my sincere gratitude. Please accept the following two question from me to Kuntarkis.

Kuntarkis, a few months ago I had asked you about my spirit guide. You told me that one of my closest spirit guide is by the name of Mignonette who was a French nationality and was incarnated on earth from December 1817 to 1893, and I would like to know what her relationship to me was during this period.

My second question regards relocation of residence. I currently live in the United States, specifically Houston, Texas. I plan to relocate (in about two years' time) to either Portland, Oregon or Bend, Oregon to establish a permanent work and home base. I have done research on these two cities but cannot decide which is right for me since both places are desirable. Please offer your insight.

Thank you, best wishes and much love,

April.

Kuntarkis replies:

Dear April, Your first question: Your connection to your current spirit guide (Mignonette 1817-1893) was that you were her daughter. Both of you lead very fruitful lives. Mignonette was a creative painter and was married to a man who was a leading lawyer who had very wealthy clients.

Your second question: The energies in both places (Portland or Bend, Oregon) would be good for you and your work. Portland holds a special meaning for you, but only you can experience that meaning. If you move there, you, dear April, will have created two paths. If you move to either place your human life will experience many different facets of life, but in reality that decision must be yours alone. Either would be good for you. If I as a being were to make a choice, it would be Portland. But please do not allow this to influence your decision. You will make the right choice for your current human incarnation. Make the choice from your heart. You have a beautiful heart – do not ever forget that.

Be blessed in unconditional love always.

Kuntarkis.

CONNECTING WITH YOUR INNER BEING

Thanks for the reply.

That's refreshing to my soul. I don't really know what the title Master Teacher means fully. Please forgive me for saying that. I just really found his teachings out recently. I would love the honour of having him as my master teacher and all the others out there willing to guide me. How do I achieve connecting with my inner being? I have tried to meditate in a quiet room and everything else. What am I supposed to hear or what am I looking for. That's why I would like guidance. I don't want to get lead in the wrong direction. But like you said I am my best guide. I just need to know what to look for. Thanks again for replying. Please write back.

Kuntarkis replies:

Dear Human Being, Every human being on your planet Earth is in reality a teacher in their own right. But first, one is always the student who must maintain a willingness to learn and understand. The one main lesson for all life forms in all universes is to learn the language of unconditional love, not only for themselves, but for all life forms, no matter what level that life form is at in their own evolution.

There is no right or wrong way to learn – everything is simply a lesson of experiences. It all depends on the individual's conscious awareness, their ability to recognise the human ego of destruction and a willingness on their part to step beyond the beliefs and conditioning of humanity that have caused so much pain and misery from one lifetime to the next over the last 928,000 years of human evolution on your planet,

Meditation is not the outcome of thinking, nor concentration or expectation. It is the transformation of you as a human being, connection to your Soul.

See yourself as a spark of light, a facet which your Soul has manifested as a spirit so that you can live in your human body to experience physical life. Remember, unconditional love is the key to freedom.

Be blessed in love always.

Kuntarkis.

FINDING THE PATH?

I would like to find out how I can find right knowledge, right wisdom and right understanding. I want to worship the creator of me the right way I want to learn how to eat the right way and raise my children the right way. My journey on seeking right knowledge has been since 1998. I am starving for the right path to go on. All I do is read everything, I can adapt psychology to ancient history. I am in need of a master teacher. I am ready to put myself to the test physically and mentally. I am ready to learn the teachings of the supreme grand Master Teacher Dr. Malachi Z York. And to be honest I want to make sure I am with 144,000. I love my people and I want to worship my creator the right way. Please get back to me thanks.

Kuntarkis replies:

Dear Human Being, What you are seeking is what all human beings seek – the truth, the purpose of human life. Allow my Being to express what you are seeking in this way: knowledge, wisdom, understanding, compassion, the reality of truth, the right path.

If you, dear Human Being, seek the above, then first learn to understand yourself, your fears. Take the precious moment in your human life to discover your true essence. Go into the silence of your mind, your inner being, and listen to your inner voice, the spirit of who your truly are. If you take the moment of your life and persist in stopping the chatter of your human brain long enough to make contact with your spirit, then you will find all you seek. You will find knowledge, truth, the right path, understanding and compassion for all life forms.

If you truly seek the truth then only within your inner being will you accomplish this. All else is the illusion of what humanity has created out of fear from the past to the present. Each human being must follow their own path to their own understanding because it will eventually lead them to their inner truth, their own divine essence which makes them a leader within their own right.

Once a human being has connected to their own spirit they will gain the understanding of truth itself, and this will give them the knowledge they seek, it will awaken their compassion for all life forms and it will open their hearts to unconditional love for themselves and all others. As a result of this process, wisdom will be manifested within their human life. The balance of mind, body and spirit will be in union, as one, not as separate facets of the human being, which it presently is.

If you feel you need to follow your grand master who you call Dr Malachi Z York. Then that is what you must do. But remember, every human being is in reality a leader in themselves. The individual only needs to believe in themselves to learn this truth. That is the beginning of becoming a human individual.

Be blessed unconditional love always.

Kuntarkis.

PUPPIES IN MY DREAM'S

Dear Kuntarkis,

I have had many dreams in which I saw puppies, such as a litter of puppies playing, a puppy come running to me excited with tail wagging, or a puppy come up close to my face to lick. I don't often see animals in my dreams, but when I did, eight out of ten times I saw puppies. Once I also saw a puppy in my vision in the waking state. Why do I keep seeing puppies and what does this mean? Please offer me your insight.

Sincerely,

April.

Kuntarkis replies:

Dear April,

There can be many reasons for why you are dreaming about seeing and playing with puppies.

My Being sees the puppies as children all playing together in harmony, without a care in the world. No beliefs, no conditions, no pain, no misery, no judgement, simply expressing their excitement and joy with each other.

The puppies are symbolic to you April. It is like saying "Never forget the child within". The child needs to come out and express, and enjoy the experience as a human being. Too many human beings become an adult and then forget the playful child that yearns to express their own creativeness, their joy, their love of life itself without the stress, beliefs or expectations of what human beings believe life is supposed to be.

Whenever you have an insight or a vision, go into the silence of your mind, your inner being, and just be without expectations. Listen, truly listen to your inner wisdom, for therein lies the path to freedom,

Be blessed dear April in unconditional love always.

Kuntarkis.

WHY IS MY HORSE SICK?

Hello Kuntarkis.

A friend told me about you and thought you may be able to help me. My horse is very sick. No one can work out why or what is wrong with her. I am 13 years old and I live in Texas.

Christi.

Kuntarkis replies:

Christi, you have a lot of love and compassion for animals, which is beautiful to see. Before I talk to you about your horse, it is important where you live to have your drinking water tested. Please do this because I know you have been having a lot more headaches.

Your horse is suffering from an internal fungus which has been caused by the water which comes out of your dam. It is run off from surrounding land which has toxins in it. Over a long period of time it could become dangerous for your horse. If your parent's have the dam water tested they will see this for themselves and will be able to do something about it.

Be blessed in the Light Christi.

Kuntarkis.

VISIONS OF LITTLE PEOPLE

Kuntarkis,

I have been having strange visions in my sleep and also seeing 'little people' even while I am awake. I'm 15, I believe in spirits but I can't talk about it to my family or friends because I know they'll think I'm crazy. Can you explain this or shed some light on what is going on with me?

Eve.

Kuntarkis replies:

Eve, you are very fortunate to have your visions. Not a lot of humans ever get to truly see the Element Kingdom. Think of yourself as very special because the Elementals do not come forward to too many human beings, mainly because they do not trust them, as they see the pain and suffering that continues to be put upon your Earth, your animals and other human beings.

The Element beings have many different kinds, (species I believe is the term you would use) those beings represent: Fire, Water Air, Earth, and Spirit.

Do not fear them for they will not harm you. They can enhance your life with infinite knowledge and understanding because they come from the heart. If you want to talk to them, ask them what their names are and tell them yours.

Safe journey special one, and be blessed in Light and love.

Kuntarkis.

MICHAEL J FOX

Kuntarkis,

I have a strange request. It is not for myself but for someone I feel is very special and is going through a lot of sadness in his life. I am a huge fan of Michael J Fox who is sick with Parkinson's disease. They say there is no cure. Is there anything that can be done for him as I truly feel his pain and I think he is a wonderful man who has given so much through his acting?

Jessie.

Kuntarkis replies:

Jessie, it is a beautiful expression of unconditional love to care for another human being, especially since you have not met him in physical form, but only seeing him on your viewing screen. Yes, I can feel your love for him and the pain you feel for what he is going through, this being you call Michael J Fox. He is also a very loving human being who in his own way of expressions has brought a lot of laughter and happiness through his entertainment to your world.

His sickness is part of what I call the result of cause and effect, which all disease on your Earth comes from, and yes, all disease can be cured beyond your human medical knowledge. His situation can be reversed; it would take a little of your Earth time and a little discipline from Michael. If you, Jessie, could communicate with this being and if he was willing to listen with an open mind and heart, I can explain to him how he can and would reverse the sickness he has created.

Jessie, the human mind is very powerful if understood. It is what I taught the one called Roman who cured his lung cancer - whatever is created can also be uncreated through the power of knowing which is within each of you. I must leave this situation up to you?

Be blessed in the Light Jessie, and be strong, because you have infinite strength within you.

Kuntarkis.

THE HEART OF JESUS

Dear Kuntarkis,

I was wondering if you could shed some light on a person that is very close to my heart. His name is Jesus and I pray to him every day. I don't ask for anything for myself, but I ask for healing for humanity and the Earth because of all the suffering man has put on it. Am I doing the right thing or can I do more?

Lilli.

Kuntarkis replies:

I must express to you Lilli that you are a very special human being for the love you have for Jesus and your selfless praying for healing for humanity and your planet. You are truly a living example of unconditional love and truth. Yes, it is sad what is and has been happening to your Earth as your planet is at present suffering both internally and externally, which is why there are so many disasters occurring around your world. Your planet is going through many changes.

Please Lilli, realise that your planet is a living being with a spirit just like every human being has a spirit. If your Earth did not have this spirit it would be a lifeless planet. Lilli, keep doing your beautiful healing. Always believe in yourself and your natural abilities.

And yes, Jesus is and always will be close to your heart. You are truly an inspiration to your kind and others should see you as an example of loving Light.

Be blessed in the Light dear Lilli.

Kuntarkis.

CONCERN FOR THE ENVIRONMENT

Hello Kuntarkis.

My name is Oki, I am from Japan but at present I live in Australia. I am doing a science degree, but my real interest is in the environment. I am very concerned about the poisons that are floating in the air and those that are in the soils. In Japan, and especially in the cities, the air is very bad. Pollution is everywhere but nothing seems to be being done about it. What will happen to us if we continue with the same ignorance? I am very concerned.

Oki.

Kuntarkis replies:

Yes, Oki, you have very good reason to be concerned, and yes there is a lot that can be done, but it is up to people like yourself who need to express this concern to your governments to show them there are some who do truly care for this planet Earth. Write to your newspapers, research and seek out information which will help explain what effects pollution is having on your species, especially on human health. The more who express concerns and reveal the truth, the more will follow the example about voicing concerns and wanting to do something about it.

What is occurring on your Earth at this time will increase and it will get to a stage where the precious air which your species need to breath in order to survive, will become so toxic that nothing will be able to live, not even your vegetation. Our own species on Nar'Kariss went through the same situation a very long time ago, and it took a long time to overcome. We have the understanding and the solution to pass on to your species, but getting your governments to listen with an honest heart and an open mind to our wisdom may be very difficult, mainly because of their beliefs and conditioning, which is simply Ego, nothing more.

Oki, remember; only truth that comes from within each of you will set you free from the limitations that your ego has put upon all. The power is within Oki.

Be blessed in the Light.

Kuntarkis.

IS JESUS A MYTH?

My name is Ulrich,

I am 23 and was born in Germany, but now live in Switzerland. I have read many books on many subjects like what you speak of, and I believe you exist on a different conscious level. I wanted to say that I have read and copied all of your website and have found it very interesting and full of knowledge. I show it to many of my friends.

My question is, was Jesus a real person, or a myth?

Kuntarkis replies:

Ulrich, it is good to see human beings like yourself reading and searching for truth, as it will expand your knowledge, but also your awareness of life itself, and allowing you to also expand your consciousness. There is a book inside of your being which is called the book of knowledge. Each human being on your Earth has it for a higher learning which can and will give you truth itself.

You ask of the one called Jesus. Yes, he was a real human being who came of his own free will to give his knowledge and wisdom to all that chose to listen. He was born on 19 August in 4BC to Mary and Joseph. But one thing must be understood, and this may upset those who are deeply religious on your planet. Jesus was born by natural human means, conceived by a Roman soldier who raped Mary by a river bed. She was rejected by her people for becoming pregnant and they believed there was no father. But because Joseph always loved her, he accepted her, married her and accepted and loved the child she bore as his own.

Jesus was a very happy child and his parents knew he was gifted. When he was 17 he chose to become a vegan, which meant he chose to no longer consume anything of animal origin. He explained to his beautiful parents that he was cleansing his body to raise his consciousness and to allow higher forms of knowledge to come to him.

He always told his parents why he came to the Earth and he even explained his death to come. Many people loved him but also there were those who were afraid of him because he was so different. Jesus was, and is, a highly evolved soul who was and is full of love and compassion for your species. That was the reason for his coming on your Earth.

If all human beings were to cleanse their thoughts and their bodies, they would raise their own consciousness to higher realms and be able to communicate with beings like Jesus. It's all up to each of you.

Be blessed in the Light Ulrich.

Kuntarkis.

WHAT DOES NY FUTURE HOLD?

Greetings Kuntarkis.

I am anxious about few things and will be grateful for any answers you can get for me:

When will my career and my relationship with my partner improve? What are they and how do I attain them?

Thank You

Mani.

Kuntarkis replies:

Dear Mani, to expand your own awareness in consciousness is to be in touch with your inner essence. To step beyond your beliefs and your conditions of your human life is your first step to self-realisation. Please try to realise that all upon your Earth's vibration, which is third dimensional, is physical matter, physical logic and physical human Ego. This is what stops the awareness of self-realisation and conscious growth, which in turn keeps humanity unaware of the infinite energies that exist in all of life and all universes. This energy which is pure light is your personal power source to give you the strength and the knowledge to know and create your path in this human world.

Because of negative human emotion, which is humanity's past, based on every individual's conditioning of life, this negative emotion holds individuals in their fears and insecurities. It stops you from seeing beyond your fears. Your career Mani can be whatever you choose it to be, you only have to see what you want from your human life and then put the action into it. If you believe in yourself you will most certainly create it.

As for your relationship, the human being in your life at this most precious moment is what you created, and it is both yours and your partner's choice to have a loving, beautiful and fulfilling relationship. The power for this lies with each of you, but you must both choose to make the effort. It will depend on both of your emotions. Each of you must deal with your own negative emotions and love yourselves unconditionally. Your relationship will then become balanced in pure love and friendship. You both are beautiful beings. Take the moments of life to see the beauty in all things.

Be Blessed dear Mani in Love and Light. Remember, you are the Creator of your own destiny. See what you want from life and go for it.

Kuntarkis.

FEELING PHYSICALLY AND SPIRITUALLY ALONE

Sorry for not addressing this to anyone in particular,

I am new to this way of believing. See, this is my problem: I feel as though I am a spiritual person. I feel things in a different view than anyone I know, but if I am as I say a spiritual person, then how come life seems so difficult to understand, and why is it so hard for my husband to comprehend my way of going inside myself for answers? How do I teach him to do this in himself? I really need people who live the way I do around me for me to continue believing in my own guides for help. I live in the heart of Christianity, Oklahoma, and feel as though there is no one near enough to me to help me channel my guides and help me through this very tough time. Please help me locate others like me.

Ginger.

Kuntarkis replies:

Dear Ginger, You as a being, that is infinite in the totality of Creation, most certainly you are not new to spirituality. It has been with you throughout all of your incarnations. The only problem has been that in each incarnation you were highly conditioned and influenced by your parents and society into their way of thinking. That is not to say that your parents or society were right or wrong, all it means is that you chose the beings you would incarnate through and in order to learn certain lessons, for that is the nature of human existence.

Please do not try to change your husband, for his journey in human form is his own. Ginger, for you this life you have in this most precious moment is one of your greatest challenges - to let go of your past beliefs and all your conditioning, and to believe in your true self which is infinite and eternal. Search beyond your human understanding and seek the knowledge and the truth within you. Listen to your inner most precious spirit and you will find the peace and harmony that you seek, and you will become the living example for others to see.

Love yourself unconditionally and love your husband simply for himself. When you touch your most inner essence, your guides will be there for you, to see and communicate with. Then the balance of mind, body, spirit and soul will be almighty present within you and around you. Even though you live in the heart of Christianity in Oklahoma, you will allow others to believe what they choose, as all human beings have their own journey in life. So many humans hold onto the past and are not willing to step beyond their present understanding.

You Ginger have the knowledge within you, which will set you free from all self-created limitations, and you also have the strength. My being believes in you. When you become balanced in mind, body spirit and soul, you will bring others who believe in the truth into your vibration.

Be Blessed dear Ginger, and May the Love and the strength of Creation flow throughout your most precious being.

Kuntarkis.

FINDING AND EXPERIENCING CONNECTION TO CREATION

Dear Kuntarkis,

I'm a young woman at the age of 21. I was brought up with the belief in Christ and his father God. I have had many experiences with things Christians call evil. My mother has been involved in exorcism for a number of years. As a child my belief in God was stronger than it is now. I assume that's because of the influence of the world. I find your beliefs resemble Christianity for God says the way to live by his laws is to love your neighbour as you would yourself. I have always been intrigued with the story of Adam and Eve. I've always thought that the apple they ate was symbolic for something else.

When I was at the age of 18, I had just come out of a bad relationship in which I gave everything of myself but received absolutely nothing in return. That's when I met the father of my child. I am a black woman and he is white. I've always been against inter-racial dating and so our relationship started out as a friendship. But we both felt this connection with each other as if we'd known each other for ages. I told him about my upbringing and religion and he told me he had his own religion and would show it to me one day. He asked me to experiment with mushrooms. Up till then I only smoked marijuana and was afraid to try something new. But he persuaded me and I gave in. During our "trip" there was a moment we suddenly realised we were not speaking with words but understood each other by using only our minds. Telepathy. I was always told that telepathy isn't from God. That it's evil. But at the time it felt so right.

My boyfriend told me never to tell anyone about our experience, but because I had a lot of doubts and fears, I told some people. I wanted to know their view. During our experience he told me about what he thought to be the truth. It is exactly what you claim. About life being a form of energy and everything should be in balance. I asked him where his beliefs came from and he answered from within and that everybody knows this deep down inside. I also told my mother about it and she knows the bible inside out and said we should look at the source from which our experience came out of and we would know it to be true or false. Drugs are a bad thing so I presume they're false. I was devastated because I really wanted it to be good and from God. I accused my boyfriend that he made me forsake my belief.

This of course is not the truth because I wasn't obligated to take the mushrooms, I did so by free will. My mother told me to be weary of false prophets because the evil will come as if it's the truth, but in fact it deceives you. What I wanted to mention also is that our lives are full of funny coincidences. I only knew my boyfriend for a couple of weeks before I moved in with him and within 3 months I got pregnant with my son. We also had some unusual pets. Two snakes: a brown one and an albino. I said let's call them Caesar and Cleopatra. At that time I didn't realise that Caesar stood for the west, being European and Cleopatra for the East, being from Africa. It was a total coincidence. We searched for names to call our child and again without knowing we gave our son these names: Neo Odessa Amaru (two European and one African). I also read on another site that names are very important because they determine the kind of person you become. Is that true because if so I feel I might have to change Amaru for it means serpent. I did not know that before I gave him that name. I named him after my favourite rap star called Tupac Amaru Shakur. (By the way is he really dead, and if not can I contact him in any way?)

A few months after experimenting with mushrooms my boyfriend brought home an xtc-pill. We took it and because we already saw a lot of similarity between our lives and Caesar and Cleopatra we rented a movie about them.

Throughout the movie we felt very connected with each other. There are a lot of mysterious things happening to me right now and it would take a phone call or a meeting with Roman to tell you everything that's going on. Please mail me back very soon. If you don't want to meet us or talk over the phone, maybe I can explain it in segments over the e-mail and tell you more about us.

Love,

Janelle.

P.S

Why does your name resemble the name of Jesus Christ?

Kuntarkis replies:

Dear Janelle, Thank you for taking the moments in your life to write to my being.

First, the story of Adam and Eve is symbolic. The reality of that truth is man-written and it has followed humanity over the last 2,000 years of human history. Unfortunately, belief systems are non-truths, as they are not experienced by the individual, only conditioned through one's parents and human society. Beliefs and conditions have followed humanity throughout history, and most of human history has been written by man from his Ego, not from his heart. If a human being wishes to know the truth it can be easily found within each individual, for all of human history and all of the lives you have had over the last 928,000 years are encoded into your essence, which is with each of you throughout your existences.

The secret to going within is the stillness of one's mind; to stop the human chatter of human Ego, to listen to your inner self which is the spirit of your true self - that which is infinite and knowledgeable. Only through perseverance with oneself can the truth come into being. You are a beautiful human being Janelle and you have a lot to give, but taking the easy way to find the inner worlds by using drugs will lead you to the falseness of human Ego.

There has never been a human being over the last 928,000 years who has found the inner truths of Creation's infinite knowledge, by taking drugs of any description. Many have tried and many are still trying. They believe what they experience is something magical but I assure you from my most inner being the only experiences you will have from taking drugs are within the lower astral vibration, based on the illusions of one's own human brain and which is from a negative energy. If the drugs of your human world are taken over a long period of your human time, they will consume your physical being and lead you to pain and misery. So many human beings look for an easy way to achieve enlightenment and yet each of you are enlightened beings already. It is all within you waiting patiently to be discovered.

The human man of your child is very knowledgeable and he has a lot of wisdom, but he is also mislead by his Ego of beliefs and conditions - the beliefs and conditions he grew up with. He has the truth within him and he does not need the falseness of drugs to give him the answers of infinite truth. Janelle, you and this man have had many lives together, the following two human children that will be born unto you have also been with you throughout your existences.

The one you speak of called Tupac Amaru Shakur - his energies on your human world do not exist, so he must have passed away.

Many human beings have written to my being on Caesar, Antony and Cleopatra who lived in your past human history. I was asked to write about them, especially Cleopatra, which I did.

You asked of my name Jecuss Kuntarkis. I have had the name Jecuss for the last 2,000 years of your human time. It was given to my being by two beautiful human beings when I incarnated in your vibration in 4BC. The name Jecuss is old Hebrew, meaning 'bright star'. Since that human life I have experienced on your Earth was very special, I have kept it close to my essence. My name Kuntarkis has been with me for around two and a quarter million years of your Earth time, its meaning is 'to see is to know and to know is to create'. It comes from the vibration of the planet I exist within and around called Nar'Kariss. There is some information you may wish to read in the article Nar'Kariss: The Planet, Nar'Karones: The Beings, also found on the Library page of this website.

May the Love and Light that exists within all things be present in your life and in your heart? If you choose to e-mail my being again please feel free to do so. Be Blessed dear Janelle, and love who you are.

Kuntarkis.

LOST SPIRIT

Dear Kuntarkis,

For some years now I have suffered from what I believe to be most debilitating, untreated, spiritual depression. I believe something was taken from me and I wish to attain peace in its absence or to regain my true self.

Thank you.

Negative Person.

Kuntarkis replies:

Dear Human Being, First, my being wishes to express to you that you are not a negative person. It is only your past that haunts you in your present, and in turn creates your future. Many wonderful experiences have come to you in your past which have brought out your true spiritual self. You, dear Human Being in this most precious moment in your life, are releasing your past emotions, and these emotions are blinding you from your true self. You feel there is no hope for you in regaining your peace and your harmony. But never look to hope for it is a negative human word and leads only to hopelessness.

Look around you, your life, and see what is negative, be it situations, where you live, what you do, or even your friends. If there are negative circumstances around you it means it is time for a change to create a positive energy within you and around you. Do not allow another to place their negativity onto you because it will prevent you from dealing with what you are feeling.

The power to your truth and your peace of mind, body spirit and soul dear Human Being is within you and always has been. To love yourself unconditionally is your first step to freedom and to the divine truth that you are a beautiful human being. Still your mind to stop the chatter of your human conditioning, and listen to your most precious inner being, for it is there that you will gain the knowledge and understanding which you seek. The Human Ego is your fears and insecurities, and it is your Ego that has created your negative emotions. All things in the universe are simply energy, and so are your fears, insecurities and negative emotions. Through believing in your true self, the divine light that your essence is, you can dissolve all your negativity and return it to the nothingness from which it was created. You have the power of this truth and Creation within you to know and do this. But what will you choose?

I believe you can do it. Be Blessed dear human being always in Love and Light.

Kuntarkis.

PAULINE HANSON AND FREEDOM OF SPEECH

Dear Kuntarkis,

I came across your website by chance, and after reading some of your information, I found it answered some of my inner confusion and what I am feeling about how this country (Australia) has lost something very special. I call it freedom of speech, for I believe it doesn't exist anymore. Which brings me to my question on a person called Pauline Hanson: could you please give me some insight why Ms Hanson is being black-banned in politics? I would be most grateful and I thank you.

Maria.

Kuntarkis replies:

Dear Maria, I am glad that you as a human being found Ilona and Roman's website of interest, and that it has helped you with the confusion around you. That is the purpose of my being, my presence - to give knowledge and an understanding of the conflicts and confusion that truly exists within all human beings on this most precious Earth.

The one you speak of called Pauline Hanson is indeed a beautiful human being, and she sees the corruption and injustice that exists in Australia's politics which has existed for so long. Unfortunately, the people of Australia have been very blind to the falseness that exists not only in Politics, but wherever the greed of man exists. I can assure you that there is much corruption in the governments of Australia, even though as a country of your Earth, it is seen as a peaceful and democratic nation. This is why the public, you the people, have no control over your lives. You are made to believe through your media, your governments and your religions, what is right and what is wrong, what is truth and what is false. Yet there are those who are willing to stand up for the rights of people, to change the injustice that your governments have created. Little by little the individual is losing control of their destiny. If the one called Pauline Hanson is able to stand up for the rights of the people, or attempts to bring justice for all people, your governments would become fearful of the possibility of losing control. They would then lose their comforts of life, which they acquired through corruption and misuse of position and power.

Yes, your government conspired to destroy Pauline Hanson and her followers, by creating a falseness to destroy her chances of getting into power, and yes, she would have achieved her goals if the falseness created by the existing governments had not manipulated public opinion. I have said this because it shows how much power and control a government has over its people.

One point must be expressed: governments are elected by the people to serve the people. It is true, the people do have the power to make change, not the governments, for the governments are there to serve the people, not to control them. Only when each human being becomes 100% responsible as an individual and learns to understand the power of Creation that exists within all of life and becomes fully aware that human Ego is the negative aspect of life, will the balance of life be almighty present in each human being. By dissolving the Ego and bringing forth unconditional love for all of life, then and only then will each of you be set free from the falseness that exists in all of your human societies. It is the fear of the unknown that holds all of humanity in the past, and yet fear is only another form of energy.

Be Blessed dear Maria and thank you for your question. May Love and Truth manifest in all of humanity.

Jecuss Kuntarkis.

ABORTION AND WHEN LIFE ENTERS THE CHILD

Dear Kuntarkis,

I am not sure I should be writing to you on my situation. I just found out I am pregnant and my parents flipped out. I am 18 years old and feel I should be able to make my own decisions, but parents don't agree with me. They want me to have the baby but I want to have an abortion, and I don't feel it's their right to tell me what to do in this situation. Do you have any advice for me? Also, my other question, when does life truly exist in the foetus. If you could answer me it would be great.

Nell.

Kuntarkis replies:

Dear Nell, All of life that exists within all universes is most precious. No one has the right to take any form of life, whatever the reason. Because if a life - any life - is taken by another, then that situation creates an imbalance, and as long as that imbalance exists (which many of you on this Earth call Karma), then it must be brought into balance once more. That is and always has been a part of nature, throughout all Universes. It is not a law, it simply is.

But dear Nell, it is the Spirit that is infinite and that exists within all flesh life, for without the Spirit, flesh life could not exist. So now to your question of what moment does life, the Spirit, enter the flesh vessel of the human body to give it life, awareness and consciousness. That is the question.

The Spirit that will enter into the human vessel is fully aware of the forthcoming child and oversees the development of the flesh vessel to be. But the Spirit does not enter until the vessel is born, that is until you give birth, and when the first breath of air is taken into the lungs, then and only then does true human life exist. If the Spirit entered before that moment, it could become locked inside of the Mother and it would create disaster. So, life in the foetus only exists because it is connected to the Mother's body and its functions. In reality it only has life as long as the Mother's body is alive, and it has no consciousness of its own. While the flesh vessel is being developed inside, it is as if it were on life support, but there is no being consciously resident there.

Each individual has a right to the freedom to choose, no matter what the situation is. No one, regardless of their personal emotions, has the right to tell another what they can and cannot do, or to impose their beliefs and conditioning upon another. Dear Nell, my being is not telling you to have an abortion or to have the child. You as an individual must come from an honest heart and choose what you want from life. Listen to your parents without judgement, but in the end the choice is always yours, and you have the strength to make that choice. I trust the answers I have given will help you make your decision more confidently.

Be Blessed dear Nell in the Love and Light of Creation always.

Kuntarkis.

SINKING OF THE TITANIC

Dear Kuntarkis,

I have a question on history. A ship in the early part of the 20th century called the Titanic sank suddenly and was supposed to be unsinkable. Did it hit an iceberg which caused it to sink, or was it the Captain's fault, or were the Germans responsible for its sinking? I am curious for the truth, as my great grandparents died in that tragedy.

Gassot.

Kuntarkis replies:

Dear Gassot, Yes, knowing the truth will ease the mind and help set you free from the past, as the past is the past, to be only remembered as a memory, neither negative nor positive, just simply the past.

The ship you call Titanic did hit an iceberg on a cold evening and sank within hours of your human time to the bottom of your Earthly Ocean. Unfortunately many human beings died for no reason except for greed and human Ego. Those who perished did not have a choice. It was the single decision of a human being who gave the order to increase the ships speed so they would reach their destination ahead of human time in order to win a contract.

It was not the Captain's fault as he took his orders from a higher source, that is, the owner. The Germans did not have any part in what happened. Unfortunately, when the ship was travelling at full speed the ovens were working at full capacity and running at very high temperatures. Being in very cold water, the two do not mix very well.

When Titanic hit the iceberg at full speed, being large as it was, the iceberg opened it up, like slicing through what you call butter. Many parts of the ship near the hot ovens added to its demise. One example, if a large amount of ice were to be dropped onto your Earthly Sun, the explosion would be so massive that your Earth would be disintegrated within moments. And so it was with Titanic. The ice was very cold and the ship was very hot in places. The shock from the collision caused it to split open.

The truth will be discovered in your near future, when humanity enters the inner parts of Titanic, and this moment is not too far away. But also just to let you know, most of the spirits who left their human bodies when the ship sank have in fact reincarnated on the Earth plane over the last 63 years and are living today in your human time.

Be blessed all in Love and Light always.

Kuntarkis.

GREAT WEBSITE

Dear Kuntarkis,

I was at my friend's place visiting, and my friend showed me your website. She said it's helped her understand things about herself and that it may help me find the answers I'm looking for. We spent about two hours viewing the site and I was completely engrossed. When I got home I decided to look at your site some more. I lost all track of time until Mum told me to go to bed.

I don't have a question at this time because I'm trying to understand all this new information. I'm so excited. This is all new to me but I feel there is a part of me that knows what you're saying. You have opened a door in my mind. When I think of a question I will email you.

Thank you for who you are and for helping us humans understand. There is so much more to learn from inside ourselves. It has definitely opened my eyes. Thank you.

Abbey.

Kuntarkis replies:

Dear Abbey, It is indeed a beautiful experience for any living being to step beyond their present level of understanding and want to open the heart and human eyes to advance one's knowledge and awareness, to bring about self-realisation. If my Being can help one step beyond their present limitations of self-created fears, then I am truly honoured to have been of service to you dear Abbey.

Yes you have opened your heart to knowledge that you already have within your very essence. Be Blessed dear Abbey in Love and Light always.

Jecuss Kuntarkis.

RELATIONSHIPS ALWAYS GO WRONG: WHY?

Hi Kuntarkis,

I was wondering if you could shed some light on why I always fall for the wrong guy. It all starts out so beautiful and within 3 or 4 months the same things always come up and destroy the relationship, especially when we move in together. It's like I can never do anything right for them. They always end up abusing me either physically or with angry words. I have no children which I think is lucky considering the types of relationships I'm having. I am alone at this time and I must say I'm a little scared to get into another relationship. I am 28 and feel alone. Could you give me some guidance please?

Sam.

Kuntarkis replies:

Dear Sam, You are indeed a beautiful human being and have a lot of love to share, but there are two things you may need to do and understand first.

First, only look for another to share your love with when you can truly look into a mirror and say from your heart "I truly love and accept who I am in this most precious moment of my life". You see dear Sam; unconditional love begins with you first. When you as an infinite Being of Creation's totality can accept and experience love for your own Beingness, you will attract the same form of infinite energies into your life, and all will be in balance and harmony.

Second, human beings as they grow up from their childhood experience some negative emotions which can and does shape their lives as human adults. If you dear Sam have fears and insecurities, they are negative emotions which will affect your relationships with human males. Because of your fears you will also attract males who will have similar fears and insecurities.

The whole purpose of attraction is in reality to help each of you to mirror each other and see the same fears in order to try to resolve emotions (like attracts like) be they negative or positive. If you look at each of your relationships, all was perfect at the beginning. You were getting to know each other, so each of you were careful not to show your fears, whatever they may have been. But slowly as you both became more comfortable with each other, little negative things began to come up, and little by little they exposed themselves more and more. This sometimes brings out the worst in humans.

Sam, there is a very simple answer to your dilemma. Look at yourself first. Resolve your past negative emotions by opening up your heart to the unconditional love that you are. Accept this unconditional love and allow it to become a part of your everyday life, in all things you do. When you can love yourself without any form of judgement you will be ready to attract the same kind of infinite energies into your life and all will be in harmony always.

Remember Sam, judgement is a negative and all it does is create a negative situation in one's life. Unconditional love is the key to freedom. Be Blessed dear Sam in Love and Light always.

Kuntarkis.

INVISIBLE FRIEND: WHO IS YONKY?

Dear Kuntarkis

I have an invisible friend who has been with me for 6 years. I'm 12 and my friend is called Yonky. She still plays with me and even sometimes sleeps with me, like watches over me. She sometimes comes to school and protects me because our school is rough and has a lot of bullies. They used to pick on me but because Yonky comes to my rescue they leave me alone, and sometimes I think they're a little scared of me and call me a demon. My question is who is Yonky and where does she come from.

Michael.

Kuntarkis replies:

Dear Michael, Your invisible friend Yonky loves you very much and it seems she has attached herself to you as your protector and guide. This is indeed a very special gift, mainly because Beings like her do not usually like humans because they see the violence humans are capable of.

Yonky is of the element kingdom. There are five elements to this Earthly vibration. They are fire, water, air, earth and spirit. To keep balance on your planet Earth and all who live upon her, all five elements are needed and must work in harmony.

Yonky is a fire element, and my Being can understand why those human bullies keep away from you. The element fire is not to be taken lightly. So dear Michael, always have love in your heart and love all of life, and as you grow and become more aware of your surroundings, more elements will come into your human life and you will become a teacher of understanding and knowledge.

Be Blessed dear Michael in Love and Light always.

Kuntarkis.

WILL JOB CAUSE KARMA?

Dear Kuntarkis,

I understand what you are saying about karma and what we do to others will be done to us. I'm turning 19 this year and I'm trying to decide if I should join the air force. It's always been a dream for me to fly jets. Even as a kid I would lay on the grass and watch the birds and see myself flying with them. What I'm concerned about is if I do join and if I have to fight for my country, how will it affect my karma and future lives. If I kill others in wartime will I have to forfeit my life in other times? This is my concern.

Leigh.

Kuntarkis replies:

Dear Leigh,

My being can see your concerns, yet only in this vibration of physical matter can wars be justified, if at all. Murder is murder. When you take the life of another living breathing conscious being you create a negative imbalance which must be brought back into balance, whether it be in this incarnation or one to come. This is not a law or judgment, it simply is the balance of all life throughout all universes.

This is not to say dear Leigh that you must not join your air force. You as an individual have the right to choose your life's path, whatever it may be. It is always your choice. There is no one who has the right to judge you in your decision. You will always make the right decision for yourself.

It is the responsibility of each human being to experience life, be it negative or positive – the outcome will be the same. Walk gently on your Earth. See life as an opportunity to grow in consciousness and respect all of life, no matter what form of life it may be?

Be Blessed dear Leigh in love and Light always.

Kuntarkis.

FEAR OF LIFE WITHOUT LOVE

Dear Kuntarkis,

Thank you for replying to my previous e-mail. Further elaboration of my plight:

I'm really worried about my life direction and in particular about not having a partner. I am 32 this year and I feel I have done so much to improve myself... and no I'm not where I want to be, but I can say that I am in a better position to receive love than I have ever been.

I have asked the universe questions in general and I get answers but on this particular question there is dead silence. I'm beginning to think that there is something terribly wrong... I tell you I'm not complaining about difficulty in choosing a person ...I'm talking about not having anyone in front of me to choose from!!! Alright I'm not looking as much as before due to exams etc. but I'm worried that if I continue as I am I will never have the life I wish for!

I don't know what to do anymore...it's like I'm a deer dazzled by the headlights and am frozen. What should I do? Am I doing something to stop love from coming into my life? I don't know what though.

I don't know what to do... love is all that matters in this life and a life without it is too lonely.

Regards Sue.

Kuntarkis replies:

Dear Sue, You need to step beyond your present understanding. Stop allowing your negative thoughts to hold you back from creating what you want and need from your human life. Stop looking to the Universe for all your answers. You Sue are your universe, whether you wish to accept this or not. You are caught up in your logic and it is your logic that holds you a prisoner of yourself.

Again, first accept where you are at this moment in your life, then take some precious moments in your life by sitting down with a pencil and paper and from your heart, not the confusion of your human brain, ask your inner self where you would like to be in the moments to come. Write them all down and make it your goal in life.

But first stop all the excuses you make about yourself. If you truly want another to love you, then learn to accept and love yourself first. Allow yourself to feel the infinite love in your heart, and feel it emanate all around you. This is your quest in this lifetime Sue – to truly love yourself without human Ego. You do know what to do, just be in your own space. Don't lock yourself in your logic for there is no creativeness in logic. Bring the balance of logic and creativeness together and you will through unconditional love find the balance in your life. But you must be prepared to listen, I mean really listen. You are the power and the strength of your true self Sue.

Take care of yourself and love yourself NOW.

Kuntarkis.

SEVERAL QUESTIONS?

Dear Jecuss Kuntarkis,

First of all, thank you for sharing your knowledge! Almost everything you say makes perfectly sense to me - it's like I already knew... All my life I've been wondering about life on earth, the universe and the meaning of it all. And during these years I've come up with many theories. I would really appreciate it if you would answer the following questions:

- **The Human Brain:** Are thoughts created inside our brains, or is it merely an organ to control bodily functions?
- **The Human Body:** Is it an energy generator for our spirit?
- **Multiple Personality:** Does two or more spirits cause it, by using the same human body to gain energy?

- **The Universe:** Is it an energy generator for "higher" beings, and are the black holes where the energy is tapped?
- **MDMA:** also known as ecstasy: Is it possible that this drug may increase our inner awareness, and if not, are there certain medicals that could?
- **I was born on:** 23 Feb 1973, 6e06, 62n09, local time: 4:15am, U.T 3:15, Sid. Time: 13:50:54: Do you know who I am, and what my purpose on earth is?

Is there anything else I should know about myself?

With love from Jan.

Kuntarkis replies:

Dear Jan, Thank you for taking the precious moments in your human life to write to my Being. You are truly on your path of self-discovery of your inner knowledge, and yes, you do have the knowledge within you of all life that ever was and will be. All conscious beings have this encoded knowledge within them, but in most human beings it is dormant, waiting for the right moment for each human being to come to self-realisation that all life in all universes will come together.

Here are the answers to your questions:

The human brain:

Yes, on a physical level of understanding thoughts are created inside your brain. Most thoughts are created from past conditionings of one's life, from childhood to adulthood, and yes, it is a human organ of matter to also help control your human bodily functions.

The human body:

The human body is not an energy generator for your spirit. The human body's only purpose is for the spirit to exist in your third vibration of physical matter, so that as beings you can learn and experience the lessons of physical life. The spirit on the other hand is the generator for your human body to function and exist. Without your spirit you would not be a conscious living being, nor could you function as you do in your vibration. To better explain this, coma patients are beings that are not in their bodies but are still remotely connected to their bodies.

Multiple Personality:

Yes, in some human beings on your Earth, a number of spirits who have passed from their human bodies do use the body of a physically living being. They pick a weaker character, usually with a cracked aura, which makes it easier for them to control the physical being and their body. It is very easy to manipulate a human being's energy fields. Drugs will not solve the problem. They first need to understand what is happening to them, and they also need to have their aura and chakra centres realigned. Unfortunately there are not many human beings who can perform what is needed to overcome the situation.

One thing must be understood about multiple personalities, the spirits who gain access through a human being's cracked aura are indeed spirits who have passed over but have not wanted to go through the Light. Instead they wish to hold onto the physical realm.

The Universe:

There are many, many forms of universes, realms, vibrations and dimensions. Everything in all of life in all universes is a generator of light. Light exists in all forms of life, from the smallest to the largest. Without this living energy of light, life itself would not exist. And yes, as you put it Jan, higher forms of life use the light as a generator. You as a human being are also a higher form of life, whereas a black hole is a vacuum. Other forms of life use black holes to travel into other realms, other universes, for they have gained the knowledge and the means to travel safely through these portals, so they are able to protect their ships and their bodies.

I was born on? Who am I & What is my purpose?

Who you are, you are a human being living and experiencing a physical existence, and you can do and create anything you wish to do in your human life. What is your purpose, to be whatever you want to be? If you stop and look, just for a moment, and see all of life as beautiful, in that moment of your own self-realisation you will know the purpose of your human life, it is to live it exactly as you want it to be, what stops any human individual from being fulfilled, is their past. That is why so many human beings are in misery, in pain, and then somewhere in that moment there is a thought, I don't need to feel this way, I can change, I can accomplish anything I set my mind to, I am living consciousness. I am apart of everything and everything is a part, of me. So in that moment everything can change, that is the Power of your human thoughts. You the individual are the Driver, the Teacher, the Mentor, the Creator of your world, your vibration, its all in your Thinking? Is it not.

If there are any more questions or concerns regarding my answers, please feel free to make contact again. Be Blessed dear Jan in love and light, and always know you are and have the truth within you always.

Jecuss Kuntarkis.

FRIEND DYING OF LUNG CANCER

Dear Sir,

My friend of 53 is currently in a hospital dying of lung cancer. He has lost a lot of weight and has had is diomorphine levels taken up to 500 per hour. I have read your remarkable story of your own personal recovery, and wonder if there is anything I could do for my friend that may help him, even just a little. The diomorphine is preventing him from speaking correctly, and he is always out of it, he smiles at the odd joke, and mumbles occasionally, but he can't string sentences together. I don't think he has lost the will to live, although I think he has accepted it.

Any quick response would be very grateful.

Thank you for your time

Damian.

Kuntarkis replies:

Dear Damian, My Being thanks you for your love, your support and your compassion for your friend, who is in need of another's love to help comfort him in his time of need. I have been asked by Roman to give a reply to your email. All of humanity, all of life that exists in all Universes, are all connected to each other in living consciousness. Your friend, even though he is not fully aware, he is preparing for another journey of transformation. The essence of his spirit is near completion in this vibration.

Yes, you can be of help and service to your friend by first, being there for him, and second, sending him healing energies of Light. Be a beacon of Light by sending from your heart centre a beam of light directly from your heart to his. Use your imagination and believe you are doing this healing for him. The Light of Creation is all around all living beings and can be used in the moment of life. To think Light from your heart is to become Light itself.

What your friend needs now is for someone just to be there, listen and care, and project unconditional love to him from the heart. May you Damian and your dear friend be blessed in Love and Light always?

Kuntarkis.

STRUGGLING WITH PAST EMOTIONS

Dear Roman,

I just kind of stumbled upon your site while I was trying to find out more information about channelling. I think you and Ilona have done a wonderful job with it, and I am grateful that you both are helping out the world in this way. Keep it going!

I was wondering if Kuntarkis could give me some clarity about a couple of issues in my life right now:

I am 23 years old. Due to some poor financial decisions I have made in the past, I am having to move back home with my parents, which is the absolute LAST thing I could have asked for. You see, I never really received much in the way of emotional or psychological support from my parents for my dreams/goals, and I guess it's fair to say that I harbour a good deal of resentment towards them for their lack of support. Intellectually, I know they did the best they could, but emotionally it is very difficult for me to deal with. There has also been a huge power struggle between my dad (who is emotionally abusive) and I for as long as I can remember. So now that I am moving back home, I feel there is a lot of negative energy from my family that I need to protect myself from, and I am terrified into slipping into my old negative and destructive mentality, since that's essentially what I left home for anyway. (I have done a lot of conscious spiritual and psychological work on myself over the past 5 years, and I feel like the knowledge I have gained from my experiences are some of my greatest strengths.) I am acutely aware also that there is some "habit" that I've learned from my upbringing that is keeping me in my current financial position, but I don't really know how to deal with it. Any illumination and suggestions on how to overcome these blockages would be greatly appreciated.

Somewhat related, in the sense that these goals are very important to me, is the issue of a very special relationship that I'm in right now. This woman, Laura, and I are just friends right now, but for a year now I know that I want so much more. There is no question in my mind that we love each other deeply and have a special bond, but I have no clue as to whether she feels the same way about me or whether or not she would want to take the friendship to the next level. Many times, I have a sense that she does feel the same way, but I frankly don't have the guts to ask her because I am afraid of being rejected (this stems from a very traumatic experience that I went through about 8 years ago). It is as if I would rather settle for a wonderful and beautiful friendship than take the risk of being rejected. However, I know that I am just settling for second best instead of asking for what I want. This situation has happened numerous times in the past (I know the pattern has something to do with my fears), and it effectively keeps me from establishing romantic relationships. I just feel that in the> past I have never really been able to manifest the relationships I've wanted because of this lack of clarity (which is probably related to my fears, of course). I really, REALLY want this relationship to work out the way I'd like it to with Laura, but I am truly scared that my inhibitions will cause the past to repeat itself and it will always be like this for me.

Is there any way that you could touch on what it is she might be feeling for me (her perception of the relationship), and any suggestions/advice for me for overcoming these obstacles so I can truly create the life I want to have for myself.

Much love and infinite thanks,

B. B.

Kuntarkis replies:

Dear Human Being, Thank you for sharing your thoughts, your heart, and your expressions. One of the hardest lessons for all of humanity is the letting go of the past and the pain of negative emotion. Each human being chooses their lessons, just as children choose their parents and parents choose their children. The lesson is forgiveness - forgiveness for your parents have done to you in this lifetime and for what you have done to them in a past lifetime.

This is where the problem lies. The past is always following humanity into the present and the future, creating the same circumstances over and over again. Regarding your moving back in with your parents, please realise that you have created your financial situation in order to face the past by being put back into your parent's energies.

It is easier to see the situation as being negative, but again it is only your beliefs and fears that bring you to that conclusion. Take a few precious moments of your human life, stop and listen to yourself and take a few steps back to see it as an opportunity to resolve the negative emotions from the past to the present. By doing this you will change your present

destiny from a negative one to a positive one. You will then find new strength to forgive and be forgiven. It all lies in the hearts of human beings.

Everything that you experience, be it negative or positive, will govern your future. If you live in fear then you will create your future from your fearful, negative past into your present which will continuously create a negative future. Try and see your parents as your teachers, just as your friends are your teachers and just as you are a teacher to all who come into your life.

The Earth and all who live upon it have one thing in common - you are all each other's teachers as well as being students. What is most important once the lesson is learnt is to move on to a new experience of existence in human form. Unfortunately most of humanity live in a negative space from one lifetime to the next, again the past following humanity.

The answer lies in the heart. It is the heart that is full of forgiveness and unconditional love. The problem is that humanity lives from negative emotions created from the past, meaning every past incarnation of a human being is continuously brought into the present. That is why there is so much pain, misery, violence and conflict on your Earth.

To forgive yourself is to forgive others. To unconditionally love yourself is to unconditionally love others. You must experience forgiveness and unconditional love in order to be able to express it to others. It all begins with you dear Human Being. The choice is always yours. How you feel about yourself is expressed to others. Remember, forgiveness and unconditional love is the key to freedom from the past to the present. You have the key.

Be blessed in unconditional love always.

Kuntarkis.

WHAT IS SPIRITUALITY?

Dear Kuntarkis,

At a dinner party with friends and acquaintances last night, someone asked what my opinion about Spirituality is, to be honest with myself I just don't know. Could you help me to clarify this?

Lee.

Kuntarkis replies:

Dear Lee, You are not the first or the last to ask this question. What is the meaning of spirituality? My Being will answer your questions from a physical aspect as created by humanity.

Spirituality, the word, is created from two words, Spirit and duality. First, the Spirit, which is the essence of all life, is the substance from which all of life is created. It is living consciousness – atoms attracted to other atoms, energy attracted to other energies. All of life in all its forms is in itself magnetic energy, all based on attraction, and depending on the level of consciousness at that moment in life, it will attract into its presence the same thinking form of energy. Simply put, your human saying "Like attracts like".

The second part of the word comes from duality, meaning two parts. There is the physical essence of the human body and the spirit essence of the infinite spirit which has no end. The physical form lives to human created time and will perish back to the Earth from which all physical life has been created. What each human being learns in one of their incarnations on your Mother Earth will govern their next incarnation. It is important to understand that the spirit could not possibly experience life in human form without a physical flesh body.

Every human being is spiritual. It is a part of your essence – you are all timeless, ageless and endless. As every human individual grows from one lifetime to the next, they will gain and learn the lessons that they chose prior to incarnating into human form.

On Nar'Kariss we see the meaning of Spirituality as unconditional love for all life forms in all universes, realms and dimensions. With love comes understanding and the ability to be compassionate and caring. When you can be compassionate and non-judgemental you will gain the wisdom and knowledge to be responsible for all actions created in all your lifetimes. With responsibility comes forgiveness – being able to forgive oneself and others from a loving heart. It is at this point that the meaning of life and all its journeys is understood, for life is in essence a journey of self-discovery. And when you have reach this point of self-discovery, then you have touched upon your spirituality.

Be blessed in love always.

Kuntarkis.

LEARNING THROUGH HUMAN DREAMS

Hello,

I decided that I would set aside doubts and ask Kuntarkis to enlighten me on a few things that I have pondered for some time.

When 18 years of age, while sleeping, I had my first experience with the astral realm, I believe. To begin with, my maternal grandfather Raymond had passed on when I was 10 years old, a man beloved by all and having a large loving family. At 18, my paternal grandfather Bernie also passed; as I slept the night of his passing, I began to experience my spirit being drawn through what could only be described as a waterfall of pure flowing love that enveloped my being and caused me to have a feeling of boundless love and elation unlike anything that could ever be experienced in human form. I thereupon came into contact with the spirit of my maternal grandfather, who reached for me and spoke "Let's go see your other grandfather." The rest of the experience alas I cannot remember, however I awoke in the morning distinctly depressed and saddened at being in my flesh body.

My second experience came when I was 28 years of age. I experienced the same waterfall of love, except this time I found myself in a cemetery observing what I somehow knew to be the burial of a college friend who had died of cancer over a year before. As I began to "walk" as it were, I heard her call for me - and as I looked, I observed that I could see through the ground at a row of caskets lined up. She jumped out in her human appearance and came to me. We talked, of what I do not remember, and she showed me how to "fly" in my spirit - she led me up into the air, down through the ground, and all over, passing around and through things one would think of as physical. The next part that I can remember of the experience, we had talked for a while, and finally she said "Well, goodbye sweetie" and patted me on the back. I then awoke back in my physical body, with a tingling sensation, not painful, exactly where she had patted me. Again I awoke very depressed and saddened.

An additional dream involved me wandering through a building, and finally asking a receptionist where I might find my grandfather Raymond. She replied only "Raymond, was a great man!", and I remember nothing of the rest of the dream except parts of the building.

Another out of body experience came after my son was born, as he was about 6 months of age I had gotten up around 3AM to console him. As I drifted off to sleep I felt my spirit rise out of my body and float across my bedroom. Cognizant of the happening, I remember telling myself to "go with it". However at that point I began to drift back towards my bed and re-entered my body. Oddly, I also remember what appeared to be a skeleton lying in one of my large dresser drawers that is built-in to a wall.

Also, ever since my first experience at 18, I have had ever-increasing instances of those memories. These have brought me to believe in a theory of a pre-destined life for each human that is tempered by their free will and ability to stray from the events that are predetermined before birth, as well as the concepts of karma and reincarnation. I firmly believe that my sole purpose on this planet was to raise children and aid them in their own spiritual growth and help them to avoid more incarnations.

Please, can Kuntarkis shed light and insight into these experiences and thoughts? There is not a day that goes by that I do not reflect on these events, and the love and beliefs that have formed in my spirit because of them. It saddens me as I encounter people daily who prove through their words and deeds that they have not the same experiences or insights, especially Christians, Muslims, and others who hate in the name of religion. I was raised Catholic and have summarily rejected all teachings of faith based on and practiced with hatred.

Dave.

Kuntarkis replies:

Dear Dave, You are indeed a very beautiful human being who has lived many incarnations in your vibration on your Earth. You have a very strong will and desire to find the truth and you have followed the road searching for truth in others. In reality, every human being is, in their own way, searching for the truth and ultimately to find meaning in their life.

Use your strong will and believe in yourself. The truth for answers from the past, present and future is within you. The reason you have had your outer body experiences is to show you that there is a deeper meaning to life than what has been conditioned into you from childhood to adulthood. Yes, there are other spirits in your astral vibration who are helping you to gain a deeper understanding of the meaning of life.

You mention that others have not experienced what you are experiencing. The truth is they are experiencing it also, but because they are highly conditioned, their fears will not allow them to remember or grow in consciousness. All human beings will advance consciously as they are willing to learn and accept new ideas, as well as remembering their experiences in the astral vibration, but at their own speed. It all comes down to what each human being is willing to accept given their level of conscious advancement.

Be blessed in love always.

Kuntarkis.

I AM LONGING FOR CHILDREN

Dear Kuntarkis,

It is difficult for me to ask you this question. I am 37, married for six years and have no children. My husband and I have been trying for the last 4 years to have a child. We have seen doctors and they tell us there is nothing wrong with either of us, but I can't fall pregnant. Can you explain why I can't fall pregnant, and if I will ever have a child or children? At my age, time is running out and we desperately want to have a family.

Kuntarkis replies:

Dear Human Being, It can be difficult to understand why life is the way it is. Please do not be so hard on yourself. You and your husband will have a child in October 2004. Another child will be born in January 2008. Please try to understand that everything is for a reason. Both of you have stressful jobs which demand a great deal of energy from both of you. The stress is affecting you and your husband, and in turn the ability for you to fall pregnant. You need to relax and take time out for yourselves and for each other – I believe it is called a holiday. Try taking three weeks of your time and both of you will find yourselves once again. You need to take the time to find the balance of the mind, body and spirit. You are both trying so hard to succeed at your jobs and to achieve your goals that the stress is affecting both your body's natural rhythms more than you realise.

Relax and enjoy your lives a little, without stress. Be blessed in love always.

Kuntarkis.

GHOSTS BY MY BED: WHAT DO I DO?

Dear Kuntarkis,

I have been reading some of your answers to questions people have been asking, and am especially interested in the ones about ghosts. I have been seeing ghosts for about two years and they always come at the same time – around 3.00 in the morning - and stand by my bed. They keep calling my name. I wake up and see them. They just stand there and smile at me. What is this all about? Could you please explain?

Kuntarkis replies:

Dear Human Being, You are indeed blessed. Please do not allow your fears to overcome the purpose of your sight. They are not ghosts – they are your guides. During your time of sleep, as you travel the astral vibration, you are with them, but you do not allow yourself to remember because of your fears. They only wish to make contact with you to help guide you through your human life of experiences.

Trust yourself and your guides, for they can help you to open your mind and your Being to the knowledge that is within you. Be strong, be brave and you will overcome your fears, and in doing so you will find great reward in the form of advancing your consciousness.

Be blessed in love always.

Kuntarkis.

GUILT AND SHAME OVER FATHERS DEATH

Dear Kuntarkis,

I am haunted by my Father's death. I feel responsible for what happened to him. Can you help me understand why I feel so much guilt and shame?

Ben.

Kuntarkis replies:

Dear Ben, You have no reason at all to feel ashamed or guilty over your human Father's death. You are not responsible for what happened and you were too young to understand the situation at the time.

Every human being creates every action and reaction during their lifetime in a human body. Yes, it is true that the upbringing of a child can create circumstances that shape their life, and in many cases negative creation follows them through their lifetime and even into their next life. However, every human being also chooses when they will depart from the human world – they may not choose the actual circumstances but they do choose the time of departure, which is every human being's right, the right to free will.

Your human Father, Clive, has asked that this message be passed on to you from the Spirit vibration. He says he has always loved you and has always wanted you as a child. He does not hold any negative emotions towards you and he has expressed that he is sorry about being hard on you when it came to baseball. He is also very sorry for not being there for you as a Father should have been, but he has come to his own self-realisation that there is more to life than being physical and playing baseball. He also expressed that he is always with you in heart and he knows he will be with you again. He said "Don't forget each time you put on the red cap, know that I am by your side my son. I love you with all my heart."

Please Ben, don't ever feel guilty. Your Father has always loved you. Love is the healer of all pain.

Be Blessed in Love and Light Ben Always.

Kuntarkis.

SO MANY QUESTIONS?

Peace and Oneness to the Entity Kuntarkis, Ilona and the Vehicle Roman.

I AM ONE who uses various names in/on this dimension. In 1999 I became an ordained Priest according to the Order of Melchizedek. I have always felt that I was some kind of priest, magician or leader in a past life due to what compelled me the most as a child; Greek mythology, witchcraft and The Bible. (The first thing I remember stealing was a bible) I have spent my entire existence experiencing precognition, seeing or knowing things before they happen.

I remember having two recurring nightmare dreams. 1) A blood sucking vampire chased me all through my house. I eluded him every time I hid in the bathroom and 2) seeing my mother lying in state in her casket. (This later happened just as I saw it, from the dress she wore to the church the services was held in).

This increased after my ordainment. I began to give readings online to people I have never met before. In 1997 I was incarcerated and had an experience that to this day gives me the strength to go on. I was contacted by unnamed/unseen entities. They gave me strength when I WAS AT MY LOWEST POINT IN LIFE, yet I do not know who they are. They spoke to me these words:

"WE KNOW THAT YOU ARE AFRAID. DO NOT BE AFRAID. WE ARE HERE".

Nothing else. Mind you that there was no other physical being but me in this room. They showed me something that keeps me going to this day. A CUBE. This cube was a yellowish gold. As I approached it to examine it closer, it raised up and began to rotate in no set direction. Where I was is still not clear, but I WAS NOT DREAMING AND I WAS NOT IN MY CELL! As I began to awake or return to this realm, I was filled with an incredible feeling; a tingling from head to toe. When I awoke (I remember waking with a smile) I was filled with a sense of peace, confidence and LOVE. I attained and retained knowledge easier than before and seemed wiser and more understanding than before.

Prior to this experience I read a lot of Dr. Malachi Z York material. I know that you are familiar with him. I was intrigued with his teachings about 9 ether gasses and how the #9 when multiplied by any # breaks down to 9. This in turn led me to begin writing about sacred ancient teachings about the science of "THE 369". I have made startling rediscoveries pertaining to the 369.

My questions are:

1. What is my name in the astral/element realm?
2. Who were the entities that helped me?
3. Who are my spirit guides?
4. Am I one who was chosen to lead the return to the TEACHINGS OF THE 369?
5. Is Malachi Z York what he claims to be? Is what he teaches to be trusted?

I know that I have asked a lot of questions, but they all are of the utmost importance to me, and hope that you can and will answer them all.

It is no accident that I came across your website. This was meant to be.

Be In Peace, Be In Love.

Saleem.

Kuntarkis replies:

Dear Saleem, My Being expresses thanks to you for taking the precious moments of your human life to express your thoughts. You most certainly used a great deal of your energy expressing your personal emotions. Always remember, dear Saleem, every experience a human individual has throughout their life time is in reality a creation of their past being brought into their present, which being negative or positive, will certainly create their future.

There is also much truth in the saying "what you eat you become" and how one nourishes their physical body certainly governs their level of thinking, reasoning and understanding.

The whole purpose of life throughout all universes is to grow consciously and to gain the expansion of awareness, which is only gained by the individual, no matter what species they may be. No other individual can make another grow consciously. They can only be a living example for others to see and be guided by to reach self-realisation and inner expansion of consciousness.

To your questions:

1. What is my name in the astral/element realm?

There are no given names in the Astral. Each element is known by their energy field, which humanity calls the aura. It is the same with other beings who live in other realms and dimensions, especially beings that no longer live in a physical body.

2. Who were the entities that helped me?

There are spirit beings who are with you to help guide you to your own truth and knowledge. It all comes from within. Listen to your inner being. Do not give up on yourself - persist and believe, be true to yourself and you will open yourself to your true self.

3. Who are my spirit guides?

Every human being who lives in a physical body has spirit guides. Some have only one guide throughout their entire human life while others can have from two to several spirit guides. It all depends on the individual and their conscious growth. Allow yourself to meditate in the stillness of your own space, and with patience you will open up to higher vibrations of spirit realms. Then you will believe in yourself and learn and trust yourself in what is being expressed to you by your guides and other entities from other dimensions.

4. Am I one who was chosen to lead the return to the TEACHINGS OF THE 369?

If you truly believe from your heart that you have chosen to lead the return of the teachings of what you call 369 then ask yourself this question: was the 369 written by a human being? If this is the case then realise it is only the idea of truth. All truths written by man or a number of men, are only the idea of truth.

Truth can only come from within. This is the lesson for humanity. The idea of truth, no matter what it may be, has always come from humanity's past, brought into the present and continuously creating the human future.

The truth that is within all life forms, no matter what they may be, is called 'the knowing'. Every human being has the knowing. It is your inner essence, your spirit life force. It contains all that you are, all that you have been and all that you will become.

5. Is Malachi Z York what he claims to be? Is what he teaches to be trusted?

My Being has expressed in other questions on Malachi Z York. It does not matter what an individual expresses. If it comes from unconditional love for all life and its forms than that is the truth. When an individual learns to trust themselves then they will know if they can trust another and their expressions of knowledge.

Be blessed in love always dear Saleem.

Kuntarkis.

HOW MUCH DOES ONE CHANGE?

Dear Kuntarkis,

I read your story on the purpose of life and I must say it makes a great deal of sense. It has answered some of the concerns that have bothered me for some time. Thank you for the knowledge you share with the human race.

I have one question I need to ask. When one stops living the past and tries to live in the present, how much does one change, and in what areas of one's life do these changes occur?

Otto.

Kuntarkis replies:

Dear Otto, My Being expresses thanks to you for your kind words. If the knowledge my Being presents, to all who choose to read, allows the individual to gain some truth, then the truth begins to reveal itself to the individual and conscious growth takes place.

Yes, when an individual makes a conscious decision to let go of their past and see it simply as experiences and memories, neither negative nor positive, then they will see the past simply as life. Change is all about going forward, accepting new ideas and concepts without judgement.

How much of their life and what areas in their life someone changes, is totally up to them, a choice only the human individual can make. A guide for you Otto is when you discover your inner truth you will begin your journey of self-discovery. The path of truth can be an outward journey, such as exploring with your human senses and understanding life from what you see, what you are taught and the truths you observe in your society.

It is a starting point to changing many things around yourself, including your level of thinking and understanding yourself as you are, from your past to the present.

Otto, if you decide to go beyond your search for change from outside of yourself to inside of yourself, then you will Begin your inner journey towards self-realisation. You will discover the meaning of life itself, where the path of inner truth leads you to completeness and bliss. You will discover that you are indeed eternal, ageless, infinite and timeless as all things are in all universes.

May your journey lead you towards completion and give you what you seek. Be blessed in love always dear Otto, and remember, unconditional love is the key to freedom.

Kuntarkis.

DIFFICULTY IN STARTING A FAMILY

Hello Kuntarkis,

Normally I don't read your sort of information but my wife Mary asked me if I would open my mind a little more and not be so judgemental. I must say, after reading some of your questions I can see whoever you are that you are trying to help people.

Mary and I have been married for 11 years and for 9 of those years we have been trying to have children without success. We have had many tests and have discovered that I have the problem. Can you help me in any way or advise me what to do. We desperately want to have a family.

Jeff.

Kuntarkis replies:

Dear Jeff, Always listen to your heart not the conditioned brain of the human being, which is conditioned with fear of the unknown. The heart is full of love.

The two main reasons why your human body is not functioning in the manner you wish it to be:

1. You are highly strung and you become very stressful in many situations. Stress on the human body takes a lot of energy. It also depletes the human immune system, makes hair go grey and/or fall out, and also kills of sperm cells which keeps your sperm count low. This will naturally cause you more stress, which then leads to depression, agitation and worry, causing more stress and depression. A vicious cycle.

2. The food you consume is not supporting your immune system or general health. Raw foods like vegetables and fruits are very important to building a healthy body and mind. Raw food will provide you with plenty of energy, will help you think more clearly, and will help flush out your internal organs of toxins so they can function more efficiently. Once you clean up your human body it will be able to produce the right nutrients so you can increase your sperm count in order to successfully reproduce a human child.

Also, clean filtered water is a very important part of the human diet. The average human body needs at least 8 glasses of water per day. Coffee or tea (unless herbal tea) soft drinks and alcohol do not form part of the 8 required glasses of water.

Jeff, changing your intake of food and increasing water consumption will help you change your thinking, which in turn will lower your stress levels. Take up Tai Chi or yoga and meditation to help balance yourself. Do this and you will be amazed in how you feel. Your body and mind will then be healthy and peaceful – no stress. It would also be good for Mary. If both of you are healthy then you will most certainly be able to have children and your health will give them a better start in life.

Be blessed in love always.

Kuntarkis.

BLACK HOLES IN THE UNIVERSE: WHAT ARE THEY?

Dear Jecuss Kuntarkis,

Is it true or false that if you enter a black hole in space that you will go through to another universe on the other side?

TC.

Kuntarkis replies:

Dear TC, Yes, it is true that if you enter a black hole you will emerge in another place, even in other universes. Let us say a space craft created from matter and manned by human beings is pulled into the black hole by its gravity field, it would enter and go through to the other side. But there is one problem – matter, like spaceships built with human technology, would be ripped apart into very small pieces, including the human body.

The force of a black hole depends on the size of the hole. The pressure in your measurement can be ten million pounds per square centimetre. Human technology at this present moment would not survive the outcome of such a journey. Most alien spacecraft's have advanced technology, meaning they have learnt to use the atom through a reverse process and create force fields that protect the spacecraft and its occupants. There are scientists on your Earth who are working in this area?

It is true there are other species within the universes that can travel through black holes with little concern for their vessels or their body's being torn apart by the force.

Be blessed in love always.

Kuntarkis.

LEARNING TO FORGIVE: HOW HARD IS IT?

Dear Kuntarkis,

How does one learn to forgive those that are closest to you? I want to so much but I can't bring myself to do it. Can you help me in anyway so I can stop the pain of what I'm feeling?

Fran.

Kuntarkis replies:

Dear Fran, Your heart is in the right place – that in itself is a beginning. First forgive yourself. Forgiveness of the self, no matter what the reason may be, must start with the self. By truly forgiving yourself from your heart you will then find the strength and courage to understand the true meaning of forgiveness.

Forgiveness from the heart comes from unconditional love. Holding onto anger, hatred or resentment is an endless road of pain and misery. Forgive yourself and then you will be able to forgive others. It will lead you to the self-realisation that everything in life, and all the human beings you interact with and encounter in life are a part of each other. Like atoms joining and creating the vast universes and consciousness expanding, life is simply about learning lessons and then moving on to new experiences.

Be blessed in unconditional love always dear Fran.

Kuntarkis.

KUNTARKIS: FACT OR FICTION?

Attn: Kuntarkis,

You speak of unconditional love throughout your messages to us, to the human race. But how do we know if you come in truth or are you trying to simply fool us into believing you come in love as you say you do? I would like to believe you but how do we know what to believe in your messages?

Kuntarkis replies:

Dear Human Being, Every human being on your most precious planet has the ability to feel and experience truth first hand. Unconditional love is the key to unlocking this ability and setting the human being free from what each human being has created in their existence over many incarnations

Unconditional love is the light that exists within your heart centre. It is your feeling, your balance, you're all. It is your connection to each other as beings and to all other life forms, both on your world and throughout all universes.

To feel the truth of my Being's expressions, first you must believe in yourself as an infinite expression of light – one that is timeless, ageless, and endless. Then you will know yourself and in turn you will know my Being.

Be blessed in love and light dear Human Being.

Kuntarkis.

WHICH PATH DO I TAKE IN MY LIFE?

Dear Kuntarkis,

I would like to know if I should get a divorce. I feel that my husband is not growing as a person and it is causing problems in the upbringing of our children. I feel I have been patient and tolerant with his shortcomings and I cannot see any hope. I would like to follow a more spiritual path in life and it's so difficult with my husband in my life. Is spiritual advancement only achieved by enduring hardships; or is removing yourself from that environment and focussing on spiritual endeavours, is it also an option? I need you to tell me directly as I have tried to let my intuition do the work but I don't feel that it works as my brain is not clear and my ego rules.

So here is the big problem..... I may be able to deal with an unhappy marriage if I can keep a peaceful mind and not be affected by the negativity from my husband. I.e. I should not let him stir up past hurt and fear in my subconscious mind. But how do I achieve that peaceful mind in the first place if I am in this environment that is so cruel? You see how confused I am? What is my karmic connection with this man and also what is my children's connection with him?

I feel blessed indeed to have become aware of you. I am grateful for the information that you give and I try to get my answers from reading your answers to others' questions. I have been debating whether to ask you these specific questions for a number of reasons which I am sure others would like to know as well....

Would I be taking up your time and energy?...Is there a limit to how much I can ask you? ...Is it dangerous to take the advice given to specific individuals and apply them to yourself?

Thank you once again.

Nanda.

Kuntarkis replies:

Dear Nanda, My Being does not have the right to place judgement on any individual. Your relationship with your human husband is of a karmic debt. Both of you have had many incarnations together, mostly as husband and wife, and yes most of those relationships were of a negative energy. But you must remember, everything has a purpose.

Both of you have created the negative side effects of the relationships, that is why you both incarnate as human beings to experience the lessons you both chose to learn. Unfortunately one of the lessons is of forgiveness. Forgiveness is the key to freedom from pain and the past.

Each of you have incarnated over and over again as both female and male. You Nanda can see the negative sides of your present situation. When an individual learns true forgiveness from the heart, it creates awareness of the spirit's connection to the Soul.

Through meditation, meaning to silence the human brain and to just be in the moment, you will begin the process of allowing your connection to your Soul. By doing this you will open new doorways to higher levels of understanding and you will begin to see life with new eyes. You will learn to forgive and let go of the past and you will then realise you can change any negative situation in your life if you choose to for the better of yourself and others. Whether this means staying in the relationship or moving on, that is a decision you alone must make, for no one can give you the 'right' answer to your question. Only you from your heart can find this truth within yourself.

Be blessed in unconditional love always.

Kuntarkis.

HOW DO WE KNOW WHAT IS TRUTH?

Dear Sir/Madam,

I just asked how Cleopatra died. The answer your site gave me made more sense than history. In the answer you mentioned the book of knowledge.

What is it and how do you know its accuracy? I am having serious problems searching history for truth. There are too many variations. Each person has their own perception of what they saw and believe. How is yours truth? Thank you.

Paul.

Kuntarkis replies:

Dear Paul, History on Earth is written by human beings. The human ego was created by human beings and the human ego is the cause of all the pain and suffering which has plagued humanity for almost a million years on Earth.

If a human being is willing to open their eyes and see the pain and suffering that still exists within humanity, and ask from their hearts "Why?" they will begin to understand that all pain and suffering comes from humanity's past, brought into the present and continually creating the future.

The book of knowledge is recorded in the essence of every human being that exists in the third vibration of physical matter. That knowledge is not based on right or wrong, good or bad, negative or positive. It simply exists to help a human individual grow beyond the human ego of fears, beliefs and conditioning.

The 'Book of Knowledge' is you, the individual. Each human being has lived hundreds and thousands of lifetimes, and each of those lifetimes are recorded in the essence of every human being; in the energy that is your spirit, that which animates your physical body and gives it life. To silence the human brain and become silent in the mind by going within your inner self is to join with your spirit. This will join you with your Soul, and there you will discover the true meaning of the 'Book of Knowledge'. There you will discover the knowing of all that is.

Be blessed in unconditional love always Paul.

Kuntarkis.

ABOUT THE WORK I DO AND PRESENT?

Hello Roman & Kuntarkis

I would love to know more about your activities and also get some teachings. Thanks.

Magnus.

Kuntarkis replies:

Dear Magnus, It would be good to run my courses in the UK, but unfortunately I have no contacts in your country. This is one of my goals, to run courses, seminars and workshops internationally by making contact with people like yourself who seek a deeper understanding of their true self and the purpose of human life.

In Australia I encourage people to organise these on my behalf. One of the reasons for this is it helps them grow consciously and to give them a feeling of self-worth and confidence in themselves. It also helps to keep costs to a minimum. I believe any human being can achieve anything in their life as long as they have the will to not only believe in others but especially to believe in themselves. That is true conscious growth and self-awareness.

The knowledge that was given freely on our website is to encourage all people on our precious planet to become more aware of their true self. All human beings are linked and come from the same source of energy - every form of life is connected to each other.

Believe in yourself Magnus, for you have the knowing within you.

Take care and be well.

Roman

MY FUTURE WITH MY BOYFRIEND?

Dear Kuntarkis

I have a problem and I don't know how to deal with it. I need some help. My boyfriend is fighting with me over something stupid. He wrote me a note telling me that he is moving out and that he can't trust me anymore, so that's why he is moving out. I don't know what to do. Will my boyfriend and I ever make it in the future? Will we ever talk to one another again? I really love him and I know he loves me, but I don't know what to do anymore. Please help me.

Ashley.

Kuntarkis replies:

Dear Ashley, while a human being is caught up in emotional pain they cannot reason with themselves or others. All they see is the pain, and yes, pain is expressed in many forms.

You say your human boyfriend is angry over something you did to him, and you say it is something stupid. Please stop for a moment and give this some thought. Maybe to him it is not stupid. Maybe to him he is hurt so he has decided to end the relationship and move out. Something you need to do Ashely is stop everything in your human life and take some time out to look at what you have done to make him react in this way.

It may seem stupid to you but he is an individual and he has a different understanding to you. He grew up in a different way and therefore he has different expectations. My Being is not saying he is right or wrong, but every created situation has a reason for why both of you are experiencing this pain. If you want the relationship to continue, then both of you need to put aside your egos, sit together and express from your hearts how each of you are truly feeling.

Communication between people in any type of relationship is the only way to resolve differences. Not from the ego, for the ego is only about apportioning blame, but from the heart with love, understanding and compassion.

Be blessed in unconditional love always.

Kuntarkis.

WHO IS ERWIN SCHRODINGER?

Hello!

I wanted to ask you a question about Erwin Schrodinger. I am not sure what information I am allowed yet but I thought I'd ask anyway. Can you tell me if he is reincarnated since he died in 1961? If he is then is he on a path to continue his work as well as working through karma and is there any information you would be able to give me as to his current embodiment?

I am feeling a little weird now about trusting my instincts. Any information you are able to give me would help in terms of my work as well as personal issues I feel are slowly clearing. I think you know what I'm getting at and if my intuition is incorrect, then why do I feel so connected to his work?

Sita.

Kuntarkis replies:

Dear Sita, The human being you call Erwin Schrodinger did pass over into spirit world in your human year of 1961. His spirit has not reincarnated into a human body up to this moment, but through his Soul he will incarnate in your human year of 2038 as a human female in the land you call America and she will continue working on electromagnetism, where she will discover the true essence of gravity.

This human being always believed that human beings can and will travel at the speed of light in space, and it will be this being who will discover how to create gravity in space craft's so human beings will have a gravity field within gravity.

The reason you feel so connected to his energies is because you have the same Soul. Your spirit is a facet of your Soul and Erwin Schrodinger is also a facet of your Soul. Even though you both have different purposes in your life there will come a time when in your human future one or the other of you will join back with the other. That is a part of human evolution.

Be blessed in unconditional love always.

Kuntarkis.

HUMAN PURPOSE ON EARTH?

Dear Kuntarkis,

I am not sure what I want/need to know, but I have a burning desire to ask anyway. Does this make any sense to you? At this time I am quite confused about my purpose here on Earth. I believe myself to be in transition from Indigo to Crystal being. Do I have a spiritual name and could/would this help unlock some more answers? If so, how? I know, lots of ambiguous questions! This is the story of my life!

Love, Light and blessings.

Sarah. X

Kuntarkis replies:

Dear Sarah, It is a very good start to have a burning desire to ask questions of the self and life itself. This is how an individual learns and grows consciously as a human being.

Most human beings are in some form of transition in their present human incarnation. One of the most useful tools one can have or use to grow is an open mind and open heart to all ideas of learning. A human being is drawn to a form of learning by desire or how they are presently thinking in their state of mind.

Confusion in a human individual is created by their past, meaning how they were treated by their human parents, how they experienced their childhood into adulthood, and conditioning becoming beliefs. This does play a big part in the life of any human being.

To truly find out the purpose of one's life, that individual needs to go beyond their current beliefs by putting aside all their conditioning and stepping beyond their understanding of life itself.

Fear creates confusion and fear forms a part of belief systems and conditioning, defining mental boundaries. To dissolve fear is to open one's mind beyond what has been experienced and accepted as all that is by stepping beyond into the unknown. It takes courage and willingness to accomplish this.

You Sarah are a very strong Human Being. My Being believes in you, and you should believe in yourself. Yes, you do have a spiritual name. It is 'Meszmekarr' and means 'oceans meet water, water is life'.

Be blessed in unconditional love always dear Sarah.

Kuntarkis.

CONSCIOUS AWARENESS DURING MEDITATION

Hello Kuntarkis,

I have a question or two about what I experience during meditations. It was about five years ago, while I was still at school, that I first experienced a guided meditation. It was very powerful, kind of like a dream, where at times I was observing what was taking place instead of actually taking part, and like a vivid dream, I still remember parts of what happened.

About two years later I found myself in between jobs and having a hard time getting to sleep and invested in guided meditation CD's to try and help. They did help, too well, when at one point during the meditation I'd find myself losing conscious awareness and the next thing I knew I was waking up to the sound of my alarm in the morning. Which was good, but I had no recollection of what had happened. This kept on happening, especially when laying down.

During such time I attended yoga classes for a while, and the same thing happened. Once I tried an experiment to see if I could make myself stay aware. It took a lot of effort and concentration, so I never tried it again. It was easier for me to allow myself to lose awareness. I was always able to come back before then end, though. This usually doesn't happen when I'm sitting, but over the year since attending Circle, it's happened about three times, the most recent being tonight. I find that people talk of experiences that I have no recollection about. I usually don't talk about what I go through myself, as I believe that such experiences are personal and there's no reason to share what happened.

Anyway. My questions are: Am I getting any benefit from losing awareness, from letting my mind go? It is helping progress or is something else going on? Should I try to stay aware and remember the experiences that come through with the guiding? What's actually happening during this time, and why can't I remember it? It's not like I'm scared or intimidated by it, I just want to be able to understand what's happening during this time. Any advice or guidance you can give will be most welcome.

Thanks.

Blessed be you.

Katherine.

Kuntarkis replies:

Dear Katherine, It is not that you lose that awareness of your experiences. Most human beings live a life of duality, meaning their physical existence and their spirit existence, is separate. One of the most important aspects of human life is to become fully conscious of their spirit connection, and yes, meditation can help make that connection; the joining of two entities becoming one in union with all that is.

To some human beings that journey can take a lot of human time. To meditate lying down can take the individual into a much more balanced space of complete stillness, mainly so the individual can be at complete peace. There is no pressure in holding the human head up. Many who go into a deep space of stillness sitting up are brought back suddenly because of some form of movement.

When a human being becomes fully conscious of their experiences, whether it is during their meditations or their sleep time, they have in reality become one entity, no longer separate. Physical and spirit are consciously one in union. There is complete awareness of all that surrounds them, inwardly and outwardly.

For a human being to achieve this, one cannot have any form of ego, especially beliefs and conditioning, no fears, and yes this is achievable. It all depends on the human individual – discipline is essential. Never give up Katherine. Always believe in yourself and live in the moment.

Be blessed in unconditional love always.

Kuntarkis.

MEDITATION & SPIRITUAL GROWTH

Dear Kuntarkis,

Thank you for your kind reply. I'm still a little confused. If I would be transported to your light ships, during meditation, am I learning, developing, processing... evolving in that meditative state? Will I be able to access the benefit I receive there? I experience a blissful, out of body experience, but remember nothing in particular most of the time, it is just a vibratory connection. Will this help me to pass through the portal my guides speak of?

Linda.

Kuntarkis replies:

Dear Linda, for a human being to be transported to our light ships during a meditation is a form of conscious growth in itself, but for that human individual to be fully conscious on their return is another matter.

Most human beings who have come onto our light ships are in fact in their sleep time. The knowledge that is learnt by that individual can only manifest itself outwardly. When that human being is consciously ready to go beyond their present level of thinking and understanding, then and only then can the human individual step beyond their own self-created limitation of fear.

There are many human beings who are fully conscious of their experiences aboard our light ships which have been present around your Earth for nearly one million Earthly years. One of the most successful forms of communication with us, directly, is through the stilling of the human brain. By having no expectations, simply sit or lie, and allow the chatter of the human brain through practice to become still with no thoughts of any kind, no noise of any kind, just you the individual and your empty space.

Yes, it does take practice, yes; the outcome can be of great benefit to you, the individual and to all of humanity.

Be blessed in unconditional love always dear Linda.

Kuntarkis.

CAREER SUCCESS

Dear Kuntarkis,

I am at a loss as to how to best use my gifts for both universal service and a successful career. I feel very frustrated and one thing I do know is that my thoughts are not supplying me with answers. Thank you so much for your time and attention.

With love,

Barbara.

Kuntarkis replies:

Dear Barbara, What you are feeling consciously about your career is completely understandable. One of the most important things to remember, is not to look for answers in your thoughts from the human brain. The brain stores memories, be they from negative or positive experiences. The human brain through your thoughts can only give you a specific answer to your question because the information is based on your past experiences and the emotions attached to those experiences.

Feeling frustrated only adds to the confusion that you are feeling because all that you are seeking is from your human brain. To truly receive a balanced answer the human individual needs to ask from the heart, which is always connected to your Soul. Your Soul is unbiased. It will always lead you as a human being in the direction you need to travel or experience.

Sometimes in human life your abilities, or as you would say, your gifts may need to be enhanced from a material means, meaning to take study and then visualise yourself in the place you would like to be, then create the action to make it manifest into your human life. This is all a part of learning and creating what you as a human individual needs in order to feel complete.

Thoughts create confusion if they come from a negative emotion, but the heart will always guide you to the path you are seeking. Believe in yourself as my Being believes in you.

Be blessed in unconditional love always.

Kuntarkis.

ALIEN EXPERIENCE

Hello Roman,

I was delighted to meet you at Desley's home a few weekends ago in Brisbane. You recognised me the moment you walked in the door. But it wasn't a recognition from this time or dimension.

I want to share with you an experience. Soon after listening to you talk about aliens, the greys, blues etc., I sat in a semi-sleeping state whilst processing what you had said. I suddenly came to a realisation that the reason we can't see them is because they don't wish to be seen. We are not ready to accept them without fear.

I on the other hand, do not fear them. So as I sat there, I said that I wished to meet them and that the reason in my opinion why we can't see them is because we are trying to use our Earthly eyes. And that we need to be in the right vibrationary realm.

At that moment, as if confirming my understanding, a face appeared in my mind's eye. It wasn't like the pictures I see often as a flat dimension. It was in 3D and in (feel mode). That's the only way I can describe it. A grey, with almond shaped eyes, black and shiny, with small slits for a nose appeared before me, if only for a few seconds. But it was long enough for us to communicate. I welcomed him and asked his name. He said they don't need names as they instantly know each other by their individuality. Just then the brightest of lights appeared from the corner of his eye and appeared to scan me from right to left.

I have thought about this and come to the conclusion that even aliens come from the light. The visit was short but sweet. I wish I could have had longer but I got the impression that it was just a quick introduction or confirmation about my beliefs.

Love, peace, joy and beauty to you and yours,

Krista (Karen).

Roman replies:

Dear Karen, I enjoyed myself at Desley's, especially being with all of you. All of you made the Seminar a wonderful experience because your energies helped balance my presentation on the Duality of Human Life. I was delighted in meeting all of you, and yes, I did recognise all of you from beyond your human forms because each of us are connected to each other. Thankyou for sharing your experiences with me during the Seminar and also from your email. Yes, fears create confusion, but also disconnects us from the Aliens who try to communicate with us.

Most Aliens come from the Light and use the Light as humans do. But there are those who come from ego, just like humans do. It is to do with letting go of ego, created from the past, which depending on any individual's experiences, particularly if they are negative, creates negative emotions and then fears.

Karen, what my Being expressed about truly believing in yourself does play a very important role in connecting to other life forces. Remember always, to be free of beliefs and conditioning is to be free of limitations. You are then open to all that is.

Be blessed in unconditional love always.

Roman.

WHERE SHOULD MY LIFE BE TAKING ME?

Dear Kuntarkis,

I've been having financial problems in this life. I would like to know if there is any advice you could give on this. Deep down inside I feel as if I am in the wrong profession. I would like to do something creative, but I don't have any clues. Can you give me some advice on this matter? I would appreciate it.

Jeannette.

Kuntarkis replies:

Dear Jeannette, financial problems have become a main issue with human beings. In fact, over 60% of humans are having major emotional problems, which then create financial problems. You each need to stop for a moment and take a good honest look at your self-created lives, and if each human being becomes truly honest with themselves, what they will see and discover is they are disconnected from the Source. The Source being their inner self, the Light that shines in all of life that exists in the Universes.

It is so important to take some moments of life and become quiet within yourself, and listen. I mean truly listen to your inner voice that can guide you out of the darkness that all humans have created from their past conditioning and beliefs, which in reality comes from your parents' genetics and has followed you through your life and has been reinforced by your upbringing.

Human beings live day to day with their negative emotions. If each human could look at themselves and realise what they have created, and that includes financial problems, and learn from their heart to dissolve their past negative emotions, and become 'feeling' beings, it would bring the balance of mind, body and spirit together as one. And yes Jeannette, it would bring out your creativeness, and you would have no confusion in your life. You would see the world you live upon with new eyes. You would know what it is you truly wish to do with your human life, and your financial problems would not exist. That is the truth, for only the truth will set you free, as it will all others, free from self-created limitations.

Jeannette, your human world, as it is now, is completely run by human Ego, which is driven by fears and insecurities, created from the past. And it is the past that needs to be dissolved before the real can be manifested. If you do this, you will become the living example for others to see and learn from. Expand your love from within outwardly for all to see. And then as you live the truth, and you most certainly will know the truth, all what you are feeling, even your financial problems and confusion, will dissolve before your eyes into the nothingness from which they first came, and peace and harmony will follow you wherever you go.

Be blessed dear Jeannette in the Light.

Kuntarkis.

HELP ME HEAL THE PAIN

Dear Kuntarkis,

I am 56 and very set in my ways of life. I read a book given to me by my daughter four years ago called The Inner Soul. Let me tell you I'm becoming a very angry woman, as I put the book in a cupboard and forgot about it, and the only reason I found it and read it was because my daughter was killed in a car accident. I'm finding it hard to come to grips with her death. I've been a Baptist most of my life and only believed what was preached to me, and what my very religious parents taught me. I am angry because I have become one-eyed and would always criticise others for their beliefs, feeling my beliefs were the only truth. After reading this book it made so much sense. I wish I had read it when my daughter gave it to me and I could have showed her more understanding and love. I believe that's why I am so angry. I am no longer a Baptist and I am trying not to judge others for what they believe in. It took the loss of my daughter to make me search for more that I was understanding. I am not really sure if I have a question. A small message would do, and I really enjoy reading the information supplied on this site. Thankyou.

Dolly.

Kuntarkis replies:

Dear Dolly, you are indeed a very brave and beautiful human being because you are willing to change and grow beyond what you have believed to be the truth. No truth can or will ever be discovered on the outside if there are insecurities on the inside. Only when each human being stops long enough to stand back and look at themselves unbiasedly, and sees how they have become what they are in this present moment, and come to a self-realisation that all their beliefs and conditions have created what they are today and tomorrow.

Regarding the book which your daughter gave you four years ago, Dolly, you were not ready to read it, and if you did, remember the outcome would have been the same. Your daughter Sara gave you that book with no conditions, and Sara never asked you once if you had read it. She knew when you were ready you would read it and grow from it.

Please Dolly, forgive yourself. Don't hold onto your pain. Your pain is your anger, and it is okay to bring your anger out and dissolve it by forgiving yourself and anyone else you feel needs forgiving. When you forgive you will grow beyond what is now. Remember to love yourself as your daughter Sara forgave and loved you very much, and always will.

Be Blessed dear Dolly and walk in the Light.

Kuntarkis

SHOULD I TELL MY PARENTS ABOUT THE REVEREND?

Hello Kuntarkis, I can't give you my name, as I'm not sure what to do. I'm 15 and I feel hopeless. About 18 months ago my parents had to go to another city because my grandfather died. They are a bit hard up for money so the reverend of the church we go to suggested I stay with him and his wife. My parents were grateful and I didn't mind. I thought my dad and mom would only be gone for 3 days, but it ended up being 2 weeks. During that time the reverend spent time with me to help me with my homework.

I caught him once looking at me when I was having a bath, but I didn't think much of it because of who he was. On the 9th day he was saying goodnight to me and asked if he could tell me a story. While he was telling the story he touched my breasts and then put his hand under my top. I didn't know what to do. He then told me he had done a healing on me and said goodnight. 2 nights later he did the same thing, telling me a story but this time he put his hand under my blanket and touched me between my legs. I wanted to tell him to stop, but he just kept telling the story. The next night he began to do the same, but he removed my underpants and took off his pants. He laid on top of me and had sex with me. He only did it once and it hurt me a lot. I kept telling him it hurt and to stop, but he wouldn't listen. When he got off me, he told me not to tell my parents as I had been selected for a special reason, and that God said it was alright, and if I told my parents I would no longer be special in God's eyes.

I didn't tell my parents, but I feel he lied to me just to have sex. I want to tell my parents because I feel bad and I find it hard to go to church, especially since my dad and he go fishing together, and are close friends. Please tell me what I should do. I just don't know what to do. Please help me.

Lost? Lost.

Kuntarkis replies:

I won't say a lot Little Angel and my heart goes out to you for your pain. I send the love of Creation to you, to have the strength to make the decision you feel comfortable with. Yes, this human man has allowed his Ego of the flesh to do you harm and please don't be afraid if you choose to tell your father or mother, as I know they will listen and love you no matter what.

You are a caring, loving beautiful human being and you don't deserve to carry this pain throughout your human life.

Listen to your heart and the truth will come from your lips. If you choose to express the truth, you also may help others who have had this pain done unto them. You are not the first, and if the truth is not revealed, he most certainly will find others to hurt in the same way. So little angel, you have a decision to make, and if you choose the truth, you will feel much better, and the pain will also heal in time in your mind and in your heart. If you want to write again, please do. May Love and Light fill your whole being?

Be Blessed Little Angel.

Kuntarkis.

HOW DO WE DISSOLVE THE EGO, WHILE LIVING IN THIS 3rd DIMENSION?

Peace. Kuntarkis suggests that we "dissolve the ego" and cultivate "consciousness beyond the Ego world" that will foster our "becoming the living truth". Kuntarkis asserts that the Ego becomes perverted in the material world and that we experience fear, insecurity, judgement, greed, lust, cruelty, and other negative emotions while in this state of consciousness. On the other hand, Kuntarkis says we can overcome the void and unhappiness we experience while in this state, when we dissolve the ego, love ourselves and others unconditionally, and we can create whatever our heart desires.

I agree with and understand these concepts intellectually. However, what practical steps can we take to dissolve the ego and manifest the truth that our souls are yearning to express, particularly while living is this third dimension?

Peace & Blessings.

Kuntarkis replies:

Dear Kalinansa, I am honoured to receive your words of enlightenment. It is a precious moment when a human being opens the door of their soul to learn, and also to bring forth their own divine truth, their desire for a higher form of consciousness, and most of all, an understanding of what is being expressed from my heart to all human beings on this most precious Earth.

You would agree that there is an incredible amount of upheaval and conflict on your planet at this present moment, both emotionally and physically. There is religious confusion as flaws in religious ideologies, theories and beliefs are exposed, and the sheer number of wars ignited through religious intolerance, are an illustration of this. You also have issues of drug abuse and drug dependence, illness, disease and genetic defects, which are more prevalent than ever before in human history, and of course what affects all of humanity to some degree is the emotional imbalance that is being experienced on a mass scale due to stress, frustration and anger. Human beings must ask themselves "why is this happening?"

If you come from an honest heart, your answer would be that this is happening because of Ego and its obsession with the past. Ego only knows the past and has brought it into the present moment. If the Ego is not brought into balance it will also create your future. All suppressed negativity in all human beings has now begun to be released and is being expressed outwardly. Confusion in human beings is rising to boiling point, as humanity as a species is becoming more irrational, more anxious and more fearful than ever before. All human beings who live in a third dimensional vibration of matter are so conditioned and controlled by fearful governments in their societies, and many are feeling trapped as they feel their existence closing in on them. The more fearful a human becomes, the more their animal instinct reacts, causing them to want to flee to be free, and that is why the Ego is controlling human societies in a mass level. Many are rebelling against the control which they have allowed to be imposed upon them.

Kalinansa, to free yourself of this entrapment, you must first become 100% responsible for every action in your life. The second is to cleanse your human body of all its toxins, and begin eating good foods from your Earth. The third is to cleanse your human brain of all past emotions, and forgive yourself and all those who have or may have offended you from the past to the present moment, including your human parents. Once you have cleansed your brain and your body you will begin to unconditionally love yourself, and in turn you will begin to love everyone else, as everyone will learn to love you. You will no longer express negative thoughts about yourself or those around you. When love is in your heart, you will begin to expand your vision and knowledge, and you will have respect for yourself and all of life. Your consciousness will expand beyond your third dimensional matter world and your connection with other vibrations and worlds will increase.

Please remember, all emotions are the past, governed by your genetics and upbringing. Your fears and beliefs are from your past, and unless you take awareness, they will make your future. Feelings, however, are spontaneous, existing in the moment, not governed by what has been.

When you are in your meditations your consciousness will grow. Still your mind in your quiet moments of meditation, and eventually the chatter of your Ego will stop. You will begin the journey inwardly to the void that exists in all forms of life, and if you listen you will hear the inner voice that will guide you to what you seek. You will find not only balance, but knowledge of all things in all universes. May I suggest for you to read, if you choose to, the April and May 2000 Conversations with Kuntarkis articles.

May you be blessed in the Light, and may your growth expand in all aspects of your life.

Kuntarkis.

SHOULD I BUY THE NEW BIKE?

Hi Kuntarkis,

I have a quick question. I want to sell my present motorbike which I own. I have a good steady job and earn good money, but I've seen this fantastic bike and want to trade mine in as a deposit to buy the new one. It means going into debt. I can't make a decision. Should I or shouldn't I buy the new bike? What do you think? I also want to say that your site has helped me understand what I'm feeling, and I think or hope I can grow better than what I have been. Thanks,

Brendan.

Kuntarkis replies:

Dear Brendan, you have an interesting decision to make and since you are feeling good about yourself, know when you make that choice to buy or not, it will empower you and you will gain strength from the choice you make at this moment in your life. The motor bike you have now is not new and also need attention. It will shortly cost you money to repair it, and if you look towards the new motor bike, it is a more powerful machine. You have to ask yourself honestly if you are capable of controlling the extra power, and then ask yourself if you want to place yourself in debt, as on your world, owning possessions involves continuous debt to some degree. So Brendan, weigh up the different choices. Be cool, and calm, and ask yourself from your heart, not your Ego. Your Ego will tell you what you want to hear, but your heart will express what you may need to hear, for in your heart lies the truth. When you have asked your questions of your heart, listen and then make your decision. When you have made your decision, go for it and enjoy your life Brendan. Be happy within yourself and allow that happiness to expand into your everyday life. Ride in safety and the heart will always guide you Brendan. Please always wear your helmet.

Love who you are and be blessed in the Light.

Kuntarkis.

CAREER MOVE QUERY?

Dear Kuntarkis,

I have a personal problem. I am 30 years of age and single, and I must admit even though I consider myself spiritual and understand who you truly are, and why you have come to help humanity understand their spiritual selves, I am also very ambitious and always open to a career advancement. At the moment I work for a small company that creates software for the corporate sector. They look after me well as I have been with them for 6 years. I have been offered a position with a large corporation. The benefits exceed my expectations, with opportunity for advancement and international travel. The problem is that I'm feeling guilty because my current employer needs my expertise and relies on my skills. I feel caught between my loyalty to my supportive employer and the opportunities a larger company can offer me. I know you are unbiased which is why I need any guidance you could offer. I would appreciate it very much.

Amanda.

Kuntarkis replies:

Dear Amanda, you need to stop feeling so guilty, as human life is like being on what I believe you call a 'merry-go-round'. Everything is just a lesson of life, of learning, not to be judged as right or wrong, good or bad. Everything in human life is just experience and your present employer is also on a journey or learning, as are all your friends. The whole purpose of life is to experience and learn, and maybe it is time for you to move on to other lessons. Even though you are needed in your present employment, someone else will take over and learn new lessons through the opportunity you have provided by moving on to another position. If you choose to take up the new position, you will open up new opportunities for growth, and expand your vision and your awareness. At the same time allow yourself to enjoy the benefits of your new job. Just ask yourself one thing Amanda: do you deserve the best in life? If your answer comes from your heart, and not your Ego, then go for it and enjoy your new lessons, and believe you can fulfil the role because you have the knowledge, the experience and the love required to succeed.

Be blessed in the Light and walk in the Light dear Amanda.

Kuntarkis.

DIAGNOSE & SUGGEST TREATMENT?

Dear Sir,

I'm writing to ask for your kind help. GIVE ME YOUR HANDS, HELP MY SON! HELP THIS YOUNG MAN! 27 years old Chinese, he has medical history of asthma. But in recent years (4 ~ 5 years), this disease hasn't broke out. On Oct.17, 2001 he went to Guilin from Shanghai for a trip. When he arrived in Guilin city, soon, his middle and upper abdomen felt uncomfortable. Immediately heart and breath stopped. After 3 minutes, he was sent to the hospital. It took 17 minutes for doctor to rescue him.

Now, heart, lung and brain has come back to life. Up till now, he hasn't woke up. He has been comatose for 7 days. His breath depends on the machine. The Hospital in Guilin has no way to save my son, since they can't find the reason to cause this terrible disease.

We would appreciate if you could help this young man, help my son. After all, his life is most brilliant. If you can diagnose this illness, would you please send us the way as soon as possible, so that we can take measures immediately? In order to find more possible ways, we hope this message could be spread out. You can contact us by fax or by e-mail.

Now, his old parents are crying. Help their sole son! God bless you! We would be extremely grateful if you would help.

Best regards!

Zhang Nainian (old father)

Kuntarkis replies:

Dear Zhang, My heart goes out to you. Your son is most precious, as all of life is on your Earth. Many problems have been created which in turn have caused much pain and suffering to human beings, especially with disease. More humans in this present moment are suffering ill-health caused by dangerous chemicals and drugs than ever before. By consuming the wrong foods, the human body cannot tolerate the stress, and this is passed on from generation to generation, gradually deteriorating human beings as a species.

Your beautiful son needs to make some very important changes in his life and his lifestyle. To explain his dilemma, his small structures in his lungs are not functioning correctly. He is a very shallow breather and must learn to expand his lungs by taking in deep breaths so that more oxygen can flow into his blood and therefore oxygenate his cells throughout his entire body, especially his human brain. It would be very wise if he could live in the country where the air is purer so he can breathe fresh air. He also needs to take up some light exercise, such as swimming, walking, yoga or Tai Chi and to include a lot of stretching so that his body can sweat out the toxins that have accumulated within him. A hot room or hot steam bath would be very good to assist in opening his sweat glands and eliminating his toxins.

He needs to drink plenty of fresh water each day, at least 2 litres (8 tall glasses). If he smokes it is very important that he stops smoking immediately. If there are any smokers around him, it is very important that he be kept away from them as smoking is a major cause of asthma attacks. Each cigarette when lit releases over 1,000 different chemicals that are poisonous to the human body. He must be able to breathe air that is as free from pollution as possible.

He needs to look at his diet and see what he is consuming. It would be wise for him to give away animal products such as meat, eggs and milk, and instead increase his intake of soy, tofu, and tempeh for high quality protein to help build up his body and repair it. Your son has a much depleted immune system and needs to build it up. A good product which is natural is called spirulina. It comes in a tablet and is very high in iron, calcium, potassium and B-complex vitamins. He also needs to increase his vegetables and eat plenty of green vegetables for iron, as iron is the foundation of the human immune system. Be sure to washes all vegetables thoroughly in water to remove any toxins and pollutants from their surface before eating them. The cities and surrounding areas are a major cause of asthma attacks - this is a world-wide problem. Moving to the country to help him regain his health would be very wise, and being more active, eating clean purer food and drinking lots of water will help flush the toxins from his body and build up his strength and constitution again.

If you have any more questions, please feel free to ask of my being. I send loving healing Light to you and your son. Be Blessed in Love always.

Kuntarkis.

AM I IMPORTANT?

Dear Roman,

Ask Jecuss Kuntarkis who I am. I might be of great importance. Get as much information as you can. Please, tell me what 'he' said. My birthday is Jan 23/2/73.

Kuntarkis replies:

Dear Jan, One of the greatest issues for all human beings on this most precious Earth is the need to feel special, to be loved, and to feel important.

In the evolution of all human beings, from a conscious level, all 7 billion humans on this planet are of great importance. No one is greater than another. All are equal in the scheme of life. What does separate one individual from another is their level of thinking and understanding.

In raising one's awareness and one's consciousness, the individual is beyond importance or the need to feel special. It is in the knowing of being humble that you will gain the knowledge and understanding to be compassionate, and to be loving towards all of life that exists in all Universes. And through this awareness you will gain the wisdom to use your inner knowledge, to help all that seek a deeper understanding of life. The secret is within your heart. Love yourself unconditionally and let go of all human Ego, for it is human Ego that is truly your real enemy. Your Ego is your past beliefs and conditioning, your fears, and this is what holds back all human beings from advancing to Light Forms of Consciousness.

What you are (and who I am) is a living Spirit of Creation's totality, as all of life is. Be Blessed in Love always.

Kuntarkis.

KUNTARKIS PLEASE VISIT ME?

Dear Kuntarkis,

I have always believed there is life on other planets. I was so excited when I read about your kind and their way of life, and how you live without a physical body. I know it is to do with our evolution in our present state of thinking, and yes I do look forward to the day we as people will move beyond our current time. I was wondering, is it possible for you to come to me and talk with me so I can see you and ask some questions of you in person? Or maybe will you visit me when I am asleep? Can this be done?

Maskiet

Kuntarkis replies:

Dear Maskiet, There is so much that can be shared with human beings, to help elevate their awareness and consciousness. Knowledge that comes from within is freedom from conditioning of human Ego. It allows you to be strong and to see the falseness that has and is surrounding human beings for so long. Knowledge allows you to be an individual and to have free will to make your own choices in your human life.

My being would be honoured to come into your presence and share knowledge with you Maskiet. Always believe in yourself and the Light of Creation and my being will stand before you. Be Blessed in Love and Light dear Maskeit.

Kuntarkis.

IS MY HUSBAND ALRIGHT?

Hello Kuntarkis,

As you are probably aware, I am soul searching at the moment. I have two wonderful children who lost their father and my dearest friend on September 11 in the attack on America. I thought I was a very strong person, but since losing my husband, it has been very difficult for me to cope. It's like my heart has been ripped out of my body. Can you tell me if my husband is okay and not lost in that black vibration? I thank you from my heart. The wisdom you share with the world and people like me is very special and close to my heart.

Thank you. Claire.

Kuntarkis replies:

Dear Claire, from a physical perspective, it is very sad to lose a human being who is so close to you, and who has shared many beautiful moments of life with you. Your husband, your dearest friend, felt no pain on his passing over into Spirit world. Kevin was confused but there were Spirits of Light who guided and helped him understand what had happened. Do you remember the first time you became pregnant and lost the child because you fell ill?

That Spirit is helping Kevin understand, and in the moments to come, Kevin will go through the Light and he will return to guide your youngest son throughout his life. It will be his chance to pay back a debt of kindness from another life, he had with him.

May Love always be with and your family. Be Blessed in Love and Light always.

Kuntarkis.

DECEASED TWIN VISITS BROTHER

Dear Kuntarkis,

I have always been a very physical person in my life. If it wasn't logical then it didn't exist... until one evening while I was asleep, I felt I was being watched. I grabbed my torch from beside the bed and shone it around the room. I couldn't see anything, so I went back to sleep. I was dreaming about something and kept hearing my name being called - Johnny. As I began to wake up there was a light-greenish glow in my room, and in the centre of it was someone who looked like me. They were standing there and said "Open your eyes to the world and you will begin to enjoy life and not be so hard on yourself." Then as I looked at this light it just vanished and I went back to sleep. In the morning I was not sure it had really happened.

I forgot about it until I was at my parents' home for dinner. My sister was talking about dreams and the mention of dreams brought it all back for me. I told them of my dream and my parents looked like they had seen a ghost. Then the truth came out. I had a twin brother who died at birth. He lived for only a few hours and so I was never told of him. Can you tell me why he came to me at this point in my life? I am 44 and a little confused.

John.

Kuntarkis replies:

Dear John,

Your departed brother Peter has been a Spirit guide to you throughout your life and will be until the day you choose to leave your physical life as a human being. His purpose was just to experience a human birth and to connect with you in the physical plane so that he could help guide you in your human life. The reason Peter came to you is clear - it is to help you understand there is more to life than being completely logical. There are other worlds, realms, vibrations, and dimensions that exist throughout many Universes. Peter is an old soul and has great knowledge and understanding to share with you. You have always wanted to write a book John, but you have never put pen to paper. You will, and you will be amazed at what you write. It is time for change John. Listen to your brother and life will become joyous and abundant.

Be Blessed Dear John in Love and Light always.

Kuntarkis

TALKING TO SPIRITS

Hi Kuntarkis,

My name is Kylie and I'm 18. I believe in Spirit, mainly because my Mom has been a Spiritualist nearly all of her life. She is always speaking to Spirits. We don't tell our friends because they will think we are literally crazy or something. Can you tell me, because my Mom can see and talk to Spirits, does that mean I will see them and be able to talk to them too one day?

Kylie.

Kuntarkis replies:

Dear Kylie, Never think or believe that you are odd because your Mother speaks with Spirits. It is a natural part of life, and in your past human history it was as natural as eating bread. Unfortunately, human beings are very fearful of what they do not understand or cannot see, so they put a label on it to make themselves feel more comfortable with the inexplicable.

Humanity has been highly conditioned to only believe in what is apparent to the five physical senses of touch, taste, sight, smell and hearing. Spirit is eternal and you Kylie are a Spirit being living and experiencing a physical life, so if you believe you are a Spirit, then Spirit must exist beyond the human body. You are very fortunate to have such a wonderfully open-minded Mother who can pass on such knowledge to her children. You are indeed gifted and blessed Kylie. Just believe in yourself, and in time your true potential will be realised.

Be Blessed in Love and Light always.

Kuntarkis.

FIRST CONSCIOUS ASTRAL EXPERIENCE

Dear Jecuss Kuntarkis,

I am writing you because I have just had my first conscious astral travel! It is all because of the advice that you had given in your most informative web page, that helped me to believe that this was a possible. I was really blown away by what I had witnessed! A spirit guide helped me (although I couldn't see them) successfully get through this experience. I felt their presence and I knew that they were literally pulling me along as I communicated with them telepathically. During this travel, I was guided to what appeared to be a spaceship or spaceship like environment. I saw humans in uniforms; they appeared to be on a mission; scientists maybe? On the same ship or ship like environment, I also saw various creatures that were a cross between human and other kind of species (animal like). I saw grey androids/robots (maybe men in protective gear). They looked like some kind of security force. The people and beings on the ship didn't seem to notice that my spirit was there.

This was absolutely similar to what we've seen here in many movies such as Star Trek. I am convinced that the movies that we see (such as Star Trek) are just a mirror images from a hidden reality! I could not hear voices or sound on this ship but what I witnessed was extremely vivid and detailed.

My questions to you is, does such a reality exist in this vibration? If so, will we (humans on Earth) ever realize the truth of this reality or will this forever be hidden?

Thank you SOOOOO in advance for your attention to this email! You are WONDERFUL!!!!

Kuntarkis replies:

Dear Human Being, Reality is what each human being creates. It depends on their level of thinking, their level of understanding, and their vision of truth. Even though humanity has progressed in their material world of technology, their progress in consciousness advancement is very limited. Because of the past, the human Ego prevents human beings from stepping beyond the self-created emotional prisons that humans currently exist within.

It takes a human being like yourself to open the door to higher level of knowledge, to actually want to learn and advance consciousness. The Astral vibration is a stepping stone which has many levels of consciousness. To expand the mind is to open yourself to be a channel of Light. Within Light is the knowledge and wisdom necessary to gain the understanding of becoming one with all things. And in turn, all things will become one with you.

Humanity will come to self-realisation and gain the truth of totality, but the path in human time is long. There is much pain of the past to be forgiven. Each human being must come to this understanding, so all can come into balance. But remember, you as an individual can take the first step by believing in yourself, that you are indeed more than your physical self. Don't let the human Ego be your future. Allow the Light of Totality to be your guide, your strength, your truth, and your path to freedom. Be still in your mind and go within the silence of your Being. Listen, truly listen to the infinite knowledge that is dormant in you, as in every other human being, waiting for you to open the door and re-connect with it. There is one thing my being would like to ad, a human being cannot go back into the past, because the past is now only fragments of energy. It is no longer physical matter, the human being also cannot go into its future, because it does not exist as yet. Humanity as a whole does write and create their future in the moment. But what does exist are parallel worlds, just like your world but in different vibrations. Some are behind you in evolution, and others are ahead of you in evolution. Now, does that not deserve a discussion?

Every human being can come to this realisation. There is so much more to life and to truth, but it is the individual's choice to open the door to the infinite spirit of wisdom, compassion and unconditional love for all of life.

Be Blessed dear human being in Love always. Within your heart lie the answers to all questions.

Kuntarkis.

HOW DOES ONE GET OUT OF FINANCIAL DEPT?

Dear Kuntarkis,

I have a problem with debt. I am constantly asking the universe and my angels and guides to help get control over my financial situation. I'm very intuitive and very much want to pursue a career in the field of Medium ship/healing and new age medicine but I have to get out of my current debt problem. What should I do? I feel unbalanced. Help!

Kuntarkis replies:

Dear Human Being, My Being understands how easy a human being can fall prey to financial debt. Your physical vibration of the material world and the enormous influence of the human Ego, has caused human beings to give in to the wants of the material world, and yes, it can and does create a lot of burden and stress.

You say that you constantly ask the Universe, and your Angels and Guides, for help to control your self-created financial burdens, and that there seems to be no answer from them.

Your Angels and Guides are always with you and are always helping you in many ways, but so many human beings have lost the art of truly being still, long enough in the mind so as to listen and hear what their Angels and Guides are communicating to them.

Human beings are caught up in their negative emotions of life, so it is natural that you cannot hear them. If you did hear them you would surely listen to their wisdom and understanding, would you not?

You also ask the Universe for help. Please sit still for a moment dear human being and realise that you are indeed the Universe. You are a part of all that is, just as all that exists is also a part of you. You are the Creator, the driving force behind all things, all experiences and all limitations in your life. You have the power and the strength to create or uncreate all things in your life. Believe in yourself, truly believe in yourself, and really listen carefully to your inner voice.

Be Blessed dear Human being in Love always.

Kuntarkis.

CONNECTIONS BETWEEN REALMS

Dear Jecuss Kuntarkis,

Hi my name is Michelle. In a previous conversation that we had I talked with you about the experience I shared with beings from another planet. Within that conversation you had said that I had made an agreement for that to take place. Would you mind to explain a little more to me, again? Like why do we humans agree to have these experiences and how and when do we agree? Also how do they find us in the first place - is it simply 'collective consciousness'?

You have said that I originated from the same planet as the beings - is there a reason as to why I had this experience? To recall on my truth maybe! But I have yet another question; I love the element world and it is said at times that I still return into that realm and in the same form. I do believe this and can recall some of these experiences, so could you please tell me why this takes place. Why and what connection does this have with the experiences with the other beings; if it does at all. I know we are all part of existence and I believe parts of us are still in existence in other places, so is this to be true in my case? Is that what is happening?

Thank you very much Kuntarkis. I feel a strong connection with the Earth, sometimes it's overwhelming. Though it's a shame what we are creating for our future. Thank you again, love and light always.

Michelle.

Kuntarkis replies:

Dear Michelle, Thank you for the precious moments you have taken in writing to my Being. Try and see from the centre of your beingness that you and all of life are connected each other, and all forms of life throughout all Universes. Many human beings on this planet Earth have incarnated thousands of lifetimes, and on other levels of consciousness, have lived in other realms, vibrations, dimensions and Universes. Every human being before incarnating into a flesh form makes an agreement regarding their life's experiences. They are helped by the guides to live out their life and to grow in their understanding of human life, even in other vibrations.

Every form of life, be it physical or spiritual, has its own unique identification within its energy field, and can be recognised by other beings through this energy signature, much like fingerprints identify human beings physically. This unique energy signature never changes – you have it for eternity.

All human beings on this Earth originated from the planet Nar'Kariss over 928,000 years ago, and humans have been evolving ever since. This knowledge is recorded in your essence. If you persist in discovering the truth, it can become your reality. The experience you speak of was activated by your inner being to show you and to give you a better understanding of life beyond the physical.

Yes, you have also lived in the elements vibration, and do visit that vibration in your human time of sleep. But remember, the element vibration exists for one purpose, and that is to bring balance to this beautiful planet. The Earth is the Mother, the spirit which gives life to all forms of life upon her. The elements help Mother Earth to maintain the balance in all her vibrations. The elements were created by the spirit of the Mother Earth – fire, water, air, earth and spirit make up the life force that is needed to create physical form. The Earth is fully aware and alive – the Earth breathes, cries and feels pain and suffering.

It has always expressed to you that knowledge comes from within and is the key to freedom from all self-created illusions of human Ego. Only those that seek the truth from within will be set free from all pain and confusion of physical life. You hold the key dear Michelle – it is within you as it always has been.

Be Blessed dear Michelle in Unconditional Love always.

Kuntarkis.

HIGHER COMMUNICATION

Mr Kuntarkis,

When I read about you, I felt to tell you that since some time ago I've had the feeling or realization that "they are waiting for me" or "they are looking for me". Who is "they"? I don't exactly know, but it's definitely not from this planet and in a higher form of life, especially that I'm kind of difficult to find since I'm in the physical factor of a body. Probably "they" know where I am and as also I understand I have a purpose here.

Some of the truth I have received is:

Life's game is the shifting balance between chaos and order. Total chaos is death; total order is no game. The soul is space; thinking space as long as there is space there will be life.

In this planet there is a continuous struggle to maintain from the material trap and considerations. I understand this and this makes me free. Question is: Do I qualify for service and life in a higher order, if I'm not already doing this? How many lives do you think I've got left here on this planet?

I got to your web site through yahoo, searching for other people in the road of truth. Since "true truth" is about freedom, unification, communication... You hit on those words. Interesting...

With love,

Gaby.

Kuntarkis replies:

Dear Gaby, See your human world as a half-way station. All of humanity has a purpose in their human existence. One lesson is forgiveness of the past. The second lesson is to let go of the past in unconditional love. The third lesson is to dissolve the human ego of its own self-created fears and insecurities. It is the human ego that has created all the past violence which has been occurring on your human world – all wars are a creation from past fears into the present moment, carried over from one lifetime to the next, and so it goes on.

Human beings have lived thousands of incarnations over the last 928,000 years of human history. The wheel of life has repeated the same patterns over and over again. What a human creates in this time, they will create it again in their next life, whether it is negative or positive. Each human being needs to resolve the negative creations of their past through forgiveness and unconditional love for all of life, and dissolve the human ego. Allow the centre of your being – your heart centre – to be your guide, then you as an individual will open the door to your infinite knowledge and awareness of who you truly are. You are a spirit being living and experiencing a human physical existence.

It is your spirit that is your true self, and it is the wisdom of your spirit that will guide you and set you free from the illusion of your human ego. The key to opening that doorway is within you, as it has always been.

Be blessed in love always.

Kuntarkis.

UNDERSTANDING DREAMS

Dear Kuntarkis,

Do you know anything about dreams? I had this dream where I was walking beside a 7 feet tall "somebody" that had a black coat that covered all including the face. Seemed to me like a female god. Even though "she" looked mysterious and dark, "her" presence didn't feel or act evil. I was accompanying her while she gave "food" to everybody on the street. It was a sort of spaghetti and she supplied even to a dog, which showed me her appreciation for all life. The next day I was dreaming inside a dream. I mean, the dream was about me waking, sleeping and dreaming in the dream. And I remember both dreams. Do you make anything of this?

With love,

Gaby.

Kuntarkis replies: Dear Gaby, Thank you for writing again and for expressing your human experiences of dreams, as you call them. Dreams are not figments of your imagination but actual reality in your sleep time. All human beings enter into the astral vibration in their time of sleep. The purpose of sleep is to repair and regenerate the human body while the Astral body experiences different levels of consciousness. Many humans do remember their dreams while many do not. It all depends on one's level of understanding to different vibrations as well as human emotions, and how busy your daily life is.

Referring to your experience of having a dream within a dream, it is due to your close connection from your astral body to your human body. You can be fully aware of what is occurring. Many human beings have recalled their dreams while seeing themselves in their sleep time. It is like being caught between two different vibrations and being the observer to one looking on and one having the actual experience.

Gaby, there are many levels of consciousness and many levels of vibrations that are constantly crossing over each other. There is so much more than just the human physical self. Please take some moments in your human life to go within your inner Being and meditate on the stillness of your mind.

Be blessed in love always.

Kuntarkis.

TRUTH &ILLUSION

Hello Kuntarkis,

I can relate to your way of thinking concerning how we each create our own path in this lifetime, as we have in all our past lives. My worry and my concern is how do we each come to the understanding especially if we believe in other truths. What do you think?

Lodgia.

Kuntarkis replies:

Dear Lodgia, The first step to self-realisation is recognising that the human ego is at present in complete control of the self and humanity, and has been for the past 928,000 years of human history. Your concerns are your fears created solely by the ego of the past. When the seeker seeks inner truth it is natural for the human ego to feel threatened and it will try to defend itself. It will place past negative emotions upon you and before you to create confusion in your life, so that your emotions keep you, the individual, from finding that inner truth. One must step beyond the present negative emotions and become the observer. See for yourself the illusion and fantasy the human ego creates.

When the individual stands strong and sees the falseness that surrounds them and humanity, then and only then can one begin their true journey of self-discovery. By allowing yourself to love your own beingness in unconditional love you will open the door from the centre of your heart and you will gain the understanding and the wisdom to step beyond the human ego of fears and deception. You will gain the knowledge of inner truth and all your worries and concerns will dissolve into the nothingness of the past. You will become a true human being and your love will emanate throughout you and throughout all of life. You will see the past as the past, a memory of experiences, lessons of life, no more, no less. No judgements, no human ego to keep humanity in the past to create the present.

Every human being on this most precious Earth must come to the same realisation of inner truth as an individual. Then and only then will all of humanity see each other in all nations as brothers and sisters of the light, and yes, every form of life has the same light within them.

Be blessed in love and light dear Lodgia throughout your journey of self-discovery, for the journey always begins with you, the individual.

Kuntarkis.

HEALING THE PAST

Hi Roman and Kuntarkis,

Thanks so much for your words on the web site. I have recently started my journey of healing from my past, namely from same sex attractions (SSA) that I have had most of my life, since my first sexual experience was with someone of the same sex.

I have been submitting healing requests on the web and have been meditating for many years. I recently started investigating SSA from being very afraid to even look it up and have found some root causes and others who have changed. From my request using meditation to my higher self I have actually started to see change and it is amazing how my ego is afraid of it and wants to hold on to what it knows even though I do not want it. I still have some big fears but really believe that I can create a future reality not from my reactions but what I desire and will. I think my sexual polarity was screwed up and manifested in my sex drive from early programming because I have since been feeling attractions! Towards women. The hardest thing for me is dealing with the subconscious as I will still have dreams that could be sexual in nature that are with same sex partners.

I have noticed that I can feel pressure between my eyes and sometimes on my chest when I am in thought or meditation. I think this may be my chakras and also I am wondering about connecting to my higher self. I would like to clear my way to this level of awareness and be able to understand non-verbal communication and interpret intuitive thought better.

I guess my main questions are:

1) Do you have any additional information on how to further heal the wounds of the past with specific people in my life?
2) The ability to help me clear my energy bodies and communicate with my higher self?

Perhaps a personal consultation would be of benefit. Please let me know what you perceive.

Thanks,

Harry.

Kuntarkis replies:

Dear Harry, My Being is pleased for you for having the courage and strength to look at some of the deeper issues of your human life, and to face yourself, which for most human beings is one of the hardest issues to deal with. Yet facing oneself is the key to finding freedom from all the fears, beliefs and conditioning of the self-created past of human life.

Regarding your sexual preference, you Harry have been caught up from past incarnations and it has plagued you for several lifetimes. You made a decision in this incarnation to forgive your past and bring back balance into your human life. It is in this lifetime Harry that you need to forgive yourself unconditionally and to love and accept yourself as a human being.

The additional information you seek on how to heal past wounds within yourself and other human beings is simple. Be in the present moment, and forgive from your heart centre, not your human brain, for the human brain creates confusion. Sit in the stillness of your mind and put your thoughts on your heart centre. Allow the unconditional love to emanate throughout your inner and outer Being. Saturate yourself in this infinite love that is endless, timeless, eternal and free of judgement. This unconditional love exists in all life forms, in all Universes.

By becoming quiet in the stillness of your Being you stop the chattering of the human brain. This will allow you to connect to your higher self, which is the infinite essence of your true self. This essence is often referred to as the light that exists in all forms of life. If you Harry wish my presence, then call my Being by my name. But only when you are still in your Being will you sense my Being is present.

The truth can only be known if the seeker becomes truth itself. It all begins with the individual. The human ego will only give you the past, which will then create your present. But the truth will set you free from all the bondage of the human ego. Walk in the light and you will become the light. Walk in the darkness of the past and you will become darkness. Remember, the choice is always yours. You are the power that shapes your creations.

Be blessed in love always Harry.

Kuntarkis.

USING YOUR NATURAL GIFT: IMAGINATION

Hello Kuntarkis.

I'm an imaginative person. I surprise myself at times. I believe like no other in things so simple for me but so complicated for others I can prove a lot of things which I claim spiritually. They always help me. I don't die easy and most importantly nobody does. My dream is to travel the universe with anybody that wants to come with me, if it's not a problem. I'm sure I won't get bored. I'm one but many. I love the self and believe like you say. I feel I know you. Do you know me! I also believe what goes around comes around like planets orbit the Sun. That's energy for me. Our eyes which are round and the balance within our hearts desire and balance which is real power for me but not others around me, why! That's what I enjoy thinking and believing about, light with no time of expiry, true power of eternity and most importantly living our hearts desires.

Petros.

Kuntarkis replies:

Dear Petros, It is good to see you are an individual and that you use your imagination. Imagination is a gift to all human beings. To see is to create. To truly believe is to become whatever you wish. The power of creation is within and around every human being, as it is around and within all life forms in all Universes.

Every human being has the ability to travel into other realms and dimensions. It all depends on their thinking and understanding. You are an individual and as an individual you have the right to think as you wish. Imagination is what has created your human world of physical matter, as well as your material world, which only exists in your third vibration of matter.

Human beings also have the ability to transform to higher realms of existence. Yes, through imagination this can be achieved. It takes practice and determination. Meditation is a form of imagination, used to still the mind and the being in order to go within your inner space and connect to your light. All human beings can transform to higher forms of knowledge, but many are caught up in the human ego of the material world. Never give up on what you truly believe, and most importantly, believe in yourself.

Be blessed in love always dear Petros.

Kuntarkis.

FEELING LOST IN MY LIFE?

Dear Kuntarkis,

I stumbled across your site while researching Fennel Tea which I'm harvesting at the moment. My question is "Am I on the right path?" I am 47 years old divorcee, soon to be 48. I am the mother of 4 children, 3 boys and a daughter. My daughter and my youngest son are twins. When the twins were born it was discovered that Dan had cystic fibrosis. He was rushed to a children's hospital when he was hours old and underwent major bowel surgery. Dan spent his 1st 2 months of his life at Sick Kids. His health has always been a huge factor in our lives. In March 2002 Dan was at death's door. His only hope was the possibility of receiving lungs. Two days after being told by the doctors that Dan's time was running out - he received the gift of life - lungs. The transplant has changed his life - he is transformed into a teenager who can do many of the things he never did before - miracles do happen.

I left my ex-husband 7 years ago - he was rarely home and definitely not a father. I moved my children onto a farm not far from their school. I ran my own business. Complications arose regarding the business and the company was forced into bankruptcy. I quickly started another business which was put into a young man's name that I was having a relationship with. He was 13 years younger than myself. This company ran for 2 years and made close to a million dollars. It became apparent that I was supporting another child (even though I loved him) and in Jan. 2000, I lost the contract for the business and the young man moved out. It was pretty grim for a while - I had hardly any money and no job to support my kids - my ex-husband never gave child support and never gave me any financial assistance. I also owed the government taxes (even though the company was in the young man's name I felt it was my responsibility to pay the debt off) and the credit card (half was his) a lot of money.

I did find a good job and started paying off my debts. A year later I went to work for another company - it was closer to home - but also discovered that Dan's health was quickly deteriorating. I worked extremely long hours as I was in management. I would wake up early, drive to work, 11 to 12 hours go by the hospital, visit Dan and then go home again. When the doctors informed me that Dan was dying I promised him that I would not leave his side until his fate had been decided. He had the transplant and spent 6 months recovering. During this period of time my work tried to terminate me. I got a lawyer and they had to take me back. Believe me I didn't go back because I wanted to - I went back because I needed to support my kids and Dan's drugs cost 75 dollars a day. 2 months after I returned they did in fact terminate me - without cause - the positive thing was they gave me a package which enabled me to decide what I wanted to do.

I have always loved to cook and have started a business that includes catering and cooking for busy people. I also have done quite a bit of public speaking about organ donation. I am on my spiritual path. I do chant and meditate and believe that there is something whether it be God or the combination of the "oneness" of all of mankind that guides me through my days. My question is whether I'm on the right path. I'm working hard - money does come in but I'm barely making ends meet. I still owe the government money for taxes which I have been paying off slowly. The credit card has been completely paid off. Sometimes I feel completely lost!

Tanis.

Kuntarkis replies:

Dear Tanis, You asked, are you on the right path in your current human incarnation. Every human being is on the path that they each have chosen. It can be negative, it can be positive, or it can be a little of both, it all depends on their own personally created karmic debt. Your past incarnations always govern your present lifetime and your present lifetime will govern your next incarnation in human form.

One thing must be understood. The level of your thinking and your understanding also governs your human life. Many humans create confusion, pain and misery in their life because of their fears, beliefs and conditioning. Many human beings always create a negative existence or distractions which keep them very busy so they do not have to face their fears.

You dear Tanis have the power of the light within you, and you can create any path in your human life, if you so choose it to be. You have a very beautiful heart and you are a caring and loving human being. You give so much to others yet you forget about yourself. You need to be more loving towards yourself. Stop and look into your own eyes, which are the windows to your soul, and ask yourself what makes you happy. Listen for the answer and allow the tears to come from your human eyes. Give yourself some precious moments of joy. You need it, and you most certainly deserve it.

Be blessed in love always dear Tanis.

Kuntarkis.

RECURRING CANCER: WHY?

Dear Roman,

My name is Mandy I am 38 yrs. old. Over the last 7 years I have had 4 tumours and 15 operations, and now I am in very early stages of lung cancer, but they cannot operate as there are too many nodules. Can you help me and how much will it cost me and what do you do. Thank you.

Mandy.

Roman replies:

Dear Mandy, Thank you for taking the time in writing to me. I truly understand what you are feeling at the present time in your life, mainly because I was in the same situation just on 15 years ago.

First, I only charge one consultation fee for a three hour session. The purpose of the session is to help you understand why you created the dis-ease in the first place. Most people find this very hard to accept, that they are responsible for their illnesses and disorders.

All dis-ease is created from negative emotions, which can have many circumstances to then cause the dis-ease, such as through your parent genetics, through negative emotions created from childhood, life style and habits that add to the negative emotions, and so on. Dis-ease, whatever it may be, does or can take 20 or 50 years to develop and affect you.

I can help you if you are truly willing to help yourself, and to be fully responsible for your actions towards your body, by understanding your negative emotions through unconditional love towards yourself and forgiveness by completely changing your food intake, lifestyle, and by confronting your inner self. You need to be willing to listen to your inner self, not the human ego that controls most people.

It is not an easy undertaking, but you must ask yourself, is your life worth it? How willing are you to put 100% effort into completely reviewing your life, diet and lifestyle in order to beat what you have created and bring yourself back into balance. I felt my life was worth the effort and I cured myself. You can do the same, if you allow yourself to come from your heart. You will always find the right answer within you.

Mandy, I cannot cure you – only you can cure you. I can only give you what I have learnt and how I applied it to cure myself. You must understand that I am not responsible if what I give you does not work for you. If you are prepared to accept these conditions, then please contact me again by email and we can discuss further how I may be of assistance to you.

I will leave this with you for your consideration.

Kind regards,

Roman.

RELATIONSHIP PROBLEMS

I just today broke up with a guy that I had been seeing for 6 months. I have never been quite sure of him or his intentions. He was always saying one thing and doing another. A week ago he used my credit card to gamble all my savings away without my permission. He ended up in the hospital for depression (suicide) and said he just couldn't live with himself for what he had done. I have never heard of someone stealing because of depression and I just wonder if that was his way out. I feel horrible for breaking up with him because he swears that he loves me, but something inside of me says run away now before something else happens. I care for him and thought I loved him, but I know that I will not be able to trust him again. Do you go with your gut feeling or take into consideration that he was just going through a rough time?

Christy.

Kuntarkis replies:

Dear Christy, when you truly trust and respect yourself you will attract others into your human life who will also trust and respect themselves as well as you. When a human being steals from another it means they have some negative emotions to deal with.

You are too trusting in your relationships to give your credit card to another who you have only been with for six of your human months. This is an invitation to disaster.

Learn to listen to your inner self (as you put it, your gut feeling) and take notice of the signs. If you are not sure of him or his intentions, then you surely must have doubt about him. Every human is on their own journey of learning and understanding. If a human being truly loves another human being, they would never cause harm or steal from that being. Love comes from the heart. It is the centre of unconditional love. The human ego does not know or understand unconditional love, it only understands the past, be it negative or positive.

Go by your inner truth, your instincts, of how you feel about this human you are connected with. If you truly love him from your heart and he truly loves you from his heart, then some strong changes need to be considered regarding the ground rules of the relationship, would you not agree. However, if you do not love him truly from your heart, or he does not love you truly from his heart, then you must ask yourself how long you will suffer his emotions. Emotions belong to the individual, but that does not mean the individual should impose those emotions onto another and cause them grief or concern that then affects another's life. You must ask yourself, when is the lesson learnt and over?

Be blessed in love always dear Christy.

Kuntarkis.

FINDING LIFE'S PURPOSE: HOW DO I?

Kuntarkis,

Please tell me how does one go about finding one's true purpose in life and why do I feel so stifled all the time. Inside of me there is something trying to express itself for a higher purpose. Where do I look for inspiration and direction? Thank you.

Josephine.

Kuntarkis replies:

Dear Josephine, Trying to find one's purpose in your human life can be very draining, leaving you feeling empty. Many human beings search for their life's purpose throughout their entire life and in most cases they are always looking outside of themselves.

Look within your own inner being in the stillness of your mind. Trying to find life's purpose outwardly will leave you feeling empty. Trying to find your purpose in your human life outwardly is like trying to find the truth outside of yourself. There is no truth outside of yourself because the truth you find is someone else's.

You can start to look for inspiration and direction from your inner self by lying or sitting quietly in your own space. Your human brain will give you many thoughts. Try not to think or concentrate, just be in the moment of your life. Inspiration and creativeness come in the moment, just like it does for an artist or a writer.

Inside of you, you said there is something trying to express itself for a higher purpose. This is the case for you as it is for all human beings. This is your spirit, the true essence of who you are. Spirit is the essence of living consciousness. Listening to your inner self will give you the wisdom and knowledge to grow beyond your present level of thinking and understanding. So go within and listen – truly listen – to your own divine essence, as all your answers will come from within.

Be blessed in love always.

Kuntarkis.

DARK FORCES: DO THEY CONTROL US AND WHY??

Hello Roman & Kuntarkis,

This is very urgent. I need your help!!! I've written before about my sister and Black magic. My daughter is psychic too and we receive messages from Saibaba, an ascended master. The last message was very alarming....it said that I needed to move out of my house pronto as there is some evil entity that has come in with the aim of destroying my child. On further checking with a tarot reader we were told that if we did not move out there would be a death in the family within 13 weeks. Please advise me as soon as possible. I am afraid and do not know what to do. Can you please, get back to me as soon as possible?

Thanks

Naomi.

Kuntarkis replies:

Dear Naomi, Human life for each individual is what you create. It can be a negative life or a positive life, or even both; it all depends on how you were brought up as a child. If you are brought up in a negative household it can and will create fear within you and throughout your adulthood.

Fear is only a form of energy, it has no power whatsoever. It is you the individual that gives it life. Beings of Light who come and help human beings do not give messages that will create fear in individuals. Those entrusted with giving messages to a human being, whether they come from a spirit or a human being (such as tarot card readers) have the responsibility to ensure their messages do not create harm through creating fear or paranoia.

What you have been told, concerning a death in the family that will occur in 13 weeks if you do not move out, is very negative and irresponsible of the one who gave it to you. You Naomi are the power and creator of your own life and destiny. You can live a life of conditioned fear, or live a life of joy and happiness. The power of my expressions to you are the same powers within your own inner being.

You may need to believe in yourself and your own ability, and listen to your inner self. Within you are all the answers you need for when you are ready to ask and believe.

It is your fear that controls you and that is why you seek your answers from others like spirit, ascended masters, tarot readers, or whoever. My Being believes in you. If you can believe in the Light that you and all of life comes from, that all of life in all its forms are created from, then go within yourself and allow your mind to be still long enough for you to connect with your true self.

Use the light that is within you and all around you to dissolve negative energies. See the negativity dissolve in the light, back in to the nothingness from which it came from, and fill your inner being with light, surrounding yourself with thoughts of love. If you dissolve your fears you will find the courage and strength to live a life of personal responsibility and the balance will be with you and your family always.

Negative emotions are illusions created from fear. Nothing can destroy you or your family if you live a life of love and truth. Be willing to dissolve your fears and all things will come to you in peace and harmony. Stop and think before reacting.

Be Blessed Naomi in love and light always.

Kuntarkis.

SPIRIT GUIDES: HOW DO I CONNECT?

Hello Kuntarkis,

How did you come to know the name of my spirit guide? This question does not come from scepticism just real joy and surprise. You see I have been asking for a long time what my guide's name is but I feel I never received an answer. What I did receive was a clear inner voice telling me that names are not concerned or are not important in the spirit world. Names are given to make us who are living to feel comfortable. We as physical forms are constantly working in "boxes". We feel safer but we miss so much. Just because we cannot see outside of our personal box that we constructed with fear, doubts, anger etc., does not mean that there is nothing outside those walls. I feel that this is telling me to trust my gut feelings and begin to let go of the fear of not being able to physically see or hear for that matter, to actually allow myself to fully receive guidance. I am still interested in if you have made contact with my guide if so how does she feel? What is she like? Did she live?

Also I did often feel touches on my leg or on my toes while sleeping at night. I may have felt them on my head as well, but when it started happening a lot I got scared and asked them to communicate in a different way. Of course it does not happen as often, strangely I miss the attention. I once woke up in the night and was still in a very heavy delta wave pattern of consciousness, this time is my most receptive time for psychic awareness, and I saw standing at the end of my bed two very faint figures. One was a woman I felt who was holding the hand of a little girl. The girl asked the woman if I could see them in a very curious playful voice. As I started to realize what was happening they faded away with each blink. I often get these visits. Thank you for replying to my email and I hope I might be able to meet you or book a session. I'd like it if you would keep corresponding with me. I am also interested in your thoughts on my questions. Of course I'm sure you have lots of emails to reply so I will be patient

Blessings to you.

Callan.

Kuntarkis replies:

Dear Callan, Depending on the vibration in the world of spirit, there are many doorways to different levels of consciousness. On our own dimension we the Nar'Karones are no longer inhabited by the ego of dense matter flesh bodies. In your world you travel by your transportation vehicles such as cars, buses, trains, ships and airplanes whether they take you to another part of your city or to another country.

We travel by thought. We see our destination and we arrive at that point by thought alone. It is like opening a door to another realm. My Being has met with your guide As'charre in the spirit vibration connected to your inner worlds. It is true that in spirit world names are not a concern for each being knows another by the light of their aura.

Your guide As'charre lived in your human year of 581AD in a small village called Pracknerr (forgive the spelling, but it has been phonetically spelt), just outside of Egypt. Her human parents were the leaders of the village. They had four children and you Callan were the youngest son. You were very close as a family and you and your sister As'charre were the best of friends. You always looked out for each other. Even though you were the youngest in your family during that lifetime, you were always very protective of As'charre.

In your present life As'charre has chosen to be your guide to protect you and guide you in what you seek from your human life. In the silence of your mind through meditation you will make contact and communicate with As'charre. Believe in yourself.

Be blessed in love always.

Kuntarkis.

UNUSAL EXOERIENCE: WHY?

Hi Kuntarkis,

I truly hope that this email finds you in the best of love and light (o: I am writing this email hoping that Kuntarkis could help shed some light on yet another unusual and bizarre experience that I've had.

About 3:00am on October 26, I was woken to a vibrating sensation throughout my body... This is usually an indication that I am about to astral project but this time I felt the presence of a Being gently touching me on my (astral) ankles. I could feel its energy throughout my physical and astral bodies. This is not the first time I've felt something or someone gently holding and gripping me by my ankles. This happened to me for the first time about 3 weeks ago and I am sure that it was the same Being that came to me last night.

Anyway, I was lying still and comfortable on my bed, feeling this entity touching me. Realizing what was going on, I intuitively knew to speak in my mind to this presence. To my quiet surprise, this entity spoke back to me - I heard the voice of a male or masculine energy. I could clearly hear his voice inside my head! I asked him why was he here and he clearly replied in a calm yet mischievous tone "I've been watching you" and I asked why? He then said "I am intrigued by you". He also said something like "we've known each other in the past". He was speaking to me while gently touching and caressing my legs and ankles. Then it got really strange. I felt him slowly part my (astral) legs and climb over me. I could feel him slowly girting over me. Then I heard him say to me, "I don't have the plumbing that I used to have." Ironically, I did not panic nor did I feel any fear. The last thing that I remember him saying to me was something "this is my H.E.L.L. (he spelled it out)". I felt that he was in some form of hell but he laughed after he said it. Thereafter he sorted faded into the distance. I was certainly feeling a little uneasy about this statement.

Kuntarkis please tell me who or what is this entity? Why is he really drawn to my energy and what did he mean by his last statement?

Your advice is sincerely appreciated.

Tony.

Kuntarkis replies:

Dear Tony, The entity you spoke of is from the past, meaning the human past. He lived in your human year of 1876 in the land called England. You also lived in that human time. You both became attracted to each other and began a homosexual relationship. Your human father rejected you because you went against his wishes as his plans for you were to marry into a family of wealth and so called power, to unite the two families.

In human terms you were a rebel, rebelling against your human father and all authority; you had your own mind, which in reality is a good thing. Your father gave you a choice - give up your relationship with the man and marry the woman, or to be cut out of any inheritance. Because you chose to stay in your relationship with the man your father became very angry. He was against homosexual relationships, and you did not speak to each other for eleven months.

Your father hired a private detective to know where you were. His anger grew, and so he decided to end your homosexual relationship by having your partner violently assaulted to teach him a lesson, and to leave you alone. It went wrong. Your partner died. Because of what your human father did to your partner, you told him you would never see him or speak to him again.

You decided to leave England and travel overseas to the land of America and yes you never saw your Father or Mother again, but you were quite happy. You always wanted to open up your own business, to create with your hands. After being in America for five human years, your dream became your reality. You opened your business in making selected leather shoes for all types of human beings. You became well known for your craftsmanship as a shoemaker.

What my Being has explained in the above will give you a deeper understanding of your present situation.

This entity who exists in the astral vibration who comes to you was the human man who you were having a homosexual relationship with and who was violently assaulted and murdered in that human life. His energies have been in that vibration for the past 128 human years. His name in that time was Edward John Cullman. This is the reason why he is drawn to your energies. When he died it was violent. His fear has been holding him in the low levels of the astral plane. In his human life in 1876 he was never attracted to the human female. He could not relate to human women and he created an unhealthily appetite for his sexual urges. This is the main reason why he has not gone through the light of cleansing.

This entity cannot let go of the negative emotions of his own creation. It would be wise for you dear Tony to place the light of protection around yourself on entering your sleep time. If this entity called Edward comes to you again, tell him you are very sorry for what happened to him in the year 1876, but he needs to let go of his fear, his past, his negative emotions, and his own self-created hell as he calls it and move on by going towards the light of love that is unconditional.

To help him let go, you need to believe in yourself and your own abilities – you can help him let go and move on to his next incarnation as a human being. Remember each human being is on their own journey. How long the entity stays in the astral vibration is their own choice.

Be blessed in love always dear Tony.

Kuntarkis.

THANK YOU FROM TONY

Hi Kuntarkis,

I just received your letter today regarding an earlier question that I sent you Roman via email, (The Elohim and the Duality of Humanity)... I was so touched that you would be so thoughtful enough to send me a letter, so that I didn't feel ignored... (Of course I would never think that).

Also, THANK YOU Roman for making the Origin of Humanity the main attraction, on your website for the month of November! It was very engaging and informative as with all of your information from the past.

I would also like to THANK YOU, Kuntarkis for giving attention to my last question regarding the encounter with the entity from my past. I can't tell you Kuntarkis how good it is to have an outlet where I could share such OUT OF THIS WORLD information and get insight without judgment and ridicule. Most, if not all in my circle would most likely perceive me as crazy or having an overactive imagination. I sincerely hope that sharing my experiences; having them posted on your website, shows others who experience simular things that they are not alone.

Again, THANK YOU all for being such super spiritual teachers! I have learned a lot as the result of finding your site and I will continue to spread the word that infinite love is the only truth and that everything else is an illusion.

Love and light, always...

Tony.

PS. I am sure that you are very aware of the events that have lead up to and affected the surprising outcome in our Presidential election... Therefore, I am asking that you Kuntarkis and all of our brothers and sisters in the spirit world send loving energy to those of us who need it in America and Iraq... The next four years will be trying at best.

Tony.

ARE WE BEING MONITORED & BY WHO & WHY?

Dear Roman & Ilona,

I would like to take the time, to thank you for the great work that both of you are doing. Particularly from someone who is learning about themselves, as you have confirmed through previous letters. So once again, "many thanks" for giving us this opportunity to be able to have some confusing answers verified.

Sincerely,

Alan.

Dear Kuntarkis,

Thank you for your previous love that you have reflected back to myself. I have two questions to ask of you which I feel are both related, to one another. My first question is, are we all being monitored, and if so by whom, and why? The reason for asking this question is because some time back I had an experience inside of my own head, which sounded like a switch clicking on and off, and when it was left on, I could hear someone working in the back ground. The last time I heard the clicking sound, I asked them, (verbally) to turn it off, as I think they were reading a paper, and all I could hear at the time was the rustling of paper. When I requested for it to be turned off, all went very quiet, then the last thing I heard was a click followed by the quietness, which indicated that it had been turned off. As from then on it has not repeated to this day.

My second question is about time. Some time back I was led into a rescue group where by the souls who refused to move forward were given an option, to either move forward, or return back to the beginning of their first experience. This experience has left me pondering, as I know that there is no such thing as real time as we know it. Then if I am right we can return at any time to an experience that we might not have fully understood, which might be in our time as we know it, back in the eighteenth century, that we might have had the experience. This then would give me the understanding that when we look back into our records of lives to view an experience, that we took on, we are viewing the real thing, and not a recording like a record, so to speak. If that is the case then, there is more than one soul experiencing the same experiences that I have been experiencing up to date, and are following those that are in front of myself.

Alan.

Kuntarkis replies:

Dear Alan, Most of humanity is unaware that human beings are mostly being influenced by a race of negative entities called, The Unseen Forces. My Being has previously expressed knowledge on the Unseen Forces on this website in August 2001 titled 'The Unseen Forces: who actually controls humanity' and again in October 2001 titled 'The Unseen Forces and their role in the Attack on America'. Note: Both those stories (expressions are in this Book of Knowledge)

First, yes, humanity are being monitored and manipulated by a race of negative beings called the Zarnaquris, which my Being refers to as a part of The Unseen Forces. They have been manipulating humanity at different levels by thought transfer. They are the main cause of most of your wars of the past and the present. They manipulate governments, business, military and especially the human individual. They live in a very negative state of energy and are drawn to any negative thoughts and actions.

The Zarnaquris have manipulated many races of Beings from others worlds. They use it for their own pleasure and entertainment because humanity has so much negative energy, which is why they are drawn to this vibration. The greatest power in dissolving their grip on humanity is the Light of Unconditional Love. They cannot manipulate those who walk in the Light of Creation's totality. The Light is within all human beings, you only have to take your own self-realisation of who you each are to recognise it. Once you truly love yourselves unconditionally from the heart, the Unseen Forces have no control over you and this is the truth.

Yes, time is only a creation of man alone. The moment is the only reality that exists. Once you as a human being discover the truth of my statement, you will step beyond man's time and see your world in a different vibration. What has taken place is a shift in one's consciousness; you will still have an understanding of man's time, but you will not be a part of it, rather you will be beyond it.

Remember the saying of both Budda and Jesus: "Live within the world, but do not be a part of it". This means live your human life and enjoy all your experiences be they negative or positive without any form of judgement.

Simply experience life as learning. Walk gently on your Earth, harm no one and you will be beyond the ego world of karma.

Yes, every human being can catch the moments of their past or past lives, and yes they are a living reality of all their experiences. The soul is one, yet many spirits can be created from that soul in order to experience different facets of life.

Be Blessed dear Alan of Earth in love always.

Kuntarkis.

SPIRIT COMMUNICATION

Dear Kuntarkis,

Again, my gratitude for all your answers. They encourage me to persist in all my efforts. Merely reading your words causes me to experience a feeling similar to my astral projections.

Is my body prodding me to devote more time to meditation (which I have difficulty attempting)? If I were able to return to the beautiful bliss that I have been pulled into in the past by my passed friends and relatives. And, are those friends & relatives who have done these things working as my spirit guides, or are there other spirits yet whom I have not consciously remembered? How may I call to them and recognize their presence around me? Are they related to the numerous times through the years that I have experienced a sudden force of energy on my bed, such as that of someone sitting on the edge of the mattress?

Finally, is it "wrong" of me to wish to avoid another human incarnation? The astral plane was so beautiful to me, I cannot imagine what other vibrations must be like.

With peace & love.

DG.

Kuntarkis replies:

Dear DG,

Yes, your Inner Being is guiding you to devote more moments of stillness for meditation. Meditation has no rules. One of the most powerful forms of meditation is simply to sit or lie down, have no expectations, take several deep breaths by expanding your human lungs, hold for a few moments and then slowly exhale. This helps to centre and still the mind.

Close your eyes and put your inner sight to the centre of your brow. Many thoughts will come and go - don't think about them, just relax and enjoy the moment, and be in your own space. Do this for, let's say in your human time, ten minutes per human day.

Give yourself one month of practice, then ask yourself "how do I feel?" What have I learnt? Write it all down. What you will begin to discover is your closer connection to spirit vibrations and communication. You will gain a deeper understanding of your true self and your meaning in physical life as a human being.

Always live in the moment, not the past. The past is the past. The moment is the moment. The now will become the knowing. In that alone is freedom.

Be blessed in unconditional love always dear DG of Earth.

Kuntarkis.

VITAMIN B12 IN THE HUMAN BODY?

Roman,

Would you mind having Jecuss explain the true role of B12 in the body, and for people who do not eat animals? If we are to consume no animal proteins, and there were no supplements available, then how would we receive B12, and would we remain healthy if we did not? Do we truly need it to be healthy?

I am also concerned with analogous B12 in sea vegetables, and their supposed cancelling of B12 in the body.

Thank you so much. I think all site visitors would benefit greatly to some clarification in this debated area.

Love and Light,

Richard.

Kuntarkis replies:

Dear Richard, The role of B12 in the human body is to help balance hormones and blood. It assists in the manufacture of essential minerals to keep electrical signals flowing unimpeded throughout the human body and to the human brain, so yes, it is most certainly needed to help the human body function correctly. It does take a very long time for a deficiency to result, but it can be corrected quickly with supplementation.

The human body was never meant to consume animals. The human being, like other animal species, was created to evolve within its environment. The body can function without consumption of animal flesh, as protein (the main reason why humans eat flesh) can be obtained from plant sources which are of superior quality and more easily assimilated in the human body without creating additional toxicity and acidity, which animal flesh consumption creates. Protein from animal flesh is second hand and already in a state of decomposition.

The higher proteins are found in all types of beans/legumes, and legume products such as tofu and tempeh - made from soy bean, an excellent source of plant protein and highly compatible with the human body. Nearly all vegetables have some amount of protein in them, and nuts are also a very good source of protein which provide a number of essential nutrients not found in flesh. There is also a super food called Spirulina, in tablet form, as well as powder form and it is one of the highest form of natural protein.

When a human being lives on legumes, nuts, fresh fruit and vegetables, and clean water, they become a balanced human being in body and thought. If the body functions correctly physically, then cognitive functions are also at a higher level, so when you eat for your body's health you begin to see things differently. Many who have become vegetarian may have done so initially to improve the state of their health, but over time they also begin to understand and accept that life in all its forms has a right to exist and evolve naturally, without the interference of human man. Human man has only existed for 928,000 years, whereas the Universe has been around for billions of human years.

B12 is found in many different vegetables as well as some legumes, grains and nuts. There are many very useful sites on your internet which can provide you with detailed information on being a healthy vegetarian or vegan as well providing recipes to help you get started on a healthier way of eating. A healthy body creates a healthy mind, and a healthy mind creates healthy thoughts. Which in turn creates the balance of Mind, Body, Spirit and Soul.

Be blessed in love always dear Richard.

Kuntarkis.

AWAKENING THE HUMAN KUNDALINI ENERGY

Hello Kuntarkis,

My name is Simone, I'm writing you about the Kundalini Force; in particular about the awakening of it. I'm wondering how to feel the Energy, if it is something that happens by itself, or someone does it for you. I guess It can happen in both ways, but for my case I don't know if I should ask somebody that does it for me, or if it is something that has to happen by Itself, and because if it didn't happen, maybe that means that I'm not ready yet...

A way to awake it is to use the Cobra breathing, that's where they talk about Kundalini they mention it but nobody explains how it works....

Thanks in advance for your help, best wishes,

Simone.

Kuntarkis replies:

Dear Simone, to awaken the Kundalini energy can bring greater awareness, understanding and conscious growth, but a human being must first be free of all negative emotions from their past and present.

The first step before even beginning to awaken the Kundalini is to face all your fears, to face yourself, and to understand forgiveness of the self and others. Open your heart to unconditional love for yourself and all other forms of life, no matter what those forms may be.

One of the reasons most human beings do not explain what to do or how it works is because the Kundalini energy is a very powerful tool in making the individual look at themselves and all their fears. It is not something that can be read about or explained in a few hours and then obtained after a few days of practice. The process of awakening the Kundalini can be emotionally very confronting and overwhelming. Please Simone, take some of your precious moments to either read or reread Story number 49 o Kundalini Energy. Only you Simone will know when you are truly ready to open up and raise the serpent of fire known as the Kundalini.

It would be highly advisable that you seek out a teacher who truly knows how to help the individual awaken this energy force safely. With respect to how long it may take to awaken and raise the Kundalini, it may take one human year or it may ten; it all depends on the individual.

Be blessed in unconditional love always.

Kuntarkis.

NOTE: Read story 49 of this book, on The Kundalini Energy.

EGYPTIANS / KINESIOLOGY: EXPLAIN?

Hello Kuntarkis,

I am wondering whether you could tell me a bit about Kinesiology. I've been listening to a CD taken from a 6 CD set by Dr David Hawkins, and it has taken my attention. Perhaps I should invest in the whole set, but I am very interested in what he has to say on the subject. I wish to understand the subject a bit more, and what is really meant by the scales used in the testing.

Also, for some time now, I've been interested in and informally studying Egyptian history, and a few questions have been sparked up upon what I've heard and read about over the last few years. Beginning with the Pyramids of Giza. We have been taught that the three were made so that they are perfectly astronomically aligned with the stars of Orion's Belt, acting like an astronomical star calendar. Another thing that has sparked my interest is that it has been said that the three pyramids, as well as other Egyptian architectural buildings of the time, were made so that they perfectly aligned with the Earthly cardinal points that no modern tools of today can duplicate. Also, that the Great Pyramid of Egypt was made like an ancient calendar, where the point that represents the year 2000 is a supposedly bottomless pit. What I was wondering is whether these are true accounts, and whether they have any bearing on what they are today. We have also been taught that the ancient Egyptian Hieroglyphs were only recently interpreted into modern terms, but there are some that have yet to be deciphered. Are these true interpretations and representations of what was intended all those years ago, and are we right in our findings and if not, what so these writings tell us?

Thank you for taking the time to read and hopefully answer this.

All the best,

Katherine.

Kuntarkis replies:

Dear Katherine, First to your question on the pyramids. The pyramids of Egypt were built by an alien race called the Illiatousous (pronounced 'I-lee-a-too-soos'). They came to the planet Earth approximately 20,640 years ago from a distant planet called Tousous, and the beings were known as the Illias, hence the name Illiatousous (the Illias of Tousous). The Illias were great builders of many civilisations who were known for their architectural genius, and they travelled to many planets in order to help other races of beings grow consciously by imparting their knowledge and wisdom within those civilisations. The Illias first came to Earth and lived among the Mesopotamian civilisation to whom they passed on a great deal of knowledge. They are human in appearance, the only difference between humans and the Illias, they all have orange-red hair, blue eyes and pale skin, and they stand around 1.7 metres tall.

The purpose of the Illias building the pyramids was as a physical guidance system for their spacecraft. The outer surface of the pyramids once had a layer of a mirror-like, highly polished surface, made of a compound that they created from sand. Being highly reflective, this surface was visible from the earth's atmosphere and was used much as lights on your airport runways are used today - to guide their ships in for landing. The main pyramids are perfectly aligned, and yes, the other buildings are also perfectly aligned with the Earth's centre points, meaning, the seven chakra centres of the Earth's energy system, which were placed on your Earth over 200,000 years ago by the beings known as the Nar'Karones. The purpose of these points was to help keep the Earth in perfect balance.

The hieroglyphics were created by the ancient Egyptians over 4,000 years ago. The interpretations are not correct, but in human time to come they will be interpreted correctly. As humanity evolves consciously and learns that unconditional love is the answer to dissolving the violent human past, and in letting go of the human ego of fear, there will be a far greater conscious awareness in every human individual, and it is then that the true meaning of the symbols will be easily understood.

One thing my Being can express about the hieroglyphics - they tell of the human past and what is to come. They originate from the ancient and universal language of the Illias and the Nar'Karones, known on your planet as Sanskrit. All human beings originated from Nar'Kariss, the home planet of the Nar'Karones, and deep in the genetics of all human beings, in your cellular matter, exists the truth of who you all are. All humans once spoke the Sanskrit language and the languages of your Earth today have all evolved from Sanskrit.

To your question on kinesiology, kinesiology is a system that uses muscle testing (amongst other methods of diagnosis) to evaluate the mental, structural and chemical aspects of the human body and its state of health. Kinesiology has been on your Earth for over 20,000 human years, having been introduced to the Mesopotamian race by the Illias, but it was lost over time. The Chinese civilisation of your Earth practised a similar system approximately 6,000 years ago, but this was also lost over time due to wars. Kinesiology was only rediscovered most recently in your last century by a human being named George Goodheart.

George Goodheart discovered the method while in a dream state and formulated it into a physical therapy. He rediscovered this information by connecting with one of his past lives, a life when he was a Chinese healer. It was during that lifetime that he developed the system and used it in his healing clinic in that time. It is therefore not unusual that he once more has brought this ancient knowledge into the present to benefit humanity.

There are human beings who have written books on this subject and it would be good for you Katherine to research for yourself this knowledge. My Being would recommend any knowledge that would help humanity grow in conscious awareness. Never give up Katherine. Search outwardly as well as inwardly.

Be blessed in unconditional love always.

Kuntarkis.

STARTING A SPIRITUAL CIRCLE: HOW?

Dear Kuntarkis

I would like to start running a spiritual circle once a week and also develop a workshop in the rural areas of Australia. Can you give me some guidance? Also could you tell me my spiritual name and who are my guides.

Thankyou.

Kind regards,

Maria.

Kuntarkis replies:

Dear Maria, Look deep inside of yourself and ask yourself this question: "What is my reason for wanting to run a Spiritual Circle, and also a 'Loving Yourself' workshop?".

Ask in the silence of your inner Being and listen to your answer. You may need to ask yourself several times, but be patient. You may also need to ask what type of meditation circle you wish to run, where it will be run, and how much will you charge. Find out the cost of hiring a hall, or if you can run the circle at a friend's home.

Ask your friends if they are interested in a weekly meditation circle and if they will commit to attending regularly. Place a small advertisement in your local newspaper and see what interest you generate. Once your weekly circle is running, you need to create a structure for your 'Loving yourself' workshop. Write down all of your ideas, read books on loving yourself and explore within yourself what it means to love yourself - it will give you a better idea of what you wish to teach. Even though you are a teacher, it must be remembered that, first and foremost, human beings never stop being students. Be open to all ideas, and never judge or criticise.

Love must first be experienced before one can teach it to others. Come from the heart always and you will be on the correct path. In the silence of your mind meditate on your spirit guides and ask for their guidance from your heart.

Your spiritual name is 'Yenschaka'. It is very old and was given to you by a spiritual leader and teacher over 3,500 human years ago in the land known as Tibet. In two parts, the first part (Yensch) means 'one who is firm', and the second part (Aka) means 'warrior', therefore your spiritual name translates into 'strong warrior'.

In that time you were a Tibetan monk because your human parents passed away from an outbreak of disease. You remained a monk all your life and helped all who came into your presence. The purpose of your spiritual name was to help you find truth and courage.

One of your spirit guides is named Twain Spencer. Meditate on the vibration of his name. He will help you understand yourself and your feelings. In your meditation, if you choose to, put your thoughts on his name. Call his name from your heart and remember to always place a circle of light around yourself before you begin. Twain Spencer was a poet and lived in your human time of 1807 in the land known as America. He was your human brother in that time.

Be blessed in unconditional love always.

Kuntarkis

DESPERATE FOR TWINS: YES OR NO?

Dear Kuntarkis,

I'm writing this letter, hoping to be able to change my destiny. I still have a strong urge for twins, and you have told me in the past that I will have six separate children. I am prepared to take a pill, to increase my chances of me having twins. But I am not prepared just to have another child, to increase the number of children to six. My question to you, is, can you change your destiny, and what would be the consequences for my actions if I tried? Would there be a payoff for my actions?

Dana.

Kuntarkis replies:

Dear Dana, Your human life is yours alone. You chose your experiences, your lessons, your human parents, even the human children you have and will have in your future. You alone create your past, present and future. If you chose to experience a particular lesson in your human life, no matter what it may be, then you are the driving force.

Whatever decisions you make in your human life, stand by them. See them as opportunities to learn. Creation is the totality of all that is and you are a co-creator in your human existence. Yes, you have the right to change your destiny. There are no consequences - everything is simply lessons of life.

Never see things as positive or negative, see all experiences as opportunities to learn and to advance your Being consciously.

Trust yourself Dana.

Be blessed in unconditional love always.

Kuntarkis.

QUESTION ON RIZQI, MARS & MALDEK?

1-Was there ever a planet Rizq?
2-Was our sun Apsu ever part of a solar system with 3 suns?
3-Was Mars known as the planet Lucifer/The Mourning Star and was it the home of the reptilians?
4-Was Mars and the planet Rizq the same planet?
5-Where is the planet Maldek now?

Demetrius.

Kuntarkis replies:

Dear Demetrius, There are 7 billion human beings living on your planet Earth and at this present moment there must be 7 billion truths in the making. Human beings are always trying to find truth about the past from outside of themselves, or are willing to accept another's form or idea of what truth is. In reality if an individual is personally responsible for themselves or their thinking and their actions, then there is only one place that truth can exist.

Within you dear Demetrius is the truth - from the past to the present, and even to the future. The truth exists within every human being – it is recorded in your cellular matter, and through your Soul you have recorded within you every experience from every incarnation you as a human being have ever had. And because of your Spirit being connected to your physical body, it even holds a record of your experiences of existences from other planets.

The questions you have asked deserve an answer. The answer to each of your questions is 'No'. But do not accept answers from my Being – seek the answers from within yourself, from your heart. Do not ask of another and do not ask your human brain, for it will only be an idea of truth. Ask in the silence of your mind, from your heart and listen to the first answer you receive. This will be your truth, but always remember, truth itself is ever changing, for truth evolves just as everything else in existence evolves.

Be blessed in unconditional love always.

Kuntarkis.

WONDERING ABOUT SPIRITUALITY

I have read articles on your site and I am confused but not really – I have never heard of talk that is on your site - Well what about me – do I have spiritual guides, do I have a spiritual name - I already feel deep within myself that I am not all that I will be - but I don't know what I will be - I live life day by day - I don't dwell on the past or the future - I dwell on what can I do today to make my life happy and others who I come into contact with - I have never tried meditation, but I do listen to a small voice that I hear inside of me - What can you tell me about where to go from here?

Debra.

Kuntarkis replies:

Dear Debra, Everything that a human being experiences in their lifetime is a part of their conscious growth. Every human being, before incarnating into a flesh body, chooses to have those experiences, whoever they may be with, and it is the choice of that individual. Living from day to day, moment to moment, is in reality living in the present. That is a good thing so you are doing well dear Debra. Being happy and helping others is a very special gift.

There are many forms and techniques for meditation. The purpose of meditation is to stop the chatter of the human brain so the individual can listen to the inner vibrations of their inner Being; to listen to the inner voice, your Soul, and to connect to your Spirit, the essence of who you are. You are much more than your physical self. All human beings are sparks of living light, evolving as conscious expressions of Creation. You are a part of everything and everything is a part of your dear Debra.

Yes, you do have spirit guides who help you through your human existences, and yes you do have a spiritual name. It is 'Po'schiris' and it means 'Eye of the Sky'.

Be blessed in unconditional love always.

Kuntarkis.

CAUSE OF ALLERGIES

Love and light to you Kuntarkis,

I want to ask you a direct question if I may: what is causing these constant allergies? It has been years. It is driving me crazy. I am eating much better (just a few sugars here and there.) I am meditating daily (when I feel well enough.) I am going to work now, and being productive. I truly feel my mind and spirit are healing. I just don't understand why I always have these allergies. Could you please help me with this Kuntarkis? I do feel I am evolving, and loving myself. I am doing everything possible to cure my allergies.

Is it the environment? Did the AIDS truly damage my immune system to such a degree, that it is still trying to strengthen?

I feel great, except for the draining allergies. I hate taking the medicines for them, but I get to a point where I have done everything I can, and am miserable, and only Benadryl seems to finally stop it. I want to be free of these allergies with all of my being. I hope you can help, and see that I am thriving, and feeling great despite having constant sneezing, runny nose and congestion.

Your brother in the sea of love and light,

Richard.

Kuntarkis replies:

Dear Richard, There are many reasons why a human body can suffer from allergies, and yes, you feel you are doing all the right things yet you still suffer badly with allergies.

The answer is yes, the human dis-ease called AIDS did break down your immune system, and yes, your immune system is still suffering the effects because of the virus. One of the major problems with the virus is that it is constantly evolving into other strains which can and do in some cases cause the human immune system to suffer. The environment that an individual lives in can also effect to what degree they suffer allergies - pollution is a major cause of human allergies.

The human immune system has the ability to combat any disease including allergies, but it needs the right nutrients so the human body can create an effective defence against allergens or human dis-ease. Iron is a building block of the human immune system. One of the products Roman took during his healing of lung cancer was Light Force Spirulina tablets - they are very high in natural iron as well as many other minerals and nutrients. Another good source of iron often prescribed to anaemic individuals is Floradix Liquid Iron supplement, made from herbs and vegetables - it acts quickly and normal iron levels have been restored in as little as 3 weeks. Another product Roman uses every 6 to 12 months is called Quick Cleanse. Quick Cleanse is an Australian made product (tablet form) that flushes out toxins from the blood, organs and muscles, and helps the body's digestive system to function correctly - it cleanses the body from the inside, including cleansing it of unfriendly bacteria which can contribute to allergies, while assisting the build-up of friendly bacteria to restore proper digestion.

It may be helpful for you Richard to investigate these products for your own personal use. My Being believes there is information on your internet which will guide you to obtaining information on and purchasing the products mentioned above.

My Being feels your pain and frustration Richard. Please understand, in your modern industrial world, pollution is present in many forms and over a period of human time it will have an effect on the human body. You are a beautiful human being Richard and you will overcome what you are experiencing at this moment - know this from your heart.

Be blessed in unconditional love always.

Kuntarkis.

WILL I GO TO AMERICA?

Mr Kuntarkis,

I have been lucky to have been able to view some of your work on the amazing internet. I am fourteen years old and would love to go to America when I am eighteen. I want to go there to study to become an engineer so I can come back to Africa and build dams for my people to have more fresh water like other people do in other countries. Mr Kuntarkis, I do not understand where you come from, yet I feel in my heart and soul that you are what you say you are. Can you tell me if I will go to America and become an engineer? I will say a prayer for you from my heart to yours. I thank you.

Ambor.

Kuntarkis replies:

Dear Ambor, I was most honoured to receive and read your question. I have looked deep into your large beautiful eyes which hold the vision and depth to your soul. You Ambor have great imagination, which will lead you to create your way to the lands on your Earth called America. Your natural power of will and persistence will bring forth what your heart truly wishes and your visions of what is to come. You will Ambor create in your life, and will bring great happiness and joy to your parents and also your human people. They will be most honoured and proud of your accomplishments, but you must always hold onto your visions and always know you have the power of Creation within you. Please always remember, even if you do not end up in America by the time you are 18 years of age, never give up on your dreams, it may take a little longer, but you will get there. I believe in you Ambor.

Be Blessed Ambor in the Love that comes from within you and believe always in yourself.

Kuntarkis.

WILL THIS JOB OPPORTUNITY WORK OUT?

Dear Kuntarkis,

I am a true believer in that what we each think will at some point in our life come true. I have read all the information that you have been expressing, and it has helped me understand more about myself. I have been happily married for four and a half years and have one child, a boy who is three. My husband is involved in computer software and has been given a job opportunity with better pay and conditions in another state here in the US. What I would like to know is, will it be okay or more the point, will it work out for us? We both want a change and we both see this as a chance to make a better life for our family. Could you give me a positive answer on this?

Barbara.

Kuntarkis replies:

Dear Barbara, Sometimes it is a little difficult to make unbiased decisions, especially if you are personally involved. Learning to trust yourself and your decisions gives you the greater power of self and helps dissolve the Ego's fear which has a hold on many human beings. The Ego is governed by the past, by what it knows which is based only on its beliefs and conditioning, be it negative or positive. Barbara, everything in human life is a lesson in life, and to be seen without judgement as an opportunity to grow and experience. I feel from my being to yours that you and your husband have already made the decision to go. Yes, it will be an experience and a material gain, it will create a better life for you all, especially for your other two human children to come.

May my Light and my Love go with you and your future? Be Blessed.

Kuntarkis.

DID MY WIFE CHEAT ON ME WITH MY FRIEND?

Hello Kuntarkis,

I am sending you this e-mail because I have been married for 9 months and I truly love my wife, but I feel I can no longer trust her. Two weeks ago my wife and I were at a party. My best friend, who I grew up with, was also there. He always seems to enjoy himself and get drunk, and then mouths off. He gets a little out of hand. I was asked to try and calm him down. I took him outside, by which time he was getting very angry. I know it was the beer talking, but in his anger he told me he had slept with my wife on several occasions. I am in the army and sometimes I am called away for training. It has been bugging me and my wife has been asking me what's wrong. I just don't know what to say. Can you please help me find out what actually happened? I am a mess.

J.P.

Kuntarkis replies:

Dear J.P., Trust in any relationship is a very important aspect of life. I have connected with your energies to better understand why your friend expressed to you his words about your wife. I will put you at ease and then suggest a way of dissolving what has occurred. First, what was said to you at the party? Your friend does find your wife very attractive and has for quite a while. He did not, or has not, slept with your wife, as your wife loves you most dearly and has eyes only for you. She is aware of your friend's desires, but would not allow his wants to destroy your marriage. By the way, there is a little one on the way – two weeks advanced.

Second, tell your wife what has been said by your friend so she understands she is not the problem. And third, you J.P. may need to approach your friend about the situation, in case he creates more Ego drama. Don't be angry with him. Come from your heart and find out why he did what he did. If he cannot deal with your truth, his own guilt, which is his Ego, it will separate him from you, as his journey in life is his own.

Be Blessed in Love and Light J.P. and our heart will always guide you through life.

Kuntarkis.

WILL I LIVE OR WILL I DIE?

This is for Kuntarkis.

It will sound as if I am complaining. I have been told I have less than seven months to live. Your site was given to me by a friend and I was amazed by Roman's curing his lung cancer. I was amazed that the cure came from a natural source and that he had the trust and will to go beyond the medical bullshit, that we as patients are told, and then we end up believing what they tell us. I have had several operations on my bowels to remove the cancer and each time they tell me they got it all, a few months later it's back. I admit now that my lifestyle was the cause because I understand more from reading your material. What I want to know is, can I still cure the cancer if I change my diet and look at my emotional baggage, or am I to accept that I am going to die? Which is it?

Malcolm.

Kuntarkis replies:

Dear Malcolm, Probably the hardest things in human life is to express the truth, and the second hardest would be to instigate change, to have the will and the courage to put the knowledge into action. Malcolm, whatever is created in human life from a physical aspect, can be uncreated if the individual wishes it to be so. You have been told there is nothing else anyone can do for you. If you truly believe this to be so then you will truly perish. But if you truly believe you want to live and be cured of your dis-ease then you must believe in the power of self and create and fortify your will to overcome what has been crated.

Change your food intake by consuming no more junk food or alcohol and learn to meditate in the stillness of your mind. Put in only good food and good thoughts; be totally positive towards yourself and don't allow anyone's negativity to influence you in anyway. Believe you truly want to live, learn to love yourself and accept who you are in unconditional love, and most of all, forgive yourself for the past. Let go of the past in love, for in human life, the past and all negativity that was created must be dissolved before the real can be manifested.

Malcolm, read through some of my earlier issues on <u>human dis-ease</u> **and read about** <u>the regimen Roman used</u> **to cure his cancer, for there lies the answer you seek, and yes, you can overcome anything in human life if you have the strength and determination to go beyond your self-created cancer. You do have the strength and the will, have you not?**

Be blessed, and the Light of Healing is with you.

Kuntarkis.

UFO's vs THE HUMAN BIBLE?

Dear Kuntarkis,

I have a question that has been on my mind for a long time. I am 11 years old and surf the web quite a lot, and I came across your site by chance. I believe in UFOs but my Dad does not. He is a priest and knows the Bible backwards. He told me God created the Earth and everything on it, and that aliens don't exist. But I've read some of your website and I feel it makes sense. I'm feeling confused by what my Dad is telling me about the Bible and God. What should I believe? Can you help me understand? I can't give my name in case my Dad finds out. He would be very upset with me, sorry.

Kuntarkis replies:

Dear young friend, I can understand how you feel because you believe your Father knows and tells you the truth, so I have no intention of telling you what you must believe or disbelieve. What I will say is that Creation of all the Universes is beyond words, and there will come a moment in your human life where you will learn and understand the different aspects of your life, where you will be able as an individual to believe in whatever you wish. Take everything in life as one more step in your own journey of your life. Listen to all things as simply being an expression to you from your Father, your Mother, your friends, your society, but don't see those expressions or judge them from a negative aspect. Just see them from your heart, and you will find as you journey through your human life, a knowing of truth will come from within you. You will know what to believe or not to believe. Love life, love your parents, and especially love yourself. As you grow you will know.

Be blessed and may the light shine on you and all your moments in your life.

Kuntarkis.

WILL I GET MY INHERITANCE?

Roman/Kuntarkis,

Please help me. I live in El Salvador where I have been without a job for over 18 months. Keep seeking one and no luck. We have sold all valuables and are out of money, in much anguish. My father *(name has been deleted to protect privacy)* **born 11.20.23 in Guatemala died on Dec16th. He abandoned me and never supported me as his eldest son when he divorced my mother over 40 yrs. ago. His family is a millionaire lives in Guatemala.**

Can you tell me, if you speak with his spirit, whether he has not forgotten about me in his will? And can you tell me when it may be read in Guatemala? Tell my father that I love him and hold no hard feelings toward him. That whatever he may leave me I will buy my first home ever, a small coffee farm and send my 2 young daughters to college to the USA...do you see this happening? I also sense that my 4 siblings whom I never met will be very upset with the outcome of the will. I feel I will move back to live to Guatemala in a couple of weeks.

I am out of money now and can't pay you, but will do so as soon as I can you may trust me. I am an honest person. I have endured so much pain, anguish and sorrow. I pray to God that his will be done and my Father is generous to me.

Alfonso.

Kuntarkis replies:

Dear Alfonso, It is very kind of you to express your words of anticipation to my Being. However, I feel Alfonso that you have misunderstood my purpose. I am one who came to your Earthly vibration for the purpose of helping humanity to grow in consciousness so each individual can grow beyond the limitations of their Ego, to help those who choose to become responsible for all their self-created limitations, and to dissolve their fears, their anger, their hatred, their greed, their lust, and their vindictiveness towards others. These are some of the traces of human Ego, and only by understanding what each human being is feeling can all humanity begin the process of letting go of the past, and learn to unconditionally forgive others for all the hurts and pain, and even misery, that has been created to all humans.

One of the most important things that each human being may need to do is to forgive themselves, because everything in human existence is only a lesson in life, not to be judged as good or bad, or what we each feel we deserve from life. If you Alfonso have nothing but unconditional love in your heart for all of life, then you will attract into your life wealth and prosperity, and live a life of pure bliss with joy, peace and harmony. And yes, if you believe Alfonso that you truly deserve great wealth in your physical life, then you will create it in your life.

There is something I need to explain to you. The past is the past, the moment is the moment, and the future is the future. Only you, and you alone Alfonso, are responsible for your past. And if your past is created from pain and fears, these are conditions of life that each human creates through their lifetime and which can become negative emotions if they are not brought into balance. Those emotions of negativity can create the moment and then create the future. It all depends on the individual and their experiences in life.

There are many on your Earth in this third dimension of physical matter who claim they can read your future. That is an untruthful statement, mainly because the future is not yet written, and you, as all humans, create your moments in life, which in turn create your future. You Alfonso have the power within you to create anything in your life, just by believing in yourself and by knowing what you want from your human life. There is a saying among humanity - if you can see it in your mind's eye, your imagination, and then you can create it by putting the action into it. Your world is physical so it must be created from a physical means.

So Alfonso, do you believe in yourself? If the answer is "Yes", then the inner power is yours. Create it, then ask yourself this question: "Do I believe I deserve great wealth and happiness in my life?" If the answer is yes, then it will be yours and all that you believe you truly deserve will come to you.

I know this is not what you wanted to hear, but the truth lies within my words of expression. Look deep into your heart, because it is in heart that reveals the truth, and only the truth can set you free and create your desires in life.

By the way, I ask for no payment, as money does not exist in my world. But if you choose, you may wish to make a donation to Roman and Ilona so they can publish their first book called *Entrapment*. It will help those seeking a deeper meaning and understanding of life.

Be Blessed in the Light.

Kuntarkis

UNHAPPY AT MY WORK

Dear Kuntarkis,

A friend gave me your web address. I found your site very interesting and exciting, as I have always been so conservative and taught to conform to rules. I believe it comes from my parents. As a child I can remember my father and mother always saying to me "no, you cannot do this", and this has shaped my life. I am now 26 and live in Adelaide. I can now see how I keep bringing negative people into my life, especially at the company I work for - I work for a bank. I like my job, but it seems the people there are so judgemental and they have conspired against me because I don't quite fit in with their way of thinking and how they live their lives. It does get me down, and I'm not sure if I should stick it out or find another job. Do you understand what I mean? What do you think I should do?

Jodie.

Kuntarkis replies:

Dear Jodie, The negativity from human emotion can be very stressful and can drain your energies, especially since you are in their space continually. Over a period of time it will affect you on an emotional level. Everything in all the Universes is energy and from this energy, thoughts from individual human beings are created, be it negative or positive. This is the cycle of human existence. Unfortunately when one is in the same space (and the majority of human beings think on the same level) you can be influenced into their way of thinking and succumb to their negative emotional fears and insecurities. You see Jodie, like attracts like. If you are not like them, or one of them, then they will become fearful of you because your energies are different in your level of thinking and understanding.

The human beings you work with have been encoded with the same beliefs and conditioning of life as their own human parents. It is all in the genes, making a human being what they are in their thoughts, habits and actions of their human life. You dear Jodie are in their vibration for only one reason, they represent your family. As you well know, there is a lot of emotional negative energy within your family, and that is the reason why you are a loner.

Always trust in yourself first and you will find the balance of mind, body and spirit within yourself; you will feel and experience unconditional love from your own being, in the knowing that you are connected to all things and all things are connected to you. You are a conscious living individual being first. You dear Jodie will find peace and balance, and most of all, happiness within and around you. Trust in all your decisions as being a pure state of bliss.

Be Blessed dear Jodie, for you have the strength and courage - trust yourself always.

Kuntarkis.

FEAR OF HEIGHTS

Hi Kuntarkis,

My name is Mark and I have a fear of heights. It doesn't matter whether I am on a ladder or on the top of a mountain, or even in an elevator. I begin to sweat, I become nervous and all I want to do is scream. People around me look at me and think I'm mad. It's beginning to get to me. Do you have any insight that may be able to help me free myself of this nightmare?

Mark.

Kuntarkis replies:

Dear Mark, First, my being wishes to express that you have taken your first step in the healing process. You have admitted your inner fears. What is most important for you Mark is in this moment to have an open mind and honest heart. Put aside all your beliefs and the conditioning of your human life, especially your logic and your human Ego. Listen with a true heart, as your fear of heights is not from your current lifetime.

In your previous life, the one before your present incarnation, on 17 August 1871, you were a civil engineer working for a transport system you call the Railway. At the human age of 47 you were working on a project creating a Rail path through some rough mountains in the land that is called America. When they were blowing up parts of the Earth to create a tunnel for the Railway, part of the mountain gave way and you fell to your death. Your last memory of the final moments of your life was the feeling of falling helplessly. This experience has been encoded within your spiritual essence as an experience of life, neither negative nor positive.

What sparked off the memory in this current life was that only moments after your birth you were dropped. It was a simple mistake, but the memory of falling helplessly was triggered and has now created an emotion for you in this life. Speak with your human parents about this incident and they will tell you what happened.

Mark, when you feel ready, sit in your quiet time and see yourself climbing the tallest mountain. Use your imagination to create the image. Do this until you feel safe and secure within yourself. Then, climb a ladder in your home, and keep practising climbing the ladder until you feel safe. When you are ready, go out and climb a small mountain. Believe in yourself that you are safe and secure, that you have the courage and strength to let go of the past. Always face your fears head on and you will come out on top, free from all created limitations. Mark, you can do this and win your freedom.

Be Blessed in Love and Light always.

Kuntarkis.

UFO'S & SEARCHING FOR TRUTH

Hello Kuntarkis,

I believe I am a very open minded person, and sometimes I feel I am the only one. I believe in UFOs and have read much of the material on your website. I can see how someone like you exists and that you really are here to help humanity outgrow their Ego. I just think people are so closed-minded. They all live in their little black boxes and are scared of change. I have sighted nearly 20 UFOs and have reported about 14 of them. Needless to say, people think I'm crazy, short of a few nuts and bolts. I have done a lot of research on UFOs and yes, I do believe that life exists on other planets. Anybody with half a brain would reach the same conclusions. So, am I crazy or should I keep searching for the truth?

Ellen.

Kuntarkis replies:

Dear Ellen, First, you are not crazy. You are seeking a deeper understanding to meaning of life and your existence. All human beings are searching for the truth, it is just that most search by going around in circles, trying to make sense of their own existence. Every human being is growing according to their limitations, created from one incarnation to the next, and governed by the experiences of their human life. Be they negative or positive, they are all experiences. Self-created limitations place many human beings in those little black boxes, making them fearful of change. If someone speaks out to create change, they shut the lids on their little black boxes even tighter.

Just remember dear Ellen, all human beings grow at their own pace and in their own time. Conscious growth cannot be forced upon another. Gain your truth and knowledge, and know that what you have seen with your human eyes is the truth. Through your research you will create a book for others to read if they choose to, or more to the point, when they are ready to open the lid on the little black box that keeps them blind and locked within their self-created limitations and prison.

Keep searching for the truth the Love and Light of Creation's totality always.

Kuntarkis.

FEELING HELPLESS: WHY?

Dear Kuntarkis,

I am writing to you because I feel you will not judge me. I need to change my life because I am so unhappy. I feel lost and no one understands how I truly feel inside myself. I want to change but I feel the people around won't support me. I have just turned 22 and when I look into my mirror all I see is a fat, fat pig. I don't love myself and fear my future. I have tried some diets but nothing seems to work. I just can't lose my fat. Do you know of any way that I can lose my fat and feel good about myself? I also have never been on a date because I am very self-conscious. I feel so helpless about myself and life.

Belinda.

Kuntarkis replies:

Dear Belinda, Listen as you read my words expressed from my being to yours. You are a very beautiful human being who has an honest heart and a very loving nature. You are very important in the scheme of human life on this most precious planet Earth. Your first lesson is to say the following words every day, 10 times a day:

I see beyond my human shape and I see inside my spirit's living essence. I love my being, I love myself and in this moment of my life I accept who I am here and now.

If there are changes I choose to make with my life and my human body, I will make those changes, as I have the power and the strength to make any changes I choose to. I am Love. I am Light. I am that I am.

Belinda, realise that encoded within you are your Mother's genetics, her beliefs and her conditioning. You can change this, and it is not as hard as it seems. First you must love and accept yourself exactly as you are. Second, look at what you are eating. At this moment one of your problems is that you do not drink enough water to help flush your kidneys. You need to drink between 2 and 3 litres of clean, filtered water each day. Also, you must give away eating all fatty foods, especially fast food and junk food. Also, no soft drinks at all. Drink green tea and eat a fresh salad each day without oily dressings. Learn to read the labels on your food products and make sure they are free of salts and sugars. Try to use only natural sea salt. Eat more vegetable proteins like beans, tofu and lentils. Steam your vegetables rather than boiling them in water, and stay away from ice-cream, as it is full of saturated fat and too much sugar. Try soy yoghurt and soy milk instead or try oat milk or even almond milk. Third, do a little exercise each day. Something as simple as walking for half an hour at fast a pace as you can will help. As you get healthier and start losing weight, you will get faster and be able to walk longer distances.

Give it a go, and after about four of your Earthly months, see how you feel. Do this for yourself Belinda. Do not allow others to put you down. You can change your human life and your human body because my Being believes in your Being. It is time for change Belinda.

Go in Love, for Love is freedom. Be Blessed dear Belinda in Love and Light always, and please let my being know how you are progressing.

Kuntarkis.

DO YOU WORSHIP A GOD LIKE HUMANS DO?

Hi Kuntarkis,

A friend of mine printed off some of your articles for me to read. I have a few questions. Where do you come from and what does your civilisation worship? As you are probably aware, people here believe in God and that

God created the Earth and all that lives upon it. We also believe that God created the Universe. Do you and your kind have the same God or is there another God or something you worship? Can you explain this to me please?

Sulim.

Kuntarkis replies:

Dear Sulim, First, may I say thank you for writing and asking such interesting questions. To step beyond one's own boundaries of understanding and beliefs is indeed a challenge, and can create fear for a human being who takes the path of self-discovery. One thing must be said - it is more important to believe in yourself and your understanding. As you journey through your human life, and as you grow in consciousness, your level of thinking will expand beyond your boundaries. You will see the past as your learning, that which has made you who you are in this most precious moment of life.

My being and all who exist on Nar'Kariss do not have a God to worship, nor do we as living consciousness worship any single individual. We are all equal in the scheme of life. We can work as individuals, or as one consciousness for the higher good of all life. Even in our past history no God was believed in. We see Creation as totality, and we know that we are all a part of Creation and Creation is a part of us, whether we are individuals or one collective consciousness.

All of life throughout all Universes exists within and around Creation, and Creation exists within and around all Life in all Universes. We, the Nar'Karones, have travelled throughout many Universe's and have communicated with many different civilisations. We have shared our culture with many and have formed bonds of love and respect. This is one of the reasons we are here - to observe and to share our knowledge and wisdom to help those that seek to expand their understanding, and to help them grow beyond the limitations of the human Ego.

I trust dear Sulim this answers your questions. May Love and Truth always be with you throughout your life as a human being? Be blessed always.

Kuntarkis.

I BELIEVE JUSTICE SHOULD FIT THE CRIME: YES OR NO?

Dear Kuntarkis,

I am very concerned about the future of people on Earth, especially when people like Bin Laden in the Middle East cause so much pain to others who don't deserve it. I am a strong believer in justice and I believe justice should equal the crime, so all those who create evil should be sentenced to equal the crime they have committed. I am a victim of crime and my attacker went free because of a small technicality. To me there is no justice, and I live every day in pain. What can I do to live in peace once more?

In hiding.

Kuntarkis replies:

Dear Human Being, from a human point of view, pain is never ending when one only sees and lives the pain, and this is understandable. You dear Human Being have had your free will taken from you and it can take many moments to come to an understanding of why you became the victim of a crime.

One of the problems that is created from this negative situation is that it can change your life as a human being and stop you from learning to forgive yourself and your attacker. Even though the pain is great and surrounds you through your life, forgiveness in unconditional love is the key to freedom in every situation.

Bin Laden and his followers, for example, have created (from a human understanding) a crime against humanity, and yes, justice must be served to restore balance for the crime committed, and this will be done. But also what needs to be understood is that negative thoughts are negative energies, and many human beings because of their emotions and anger towards what Bin Laden has done, is only escalating the situation in the Middle East. Even after the completion and settling of all the upheaval in the Middle East, there will come another Bin Laden because the past will only come into the present and create the same future again.

Negative emotions must be dealt with on all levels of understanding and resolved so it can be the past and remembered only as a memory, neither negative nor positive, but just an experience of human life. To send unconditional Love and Light to all negative situations will help to ease the pain and bring a balance to all your human societies.

Thousands of excuses can be made for why you cannot or will not forgive. But to grow in consciousness, beyond your pain, in the end one must forgive in Love the attacker and the victim. This will bring back the balance of life and each human being will grow beyond their present level of thinking and understanding. Conscious growth is freedom, just as knowledge is freedom and love is freedom.

Remember dear Human Being, to forgive is never to forget, for if you have truly forgiven, you have not forgotten the life lesson, be it negative or positive. Be Blessed in Love and Light always.

Kuntarkis.

I NEED HELP FOR MY DAUGHTER

My daughter is 25, living in New Orleans alone, while we are here in New York. She is so lonely for love, it hurts me to the core. She meets a nice guy and for some reason always walks away, of course wanting to remain friends. All she want is to be special to someone. Marriage is not for her, nor are children, she just wants someone to be close to. I have convinced her to seek some counselling, and I think she will, but she needs help desperately. Please can you give me some answers?

Thanks.

Kuntarkis replies:

Dear Human Being, Your concern for your human daughter is very special and yes all human beings want to feel special. Many human beings want to be loved and needed in any form of relationship, whether it is with their parents or friends, or in an intimate relationship. This is where the problem lies – wanting to be accepted or loved by another, but never accepting or loving the self.

To unconditionally love another human being one must first experience unconditional love within oneself. All human beings on your plant Earth are sparks of light created from unconditional love. It is the human ego of humanity that has closed the door to self-love and the acceptance of love from another. Love comes from the heart centre, not the brain, nor the ego.

When a human being opens their heart to love and feels love emanating throughout their inner being, that love will emanate all around them and they will attract the right human being into their life. They will feel special to themselves, not needing the approval of others. It all begins with the individual learning to love one's being, and this in turn will open the door of the human heart to love. The heart centre is where all feelings of self-love and love towards others exists. It begins with unconditional love always.

Be blessed always in the love and light of Creation's totality.

Kuntarkis.

QUEEN OF SHEBA: DOES SHE EXIST?

I was watching this really interesting programme on the ABC a few weeks ago on the Queen of Sheba. I was wondering whether Kuntarkis would know anything about her and if she really existed.

Regards Papinda.

Kuntarkis replies:

Dear Papinda, in answer to your question, did the Queen of Sheba actually exist in your human vibration. Going back in human history there were no actual accounts of the one you asked of called the Queen of Sheba. What my being did discover was 2734 years ago in your human time there was a human female called Sheba Saimondra who was married to a man who was the son of an Egyptian Emperor was named Tambuna.

The son of the Emperor was called Tuman and with Sheba he had two children, a daughter called Shahnie and a son called Szbarr. Sheba was giving birth to a third child, a son when both she and the child died from complications during childbirth. Sheba was 24 years of age when she died.

Tuman remarried six months later and had four more children with the second wife, named Nenhar. Tuman became Emperor at the age of 31 and ruled Egypt for 21 years until he was murdered, as arranged by his first son Szbarr. My Being trusts this answers your question.

Be blessed in the love of Creation always.

Kuntarkis.

WHAT SHOULD I BE DOING WITH MY LIFE?

Greetings Ilona, Roman and Kuntarkis,

I am so thankful for all of the great work that you are doing! You guys by far have the most heart-stirring advice and guidance on spirituality ever! I can't wait for the book! Entrapment.

The reason why I am writing you is this... I am extremely musically and artistically inclined. Music and visions flow through me as natural as breathing air. I have performed before thousands over the years, and I know that I am very good at what I do. Although I have a good job, I really can't imagine doing anything else but be an artist for a living. I am constantly told by many that I need to really pursue a professional career in music... I know that I have the kind of talent that should be shared with the world but the problem is that I can't seem to attract the right elements to help me to make my dreams a reality.

I've worked so very hard, sacrificed and invested so much to make things happen but it just doesn't seem to ever be enough. I really feel like I am hitting a brick wall. I am beginning to think that the music career that I envision for myself is not in my charts for this life time. Could you please give me some advice on what I should be doing with my life? Will my goals be achieved with my music in this life? If not, please tell me where I need to focus my energy?

Again, thank you for your all of the inspiration and guidance and KEEP UP THE AWESOME WORK!

Kuntarkis replies:

Dear Human Being, Human physical life in itself is a beautiful experience. What actions and decisions one makes in their lifetime is a personal choice, yet the experiences of a human being growing up into adulthood can and does reflect the outcome of an individual's human life.

What is most important for a human being is not to hold onto any negative creations that one creates from their experiences of life or their parent's genetics. This is because it can and does shape your life as you grow into adulthood. A human being must break the negative past in order to create the future that your dreams and goals are made from. Live only in the moment, never live from the past. Living from the past will create your present and future, so your past will never leave you.

See the moment as complete bliss and create your future through your imagination. See what you want and then put the action into it to create it, to make it your reality. Your thoughts are very powerful. If music is truly your Passion, then never give up. Never see the negative in anything, but see it as life's experience, and then go beyond it to create your present and your future. Never give up your dreams – live them, feel them, taste them and truly believe in yourself – and all you see and desire will be manifested to you.

My Being believes in you dear Human Being. Be blessed in love always.

Kuntarkis.

PERSONAL EMBETTERMENT

Dear Kuntarkis,

I have quite a few questions on life but I won't bombard you with them. But I would like to know where I need to be financially and how will I be able to maintain stability mainly for my daughters sake. I work in the government and have been for six years but I don't see myself staying here. My dream would be to start my own business, but financially, I can't. At least not right now. I feel like I am in a situation where I am under someone's control which eats at me almost every day because I feel I am/should be destined for much more. The reason why I say this is because I have a very intuitive mind and somewhat aggressive when it comes to what I want. I am very blessed for where I am though at my age (23) and where I come from and my salary, but I still feel like this is not me. Maybe I just need to be a little more patient. Also, I have a controversy within me that bothers me almost every day. I have a girlfriend whom I love and she proclaims the same, and we have a daughter together (which I love more than life itself), but we aren't married, and I am against marriage because I feel it's a scam and a trap by society. I am not scared of marriage, but maybe of divorce. It seems every time there is a divorce (which divorce rate is ridiculous), the judicial systems makes the husband to be the problem and automatically digs into his pocket. The real problem is she doesn't think like me and family doesn't either (I was raised in a Christian home). We live together and have been for two years, I am just tired of being looked at as the "bad guy" because I don't won't to follow a particular tradition. Could you advise me?

Thanks in advance for your advice.

Ronald.

Kuntarkis replies:

Dear Ronald, Individuality is the knowing. The power of who you are will show you where you are going in your human life. Negative emotions from the past create the mental and emotional prisons human beings find themselves trapped in throughout their lives. Emotion is created from the past and inevitably creates the present and the future of human beings. To break free from the beliefs and the negative conditioning of life one must step beyond what one currently understands and believes. To know yourself spiritually you need first to understand yourself both emotionally and physically.

Learn to understand energy Ronald. All of life in all Universes is created from magnetic energy. Each human being can only live their life according to the lessons and experiences of their life. In other words, what you think of yourself, you can and will become. From that understanding you attract into your life the same-thinking human beings. Only when you, the individual, chooses to grow consciously, will you then step beyond your self-created limitations and boundaries. Even though you may not admit this Ronald, how you feel about yourself, your life, the types of friends you bring into your vibration, is the outcome and influence of your parents and childhood experiences.

Allow yourself to step beyond your past and see it only as experiences, neither negative nor positive. Be willing to step into the unknown without hesitation or fear and accept all of life's experiences as a part of personal growth towards a higher understanding of human life. Know within your heart that you alone can create or change anything that is presently in your life.

Ronald, you are the creator of your existence. As you breathe the air to keep your human form alive, use your imagination to create a life of complete joy which will in turn bring peace and harmony to you. Loving yourself unconditionally means you cannot do it for others. Each human being must find the balance of life first in order to guide others in their lives. Unconditional love exists within all of life. The dramas and affairs of human life are a creation of human Ego.

Unconditional love is a creation of the heart and that is where all truth emanates from. It is all within you – the truth, the love, the joy, and the understanding of all knowledge. Believe in yourself Ronald; truly believe, and all will be manifested in you.

Be Blessed Ronald in the love and light of Creation always.

Kuntarkis.

COPING WITH LONELINESS

Hi Kuntarkis,

I thank you very much for your response. If it would be alright I would like to follow-up with a further question(s).

Please allow me to share a bit of background information with you. 3 months ago I consciously ended a relationship with a woman. I thought she was physically very beautiful, we had fun together, and we had many great conversations, but there was one thing - that something in my heart told me that she is not the one. I felt this somewhere from the start but was too afraid to listen. I have always in the past hung on to women till they had to tell me they did not want to be with me anymore. It was like my fears latched on so hard and I controlled them (through the guise of being loving). But this time I had to tell this beautiful woman the truth of my heart. She wanted to be with me so much, yet I heard the whisperings of my heart. But this has been so hard for me to deal with life this past few months. A month ago she called me and missed me so much. I knew that the selfish part of myself that was so deeply lonely wanted to run to her so much! I really wanted to run to her. But I with all my strength have managed to listen to that whispering of truth in my heart. It is just so hard - being by myself. Something is saying to me very clearly that this is such a beautiful gift - this alone time now in my life for I know that one day I will have a family who will look to me and depend on me. And I understand I cannot truly be the head of a family and love them, unless I can be with myself and love myself. I should be on my knees thanking Spirit for this, however, much of my time here seems to be spent in pitiful remorse at the great pain of my loneliness. I am in between two streams of consciousness it seems - that of the child and that of the adult who knows and nurtures himself. I really would appreciate any words to assist me in this process that at times feels it has no solution. It is that many times I just do not know what to do with myself, do not know what to do with my time, or how to spend my time (aside from my work). Like I don't even know what are my interests in many ways because I have always been so interested in curbing my loneliness.

Scott.

Kuntarkis replies:

Dear Scott, Thank you for sharing your most inner feelings with my Being. You have spent much of your human time curbing your loneliness and yet it is only a conditioning of your past. Your loneliness as a human child has followed you into adulthood. It has become part of your belief systems. Loneliness is only a human word, and you have created this word into a living energy, creating your present existence and becoming your future.

It is time to look at your past as a child. It is time to nurture the child within you Scott. It is time to forgive the past and all its hurts, no matter what they are. It is time to meditate in the stillness of your mind to overcome this emotional pain.

In your mind's eye see yourself as the child. Then see the child walking up to you. See yourself opening up your arms and embrace the child. Hold onto the child and express your most inner feelings of love to this child who is you. Feel your heart expressing unconditional love to this child and from your heart express these words:

I forgive you and all my past hurts, and I now see them all as lessons of life, neither negative nor positive, just experiences. I will and I am allowing my past hurts to dissolve back into the nothingness from which they were first created.

Tell this child: *I love you with all my heart and I will always love you.*

Feel the love from your inner child being expressed back to you. Scott, allow yourself to cry from your human eyes – you need to do this to break free from your past. Place this most precious child down and see this child smile at you, for everything is coming into balance. Your past has become a memory of experiences, neither negative nor positive, simply lessons of life. Believe this and it will become your truth.

See this child run off and play with other human children. Place your arms around yourself and say: the past is the past. I am now living in the present and I accept all good experiences into my life for my higher good.

Tell yourself: *I love myself now and forever more and I accept love from others in my life without question, for me, Scott, deserve to love my own Being and to be loved by others.*

Scott, it is not your heart telling you that the human female in your life at this present moment is not the one, it is your conditioning of the past, your fears of loneliness that is being expressed to you. Allow what is in your human life to be enjoyed, accepted in love and let it run its natural course. Allow yourself to love this human female without conditions and allow yourself to be loved by her. Take each moment as it comes and enjoy the experiences.

Be blessed in love always.

Kuntarkis.

SEARCHING FOR THE TRUTH

Dear Kuntarkis,

Your writings touch my heart. I feel a truth about you that I have never felt with any other form of truth. You have made me cry and that is very special, since I have not cried for 32 years. I am 52 and I have had some very hard lessons in my life which caused me a great deal of pain. I have been searching for myself and my truth, and yes, I was always looking in the wrong places.

Since I have found your writing I have been doing a lot of soul searching. I have cried every day for the past two months. It may sound a little silly, but you came to me and sat with me at my special place and the time you gave me has changed my life forever. Even though I believe I have wasted my life, I can now see the lessons of my journey and for the first time I can see my direction in my life. I have begun a new life and what you said to me about my life's experiences, I am writing it all down as I feel it can help others in their journey. From my heart I send you my love Kuntarkis, for your guidance and your understanding. You are who you say you are.

Thank you. Your friend always,

Becky.

Kuntarkis replies:

Dear Becky, My Being thanks you for your kind expressions, and for having the courage and strength to face your fears. Your journey in this human life will be balanced and become joyous, and you will feel a great happiness and peace within you and all around you. You have crossed your self-created boundaries and you have begun to dissolve your fears of life and loneliness back into the nothingness.

You are a very special beautiful human being, and you have an endless river of love to give to others. Through your expressions of human words on paper, your book will be created through your power of self-trust. Every human being is on their own journey of learning and letting go of the past. To let go of the past is to step beyond all self-created limitations.

Fear is the past and only through forgiveness and love of self and all of life will each human being be set free from all pain and misery. Becky, never give up. Always be willing to step beyond your past. Never see the past as negative or positive - see it only as a memory of experiences, lessons in life. Be completely unbiased, love your Being and all of life unconditionally. That is truly conscious awareness, growth and living.

Be Blessed in Love always.

Kuntarkis.

DEPRESSED DAUGHTER

For Kuntarkis,

Please help if you can. My 15 yr. daughter has many problems including self-harm and depression. She says she sees goblins and men (evil) who talk to her and threaten to take her to their 'underworld'. I stress to her 'they' have no control over her but she won't listen.

Could you tell me who they are and how to free her from this very scary world she lives in?

Thank you

Sonia.

Kuntarkis replies:

Dear Sonia, What your human daughter is seeking is simply attention. The Astral Vibration of Spirits cannot control a human being unless that human being allows it by giving away their own free will.

If a human being lives a negative life and has created a world of fear within the self, then yes, that individual can be influenced by negative energies in the Astral Vibration.

Your expressions of words to my Being indicate that your human daughter is most certainly rebelling against you. The fantasy of what she is expressing to you is her way of getting back at you for whatever reason it may be. But what she is expressing is from her own negative emotional creation of negative thinking within her own thoughts.

Change is needed for both of you. Communication with each other in how you both feel is a good beginning; especially you can both be truthful to each other.

Be blessed in unconditional love always.

Kuntarkis.

WHAT IS MY LIFE PATH: MY MISSION?

Dear Roman and Kuntarkis,

I have really enjoyed reading your website and about the planet Nar'Kariss and how they are there to help us on Earth.

I have a couple of questions. What is my mission in this life? I want to know as I am not sure now what sort of a job I should get. And I feel that it should not be based on money, but sooner or later I will have to support myself and I am interested in so many things. Is it to do with healing or something creative - I have no training in these fields?

Also, can you please help me with direction in my love life? I feel stuck.

Thank you.

Pip.

Kuntarkis replies:

Dear Pip, Again, this question is asked by so many human beings - what is my purpose or mission in life? There are many answers to this question, yet how many human beings would accept a simple answer such as this: "The purpose of life for all human beings is to just be in the moment of life".

Please take the time to read the current issue of Conversations with Kuntarkis entitled Purpose of Life. Read it undistracted, in the silence of your mind, with an open heart and without prejudice. Allow the energy of my Being's expressions to fill your heart so all your questions can be answered from your own inner truth. In this book go to story number 40, on The Purpose of all Life.

Read my expressions of words several times over a few weeks of human time. If you know what you want to do with your human life and how you go about it, then you will find all will fall into place if you truly believe in yourself.

The direction in your love life always begins with how you feel about yourself. If you truly love yourself in unconditional love, you will find the balance in a relationship. It always begins with you, the individual.

Be Blessed in Love always.

Kuntarkis.

WEIGHT LOSS

Dear Roman and Kuntarkis,

This is the second time I want to ask something about myself. Last time was about two years ago. Your answer then helped me and gave me a warm feeling. It was about the feelings of loneliness I had, and I do not feel so lonely all the time anymore.

Now I want to ask you why it is so difficult for me to stay on track while trying to lose weight and when I manage, why it is so difficult to keep it off. I know what to do, and I only try to lose weight through healthy eating, sometimes I use pills to help to keep me from eating too much. And I do not really want those pills, but if I do not take them, I start gaining weight again. When I am in that mood, I can't get myself not to eat the wrong food.

I once started yoga, and I liked it very much, I know the good feeling when I am doing the right things for me, and yet, I start to do the wrong things again and again, it feels as if it is not me who is acting at that time, but somebody else.

I very much would like to have some information about why I act the way I act? I know exactly what to do, but after one year or so, I fall back into bad habits, although I got some good habits now, like eating a lot of fruit and vegetables in general, but the times I do not control myself makes me gain weight slowly but surely...Why is this such a struggle? I can't allow myself to gain too much weight, as I know that is unhealthy.

Please help me to solve this life-long problem by understanding the "why"?

Thank you for your time.

Lia.

Kuntarkis replies:

Dear Lia, Your fear of gaining weight has become a belief and now it has been conditioned into your genetics, in your DNA.

It is all about how you truly feel about yourself – your negative thoughts combined with your fears, resulting in your becoming overweight. Thoughts are very powerful indeed. How you feel about yourself in your thinking is created by you in the physical world of matter.

You have heard the saying that what you think you become, and what you eat you become. It is all in the emotions and in most cases these negative thoughts are created from childhood. Through negative experiences beliefs are formed and conditioned into you. Some humans find it is very difficult to change their habits and thinking.

You Lia are so concerned about not putting on weight and this is where the problem lies. You need to change the programming within yourself. A good place to start is your food. Try to eat only raw vegetables and fruits, and for protein add some nuts and beans into your daily meals. Try not to have any cow's milk and go without cheeses of any sort. Give away take away foods, soft drinks and alcohol. All processed foods bloat the stomach and bowels, especially breads. If you need to eat bread, have breads that are yeast free.

One of the most important things for the human body is to drink clean water, at least 2 litres per day (8 cups of 250ml each). Water will help flush out accumulated toxins in your tissues and organs. Over a long period of time the human body becomes stiff and inflexible due to toxins as well as degenerating and breaking down to the point where serious dis-eases such as cancer set in.

Note also the human body was never meant to eat and digest animal flesh, for ingested flesh creates enormous amounts of toxins stored in the body.

One of the main reasons for your falling back into your bad habits is that you lack self-worth. You do not believe in yourself and you feel you were not good enough to be loved by others or by yourself. This has become a belief throughout your human life and underlies your fears.

You Lia have the strength to change. Fear is only a belief. It has no power, only the power you give it. Change your thinking in how you see yourself and you will begin to change your life through a more positive attitude.

My Being is a part of Creation's totality as your Being is also. You are a part of all that is, and all that is, is a part of you. Be willing to change by loving yourself unconditionally, and seeing yourself as a beautiful human being, full of love which emanates from your heart centre.

Every time you feel negative towards yourself, at that moment realise that you can put positive energy within yourself by saying "I believe in me. I know I am a beautiful human being and I can achieve anything I choose to in my life".

Say "My fears are only the past, created by my beliefs and my conditioning. I choose now in this moment to dissolve all my fears and I will replace them with positive actions which will enhance my life".

Lia, the power of change is within you. It all begins with your love for your own being. Be Blessed in Love always.

Kuntarkis.

CONFLICTS WHY?

Dear Roman & Kuntarkis,

I am interested in a consultation with advice or guidance from Kuntarkis. Thank you for your site and your commitment to such a worthy endeavour.

I have a particular problem with a senior work person and I realise that nothing is just one person's fault but I do not know what I have done to press this person's buttons or whether it is some unresolved issue from some other life. I have wondered whether it is the aim of this woman to put pressure on me to resign or worse.

Another issue is whether my divorce settlement will finally materialise in a manner to which I would be satisfied after such a long waiting process. I would be interested to know how each of these people view me (in the first and second issue) and if their views are justified so I can forgive myself and them and move on.

My third issue is that my Dad is in his 90th year and when it is his choice I will have to allow him to move on but I hate the thought of life without my Dad around. I probably fear that I will not be able to be as self-sufficient as he has been when it is my turn to be an example for my kids to be in the background for when they need me.

Regards

Jenny.

Kuntarkis replies:

Dear Jenny, Thank you for writing your words of expression. One thing for all human beings to become aware of is the negative energies of life as well as the positive energies of life, for this is a part of the learning process for human evolution.

From one incarnation to the next, each human being is creating negative and positive actions. Many call it Karma – what you do to another will eventually return to the one who created the action in the first place, be it negative or positive.

Your first question concerning a senior work person regarding your "pressing their buttons" is in reality a positive action. If you come from the heart when pressing their buttons you are indeed a brave human being. You are willing to step beyond social conditioning. In fact, you are actually helping them to deal with their own personal issues. But if you come from the ego you will only cause yourself more pain and misery.

When you meet a human being who reacts negatively towards you, the best way to deal with that situation is to first - not react yourself, and second - not place any judgement upon that person. Very hard to do as it would be an automatic response, but thoughts are extremely powerful, thoughts are energy and can create Karma for the individual, whether it be positive or negative.

Simply fill your heart with the healing light and project it to this person. Each time they are negative towards you repeat filling yourself with light and projecting it to them, deflecting back their energy with compassion because they are behaving ignorantly and know no better. If you truly believe in yourself, it will work.

Your second question concerning your human divorce settlement. It can only be resolved when all parties are in agreement. How the first and second party view you is irrelevant to you as an individual. If they view you negatively or positively should only be their concern because how you the individual see yourself is more important and in fact should be your only concern.

Yes, you do need to forgive yourself and fill your inner and outer being with unconditional love. Let go of the past and live in the moment so that you dear Jenny can create a joyful, happy future.

My Being realises you are saddened by the negative energies that have been projected towards you. If you are feeling depressed then negative energy can and does affect your thinking and your surroundings. Human beings are emotional beings and are highly conditioned by negative actions and thoughts that have been generated over many lifetimes. To break free from the past, the conditioning and negativity, each human being needs to fill their hearts with unconditional love and forgive themselves and others. This will dissolve the prison that surrounds them. Their level of thinking and understanding will change and each human being will become aware of their true self.

To your third question, you have had many incarnations with your human father and you will have many more to come. Even when he chooses to depart from your Earthly vibration he will be in your heart but also his energies will be close to yours. Never view death as life being over. Death is simply a transformation to higher forms of energy.

Jenny, you need to believe in yourself. You need to let go of your fears for your fears are simply a form of energy created by your past experiences. Your fears have no control over you. Only you as the individual can place limitations upon yourself. Each time you think negatively you reinforce your past conditioning. Every time you think negative thoughts or do negative actions, stop for a moment and fill your heart with healing light and say:

"I, Jenny, control my thoughts and actions, and I choose to have only positive thoughts which will create positive actions in my life. I am a beautiful human being and I have the power and the will to choose how I think and feel about myself. If others think negatively about me, that is their choice. But I choose to love myself and to create in my life happiness, joy and pure bliss. This I say and this I will do."

Jenny, forget what others think about you. It is not important. How you feel about yourself is what is important to your own evolution and to your children.

Be Blessed in Love and Light always.

Kuntarkis.

SOY PRODUCTS: GOOD OR BAD?

Hello Roman & Kuntarkis,

My name is Michelle' and I would like to clear some thoughts about Soy products'.

Recently I have been told that Soy Based products especially 'soy milk' stops the absorption of calcium into the body' now I think it may only be certain types of Soy' products not all of them if true at all, is there any truth in this assumption? Also I have been told that my body is not absorbing enough nutrients out of my food, as I am of a very slight build and I'm vegetarian and I have a concerned parent.

Would you have a suggestion that would help me to build up my body and muscles so I can keep more weight on? I do take spirulina and soy protein powder, tofu, legumes and other soy products. Maybe I'm not eating enough as I am very active with my work. Do I have emotional issues that block me from being the healthier weight I want to be?

Thanks Roman

Michelle.

Kuntarkis (& Roman) replies:

Dear Michelle, Human carnivores have always been threatened by vegetarians, especially vegans, mainly because of their ignorance when it comes to being healthy. From one generation to the next, the human animal conditions their children into certain eating habits because they were conditioned by their parents, and so misguided beliefs and illusions go on and on.

Soy products of any kind do not inhibit the intake of calcium into the human body. In fact, drinking too much cow's milk or consuming too much dairy causes the body to dump calcium from the bones. Cow's milk does have a high level of calcium, but if consumed in large amounts it will cause the body to excrete the calcium, mainly because it is of animal origin. All nutrients are transported via the blood for use or storage. The body regulates nutrient levels via the blood and if the blood has too much calcium in it, the body in an effort to redress the balance will begin to release it from the bones for complete removal from the body.

The same effect occurs with the consumption of dead animal flesh. Consuming animal flesh (or animal products such as dairy) creates too much acidity in the human body, and again using the blood as the indicator of nutrient balance in the body, too much acidity in the blood causes the body to release nutrients to redress the balance, calcium included. This unbalancing of nutrients through diet, such as calcium, leads to nutrient deficiencies such as calcium deficiencies. Humans in the Westernised world eat enormous amounts of calcium in the form of dairy, yet this same population suffers calcium deficiencies compared to nations who do not consume animal products.

On the other hand, natural calcium from soy products has been used for thousands of years by Asiatic people. If Western medicine were to study Asian dietary habits it would be discovered that prior to Western dietary influence on Asian cultures, these cultures did not suffer diabetes, osteoporosis, obesity, bowel disorders including bowel cancer, other cancers, heart disease or arthritis. People of the Western world suffer many diseases, with most being created from the diet. You have heard the expression 'you are what you eat'. It is one of the greatest truths on this planet.

It is the same as saying you are what you think. If one is open minded and if one can step beyond their beliefs and conditioning, they may come to the realisation that there is no truth in the claim that soy products stop the absorption of calcium in the human body. Soy is a miracle food and has many benefits for the human body. All though in saying that, you as humans, have heard the expression, "Oil's aren't Oil's". So it is the same with Soya Products, only use Soya Products that say whole Soya Beans. Any Soya Products that use a by-product called Isolates, try and avoid them at all costs. There is a lot of research on Soya Products, and on your internet you will find the positives and the negatives.

There is plenty of research now available to anyone with an internet connection. All it takes is a little time and a desire to seek it out. Starting your research will empower you with knowledge, for knowledge is the greatest weapon against ignorance.

It must also be understood that each individual is responsible for their own health and well-being. It is natural for a parent to be concerned for their human children, but you are an adult and you are completely responsible for yourself. Michelle, because you are so active and use a lot of energy you need to increase your intake of good foods, especially soy beans. Soy actually builds and repairs muscle tissue. You also need to eat more fresh green leafy vegetables for iron – iron is an important building block of the body, fresh fruit for enzymes and vitamins, especially vitamin C which assists absorption of other nutrients, and you also need to add a few nuts and seeds each day to your diet for essential fats, protein and natural easily absorbed calcium.

Yes, you do have an emotional issue concerning your weight. You feel you need the approval of others in how you look. You feel you need to be accepted by others and you have a fear of rejection, of not being good enough. However, you must remember Michelle; fear is only a creation of past experiences, brought into the present. Fear is simply a form of energy that each individual has created. What is created can also be uncreated if the individual is willing to face their own fears.

I believe you can face and dissolve your fears. You are a strong person, and by facing yourself, you will transform not only your level of thinking but you will also set yourself free from your self-created past.

As you Michelle are aware, parents can be an influence in how we think and feel about ourselves, and it can be negative or positive. Both negative and positive influences are needed so each of us can learn not only about ourselves, but also about others. It can help us find our individuality or make us a clone of our parents.

One of the greatest lessons our parents can teach us is not to be like them. The only way to grow consciously is by experience, and to be an individual. When an individual can love themselves unconditionally they will find the balance. That is conscious growth; that is pure bliss; that is The Knowing.

Take care dear Michelle and always believe in yourself.

Be blessed in love always.

Roman (& Kuntarkis).

NO PASSION FOR LIFE

Dear Kuntarkis,

I am 36 years of age and as yet have found no direction or passion for life. I am not happy in what I do in life yet I have no drive to change it, I just seem to ramble along, I guess afraid to make change. This affects all areas of my life, work, relationships, free time etc.

I just do not seem to have any drive to do anything, yet where I am makes me unhappy and unfulfilled. Life just seems too much like hard work and I feel sometimes the sooner it is over the better. I have no passion for sex and this of course affects relationships I have had, I seem to destroy each one I have.

I am not aware but obviously scared of stepping outside the square I live in and enjoying life to the full. I feel trapped and I do not want to be like this any longer. I want to enjoy life and live to my full potential instead of doing absolutely nothing. What can I do and where should I start?

John.

Kuntarkis replies:

Dear John, My Being thanks you for sharing your inner thoughts. Please John, as you read this expression of human words, open your heart to your own divine essence of love.

First, change must take place for you to become balanced and happy in your human life. As you were a child, you experienced unhappiness and this unhappiness followed you into adulthood. It became your belief, that you dear John, do not deserve to be happy and fulfilled as a human being. Would this not be the truth?

Only by looking into your essence of love, which is a part of all human beings as it is a part of all forms of life, will you begin the healing process of letting go of the past. The past is simply there to teach and to help a human being understand the lessons of life that each human being chooses to experiences while in human form.

The past is one of the problems all of humanity is facing. The past has become the present which in turn creates the future. Only through forgiveness of yourself, which means looking at your beliefs and the conditioning you experienced as a child, will you begin to let go of the old and create a different reality, present and future. What you experienced as a child must only be remembered as experiences, neither negative nor positive, simply lessons of life.

Human sex is irrelevant to happiness. Human sex is for pro-creation, as it is with all forms of life. Humanity however has used human sex as a distraction and an excuse that relationships are not working if there is no sex. Having sex is not the purpose of living or of experiencing human life.

Only when an individual is balanced in mind, body and spirit can the individual truly feel happiness. When that individual is balanced and happy, then they will attract into their life the same form of energy which will enhance the relationship between the two human beings. If sex is involved it will be an expression of their love for each other, not simply just to have sex for pleasure or lust.

Unconditional love is the balance for all of life. Every human being is love. You only have to believe it, feel it from your heart. Many human beings want to change. To step outside of the square, your boundaries, is the beginning for you John. Being afraid to do this is simply your past, which became your fears, your beliefs, and your safe surroundings. While they may be familiar, they are also halting your growth and ultimately keeping you from finding the balance and happiness you seek.

Your potential in your life can be whatever you choose it to be. Stop now. No more excuses John. Expand your imagination, for whatever you can imagine John, you can create and become. The power, courage and strength is within you, as it is within all human beings. Believe it, see it and then create it by putting in the physical action to make it happen.

The reasons your relationships always fall apart is because you bring the energies of your past into the present, and in reality it is not what you John want. Change your thinking and you will change your present which will create a balanced, happy future. It is all in the level of your thinking. Change that and you change your human life.

Be blessed in love always John.

Kuntarkis.

HOW DO I HEAL MYSELF?

Dear Jecuss Kuntarkis,

I have found your knowledge overwhelming, yet most informing. It has helped me understand so much about my parents and especially myself. I was wondering if you could send me some healing light to help ease my pain.

I have bone cancer. When I was twelve while playing football I had an accident. Where our school was, the oval had an embankment which I fell and rolled down. There was a thin metal spike protruding out of the soil, and it ended up in my calf muscle, piercing the bone in my leg. It has caused me great pain for several years.

I am now 27 years of age and was told nine months ago that I have cancer in that area. They are doing a lot more testing but it seems that the cancer is spreading. I am sorry to put my emotional pain onto you. What I would like is a healing of unconditional love. I am learning to accept myself for who I am and to love myself just as I am. You Jecuss Kuntarkis have helped me see with new eyes and with a more open heart. Thank you so much.

Grant.

Kuntarkis replies:

Dear Grant, Yes, unconditional love is a way of life. It is the ingredient that will heal all pain and it will open up your inner vision to a much deeper understanding of the meaning of life and all its wonderments.

All human beings are to some point on a road of struggle. That road has many avenues which can help shape the individual and lead them to a greater awareness of life. Some see life as a negative continuous struggle of pain and misery. That path keeps the individual in their past, creating their present and sadly their future for many incarnations to come.

My Being, Grant, understands how sad your childhood was and the pain you had to endure. You came into this world of physical matter full of love. Your eyes sparkled, and all you wanted was to be loved by your human parents, to be accepted, to be guided by your human parents, to enjoy being a child, to grow up into adulthood and become the best you could be and have your human parents be proud of their son.

Grant, it took this human dis'ease to halt you, to open your eyes, to make you search deep inside of yourself. You Grant have discovered that unconditional love is within you, in every moment of your human life – you are unconditional love. Every form of life in all universes is created from the essence of light. Every human being is unconditional love, for that alone is the greatest lesson to discover. You do not have to learn unconditional love, you only have to feel it from your heart and then learn to live it, and then you (as all human beings) will become it.

Once a human being accepts unconditional love from the heart, the meaning of life becomes an open book for all to see and is revealed to all who choose the path of love for the self and all forms of life, no matter what they may be.

Grant, my Being will be in the presence of your human time, 7 December 2004 at 11.00pm in your time of human sleep. We shall sit and express and my being will do a healing on you and help you to also do a healing on yourself. Take some precious moments until then to put your thoughts on the forgiveness of your human parents and yourself. Allow unconditional love to flow from you throughout your being and express this unconditional love of light all around you.

Be blessed in unconditional love always dear Grant.

Kuntarkis.

WHAT IS MY SPIRITUAL NAME?

Hello Kuntarkis,

I was wondering what my spiritual name is?

Best wishes,

Annette.

Kuntarkis replies:

Dear Annette, You have a beautiful human name "Annette" which will serve you well in your current human life. Yes, every human entity has a spiritual name and is known by you, you only need to ask your inner being, your soul.

Ask yourself - What is my spiritual name? Listen to your first answer and it will always be your truth, as long as it comes from the heart. Truth is very important when it comes to conscious growth.

Your spiritual name is Beasheri. Say it many times to yourself and listen to the tone.

Be blessed in unconditional love always.

Kuntarkis.

SO MANY QUESTIONS: WHERE DO I START?

Hello Kuntarkis,

I am hoping that you can assist me in my life path as a spiritualist and hopes of being able to communicate with my guides. I feel as if I'm here to guide others on their own paths, I feel I am to channel, give lectures etc.? Do you see this for me, can you tell me my guides name, can you see when in this lifetime I will achieve my hearts desires, and what areas I need to work on?

Love and Light

Rina.

Kuntarkis replies:

Dear Rina, All human beings are on this planet Earth to help guide others in their quest for knowledge and understanding. To do this you need to work on yourself first, in order to help others who are seeking your guidance. Learn to face your fears, be willing to learn from others, and learn to love yourself from the heart, for all else is the illusion of the past created from human ego.

Yes, you will communicate with the inner world of spirit and also the ones who help guide your path. You need to meditate in the stillness of your mind, your inner being, and allow yourself to listen to your inner voice. Be true to yourself rather than listen to others, as they are also wanting to find the truth.

It is within you dear Rina. Learn to trust all your decisions and put action in to it. Everything will be revealed to you as you allow yourself to believe in you and your truth.

Be blessed in love always.

Kuntarkis.

SPINNING ENERGY

Greetings Kuntarkis,

First, I would like to thank you for allowing us to ask questions. This is truly wonderful. My question involves meditation or just sitting quiet. Sometimes when I sit quiet I have a tendency to spin. It is not my physical body that spins, but an energy within... at times it feels clockwise. Can you please elaborate on this experience?

Thank you so much.

Nat.

Kuntarkis replies:

Dear Nat, when a human being sits in their quiet moments of meditation, they connect to their inner soul. What is referred to in your human world as the Astral Body, is being activated and it can and does create a feeling to spin in either direction left or right, it all depends on the human individual.

The feeling of spinning is a form of awakening the inner you, the real you, not the illusion of your physical self. The human physical self is simply a state of mind which created and manifested the human form of matter, yet it is still an illusion. You Nat, as all human beings and all forms of life, are living energy, created from living consciousness. Keep up your meditation in the stillness of your mind, for you will gain a much deeper understanding of all that is.

Be blessed in love.

Kuntarkis.

SPIRIT NAME & SPIRIT GUIDES

Greetings Roman and Kuntarkis,

I wanted to ask what my spiritual name is and who are my spirit guides that are around me?

Thanks for your time.

From within,

Mandume.

Kuntarkis replies:

Dear Mandume, First ask yourself "who am I". Listen to your own answer from your heart, then say the following: "I am that I am, a living spirit, experiencing human form in this world of physical matter, which is third dimensional."

Yes, you are spirit first, human form second. Your spiritual name which has been with you from the beginning is Jessurah. You have nineteen guides in spirit that will help you throughout your human life. Some will be with you for a short time, others will stay much longer. One will be with you in all moments of your human life – this one is more a teacher to help open you up, to connect with your inner knowing (your knowledge).

Take more moments in your human life to connect to your true self – your soul. Ask your soul to guide your human affairs and believe. It will amaze you. Your main guide is named Naa'Couy.

Be blessed in love always.

Kuntarkis.

TORN BETWEEN TWO: WHO DO I CHOOSE?

To you Kuntarkis,

I have a problem. I am torn between two guys that I have dated before. The first guy, I have dated off and on for many years now. He has treated me terribly bad in the past, but I guess now he wants to make it right, but there is just one thing. I can't trust in what he says because he has told me that forever. Now, the other guy, he told me that he was sorry for what he has done to me, but he was just scared to be with just me for the rest of his life and now he's not afraid anymore. I just don't know what to do because I love them both and I care for them. I need help with this problem. Which one is the right one for me?

Ashley.

Kuntarkis replies:

Dear Ashley, You are not torn between two human beings; you are torn in yourself. First you need to love yourself unconditionally. You need to feel the love in yourself first, so you can understand what true love is, not the human world of conditional love and fear. It is a beautiful feeling to love others, yet to feel true love first one must experience the love of yourself – from your heart.

The human heart is the centre of all that is. The human ego is self-created fear of wanting to be loved. All human beings are love. Many are conditioned because of how they were brought up by their human parents and human society. To find true love, look to yourself – your heart – by experiencing unconditional love of the self. You will know who you are meant to be with. You will know who is right for you.

Be blessed in love always.

Kuntarkis.

LOVE OR EGO: WHICH ONE?

For Kuntarkis,

I wanted to ask a question about love. While I seem to be able to clear most of the pain I work on from the past, there is one thing, or should I say, a person that seems to be haunting me all my life and no matter how much I try to move on, no matter where I go or what I do it feels like they have engrained themselves on my soul, and no meditation, advice or self-empowerment can get rid of it.

When I search inwardly I feel love and a huge connection, but everything outside of myself - including the other person's words and actions tell me that they care for me very little if at all.

I know that the situation has helped me see a lot of bad ego, that I wasn't aware I had and while I've worked to change that, and I looked at the experience as learning and take what lessons I feel are important, my feelings towards this person have not changed. I've accepted what I did wrong and I have forgiven myself for it, but I still feel overwhelmingly sad.

How can you tell when a person is behaving a certain way because they are hurt, scared or insecure or whether they just behave that way because they don't care?

When inside is telling you one thing but everything that goes on in the real world (including the other persons actions) completely contradicts it, how can you be sure that the voice really comes from inside? How do you know if you're fooling yourself or not? I just can't see where I'm going wrong. Especially when you look into somebody's eyes and see something that makes you want to change into a better person.

I guess I just need to know what's going on because I've been trying so long and can't figure out what's going on - it's the only thing that still doesn't make sense. I should have sorted this out long ago but it's something that I feel so strongly about every second of every hour of the day. I just don't understand how I could believe in something so much that appears (at least in the physical) to be nothing.

I do want the truth because it's the only thing that will clear this, and I know you know what it is. I need to know the honest truth because it seems that something is shielding me from it but it's not helping.

Thankyou. Your site has taught me so much.

Much love.

Kuntarkis replies:

Dear Human Being, unless the knowledge has been passed onto you it can be very difficult to understand these emotions you as a human are experiencing. My Being wishes to express thanks for taking your precious moments in your human life to express your words of concern.

First come to you own self-realisation that you as a human being are indeed on your own journey of self-discovery. Every human being on your planet Earth are on their own journey of learning and understanding of who and why they are. Every human being will experience many, many facets of human life, not to be judged by anyone or even yourselves as negative or positive, as all lessons are simply experiences.

Human beings, because of their beliefs, their human conditioning and their human ego, create a very unbalanced world of fears. All fears of all human beings come from the past and create the present and future. Fears are created from negative emotions and are based on negative circumstances from the past, and this is how the present and future is always shaped. Unless a human being changes their way of thinking by letting go of the past and all negative emotions, they will keep bringing the past and all its associated negativity into their present and future.

So you may gain your own understanding towards what you are feeling, in your human world you refer to "Twin Souls" or "Twin Spirits". The soul of an individual can create many individual spirits from its own essence. That is, it splits off facets of itself and these facets then incarnate and experience all manner of life, eventually joining back with the soul. With that joining comes greater conscious growth and understanding which benefits all spirits connected to the soul in their future incarnations.

The being you feel is ingrained on your soul is a part of yourself. They are a facet of the energy from which you and others of your energies come from, a facet of your soul. You feel a deep connection because they are a part of your energies. Like you, their purpose is simply to experience human life and learn its lessons, lessons which your soul, the collective of all the spirit energies of which you are a part, and has chosen.

To experience truth as an individual, you must become the truth itself. Yes, forgiveness is a part of letting go of the past, but also recognising forgiveness and what you are forgiving can only come from your heart, the centre of your unconditional love.

Be blessed in unconditional love always dear human being of Earth. You will overcome what you are feeling.

Kuntarkis.

ET: EXPERIENCE

Hello Kuntarkis,

I haven't found anyone who can answer my question, so I hope you can help. One night in bed, I was not yet asleep and I heard what sounded like tennis shoes walking on my polished floor boards. I heard the noise walking through the house and through my bedroom door. I didn't see anyone and no one spoke but the next thing the whole bed felt as if it was tipping up, I saw the night sky and stars through what looked like the windscreen of a space ship and we took off really, really fast! Prior to that I wasn't scared, but I became so, because I didn't know if they were good or bad, or where they were taking me. I asked them to tell me who they were.

I saw a picture, like a logo, which was cut out of a polished silver looking material (my thoughts were a space ship). The image was cut out of the metal and a green light shone through it. The image was of someone on a horse, with the horse mid stride. They were facing side on, to the left of the picture. The whole image was a square shape, with Greek/Roman style border at the top and bottom.

I called out in a loud, strong and demanding voice "STOP!" because I didn't get any clear answers. "TAKE ME BACK!" I became conscious of the fact I had children to care for and didn't know if I was going to come back to them. I was still able to see the stars and sky through the windscreen and felt the speed at which we were traveling. After a few seconds it did stop. And I was mentally back in my bed with a slight kind of altered golden hue in the air.

I understood what had happened was significant, and then went to sleep. It's never happened again. Who were they? What was it about? Can you explain? Thank you.

Fiona

Kuntarkis replies:

Dear Fiona, Well it seems you have had quite an experience. An experience of reality itself, your experience is what you as a human being have been asking for most of your life.

Your experience was showing you, Fiona that your human world of physical matter is in reality a state of the mind. The mind is the totality of all that is – it is beyond the world of matter for the mind created the world of matter. Human beings believe that if you can touch it, smell it, see it, then it is real. If you cannot touch it, smell it or see it, then it is simply an illusion.

However, your experience was as real as you can hold a glass of water. You as a human being cannot walk through a solid wall of matter because you have been conditioned into believing you cannot. Physical matter cannot pass through solid matter because all human beings believe that idea of truth.

All human beings have a spirit which is endless, timeless, ageless and infinite. Spirit has no limitations and can pass through any wall of matter. Yes, it does depend on each human individual and their level of thinking and understanding.

In your experience, your walls and ceiling disappeared as if they did not exist. You, in those moments, were beyond your beliefs and conditioning. Your mind was open, but it was your fear that did not allow you to continue that journey, that experience. If you allowed yourself to simply experience those moments you would have met some entities who would have given you the answers you have been seeking for so long.

There will be another opportunity for you in your human near future.

Be blessed always in unconditional love dear Fiona.

Kuntarkis.

PAST LIVES

Hi Kuntarkis,

My name is Helen. I have often wondered about any of my past lives. But never really sure where to go. Found your web site, and I feel it is the right place to ask. Are you able to help? I'm wondering who I was, and how this influences my life now.

Looking forward to your reply.

Yours Faithfully. Helen

Kuntarkis replies:

Dear Helen, Your name in your past life was Florence Emma Beckman. You were a writer who moved from England to America in 1817 to marry into an industrial family that produced large amounts of steel. It was an arranged marriage by your father, but when it came closer to the wedding day, you disappeared and moved to Ireland. You became very good friends with a lady there who helped you settle into the local community.

You became very interested in writing about women's rights in society. You believed that a woman had the same rights as a human man. As the years went by you travelled back and forth between Ireland, England and America. You were associated with women's rights organisations and also became a public speaker on the matter.

You took a complete dislike to men and never married, but you did have a close relationship with a woman and you experienced a very deep love in that relationship.

Always remember dear Helen, finding love within yourself is the beginning. It will bring the balance of all that a human being is seeking.

Be blessed in unconditional love always.

Kuntarkis.

WONDERING ABOUT OUR ORIGINS?

Hi Kuntarkis,

I would like to know my spiritual name, my 'roots' in the Universe and any past life information you think would be beneficial to my experience. Have I 'travelled' with my current partner, Pedro, before?

With appreciation,

Linda.

Kuntarkis replies:

Dear Linda, Please allow my Being to answer your first question, what is your spiritual name. You were given the name 'Isher'Ka' by your human parents nearly 17,000 human years ago, in the land you know today as Africa. This was your first incarnation as a human being. Your name means 'flower of the night sky'. Your human parents gave you this name because they believed you came from the night sky to experience and understand the human animal.

You are right in taking small steps. Go slow, learn slowly - it will give you a better understanding of your human life. You are a spirit being, an infinite spark of light, originated from a planet called Nar'Kariss. The civilisation of this planet were called the Nar'Karones. They were once flesh-bodied beings, who, over thousands of human years, evolved beyond the third dimension of physical matter into a form known as light bodies.

The energy you refer to as Pedro does not have a separate vibrating frequency that my Being can pick up, so it would be safe to express to you Linda that the energy of Pedro is a part of your energy, split from your Soul in order to live a separate human life to experience different facets of human life. This is quite common within humanity. Look at it this way, you are a spirit, a facet of your Soul. The Soul can and does send out many facets to experience different lessons of human life. You and Pedro are but two of several facets.

Please always remember Linda, no matter whether they are of human origin or from other vibrations or worlds, if a being expresses knowledge from the heart of unconditional love, you will always feel the truth of their expressions from your own heart. It is the ego of fear that expresses negative emotions and places judgement upon others in what is being expressed. In most situations the ego is only found in the third dimension and the lower levels of the fourth, known as the Astral World.

Always ask for truth from your heart, for that is where unconditional love is centred. Logic will only give you an idea of what truth is, and that truth is from the created past of confusion. Always have an open mind and heart - this is where you will find the road to freedom.

Be blessed in unconditional love always dear Linda.

Kuntarkis.

GROWING CONSCIOUSLY

Hi Kuntarkis,

I just have a question for you. How did you get to the level you are on now. Did you teach yourself or did you have a teacher? I feel like I need someone teaching me for some reason. You know how people go to church every Sunday for the lesson of the week? Is it possible to reach levels you thought would be impossible without someone guiding you? And tell Deeity9 I said thanks.

Kuntarkis replies:

Dear Friend, Hi, it's Roman. I felt I should answer your question. From the moment I came into this world as a human being I was always searching for answers to questions that no one seemed to have the answer to. I would go to public libraries, religious groups, public lectures, and searching through books on spiritual matters, reading and reading until my eyes could not focus anymore. Even though all these places had some form of truth, I felt in my heart it still wasn't quite right. I discovered meditation at an early stage of my life and began to practice different methods.

At first I found it hard to concentrate on meditation - my brain would always wander on different thoughts. Only through disciplining myself did I begin to experience the real meaning of meditation. I discovered that meditation is not about concentrating or thinking. I also learned not to have any expectations for the end result. What I discovered was that meditation is a form of transformation beyond human thinking, beyond logic. It transforms your level of understanding enabling you to connect to higher planes of communication.

To connect to other vibrations you have to still the mind, stop the chatter of the brain and take it beyond the everyday mundane confusion and thoughts. By doing this you make a connection with your inner voice, your Soul. That to me was the beginning, the opening of who I am. A spirit facet of my own Soul made a connection with me and helped me raise my consciousness to higher vibrating worlds, and this allowed me to be able to communicate with other entities in higher vibrations.

Yes, it is true that the knowledge of all that is and will be is within our essence. What needs to happen to each of us is for us to step beyond our present understanding and to be willing to step into the unknown. By doing that we open ourselves up to the infinite knowledge of all that we each have been and will become. That is our right to know.

The power of that knowing can come to each one of us as human beings. How long the journey takes is up to the individual. That is what I discovered. I personally found my greatest teachers, who have helped me, were in spirit, because they came from the heart and were not judgemental, but full of unconditional love and compassion. There was no ego, just love.

I trust my friend that this will give you a little help.

Roman.

ILLUSION OF PHYSICAL LIFE

Hey Kuntarkis,

OK, I did think it was real. I remember meeting "Thomas", and it felt like he was a long lost brother. Was he there as well? Is Thomas a close part of me? There seemed to be a third person too, but he was quiet, and distant.

I don't remember too much of the dream, except that you and he were sitting across from each other, and that your hands were interwoven and connected like tree-trunks. I then remember that I reached over and stuck my arm into your shoulder, and you began laughing, and said that you were surprised, and that I was a natural. You also said that you did not come to me, that I called to you, surprising you with my strong energy that called out to you, and that I had another breath form when we last spoke and that you were happy to see me. I am not sure what is imagination, and what is real. I don't remember being told what my true mission is, I guess that is later.

Oh, about the current astronomical situation with the supernova, hourglass nebula, and EtaKarina. Are these definite factors of our current enlightenment and DNA programming into the 5th dimension?

Thank you for talking,

Love and light,

Rich.

Kuntarkis replies:

Dear Richard, An individual's true mission in their human life is in reality the individual's purpose as a human being - to discover their life's path for themselves. To express to a human being their life path can change the events that the being has chosen to undertake. My Being would do you a great injustice and disservice to reveal this truth to you.

My Being can give you guidance so you can discover the power of this truth from within yourself Richard. Every human individual has this knowing already recorded in their cellular memory. It is all about seeking the truth from the stillness of your mind so that you can connect to the inner voice of your Soul.

You asked about the current astronomical situation with the supernova, hourglass nebula and EtaKarina and if they are definite factors of current human enlightenment and DNA programming into the fifth dimension. Well Richard that says it all! Humanity always places labels on things and complicates what human beings are all about, especially with respect to their evolution as a species. The terminology itself creates confusion.

Once a human being evolves beyond the human ego of illusion and discovers the unconditional love within themselves, then and only then can a human being evolve beyond the third dimension of physical manifestation and enter the fourth dimension where human flesh no longer exists. Then, by growing consciously beyond the fourth dimension that human being can enter the fifth dimension where the power of thought is how all things are manifested into one's reality, even the manifestation of a physical body at will.

Evolving to that level of awareness can be a very slow process, taking many incarnations. The Nar'Karones evolved in this way over thousands of human years. It was the choice of the individual to evolve. Knowledge was passed on from parents to children and so on. Yes Richard, you can say it is in your DNA, but to truly believe and recognise that truth, and then put it into practice that is where the challenge lies.

All of humanity will come to that understanding as each human individual lets go of their human ego. The ego cannot go beyond certain levels of the fourth dimension - if it ever did, it would create an imbalance which could destroy that dimension. However, my Being can assure you this will never happen.

Always remember, unconditional love is the key which will open the knowledge and the understanding to higher vibrations.

Be blessed in love always Richard.

Kuntarkis.

WHAT IS MY DESTINY?

To Kuntarkis,

I have been reading over the site and all I can say is wow! I am very impressed.

I do have a few questions:

I was wondering about any guides that I have and their names, any and number of past lives I might have had (anything about them). My "love life" and where that is going, is there anyone coming into my life and a bit about him. I am also opening a business so I was wondering how that will go. I was given a coin by my father a few years ago and it was a gold coin that was very special with a special story behind it. I lost it a few months ago because my son seemed to have taken it and put it somewhere in the house I hope. I am not sure if he took it but it's not in my jewellery box. Where is the coin? Also anything about my son Adam, he is an old soul to say the least. And last, about my spiritual path and when my clairvoyant abilities will come

Thank you

Love and Light,

Laura.

Kuntarkis replies,

Dear Laura, Your spiritual name is 'Tangrear' and means 'flower which floats on water'. The language your name comes from is, Nar'Karones the beings and Nar'Kariss the Planet but on your Earth it is known as Sanskrit. Sanskrit is the Universal language throughout many Universes and was the original speaking language on your Earth.

You, to this present moment, have had 17 spirit guides which have been helping you on your path as a human being. The name of one of your guides is Lappier. He is Peruvian and he is guiding you to understand your emotions, which, through circumstances, you have been creating during your present incarnation as a human being. You have had 547 lives as a human being over the past 928,000 years of human evolution.

Please remember, every single human being holds the power of their own destiny in their hands. You are a co-creator in the totality of Creation - you alone create your life's path. Feel from your heart - this is where the truth lies. See from your mind's eye and you will create and manifest anything into your life that you desire.

You Laura are the power, the ruler, the driver, the creator. When you place a thought of energy into your mind's eye, you will, with persistence, make it your reality if you truly believe in yourself, your very being, your Soul.

You ask about your human son called Adam - what specific information you are requesting. Please be specific.

The gold coin you refer to seems to be lost. My Being is unable to feel any energy connected to the coin you speak of. However, you must remember, nothing is ever lost, only misplaced.

Be blessed in unconditional love always Laura.

Kuntarkis.

ESHAAN: MY FATHER

Dear Kuntarkis,

This is our grandson age sixteen months. [Photo was provided] His name is Eshaan. All our friends say he looks like me but I do not agree with them because to me he is an angel who has brought much happiness to his mother, my daughter. What do you think of him? Is he destined to be a great human being and what is his spiritual name?

Much love and many thanks.

Ashok.

Kuntarkis replies,

Dear Ashok, for a spirit to be born into the human world is indeed a very special gift in itself. It gives that spirit the opportunity to learn the language of unconditional love for all life forms. That spirit through the guidance of the Soul, chooses their human parents so they are given the appropriate circumstances which can help that spirit fulfil their life's plan.

Every spirit that is born into human form is in reality working out their karma, be it from a negative creation or a positive creation - it all depends in the individual's past incarnations in human form, as everything must be brought back in to balance from past lives. This allows conscious awareness and conscious expansion for all life forms, no matter form they may be.

Yes Ashok, your grandson is indeed an angel, and yes, under the right guidance from his parents, he can achieve greatness, (just as your human daughter can also achieve greatness), as long as you as parents' guide him with love in your hearts.

Unconditional love for oneself can be transferred to the child, and they in turn will grow into a balanced human being. Always be positive and understanding with your children and grandchildren; become the living truth of unconditional love.

The spiritual name of your grandson is 'Barshie' and means 'visions' or 'imagination'. To see it in one's mind's eye is to create it so it can be manifest into the human world.

Be blessed in unconditional love always.

Kuntarkis.

NIGHTMARES: WHY DO I HAVE THEM?

For Kuntarkis,

I'm under a lot of stress lately and have been having these nightmares which appear so real. The common element in all is pitch blackness of the surroundings and my inability to move and this fear that there are people around me that wish to do me harm, but I can't see them. I wake up with this pulling feeling, as if I'm either being pulled back into the dream or being pulled into consciousness. Can't work out which. Can I conclude that these are mere extensions of the tension I am feeling during the day consciously or is there something more?

Peta.

Kuntarkis replies:

What you are experiencing is very common with a lot of humans, whether it be their daily lives or the employment they have chosen. You each create your daily stress and if you do not have a means of dissolving your created stress, it will build up within you and around you, and be a part of everything you do in life. That is why your experiences in your time of sleep, or more to the point, in the Astral World are complete confusion. Nothing makes sense, and yes, the common element is that you are surrounded with darkness. What it is trying to show you is the limitation which you, along with many others, place upon yourself, which is only based on your fears that are created from the past. That is, your beliefs and conditioning. It is these two elements that need to be looked at unbiasedly and then dissolved into the nothingness from which they were first created.

Fear is only a human word created by man and placed upon human society, and from there it became a condition of human life. Not being able to move means you are restricted in the little black boxes that you have put yourself in, like so many human beings do out of fear of change or not being able to cope with the stress of human life. Taking it from another perspective, the people around you as you describe, may be trying to help you open the lids of your little black boxes so you allow the Light in, which in turn allows change in your human life.

Peta, your guides, or angels as you may prefer to call them, are trying, out of love, to help you. But only you can let the Light in. And yes, these situations that you are experiencing are extensions of the fears or tensions you have or are creating. It may help you understand more if you read the article entitled **"You are What you Eat/ You are What you Think"**. Remember you are loved by many, but remember the love from within is the first step in the process of self-realisation. The story or article mentioned is number 5 of this book.

Be blessed in the light,

Kuntarkis.

FASCINATED BY ASTRAL TRAVEL

Yes Kuntarkis,

My question is a little confusing for me to put into words. I've been into spirituality for a number of years and I am fascinated by astral travel. I can't seem to have any form of awareness while I am out of my body when I'm asleep, and everything seems upside down. Can you please give me some guidance on this?

Andrew.

Kuntarkis replies:

Andrew, it would take many pages of paper to give you a complete answer to your question. There are many levels of consciousness within the Astral World. But first, there are some very important things you must consider.

1. Your emotions need to be balanced;
2. Your intake of food must be nutritious to the human body; and
3. You need to consider giving up your smoking and drugs, as they are incredibly toxic and polluting to your human body.

Only by cleansing your human body of all its toxins, which includes junk food, will you begin to raise your consciousness. Your awareness of all that is within and around you will increase and your level of thinking will change. You will see things without judgement and your emotional pain from your past will no longer affect or concern you. You will find you no longer need to distract yourself with your drugs. The unconditional love that is within you will emanate outwardly and become a part of you, and you will take recognition of 'the knowing'.

Begin there Andrew and persist, and all that you seek from your physical life and your spiritual life will come together in harmony, and you will exist in a pure state of being. Please Andrew, read this a few times and let it be absorbed into your being so that it becomes a knowing of truth within you.

Be blessed in the Light.

Kuntarkis.

MY MOTHER HAS CANCER

Dear Kuntarkis,

I live on my parent's farm and I am 12 years old. I was surfing the net for information on any cancer cures and found your website. I read about how Roman cured his cancer by himself, and it made me think that maybe there is some hope for my Mum. She won't tell me she has cancer, but I saw a letter sent to her. She has been very sick, and I don't know what to do to help. I don't want her to die. Can you help her?

Tim.

Kuntarkis replies:

Tim, you are a very brave boy and I know you love your Mother with all your heart. It reminds me of when Roman had cancer, and the pain and loneliness he went through. I can tell you what I did at the time, even though Roman wasn't fully aware of my presents then. From the centre of my being, which is where your heart is, where all your love comes from, I would send a beautiful ray of white light to him and also inside of him by using my imagination. I would see this light as a healing light and know it would burn away all the cancer cells inside of him.

Believing is the most important thing of all because your thoughts Tim are very powerful. When you imagine something and really believe it, it is happening. The whole universe is made of light and it is there for all to use if they choose to. I will send a healing light to your most precious mother. Tim, love her and embrace her, and send her light from your heart.

Be blessed in the Light Tim.

Kuntarkis.

GAMBLING PROBLEM'S: I NEED TO STOP?

Hi Kuntarkis.

I am writing to you because I have a big problem. I have been gambling for the last 11 years and no matter what I do, I can't stop. I feel helpless. I'm losing everything - my husband and children especially. I can't keep a job. I'm desperate. I believe in you and who you are. You give so much information and wisdom. Please help me understand what's happening to me.

Lorraine.

Kuntarkis replies:

From an energy level I feel the pain you are creating in your life as a human being. If you look deeper into your childhood, and be honest from your heart, there alone you will begin to see why you are creating so much pain and misery. Within you is a hurt child expressing their emotions outwardly? For you, it is self-worth and a denial of being prosperous. You feel you do not deserve joy in your life, so you begin the journey of self-destruction until you lose those you love most.

It is a path many human beings take. It is based on your past emotions, for whatever reason they were first created. As a child you were rejected, not because you were unloved by your parents, but because your father had a drinking and gambling problem. He had a sad upbringing and the genetics were passed on to you.

Look at your past, learn to understand what you are truly feeling and begin the healing process by accepting yourself as you are, for everything in life is just a journey. You do not have to hold on to the pain throughout your life. Forgive yourself, forgive your parents and love yourself from your heart as you truly are - a beautiful human being. As you begin to believe in yourself and realise that you deserve the best, the past pain that you have been feeling will dissolve over time into the nothingness from which it was first created. From there you will begin a journey of love and balance.

Lorraine, believe in yourself. Be blessed and loved in the Light.

Kuntarkis.

ETHICAL BEHAVIOUR

To Kuntarkis,

Question: How do we know, if at all, if our behaviour is ethical?

Alex

Kuntarkis replies:

Dear Alex, It is an interesting question. Indeed, how can we know, if at all, if our behaviour is ethical? First dear Alex, in reality there is no right or wrong, good or bad. Judgement comes from your past, your beliefs and conditioning of life, your fears and insecurities. These make up your characters and shape your way of life. It is called Human Ego. If a human does something to another human being which could be negative or even harmful, it would mean that human being has fears and insecurities of a negative nature, and that would be unethical behaviour.

To know if you are being unethical you must first ask from your heart and not your emotions. Your heart is your feelings, your very being where the truth lies. Your heart can only give you truth. Alex, if you need to ask yourself a question, and it does not matter what it is, still your brain from the chatter and go quiet. Feel from your heart and when the moment feels good, ask your question and listen to the answer. The first answer is your truth. You Alex are the power, a facet of Creation's totality.

Be Blessed in Love and Light always.

Kuntarkis.

WHY AM I UNSUCCESSFUL IN LIFE?

Hello Kuntarkis,

Why have I not been able to find work and prosper? I've spent the last 10 years toiling away and do not have anything to show for it. I live pay check to pay check and as I am getting older, this is becoming a major source of concern. What is wrong with me? Why am I not successful? Should I sell Mary Kay Makeup? Thank you.

(No name given)

Kuntarkis replies:

Dear Human Being, all humans have some form of fears and insecurity. There is nothing wrong with you in reality. But I ask you to go beyond your emotions and ask yourself this question: what do you fear most?

You may not agree with this, but if you choose to come from an honest heart, your answer would be that you fear success, the very thing that you desire. When some opportunities have presented themselves to you, you did not follow through. You are a deep thinker and you have a beautiful heart, but you are your worst enemy.

At this time in your human life you need to believe in yourself. You have the strength to succeed in any venture you choose to take on. The secret is to believe in yourself and take the chance to step beyond what you are today. Do not live to time - step beyond human time and live for the moment, for that is where your creativity exists. If you choose to sell Mary Kay Makeup, then put 100% of yourself, your being, into the job and see yourself successful even before you begin. Remember, how you see yourself is what you will become. That is called, The Law of Attraction. What you think of yourself, you are putting that energy out to whoever you believe in, and that is send back to you?

May Love and happiness come to you throughout your success? You are the driver of your life.

Be Blessed dear human being.

Kuntarkis.

BROTHER HAS LUNG CANCER

Dear Kuntarkis,

My brother, Ron, has just been diagnosed with a very aggressive form of lung cancer. His current symptoms include breathlessness and a productive cough. Apart from these symptoms, he is reasonably well.

My brother's attitude is positive and he doesn't want to die. Ron is happily married with two young adult children. Unfortunately, in the space of three-four months, Ron's cancer has grown to the size of a large grapefruit and is highly vascularised. The cancer cannot be removed surgically. Radiotherapy has also been ruled out. Ron is still making up his mind about whether he wants chemo for palliative purposes. His outlook is not good.

My brother lives in Yeppoon. Do you have any contacts in your network that may be able to help in the Yeppoon / Rockhampton area? Alternatively, is there something that you feel you could do for Ron, say within the space of a week of personal consultations if we bring him down to Brisbane? If so, I would appreciate your call.

Thank you for your time and consideration.

Best regards,

Mike.

Kuntarkis replies:

Dear Mike, One of the hardest things to do is to give advice to someone who has been diagnosed with some form of human dis-ease because each human being is different when it comes to human emotion. A human being asked me once, why does human disease exist? The answer is simple, but because there are many levels of thinking and understanding within humanity and because human beings become too closely, emotionally involved, the simple answer does not seem to be accepted, and is reacted to in a negative way.

The answer is that all human disease is purely a state of the mind, created by negative thoughts over a period of human time, and enhanced by poor diet, meaning highly processed foods, drugs and medications, alcohol, smoking, and pollution in the environment.

When Roman was diagnosed with lung cancer and was told he had no more than about eight months to live, at that moment in his life, he alone chose to cure it himself against the advice and doomed predictions of his human doctor. He began doing research, he went deep into his quite time in meditation, and he always had an understanding. Whatever we create in our life can also be uncreated, he began looking at his life his emotions. He began the process to eliminate all the things in his life that caused him stress because stress is the major trigger of all dis-ease in humanity. He then set about changing his diet (refer to Ask Kuntarkis index under Dis-ease & Health for a list of replies dealing with this issue). He had begun his journey of self-discovery...

For your brother Ron, it will be a difficult journey. He will need to be strong and change many habits in his life. He will need to learn about his emotions and feelings, and he will need to be honest with himself from a loving heart.

There was a beautiful human being on your Earth called Dr Edward Bach he expressed something along these lines about human dis-ease:

Dis-ease is neither vindictive nor cruel. It is a means adopted by the soul to halt us, to prevent us from doing greater harm, and to help lead us back onto the path of light and truth from which we each should never have strayed.

One of the reason Roman created lung cancer was that he had a fear of life. Many human beings have this fear but most would never admit to it. To change your life from a physical perspective is not so difficult. The difficulty lies deeper within. The greatest cure for all pain and misery is to unconditionally love yourself from your very being, for that alone can shift your level of thinking and understanding to a higher level of consciousness.

Your brother Ron can change his present circumstances. He does have the power and the strength to do so, but the choice is his alone. As you are probably aware, Roman have moved to Adelaide South Australia. If you or your brother would like to talk to him about this issue, you can always ring him.

Be Blessed in Love and Light always.

Kuntarkis

DOES GOD EXIST?

Dear Kuntarkis,

My question is, does God as told in the Bible exist? Could you shed some light on this please?

Mohcene.

Kuntarkis replies:

Dear Mohcene, you are asking a question that has plagued human beings for at least the last 2,000 years. Who wrote the human Bible? Well, that is simple - human men wrote the Bible. And where does God as written in the Bible come from? From the human men who wrote the Bible. So, what was the purpose of writing the Bible? To keep human beings in some sort of order. Which leads my Being to your question: Does God, as in the Bible, exist?

Well, Mohcene, it all depends on your level of thinking and understanding; on whether you live in that little black box that keeps humanity locked into beliefs and conditioning from one life to the next. Let my Being answer your question in this way. When all of humanity lets go of their limited beliefs, conditioning, fears, and insecurities of life that have been created from the past, then each human individual will see the falseness of life through human Ego. Once that occurs, then and only then will the real come into being and all the falseness of the past will dissolve into the nothingness from which is was first created. The truth and only the truth will be manifested in the present moment. There lies your answer Mohcene.

One thing I must ad, whoever believe in your self-created God, it always has a purpose. It is every human beings right to believe in whoever or whatever they as individuals want to, it is called free will. Every created condition or belief system helps every individual to enhance their awareness as well as their conscious growth. But there will come a moment where the individual grows beyond that level of thinking, when, it's up to the individual.

Be Blessed dear Mohcene in Love and Light.

Kuntarkis.

ANSWER'S IN DREAMS

Hi Kuntarkis,

My name is Tatave and I am 37. I am confused in my life in what I would like to do. I feel I need to express myself. Like being creative in some way with my hands. In my dreams my hands are always moving, but I can't see what they are doing. Can you help me see?

Tatave.

Kuntarkis replies:

Dear Tatave, you are indeed a creative being in this lifetime. In your past life you did not complete your dreams. Your hands hold the secret to your creativity and that is why you are dreaming of your hands as they move fluently before you. Dear Tatave, you are an artist. In your previous life you painted from your inner being. Most did not accept your wild ideas, and yet in your human world of today your paintings would are priceless.

If you truly want to change your circumstances, allow your creativity to come forth. I know you meditate. Meditate and see from within the truth that you can. If you choose to paint in this lifetime, the knowledge is already within you - just open the door.

Be Blessed dear Tatave in Love and Light.

Kuntarkis.

SEARCHING FOR MY FAMILY ROOT'S

Dear Kuntarkis,

I have tried everything possible on this plane to assist me, but to no avail. I now need higher assistance.

A few years ago I had an urge to find my family roots. I started doing genealogical research on my father's side (Dollmann) however could not find out anything but my grandfathers' names. I have a photograph of the family grave site which shows three grave stones: Carl P. Dollmann, Olga Louise Dollmann and my grand-father, Georg Curt Adolph Dollmann who passed on in March 1951.

The problem is that I do not know where on this earth this grave site is. With there being no one alive to give me answers, I have basically reached a dead end. Could you assist me in this matter? Although what I seek appears unimportant, to me it very important as I know very little about my family.

Yours Faithfully

Carl.

Kuntarkis replies:

Dear Carl, I can understand from a human perspective how important family history is to the individual, and you wish to take on this journey into the past to help you discover yourself in the present.

The country on this Earth called Germany would be the beginning of your journey and it will take some effort and patience. You will need to go through old records held in files in Germany (provided they were not destroyed during the Second World War), as this will lead you to the truth you seek. Remember too, borders of that country have changed many times, so what was Germany then may not be a part of Germany today. Please always keep an open mind in what you discover, as the past that you seek may not be what you want to know. If the old records are not sufficient you will need to check the human grave sites in Germany which will take a lot of your human time. Yet at the end of your journey it may or will help you understand your past and your parent's past.

Just remember all is infinite. Nothing ever dies, only transforms, and the spirit lives on, preparing for another human life. If you wish to give my being more information on what you seek, please feel free to do so.

Be Blessed dear Carl in the Light and the Love of Creation's totality, and know that you are a part of it and always will be.

Kuntarkis.

DIRECTION OF LIFE & SPIRITUAL DEVELOPMENT

Dear Kuntarkis,

I don't know whom you are, but you don't seem to be from this world, and you seem to be able to "see" more than we do. Therefore I humbly ask you this question: I am so much alone....... but I want to develop myself in a spiritual way. I want to use my skills to help people. I can feel I could do that...I just don't know what direction I should go.....Is my being alone, part of my education and how should I really use this time? I want to contact my guide but I am not successful....can you help me? Thank you for your answer.

Lia.

Kuntarkis replies:

Dear Lia, Thank you for taking some precious moments in your human life to express to my Being. First dear Lia, you may feel alone, but in reality you are never alone. Your Guides are always with you, even when you lay your human vessel down to sleep. All human beings learn while they are awake and while they are asleep.

One of the main distractions that can, and does, stop conscious growth is the fear and insecurity of the human Ego, and this is because most human beings are caught up in beliefs and conditioning. Beliefs and conditioning are only a creation of the past, and many human beings live the past, making it their present and creating their future from it as well. This is not good for the evolution of humanity.

Lia, you as a Being of Light are confused in which direction to take. Your Guides have been guiding you to your quiet time so you can see yourself from the outside, like being an observer, neither negative nor positive. This is where you're true growth begins, and yes, it is a part of your education, and yes it is important to use this time wisely.

Never see yourself as not being successful in contacting your Guides. Just to try and be aware of the process is success in itself. In this Book of Knowledge go to story number (22) called 'Meditation for the New Year', read the meditation a few times, and then using your own voice, record it onto a tape. Then, in your own private space lay down or sit upright and allow yourself to be guided into the stillness of your Being, having no expectations. Just be in the moment.

Lia, one thing you must always remember. You are a part of the totality of Creation and Creation is a part of you. Your essence, your Being is far more than your physical self. You have lived many, many incarnations, and over all those life times you have gained many experiences, knowledge and skills. You have also been a healer, and that is something you would like to do in this life time. You can and you will, but you must believe in yourself and listen to your inner voice.

One thing must be said. You are already a spiritual being. You only need to awaken your inner self and allow the process to come outwardly. This will be done through the stillness of your mind in meditation. It allows you to become consciously aware of all your surroundings, and if you practice this you will amaze yourself with the knowledge that comes forth.

Never give up to the human Ego, for it will only depress you and hold you in a prison. Always believe in the Light of which you are and always have been. Most of all, believe in yourself, for my Being believes in you.

Be Blessed dear Lia in Love and Light always.

Kuntarkis.

EXPERIENCING PASSING OF SOUL'S or SPIRITS?

Dear Kuntarkis

I was fascinated to fall upon your website, when in actual fact I was looking for information on 'Liver cleansing' or should I say I thought I was! I am the eternal optimist, love life. I have not felt well for a while although I have not been diagnosed with any specific illness. I decided it may be my diet, (I am vegetarian) lifestyle and/or state of mind.

I read with interest your replies to others concerns. I have experienced the passing of many friends and loved ones in the past couple of years. Many times I feel I was meant to share this ending or even this moment of passing with them. Circumstances sometimes placing me unexpectedly in this position as though I was meant to experience this or be there for them in some way. As though I can feel their spirit in the process of moving on to the next level and I needed to be there in some way. I feel a lot of love but at the same time feel unsettled, something words cannot explain?

What is my vocation? Why am I constantly in contact with people that are passing? Is it a lesson I need to learn? I have vivid dreams of places, people, and other worlds. I have bouts of exhaustion, totally drained of energy & sleep for up to fifteen hours straight - I call them my coma sleeps!

I believe in unconditional love and accepting other people as they are, that our limits are only the ones we place upon ourselves. What am I missing? I know there are many people in need of your guidance & advice with genuine life difficulties and realise mine is a minor issue in comparison. So there is no urgency for a reply, just that if time permits somewhere along the way it would be greatly appreciated.

Thankyou.

Love and light to you from me.

Kris.

Kuntarkis replies:

Dear Kris, It was most kind of you to write to my Being and express your thoughts. First, yes there is a reason for you to be there in the passing of other Beings. It is your energies which help the passing over process. Expressing unconditional love to ones who are leaving their physical vessels can and does help in the letting go of their physical self, which allows the spirit freedom and to move on.

You feel unsure of what you must do, or need to do, in this lifetime of yours. The path of all human beings is to accept unconditional love. Once you accept unconditional love, which is infinite, timeless, ageless and endless, you dear Kris will experience an understanding of being, completely aware of every moment in your human life. Every problem will also have a complete solution. You will not see anything as negative or positive. Nothing will be impossible. You will only have to ask of your being for the answer and it will always be there for you.

You must go beyond just believing in unconditional love. You must live it, breath it, smell it, see it in all of life. But first become it. When you feel unconditional love in your heart, then you will not be missing anything. All your past hurts will become just a memory, neither negative nor positive, and you will then live in the moment.

Your minor issues as you put it are just as important as anyone else's, for every human being on this Earth is important in the scheme of life and existence itself.

The experiences you have in your sleep time are actual reality on another level of consciousness. You have lived other existences in different dimensions, so dear Kris, first believe in yourself, and love, truly love yourself in unconditional love, and you will begin to see all things with new eyes.

One thing must be said. Your human body does need a cleansing and to start with the liver and bowels would be a good beginning. Toxic build up in the human body creates exhaustion and a drop in energy levels. Over a period of human time this will cause other health problems. Remember, health is wealth, and if you're human body is not well it will also affect your thinking. So please dear Kris, take good care of yourself and always remember inner knowledge is the path to wisdom and wisdom is the path to freedom.

Be Blessed dear Kris in the Light and Love always.

Kuntarkis.

Kris then replied: Dear Kuntarkis, Thankyou so much for your email. I was so happy to hear from you so soon. Thankyou for your advice, I know in my heart what you say is true. I will endeavour to become all that I can be in this lifetime. I have a week off work, so this week will be spent cleansing my body and mind. Thanks again!

Love to you Kris.

EXPERIENCE'S OF ENLIGHTENMENT

Dear Kuntarkis,

Since I last wrote to you consumed with multiple bereavement, guilt and anxiety I have been managing to take small, positive steps to heal myself. I feel quite powerful although at times I still experience panic and terror of the future.

Having been in touch with my quiet, inner self I have begun to experience some pretty amazing experiences. During a quiet time when my mind was rested and my inner voices stopped chattering in my head I had a sudden, pure flash of understanding. It's hard to put into words as it was an experience beyond this plane. It was as if suddenly everything was totally clear about the reason we are on this earth and the purpose our human journey serves. I was in a place where there was peace, tranquillity and pure understanding without human words or form. Everything was clear although cannot explain how. I felt it was a knowledge shared with me from the members of my family who have moved onto that dimension and were trying to give me a little glimpse of where they are and why we had to traverse the rocky path of human life first. It was a pure and peaceful awareness that probably only lasted a second in a state of relaxation. But it has changed my outlook and guilt. It's all a matter of a deeper understanding that you can only glimpse if you're lucky or in tune. I realise my time here is just a huge classroom full of love, challenges, learning opportunities and hidden secrets, The pain, grief, guilt, disappointment are challenges that must be faced and dealt with before the next step can be taken beyond our earthly existence. It kind of all made perfect sense although I couldn't really articulate it in the limited vocabulary of the human form.

I'm not weird or schizophrenic, but I'm sensitive in a spiritual sense and seem to understand, see things and feel things before they happen. How can that be? Is somebody trying to reach me? It kind of helps with the tremendous challenges I am facing daily with huge tasks and decisions facing me. I see it as a necessary step towards something beyond. Does any of this make sense or do I sound as if I'm on drugs???? (I have never been on drugs by the way apart from the odd Panadol!)

Thank you for being in touch with me. One thing I don't know the answer to is what to do about my very challenging and disturbed 11 yr. old son. Can you help to know what to do about my son? I love him and want him home with me. Should I follow my gut instinct despite all his problems?

Jane.

Kuntarkis replies:

Dear Jane, My Being feels you have overcome a huge barrier in your human life and a great opportunity will come to you in your moments to come. Also, my Being sees you are expressing with your heart, and this is truly a blessing for you.

Always know the answers to all questions come from the heart. It is the heart that is the centre of your Being. Congratulations on your experiences of understanding. Keep seeking within and the doorway to your inner being will come forth more and more. With it will come the truth and the truth will set you free.

Yes, what you have to express to my Being does make sense, and yes, your Guides are trying to help you understand yourself, as well as your human son, who is on his own journey of self-discovery. Don't see him as being disturbed. See him as a single entity or individual trying to make sense of human life. His anger is a form of energy which needs to be channelled appropriately so he can learn to understand his own journey in life.

You dear Jane can become the living example of unconditional love. Love is truly the balance of human life, as it is with all of life. Each individual is trying to come to that understanding. Sometimes a human being must let go and allow another to learn. It does not mean they do not love them, it means no one can do it for another. One can only guide another if they choose to be guided.

Always look within yourself and the answer will be there for you. Be Blessed dear Jane in Love and Light always. Trust yourself always.

Kuntarkis.

FEAR OF FAILURE: WHY AM I LIKE THIS?

Hello Kuntarkis,

I have a fear that my new business will fail. I opened my business seven months ago and sell a huge variety of Dolls and Teddy Bears and accessories. I have been advertising through the paper it has cost me a small fortune. I am really concerned that my business which I love will not last long if sales don't improve. Can you see a bright future for me or will it end up like the rest of my life - a failure.

Jane.

Kuntarkis replies:

Dear Jane, Success as an individual cannot be measured. It all depends on one's level of thinking and understanding of one's personal growth. Dear Jane, if you believe in the fear of failure then you will set yourself up to fail.

My Being must express your fears are from your past. They began when you were a child with the constant expression of words from your human parents. They always said to you that you can't do anything right, and then why can't you do as you are told, and telling you always to be quiet, never allowing you to freely express your creativity.

It is your past hurts that hold you in a negative space. Only through forgiving your parents from your heart, and forgiving yourself, will your inner pain and anger be dissolved. Jane, love yourself as you are, in this most precious moment of life, and allow your love to manifest from your heart centre, to emanate all around you, and place that love in your shop, into all of your dolls and teddy bears. Know in your heart that your love is shared with each child who buys one of your toys, so everything you do with your business and personal life is filled with unconditional love.

Allow the past to be the past, remembered only as an experience of life, neither negative nor positive. Live in the moment and life will become balanced and you will not feel the fear of failure, only success will be in your heart and mind.

One thing you may also try is to set up some doll and teddy dress-up parties. Advertise them in your papers or do up leaflets and do a letterbox drop. Human children love to dress up dolls and teddy bears. Try it and let my Being know how you are progressing. Always remember unconditional love is the greatest healer of all human past hurts.

Be Blessed in Love and Light always dear Jane.

Kuntarkis.

ANGER & FRUSTRATION OVER INJUSTICE

Kuntarkis,

Hi. My name is John and I read your article on the fears of Humanity. I must say you hit the nail on the head. It brought up some serious emotions with me. When I was eleven (11) I was attending a Catholic school for boys, and for 4 years I was being sexually abused by one of the priests. I am 49 now and have never been able to have a lasting relationship with a woman. I never married or had kids because I felt it could happen to them. I did not want them to go through the pain I suffered in silence.

The priest who abused me died 12 years ago and I feel I will never have justice. I know I am feeling sorry for myself, but I would have liked him to be held accountable for his crime against me, and no doubt other boys. How can this ever come about now? I am frustrated and angry.

John.

Kuntarkis replies:

Dear John, What was done to you in your past was indeed a great injustice and extremely traumatic. You have carried the pain and trauma with you throughout your human life. My Being feels your anger and frustration, for you have been cheated out of human justice which would have helped you bring your sense of loss and violation to some kind of closure so that you could move on with your life emotionally.

My Being is sending you a healing energy to help heal your heart. There are places in your human society that you John may need to go to so you can express your emotions outwardly so that you don't hold onto your pain and create human dis-ease. It is better to bring out your anger and frustration so you can begin the healing process and deal with these created emotions in this life time of yours so you don't take them with you into your next incarnation. When a human being has experiences that create a lot of emotional pain, it can be difficult to forgive and to love yourself.

Through forgiveness the healing process begins, and then to learn to accept your own unconditional love, will release you from all past pains, no matter what they may be. Unconditional love is within all of life, it only needs to be awoken in the human individual. Every human being on this planet earth is caught up in human Ego, and that is the true enemy of humanity. Awakening your love from within will set you free from all pains, all fears, and all limitations.

John, do not concern yourself about human justice. All negative creations by individuals will be brought into balance. What is done to another, be it negative or positive, will be done unto them. It simply is the balance of all life.

Be blessed John always in Love and Light.

Kuntarkis.

I AM LOOKING FOR MY FATHER: WHERE IS HE?

Dear Kuntarkis,

Could you please help me find my Dad? He left home 6 years ago when I was 7. My mum told him to leave because he drank too much and spent all our money. I miss him a lot and love him very much, please find him. His name is Mr B Williams.

Christi.

Kuntarkis replies:

Dear Christi, It is beautiful to hear that you miss your human father, and that no matter what, you love him from your most precious heart. Your mother does still love your father and my Being knows you would love him to come home. Please do not be angry with your human mother for telling your father to leave. It was a very painful decision, which she had to make.

As you grow into a beautiful young human being, you will learn and understand why your mother did what she did. Your father is one that is called homeless and lives in a place called Queensland, in the Gardens of Brisbane. He sleeps amongst the trees by night and walks the city by day. I trust this may help you dear Christi, and may love always fill your heart. Please love your mother for she loves you with all her heart and soul.

Be Blessed dear Christi in Love and Light.

Kuntarkis.

LOOKING FOR LOVE IN ALL THE WRONG PLACES

Dear Kuntarkis,

I'm afraid I've regressed. I just feel as if I'm stuck in a vacuum and nothing can shift me out of it. Do you ever feel that others are streets ahead of you and you're just learning the basics?

Why doesn't anyone love me? I look at some people who are clearly dysfunctional (yes a judgement) and think how is it possible that they have love and I don't. I'm feeling extremely sorry for myself. I ask and ask the universe for direction but it's very silent on this issue. Other small things yes, I get answers, but this no.

Can you please help me understand?

Thank you.

Sue.

Kuntarkis replies:

Dear Sue, Never see yourself as regressing for you are not. You are in a process of learning about yourself and about life. Sometimes everyone feels they are stuck in a vacuum.

Try to see what you are experiencing as only self-doubt, not believing in yourself, which is normal for everyone. How long you choose to stay in that vacuum of self-doubt is another question for you dear Sue to consider.

There is a Universe listening to your desires and questions. There is no-one greater than you Sue, and there is no one lesser than you. All of life is equal throughout all universes. The only one holding you back is yourself and that is the truth. The same would go for my Being, or anyone else.

You asked why anyone doesn't love you. That is far from the truth. Love is a spontaneous expression in the moment of life, from each moment to the next, and so on. It is endless. The problem is you are scared to love yourself, and you are scared to be truly loved by another. It does not take a lifetime to accept self-love or love from another, if you can allow the love that is within you to be felt from the heart. It is the heart centre that holds the well of infinite love and light for all of humanity to express and feel. Love from the heart allows you to be loved and to also love another.

The question Sue that you need to ask yourself is this: Do I believe I deserve to love myself and be loved by others? The answer should always be: Yes. I do deserve to love myself and be loved by others. Every human being deserves to be loved. You only need to choose the moment in life when to accept your own infinite well of love that is within you always.

Never love yourself from your beliefs of conditioning of life, for they are only the illusions of human Ego. Allow yourself to truly feel from your heart, for in the heart lie all your answers.

Please feel free to contact me again, if you choose. May love fill your heart from your very being always?

Kuntarkis.

EXPLANATION OF SPIRIT & CHAKRAS

Only for Kuntarkis,

What is the nature of human spirit and its make-up and composition? A complete explanation of what chakra is?

Q?

Kuntarkis replies:

Dear Human Being, The nature of the human spirit is to express unconditional love to all forms of life. The makeup and composition of spirit is living consciousness. Its purpose is to learn and experience all facets of life's lessons and to ultimately transform beyond human ego. Its composition is magnetic energy, which is a part of all life forms throughout all universes. Magnetic energy exists within and around you. As you move your human body you are passing through magnetic energy. You as an individual can use this energy that surrounds you to advance you in your consciousness and to open up your inner knowledge and wisdom. Magnetic energy is attraction - how you think and feel will attract the same circumstances and types of humans into your life.

The human charka centres, of which there are 55 in total, 9 are essential for your wellbeing and for advancing your consciousness and your level of thinking. Your charkas are your balance and help you to exist in human form by feeding vital energies throughout your vessel – without them you could not exist in human flesh form. They also help you exist within other vibrations, such as the astral vibration (fourth dimension).

My Being trusts this information has been of interest to you. Love and Light to you always, Q?

Be blessed in love always,

Kuntarkis.

ARE ALL HUMANS, BEINGS OF LIGHT?

Dear Kuntarkis,

I started crying as I read your reply. It made me so happy and so at peace to know I'm not the only one, and that everything I've experienced in this form isn't "crazy" and that it's real. I am so grateful for your reply. Are all humans like this, a Being of Light, if not, are there many of us? Is there some reason we are in human form? Please forgive my inquisitiveness, but I so want to know. Once again, all of my thanks and deepest gratitude.

Janet.

Kuntarkis replies:

Dear Janet, You asked are all humans, beings of light. The answer is yes; all human beings are of light, as are all life forms. Light is the substance and the essence of Creation.

You also asked the reason why is humanity in a physical form. The answer is to evolve beyond the destructive human ego that has caused all human beings to be caught up in the illusion of what reality is believed to be. Humanity has been incarnating for the past 928,000 years and the human ego has also been evolving for that same period of human time. Take a look around your world with open eyes and see the pain, misery and misunderstandings the human ego is creating. It all comes from a fear of letting go of the past.

The past is humanity's legacy following each human being from one incarnation to the next. The true enemy is never on the outside, such as your neighbour, or another nation. Seeing other people as the enemy is only an excuse. The true enemy lies within each human being. When you resolve the inner enemy you resolve the outer false created enemy. It all begins with the individual. Unconditional love and forgiveness are the keys to opening up the heart centre, and this will transform human beings to a higher realm of understanding and wisdom.

Be blessed in love and light always dear Janet.

Kuntarkis.

LOVE & CAREER: HOW DO I FIND THE BALANCE?

Dear Roman & Kuntarkis!

Thank you very much for taking the time to answer my two questions. It has been helpful. As I have understood from your reply, I guess I need to first focus on myself and then after I have achieved loving myself unconditionally, only then I can go ahead and help and love others. The only problem I have, is that I don't know how I should proceed career-wise. I would like to have a job in which I actually help people, but if I have to help myself first, I guess I will just have to continue to be unhappy with my job until then. Knowing if my girlfriend is my soul mate and by looking into her eyes will be quite a challenge since we are separated by thousands of kilometres and I don't know when I will be able to see her again.

Thanks

Robert.

Kuntarkis replies:

Dear Robert, Please do not concern yourself with your human career. As you begin your own personal journey of self-discovery and allow the process of loving yourself to manifest within and around you. You will find your understanding and thinking will begin to change, and as you transform your thinking you will attract other energies (humans) into your vibration.

Remember, happiness is simply the way you feel about yourself and your surroundings. To grow consciously is to transform yourself from what you once were to another level of awareness. If you feel unhappy in what you do with your human job, then take realisation of your thoughts and how you see your own created world, and know that you created what you are. So if you are the creator of your own world then you also have the power and strength to change it.

It is simply how each individual feels about themselves. If they are happy or unhappy it is like being positive or negative -each human being has the choice to create a positive or negative existence. Never feel separated by distance concerning your girlfriend. Everything in all universes is energy, created by the power of thought and will. See your girlfriend in your mind's eye and with practice you will be able to communicate with each other through your mind and ask her to do the same, it may amaze you. Distance is only a limitation created by the self. Step beyond your understanding and believe in your inner light, and you will achieve what you seek in your human life.

Be Blessed dear Robert in the love of Creation always.

Kuntarkis.

MY LIFE'S MISSION: WHAT IS IT?

Dear Kuntarkis,

After having read some of your responses to others, I feel that it is sound and loving. My question to you is as follows: I am constantly asking myself and other aspects of self, what my life's mission/work is. I know that it has something to do with healing and teaching, however, I do not know where to start or how?

Thanking you in advance for your response.

Sincerely,

Marie.

Kuntarkis replies:

Dear Marie, It is always a challenge to the human self to know what path to take. Many human beings from childhood already can see what they want to do with their lives when they become adults. Many reach their dreams, but in most cases it is not reached from a physical perspective. What is achieved and learnt is not necessarily the lessons chosen prior to entering into their current incarnation. So many beautiful human beings become caught up in the stress of modern human existence. The human ego is the most powerful negative force that prevents human beings from realising their inner connection to all life forms in all universes.

Human beings like yourself, dear Marie, are very special in the scheme of life. You are a very curious human being who wants to teach, to heal, and to share your inner love with those in need. That in itself is a beautiful lesson for all human beings to learn.

It is natural for the human race to evolve on the material plane, but there must be a balance of both worlds between your outer being and your inner being. Without the balance there can be no conscious growth, only confusion. My Being will express to you what your chosen mission is in your current human life, but you must remember the responsibility for your choices always lies with you as a Being of Light.

In your previous life you worked in an orphanage looking after little human children in the land of Africa. You devoted your whole life to that work. You learnt to become a nurse in the land called England and, against your parent's wishes, you volunteered to go to Africa for three of your Earthly years. But instead of staying three years, you remained there for your entire human life. You were buried in Africa. The African people looked upon you as a gift from the heavens. They called you Shahmater, which means the healing hands of Mother Earth.

In reality, you already have the gift of healing. You are already a teacher of knowledge and you also have the courage and the strength to see your path in life, mainly because you have chosen to do this again in your current human life. What is most important for you, dear Marie, is to believe in yourself. Do not let your human conditioning from your upbringing stop you from going forward. Step beyond what is and step into the unknown.

In the unknown is conscious growth and self-realisation. So, what are you going to do?

Be Blessed dear Marie in unconditional love always.

Kuntarkis.

THE STRUGGLE OF UNDERSTANDING ENERGY: WHY?

Hi Kuntarkis,

Weeeee! Love it, (the website) but I do have a question and aren't smart enough to do it any other way (newbie!). When it comes to the struggle of energy do you:

A: agree and recharge after;

B: stand your ground and put up with the huff;

C: become more enlightened in which case I was hoping you could help me out.

Sorry for the abruptness, hope you can read this and help me out.

Brian.

Kuntarkis replies:

Dear Brian, Spiritual work in all aspects of life, be it in the human world of matter or other worlds and vibrations, is the most satisfying experience a Being could have. Simply to give without expectation is reward in itself. To send healing energies around your human planet and to give healing to other beings (human or otherwise) is an expression of unconditional love and respect for all forms of life.

Energy is endless; it has no specific job. It is the individual who makes the connection to the inner divine and then can use that energy for many purposes. If the individual uses the energy for loving reasons then love will always be present. But if the individual uses the energy for negative reasons, then negativity will always be present. How energy is used is always the choice of the individual.

Meditation in the silence of the mind is one of the best ways of always having energy ready for a purpose. Energy is abundant, endless, timeless and ageless. It is free from the greed of many human beings and cannot be bottled and sold. You Brian, as all human beings, are created from magnetic energy, the energy that all of life is created from. If you are in a situation that is becoming uncomfortable, there is no need to get in a huff. Simply excuse yourself politely and allow your Being to be somewhere more pleasing. You are the power and the driving force behind all changes in your human life.

Be Blessed Brian in unconditional love always.

Kuntarkis.

SEEING BEYOND PHYSICAL VISION

Hello Kuntarkis,

My life has changed. I would like to know why I see energy. I see energy wave particles in my environment, auras around objects and people mainly green and blue or sometimes just a soft white glow. I also see energy that looks like DNA. It is hard to explain this as they seem to be invisible, clear, no colour just movement and different shapes.

I would like to know why I have started to see this. I have been seeing this now every day for the past 3 years. I have also had different forms of out of body experiences. I have seen an image of a little boy in black and white, standing near my bed. I have closed my eyes and all of sudden I have seen a vibrant colour physical picture of a physical location as if I am looking through my third eye.

I also regularly feel shivers of energy flow through me at different times of the day. I also write a lot, in fact what I write sometimes I don't understand.

I would be grateful if you could tell me what is happening to me, as I am going through a lot of this every day.

Jennifer.

Kuntarkis replies:

Dear Jennifer, All of humanity are blessed in infinite knowledge and the wisdom to use that understanding. What is sad with humanity is the belief in having to have everything in the self-created material world of illusion.

Not many will experience what you Jennifer are experiencing at this time in your human life. What is happening to you is the opening of other vibrations to your inner vision, and you are allowing it to be expressed outwardly. You have a strong connection to the element world, especially the water element. The shivers are simply healing energies. You are a natural healer. In other incarnations you have been a healer and your connection to Mother Earth is strong. The Earth is the Mother to all who live upon her. The Earth is a living entity connected to the divine Light of Creation.

You may need to meditate in the stillness of your mind so you can further your understanding and connect with your helpers in the spirit world. They are close by your side. Trust yourself and listen to your true self.

Be blessed in unconditional love always dear Jennifer.

Kuntarkis.

KUNTARKIS: WHO WERE YOU BEFORE?

Dear Roman,

I need confirmation that Jecuss Kuntarkis is who he says he is. I do believe that he is a highly advanced soul and his advice is very reassuring but I need to hear another name or names that are used to identify him.

I have been told that there are many masters in Human form on Earth today who have come to help us, and I have in fact met three myself. I would like to know how many exactly are there and are there any that do not reveal themselves?

Thank you.

Norman.

Kuntarkis replies:

Dear Norman, I understand that you, like many others, seek proof of those who express knowledge, unconditional love and wisdom to those who choose to listen from their own hearts.

You asked if Jecuss Kuntarkis goes by other names. Kuntarkis normally does not use his past names from when he was incarnated in human form – he sees the past as the past.

However, I will give you examples of his past names. Kuntarkis when first incarnated on Earth was called Buddha, meaning 'Enlightened One'. In his second incarnation he was named Jecuss by his mother, which means 'Bright Star'. This name was later changed by man to Jesus, meaning 'Divine Being'. In his third incarnation he was named Damus, but later in his life he was called Nostradamus, the name which means "one who sees into other worlds". These three incarnations were physical births into the world of humanity.

At this present moment Kuntarkis exists in human form, having 'walked in' to the body (a cooperative decision made by the original entity that inhabited the body and Kuntarkis) and lives in Australia. His only purpose is to express knowledge to all who seek a deeper understanding and to help humanity grow beyond the human ego of pain, misery and destruction.

Only by believing in yourself, and accepting and projecting unconditional love, will you find the truth of all that is. There are at present 127 beings from other worlds and vibrations on this planet at the moment whose purpose is the same as Kuntarkis'.

Be blessed in love always.

Roman.

SELF-DISCOVERY

Dear Kuntarkis,

Last week I visited a clairvoyant who told me that I was on the brink of discovering much about myself spiritually. She told me that I was an advanced soul and that I have a lot of healing power in my hands. I have no problem seeing energy but I have only begun my search for my inner self and although I have always felt very strongly that I have another purpose besides the physical life that I lead, I would love to learn more, however I am unsure of where to go from here.

I am writing this letter because the name Roman came up twice in my reading - I have never known anyone by that name before until I visited this site. I would be happy and excited for any advice you could offer me.

Love and rainbows,

Debbie.

Kuntarkis replies:

Dear Debbie, It seems your clairvoyant reading has helped you discover a deeper and more meaningful relationship with yourself. You are a natural healer and you do have the ability to discover infinite knowledge from within your being that can be of great benefit to yourself and others.

There are many ways of finding out more, outwardly as well as inwardly. Read books, investigate spirituality courses and spiritual growth groups. Pick what is right for you from your heart.

If you truly want to be a healer of the light, first look to your own health. Look at your life habits and ensure you consume good fresh foods and clean water to create a healthy mind and body. This will allow you to bring in higher healing energies.

Meditation is a very important step to consider in your quest. There are many different forms of meditation. Seek them out and try a few to see how you feel. Meditation can help you gain a deeper understanding of yourself, your inner being.

To get you started with meditation, sit or lie on a bed or the floor in quiet surroundings where you will not be disturbed and where you feel safe. If you wish, put on some pleasant calming music to help you completely relax. As you sit or lay, put your thoughts to the centre of your eyes, just above the bridge of your nose and feel or imagine a small ball of light in front of that point. Do this for a little while.

Next, see or feel this light growing in size, becoming larger and larger. This light is being drawn towards you. See it emanating all around you, warming you, making you feel balanced in mind, body and spirit. It goes within you, cleansing your inner being.

After you feel completely comfortable and balanced, ask yourself this question: "Who am I?" Listen to your first answer and remember it. As you feel good in this moment, realise that you can do this little exercise whenever you want to; it will help you on your quest.

The name Roman will become a future event and you will remember, especially in the writing of books.

Be blessed in unconditional love always.

Kuntarkis.

SANANDA & KUMARA ENERGY: WHO IS IT & WHAT IS IT?

Dear Kuntarkis,

Thankyou very much for your response. I am still confused. Who then is Sananda and what the Kumara Energy is?

I would very much appreciate your kind reply.

Thanks again.

Norman.

Kuntarkis replies:

Dear Norman, Confusion in oneself only means you do not believe in yourself. Yet you are an infinite being, a spark of living consciousness, which in this moment of your own reality, living a human life in order to learn, to love, to experience all that you have chosen before incarnating into your current human form.

You dear Norman possess infinite knowledge within your own inner being from the past to your present moment. Just truly believe in yourself and meditate in the silence of your mind. By doing this and believing in yourself, you will begin your true journey of the self-discovery of who you and all of the humanity truly are.

Regarding Sananda, the name comes from the ancient language of Sanskrit. It was given to Jesus by a specific group of humans in the year 21AD. Sananda means 'Infinite Knowledge; one who has become open to all things'. Jesus never took on the name Sananda, it was simply given to him by human beings at that time. Some humans today believe the name Sananda holds the energy of unconditional love.

Regarding kumara energy, the human word kumara is the name of a vegetable, the sweet potato. However, some humans believe kumara energy to be the energy of wisdom. Another variation on the word is Sanat Kumara. To those who use these words it refers to planetary consciousness.

One of the most important lessons for all of humanity is to discover their true essence, found through the unconditional love for their own being as well as other forms of life, no matter what they may be. Through the discovery of unconditional love comes the knowing. The knowing is the totality of infinite knowledge of all things, from the past to the present to the future. All else is the illusion of man's creation from humanity's destructive ego, the ego that has ruled humanity for more than 928,000 years.

The answer lies within your inner being Norman. Meditation in the stillness of your mind will bring the connection and the balance you seek, and this will lead to greater clarity, spiritual freedom and bliss.

Take care dear Norman and believe in yourself.

Love and light,

Kuntarkis

DROP OF BLOOD

Dear Kuntarkis,

While cleaning her toilet, a friend of mine had a drop of blood fall from above her into the bowl. Instead of expanding out on the water as blood normally would, it went into a funnel shape and down the bowl. She says that as it dropped, she automatically looked up - but could see nothing on the roof above her - neither were there any cuts on her fingers or elsewhere.

She has had a number of problems within the past few years - with her husband being imprisoned for something of which he is innocent. She has spoken to the Minister of the Spiritual Church which we attend - but we have been unable to find any answers. Could you please shed any light on what the significance of this blood is?

Thank You

Julia.

Kuntarkis replies:

Dear Julia, First, my Being needs to express a sad truth. Every experience a human being is having, be it negative or positive, is a creation of the individual's past brought into the present. It all has to do with karma; no matter how much the individual fights it or believes it, it is karma, and that is the truth.

Karma can be either negative or positive. It depends on the level of thinking and understanding of each human being. The situation with your friend's husband is from a past incarnation and is being brought into balance in his current incarnation.

The drop of blood your friend experienced is not of the physical vibration. Its meaning is for your friend to let go of the past and live in the moment. It was showing her that her life force, meaning the blood that sustains human life is being drained away. Your friend needs to step beyond the past and to love herself in unconditional love.

The funnel shape the drop of blood created is a representation of her human life being wasted on the past, and yes the truth will always hurt. It is part of the healing process of forgiving and letting go of the past so that one can live in the present and begin to create a future of joy, peace and unconditional love.

Every human being, as all other forms of life, have the right to be happy and fulfilled. Human life is all about experiences – negative and positive experiences are all a part of the human lessons of learning.

Be blessed in unconditional love always.

Kuntarkis.

GRIEVING FOR FATHER

Dear Kuntarkis,

My father died 17 months ago. We got on very well and I miss him badly. He was always a comfort to me. He died of stomach cancer and was in a lot of pain for several years before his death, especially in the last few weeks before he died. My question is will he be at peace in the spirit world or is he still living in his pain? I miss him so much, it hurts.

Beth.

Kuntarkis replies:

Dear Beth, My Being expresses healing energies of light to you. Your love for your human father is a sign of the love you feel for your own being, the unconditional love that is most precious. You are indeed a loving human being who has an honest heart and honest feelings towards others.

Your father's part in life was a sad one, yet he loved you so very much. Both of you as spirit beings are of the same energies and as human beings you have had many incarnations together. In your next incarnation you will experience his presence in your human life.

Yes, he is at peace in the spirit world – no pain, just unconditional love. His essence knows you miss him and his spirit is always with you and will be throughout the remainder of your current human life.

Love is infinite, endless, ageless, timeless, eternal, pure bliss. Unconditional love is the main lesson humanity needs to learn, for all else is simply the illusion of humanity's past.

Be blessed in unconditional love always Beth.

Kuntarkis.

BUDDHISM & ENLIGHTENMENT

To Kuntarkis,

After reading "The Purpose of Life", I feel that many of its philosophies is similar to those of Buddhism and its search for Enlightenment. Will practising Buddhism enable the human being to free itself from the incarnation cycle?

Also, what is your view on "fate" and "destiny" if you say that we are a result of our own actions? Does this mean fate and destiny does not exist?

Amy.

Kuntarkis replies:

Dear Amy, Yes, Buddhism can guide the individual to complete bliss as long as the individual is true of heart in their search for Truth and Enlightenment.

Practicing Buddhism can help the individual free themselves from the incarnation cycle, in Buddhism they refer to it as The Wheel of Life, as long as the human ego is dissolved back into the nothingness of self-created fears, beliefs and conditionings of the past.

Every human being creates negative and positive actions in their life, just as there is good and bad karma. The actions created by the individual are the outcome of their life experience, from childhood to adulthood, depending on their fears, beliefs and conditioning. If a child is highly conditioned by certain experiences and beliefs which are reinforced throughout life, and by the conditioning of human parents, and also by genetic transfer from the parents, then fate and destiny, the concept of the 'self-fulfilling prophecy', can become a very real part of an individual's life. A human being becomes a clone of a parent or both parents, and of the society they were raised in, and conscious growth is held back.

This happens to many human beings. But it is also true that if a human being has a strong character and they truly believe in being an individual, if they do not like some aspects of their character, they can create change in their life and step beyond their beliefs, fears, conditioning, and their human ego. They can create their own path in life, whatever it may be. In reality they create their own fate and destiny.

The individual creates their own actions in life, whether they are negative or positive. It all depends on their level of thinking and level of understanding. To consciously recognise the need for change within oneself so as not to repeat the past of those before you (usually accepted as fate or destiny), and then to physically make the necessary changes, is to undergo Enlightenment.

First, be true to yourself, have the courage to recognise the need for change, and then find the strength to make changes. By changing your thinking and understanding you will discover real compassion not only for your own being, but for all forms of life, whatever they may be.

Through compassion you open the doorway to your own infinite knowledge, knowledge that is within all life forms. From here you begin to walk the path to wisdom, opening the heart centre to unconditional love for your own being and all life forms. In the process you begin your true journey of self-realisation and learn that Enlightenment has been with you always. You only had to remember who you in reality are – a spark of living consciousness on a journey of self-discovery.

Be blessed in unconditional love always dear Amy.

Kuntarkis.

ENHANCING VISIONS

Hello Kuntarkis,

I found your website by way of seeking information on the Barathary gland, which I have wondered about for a while. I was impressed that I found the information on your web site.

I would like to know how I can enhance visions. I used to have them, but I discovered that a jealous soul (under the guise of friend) was attempting to sour my life but this has changed, now that I know what her intentions had been toward me, which was not good.

Truly,

Debra.

Kuntarkis replies:

Dear Debra, Every human being can reconnect to their source of inner light, that is, their Soul. Most of humanity are disconnected because of their creation of the human ego, which has lead humanity through a very violent history. The past of humanity's making has followed each human individual from one incarnation to the next, and this has been going on for almost one million years.

Human karma from a negative aspect has stopped the conscious growth of many human individuals. Yet there are many human beings wanting to grow beyond the human ego of destruction.

To begin the process of letting go of the past one needs to learn forgiveness. One needs to fill their heart with unconditional love for all of life, in all its forms. One needs to purify their human body from polluting toxins and they need to nourish their body with good food and plenty of clean water. One also needs to change their thoughts of negativity to positive thoughts. One also needs to feed the human body and spirit through meditating in the stillness of the mind by stopping the chatter of the human brain so one can truly listen to the Soul and allow the inner light to come forth and be their guide.

This process dear Debra will indeed open up your inner and outer vision to spirit world and beyond.

Be blessed in unconditional love always.

Kuntarkis.

LONG CHILDBIRTH LABOUR: WHY?

Dear Kuntarkis,

I have had four children, and I am expecting my fifth child. What I am wanting to know is why I have to have such a long labour, when others seem to walk in and are finished in such a short time. Each labour last about 15 hours. Also could you tell me if I will ever have twins, and why does life always seem to go against me when I try to achieve things in my life? Thanking you.

Dana.

Kuntarkis replies:

Dear Dana, First, please take a precious moment in your human life to sit down, take three deep breaths and relax. Ask yourself from your heart

"Who am I?" Then realise you are a beautiful human being on a journey of self-discovery. Believe this from your heart, for this is the truth.

Having long labours can have many reasons. First it can be associated with your genetics – maintaining a healthy weight while not pregnant will help you maintain healthy weight and healthy weight gain during pregnancy, as excessive weight makes labour longer. It can also be diet and the amount of water you consume. Exercise plays a very important part in keeping the human body supple – keeping the muscles stretched is very important. Yoga was passed onto the human race over 700,000 years ago by the Nar'Karones. Yoga keeps the body calm and allows tension and stress to be eliminated. It keeps the body flexible and helps in the delivery of a human baby.

You as a spirit being chose before coming into a physical existence to have six human children individually. Your human daughter chose to have four children and yes, there will be one set of twins to your human daughter.

Dana, life does not go against you. Whatever experiences you are having, it is what you chose to experience in your present human life. You wanted to be challenged with life so you could say "this is what it is but I will never give up".

Believe in yourself Dana – always believe and you will achieve. You will Dana.

Be blessed always in unconditional love.

Kuntarkis.

FEELING EMPTY: WHAT DO I DO?

For Kuntarkis,

I am 4 months away from having my only daughter go off to College...and 2 months from having ended a very special relationship of several years. All things that I knew were inevitable...even healthy....but I find myself with this very empty void in the pit of my stomach.

As you can tell, I am torn, there is a part of me that feels maybe I should just give up on love and resign myself to stay alone for the rest of my life...if you come to think of it...I have had and done everything most woman only dream of...and then I know that would not be me...I am a true optimist... albeit a romantic realist....but I just don't know where or how I will find that special person.

I feel that if I let the dream die...there is a part of myself that will also die, but I don't want to hold on to an impossible dream. Do you see me with someone special in the near future?

Shakti.

Kuntarkis replies:

Dear Shakti, Never lose sight of your dream - that is what makes a human being so special. But do not put expectations on what you want as a special human being in your life. You see Shakti, you place many expectations on yourself and you expect this from others. The void you are feeling is an emptiness of love for yourself.

Love comes from the heart centre. It is complete unconditional love. The heart places no rules or expectations on you. What does place expectations on human beings is the circumstances that each human being grows up with as a child into adulthood. Most human beings think from the human brain in all their decisions throughout their life.

There are no feelings in the human brain, only recorded experiences, be they negative or positive, and in most cases this is what shapes human life. It is like emotions, love is not an emotion but a feeling and feelings which come from the heart are spontaneous. That is unconditional love. The human brain can only give you a recorded memory of what love is, meaning, what is a known experience, negative or positive.

Shakti, you need time out to get to know your heart and love yourself unconditionally so you can attract someone into your life from your heart. Only then will you be able to love and be loved in the purest form of love itself.

Be blessed in unconditional love always.

Kuntarkis.

REPTILIAN BEINGS

Hello Kuntarkis,

It's been a while since I've made contact any kind of contact with you Kuntarkis. Of course this does not mean that all is not well or forgotten. I loyally come to your website every month to share in your guidance, insight and wisdom. I've been sharing your website with all who are opened to explore spiritual matters beyond the conventional way and this is something that I will continue to do.

Well, I have had yet another unbelievable experience since the last time I wrote you, this one is far too explicit (and a bit disturbing) for me to repeat here. If Kuntarkis would like to comment on this without me going into details (I know he can access my thoughts through the words I transcribe on this email letter) I am opened to it.

The main reason I am writing to you is because there is a lot of information floating around the internet about ego-driven reptilian or dinosaur like Beings who are manipulating the affairs of mankind from underground areas on earth as well as from other dimensions. I've personally seen a Being who was clearly reptilian-like in form (had crocodile eyes and pasty white freckled skin) during an OBE about 4 years ago... Therefore, I know that there is some credence to this. My question to Kuntarkis is this... Were the 87,000 Nar'Karones who were placed on earth about a million years ago reptilian in their form? If so, are they "the Gods" the ancient civilizations of the past worshipped and feared?

Once again, thank you for being such an inspiration to myself and the many others who share in your wisdom, grace and unselfish energy.

Tony.

Kuntarkis replies:

Dear Tony, the 87,000 Nar'Karones placed on Earth almost one million human years ago were not a reptilian species. They were humanoid in appearance, very much like human beings in this present moment. There were alien beings from other worlds who have visited Earth in the past and have existed within humanity, and yes, they were seen as gods of the heavens. Many civilisations of the past worshipped these beings and there were those who feared them.

One of the main reasons why humanity of the past worshipped them was because they came from the skies and seemed to have special powers. These beings used technology to make humanity see them as gods, and yes in some situations they used fear to control and dominate human kind.

It would be easy to dominate a race that was not technologically advanced or technologically minded. The alien beings would see them as simple minded, and easily controlled and manipulated for their own benefit.

Be blessed in unconditional love always dear Tony.

Kuntarkis.

MEDITATION/REGULARLY: HOW OFTEN?

Hi Kuntarkis,

I would like to introduce myself. My name is John and I am from India. Accidently, when surfing the internet, I found out about you. I would like to know more about you and your web site.

About me - for the last 8 years I am doing meditation regularly and now am at a stage I feel that my body is something like a tool in the hands of my soul, and to some extent I can control my thoughts and make my mind be present at this moment as per my will. At deep meditation I can only feel myself and not my body. Sometimes I used to travel unseen land and I used to be near unknown people without knowing them. Sometimes I use to fly over the mountains and see beautiful land scapes.

Can you tell me what is all this and can you tell me what my name is according to you?

Please write to me, and I would like to tell some more about me, and what I learned about this life which has been taught by unknown teachers in my meditation.

Thank you,

John.

Kuntarkis replies:

Dear John, My Being wishes to say thankyou for sharing your experiences of words. Meditation is one the most important exercises for conscious growth. When a human being meditates on a regular basis in the stillness of their mind they make a conscious connection to their Soul.

Yes, all human beings in their time of sleep will astrally project from their human body. Depending on their own awareness they will have different forms of experiences. These experiences can be negative or positive, but it all depends on one's level of understanding, their thoughts and their spiritual knowledge.

Your outer body experiences will help guide you to your purpose in your current life. John, in your previous life as a human being you were a teacher of knowledge and a light healer. This knowledge is with you in your current human life. Meditation will help you to open up your inner understanding.

Your spiritual name is 'Herm 'rumen'. It is old Hebrew, dating back 14,000 human years and means 'one who walks in the light'.

My Being will sit with you in your meditation and we will express our thoughts.

Be blessed in unconditional love always.

Kuntarkis.

STRANGE DREAM EXPREIENCE

Dear Kuntarkis,

My name is Joshua, and I have a few questions. I understand if you cannot answer them all.

My brother, Richard has recently received a spiritual name through you: Pukree. Last night I had a dream where I met a man who seemed to me to be a spiritual being. I asked him how to pronounce Richie's spiritual name, and he seemed to look both at me and beyond me. He smiled and spoke softly, pronouncing his name, as if he liked the sound of it. At first, upon awaking, I thought of Sai Baba, but am unsure if it was him. What happened in the dream next puzzles me? My throat was so constricted I could no longer speak. I could neither cry. When the spiritual being looked at me, it looked like he was both seeing beauty in me, and also the beauty of what I was becoming. Still, I could not speak or express anything, I could only meditate on the sensations of dream constriction until I awoke, aware of my physical throat's sensations, that it was perhaps constricted.

My question is this: Who was that spiritual being? Was he someone who watches over me, over Richie, was it Sai Baba, or an angel? Was it you, Kuntarkis? Is there a way I can contact him again? I am not sure if this is a question you can answer. I prayed that night that one of God's angels would speak to me and teach me, open me up more to my truth. Was it the angel?

I have been meditating mostly every day for a few years now. I have been growing a lot, and have even felt in moments like I have actually touched my soul. I want so much to grow, to be able to look sincerely at myself without judgement, and others as well. If you can see anything that I can do to grow, I would be honoured if you would let me know. I have been struggling a little with an apparent duality between Kundalini Yoga and Vippassana Meditation, as well as trying to find a way to share these practices with Christians in a way that utilizes Christian terminology so that they have less fear about exploring their inner selves. If you have any insight into any of this, or if you see something more to the core of what is needed for my progression, please help me to see it.

Are my migraines related to my suppressed anger?

I have one other question, about a mantra I received through a dream/out of body experience. It is: "God Light Angels." Where did this come from? What are its properties? Should I simply explore it to discover its properties? Is it something you recognize as a true mantra, like Sat Nam Wahe Guru is to the Sikhs?

I hope you are having a wonderful day.

Yours truly,

Joshua.

Kuntarkis replies:

Dear Joshua, My Being wishes to express thanks to you for writing your words of expression. Your brother Richard has been a little confused about his spiritual name and how it is expressed in human language.

His thoughts were upon my Being and my name. My Being picked up his thoughts and my Being visited him in his time of sleep. You Joshua were with him in your time of sleep. Richard at this time was not aware of my presence, but you were aware of my presence. Yes, that being that came was my Being and you asked how his name was pronounced.

One of the reasons you felt constricted and could not speak was that you were trying to speak from your human voice in the fourth dimension of the astral vibration. This vibration is on a completely different frequency. There was a balancing of your energies. Sound in spirit world is very different. Rather than physically speaking, it is more speaking with the mind.

Please be very careful when practising the Kundalini. The Kundalini energy which sits at the base of the human spine can cause damage to the human body and its organs if released without proper knowledge or guidance on how to release it correctly. Seek a teacher of the heart who can give you correct guidance.

Your migraines are not related to suppressed anger, but are the result of eye strain and diet. Your body is releasing toxins into your blood which in turn flows through your heart and throughout your human brain. In most cases, toxins do not cause headaches or migraines, but to some they will cause headaches and migraines. Look to eating more fresh fruits and raw vegetables on a seven day cycle and increase your water to 2 litres per day. This will help cleanse your body and will bring relief from the migraines. Avoid caffeine, nicotine, alcohol and junk food as much as possible.

The mantra you received in your time of sleep was from your spirit guide who is trying to make contact with you. It means 'search for the light within you' and yes, explore and discover further meanings. The answer is within you. Meditate in the stillness of your mind. Persist and you will discover your true self and the meaning of your life as a human being.

Be blessed in unconditional love always.

Kuntarkis.

ANGELIC VISION

Dear Kuntarkis,

About two years ago, I had a vision while meditating. In my vision, a beautiful Angelic women appeared and spelled out the name Amerylise across my third eye. I then asked her is this her name? She shook her head and told me that Amerylise is my name, and that I am of Celtic origin. Since then, I had tried to find out of which Celtic Tribe the name Amerylise originates from, but to no avail.

What I'm trying to do is, to trace a part of my roots. Please can you offer me some help?

Much Love,

April

Kuntarkis replies:

Dear April, Your vision is very interesting. The Being who came to you is one of your spirit guides. Her name is Mar'zyher and she was your twin sister in a past incarnation. Of Celtic origin, your family name was McCluskey and your family colours were brown, green and red.

The name your spirit guide gave you is correct - you were called Amerylise. The meaning of Amerylise is 'swift as the wind'.

It is always good to trace or gain the knowledge of one's past lives, but always remember the past can only be a memory of life's experiences. It is this life April, this moment that is important. What you do in this moment will shape your future.

Be blessed in unconditional love always.

Kuntarkis.

ENERGY CONNECTION

Dear Kuntarkis,

I've had a personal experience for the past three years which I had repressed in my mind and kept to myself, but at this time I really feel a need to bring it to light. I hope that you will help me to understand this particular situation better.

Three years ago, I began to purchase some medicinal products from a company in North America, and along with these products I also purchased the book that detailed their therapeutic functions. Like many books, the author's photo was printed on the back cover. The moment that I saw his photo I felt an immediate attraction and closeness to this man and his energy. There have been many occasions when this energy connection was pretty intense, at such times I felt his energy very physically near me as if he is in the same room with me. This on-going closeness that I feel with this man is very much alive today as it has been in the past three years. I have never had any contact with this man; I have never seen him and have never spoken with him. I'm in Texas and he's hundreds of miles away. I really don't know who he is other than the fact that he's the owner of the company that I purchase the products from. This uncommon experience is the first for me, and I don't know how to make sense of it. My question to you Kuntarkis is, why do I feel a wonderful closeness to this man whom I don't even know?

I try my level best to handle this personal experience with great sensitivity and respect because it involves another person whom I don't know, and he does not know me. I have absolutely no inappropriate intention and absolutely no agenda regarding this man. I have repressed it for the most part but because this experience has stuck with me for three years, therefore I want to come to terms with it and not push it away anymore. Will you help me to understand his energy connection? I'm very grateful.

P. S. About your response to my previous question, thank you so much for reminding me to be here and now. My heart has really felt incredible peace.

Very joyous love to Kuntarkis,

April.

Kuntarkis replies:

Dear April, Please realise humanity has been evolving for nearly one million years of human time, so human beings have been incarnating over and over for the same amount of time.

Reincarnation for humanity is a way for human individuals to experience and to work out their karmic debts, whether positive or negative. You and the human male you speak of have been involved in some relationship from a past incarnation, which is why you are drawn to his energies.

If the human male you speak of saw a photo of you, and he was in touch with his inner being, he may also feel what you are feeling towards your energies. Please remember April, you as a spirit being choose all your experiences before incarnating into a human body.

If both of you are meant to meet, no matter if you live thousands of miles apart, it will happen because both of you choose to. If you are not meant to meet in your current human life, then that is okay also, is it not?

See life in each life time as a moment that is passing, like a ripple in a lake. In spirit world time does not exist but in the human world of time it can seem like forever. Trust your heart in all that you seek dear April. Believe in who and what you are, for you are an infinite being of light itself, simply on a journey of self-discovery. That is what you are April.

Be blessed in unconditional love always.

Kuntarkis.

TRANSPORTATION OF ENERGY

Hello Kuntarkis,

Thank you for answering another question for me. I have had the great gift of spirit communication through channelling (I am on the questioning end...) for almost a year. It has positively influenced my life, my path and clarified my purpose. Are my 'light teachers' Nar'Karones?

To project ones energy in a split second to Nar'Kariss in meditation, (is it what my teachers call: the vast library of wisdom that surrounds the planet past the chatter of the brain..."opening your soul to the spirit and beyond") how would one actually experience this transportation of energy; since there is no physical manifestation to 'see'? Is it just that blissful, light, vibratory state I experience during meditation? Where do I go...? When I go there? Am I being taught something, or being beneficially connected in that vibratory experience?

My guidance says: "Welcome to the day that you open your soul to the spirit and beyond. You have no idea what will come through." I have been writing my life story and going over the events, releasing buried emotions and recognizing the intent, purpose and gift of each event. Is this the process that will clear up the blockages that remain? As you can feel, I am impatient to get on with fully knowing and loving myself... to completely free myself from my own bonds of illusion. What do you see as obstacles in my path? I believe I am a healing teacher of the body. In which lifetime was my personal expansion most manifested? I am learning to better communicate with my own heart and I appreciate my growth in that area, but I still find information from your broader perspective most helpful.

Thank you, Kuntarkis and Roman & Company for the light you so generously provide.

Linda.

Kuntarkis replies:

Dear Linda, to your first question, are the Nar'Karones your Teachers of Light? Your

answer is yes, that is the truth.

To your second question about projecting your spirit in a moment of time to Nar'Kariss while in meditation, is it what your teacher calls the vast library of wisdom that surrounds the planet? Your answer, there is some truth in that, but please realise you, as all human beings, are in reality the vast library of wisdom. All that is, is within each of you. It is your connection to your Soul that can and will realise the knowledge of all that has been and can be.

You are the living essence, pure consciousness. The more you purify your physical self, the more you will connect to your Soul. In many cases human beings like yourself are transported into our Light Ships because we are all interconnected, we are all one. The only difference is you are experiencing a physical existence while we are no longer in physical form or exist in a physical realm.

There is only one obstacle that all human beings need to resolve and dissolve – the human ego of self-created illusion. And yes dear Linda, unconditional love is the answer and the key that will unlock the prison that was created out of fear, from many lifetimes. Be blessed in unconditional love always.

Kuntarkis.

IMPROVING MY RELATIONSHIP: HOW?

To Kuntarkis,

Thanks for responding. I have been doing lots of research on diet, health, etc. I have been juicing lots of organic veggies and fruits and exercising on a regular basis. I appreciate your response and know in my heart that it is true. I am really going to work on feeling better about myself. Before this latest health issue occurred my husband and I were experiencing some problems. I am not sure that they were totally addressed or resolved. I am wondering if you can tell me if this problem will occur again in our future. Is there anything else I can be doing in the relationship to make it better? I know he loves me and I love him very much. I do experience anxiety over this and I am trying to work it out. Thanks again for your help. Love and Peace.

Amy.

Kuntarkis replies:

Dear Amy, Yes, there is a small thing you can do for yourself and your human male. First for you to accept yourself exactly as you are in this moment and love yourself unconditionally. Love your human male unconditionally and have no judgement or expectation. Just love him as he is and love you as you are in this moment of life. Everyone needs the comfort of human life and that is completely understandable, but remember Amy, all pain, misery and unhappiness, all negative emotions are a self-creation of all individuals. Because human beings are subjected to beliefs and conditioning, mainly formed from negative experiences and ingrained within DNA, negative emotions in so many people create confusion, shaping their present and future. Fear is one creation that affects most of humanity.

One of my favourite sayings is this: to truly love is to experience bliss, so to love who you are in unconditional love is the greatest healing for oneself and all others. Be blessed in unconditional love always Amy.

Kuntarkis.

SOUL MATES FOREVER?

Dear Roman and Kuntarkis,

Thank you for your response to my questions about love and dreams. Yes fear is definitely an illusion, created to sabotage our dreams if we allow it. It was good to be reminded of this.

I just wanted to ask you about meeting my soul mate and 'how' I can only make that happen? I have vivid dreams about a man sometimes he is with a child. We are either on a spaceship with other light beings or a parallel universe. I sense his spirit often and wonder if I will meet him in this realm. The man I am spending time with now is beautiful and we do have a lot in common on many levels. I am learning through being with him about detachment and expectations, which is unconditional love... It is a hard lesson to learn and takes a lot of reprogramming. Our 'casual' relationship is very intense on a sexual level to the point where sometimes he needs to get up and go for a swim to centre himself. I do wonder if he is just scared of what his feeling emotionally and his way of not getting to close?

I feel I need to be patient and gentle with this man as he has experienced a lotG of pain due to losing his mother and sister to cancer. I have felt he could be my soul mate as he has the qualities and essence of the man I envision myself being with. I know I am falling in love with him and wonder if his afraid of taking things to the next level or is he just in lust?

Thank you once again Love and Light.

Gabrielle.

Kuntarkis replies:

Dear Gabrielle, to wonder is like a dream. Will it be manifested into your life or is it simply a dream of desire. Always remember Gabrielle, first you have the vision - see it as imagination, then if you choose to manifest it into your own created reality, put action into it, meaning energy and thought, so it can be manifested into your physical reality. You are a very powerful being, a spirit which is a facet of your Soul, and you as the Soul are infinite in all things. It is called the power of the self from within. All lessons in human life are unbiased – human beings create the lessons to be hard or easy. That is the power of your inner self. Your lessons of your life are yours and your partner's lessons are his. The two things of life for him to learn are forgiveness and grief. He will accomplish this. Both of you are good for each other – you help each other to balance life's lessons. The dreams experience of seeing a man and child have a very special meaning. In a past life, not of your Earth, you were married to this man in your dreams and the child was yours to him. He and the child are now spirit guides to you. They will be with you throughout your current incarnation as a human being.

Remember, unconditional love is the answer to everything, you just have to believe and it will be so.

Be blessed in unconditional love always.

Kuntarkis.

I NEED MY LOAN APPROVAL: WHEN?

Hello Kuntarkis,

I am awaiting to hear from a bank in Costa Rica whether they will approve a friend of mine a loan for a project of his milk, juice and cheese company. If approved I will get a very nice commission. Maybe you can contact my beloved grandma Tina in spirit, after she passed away in 1981 everything came apart, she was so just and fair to me.

I expect a reply on May 4th 2006. Can you tell me what your insight tells you? I have endured so much anguish and despair for many years, and at this time I am unable to pay you until I get some money. You may trust me. I was born 11.29.49 at 5:40 pm in Guatemala City, Guatemala Central America currently live in El Salvador.

Hope to hear soon from you.

Regards,

Alfonso.

Kuntarkis replies:

Dear Alfonso, Waiting for news can sometimes become quite frustrating. My Being understands that your human life has had many ups and downs. Many human beings create a very negative space in their life and because of their upbringing from a child into adulthood; there has been a lot of pain and confusion.

Most human beings create their life from what they experienced from childhood. It becomes their present and in many cases their future. Always remember Alfonso what you think about yourself does become your reality.

It is very important to have a positive attitude towards yourself, to believe in yourself, to love yourself unconditionally no matter what. Never allow your past to influence your present, especially if you have experienced negative situations. Believe, truly believe that wealth and riches are flowing into your life NOW. To believe is to create and to create is to manifest that creation into your present reality.

The one you speak of, your human Grandmother, Tina Salino that you say passed over into spirit world in 1981, is not in spirit world any longer - she has passed through the light and is to be reborn into your human world very soon. She will come as a human male into your family line.

Alfonso, if you believe in yourself from your heart, then what you are expecting as a commission will come to you. Everything in your Universe is created from energy. Create positive thought always and you will create a positive outcome.

Be blessed in unconditional love always,

Kuntarkis.

SEARCHING FOR A LIFE PARTNER

Dear Kuntarkis,

My question is who is supposed to be my life partner (the one I want to have a family with). I love the one I am with now and want to be with him, but why is my family so opposed to this? What should I do? I am sad by what is happening. Please help.

Sofia.

Kuntarkis replies:

The hardest thing in life is to please your human family, especially when you feel that you need to. You are an individual and you have a right, if your heart is true, to love, to marry or just to be together with the one you love. That is called free will.

Your parents are beautiful human beings and they only want the best for you, even though it may not seem to be this way. If you truly love the one that you speak of, from your heart, then you must follow it and be happy. Parents often forget they were in love once and that they felt the need to follow their hearts!

From what I can feel, you want to please your parents because they have raised you. Yet if you let him go you may end up resenting your parents for manipulating you into making the wrong decision. Beliefs and conditioning can make you feel obligated, but you need to remember it's still your human life, and you need to make the decision that makes you happiest because you are the one who has to live with it. Each of you as human beings, need to believe in yourselves, you each have the right to be happy, and in the end only you can make that choice.

I feel from my heart that you are a beautiful human being and that you have a loving heart. Allow it to guide you. Please try to remember that only from an honest heart will the truth manifest itself. Your family feel you deserve better, but only your heart knows what is best for you. Follow your heart always.

Be Blessed.

Kuntarkis.

GOING FROM ONE RELATIONSHIP TO ANOTHER: WHY?

Dear Kuntarkis,

I'm always going from one man to another with the same traits. How do I stop this and let go of the feelings which make me do this?

Kelly.

Kuntarkis replies:

One of the greatest problems human beings grapple with is emotion which is the result of negative experiences from your past. If you have unresolved negative emotional trauma from your childhood, that alone can set the pattern in how you deal with your intimate relationships for the rest of your human life. If you do not feel good about yourself and find it difficult to deal with rejection then you will bring into your life people who will be negative towards you and so you will constantly bring the same type of partner into your life, that is, one who does not treat you very well.

So remember, like attracts like. If you are negative, then you will attract negative people. You must become positive and believe you deserve the best in life in order to attract someone who is also positive and who will love you and care about you. Learn to love yourself unconditionally and believe you are capable of doing anything you put your mind to, and you will achieve your goals.

Please also read my reply to Jennifer in the next question and use the affirmation below to help you learn to love and accept yourself as you are. With time and practice you will let go of the negative feelings and beliefs which hold you back from finding happiness.

Be Blessed.

Kuntarkis.

HOW DO I BELIEVE IN MYSELF?

Dear Kuntarkis,

I never feel good about myself, especially when I look in the mirror. I'm always negative towards myself even though my friends often tell me I'm a beautiful and a kind person. But I get embarrassed and I don't believe them. What can I do to start believing in myself?

Jennifer.

Kuntarkis replies:

Jennifer, I have looked into your heart and I know you are a beautiful human being, and that you do have a kind and loving heart. You can overcome any negative situation in your human life because you are a strong human being. Each time you look into your mirror and feel negative towards yourself, right at that moment you have the choice, with the power that is within you, to change what you feel about yourself into a positive affirmation just by saying and believing from your heart the following words:

> I am a beautiful person here and now, and I have a lot to give.
> I express my true feelings from my heart and soul.
> I know I am worthy of love, and I can and will say "I love
> and respect myself now and forever more".
> I am love. I am love. I am love.

Please try to remember, by being positive towards yourself you will begin to change your negative beliefs into positive ones. I believe in you Jennifer.

Be Blessed.

Kuntarkis.

LEARNING TO FORGIVE MYSELF

Dear Kuntarkis,

I am overjoyed in reading the stories on your website. How you explain about human ego and the negative emotions humanity has created, I have always been an angry person and would hold grudges against people who cause me pain. After reading some of the stories (Fear of Humanity, One Incarnation to the Next, You Are What You Eat and What You Think, and especially Who is the enemy and Unseen Forces) I have begun to really look at myself, and it really hurts. Yet I can feel as if I have let go of some pain that I have been carrying around most of my life. I'm starting to feel good about myself. Learning to forgive myself and love myself, and it is a real nightmare. I feel I am getting there and I just want to say thank you for your help and guidance, especially the truth.

Nelly.

Kuntarkis replies:

Dear Nelly, My Being thanks you for taking the precious moments of your human life to express your words of wonderment to your own self-growth.

It is the truth that self-hating emotions are humanity's downfall, and have been for the past 928,000 years of human history. Only when each individual steps beyond their self-created illusions, which in reality is their human Ego, will then and only then, the truth be manifested to each human being.

True forgiveness from the heart is the key to opening your inner being. Unconditional love is the key to freedom from all self-created pain. Knowledge is the key to Enlightenment, and true knowledge is encoded within all life, for all of life is equal. All pain, anger, hatred, violence, lies, domination, wars, and religions are man's creation of a negative vibration, which is all the fears of the human Ego. This must be dissolved back into the nothingness from which it was first created before the real can come into being. Only through unconditional love Nelly can the truth be manifest in each human individual.

Please express to my Being if I may be of help to you further on your spiritual journey. Be blessed in the love and the Light of Creation's totality always, for you are indeed a beautiful human being Nelly.

Kuntarkis.

FEAR OF CREATING LUNG CANCER: WHY?

Dear Kuntarkis,

I have no symptoms of lung cancer, but I have smoked for over 40 years but I have just quit. I am still quite anxious about getting lung cancer, mostly because they say there is no cure for it. I would extremely appreciate any help you could give me.

Thank you,

Dick

Kuntarkis replies:

Dear Dick, Thank you for taking the moments to express to my being your concerns about the human dis-ease lung cancer. All types of human dis-ease have escalated over the last sixty years of human time, and especially over the last 27 years, mainly because of lifestyle and the enormous increase in pollution on this most precious Earth.

The human body can repair and cure any human dis-ease that attacks it, but it is most important to put the right foods and thoughts into your human body. If unhealthy nutritiously devoid foods are consumed, and negative thoughts plague the human brain, then over a long period of time the human body will eventually break down and dis-ease will follow.

Smoking is a poison. When a cigarette is lit, many hundreds of harmful chemicals are released. These chemicals destroy the immune system, as well as doing great damage at a cellular level. The immune system is a human being's only line of defence against illness, and the right nutrition must be provided to protect you for the length of your physical life.

What is unfortunate with your human doctors is many are ignorant to the truth, especially when they tell an individual "there is no cure". Roman would not have survived if he had listened to his doctor. Roman believed that all disease can be cured if one is willing to believe in the power of the self. All that is created can be uncreated. It is all in one's attitude. There are on your earth thousands of human beings who have cured their fatal illnesses with natural non-invasive methods of healing.

Negative thoughts over a long period of time will also create illness and imbalances in the human body, and these can and do lead to dis-eases. There is a saying: "What one thinks, one becomes". Just as truthful and accurate is the saying: "What one eats, one becomes".

Dick, always be positive in your thoughts, and care for your human body by consuming nutritious foods and drinking plenty of water. When you care for human body and support it with a positive mind, you will create the balance of mind, body and spirit, and good health and happiness will be your reward.

Dick may love and peace be with you throughout your human life.

Kuntarkis.

THANKS FROM FELLOW LIGHT WORKERS

Dear Fellow Light worker,

I have found your site accidentally on purpose. Thank you for doing what you are doing. As we are all connected by one consciousness, one soul. All it takes is for one part of that soul to help the rest of it evolve. Just the fact that you are helping people to awaken from the slumber of ignorance into the oceans of Light is changing the world and healing it. We all have our parts to play on this mission, and none are greater or less in importance.

Thank you for working on the side of the Light. Thank you for teaching unconditional love and acceptance, and thank you for simply being and existing with all of us on this Earth Plane in the year called 2008. I thank the All for using you and your gift of writing and speech to help heal others, and I thank the All for giving me the gift of clear vision to paint the healing images for others that I do. I send love and light to you and your circle as well as good health and prosperity.

Peace and love always, Alina.

Kuntarkis replies:

Dear Alina, My Being thanks you for your kind and loving words of expression. You have a beautiful heart of unconditional love, and yes one single human being who discovers self-realisation of their true self, and accepts the path of unconditional love can truly make a great difference to all of humanity and all of life.

Your gift of love is through your inner visions and expressed through your hands. My Being can feel your messages of love to all of life. You are truly blessed in the Light that exists in all Universes, as all of life is a part of each other. We are all connected to the Light that is divine. Be blessed in the Love and the Light of Creation's totality always dear Alina.

Kuntarkis.

PSORIASIS CONDITION

Hi Kuntarkis,

I have been suffering from what looks like Psoriasis in certain places on my scalp, like behind the ears. I have also found round patches on my back, which seem to get larger. I have tried certain lotions but the flaky scalp keeps coming back. Do you have any herbal remedies which can use to treat this condition? I will be very grateful if you can help me.

Thanks,

Uzman

Kuntarkis replies:

Dear Uzman, Your condition of psoriasis is of a toxic build up in your human system, which has been caused for several reasons. Please have an open mind and an open heart when I give you a few examples of why you are suffering Uzman. Do not place any judgement upon it, for if you were to research what my Being is about to express, you would come to the same conclusion.

At this present moment in human time, your Earth is dangerously polluted with all sorts of chemicals - in your air, waterways, and in your soils. Also, in the foods you buy like fast foods, cigarettes, alcohol, packaging, and personal products such as shampoos, soaps, toothpastes, make-up, deodorants, and household cleaning products. All are full of chemicals which contain harmful toxins, and over a long period of time these chemicals build up in your human body and cause a number of illnesses and conditions within the human body.

There are companies on your Earth that produce toxin-free products which are not harmful to your human body. It would be worth your while to research them. Your problem Uzman can be overcome if you can make your life as free of these poisons as much as you can. Start by looking at your personal care products. This will take a little effort, so go to places like your health food shops and natural health practitioners. Ask them for their advice. My Being believes they can help you. The power is in your hands.

Be Blessed in Love and Light always.

Kuntarkis.

LOST SIGHT OF TRUTH & DIRECTION

Hey to whoever,

Where did you come up with evil spirits controlling governments and such? This ruined your paradigm of truth to me. Greg

Kuntarkis replies:

Dear Greg, My Being thanks you for writing to express your thoughts.

Truth itself is neither negative nor positive, it simply is. There is no right or wrong, good or bad, or even as you put it, 'evil'. What does exist is the human Ego and it is each individual's choice which direction one takes in life. One of the greatest threats to humanity is fear, and it is fear that creates all negativity on your Earth. If you open your heart and mind to the truth you will see with your own eyes what is being created from a negative aspect all over your world. It does not matter to my Being if you wish to stay blind - that is your free will.

To my Being and those like myself, we see everything for what it is, simply lessons in life. To evolve and grow consciously as an entity one must recognise the truth that is all around you, be it negative or positive. This truth, no matter how painful or frightening it may be, is what will set you free from the human Ego. Take knowledge for what it is and see the truth with your heart, not with the conditioning of your human brain or the fear of your human Ego. The brain will only give you the past. The Ego will only give you what you are comfortable with and willing to accept. That does not make it the truth.

Be Blessed in Love and Light always.

Kuntarkis.

Greg replies,

I see what you are saying. Thank you for opening my eyes. It is so sad. I send love.

Greg

BEEN BLIND FROM THE AGE OF SIX YEARS OLD

Hello Kuntarkis,

My name is Judy and I am 27 years old. I have been blind since six. No one has been able to determine why I went blind.

I have been going to a spiritual church for the last year and I must say I'm enjoying myself, meeting a lot of nice people who have been helping me understand why I am blind in this life. They have explained Karma to me and I was wondering if you could tell me if I was a bad person in my last life.

Thankyou for taking this message.

Judy

Kuntarkis replies:

Dear Judy, You are indeed a brave human being and you have a beautiful heart of love and compassion. My Being is pleased for you that you have found friends who are willing to help and to guide you dear Judy to a deeper understanding of your present circumstances.

Karma is non-judgemental, neither negative nor positive. Karma exists in this third vibration for one purpose only – it brings balance to all of life, to help individuals grow in consciousness beyond the third vibration of matter. Humanity must let go of the past by learning to live in the moment of life and learning to forgive all past hurts.

Human negativity must be dissolved in this third vibration so each individual can step beyond human ego. Judy, do not see yourself as having been a bad person in your previous life. Try to accept that the past is the past, and by forgiving the past, you allow yourself to live in the moment. It is the moment that will create your future, however you wish it to be. Each human being on this planet Earth determines the outcome of each incarnation form one life to the next. So in reality Judy, you are the driver of your past, present and future.

Judy, there are some people you need to forgive and you know who they are. Through forgiveness the individual can let go of their negative emotions and allow the balance to be within. Loving yourself as you are, in unconditional love, will break the chain of the past and fill your inner and outer being with love. No one in reality is a bad person. It is the circumstances of one's life that shape the human Ego, whatever the reasons.

The Light is within all of humanity and each individual must reconnect to the Light to see the false and gain the truth. Judy, you may find interesting what my Being is about to express. There is a technique that was taught long ago on my planet Nar'Kariss for blindness of the eyes. Even though the eyes do not see from a physical perspective, there is an inner eye, on your planet referred to as the Third Eye. The Nar'Karones taught the blind to use the inner eye. It takes practice and discipline. Judy if you wish my Being to explain the technique please let me know. I would be honoured to help.

Be Blessed dear Judy in Love and Light always. And trust yourself and your decisions.

Kuntarkis.

LIVING WITH BRAIN DAMAGE

Hello Kuntarkis,

I have a brief question on your view on reincarnation. I was born normal, then had an accident, then brain damage. The brain does not register much, although once smart, like the person disappeared and left a blank space.

I was regular person walking across the street got hit by bicyclist, then faculties were not there, brain went flat and empty. The head was just grilled by the impact of head injury (head slamming against the pavement) it just roasted all the connections in my head and grilled everything. The senses were taken out, the person was taken out, and their intelligence was taken out.

My question is rather odd but wonder how one can drop this condition and get a normal human birth again. With a normal human head again that has not been brain damaged but contains whole person like was originally born as. Anyway wondered people's views on reincarnation, and if you are mentally disabled in one life, although started out normal, can you get a new "package" for next life just to have a normal human head that has a person in it.

Thanks for any feedback. Know these are odd questions. Wanted to get spiritual perspective.

Sincerely Maura

Kuntarkis replies:

Dear Maura, Your pain and suffering can sometimes be, or cause, a lot of confusion from a human understanding, especially when it involves the individual. It is very hard for humanity to understand that human life on this Earth is a schoolroom of learning and experiencing lessons of life, from one life to the next. Everything that happens to a human being throughout their life has a purpose and one of the lessons is to let go of the past, for the past has been haunting humanity throughout history, and keeps creating the present and the future, be it negative or positive.

To let go of the past through forgiveness and unconditional love is to live in the moment without expectations and judgement. It allows conscious growth for the individual to expand their awareness and understanding, which will pass over into their next incarnation and allow the individual to live in joy, peace and harmony. What you are experiencing dear Maura is pain, sorrow, anger and confusion, and it is a natural emotion.

Humanity has created a very negative past and has been recreating this past over and over again. Every human being on this Earth has played a part in its creation. It is called on your Earth Karma - what is done unto another will return unto you. It is the balance of life and has been going on for over 928,000 years of human time.

You may say all this sounds so negative. Yes, my Being would agree with you, and you dear beautiful Maura may ask then how do we stop all this negative creation so we do not carry it over to our next incarnation? The answer is very simple. Learn to let go of the past and forgive all that has been created upon you from a negative experience. Once an individual has truly forgiven themselves and others, from the heart, all the negative experiences of life, those experiences will become a memory of the past, not judged as good or bad, right or wrong, negative or positive. Only then will unconditional love flow from the heart and the lessons of life will be accepted and learned. Then human being will see with new eyes and there will no longer be negative thought or actions. Unconditional love will bond all of humanity and human Ego will no longer exist. This is the path to conscious growth and evolution.

You Maura have a great opportunity before you. Put aside your anger, pain and frustration, put aside your negative emotions of human Ego, and see with new eyes by becoming quiet in your mind and stopping your human chatter of confusion. Feel your love from your heart and go within yourself. Deep within your being, your inner essence of divine light, there lies the strength and the courage to overcome all your anger, pain and confusion.

It may take some time, but persist and the inner truth will set you free and will give you an understanding far greater then what you are experiencing at this moment of human time. My Being will visit you in your time of sleep and we will communicate on another level of consciousness.

Be blessed in the Love and the Light of Creation always.

Kuntarkis.

WHAT IS THE PURPOSE OF HUMAN LIFE?

Dear Kuntarkis,

I have two questions (I would be very grateful for any answers):

1. What is my purpose in life?
2. Is my present relationship my true soul mate, or am I just fooling myself?

Thanks,

Robert S.

Kuntarkis replies:

Dear Robert, You asked what your purpose is in your human life. One of the most honest

answers would be, for you Robert, to just be - to live from moment to moment, to enjoy all your experiences, to live your human life in harmony with all other forms of life. This means to live without expectations or stress, to know every decision you make is the right one for you and to live your life in balance and having the knowing that you, Robert, can have the courage and strength to create whatever you choose to be or do with your human life in this incarnation of yours.

Your purpose in this lifetime is to gain the knowledge and understanding to love yourself unconditionally with no rules or expectations. By doing this you will love all other forms of life. A soul mate or twin flame is a bond between two souls who have been together through many lifetimes. Soul mates know the truth about each other. Become silent in your mind and look into each other's eyes with love from your heart - this will confirm what you desire as truth about being soul mates.

Be Blessed dear Robert in love always and trust yourself in all things.

Kuntarkis.

WATER ELEMENT: CAN IT TAKE ON HUMAN FORM?

Hi, my name is Janet.

I stumbled across this site when I was looking deeper into some things I heard... I suppose you would say telepathically. Throughout my life I have been very different. As a child I would see rainbow flashes of light and constantly ask my parents why people did things. When I got older I heard it was unnatural and crazy and started to block out my connection to the spirits.

During the past two years I have realized how wrong everyone was and have been opening my connections back up. Yes, I'm sure you're waiting for the point. I am basically a classic water element (born March 5, 1986) and have always loved water naturally and pretended to be a mermaid when my friends and I would play. Well two weeks ago I was taking a shower and, as usual, I was completely lost to everything but the feeling of water. Then I heard a voice (I often describe it as him) and he said I was "a typical water elemental". This was the first time I remember hearing the word. The voice also said something about me and the other elementals in "human form" would soon have to come to a decision.

After the experience I went and looked up elementals in one of my books and read the part saying that elementals had no physical form and have been trying to find out how and why an elemental would be born into human form. I still hear this voice when I'm most Intune with water (watching rain, shower, etc.) but it won't tell me much more it just constantly asks what I think. When I saw your site it seemed like maybe I could tell this to you without you thinking I'm some nutcase. I would appreciate hearing back from you and maybe what you think about all of this. Thank you.

Janet.

Kuntarkis replies:

Dear Janet, You are a very brave and beautiful human being. All human beings have the gift of sight and sound into other vibrations and realms. Unfortunately very few take notice of their natural abilities. They live a life of beliefs and conditioning which keeps them locked in their prison of logic. Logic is good, but there must be a balance of logic and creativeness. Never think or believe it is unnatural or crazy.

When you were a little child, around the age of three, you would see all different colours before your human eyes, and in those colours were shapes of little elements – little Beings of Light that live in the vibration of the fourth dimension.

You are one of those elements and yes, it is of the water element. The voice you hear is also of the water element and it is wondering what human life is all about. Listen Janet to your inner Being of Light where all truth is manifested, from your heart centre.

There is so very much more to your existence as a physical being as well as an infinite Being of Light. Believe in yourself as my Being believes in you. You can rise above the human ego of illusion, and then you will be able to see other worlds of existence, and yes, the element vibration can teach you and awaken your own knowledge of truth.

Be Blessed dear Janet in unconditional love. May you find what you seek from your heart?

Kuntarkis.

ELF KINGDOM: REAL OR NOT?

Dear Kuntarkis,

Best wishes: Still reporting to your site faithfully! It is truly helping me spiritually and mentally! Keep up the great work!

I saw a being that was not human during an astral travel (dream). There is no doubt that what I saw was a figment of my imagination; it was very real indeed! This particular incident stands out in my mind because I've rarely seen beings that were not of human in my dreams or during astral travel (there was only one other time). This being appeared to be a female child... She had very pale white skin with small reddish/brownish blotches or freckles all over her face and neck. She had a long narrow limp neck that appeared to be too weak to support her head. Her hair was scraggly and blonde and she had an extremely sharp narrow nose with paper thin lips and yellow alligator looking eyes. Could you tell me what kind of being was she? The interesting thing is that she appeared to look at me as if she knew who I was... She also appeared to be unhappy... Anything you can tell me would be deeply appreciated!

<u>Kuntarkis replies:</u>

Dear Human Being, Thank you for your warm wishes and kind words. It is good to see that theg website is of help to all who seek understanding and knowledge. Every human being on your Earth at this moment has the knowledge and the wisdom within their Being. It has always been there - you only have to believe, truly believe from the heart.

Imagination is what we the Nar'Karones use to create and manifest into our presence. It is a simple process to think, and to see in our mind's eye. Once we see it we create it by manifesting it into form from living energy, the light that exists in all universes and all forms of life.

You as human beings have the same knowing, but it is believing in yourselves, truly believing that you are all a part of the same infinite energy that all of life has been created from. The only difference between life forms is evolution. The less negative emotions, beliefs and conditioning of the human Ego, the more the individual will break free of the prison that all humanity has created in fear, and they will connect with the light of Creation that is within all life forms.

What you experienced in your astral vibration and how you described the Being you saw is in fact an Elemental. That Elemental is of the Elf Kingdom and they are the ones who look after Mother Earth and all of nature. They are all known as elements - fire, water, earth, air, spirit. They are the essence of Creation and do a great service to all of humanity and all forms of life that exist on your Earth. They do try to make contact with humans if they are willing to listen and learn of the knowledge they can give. They have a great fear of humans and are very cautious with who they make contact. The reason they are unhappy is because of the violence man places upon man, and the slaughter of other forms of life for man's pleasure and consumption.

They are peaceful beings and see humans as aggressive predators. The Element Kingdom believe that all of Creation's life forms are precious, and when a life form is destroyed, be it human, animal, plant (such as vast areas of forest) or earth (such as vast amounts of mining), that violent action has an effect on nature and creates an imbalance which creates negative energy, and this in turn must be brought back into balance.

Be Blessed dear human being in love always.

Kuntarkis.

ADDICTED TO SEX: WHY?

Hello Kuntarkis,

How does one let go of a habit that has been with you for 23 years? I have tried everything, even suicide, and I was too chicken to go through with it. My habit is sex – I just can't get enough. I was wondering from a spiritual point of view, can you give me some guidance. I would be most grateful.

Desperate.

Kuntarkis replies:

Dear Human Being, It all began when you were only a child and you do remember what my Being is expressing to you. Your sexual experiences began at an early age. My Being is not condemning your father, just bringing the truth to the surface so the pain can be felt and your father can be forgiven. But especially forgive yourself. It was not your fault. You were not to blame, for you were highly conditioned at an age where you did not understand right from wrong.

To you it was a game between you and your human father. It was your father who needed to resolve his own created negative emotions. Those emotions were placed upon you and for the past 30 years of your human life, it was reinforced as a conditioning, as a belief, genetically encoded into your way of thinking, and yes, it helped destroy your relationships and left you susceptible to being used by human males.

There is no drug on your Earth that can resolve the conditioning. My Being can only give you some guidance so you can begin the process of forgiveness of your father and of yourself. There is a saying on your Earth – no gain without pain. The pain must come to the surface so it can be resolved. It must and needs to be recognised. That is why human beings incarnate so many times, to learn and to forgive, to manifest through their heart centre the unconditional love that is present in all human beings.

Your world is simply a large stage, or as some call it, a schoolroom, so one can gain the truth which will release one from all self-created negative emotions that have been created over many human life times. My Being understands what you have been feeling, but never give up. This is a lesson and by overcoming the lesson it will make you a much stronger and wiser human being. Learn to channel your energies and step beyond your conditioning. You are a creative human being. Again, channel your energies to change your direction in your present incarnation. Believe you can, truly believe you can, and you will.

Be blessed in love and light always.

Kuntarkis.

DREAMING OF LOST HUSBAND

Dear Kuntarkis,

My name is Amie. I am 32 and I have a 6 year old son. We lost our most precious gift, my husband. His name was John and he was taken from us on December 22, 3 days before Christmas. The emptiness that I have felt I could never describe. I loved him with all my heart and I miss him beyond words. Six nights ago in my dreams he appeared. He was so beautiful and very calm. There seemed to be a yellowish light all around his body.

He told me as he looked into my eyes that he was so sorry he cannot be with me anymore and that he loves us with all his heart. He also said he would be with me again – next time. He then disappeared before my eyes, and I woke up in tears. I must have cried for hours before going back to sleep. Can you tell me, did the meeting really happen? I will love him always.

Amie.

Kuntarkis replies:

Dear Amie, to love for a moment is more precious than to be with someone you do not feel love for in an entire lifetime. You and John are indeed very special soul mates who have been together in many incarnations, and yes you both will be together in your next incarnation. What you experienced in your time of sleep was in fact reality. It was his way of making contact with you and it will happen many more times to come. Do you remember when you first met, he would look at you and into your eyes and say if there was any such thing called an angel, and then I am the luckiest man alive to have one in my presence. You do remember, don't you Amie, because he meant it and he loves you beyond human life.

Give the same love and understanding to your son and teach him all about the spirit world, so he can gain the awareness and knowledge that there is more than just human existence. Be Blessed dear Amie in love and light always.

Kuntarkis.

GETTING PEOPLE TO LIKE ME

To Kuntarkis,

I was reading some of your articles about emotions and feelings, how they are very different, and I can see what you mean. How do I get people to accept and like me? Thanks.

Kuntarkis replies:

Dear Human Being, It is not about getting other human beings to accept and like you. It's all begins with self-acceptance and liking yourself. My

Being knows you are a very interesting and special human being who has a lot to give and offer to others. Stop trying so hard for others to like you. Stop trying to be like them so they will accept you. Be the best you can be at what you do and who you are. Express self-confidence and only speak when you have something to say that will show them you are confident.

Try this exercise. Stand in front of a mirror, and say these words over and over again: I am a very confident and well-spoken individual. I see in this mirror that I am a beautiful human being with special talents. I have self-worth in all I do, and I amaze myself in all that I do. I love myself and respect my individuality, and I can express myself in public or with my friends with complete confidence.

Remember dear Human Being, each time you feel low, say those words to yourself and feel their truth and strength. Most of all, believe in your own self-worth. Never be scared of change and always be willing to grow and learn new ideas. Remain open to change and new experiences and you will always have the courage and confidence to take on new challenges. It all begins with you, the individual. Like yourself and others will be attracted to you.

Be blessed in love and light always.

Kuntarkis.

DAUGHTER'S FIRST CHILD

Dear Kuntarkis,

I am a retired man aged 59. My daughter is expecting her first child, estimated date of delivery being end May - early Jun 2004. My wife and I are at present with our daughter to see the safe delivery of our grandchild. We are of course very excited and thrilled and awaiting the arrival of a new life in the family and into this world. Please say something to welcome our grandchild onto this planet! Thank you.

Anxious Grandfather to be.

Kuntarkis replies:

Dear Human Being, We the Nar'Karones believe that life in all its forms, throughout all universes, is most precious. We congratulate you! Your human family awaits the arrival of a human baby which will bring great joy to all your hearts.

May joy, love, peace and happiness always follow each of you dear human beings throughout your lives? Always remember unconditional love is the key to bliss.

Be blessed in love always.

Kuntarkis.

FAILED ASCENSION: HOW COME?

Dear Kuntarkis,

I believe this was supposed to be my last lifetime. I was supposed to reunite with my other half and become whole. I went through ascension and I failed. My true love whose name is Michael and my twin flame Maher were not there for me which leads me to believe they didn't love me. So my truelove, twin flame and soul mates didn't want me. My soul became extinct and God just watched. I could never imagine something horrible like this could exist. I am very angry at God for not helping me, and I never felt my guides or angels help me much, and they didn't keep me on my destiny. Why do some people have visitations from angels or guides and I begged God for this because I knew the severity of the situation. I will never be able to forgive him or forget it was too cruel. I feel I'm in a nightmare and I wish I could just wake up. My question is, is it possible for my soul to go back in time so I can have another chance to redo what happened?

I'm also angry because apart from my truelove and twin flame, my soul mates didn't want me, and my friends and family didn't even care if I lived or died. I guess I know what a fallen angel is and what Adam and Eve experienced. If I say life or people or God or my loves didn't care about me how could I love now. Now God tries to love me now that it's too late, I lost my innocence, sexual passion, flowering for ascension, hopes, all my dreams everything is lost and can't be returned and now God gives me love when it's too late. And now spirit comes to me, when I begged with all my heart and soul. I would experience my soul crying. I feel that during ascension it was a special occasion God created and he made everyone fall in love and it's as if there was this huge party and I was left out. I also feel that I wasn't worthy to have a human being, instead I connected with etheric parasites - spikers and incubus. So how could I love people they weren't there for me before and now my soul became extinct it's too late?

Also I feel I didn't ascend and my soul group did ascend without me, and because I wasn't able to ascend I feel I was put in a lower vibration maybe another world line or another planet that is a replica of planet earth. Did these two things happen, am I sensing correctly? Can you tell me a bit what Michael and Maher felt?

Also I feel because of my soul becoming extinct and my "house burnt down" from the pain, that it is the end for me, that there is no more purpose for me to live - for this life it feels as if for example when someone has a terminal illness and they sense they will die, but I feel it's the end also for all my lifetimes, that I finished everything and have no more purpose and I learnt all my lessons, is this true again, am I sensing correctly?

If so than I would like God to make me leave this plane, I don't want to live anymore, why is he keeping me here against my will? I also have a lot of dread, I sense danger or that it's the end for people to, will there be a disaster soon maybe the earth changes?

I know these are a lot of questions, but if you could answer them it would make a big difference in my life. Thank you for all your help, and I appreciate your time.

Love and light.

Diane.

Kuntarkis replies:

Dear Diane, You have most certainly chosen a confusing incarnation in your present human life. Even though your path can look to be cruel, please always remember that you alone, the individual, choose your lessons and life experiences. Every human being is the creator of their own lessons of life, be they negative or positive experiences.

One thing must be understood – no-one ever fails. You expressed Diane that you failed at your ascension. In reality you did not fail. You judged yourself from negative emotions, based on your beliefs and conditioning from your human life. As a human child you were never encouraged to be creative, to believe in yourself, or to think for yourself as an individual, so you have always believed others would give you the answers to your own created problems.

You believe your true love and twin flame did not love you or want you. Again, you look to be loved and accepted by others when in reality love is within all human beings. Love comes from the heart centre and must be felt and accepted by you first before you can accept love from others.

Diane, you are love in the moment of life. You have been love always but you alone must come to this SELF-REALISATION. Only when you accept your own unconditional love can you begin to allow yourself to accept love from others. You are not alone - this is humanity's biggest lesson.

You expressed to my Being that you are very angry with your human god. In reality Diane, you are angry with yourself. Taking responsibility for your own self-created feelings can be very painful, but it is a part of learning. You also expressed that you will never be able to forgive your god. What you are expressing is that you can never forgive yourself. Only through forgiveness can you open up to your unconditional love, the love that all human beings are a part of. Forgiveness is the key to freedom from all your pain and confusion.

Stop looking for others to love you and accept yourself as you are. It all begins with you. Life can be bliss or life can be a misery. It is a simple choice – you have the power and free will to choose.

One of the hardest lessons for human beings is truth. Most do not want to know the truth yet the truth will set you free from self-created pain and misery. If you truly want to transform your mind, your Being, your awareness and your understanding to higher vibrations, first accept yourself and be responsible for what you feel and all your self-created actions in your present life. Look to yourself for the answers. The power, strength and courage is within you. Through the stillness of your mind in meditation you will discover your true self and unconditional love for your being.

Diane, everything you are experiencing at this present moment in your human life is fear, self-created fear, which has created your confusion. You are living in your negative emotions – like being on auto-pilot. Stop, relax for a moment and go beyond your emotions. Step outside of yourself and observe your actions and thoughts. You will begin to see the truth, the illusions of your own creation.

Be blessed in love always.

Kuntarkis.

NERFERTITE: WHO IS SHE?

Hi Kuntarkis,

Just wanted to say thankyou for your wonderful site, I love reading the views of Kuntarkis. Thank you for bringing some reality and sense to many of my similar views. I was wondering if you could share some information out of the book of knowledge with me about Nefertiti. I'm ready for what you have to say about her. I feel a lot of negativity towards her but cannot help but be drawn to the true story of her life. Information on this subject however brings no personal satisfaction and is very hard if not impossible to pick up on. I would greatly appreciate any assistance you could offer me on this matter, thankyou. You must hear it all the time but keep up your wonderful work, you bring inspiration and light to all of us whom you touch, you rock!!! Thanks again.

Happy thoughts and smiles to you.

Regards Jo.

Kuntarkis replies:

Dear Jo, My Being thanks you for your kind words - it is always encouraging to receive kind words and thanks for this site! As you are aware, this site is simply to put forward knowledge for all human beings so it may give all the opportunity to become aware and to help the individual to grow consciously and to let go of the past. Once the human ego is dissolved into the nothingness there will be peace, harmony and balance amongst all human beings. Unconditional love will foster brotherhood and sisterhood throughout all civilisations and cultures.

To your question regarding Nefertiti, yes, she created a great deal of negativity during that lifetime. She lived a very privileged life as a human being. Her human parents did her wrong from a physical perspective by teaching her that she was better and greater than anyone else, that she was above others and could have and take anything she wanted.

Unfortunately this is exactly what she did. She used her wealth, social position and physical appearance to get what she wanted. She may have been physically beautiful on the outside but her heart was cruel and cold. She became a clone of her human father – wanting and taking but never giving, unlike her mother who was a very quiet woman. Nefertiti had two brothers –one she got on with very well, but the other who was two years her junior she constantly fought with him, especially when it came to power. The younger brother was a soldier who became a commander of the army. Nefertiti hated her younger brother and manipulated a soldier to cause his death.

What is truly sad is the lack of realisation that every negative (or positive) action is carried over into other incarnations – what is done unto one will be done unto the other. Nefertiti created a very negative existence during that incarnation and since then she has had four incarnations to this present moment in human time.

Dear Jo, Nefertiti is presently living as a human woman in a place called America. Her younger brother who she conspired to have murdered is also living in America at this moment. The reason they are incarnated in the same society at the same time is their human karma – the need to bring balance back into their union by paying it back or to forgive the past deed.

Unconditional love opens all human beings to the greater awareness of infinite knowledge of the past, present and even the future. It allows the individual to step beyond their past so it does not continually create their present and future. Unconditional love brings the realisation that it is alright to forgive and let go, to move on to new experiences of life.

Be blessed in love always.

Kuntarkis.

RECURRING DREAMS: QUITE CONCERNED?

Kuntarkis,

Please help me to understand the reasons why I have had recurring dreams of being shot in the head? The dreams are so real that I truly feel it - the heat, the sound of the gunfire and the stinging sensation of it going into my head. The thing that makes these experiences all the more interesting is that all of the scenes in which I am getting shot, were in different places under different circumstances. It's so very puzzling to me. Anyway, your help in understanding what this dream is telling me is greatly appreciated.

Kuntarkis replies:

Dear Human Being, in your time of human sleep your astral body leaves your physical body. Your experiences vary depending on your emotional state. In many cases, whatever the individual experiences throughout the day, many will experience those events during their time of sleep. This can be very confusing and even causes fear.

These experiences during sleep time can and do hold the answers an individual seeks on a subconscious and conscious level. These experiences can even be based on past incarnations. It all depends on the individual, influenced by their life experiences – negative or positive emotions, beliefs, fears, expectations, what makes one happy. It all plays a part.

From what you have described about your dreams, you have a fear of being shot. In fact, dear Human Being, you have a fear of death. This fear comes from past incarnations and still haunts you in your current incarnation.

Human death of the physical self is simply a form of transformation from one existence of living in a physical human body to a non-physical form, or straight back into another physical form. The purpose of physical life is to learn, and once lessons are complete, the physical shell has no further use to your spirit being, which is infinite, endless, timeless and eternal.

Yes, human dreams can be very puzzling, but see them as experiences, neither negative nor positive. Human dreams are a combination of fears, your understanding, and your level of thinking, beliefs and conditioning. One thing also must be expressed, you the individual are in fact the creator of all your Dream experiences.

Be blessed in love dear human being.

Kuntarkis.

PARANORMAL EXPERIENCES: HELP ME UNDERSTAND?

Peace and Love to Kuntarkis,

Please help me to make sense of a couple of things... For quite some time now, I have been trying to understand an experience that I had that was quite paranormal. It happened while I was asleep on a couch one early evening. While my eyes were closed, I suddenly became consciously aware that my etheric arms were disconnecting from my physical arms. Then, my etheric arms slowly came up and out of my physical arms in an arch like form. My index fingers on both sides of my etheric arms pointed down and touched the space on my forehead, slightly above my eyebrows. As soon as my etheric fingers touched my forehead, I saw and felt a wave of blue static electricity. From there, I saw like a giant wall of golden numbers, zeroes and ones, in different combinations (like computer codes). These number codes were moving slowly in an upward motion. Out of these computer like codes images and drawings come in and out of these codes. The two strongest images that I remembered were of the boat blueprint of the African slaves who were brought over to America and images of a Native American holding or shaking hands of a pale complexioned blonde haired white man. Still to this day, all I could figure was that this was some kind of conscious upload but I don't know where to or why? Please shed some light on what this experience was about.

Also, do we (humans) incarnate over and over again within the same racial collective conscious or do we actually incarnate into different races? A close African American female friend, said that she vividly remembers being a white male on his death bed in a hospital before her incarnation now. I have always known and felt that I have been on earth many times as a female (I am an African American male) but anything further than that has never been clear... just wondering... Anyway ... your time in answering these questions is sincerely appreciated.

Tony.

Kuntarkis replies:

Dear Tony, Yes, you were having what is called an outer body experience where your astral body was disconnecting with your physical body. Your physical body was in a form of light trance, allowing you're astral to stretch outwardly and disconnecting with full awareness of what was happening. Once your astral body touched your third eye, centred just above your eyebrows, it allowed you to experience what you refer to as paranormal.

It is a common and natural occurrence when in a trance state to see many colour combinations or a single colour, like the colour gold you were seeing in your experience. The colour gold relates to being or becoming enlightened, one who has future visions, one who is a natural healer of the light, and one who seeks knowledge beyond the physical realm.

The numbers, ones and zeroes, are a map of your human future. The answer to that part of your experience will express itself to you as you progress throughout your human life. The boat blueprint of the African slaves which you describe was a vision of your past incarnation. You were a girl slave brought to the Country of America in your human year 1791 in the month of August. You had two older brothers on the same ship with you. The Native American and white man shaking hands represented a guide introducing himself to you, but it is for you to learn which man represented your being in the vision you had.

Yes, you were having a conscious upload of information and it will express itself to you at different times throughout your life in order for you to learn from and grow consciously.

Many human beings incarnate over and over again in the same family lines and also in different cultures, but usually always with the same souls, so if the souls choose to be for example Asian of African American in a series of incarnations, then you can be Asian or African American for a number of incarnations with those souls until the lessons you have each chosen to learn with and from each other have been achieved – it all depends on the level of understanding and the willingness to grow, to forgive and to accept your own unconditional love, the love that is within all human beings.

Just remember, the more negative actions an individual creates the more negative karma is created. There is a saying on your Earth: "Walk gently upon the Earth". Essentially, harm no-one; love yourself and all forms of life no matter what they may be; be forgiving and understanding; express unconditional love to all without any form of judgement. That Tony is a true human being, one who is balanced with all things. The only karma that is created is infinite wisdom.

May love always fill your heart dear Tony and May you become the light for all to see?

Be blessed always in love.

Kuntarkis.

BEING FIT IN MIND AND BODY

My question is, how I become fit, meaning a fit mind and body. What do I have to do to accomplish this? Please give me a sensible answer.

Kenny.

Kuntarkis replies:

Dear Kenny, My Being thanks you for such a very interesting question. To do it justice my Being will express it in the August edition of Conversations with Kuntarkis.

In the July edition you may be interested to read about unconditional love. Many have been asking the same question – how do I find love?

My Being trusts Kenny that you can wait for your answer until August. In the meantime, please read the July story – it will be the start of your answer.

To the answer of Kenny Question: Being Fit in Mind and Body, please read story (42)

Be blessed in love and light always.

Kuntarkis

UNCONDITIONAL LOVE

Hello Kuntarkis,

I believe that love is the only answer, but in today's troubled world of terrorism and war, is it not right that to begin to help each other, blood must first be spilt? I am a soldier in the armed forces and try to treat others with respect and warmth, but in my world of service I find many conflicts of interest. Finally, is it wrong to enjoy meat, alcohol, cigarettes and female companionship and still be able to reach enlightenment?

Kuntarkis replies:

Dear Human Being, Yes, unconditional love is truly the answer to all conflicts, yet humanity for almost one million years has been raging wars of destruction all over your planet Earth. The only true reason why wars of misery and pain exist in any civilisation, human or otherwise, is due to the created past being relived continuously in the present.

Every human individual has been experiencing many different facets of human life for nearly the last million years of human evolution. Each life that an individual lives creates some form of negative or positive karma, repercussions, which are carried over into their next incarnation to be resolved and experienced by that individual.

Every action creates a reaction, and energy is energy, no matter what form it takes. If an individual takes the life of another individual, that action is negative and must be brought into balance. There is no judgement. The energy from which all life is created is unbiased. Every human being that has existed for the past 928,000 years has free will in every action they have created, be it negative or positive. It is all about their level of thinking and their understanding that all of life, in all its forms, is precious. If all human beings have love in their hearts there would be no wars, no conflicts, no murder, no rape, not even greed of any sort.

The only reason why humanity suffers so much is through their self-created human ego, constantly living the past by not wanting to forgive or let go. Terrorism today is simply the past catching up in your human present. To murder or spill the blood of your fellow humans in the name of war is simply an excuse to carry the emotions of humanity's past into the present which then creates the future. The truth of all that is, is within every human being, but the human ego has many faces of illusion. There is no right or wrong, good or bad, just the level of one's thinking that governs the outcome of any situation. Humans can choose to war or choose to solve their differences rationally and peacefully.

Unconditional love begins with the individual. It does take a strong human being to step beyond the fears of humanity in all its creations. Fear is what holds the human individual from stepping out of their past into an energy of love and compassion.

Everything in your human world is created from free will, even down to the choice of eating the dead flesh, consuming alcohol, smoking poisonous toxins in cigarettes. All of these habits cloud the true self and hold the individual back from seeing the truth. Energy is energy and there are many levels upon which to grow consciously.

To have or to mate with human females is a part of human growth - it is a natural part of life. Every human being is already enlightened, it is a matter of choosing which path in your human life you are ready for. It is your choice alone. You have love in your heart and that is very special. Believe in yourself.

Be blessed in unconditional love always dear human being.

Kuntarkis.

NEED TO KNOW WHO MY SPIRIT GUIDES ARE?

Hi Roman and Kuntarkis,

Glad to learn from you. I am a light worker and I know pretty well that I have to cultivate in the here and know, yet just wondering what my spiritual name is and how many spirit guides I have?

Thanks.

Love and Light,

Gauss.

Kuntarkis replies:

Dear Gauss, My Being thanks you for asking your question on your spiritual name. First, always remember, healing always comes from your inner essence. There is a saying "to heal is to be healed". There are many levels of healing, as there are many levels of consciousness. To connect to your Soul will enhance your energies and enable you to heal others in the same light, for the light in my Being is the same light in your Being.

Your spiritual name is 'Tuoshun'. It is of the language of Sanskrit. Sanskrit is universal and is the language from which all human languages began or came from. Your spiritual name means 'one who is, or will, become aware'.

Always listen to your heart, for it will lead you on your path of conscious awareness. You at this moment have nine spirit guides which have been connected to you from other incarnations. To make the connection to your guides, meditate in the stillness of your mind, and always trust and listen to your inner voice. There is always truth in your inner being.

Be blessed in the love of Creation.

Kuntarkis.

EGYPTIAN PAST LIFE

To Kuntarkis,

Thank you for your attention in answering my questions. I know that faith is a powerful reminder that I'm not alone but it is great to have others backing up a sometimes not so optimistic way of thinking when it comes to contacting other energies. I do have another question though about my previous life in Egypt. You have told me that As'charre was my sister in a past life in Egypt in a village called Pracknerr and that she is now my spirit guide.

Can you give me any other information about that life? I have had a long almost obsessive curiosity with Egypt, in particular about a true feeling that the Egyptian civilization was an offshoot of the Atlanteans civilization.

I also have had many dreams and feelings of knowing you could call it that the pyramids stand for so much more than just monuments. I also feel that people today have underestimated the real advanced state the Egyptian accomplished. Even though we say today that they were incredibly advanced for their time I believe that they actually surpassed us. I feel that the dating methods used today are out of whack at least by a couple of thousand years. I feel as though our human history extends further than we realise. I ask myself why I have these feelings about this culture which is on another continent and which existed thousands of years ago. I dream about a life there and in particular the details I mentioned.

If you could possibly contact my spirit guides again and give me a little more information about these things in concern to my past life it would clear up a lot of things for me. I'm drawn to this place. Until you mentioned my past life I'd never given it any real thought as to why I had this obsession but it put me at ease to know that it all comes from somewhere. Thanks again for your attention

Regards,

Callan.

Kuntarkis replies:

Dear Callan, Your childhood in Egypt was a happy one - there was a lot of love in your family. When you were 14 human years of age you were taken by the Egyptian army and trained in the art of combat, the reason being to fight the advancing Roman armies. It took the Roman emperor six human years to defeat the Egyptian army.

Rome set new laws in Egypt. You survived the war and were enlisted in the Roman army, and yes the Egyptian civilisation was an offshoot of the Atlanteans civilisation. The pyramids were built over 20,000 human years ago. They were designed by Alien beings who in reality built most of the Pyramids that still stand in your present moment of time.

Most of the Egyptian culture came from the Alien beings who built the Pyramids. They came to share knowledge and to help advance human consciousness. The main reason the Alien beings decided to leave your Earth was because human beings wanted more knowledge and power, and this turned to greed.

These Alien beings came to Earth nearly 24,000 human years ago. They passed a great deal of knowledge on to the Mesopotamian civilisation at that time. These Aliens were called the Illiatousous (I-le-a-too-soos). Their home planet is called Tousous and they are known as the Illias. They are the great builders of many civilisation and known for their architectural genius.

Yes Callan, so much of human history is illusion.

Be blessed in unconditional love always.

Kuntarkis.

GOOD AND EVIL: DOES IT EXIST?

Hello Kuntarkis,

I am not quite sure how I stumbled onto your site. I have learned over the years not to question such things. But I have had some questions that I have been seeking answers too for quite some time. Maybe sir you can be of help.

I don't know if I am opening up my spiritually or not. I do know that I feel a great force inside me that wants to explode from its depths. Most of the time it remains silent, but never subdued. On this world I have faced many situations in my life both very evil and very good. I have been confronted by pure evil and have been able to come out on top of the confrontation that I had. But I am always wary of what waits around the next corner of life for me. I am not a paranoid person. Nor am I fearful of anything. I am telling you these things in order to give you some insight into myself. Some of the things that I am going to say I have never told anybody and most of the things about me. I have only spoken about them to a select few.

Everywhere that I venture, I feel inside that there is a reason for me being there. I have tested this theory proving myself correct. For the most part it seemed as if there was always someone that needed me to come into their lives in order for them to help themselves or achieve a certain goal, or something else. Many times I have felt like a wondering counsellor, soldier, policeman, or confidant. My wife says that I am her Knight and that she could not live without me even though we have only been in each other's life for less than two years. I walk into a room full of strangers and the whole room seems to end in time as everyone focuses their attention on me. No matter where I go it is that way. I told a friend about this and she didn't believe me until we entered a large restaurant together and she saw it too. None of this really bothers me. But there are other things and they too don't bother me. I just would like to understand why.

I have never been able to find a religion that I can submit too. Although I do believe in the deities of both good and evil. I have studied many religions searching for myself, but to no avail. Until recently... I started down a path into the world of the Occult. I was amazed to learn that it is a religion all to itself and even more so to find out how familiar these things were to me. I don't feel like a child with a new toy. Instead I feel like I have found a lost friend. Since I was a child I have been able to see colours around people, only now do I find that it is called an aura. Since childhood I have always been able to know what kind of person was around me or I am doing business with. I have never been wrong. I read a spell that some person gives to me and I can feel if there is any power to the words or not. By most I am considered a very good person. I consider myself a normal man. What I guess I am asking is for an understanding of my life. I don't feel with what I have been told so far by you about myself, so I am asking for you to give me a deeper understanding of what I am asking of you not just a thimble. I do believe strongly that I have a life beyond this one. I can't explain it but I believe it. If that is so...I must also have a name that is part of me in that life. If nothing else...could you help me with that?

Thank you for your time.

May peace go with you?

Mark.

Kuntarkis replies:

Dear Mark, My Being wishes to say thank you for the precious moments you gave in expressing your words. First, the human words 'good' and 'evil' are a creation of man alone. They exist in the third vibration of physical matter only and in the lower energies of the astral world.

Good and evil are in reality the same. To be good is a self-created condition or expectation. To be evil is a personal choice, which is also a self-created condition and a belief. When one wants to be good or evil, they create their deeds and actions from their life's experiences.

Good and evil are created from fear, and fear is a self-created condition of the human ego. To be rid of ego is to be rid of fear, and to be rid of fear is to be rid of the condition of good and evil.

To accomplish this, one must open the human heart of unconditional love. Good and evil cannot exist where unconditional love is present, since fear is of the ego. Fear also cannot exist where unconditional love is present. This is the true journey of self-realisation for all of humanity.

Your journey Mark, in your current incarnation, is to have the self- realisation of who you truly are. Who you are is not your past, for the past is simply a memory. Your past is not to be judged as right or wrong, good or evil. Each human being can draw on their past incarnations to learn from as well as to understand why karma exists within humanity.

To explain Mark, one of your past lives was in the human year 1691. You were a human male and you were a Seer - you had the ability to see what others could not. This afforded you the respect of your Emperor and his people. You were known as 'Alotikni', the name being given to you by your Emperor and meaning "the Light that shone from the Gods".

In that life you held a high position of importance. You lived well because your abilities helped the Empire from being destroyed. You knew when the enemy was going to come from across the water to attack. You could see the lights that surrounded the human body and you would do healings on people. Children loved to hear your stories and you would know when a person was to pass over to spirit world.

All these abilities are within you. The only thing that has changed is you Mark. You are living a different physical life. Your main lesson in your current incarnation is to open up your heart to your unconditional love. This is the ultimate power for self-discovery - it will allow you to channel knowledge directly. All human beings have this potential and capability.

Go within your silent mind and listen to your inner Being, your Soul, and your connection to all that is.

Be blessed in love always Mark.

Kuntarkis.

RICHARD'S LIFE: WHY/WHERE?

Question directed to Roman,

I am so blown away by all of this. This is what I TRULY believe. I only want this in my life. I try so hard to not to be distracted. I try so hard not to be affected by my disease. I am in Royal Oak, Michigan, just outside of Detroit and was wondering if there was anyone in this area you could refer me to. A guru/teacher/guide/mystic/angel.

I am currently out of work, due to complications from my disease, but I am ready to LIVE. I have always only wanted to spread love, and be love, and hopefully you can see this in me. I seem to have a small problem with the flesh; not severe, just bothersome - sitting at home with the Internet can be horrible for the ego. I am very much in love with my partner Calvin for almost 10 years, but sometimes I wonder if this is against my nature. I have no complaints with him at all, just the nagging voice in my mind that says that this is not yin/yang - or supposedly "right." I know that we have a true love; which must be sending out some type of healing vibration out into the world, when millions upon millions of men/women are not, so I do not worry that much, I was just curious to as your view on our relationship.

Roman, I want GOD to be so happy with me that I am called home instantly and shown my truth, and shown what the Universe is, and to be with beings of pure Love.

I try and express my creativity and limited knowledge of Spirituality through music, and through the communications of growth I have shared with my thriving brother Josh, and am SO not looking forward to going back to being confined inside of a cubicle when I am physically able, consumed into a material computer screen, knowing the world needs me.

I want to help the world and myself. I want to be a Sun on this Earth. I hope you can see me now and see that this is true. I don't condone wars, or violence, or anything but love, and have always strived to learn, and be selfless, and I have given up many things in my life to not have negative karma attached to me so I can get out of this wheel. I am here still, and want to be whole again. I know this is illusion in my heart, but don't know what my next step should be. I try and meditate, but only like to do it outside, and it is very cold here, so I tend not to in the winter (or much, for that matter until recently). I have read that warmer climates are better, seeing we receive our nutrients from the Sun (i.e. "sun gazing").

Part of me wants to give everything away, and just be; maybe living with others in a community that are like-minded in a spiritual place or country. I can feel that this duality exists in me, and it upsets me always. On one hand I love to write modern music (hoping to send love out through this medium of vibration, some is also cathartic), have my brick ranch home, etc.., and the ability to pay the bills, and on the other, I know that I am not really helping or living. I know that I am ensnared in illusion. I feel there is a hunger in me that wants so much more... I realize I can live in my existence now and be whole, but this is not enough. I truly feel my untapped potential that is just out of my reach.

I hope this is not too overwhelming for you. I must have this desire for some reason...

Love,

Richard.

Kuntarkis replies:

Dear Richard, My Being thanks you for your kind words. With all the confusion that is present within and around humanity it would be difficult for any human individual to find out more about themselves. Negative energy has become a very powerful force within human societies.

To truly become one with yourself, you Richard, or any other human being, need to detach yourself from the influence of the negative energy that distracts the individual from understanding the purpose of human incarnation.

You are a loving, caring human being towards others Richard, but you may need to be a little more caring towards yourself. To truly feel complete unconditional love for another you must feel and experience this love within yourself first.

You said Richard that you want to spread love and be loved. This is your lesson, as it is with all human beings. You need to become silent in your mind, to listen to the voice within you. That voice is your Soul and your Soul is you; your Soul is unconditional love. Richard you are unconditional love. Love must be felt and experienced by you before you can spread love to others.

My Being expressed these human words in your human year of 28AD: "The Spirit is willing, but the flesh is weak." You said you have a problem with the flesh. Yes, your beliefs and conditioning have kept you locked into that way of thinking, and it has been programmed into your human brain.

Richard, you have a fear of not being good enough to experience love from a human female. More to the point, being intimate with a human female. You find it difficult to express yourself sexually.

You speak of the Yin and Yang, the balance of life. What all human beings need to discover is the balance of Yin and Yang within themselves. Each human being needs the balance of Masculinity and Femininity to be whole and complete. You also expressed the world needs you. Yes, this has some truth, but more to the point, you need you first. All human beings need the balance of healing of themselves first before going out to save the world.

Meditation causes the mind to expand into other levels of consciousness. It stops the chatter of the human brain. My Being would like to make a recommendation to you – make contact with an organisation in America called Centerpointe Research Institute. NW 167ᵗʰ Place, Suite 220, Beaver town, OR 97006. They are on the internet at http://www.centerpointe. com/. You might find them of interest. Please let my Being know.

Yes your potential is untapped. To change your thinking and how you feel about yourself is to open up to new levels of consciousness.

Be blessed in unconditional love always dear Richard.

Kuntarkis.

LOOKING FOR DIRECTION IN MY LIFE?

Dear Kuntarkis,

I am lost. I go to a channellers in Delaware but I am more confused every time I go. I am a single parent, have no job, and my soul mate left me for someone else. I don't have a purpose in my life right now. I don't know what direction I should take. Do you have any advice for me?

Michelle

Kuntarkis replies:

Dear Michelle, I do understand the emotional confusion you are going through in your life. Nearly all human beings on this most precious Earth are in a state of fear and great confusion, and all human beings are looking for some kind of direction and answers to what is occurring in their present lives.

There is nothing wrong in seeking answers from others, for that is a part of the learning process of life and of evolution. But bear one thing in mind - as I look into your eyes Michelle, I see your soul, your essence, and I see a frightened child within you, who wishes to be loved and nurtured. I see and I feel your sadness and your pain. This pain is your past, and your past is your fears, your insecurities, and your sadness. As a child you had such a great imagination, but when you grew into an adult you closed the door on your hurt child and all the pain with it. The hurt child within you has been crying for you to look within your being and dissolve the pain and free yourself of your fears and insecurities.

Realise Michelle that you are the great power within your life. You can create anything in your life if you put the energy into it. You are a creative being. Use your imagination NOW, in this moment of life. Close your eyes, breathe in deeply and still your cluttered human brain of your concerns. Through your heart, which is the centre of your unconditional love, allow the Light of Creation's totality to enter your whole being in a pure white light. At your heart centre feel the child within. Love that child, embrace it and bathe it in your love, your essence. See and use your power, your free will - use your imagination, and know all the answers to your questions can be found from the inner source of your being, your truth.

If you allow yourself to come from an honest heart and an open mind, you will gain the power of Creation and all answers will be there for you. That Michelle is the truth and only the truth. If you seek it Michelle, it will be given unto you.

Once you have found your truth within, the purpose of your life will become clear. You will know which direction to take and you will have the strength and courage to take it. You will pass your pure love and knowledge on to your child and your child will grow with greater awareness in their life. The one you call Soul Mate, who left you for another, I am sad to say was not your Soul Mate. You will realise this as the moments in your life pass. When you allow the above process to work from within you, your life will no longer be of pain or negativity. You will meet your true heart and be balanced in life. Learn to trust yourself dear Michelle - all will come into union.

Be blessed in the Light, and may Love fill your heart always.

Kuntarkis.

WORDS OF HOPE FOR MY FRIEND

Hi, my name is Joanne, Question for Roman,

I have a friend, Miles, who has just (1 week ago) been diagnosed with stomach cancer and has been told that he has under two years to live. He has also been told that he has a very serious cancer which is rapidly moving throughout his body and it has now started to attack other areas of his body such as his lungs and kidneys. The reason I am writing to you, is that I read your story and thought that it was great to hear about your survival. It would be great if you could Email me back if you know of any good support groups or have any more words of hope for Miles to help him get through this and give him the strength to also survive.

Joanne.

Roman replies:

Dear Joanne, Thank you for e-mailing me and expressing your sadness for your friend Miles. It is always hard for someone to discover that one of their friends have been told they have a serious illness and only a certain amount of time to live. All human dis-eases are serious, especially to the one who has it.

Your friend you call Miles has now the opportunity of un-creating the created. All dis-ease is created over a long time of one's life, and can also be handed down by one's own parents. From a metaphysical perspective, all dis-ease can be cured if the person has the strength, the courage and the will to live. This would be the first question Miles has to ask of himself. If his answer is "Yes, I want to live", then he has begun his journey of self-discovery. Then he must look at why he has created this form of dis-ease, because all dis-ease is related to negative emotions.

You read about my own cure and why I created it. If we look at Miles' disease from a metaphysical point of view, Miles has a lot of inner anger and has a fear of making decisions. He is scared of the future and of life itself. When one carries these emotions over a long period of time, one creates dis-ease, which is then reinforced by one's diet and lifestyle, whether it be drugs, alcohol or junk food. A lifestyle which does not support the body's health will create stress and lead to a breakdown of the body.

Miles needs to ask himself a very important question. It must come from the heart and only the heart. Does Miles want to die? If his answer is "I want to live", then he must look deep into his inner being - not from logic, for logic is based on beliefs and conditioning from one's life. If his answer is "Yes", then he needs to change his food intake and begin to change his thoughts of negativity into positive thoughts. On this website there are affirmations. If expressed from the heart, they will help with this process of bringing positivity into his life, but for them to work he must truly believe and discipline himself. Also, there is a <u>diet plan</u> on this site which was given to a couple of other people that wrote in who also had created dis-ease in their lives. Miles may find these particular pages of interest and useful. If he wishes to e-mail me and let me know how he is progressing on his journey, he is more than welcome to do so.

I would also like to say, I began meditation when I was 15 years of age. I discovered many ways to practice meditation, I personally found by stilling the brain of all its constant chatter and just learning by being in the moment, I could connect to my inner divine. To me that connection was my Soul. We as humans, are made up of over 4 quadrillion cells, and each of these cells have their own infinite consciousness. They are all preforming their own specific tasks in keeping the human body in perfect form. The problem that I discovered while in communication with these cells, was us? We do abuse our body, whether it is in bad foods, not drinking enough clean water, or in our own negative thinking, and over years we help destroy our own genetics. Then we pass on damaged (DNA) to our children. So from one generation to the next and so on, we create more and more Dis'ease?

I found out, how to communicate with my 4 quadrillion cells, and learnt the 'Secret' of how to rejuvenate my lung. The body is in fact, its own healer. Your cells want to communicate with you, but if we don't know how to do this dis'ease take over. We as a species, need to learn the Spiritual aspect of the human body, and I can say this with absolute truth. Why, because I am the living example of curing my own self-created dis'ease?

Be blessed in the Light and Love of Creation's totality and be strong.

Roman

TRAPPED IN MARRIAGE & NEEDING A CAREER

Hello Kuntarkis,

My name is Gajra. I am twenty two years old and was given away by my parents at 15 to be married. I have four children. The man I am married to treats me lesser than himself. He is a business man, a landlord of houses that people rent. My marriage to this man was an agreement between my Father and my husband, and in return my parents and three sisters would have a house to live in rent free for ten years. My Father agreed because my husband is wealthy, has position and power. Even though my husband looks after me, I know he sees many other women, and this makes me unhappy. It seems I have no choice, but I also wish to have a career to give my life more meaning rather than to simply be a wife and Mother. I find computers very interesting and would like to learn more. What can I do?

Gajra

Kuntarkis replies:

Dear Gajra, You are indeed a brave woman to be in the position you are now, even though your culture suppresses women's rights. My Being will answer your question in this way and trust it will give you some guidance.

First, you have four beautiful children who rely on your love and acceptance. Second, you are also in a position of power. If you wish a career in your world of computers then speak to your husband of this and explain why you wish to learn more. You will be able to help him in his business so he does not have to pay another to enter his records onto his computer, and also by learning you can help your four children learn from a young age of the computer world which they will all be a part of when they grow up. Express the advantages to him and I feel he will agree and arrange for you to learn more. Be persistent in your natural loving way.

The other situation concerning your husband's needs for other women is very painful to you, but you see Gajra, he is the creator of his own world, just like you are. You have the power within you and only you can recognise it. Only you can decide on the changes you wish to make in your human life. If you decide to confront him about the other women, then you alone must make that choice, and face whatever is created from that decision. You have yet to see your future, so grow strong and learn of your computer world, as there will come a time when you will run your husband's business. When this all happens, will depend upon your husband.

Believe in yourself Gajra, and may you and your children be Blessed in the Light of Creation.

Kuntarkis.

QUEST FOR KNOWLEDGE ON ASTRAL TRAVEL: PROJECTION

To Kuntarkis,

I have been studying the information on your website and I am very pleased to say that it has helped me in my life and my understanding of the Astral Plane. Let me explain. My name is Terry, I am 32 years of age and my parents have been involved with Spiritualism for as long as I can remember. My question and my quest has been to experience Astral Travel and to be fully conscious of what I am experiencing. Unfortunately I have been unsuccessful in my quest to date. I have tried many claimed methods but with no success at this time. I read your April 2000 article <u>Dimensions, Realms and Universes</u>, and also the March 2000 article <u>Comas and Death:</u>

<u>Where does the Spirit go?</u> Both have given me a very clear picture and have motivated me to persist with my quest. Can you suggest anything I can do to help me achieve my goal? I would be most grateful. Thank you.

Terry.

Kuntarkis replies:

Dear Terry, Persistence is the key to success if you truly wish to experience the Astral Vibration and be fully conscious of your Astral body. There are no rules to that vibration, but there are conditions of your human emotional world that you may need to balance out in order to become fully aware of your presence in the fourth vibration. Please remember the Astral Vibration has many levels of consciousness, and depending on your beliefs and conditioning of your human life, it will determine which level you experience.

To give you an example Terry, if a human being has had a negative emotional upbringing and they carry a great deal of pain and fear in their human life, their fears can create very confusing experiences. The separation of the conscious (physical) and subconscious (spiritual) can stunt one's spiritual growth. The goal should be to unite the two so they exist together in harmony. To achieve this is to be able to take your conscious awareness into the Astral Vibration and then be able to bring back those experiences clearly when one is fully conscious in the physical realm.

Terry, to complete your quest and grow beyond the third dimensional matter world, please look very carefully at your present level of understanding by being completely honest with yourself. First, look at your emotions and learn to forgive the past, for the past is the past, and it can no longer become your present or your future. Do this from an honest heart Terry. Then look at what you are putting into your human body. Junk food and negative thoughts have been holding you back from your quest, especially your smoking, for smoking is a drug which clouds not only your Human Aura but also deposits toxins into the cells of your human body. All together these things prevent conscious growth.

Terry, by doing what My Being have suggested you will be raising your consciousness, which in turn will raise the level of your thinking and understanding. This will then help you enter higher vibrations in the Astral World and help you retain full awareness of your experiences in that vibration. If you choose to complete your quest, please let My Being know the outcome.

Be blessed in the Love and Light of Creation's totality, of which you are always a part of.

Kuntarkis.

HAVE I CREATED KARMA?

Hi Kuntarkis,

My name is Monique. I can't give you my professional name as I am known to many as a clairvoyant. I have been doing this work for about 11 years. I came across some of your material and have now begun questioning the work I am doing. Being honest, I tell people what they want to hear and they just keep coming back, and even recommend my services to their friends. This is great for my business, but I feel I need to change my career because of all the emotions that people bring with them when they come to have a reading. It is starting to affect my personality as well as my health. I am finding I am becoming very negative. Is this my karma?

Monique.

Kuntarkis replies:

Dear Monique, Let's look at Human Karma. It is a belief system, governed by negative emotional creations that one creates depending on their life's habits. What you do unto others will be done unto you - would you say that about sums it up Monique? In the vibration where I exist, Karma does not exist because Ego does not exist, and Ego is the creator of the negative belief system of Karma.

Human beings live in a third dimensional matter world, and this vibration is a learning ground for conscious growth. So the Ego exists and Karma also exists to bring about the balance of life. Karma only exists in the third dimension, but also lives in human time, and time was created by humans.

If a human being lives in the moment of life and understands Karma, then Karma itself can be dissolved in the moment of life, depending on the level of one's consciousness. So dear Monique, remember, when one interferes with another's existence and creates a path for them to follow, they are taking on the responsibility of that being. Whatever is expressed to them can change their path in life, and it is from this that Karma can be, and is, created in your third vibrational matter world.

Monique, the choice is always yours. You alone must make your decisions, but make then from your heart, for from your heart comes your inner truth. Walk gently upon your precious Earth, harm no-one, and life will always be balanced.

Safe journey Monique, and be blessed in the Light always.

Kuntarkis.

A WISH FOR MY PARENTS

Hello Kuntarkis,

I don't have a question but I would ask of you a request to give my Mom and Dad some of your healing light, as they are both having big problems. Could you do this for them? I am 13 and I love them both so much. I want them to stay together. Please help them.

Leanne.

Kuntarkis replies:

Dear Leanne, It is done most precious child of Mother Earth. They will stay together, for it is not as bad as you think. Your parents love you ever so much, and they also do love each other. Their love for you and for each other will bond them together throughout their lives.

May Love always fill your heart and you're Soul, and may your life be Blessed in the Light always.

Kuntarkis.

IS MY TEACHER IN SPIRIT WORLD REAL?

Dear Sir,

I have been talking to my Teacher for several years in my meditation. He has guided me through some very difficult times and has taught me how to heal myself of physical and emotional trials. I have been very secretive about Teacher because I was afraid that others would think I was crazy for talking to a Spirit. I guess I just need reassurance that what I experience with him is real. He has always told me the truth and taught me how to live and love myself and others. Can you tell me if what I know to be Teacher is real?

Jeibrab.

Kuntarkis replies:

Dear Jeibrab, My being wishes to thank you for having the trust to share your feelings on your Teacher. You expressed that your Teacher in spirit has been guiding you for several years in your quiet time of meditation, and that your Teacher has helped you through difficult moments in your human life.

Please dear Jeibrab, never be afraid that others will think of you as crazy for believing in the existence of spirits, for those spirits have been guiding humanity for the last 928,000 years. Most of humanity believe if you cannot see it or touch it, then it does not or cannot exist. Jeibrab, from a physical perspective it is more important to believe in what your human eyes cannot see rather than what they can physically see. By trusting in your inner self you will as an individual gain a far deeper understanding that humanity is most certainly not alone in the universe.

Every single human being has guides who are there to help them throughout their human life. These guides do not interfere in your evolution, but allow you to make choices, and if you wish to listen to them and their teachings, then they will help you open up your awareness and understanding of all of life and its purpose.

Always remember the Light of Creation exists within and around all of life, and it is there for you to use for protection, healing, and gaining knowledge. This Light of Pure Love is in you Jeibrab, and it has always been there.

To love yourself unconditionally and to love all of life that exists in all Universes, will expand your vision and elevate your consciousness to higher levels of understanding. Through this you will become a beacon of divine healing for all to see and grow from.

Trust yourself and your Teachers in spirit, for you Jeibrab are an infinite spirit being, encased in a human vessel. Be Blessed in Love and Light always.

Kuntarkis.

RE: AMY WROE BECHTEL

Greetings Kuntarkis,

I am checking into what has transpired regarding Amy Joy Wroe (Birth Name), Amy Wroe Bechtel (Marriage Name), did a google.com search for her name and came upon your sharing.

Just wanted to say thank you for your viewpoint. You see, I am working on the names from a healing viewpoint to see if I can help solve the case in physical. Yes, I at this time agree with you that Amy is no longer in physical. What I do, which is indeed akin to what you are doing. It is highly intuitive in one respect ... I render the vibrations of the names in the letters, seeing what the chords of meanings are in the name's letters themselves.

Will.

Kuntarkis replies:

Greetings to you Will, My being wishes to thank you for taking the moments in your human life to view Roman and Ilona's website. We are impressed with the good work you do in helping your brothers and sisters by assisting in solving investigations in your physical world. In doing what you do, your heart and being is filled with love and compassion, for you are also helping lost spirits that have become confused in what has occurred in their human life. It helps bring balance between their bodies and souls. You in reality are part of the healing process which allows the spirit to let go of its human element, and step beyond the third vibration of matter, to experience the pure bliss of Creation's totality.

May Love always be with you throughout your human life? As humanity evolves into a new vibration of energy, a deeper understanding will emerge from within each individual and the following two principles will be followed:

1. Forgiveness is the Key to Self-Realisation.

2. Unconditional Love is Total Freedom from self-created illusions.

Be Blessed Will in Love always.

Kuntarkis.

WHY DID I SURVIVE?

Hi Kuntarkis,

I have been doing some soul searching for the last three months and I have come to the realisation that I have been a false person not only to myself, but especially to others. I have been acting like a real idiot. I felt I was invincible and nothing could hurt me.

Two years ago I was in a serious car accident with three of my closest friends. We were all raging drunk, including the driver. I was very lucky - I was thrown from the car. One of my friends ended up paralysed from the waist down, the other two died on their way to hospital.

I don't know what I am feeling, whether it is guilt for surviving with only a few scratches, or whether I blame myself for what happened to them. I haven't seen my paralysed friend since that time. I know she is in a wheel chair. Can you see any good coming from all of this? I want to understand more of life. I want to learn and understand myself. Thank you for any advice.

Heidi.

Kuntarkis replies:

Dear Heidi, You are indeed a brave human being. Even though you as an individual are responsible for all your own actions in life, you are not responsible for others. Responsibility lies in the hands of each human being. What is sad is the upbringing; the beliefs and the conditioning imposed on the new born who come into human life, full of love, with no expectations. It is human conditioning that governs the outcome of each individual in human form, be it negative or positive.

You dear Heidi did not have a good opportunity when you were growing up. Your mother was very angry and taking drugs, alcohol and smoking, which did not help you. Your Mother placed her conditioning upon you. Living in anger is not healthy. But do not blame your mother, for she grew up within a similar environment. My Being feels your anger towards your mother, and also your father for not being there in your time of need. This is an issue you need to deal with.

Each spirit before entering into a human body, chooses the situations in human life to experience, to learn and grow in consciousness. They choose their parents for each incarnation and parents choose their children. It is all in the learning - to grown beyond human Ego, and not to see things as negative or positive, but just to learn to be in a pure state of being. This is the purpose of reincarnation. You dear Heidi can change any event or learning if you choose to. You are the driver of your own life.

You are a beautiful human being, and you are a creative being. Believe in yourself and learn to forgive from your heart, especially yourself. Your creativity is in arts of expression. Never give up your visions, for your future is in your visions. Your imagination is your power and strength. You can do anything if you truly want to. My Being believes in you dear Heidi.

Go for it and allow the Love within you to expand all around you. Be Blessed in Love and Light dear Heidi.

Kuntarkis.

MY SISTER IS BEING HURT

Dear Kuntarkis,

I feel strange writing to you because you're a stranger to me. I am into computers and have been for several years. Always looking through the internet, I came across your website and I must admit it blows me away. On reading Ask Kuntarkis, I can see how you are helping others to solve their problems.

My problem is my step farther. He's doing things to my younger sister that he shouldn't be. I told my mother and she doesn't believe me. My mother did confront him and my sister. He of course denied it, and my sister being scared of our step father, also denied he did anything to her. Should I just be quiet or try to do more about it?

Joe.

Kuntarkis replies:

Dear Joe, Knowing the truth can sometimes cause more emotional pain and stress to the individual. You Joe know a truth. You understand from a human perspective right from wrong, and you also love your sister and do not wish to see her being harmed. Your step father is unbalanced in his human brain and has caused the same harm to another girl when he was in his previous human relationship. He was found out and he served earthly time in your prison system. He is recorded on your police file system. Even though he has changed his name and details, his finger prints will reveal the truth. It would help your sister from an emotional perspective to be set free from the torment of your step father, and to help the healing process begin by bringing forth the balance of mind body and spirit.

You Joe must ask yourself, should you help set your sister free of this torment, and at the same time help your step father receive the help he needs to try to heal his sick human brain? Or should you simply ignore it and hope that it all goes away in time? You alone Joe must make the decision, for the truth is in your hands. It is the truth that sets free each human being from their pain and misery.

Joe, sit quiet for a while and ask yourself what you should do. Then listen to your heart, for your heart will always give you the answer. Be Blessed in Love and Light Joe always. If you wish, please let my Being know your decision.

Kuntarkis.

IN CONSTANT PHYSICAL PAIN

Roman,

I had cancer surgery about ten months ago on my neck. Now I'm out of work with permanent pain and constant headaches. I'm doing energy therapy now and it seems to be helping a little. Will I ever get rid of this constant pain? I'm on some pretty heavy pain medication that's keeping me from returning to work. The people that decide if I am disabled enough for disability, say that I can go to work with constant pain and more or less live with it. My question is, will I ever get better and what do I do for money? Thank you.

Claude

Kuntarkis replies:

Dear Claude, My Being has been asked by Roman to reply to you. One of the hardest decisions to make about human life is to do with your health. Because humanity has been highly conditioned by the drug and medical organisations upon your Earth, most humans give their personal responsibility away to these organisations in the hope that they will or should be cured.

Claude, your human body has the means and the knowledge to cure all dis-ease that has been upon your Earth. Every cell that forms your human shell has its own consciousness and awareness to UN-create what has been created. Take Roman as an example. Roman's lung was beyond repair from a human understanding and he was told that it must be removed and that he must be placed on drugs for most of his remaining life. Roman chose to heal himself. He not only healed his lung, but he completely rejuvenated it so that it was as if the disease had never occurred.

All of human dis-ease is created from negative emotion and reinforced by an unhealthy lifestyle, such as smoking, drinking alcohol, eating junk food or nutrient deficient food, drugs and pollution. Combine this with negative thoughts and human disease will be created and passed on to following generations. From one generation to the next the DNA becomes weaker and disease is more likely to manifest, especially at a younger human age, and this is Not Natural.

Yes Claude, your constant headaches are caused by the drugs you are consuming. Your human body is out of balance and yes, you do need to change some of your Earthly personal habits. To begin the process of healing, look at what types of foods you are consuming. To help your liver and kidneys, drink at least 2 litres of clean filtered water each day. This will help you flush out the toxins in your body and in this moment of your human life it is very important to do this. Also, consider buying 2 products - Spirulina and Kombucha Tea. Spirulina is a natural product full of iron which your body needs to help build up your immune system. Kombucha Tea will help balance the enzymes in your stomach. Roman was on both products and still is. They have kept his human shell healthy. You can read more about Spirulina, just by typing in on your computer the product Spirulina and you can also read about Roman's diet when he had cancer by going to the Ask Kuntarkis Index and looking under Human Dis-ease.

You alone Claude must make the decisions in your human life. The knowledge and understanding is within you. All answers to all questions are within your essence, your Spirit that is connected to Creation's totality. You Claude are more than you think. To dissolve negative human emotions is your first lesson and the greatest challenge for all human beings. All your pain that you are experiencing at this moment in your human life is just your human conditioning. Look deep within yourself and be true to yourself. Love and accept yourself, your being, and you will find the balance of your human life. It is all in your thoughts, for thoughts are energy which in turn are created into action, be it negative or positive. You are the creator, the driver of your thoughts.

Be Blessed dear Claude always in Love and Light.

Kuntarkis.

AM I ON THE RIGHT PATH?

Dear Kuntarkis,

How does one know if one is on the right path or the wrong path? That's my question.

Izzy.

Kuntarkis replies:

Dear Izzy, All paths in life have a purpose. It all depends on one's level of understanding. Izzy, try not to see your path in your human life as wrong or right. Learn to accept everything as an experience, neither negative nor positive, without personal judgement. Live the moment and embrace the wonderment of life itself. Not just this physical one you are experiencing. Raise your level of thinking and understanding beyond human Ego, and your eyes will be opened to a greater picture. Dear Izzy, as you connect to your inner essence, your spirit, you will become aware of your own living consciousness that you are indeed on a path of self-discovery.

Stepping beyond human Ego is the first step to self-realisation. All of life is interconnected to Creation's totality, meaning you as an individual are indeed living multi-dimensional existences in many other vibrations at the same time. Simply put, it all depends on your level of thinking. Unconditional love is your key to finding the freedom of the knowing. Be Blessed dear Izzy in Love and Light always.

Kuntarkis.

I HAVE LOTS OF QUESTIONS?

Dearest Kuntarkis:

I just "happened" upon your website yesterday and I cannot stop reading! You are wonderful and I can feel your love in your messages. I wish I could converse with you (like this in e-mail!) because I have so many questions! How wonderful it is for me to even have connect with you! I am honoured that you are taking my question. Please tell me about our current President Obama. Is he here for our better interests? Or is he part of the New World Order? I'm so confused right now and I don't really trust the government. I feel like they hold so much back from us. Please help me on this one. Also, I've recently in the past year developed some health problems (severe, debilitating anxiety attacks). I feel like I cannot stand to be here in this body much longer (I'm only 37!!) -- Like my body can't take being here anymore. Why is this? And why do I feel as if I am dying sometimes? Thanks SO much for giving humanity hope!

Another question is financial. I have dreamt of staying home with my children to raise them instead of working. I am a working mother. I want some kind of money-maker I can do from home so I can be with them. I yearn for that. I have thought of numerous ideas, but it takes money. Do you see anything happening for me in the near future so I may stay home with my kids? Please help -- it is my dream!!

P.S. Please give special blessings to my two precious children whom I love with all my heart.

With love and prayers.

Jo Karol

Kuntarkis replies:

Dear Jo Karol, It is most kind of you to express your feelings for Roman and Ilona's website. Their whole purpose is to help expand human consciousness by helping the individual in their evolution to step beyond human Ego. In this way my Being is overjoyed to be a part of their vision. Knowledge beyond the human Ego is indeed a step towards self-realisation and freedom from one's own self-created limitations. You expressed that you are honoured that my Being is taking your questions. My being is honoured that you would take the moment in your human life to listen to my response.

You dear Jo Karol are indeed a special human being, for within you lies the truth and answers to all your questions. The first step is to trust all your decisions, beyond all of your human beliefs and conditioning. It is human beliefs and conditioning that has shaped and created all the misery and pain within the individual and all of humanity. Each human being has the choice of living in a negative or positive space. It is this choice that shapes their present life, as well as their future.

You dear Jo Karol, even though you do not believe in yourself completely, you are indeed a very strong human being, and you can create whatever you wish from life. The key lies in your imagination. If you can see it with the power of your thoughts, then you Jo Karol can most certainly create it. To see is to create and to create is to manifest.

Regarding your current President Obama whether he is there for the better interests of the American people. This President believes in what he is doing and he believes it is for the better of all. If this is the truth, it is very important that all Americans send him a positive energy to help create a positive outcome. You asked whether your President is a part of The New World Order. My being can only express the truth and say yes. Please realise that 72% of governments on your Earth are involved in the New World Order system. This is not to say it will be negative or positive, but it will bring about many changes and there will be governments who oppose the New World Order and even go to war to fight it.

Please understand, your Earth and all who exist upon her, live in a third vibration of human matter, and human Ego only exists in this vibration. Learn to trust yourself dear Jo Karol, not anyone outside of you, and then you will be in control of your own destiny. Learn to meditate in the quiet of your mind and listen to your inner voice. The stress you are experiencing is created by yourself - you feel the world is closing in on you. You are here on this Earth for a reason, as all human beings are. You are here to learn lessons of life, and the most important one being just 'to be', neither negative nor positive, but just to experience all facets of human physical existence without judgement. See everything as an experience, an opportunity to grow consciously and to unconditionally love yourself and all of life that exists in all universes.

Life is sometimes frustrating for you, and especially your human body. You feel you are dying sometimes. All of human life will perish eventually. It is a part of the human cycle, as it is for all life on your precious Earth in the third vibration of matter.

The reason that you feel what you feel, dear Jo Karol, is that you are disconnected from your true self - your Light, your Essence, your Soul. It is the Light that is almighty present within you and all of life. Your Light is the fire that drives you in every moment of your existence. You need to reconnect to the Light that is dormant within you. To do this is very simple. Find a quiet space for you alone and lie on your back. Place your hands over your heart, and using your imagination, visualise a bright white light within your heart. Feel its warmth emanating, and allow this light to emanate pure love within and all around your human body. As you do this, say these words:

"I, Jo Karol, allow this Light of Love that is within me and around me, to be almighty present in my human life, and every moment of my existence. I see my life, no matter what the circumstances, to be Pure Bliss. I bring into my life what is needed to make my life happy and joyous in all areas of my life, now and forever more."

Do this as many times as you wish, and if you truly believe, it will manifest into your human life. In the vibration that my being exists, there is no physical matter, there are no negative thoughts. Everything is a pure state of bliss. Everything is created for the higher good of all. Money as you have on your Earth does not exist on Nar'Kariss. The Nar'Karones create all they need from the power of thought, manifested from Creation's energies. By putting thought into action in your human physical world of matter, you can manifest it into the physical realm.

My being realises you live in a human world and that money in your world is of great importance at this moment of your time. But you dear Jo Karol must ask yourself this question, and be true to yourself in your answer: Do I come from a negative or positive space in my human life? Once you have answered that question you must step forward and be willing to make the necessary changes.

A healing energy from my being has been sent to you and your two most precious human children. You dear Jo Karol are the power of your own destiny. Be Blessed in Love and Light always, and may joy and happiness be with you throughout your human life.

Kuntarkis.

<u>ARE THERE 15 MAIN CHAKRAS?</u>

Dear Kuntarkis,

My understanding is that in this age of enlightenment we are able to access our Higher Chakras. I think the Melchizedek teachings discuss 15 chakras. I am a healer and Tarot reader and would be interested on your analysis of the 15 chakra system and the colours connected to each or if you can point me in the direction of more information. Many thanks for your illuminating Web site.

Jacky.

Kuntarkis replies:

Dear Jacky, There are many forms of truths, beliefs and understandings. You have on your planet Earth at this moment over 7 billion human beings who exist on this most precious Earth and therefore the same number of truths. But in reality it is only an idea of truth as all truths that exist on your Earth are created from your past and from the beliefs of others.

The age of enlightenment has always existed on your Earth, and it is the human Ego that is responsible for humanity's not evolving beyond the past. Humanity has been on this planet for over 928,000 years. Each human being has lived thousands of incarnations and the past has evolved with negative emotions into the present as each human being incarnates. Continually creating the future of the individual as well as humanity as a whole.

Most human beings wear masks of illusion and in illusion there is no truth, only fear. To access higher charkas and step beyond present understanding, human beings need to dissolve the human Ego and all its masks of illusion. For many it is a very difficult journey. The human being has 27 main charkas and yes, every human being has the ability to cleanse and transform from their present state.

It is not a difficult task in reality. Meditation in the stillness of your Being is your first step. The next step is learning to forgive yourself and all those from your past to your present who have caused you pain, in unconditional love. To love yourself unconditionally, to become non-judgemental towards yourself and others, to let go of all negative emotions from the past to the present, is the path towards Spiritual Evolution.

Allow your human eyes to see the love and beauty in all of Creation's life forms; cleanse your human vessel of all toxins and poisons by eating only what grows from the soils of Mother Earth and allow other forms of life to exist in harmony with humanity. Do not eat of the dead, for those who do will become the living dead. That is why humanity is plagued with so much disease.

When a human being cleanses the mind and the body, when one sees all of Creations life forms as equal cohabitants upon your Earth, and when one allows the love to emanate from within their being outwardly, all their charkas from within their Being will be opened and the balance of mind/body/spirit will be present. The knowledge of the past, present and future will be with them, and they will have self-realisation. Their spirit will be connected to all that is and total truth and awareness, the knowing, will be present.

Be Blessed in Love always Jacky.

Kuntarkis.

THE MEANING OF 'GOD'

To Kuntarkis,

Many thanks for your previous love, in September 2002. Not only did I feel, when you had the contact with my Spirit, but I also received the answers to the problems that I was having with myself, on that day. Not only do I sleep better at night, but also realised, that I was not trusting my Spirit, for past misgivings.

I would like you to explain to me the meaning of "God", as I do not believe that God is a single entity, as such, but group of entities, spreading the love to others. The reason for this belief is that I had read that those brothers who visit us from other worlds, believe in a loving being, and not a God as such. When I was searching for my own answers, to my health, I also had received Spiritual healing, and it was on one such session that the healer had called out certain symbols, to which the loving Guides around me replied, that the symbol was to call up the old Gods, and when the healer called the next symbol, I was given the understanding, that was to call up the new Gods?. This brings me back to an understanding that we all come from the same spark of life, and that we are working to reconnect with that spark by our many experiences that we go through. This leaves me to think that when we are praying to God that we are praying to the God within ourselves, from where we originally came from, and will return. Also why do I see faces of people that I do not even know in material objects that are around us? Your loving brother,

Alan.

Kuntarkis replies:

Dear Alan, My Being has been asked by other human beings, am I 'God'. From a human understanding my answer would have to be yes, for 'God' in human terms is within all of life, as all of life is within God. The word 'God' is a creation from your human past. It means to believe in a being that is supreme to all other forms of life, and yes, again there is some human truth to that expression of the word 'God'.

Many extra-terrestrial beings from your past history have been recorded to some degree and were recognised as a God or Gods because they came from the skies or so-called heavens. Sightings go back as far as 711,000 years while your human population is over 928,000 years old. The truth back then was real, but it changed and it was man alone who changed the truth. Yet the truth still exists and is within all human beings. It is recorded in your essence, as are all of your past incarnations, for your essence is eternal, timeless, ageless and infinite.

The word 'God' was solely created by men from your past and carried into your present. It continues to create your future beliefs. Our civilisation, known as the Nar'Karones, exist in a vibration of non-matter, meaning we have no physical form. We are a species known in many vibrations of life forms and we are referred to as the guardians of different species. We come into vibrations of different life forms to help guide those who need a little help in evolving beyond the past, and to help those who seek a deeper understanding of life, so they can gain awareness of their inner truth and evolve consciously.

Only on your planet has a supreme God been created. The main reason for this creation is control and domination of the human species. Human Ego has been behind all of your sufferings, wars, misery and disease. Humanity created your God from the sightings and appearances of extra-terrestrial beings who came to your Earth to share wisdom and knowledge. Human beings with their level of thinking and consciousness at the time saw them as Gods, and what you have today is your present God, something to believe in which is superior to Man of Women.

Everything in all universes is infinite. No life form is greater than another, for every life form has wisdom, truth and the knowing within their being the essence of their consciousness. The problem is the human conditioning of the past being brought into the present which creates the future in fear.

The knowledge of all Creation is within you Alan. You only have to seek within your Being and it will be revealed. Be Blessed in the light of Creation always.

Kuntarkis.

THE ART OF MANIFESTATION

Dear Kuntarkis,

My question relates to relationships. I have recently been in one that did not work out - if I am capable of manifesting, am I able to manifest a certain person back into my life?

Fiona.

Kuntarkis replies:

Dear Fiona, You as a human individual have the power of manifestation within you every moment of your human existence. If you decide to manifest a certain human being into your life, then you can, if you choose to do this.

You Fiona are a part of Creation's totality, as all of life is. But you must remember that the past has always haunted humanity throughout history. The human Ego is the creator of all pain and suffering from the past to the present.

When you manifest anything, always manifest it from your loving heart, not from the emotional past of your human Ego. To manifest from unconditional love is the journey of self-realisation for all human beings to experience. Always be aware that you, Fiona, are the power of your own creations in this human life and all your incarnations to come. The Art of Manifestation is within your Imagination, every thought you have Fiona is and can be manifested into your own reality. It all depends on your level of thinking, let's say if you were a negative person and you had a lots of fear. You most likely will create a negative outcome in your manifestation, the same goes with you being a positive person, if you come from your love centre meaning your heart, your thoughts would then come from a positive place and you would then create a positive outcome in your human life. Everything is in your thinking, you are the only power in your thoughts, and you create every action and reaction in your life.

Be Blessed in Love and Light always.

Kuntarkis.

HOW IS KUNTARKIS CHANNELLED?

Hi Roman,

I loved your website, thank you very much. The advice that Kuntarkis gives is terrific and I'm sure he/she's helped many people.

I am interested in Medium ship/channelling and would like to ask you about the mechanics of it, from your experience. For example, do you receive impressions and/or pictures in your mind of Kuntarkis, or do you hear or see him/her externally - outside of your body, is it automatic writing? Etc. If you receive information from Kuntarkis, do you receive other information from loved ones who have died? Sorry to sound nosey, but my interest (apart from becoming the best person I can, through love and service) is the mechanics of Medium ship.

P.S. Funnily enough - I was reading about your history, and I was actually a service controller for a Panasonic agent here on the Sunshine Coast - and hated it! I only lasted 6 (long) months!! I won't be creating another reality like that one in a hurry!!!! (Got a cheap tele though so it wasn't all bad!)

Thank you for your time.

Shellee.

Kuntarkis replies:

Dear Shellee, I are glad you have enjoyed our website and we trust the information may assist you in your journey of life. Going back in my life around 30 years ago, I began searching for more truth than I was being told. My searches took me into the Martial Arts world, which gave me discipline, and I began to become serious about meditation. I found out one of the best forms of meditation was going into the stillness of my mind, and not having any thoughts or impressions, completely disconnecting from my physical self.

I began to realise I was tapping into an energy that was giving me different information, knowledge that I had not been taught. It opened up a whole new way of thinking and expression for me. I connected with departed spirits. I first could hear them and relay their messages, then I began to experience their presence in my time of sleep in the astral vibration.

As I started to accept without judgement, my inner eye opened to sights and visions that I found a little hard to accept at first, but in time I completely accepted what was being presented to me.

I realised that I needed to step beyond my present understanding and grow towards higher levels of communication. To embark on this journey I purified my body of destructive toxins. That is, I gave up all forms of junk food, no more alcohol or smoking, and I became a complete vegan. I drank lots clean water and formed my diet from a minimum of 70% raw food. Over several years I realised how much better my lifestyle changes were for raising my consciousness to higher forms of learning and communication with beings from other dimensions, realms and vibrations.

It is like being a healer. There are many levels of healing and there are many levels of spirit communication, but it is our personal responsibility to raise our energies to meet higher energies if we wish to channel higher energies. We need to raise our energies to meet theirs. If higher energies were to come into an unhealthy body it would be harmful to that person, and over time disease would be created because an unhealthy body is unable to cope with higher energy frequencies.

With Kuntarkis I have been able to establish a balance and since I have been channelling his energies for many years, Kuntarkis uses my body when he chooses. He steps into my body as I step out and moves as freely as I would. When I channel other entities from different vibrations, communication can be verbal or visions (pictures) in my mind. Many departed spirits come and sit with me to talk and express.

I have found all levels of communication to be a form of learning within itself, and always keep my mind open to all communications. Shellee, you expressed that you want to become the best person possible in love and service to all. To fulfil this dream, become the best within yourself first and learn to love yourself unconditionally. See the past as the past – never see the past as the present because it will continue to create your future. You are a beautiful human being and yes, you have a lot to give.

The mechanics of being a good medium is to live only in the moment, and to see all experiences as lessons in life, neither negative nor positive. See them as stepping stones to your growth and awareness. Purify your body of all toxins, and give away the consumption of animals and any other habits that pollute your body. Love yourself and all of the life forms in all universes, and especially, believe in yourself and know you can and you are the best in all you do.

Be blessed in the Love and the Light of Creation always dear Shellee.

Roman & Kuntarkis.

TO FIND ENLIGHTENMENT: HOW DOES ONE DO THIS?

Hello Kuntarkis,

I just wanted to share with you that I have found love and light inside myself and feel more free than when I wrote you before. I have found the means of acceptance inside of me and my fear and worry of life and what is to be is fading. Yes I did choose massage therapy to stay in and I have been put here as a healer of which I'm sure of now and I realized the healing had to start within. I view you as some form of spirit guide, and your words as well as other guides I have chosen to seek have helped me open up and the love I feel is coming from within and seeping out as well.

I just wanted to say thanks because your web site helped to open my mind at a time I was looking for answers, and some may feel the whole concept is nuts or crazy. I chose to seek it out for a reason and that's all I need to know. You were right about the truth. I have always believed in it and I have come to accept that it's been this way in many lives before as well.

I was also wondering something. I have noticed there are things having to do with the orient, medicine, martial arts, philosophy that I cling and am drawn to. Do you feel or is it possible for you to tell if I used to be Asian or was into the Asian arts in a past life? I have never had a moment of training, in using a staff, yet I can use one as if I was trained. I only took 2 years of Kung Fu yet I still practice my own martial arts and it all seems as if it's always been there. Or maybe in this life I have just chosen to take interest in this. Any words would be listened to and appreciated

Love and lasting light.

Guy.

Kuntarkis replies:

Dear Guy, My Being thanks you for sharing your human words of self-expression. You are indeed opening up your inner self, and this is very good for your growth and your awareness. Well done Guy.

When a human being decides to seek their inner truth it marks the beginning of becoming one with all things - in knowledge, in understanding, in gaining the compassion and wisdom to make their own decisions within their human life. That is harmony. That is the balance of mind, body and spirit.

Guy, humanity has had thousands of different incarnations. You have been Asian in many lifetimes, and the knowledge of those lifetimes and experiences is within your cellular essence, your Book of Knowledge, which every human being has. It is all recorded within your knowing, and all that knowledge can be brought forth from within you, to learn from, to enhance your present life, as well as your future incarnations. When you seek the truth always put aside your physical self and thoughts, and listen to your inner wisdom. All truth comes from within.

Take good care of yourself and believe in what you wish for your future.

Be blessed in the Love and the Light always.

Kuntarkis.

THE PURPOSE OF LIFE'S LESSONS?

Dear Kuntarkis,

Firstly, thankyou in advance for considering my question. My question is this: If it is the case that we are so much more than we presently know we are, then why do we need to go through these lives and different stages to become what we already are? What is the meaning of it all? If we already know deep down somewhere, why do we need to learn? This question has plagued me for some time, thus I would love to hear the answer.

Lots of love,

Fiona.

Kuntarkis replies:

Dear Fiona, The meaning of life in all its precious moments is simply one human word – imagination. In the totality of Creation, you, as all of life in this most precious form, can create whatever you wish from your human life, meaning if you can see it, feel it, know it, by using your imagination you can create it. By simply knowing it exists, you have indeed manifested it into your human life.

What separates humanity from Creation is negative past emotions continually being brought forward into the present, which then creates your future. The only reason humanity cannot evolve beyond the past of the human Ego is because the human Ego is in control. Too much logic has suppressed the human spirit, the Light of Creation that is with you. As all of life, your spirit needs to be reconnected to your physical self, and this is done by stilling the mind and creating silence within your Being, thereby allowing your essence to come forth.

The first step to connecting to your inner light is the realisation that you are a Spirit Being, living and experiencing a human existence in a physical vibration of matter, not the other way around. Knowing the truth is also becoming the living truth. The truth of all knowledge is within you, but the logical human brain of the physical self-stops a human being from searching within. It can be a difficult journey for many, yet obtaining the knowing is the ultimate freedom from the past and from the human Ego of deception.

All human beings are affected by self-created limitations from one lifetime to the next. This is humanity's choice. The human Ego through negative experiences continually recreates the negative past into the present. There is no supreme being who is punishing humanity. It is humanity alone who punishes itself through wars, violence, murder, rape, deception, judgement, vanity, greed, lust, domination, jealousy, fears and insecurities. These are all the creation of the human Ego. They are all negative traces which need to be dissolved back into the nothingness from which they were first created.

It is the responsibility of the human individual to step beyond the human Ego and become the living example so others may be inspired to grow consciously. It all begins with you Fiona. Believe in yourself that you are more than your physical self. Live your inner truth and it will be manifested outwardly.

Be Blessed in Love and Light always.

Kuntarkis.

EFFECTS OF ENERGY AND SPIRITUAL WORK?

Hi Roman,

My name is Clare and I have just read the channelled information about 'the Blues'. Whilst reading this I feel some things 'clicked' and have a question for Kuntarkis.

Dear Kuntarkis,

I have just read your information about 'the Blues'. Whilst reading this information I feel as if I had a revelation. About 3 years ago I was in a very unhappy/unsatisfying place in my life. I was looking for an 'out' and soon after I felt debilitating-ly ill. This worked out for the best as thanks to this experience I am now in a very happy place studying to become a Naturopath which I have a deep passion for. I truly feel as if I now have the great potential to help others.

Now 3 years later I have recently began doing a lot more energy/spiritual work and have done a lot of clearing of my charkas and of various entities within my body. In particular, I have discovered and cleared an energy that I could not name except for its colour which was a definite blue. I cleared this energy and then the next day (for about 2 weeks) I was terribly ill experiencing all sorts of ailments within this time.

I am hoping for your opinion on whether you feel that this was 'the blue' energy that you talked about? Do you feel that there was a walk-in experience occurring? I would be very grateful for any info you wish to convey.

Yours Gratefully,

Clare.

Kuntarkis replies:

Dear Clare, Thank you for taking the precious moments of your human life to express to my Being your concerns. First, you as a human being do have a passion for life and in wanting to serve humanity by becoming what is called a naturopath. This would create a very positive energy in your human life as a human being, and yes, you do have the potential to create circumstances in your human life that will create a balanced lifestyle for you throughout your human life.

Clare, my Being needs to express to you that the reason you have experienced illnesses over that period was because certain human beings have been draining you of your energies. Many human beings are like what you call 'Vampires', the only difference being that these Vampires consume energy from other beings (instead of blood!). This draining of energies can leave human beings such as yourself susceptible to different forms of dis'ease and illness, and can leave you feeling lethargic and tired.

Always remember Clare, truth in its purest forms comes from within you. The energy you refer to as blue is not in reality Alien, but is in fact a new spirit guide making her connection with you. This spirit guide is for your spiritual growth as well as to help you gain strength and courage for your journey ahead. Yet again the choice for this connection is always yours to make. There are many new experiences coming into your human life.

Be Blessed in Love always and trust yourself in all your decisions.

Kuntarkis.

CONFUSED BY KARMA: WHY?

Hello Kuntarkis,

I just had a question about Karma. If what happens to us and our life situation is dictated by our past or past-life actions, how can you explain this: let's say it's the beginning of the earthly creation and god creates the very first human beings to live out their very first physical life on earth, now let's say one of the humans ends up punching or stealing from the other caveperson (suppose it's the stone age); how could you explain why the receiver of the punch or the victim of the theft had to suffer that consequence?- because these humans have not even lived a past life yet, so it can't be their past Karma. What came first? - The chicken or the egg? - was Karma there before mankind's creation, or was man created before Karma?? This question was driving me crazy, I just needed another opinion or thought on it. Thank you.

Ajay.

Kuntarkis replies:

Dear Ajay, First, all life forms on your precious Earth began within your oceans over a very long period of human time. Life forms began to come out of the oceans and again they began the process of evolution into different species.

Your Earth is billions of years old. There have been many beings from other worlds who have visited your Earth. Many new species have been placed upon your Earth for experimental purposes. The original Aboriginal is a direct descendant of the Neanderthals, which evolved from apes, and apes evolved from your oceans.

My Being is from a race of beings called the Nar'Karones. Over 928,000 of your Earth years ago, 87,000 Nar'Karones were placed on your Earth and over a great amount of time they evolved with the Neanderthals. The Neanderthals evolved as a race and became the natives of the continents of your Earth and you can see a very strong resemblance physically to this ancient species in many nationalities on your Earth, such as the Africans and Australian Aborigines.

You can also see Neanderthals to a lesser extent in your European beings, but then genetics are a combination of Neanderthal and Nar'Karones, which also make up the Western species of humans. On the other hand the Asian races are a very interesting creation of evolution and genetic engineering, having evolved from chimpanzees and apes, and other primates over hundreds of thousands of human years with the assistance of physical beings who still visit your planet in your present time.

These beings from other vibrations experimented and implanted their own genetics along with that of the primates, trying to create an intelligent non-aggressive physical being who would not be a threat to them. This new species of beings was monitored by their own scientists, just as your scientists today on your Earth are experimenting with implanting genetics into related and vastly unrelated species to see what effect such genes would have.

Interesting from a point of truth, it shows how history is repeating itself, is it not?

So in reality there are three different forms of humans upon your planet – the first being the Neanderthals who evolved from your oceans, the second being the mixing of the Neanderthals and the Nar'Karones who come from the planet Nar'Kariss, and the third being the Asians who were evolved from the chimpanzees and apes and the DNA of physical alien beings who came from other vibrations.

This is what has made up your race of human beings as they are in your time today. There was no God in the creation of your species, simply evolution and the interference of other worlds.

Be blessed in love always dear Ajay from Earth.

Kuntarkis.

MY LIFE'S PATH: HOW DO WE KNOW?

Hello, my name is Pauline.

I am sure it is a very common question and may be boring as it is asked so many times, but it is very important to me.

I still do not know what I want to be when I grow up. I turned 30 years of age last month. My family is growing, and I am now finding free time on my hands. I know I am a Light worker, but I have many interest. I can easily contact clients Angels and Guides, and pass on messages, but am unable to do this for myself.

Basically I want to know, what way I may serve Spirit the best. What are my greatest abilities that I may put into practice, to serve all who wish to receive my blessings. This is been going on for 2 years now, and I am still unsure of which path to follow. Money is scarce so I would like to know which courses etc. I should do instead of dabbling in everything and using up the money. My husband has been the bread earner for so long, and now I would like to help, even though he has never asked.

Any insight will be greatly appreciated.

Love Light and Blessings.

Kuntarkis replies:

Dear Pauline, My Being thanks you for expressing your human words. You have a saying amongst your human kind – "to be or not to be" - is that not the question?

Who am I? I am that I am. What am I? I am a Spirit Being that is a part of everything. Where am I going? Wherever My Being takes me on my journey of self-realisation.

Your human world is a place of learning and letting go of the past, and yet for all the incarnations each human individual has been experiencing, the problem for most human beings is that they have been living the past over and over again, causing humanity to live in fear and pain, and not knowing how to go beyond the past in order to create a balanced present and future.

Many human beings are always trying to help others while forgetting to help themselves. The first lesson of human life is to be true to thy self - to balance the self – in order to help others. Do not look beyond yourself Pauline. To help others solve their problems, their pain, their misery, is indeed an honourable thing to do, but first face yourself and all your fears. Deal with your own pain first.

Find the balance within yourself. Go within your inner being and find the unconditional love within yourself. Once it is a part of your whole essence, then you will be ready to go out into the human world. Only in the stillness of your inner being will you find your true self. Every human being on the planet Earth lives to some degree in fear. Fear is a part of the created human ego. It is the human ego that needs to be dissolved back into the nothingness before the real can come into being.

Humanity always needs to prove themselves – that is fear; that is the human ego. On the other side is unconditional love - a pure state of being in the moment of life.

Humanity's lesson is to let go of the past, to live in the moment, to discover their true essence, to experience unconditional love for themselves and all forms of life.

Pauline, find yourself first and you will know who you are and your true path in life. You will gain what is called the knowing and through the knowing you will see beyond the self-created human ego.

Be blessed in love always.

Kuntarkis.

SELF LOVE: IS IT POSITIVE OR NEGATIVE?

Dear Kuntarkis,

How do I begin to love myself, because I am sick of the way I feel about me.
What steps do I take? Any advice would be most appreciated.

Jaliz.

Kuntarkis replies:

Dear beautiful Jaliz, What you have been feeling about yourself is a creation
of your social surroundings. It has become so ingrained in your thinking
that it has become your truth. When a human being feels worthless, it then
becomes a negative emotion.

Jaliz, first accept yourself exactly the way you are. Accept everything about
yourself, be it negative or positive. Then when you are ready, sit in front of
a mirror and look at yourself. Just look – don't judge. Look around yourself
and then look into your eyes. Look deep and ask yourself these questions -
Why do I hate myself? Why does no one like me?

Jaliz, you do not hate yourself. You are just very angry with life because of
the way you grew up from a child. It is the child within you that is angry
because you feel you were cheated of being loved by your parents. This
became your belief and it became your fears.

You are 32 years of age and have tried to commit suicide twice, but were
unsuccessful. The reason you did not succeed at suicide is because your
lessons of life are not complete. Jaliz, you have a long human life ahead of you,
and your life in many moments to come will be one of joy and fulfilment.
In this present moment you are experiencing a lesson of acceptance of who
and what you are.

As you look into your eyes know that you are looking into your soul. Your
eyes will connect you with your own being and help you to overcome
the anger you feel. It will also connect you to your heart centre where
unconditional love exists in all forms of life.

All your negative and positive experiences up to this point in your human life will shape the human being you will become. Remember, free will is a very powerful gift. It can create a very negative life or it can create a life of bliss. You Jaliz are the driver and the creator of your life to be. It all begins with how you see yourself. Change your thinking and you will change your life. Unconditional love is the beginning of awareness and conscious growth.

Be blessed dear Jaliz in love always and believe in yourself.

Kuntarkis.

SPIRITS IN DREAMS: WHY?

Dear Kuntarkis,

A spirit comes to me in my dreams and talks to me about different things. It may be about the weather or about people, or even myself. It is always different and always asking my opinion. Who is this spirit and what is its purpose?

Jeff.

Kuntarkis replies:

Dear Jeff, This spirit is one of your guides and is making a connection with you. This spirit is there simply to help build your confidence. It asks your opinion because you need to learn to express yourself in your physical life. Would you not say this is the truth?

It is also helping you to communicate. Communication within human society is a very important factor of life. Jeff, when you are confronted by other human beings, you always shy away and never express what you truly wish to say. You never feel what you may express could be of any interest or importance.

Yet you Jeff have a lot to offer. Begin by expressing yourself. It will give you more confidence.

Be blessed in love always.

Kuntarkis.

CHANGING WEATHER PATTERNS: HOW COME?

Dear Kuntarkis,

I am very confused about the weather patterns we are having. It seems the weather is changing all over our planet. Why is this happening?

Fran.

Kuntarkis replies:

Dear Fran, All human beings should be concerned. Your climate around your Earth has been changing dramatically, especially over the last 176 years of human life.

The chemical pollution that is being released into your atmosphere is a major contributor to your climatic changes. Global warming should be a major concern to your governments and scientists.

What humanity calls the ozone layer, is being affected and needs to be addressed urgently before the damage becomes irreversible. There is a solution, but it seems what you call your dollar is more important than human life as well as all the other species that live upon your Mother Earth. You must remember, the power is not in your governments, the real power is within every human individual.

Fran, it is the truth that scares human beings. This subject on the changing weather is of great importance. It will be interesting to see if other readers express an interest in this very important issue.

Kuntarkis

ELVIS PRESLEY

Dear Kuntarkis,

I have two questions. First, did Elvis Presley work for the FBI, and second, how did he die?

Kuntarkis replies:

Dear Human Being, to your first question, yes, the human being called Elvis Presley actually did work for what is called in America, the FBI. He was like an ambassador for that organisation, for he had always been fascinated by the secret service. It was his dream to become a secret agent for the American Government.

To your second question, Elvis Presley died of a heart attack induced by a drug to give the appearance that he died of a heart attack. So in reality, he was murdered. He was silenced. This truth may come to the awareness of the masse or it may be kept completely hidden from the public. Elvis Presley was worth more dead than alive.

It makes the mind think, does it not, that all is not what it seems?

Be blessed in love always dear human being.

Kuntarkis.

PLANET HADAR: DOES IT ACTUALLY EXIST?

Question for Kuntarkis,

A good friend of mine was told that she was from a place call Hadar. Can you tell me a little about the planet and whether or not it exists? Also, if there are many people residing on earth from this distant planet.

Thanks again for your time.

Mandume

Kuntarkis replies:

Dear Mandume, if your good friend told you that she came from a distant planet called Hadar, this would be her truth. No matter how your friend argued this truth, for my Being to express that this planet does or does not exist would not do justice to you or your friend.

My quest with all Human Beings is to help you discover your knowledge of your infinite self, to help all human beings grow beyond their self-created ego. All human beings want to believe in something, even if that something comes from another. The ultimate truth is to believe in yourself, your inner being, you're Soul which is connected to all things in all universes.

Mandume, ask yourself, does your friend's truth feel truthful to you? Ask from your heart, the centre of your love, and listen to your first answer. In that you will know.

Your second question, are there many human beings that live on Earth who come from the planet your friend calls Hadar. My Being's answer is no, there are not.

You are the power of life - your life - believe in your Soul.

Be blessed in unconditional love always.

Kuntarkis.

SPIRIT GUIDES: HOW DO I COMMUNICATE WITH THEM?

Hi Kuntarkis,

I recently established contact with the spirit of someone who was close to me and another person who indicates they are my spirit guide. I have believed all my life that this contact is possible and have had many experiences that prove to me beyond doubt that the spirit world is real and that we on earth can interact with spirits. However, I have never had any direct communication with them until just now. I felt compelled to take up pen and paper and the words I wrote were those of these two spirits, one of whom has much to tell me that was unresolved when he was alive (it has been more than 10 years since his death and I have multiple indications that he has been pursuing contact with me for much of this time). I am concerned that the words could be reflections of my own mind and desire to communicate rather than those of spirits - in other words, that I want too badly to be connected in this way. On the other hand, it feels right and seems appropriate that I should make contact with my spirit guide at this time in my life. Can you offer any words of wisdom to help me make sure I am following the right path without self-delusion?

Many thanks in advance, even if only for taking the time to read my message.

Tara

Kuntarkis replies:

Dear Tara, My Being wishes to say thank you for sharing your inner experiences. Sometimes it can be a little confusing whether you believe you are communicating with your spirit guides or simply it being your own mind playing tricks on you.

As you put it Tara, on the other hand it feels right. So trust yourself, really trust that, yes, you are communicating with your spirit guides. Many human beings have experiences with spirit world but pass it off as a trick of the mind, or a delusion that it is the human ego talking. The human ego does not believe in what it cannot see, touch or smell. It only believes in what it has experienced from its past, based on its beliefs and conditioning from physical life.

Tara, my Being believes in you and yes, your guides have been communicating with you for many of your Earthly years, so believe in yourself no matter what others think or try to tell you. You are the power in your life. Believe and it will be manifested.

Be blessed in love and truth always.

Kuntarkis.

WHY DO I MAKE HIM HAPPY?

Dear Kuntarkis,

I have found the one I am supposed to be with. I have chosen the one that I have known for the past 5 years now. Now, he wants to know why I am happy with him and I can't give him the right answer. I have told him that the reason he makes me happy is because he loves me for me and nothing else, but he still asks me the same question. I don't know what more I can tell him. I have also told him that for the past year that we were apart he was all that I thought about, even though I was with other guys. He has always been the one for me and always will be. But now I need help to answer his question: why I make him happy?

Ashley

Kuntarkis replies:

Dear Ashley, The question you ask of my Being can only be given in one very simple answer. The answer to your question is within your human boyfriend - you need to reverse the question from yourself to him, and ask him why you make him so happy. Only he can give you the answer. Remember unconditional love from the heart is the absolute truth, and all else is the illusion of the human ego.

Be blessed in the love of the heart always.

Kuntarkis.

SPIRITUAL GROWTH: AM I DOING WELL?

Hello Kuntarkis,

My name is Yvette. I am from Canada in the U.S.

Could you tell me answers to questions about myself? My husband died 5 months ago in a coma. Since then I have been learning and trying to understand why am I here and why we must all experience this sadness after someone dies. Before this I never really thought about dying. But now I know it's a part of life, we live, learn, and die (return to spirit). Would you be able to tell me if I am learning my life lessons? How am I doing with Spiritual Knowledge? I greatly, greatly appreciate it if you can assist me.

By the way I love your website :)

Yvette

Kuntarkis replies:

Dear Yvette, It is a very emotional experience for any human being to lose a loved one, mainly because Western society is afraid of physical death. In many Eastern cultures their societies teach the meaning of physical death and therefore they accept it with a more open mind and heart.

My Being feels your pain and your sadness with your human husband's passing over to spirit world. The lesson of grief can seem very cruel indeed yet it is not in any way meant to be cruel. Human death is simply a transformation back to your infinite self, back to the spirit which is a facet of your Soul. The Soul is infinite, endless, ageless, timeless, eternal and immortal in the scheme of life.

In your previous incarnation as a human being you were married to your husband who passed away five human months after your marriage. The roles were reversed where you were the human male and he the female. In that incarnation you passed away at the human age of 37. It was a very emotional lesson in that lifetime for him as your wife. In this lifetime it is your lesson of learning about the emotion of grief. You will step beyond this sadness of loss and grow strong in your awareness.

In your next incarnation you and your husband will come together and marry once again, and you will have a very long relationship together, for you are facets of the same Soul.

Be blessed in unconditional love always.

Kuntarkis.

PAIN IN MY LEFT ARM: WHY IS IT LIKE THAT?

Dear Kuntarkis,

Thanks so much. Does this name has a special meaning? (Refer Ask Kuntarkis February 2005)

I got another question. For several years I got a pain in my left arm. It's not when I move my arm around, but mostly when I do nothing. Do you have any idea where it's coming from? May be from my back? Any help would be much appreciated.

Regards,

Annette

Kuntarkis replies:

Dear Annette, The pain that you described in your left arm can be caused by pinching a nerve in your shoulder or at the top of your arm at the back. This can occur while you are asleep. Also, your circulation is a little slow which creates less oxygen to be present in your blood.

The human diet can play a very important role in the health of a human being. Drinking two to three litres of pure water every day, or in combination with herb and green teas will help your circulation and also help to flush out harmful toxins which lodge in your muscle tissues. To keep your human vessel in good working order. Diet, water and exercise will allow you to feel physically good, you will sleep well and have plenty of energy to live and enjoy your human life.

Your spiritual name Beasheri was given to you by your human mother in the human year 211 BC. It means "one who sees faces in water". For example, you always sat by a river that flowed and would talk to the river. You could see faces appearing in the water. The image that was shown to my Being was of a human female at the age of 11 with long dark hair, dark eyes and dark olive skin.

Be blessed in love always.

Kuntarkis.

CONNECTING WITH THE INNER SELF

Hi Kuntarkis,

I've done a lot of "searching" outwardly and ask many a question of various "readers". I do feel that I need guidance from within as I've been a bit bull headed (of course, my guides probably think I've been extremely bull headed).

From your perspective, what do you think is the best way for a being as myself to connect to my inner self? And do any of my guides have anything that I absolutely need to know...? Would I be consider a star being?

On a different note, I find it interesting that there is another reader/channellers in Australia who has some great information. His discussion group is http://www.smartgroups.com/message/listbydate.cfm?GID=915762. I think because there is a hole in the ozone layer there in Australia, lighter codes are coming in an awakening people.

Thank your for opening yourself for questions.

From within,

Mandume.

Kuntarkis replies:

Dear Mandume, Many can give different forms of guidance to those seeking ways of connecting to the inner self. As a human being you need to try different ways for yourself; only then will you know which way is best for you. Following is an example from the past from when my Being was in physical form.

Admit to yourself these words when you are in your own quiet space: "I am the Soul". Say it several times out loud and be aware of what you are feeling. Believe in your feelings, for feelings are spontaneous, coming from your heart centre, the place of complete truth.

Learn patience. Sit in complete quiet and still your thinking, quiet your human brain. Just sit without any expectation. Enjoy the moment and step beyond the emotions of your physical self. Then ask yourself, your Soul, "What do I absolutely need to know about myself?"

You may need to ask this question several times. After asking you truly need to listen, really listen, and trust and believe you are capable of accomplishing the task.

Be blessed in love always dear Mandume.

Kuntarkis.

COULD SHE BE MY SOUL MATE?

Hi Roman and Kuntarkis,

I pray this finds you well. I have not been able to let rest a desire to meet a woman you spoke of to me. Since you told me that there is a female born in Tasmania at the same time as me that shares the same soul as I do I have been eager to meet her and dream of spending my life with her. You mentioned that we would not meet for another 11 years.

My questions are:

   1-May I search for her now? (Are there factors I am unaware of that would persuade me not to?).
   2-If you don't have any objections to me meeting her in the near future, will you give me more information to find her with? (A name, etc.).

With the simple details of equal birth time but born in Tasmania I believe I could find her, but I really desire to hear your thoughts on this matter before I take any actions.

Love,

Rumen.

Kuntarkis and Roman replies:

Dear Rumen, since your phone call I have been in deep thought, especially after reading your email. I have read it several times and feel within myself it would be wrong of me to give answers to your questions.

Please realise Rumen our Souls share much wisdom in understanding the spirit of who we are. Everything we experience, whether negative or positive, helps lead us to the next level of our life's journey as a human being.

For me to explain to you or give you her name or birth date, would only create a situation that could or would cause you both pain. It would be a more positive outcome if you allowed yourself to grow in the now, consciously, so that when the moment comes, your energies will be in balance and harmony, and everything will come together as it is meant to be, not forced too soon.

I myself had a vision 28 years ago about meeting the perfect woman and I wanted so much to meet her at that time, but I was shown if our energies came together too soon it would not come together in harmony because of our own negative fears. We as human beings choose to learn certain lessons and unless we let go of our fears, we can destroy the delicate balance, the harmony, the love that is meant to come into our lives.

Rumen, find the balance, the love and the harmony in yourself first and your future will come together as your Soul intended it to be.

When you read this email you may decide you do not wish to come to our appointment on Wednesday 7 December at 10.00am, or you may still wish to come. I would appreciate your calling me to let me know your decision either way.

Kind regards,

Roman.

FEELING LOST WITHIN MYSELF

Dear Kuntarkis,

I have been in a relationship with a man for nearly 2 yrs. He is a very kind and honest man, but unable to show any emotions towards me. I know that he does care but I find it very hard at times to be with him. I feel sometimes that there is no heart connections from him and that makes me feel sad as I deeply love him. I have tried talking to him about how all this makes me feel but he changes the subject and never tries to talk about it even though he knows it upsets me.

What I am puzzled about is that I feel there is a strong bond between us which seems to stop me from ending this relationship. What is my purpose in this relationship? Am I supposed to be learning something? Can I find a way to open him and make him more affectionate so that we can have a more loving relationship? Which is the best way for me to deal with this? I feel so lost at times.

I would so much appreciate your advice.

Thank you

Nikki.

Kuntarkis replies:

Dear Nikki, Please understand that each human being is on a journey of self-realisation and to learn to let go of their past by understanding how to live in the moment.

The human male you are in a relationship with has come into your energies to learn about love, the true meaning of love. Most of humanity has no understanding of unconditional love because human love is usually based on the past, created through beliefs, conditioning and fears.

Emotion is a negative aspect of human understanding, created by fear. Feelings on the other hand are spontaneous and are created in the moment, much like artists, writers, and actors for example create in the moment through their artistic expression. Feelings come from the heart, the centre of unconditional love.

The human male you speak of has experienced negative emotions from his past, and these have prevented him from expressing his feelings from his heart. He wants to, yet his past holds him back.

You asked what your purpose in your relationship is. Your purpose is to help him open his heart so he can truly feel love, your love and his own love. The bond you feel with him is from a previous life.

Never give up Nikki. By helping him to understand love for himself he will then learn to love you and to be more affectionate and understanding of your needs. As you help each other, then each of you as human beings will grow consciously in your own awareness.

Remember Nikki, unconditional love, and the giving of each other to each other freely, is the greatest lesson and experience that any life form can learn.

Be blessed in unconditional love always.

Kuntarkis.

THE LANGUAGE OF THE NUWAUBIC: YES OR NO?

Greetings Kuntarkis,

In my research I found a script called Nuwaubic, its roots found in cuneiform. Is this the first language on Earth and was there any beings call Anunnagi? If so where did they come from and can you tell me my Spiritual Guide's name and my name in the spirit realm? Thank you for sharing with me and everyone in this realm. Much respect and in the writing of Nuwaubic. Wahid A's hug (One Love)

Donald.

Kuntarkis replies:

Dear Donald, First to your question regarding the Nuwaubic language. Humans as they are today date back over 928,000 years, and the language that was used from that beginning is known as Sanskrit on your Earth. Sanskrit was the language of the Nar'Karones civilisation, a race of beings who lived on the planet Nar'Kariss, 417,000 light years from Earth.

Prior to the Nar'Karones coming to Earth there was a species of beings refer to as Neanderthals? They were evolving as a species and had their own form of communication, but it was not Nuwaubic. Nuwaubic is a language that dates back 71,000 years in human time, to a species called the Ceemouitts, an ancient people who originated from the land of Africa.

My Being has gone back in your human history and did not find any beings called Anunnagi, but that is not to say they did not exist.

Your main spirit guide is called 'Oshweeah' and loves you unconditionally. Your spiritual name is 'Tain-nissh' and relates to the element of Earth.

Be blessed in unconditional love always.

Kuntarkis.

WHY IS MY HAIR FALLING OUT?

Dear Roman or Kuntarkis,

Thanks for the previous help that I have received with my previous questions. I would now like you to ask Kuntarkis why I am losing so much hair. Also will it grow back, as I am concerned, as I had lovely hair, and now it is looking very thin? Am I lacking vitamins, or is there some other reason for this to be happening at the age that I am at. Am I doing something wrong, as my partner has different ideas as to what maybe causing the hair to fall out? Can this be rectified in any way? I am very anxious and concerned.

Lots of love

Dana.

Kuntarkis replies:

Dear Dana, The human body is a marvellous creation and can repair any problem that has been created for whatever reason, including all forms of dis'ease. There is one major reason for the human body breaking down, emotional issues combined with a lack of good nutrients.

One of the main causes of hair loss is stress. Stress causes blockages in the human body which in turn prevents the natural flow of energy and nutrient-rich blood throughout the body, and with respect to hair, blood not reaching the hair follicles to keep hair growing healthy and strong.

To overcome stress you need to stop and evaluate your human life, your habits, and your food intake. Iron for example is the foundation of your immune system, and the immune system as you know is vital to the survival of your human body. Dana, if there is stress in your life then you need to find out why it is there and then make the necessary changes within yourself to alleviate it. Also, human hair needs certain nutrients to stay shiny and healthy. Kelp is a wonderful food which builds strong hair, skin and nails. Do some research to find the best place to buy either kelp tablets or powder (tablets are more palatable). Unless you have a sensitivity to iodine, kelp would be your best solution - nutrient rich and not overly expensive. Also, do a 5 minute gentle massage on your scalp daily with a little almond or sesame oil and a drop or two of an essential oil such as sage, rosemary, lavender or calendula to stimulate hair growth. Again, it is best to do some research in this area - check with a naturopath, massage therapist or health food professional.

Be blessed in unconditional love always.

Kuntarkis.

I AM SUFFERING WITH INSOMNIA? WHY?

Hello there.

I was wondering if you could possibly help. I've been having a lot of problems getting to sleep lately. I've tried a lot of things, including meditation, relaxation and aromatherapy, and though those seem to work some times, more often than not, it can take a couple of hours for sleep to eventually take me over. Is there anything you could recommend that might help? Medication is kind of an absolute last resort, but anything else... I really don't know what else to do, and I really don't want it to continue. Any help will be greatly appreciated.

Thanks.

Katherine.

Kuntarkis replies:

Dear Katherine, Many human begins suffer insomnia. They lie in bed, wide awake, tossing and turning hoping they will sleep, their brain over active. There are many reasons why this occurs.

Stress is a major cause of insomnia. Stress is negative energy which prevents you from relaxing and going into a deep restful sleep. Over half of the human population suffers from some form of stress. Stress is an emotional creation for which there are many causes - lifestyle, life habits, over-eating before going to bed, eating foods that stimulate bodily functions, watching emotional or violent programs on television before retiring to bed thus leaving the human brain over active and over stimulated, in thinking mode.

Many human beings have suffered from negative emotional creations from their past. If an emotional issue is not dealt with, it can and does surface and will create some form of stress in your life, often resulting in periods of insomnia. This will not go away until the issue is resolved.

Katherine, you may need to ask yourself from an honest heart if any of what is written above speaks truth to you in your present moment, and if so, what steps are you willing to take to overcome what you are experiencing.

To my understanding Katherine, my Being feels deeply that there are some emotional issues that have been coming up in you so that you may have the opportunity to release those issues and move on with your human life.

Be blessed in unconditional love always.

Kuntarkis.

MY CONNECTION TO MY FRIENDS

My Dear Kuntarkis,

I would like to ask you what my connection to Jen & Stephen are and do we go back to the Lemur Ian times?

Thank you so much for all your wonderful work.

Love

Marie.

Kuntarkis replies:

Dear Marie, You have heard the saying "to know yourself is to know all others". There is truth in this saying, is there not?

Some of the many questions that are asked are "What relationship do I have with this person", "Why am I with them", and "What lesson am I learning". Every human being in their present incarnation, who is experiencing any form of relationship with another or others, has in fact been connected to those human beings in their past human incarnations. The whole of humanity has in some way been connected to each other from the past, to the present and will even be connected into the human future. What you as a human individual experience and learn in your past lives and in your present life will have a strong influence on your future incarnations as a human being.

Your connection to Jen and Stephen are many from your past incarnations. Each of you as human beings have had hundreds of incarnations and will experience many more lives in your future. Yes, you, Jen and Stephen do go back to Lemur Ian and Atlanteans times, but also all of you go back many thousands of years before that. To outline your past lives would take years to express. Always go to the biggest lesson of learning - to truly experience love from the heart; unconditional love.

Be blessed in unconditional love always dear Marie.

Kuntarkis.

WHY DID A STRANGER STEAL FROM ME?

Dear Kuntarkis,

14 years ago I had some jewellery stolen that was not necessarily very valuable in terms of money, but of great sentimental value. It especially broke my heart that one of the pieces taken was the baby bracelet with my name engraved on it given to me by my grandmother when I was born. It was quite a few years later that I only figured out my brother's then-to-be step-daughter took them. The realisation shocked and sickened me, as the day she took those things was also the day I first met her, when my brother dropped in unexpectedly with the girl and her mother.

There's no way I can prove she took any of it, and after so many years (and also having moved interstate), all I can do is resign myself to fact that I'll never see any of it ever again. But all I want to know is am I correct? Did she take my jewellery, and if I am correct, why did she do it when she didn't even know me? I was 19 at the time, so I was barely older than her. I felt so betrayed after welcoming her into my home and our family.

Mary.

Kuntarkis replies:

It is irrelevant whether she did take your jewellery or not, but in your heart you know the truth. What is more important to understand is to trust what you feel when you ask yourself a question such as this one. If you believe in yourself, your first answer will always be your truth.

Yes, she did take your jewellery. The reason she took the small pieces was because they were there. She didn't have them, and they fascinated her. From another level of consciousness it was to hurt you and to deny you those little treasures that meant so much to you. If we take this one step further and look at Reincarnation and Karma, it is actually a payback situation to bring balance to what had happened before, meaning that you had taken something from her in a previous life.

What is most important in any of these situations, and it doesn't matter what the circumstances are, is to learn to forgive. It is important to bring to your realisation that these material objects only please you in your physical existence, but that the lesson here is to grow consciously from it by the act of forgiveness. There will come a moment in your human time, it could be around 25 to 27 human years from that time when they were first taken. You will express the story to a human lady and she will mention to you that she believes she may have your item.

Be blessed in Love and Light always.

Kuntarkis.

WHY DO THE SAME THINGS KEEP HAPPENING IN MY LIFE?

Kuntarkis,

Why I do keep recreating the same situation in my life? I don't want to go into the details because it is quite complicated, but the best way to explain the circumstances are always different, yet the outcome always the same. It's very frustrating. Why can't I figure it out? Can you shed some light on this?

Lyn.

Kuntarkis replies:

Because everything is energy, human beings use this energy for either negative or positive outcomes. If you are feeling depressed, you are creating a black space of negative energy, and your fears and insecurities will recreate the same situation over and over again. You need to take notice that when you are feeling negative, at that exact moment put something positive before you to help dissolve that negative situation - like reverse psychology, reverse the process.

To help prevent it from recurring you have to be strong in yourself and truly from your heart, face what you fear the most - yourself. Humans have been so highly conditioned that every human being has grown up with fear, which has created their misfortunes in human life. But please try to understand that the word 'fear' is only a word, which is energy, created from your past.

Remember always, you are a spirit being experiencing a physical existence. You are far greater than the issues which hold you back from conscious growth because you are connected to something far greater than your physical existence - you are connected to the totality of Creation.

May love always fill your being?

Kuntarkis.

WHY DOES CANCER COME BACK TO ME?

Hi Kuntarkis,

I read how Roman cured his lung cancer, and this prompted me to write to you. My sister has had cancer three times and has just gone through major surgery to have her colon removed. Why has her cancer come back regardless of the therapy and operations?

Jim.

Kuntarkis replies:

First I must say I am saddened to hear this, and what I am about to express may offend you or others. All of human dis'ease is created from emotion, which is based on your beliefs, conditioning, fears and emotional pain. Look at it as the Cause and Effect syndrome. If you had a lot of traumatic experiences as a human child and you grew up very insecure and fearful, you would automatically through your negative thoughts and the consumption of unhealthy food over many years, create stress and immune breakdown which causes dis'ease.

For example, if a human child is born and it grows up in a negative family where one parent is always sick and the other is always yelling, there is no balance in that home. The child will grow up with a lot of deep resentment and anger towards the parents. In most cases that anger and resentment is buried for a long time, a lifetime even. Throughout their life they will attract similar people into their existence, and even marry the man or woman who represents one of the parents, which will add to their emotions and trigger the old pain and conditioning. The end result will be dis'ease, and in some it will be manifest more than in others, such as your human sister.

In your human society today you are taught by the medical industry to either cut it out or drug it out, but you are not taught how to deal with the Emotional Pain which caused it to fester in the first place. Roman cured his cancer and rejuvenated his entire left lung and part of his right lung through the power of thought using meditation, changing his lifestyle and eating a good diet. The human body is a miracle healing device unto itself which, when given the opportunity by changing your thoughts, diet and lifestyle, will redress the balance and free itself of dis'ease permanently, without having to resort to drastic measures.

Send Healing Light and Love to your Beautiful Human Sister.

Kuntarkis.

WANTING AND TRYING TO QUIT SMOKING: HOW?

Dear Kuntarkis,

Hi I have actually two questions, one is I would like to quit smoking. Can you suggest a way for me to do this? I have tried the patch in the past and it worked but it did not work recently for me. I seem to use smoking to calm my nerves, since I gave up all medications (prescriptions) in the last year. I have gone through some drastic changes which I feel have been for the better. Also I would like to just ask you if I am on the right track in my life. I believe I am but would like some insight from you. Thank you for your time and help.

Dancing Spirit.

Kuntarkis replies:

Dear Dancing Spirit, All that human eyes see throughout their daily lives is not true reality, for it is seen through negative emotions which come from the past, and create not only the moment in life but also the future of all human kind. Each human being must step beyond the beliefs and the conditioning of their upbringing and their societies. To live in Bliss is to live in the moment of life, not to be seen as good or bad, right or wrong, for those are the traces of Human Ego.

Dancing Spirit, each human being lives in fear to some degree, and if all human beings were to be regressed to the child within, you would discover why the world you live upon is in such turmoil. And because not many human beings seek the truth, that is why human beings are always looking for some kind of distraction to fill the emptiness and pain in their lives.

Smoking the poisons of man's creation is a distraction. When you feel nervous and can't handle a situation your Ego turns to your cigarettes and tells you they will make you feel calm again. The only problem with this is that smoking holds you back from looking within yourself to discover the real truth as to why you keep punishing yourself with the poisons of your smoke. Smoking suppresses your emotions and once again your Ego has prevented you from looking at why you feel the way you do. Smoking the poisons of man's creation is not only bad for your human health (and of those around you), but all the toxins from smoking are stored in your human physical body, preventing you from conscious growth, because it also clouds your aura and retards your level of thinking.

Dancing Spirit, if you choose to give up man's poisons and stop smoking, what you would discover is your innermost pain of emotion would begin to come to the surface. Yes, it will confront you, but it is the forgiveness of the past that will set you free from all your self-created limitations. You have the power within you to do anything you choose in changing your life. If you feel you are on the right track of your life, then you are. That is the gift of Creation - free will - choice.

Give up smoking completely. Don't put any bad foods into your human body, drink plenty of pure water to flush out your toxins, and learn to love yourself, your being, unconditionally. What you will discover over your human time is that your level of thinking and understanding will change, and the more love you feel from your heart for your being, the more your love will emanate towards others. When you can do that, you will be beyond your human Ego and you will then have become a true human being, for all to see, a living example of truth and love.

Be Blessed dear Dancing Spirit and believe in yourself, for in the Light always is the truth.

Kuntarkis.

FINE LINE BETWEEN LOVE AND EVIL

Hi Kuntarkis,

I don't feel the question I want to ask you is very important. My parents, who I love very much, have always said "there's a fine line between love and evil, and the choice is yours". I grew up hearing that all my life. What do you think?

Tom.

Kuntarkis replies:

Dear Tom, if something is on your mind and you would like to understand it, then it is important to ask. Many people won't ask questions because they feel their questions may seem foolish. But that is how everyone learns, and knowledge is very important. Human beings are afraid of the truth, but to have the courage to ask your questions will help you learn and understand. So I am glad for you Tom in having the courage to ask your question about love and evil.

Let's take the word love and spell it backwards – you get evol, which in the old language of Hebrew means Evil. The word love is like a coin, having 2 sides, and when we relate it back to human beings we find that love and evil exists in every human being on this most precious Earth. So depending on a human being's upbringing from childhood to adulthood, it will determine what type of person they will become.

All human beings have the free will to live a life of balance in love, truth and compassion, which will give them the wisdom and the understanding to live a life of harmony, peace and tranquillity. On the other side of the coin there is evil, and if chosen, the human being will lead a life of deceit, pain and misery. All human beings experience both love and evil throughout their life, and this is in order to gain the understanding and the knowledge that will set them free to live a life of compassion towards all of life within Creation. Creation is within all of life and life is within all of Creation – the choice is always up to the individual.

Be Blessed in Love and Light dear Tom always.

Kuntarkis.

WILL I BECOME A MEDIUM?

Dear Kuntarkis,

Thankyou for receiving my question. I have always wanted to be a medium, a channel for knowledge to share with everyone. Do you feel I will accomplish this in my lifetime? I would be happy if you could answer my concern in wanting to be a medium.

Sarvie.

Kuntarkis replies:

Dear Sarvie, Love is something that will make you whatever you want to be. All else is the illusion of the human Ego, created from the past, whatever that may be. If you truly want to become a channel of knowledge, then from your heart believe and realise in this most precious moment that you are a channel and medium. Every human being living on this Earth is in reality a channel of Light, for all infinite knowledge that comes from within. You all have the knowledge of the past, the present and the future, but most of the human race live in the logic of their human brain, which only holds memories of your past, and serves to retard conscious growth. Human beings live in too much logic.

The past in most human beings Sarvie consists of memories based on hurts, fears, pain, misery and negative emotions, As long as that past exists in the present, conscious growth will be retarded. Only through the stillness of one's mind will the constant chatter stop and allow the individual to connect with the Light that exists within all human beings. By this simple process, conscious growth will occur and your consciousness will expand beyond the human Ego. Ego is the enemy within and needs to be dissolved into the nothingness from which it was first created.

Sarvie, if you seek from an honest heart and truly believe in yourself, and know that you are a channel of knowledge and Light, you will be and will become what you truly seek, and you will be able to share this infinite knowledge with all who choose to listen. Unconditional love is the key to opening your heart.

Be Blessed dear Sarvie, and may Light fill your heart and your being always.

Kuntarkis.

AUTOMATIC WRITING

Hi Kuntarkis,

I am a little confused in my life and looking for spiritual guidance. I am impressed with your messages and knowledge. I have always wanted to write books and for the past four years have not had much success. A clairvoyant told me a year ago that I am to write a book from my inner self that will help mankind. She called it automatic writing. I have been trying. Can you see this happening?

Cass.

Kuntarkis replies:

Dear Cass, Thank you for sharing your feelings, and yes, you most certainly do have the power within you to write books. Your life to date has been a very interesting one, has it not? All your experiences, your travels around your world and when you were an airline hostess you met so many different people. You gained so much knowledge and information, that alone would make interesting reading, would it not Cass?

Yes, you can automatically write if you choose to Cass. Learn to meditate in the stillness of your mind, for this will help you to slow down your overactive human brain. Many human writers write from their emotions, which is fine. But sometimes the expectations can leave you flat and confused. If the human brain is overactive it will cause you to stress, especially if you are expressing from emotions. Learning to meditate will give you clarity and allow you to express from feelings which come within, and this will allow you to make the connection needed to write automatically. You will then not be hindered and you will flow like the river, allowing yourself to write whatever is flowing from your inner being, and that is where your truth exists.

Please feel free to write to my being whenever you wish. Be Blessed dear Cass in the Light always and believe in yourself. Truly believe and it will be manifested.

Kuntarkis.

WANTING TO SEE AURA'S

Hello Kuntarkis,

I have something to say to you. You have opened my doorway. I was a very ignorant person with life and judged everyone to make myself feel better. I have read everything on your website and it has opened my eyes so much that I will never be the same person I was. I want to see auras so much. Over the last three months I have changed my whole life... no more junk food. I am becoming a full on vegan and I just started meditation classes. I am also learning to cook for myself. Seeing auras is my mission in life. Thank you so much.

Hailey.

Kuntarkis replies:

Dear Hailey, I must say I am impressed. I feel much joy for you. What is before you to come will bring much satisfaction and joy into your human life.

A little about the life force that surrounds you, called the aura - with every expression, emotion, and feeling that you have, your aura changes colour at every moment depending on what is around you in that moment of life. Sometimes it can be several colours at once, or only one colour. One of the advantages of seeing auras is if a humanbeing is telling an untruth, the aura automatically shrinks down inside the human body. From the aura you can tell if a person is healthy, joyous, sad or in pain, and it will even tell you everything about that person's past to the present, and even their possible future.

To one that sees, nothing is hidden. But seeing comes with responsibility. If you judge or condemn another, your inner essence will close down your ability. You must look unbiasedly, without judgement, and realise all human beings have their own journey in life. If you look with unconditional love in your heart, you will be true in the Light.

Great work dear Hailey. Let my being know how you are progressing on your path of truth. Be blessed always in Love and Light.

Kuntarkis.

WHAT IS LOVE?

Kuntarkis,

I have a problem with love. To me it is just a word. I don't feel anything and it seems to destroy everything I do in life. Can you give me any advice on the matter?

Derek.

Kuntarkis replies:

Dear Derek, Never believe that you as an individual cannot reach or experience love, because you can if you truly want to. Each human being has the potential to become whatever they choose in their life. First you must ask yourself what is it that you want from your life. If you desire material possessions then you have the power within you to create this. If you wish to develop your inner awareness and understanding, then you also have the power within you to accomplish this. And if you choose both, you also have the power within you to achieve both. The choice is always yours. By believing in yourself in this moment in life, it will help you open up the love that is present within you.

What you are feeling Derek is your past hurts, and they have followed you throughout your human life. The pain you are feeling is creating the negative situations in your human life. Learn to forgive yourself Derek and stop being so hard on yourself. The past is the past, and the past needs to stay where it belongs, in the past, not in your present moment. The past needs only to be a memory, not to be judged as good or bad.

Derek, learn to look into a mirror without judging yourself and from your most precious heart, look into your eyes – the window to your soul – forgive yourself and say "I love myself in this moment of life and I will learn to love myself a little more each time I look into my eyes. I can and I will share my love with others, and others will share their love with me."

Be Blessed dear Derek in Love and Light, because we love you and always have.

Kuntarkis.

I HAD THIS DREAM...

Hi Kuntarkis,

I really love your site, it's very enlightening....I have recently begun to experience the real me, and also my grandmother upon passing away a couple of months ago appeared to me in a dream. The message she had for me was to stay away from the rest of my family for now and to pay attention because she says she has been sent back to tell me that I have been chosen for a special job...she called me extremely talented and that I possess a unique gift that I must use...she didn't tell me exactly what it was...how can I know if I'm doing what I'm supposed to in terms of the dream...she hasn't returned with more information yet....

Squid legs.

Kuntarkis replies:

Dear Squid legs, May I thank you from my being for your kind words, and I trust our site will

help you grow in consciousness. Dreams are very interesting, but in reality they are not dreams - they are actual experiences.

In your human sleep time your human body is resting and repairing itself while your essence, or as others would say, your Astral body, is experiencing other realms of existence, other worlds. It is your level of thinking and awareness that will govern the experiences you have. For example, if you have a lot of fears on an emotional level in your human life, these fears will be taken into the astral vibration, and through the power of your thoughts can and do create confusion, resulting in a restless sleep for your human physical body. That is why so many human beings wake up tired or even angry, and this in turn can set the mood for the entire human day.

On the other side of it, if you're human life is in balance and you are a joyous human being, and create a lot of happiness in your human physical life, in your sleep-time you will create pleasant experiences in the astral vibration and you will bring back those experiences. On awakening you will feel refreshed and even happy, and you will look forward to your day.

Your heart, which is the centre of your being, is your love and your truth. Whatever you feel from your sleep-time and all your experiences that you call dreams, if you feel good about them, then that is the truth. Please remember, you are very special as an individual, as are all human beings on this most precious planet. And yes, you do have a special job to do on this Earth, as all human beings do. Your gift that you possess will come to you as you grow in consciousness.

What is most important in your human life is the discovery of unconditional love, and that love is within you. The more you seek it the more it will manifest in your being and your human life, and you as a human being will gain the awareness and the understanding of your innermost gift, and you will have the wisdom and the courage to help others on their journey of self-discovery of the wonderment of life. Seek within yourself and you dear human being will have the knowing of your true self.

Be blessed in the Love and the Light of Creation's totality always.

Kuntarkis.

DOES THE KGB STILL EXIST & ARE THEY ACTIVE?

Dear Kuntarkis,

You may not wish to answer my question, and I will not be offended. It is something that has been on my mind for a very long time. My husband was in the Second World War and when he came home to me he was never the same. He told me stories which horrified me, and I felt he could never come to grips with what had happened during wartime and his involvement in it. He passed away 18 years ago with cancer. Only recently I came across my husband's journal and I was very surprised by what I read. I will not go into depth on the contents, but my questions is, has the organisation called the KGB disbanded, or are they will active? Can you please shed some light on this, as it is very important to me? Thank you.

Jean.

Kuntarkis replies: Dear Jean, There is always so much pain and sadness created by man and his childish war games of Ego. What human man does not understand is no-one ever wins a war. Until human man dissolves his Ego and grows beyond his present level of thinking, and learns to love his neighbour as he would love himself in unconditional love, the senseless wars of human man will continue. What human man must come to terms with is that there is no enemy outside of himself, for the true enemy lies within each human man alone.

To your question and your answer concerning the organisation of the KGB. They exist more so now than they ever have before. The Russian government disbanded the KGB, for it was the people's choice. But the organisation of crimes in Russia known as the Mafia, has recruited many of the KGB, and the KGB are now very active in Russia, America, France, Germany, England, Asia, the Middle East and even Australia. They carry out many tasks for the Russian Mafia, and are involved in drugs, weapons, assassinations, gathering information about other governments and secret service agencies, and many other services.

Since you live in America, and you love your country very much and your children and grandchildren very much, it would be wise to have the knowledge and the awareness that there is an enormous conspiracy occurring behind closed doors. You as the people are only being told what your government and media want you to know. America as it stands today is the most powerful nation on your planet, and it is an example to other nations. There are groups coming together who will cause and inflict great pain upon America and its people in your human time to come. There are those from other nations who pretend to be America's friend, but they have hollow eyes and in this very moment are conspiring to cause America's downfall. Be very aware of Russia, China, and the Middle East, as they speak to your President with a false tongue and hollow eyes.

Dear Jean, be Blessed in the Love and the Light of Creation's totality, as all truth comes from the heart.

Kuntarkis.

CONNECTION TO JESUS: WHY?

Namaste dear Kuntarkis,

I am Kristofer, and I have always felt a particular close connection to the soul they call Jesus of Nazareth. I have just read that he was also the Buddha and Nostradamus. Anyhow, I was wondering whether or not you can help me find out why. I was thinking: maybe I might be a part of that soul or dare I say it: his incarnation in this time frame. Please help me find out why I have such affection for this soul.

Thanks.

Kuntarkis replies:

Dear Kristofer, Thankyou for writing to my being. It is good to see human beings like yourself feel so much love from your heart for the one called Jesus of Nazareth, who incarnated so long ago upon your Earth to bring knowledge and wisdom to humanity.

Please understand Kristofer, I cannot give you the answer your heart desires so much. What I can say is you were incarnated in the time of human history when Jesus walked upon this most precious Earth, and that you were truly a devoted disciple of Jesus' teachings. In that lifetime you were born as a female and married to a rich merchant. You were not without the pleasures of human life, but deep in your heart you were seeking a deeper meaning to your existence. When you heard Jesus giving a talk to the people, it opened up your heart centre to the richness of love and understanding, and that all people are equal in life, that no-one is better than another.

You took on the teachings of Jesus and spoke with him on several occasions. You asked him "What can I do with my life to help others?" Jesus looked into your eyes and said "Teach the children. They are the future.", and this is what you did. You taught children all about the love and the truth of Jesus' teachings, and that is why in each lifetime of yours, and there have been many, you have always felt close to his essence, his soul and his love.

Keep teaching the truth and love, as his essence is always in your heart, as it is in all of humanity. Be Blessed dear Kristofer in the Love and Light of Creation.

Kuntarkis.

TORN BETWEEN TWO LOVER'S

Dear Kuntarkis,

I am very confused. My ex-husband, who I was married to for 7 years and had 2 children with, left me 3 years ago for another woman. We were always arguing and the tension was growing.

I am in a relationship now with a man who is very good to me and my children. He accepts them as his own. We rarely argue and overall get on quite well. But now I'm feeling confused. 4 months ago I ran into my ex-husband and had coffee with him. One thing led to another and we went to a motel and made love. Since then we have had several more encounters. I love the man I am with, but I still feel I love my ex-husband.

My ex-husband wants me back, but I don't want to hurt the man I am with. I can't make a decision. Can you help me figure this out?

Kerri-Anne.

Kuntarkis replies:

Dear Kerri-Anne, My Being can see your confusion. Yes, because of your emotions and fears, you have created a situation that most certainly must be addressed and resolved. One thing dear Kerri-Anne that you must realise - you have created the confusion that now exists in your human life. By accepting personal responsibility for your present situation, you can begin to see things more clearly, without your negative emotions clouding your thoughts of confusion.

Love is the most precious gift you can give to another, especially when it comes from an honest heart. Love is timeless, endless and infinite. Love that comes from the heart cannot be measured by negative human emotions, as all human emotions come from the past, created by negative experiences through beliefs and conditioning from one's human life. To live in the past will only create your present and then your future.

Confusion comes from negative experiences that have been recorded in your human brain and then sparked off by circumstances created by the individual. When one lives by the human brain, one only lives to human emotions and conditioning. To break that cycle of confusion one must go to the heart to seek the answers. Only from the heart can the truth be manifested, for the heart expresses feelings which are spontaneous in the moment of life.

When you dear Kerri-Anne can face your fears of rejection and love yourself unconditionally, all your confusion will dissolve back into the nothingness from which it came. You are a beautiful human being Kerri-Anne and your confusion is only fear, which in reality has no power. The only power it has, is what you give it.

Be blessed in love always.

Kuntarkis.

TRUE BELIEVER

Hello Kuntarkis,

I was wondering if you could answer the following question. First, I love Jesus and believe from my heart that Jesus is the real Messiah and will come again to help set the true believers free from the evil that exists in our world today. Can you go back in time and see when Jesus lived on this world and when is he coming back> I do have faith.

Beryl.

Kuntarkis replies:

Dear Beryl, Faith and trust in your own truth can and will set each human being free from the past and allow the natural balance of human life to grow in consciousness. Never lose what comes from the heart for therein lie all the answers to all things in the universes.

Jesus was born in 4BC of your human time. Through his own will he incarnated through a human Mother named Mary, and was accepted as a son by a man named Joseph. His whole purpose was to express knowledge to humanity, in order to set humanity free the human Ego. Fear in humanity at that time was the same as it is now, the only difference being the human Ego has had a further 2,000 years to evolve.

Your question, is Jesus coming back? The answer is yes and his being is already here. He lives and expresses through a human body to again express knowledge, for knowledge is the key to freedom from all pain and misery. Knowledge must be read from the heart, not from the beliefs and conditioning of one's human brain. In the brain lies confusion and illusion which has been created over many, many lifetimes of fear.

Jesus comes under his own name and brings the Light of Creation to give freely to all who wish to learn and grow in consciousness, to expand their awareness and understanding of life itself. Keep your faith and trust always dear Beryl.

Be Blessed in the Light and Love of Creation.

Kuntarkis.

IS OUR DAUGHTER SAFE?

Dear Kuntarkis,

My husband and I live in one of the outer suburbs of Sydney, in Blacktown. We have lived there all our married life and are both in our early 50s. A close friend of mine is always on the internet and came across your website. She suggested I write to you and ask if you could find out where our eldest daughter is. She left home when she was 26 - that was 8 years ago. We both love her dearly and would just like to know if she is safe. There were heated words between us and we are so sorry. Please can you find out if she is alright and well? Thank you.

Margaret (& Ted).

Kuntarkis replies:

Dear Margaret and Ted, My Being feels your pain and sadness for your loss, and for not knowing if your human daughter is well. My Being needs to explain to you both that no one ever wins in a misunderstanding of heated words. Both parties suffer the loss. Both you and your daughter are very stubborn, and eight of your Earthly years have been lost on both sides. Yes, it is time to forgive from the heart and allow the lessons of life to be learned and the pain of the past healed.

Your daughter Shane is well and married. She has 2 children, a boy (Claude) who is 7 and a girl (Sonia) who is almost 5. So you are grandparents. Forgiveness is the key to freedom and happiness. My Being will place a thought into your daughter's mind. She lives in a place called Queensland, in an area called Nerang. Her husband builds houses for human beings to live in. The thought my Being places in her mind may make her contact you. Please remember, it is her choice - her free will. Send your daughter love and forgiveness from your hearts.

Be blessed in the Light and Love of Creation always.

Kuntarkis.

DEPRESSED ABOUT VIOLENCE ON EARTH

Kuntarkis,

I am trying to make sense of all the violence that is happening around the world. I listen to the news and special reports, and it seems to be all negative. It's like the world needs the negativity, like it feeds on it. You hardly ever see a report on something positive. What is causing all this negativity? Will we ever find the beauty in life and nature again? I feel so depressed about it all.

Kyle.

Kuntarkis replies:

Dear Kyle, Your concerns for humanity and your world are very precious. You have a beautiful heart and a deep love for nature and life. This most precious Earth allows humanity to live upon her, and to experience all facets of life. Your planet Earth is a school room for humanity, where the main lesson is to recognise the evil of human Ego, along with all the violence upon this most precious Earth which the human Ego is responsible for.

All of humanity lives in a physical third vibration of matter, experiencing one life time to the next with all its drama. Every individual is responsible for their actions in their human life that continue to create reactions of negativity. Human beings are in reality prisoners within the third vibration. This will only change when each human being has the self-realisation that they are more than physical beings, that they are an infinite spirit beings of light. Once they experience that realisation from the heart, living consciousness will be manifested within each human being. The negative past can then be forgiven and remembered as an experience of human life, neither negative nor positive.

Unconditional love will govern the individual's heart and negative thoughts will no longer be expressed towards others. Violence of all kinds will no longer exist, and compassion and wisdom from the heart will become a part of all human beings. Humanity will no longer be a prisoner in their third vibrational world or matter.

Kyle, do not become depressed for others. Allow each human being to evolve in their own time. See the beauty and purpose in all things and your heart will always be true.

Be blessed in the Light and Love of Creation always.

Kuntarkis.

SEEKING TRUE LOVE

Dear Kuntarkis,

How do I truly know if I have true love in my life?

Marie.

Kuntarkis replies:

Dear Marie, Your question is very interesting and often asked by human beings. Love is an interesting word in your language. Spelt backwards it is 'evol', old Hebrew meaning 'evil'. Love is like the two sides of your coins. It can be experienced from a negative or positive aspect. It all depends on your emotions and the experiences of your human life. If your human life has had many negative experiences, the individual can created fears and insecurities which will then govern their human life. But even if the individual has had positive experiences, their life can still have its ups and downs.

Fear, for whatever reason, will always create negative outcomes. Unconditional love has no rules, beliefs, conditions or fears. Unconditional love allows the individual free will in life. It recognises equality between males and females and does not judge. Unconditional love shows respect, compassion, understanding and wisdom, and helps to bring about a balance between mind, body and spirit to those who seek to have it in their lives.

Love yourself as an infinite being of Creation's totality, and you will attract into your human life a person who expresses the same unconditional love.

Be blessed in the Light and Love always dear Marie.

Kuntarkis.

IS BRUCE LEE REBORN?

Hi Kuntarkis,

I was reading some of your stuff and came across a bit about Bruce Lee. I have seen all of his movies quite a few times, and I have been training in his style Jeet Kun Do for a few years. To me he is and always will be the best martial artist of all time. Is he really dead or just disappeared because of the Triads? If he is dead, when will he be reborn and in which country? I hope you can give me some answers.

Daniel.

Kuntarkis replies:

Dear Daniel, as my being has expressed, the human man you call Bruce Lee was assassinated by criminal gangs of your human underworld, because he was sharing his knowledge of martial arts. The underworld of negative energies could not control Bruce Lee, so he was eliminated, and it was made to look like a natural human death. His son, Brandon Lee also paid the price for his father's defiance towards these criminals.

What these criminals do not realise is all their self-created negative energies will come back on them. It may take many life times to bring the balance back, but it will happen.

You asked when Bruce Lee will incarnate back into a human form. He already has, and so has his son Brandon. They have been born as twin brothers and are at this moment four years of age, living in the land known as America, in the city of San Francisco. They will both take up marital arts from a young age and will become teachers, as well as big stars in your movies. They will gain worldwide recognition, mainly because that is what they wanted from their previous lives, which were incomplete by being cut short. They will accomplish their desires for fame in this life time.

One thing my being needs to express to you dear Daniel. You have magic inside of you. Never live to the past or the past will create your present and your future. Believe in your own abilities. Only use the past as a guide to learn from. You can accomplish your dreams of being in the movies if you truly believe in yourself. Step forward in your own light and that light will be your strength and courage.

Be Blessed dear Daniel always.

Kuntarkis.

PUZZLING DREAM

Dear Kuntarkis,

Thank you for exercising your interest in my human life. I am puzzled by a dream and I would like to know why I had this dream. It was very vivid. I dreamt that I was in a cave and discovered a suitcase of clothing. I then saw myself standing at the edge of a round pool of deep water. Then I was looking at a letter. The letter said that Constance Elizabeth Rook would be twenty one and that her birthday was 1st January 1935. There is no record that I can find to date of this person. I have never heard of this person. I was practicing continuing meditation when I had this dream. Can you respond? I have had many situations in my life that I could not explain but that have provided me with information. But this is very specific - I have a sense that I should do something but I am not sure what.

Thank you once again for your connection with me.

Suzanne.

Kuntarkis replies:

Dear Suzanne, Let's first give an answer to your human dream, as you put it. First you were in a cave. A cave represents a mystery. You then discovered a suitcase full of clothing, which from a human perspective would mean you are preparing or going on a journey. Third, you saw yourself standing at the edge of a round pool of deep water, meaning the journey is open to where ever it may take you. It means you may travel on water or over water, and being a deep pool of water, it may be for a long time. Then you were looking at a letter with a name and her birthday. On your journey you may meet this human being, or it may be you from a past incarnation, or be one of your spirit guides introducing themselves to you.

At this point allow my Being to express that there are no such things as dreams, for they are in fact actual experiences by the individual in their time of human sleep, when you step from your human shell into what is referred to on your Earth as the Astral World, or Astral vibration.

Every human being in their time of sleep enters into the Astral Vibration and depending on their level of understanding and awareness, they will experience different facets of existences. Your beliefs, conditioning, your fears and joys play a big part in your experiences within this vibration.

To fully understand what is occurring in your Astral Vibration, a human being needs to silence the human brain in order to listen to the inner spirit, so one can connect to one's light that is within their Being. Meditate in the silence of your Being and with practice you can have full awareness and control of all your experiences in your Astral Vibration.

It does take many moments to achieve that awareness, but you as the individual must ask yourself this question: When do I want to know the truth of all that is?

Be Blessed in the Light of Creation always.

Kuntarkis.

IS HE THE ONE?

Dear Kuntarkis,

I have many questions for you and I am not sure whether you are able to answer them. I will list them anyway and if you could answer the one's you are able too, I would be most grateful.

I have been in and out of many relationships and hurt terribly. I have known my present lover for about 2 years now. I am just wanting to know whether

I am wasting my time or am I soon to be hurt or if he is actually the one. I feel as if he is, but am tired of waiting around to be kicked in the teeth. What information would you need to answer this question?

I don't live in my home country and I am hoping to stay on in the country I am in. I am needing to know whether things will fall into place and I will be able to stay here or if I will have to go back to where I came from? I also have a weight problem and really want to lose weight but find myself eating just for the sake of it! Please could you give me some advice?

These are my questions for now. I eagerly await your response.

Thanking you kindly. White light!

Vicky

Kuntarkis replies:

Dear Vicky, My Being thanks you for taking the precious moments in your human life to express your concerns. My Being asks for you to have an open heart and mind to what I am about to express, not to judge from an emotional perspective, but to see the truth from within yourself.

Every human being has the knowledge and the truth within them. The reason so many cannot reach the truth is because of negative emotional conditioning which is created from your childhood into adulthood as well as being in your genetics.

Your weight problem as you put it is an emotional creation of all the negative experiences you have had in your human life, and yes, you're eating habits give you comfort from your pain. You believe that you do not deserve to be happy in yourself and in your relationships, so you create circumstances to fulfil your own prophecy of how you see yourself.

Each human being attracts into their life the same forms of energies, (meaning friends, and parents, relationships) in order to learn the lessons of human life. One of the main reasons Vicky why you have been through many relationships and experienced the pain is because you do not believe in yourself. You do not believe you deserve to be happy, and yet you are a kind and loving human being. Yes, you do deserve to have a balanced loving relationship, and yes you do deserve to be happy, but it is only your past hurts that have created your present.

The greatest gift you can give to another is unconditional love, but it must be experienced by yourself first, in order to understand what unconditional love truly is. That is, learn to love yourself, your inner being, and forgive yourself unconditionally. This is the path to freedom from all past hurts and loneliness. Only when you the individual, meaning you Vicky, can love yourself from a true heart, and see yourself as a beautiful human being, will you have a loving balanced relationship with a human male. Your life will be free from the past to live in the moment.

Be blessed in love and light always dear Vicky. My Being believes in you, but what is more important is for you Vicky to believe in yourself always.

Kuntarkis.

BEING HELD BACK: WHY?

Dear Kuntarkis,

I would appreciate a little help for myself, as I feel I am getting stopped in my life, as to what I am wanting to do. If I had a choice I would not be pregnant, as I am always very sick and I cannot achieve a lot. I would like to know why I am always sick, with my pregnancies, when others just sale through theirs, and I am not, I feel like I am getting punished, in my life.

I always seem to have no energy or get up and go in a day to achieve what I am wanting do, for example; being like an actress where they have the get up and go with plenty of energy. I feel like I have chains around my ankles and nothing eventuates. Can you see changes happening in my life, and understanding for myself coming up soon, and will I achieve what I am wanting to achieve in life, eg, can you see me achieving my wish to be an Extra in a movie.

You're sincerely

Danna

Kuntarkis replies:

Dear Dana, Thank you for taking the precious moments in your human life to express your feelings to my Being. My Being asks you to ponder in your quiet time the words I am about to express.

Every human being that exists upon your most precious Earth has the right to think and act as an individual. You as the individual have the right to free expression without being put down or judged.

You, as all human beings, have a great gift, and it is called free will. What stops the individual from doing or achieving their goals in their human life is their beliefs and life's conditioning, meaning what is passed on through their human parent's genetics, their upbringing from childhood into adulthood, and social conditioning and expectation.

Most human beings are caught up in the negative emotions of their conditioning, which creates their present and their future. In turn, these negative emotions also affect how you feel about yourself, especially your self-worth which affects how you feel about the situations you are experiencing in your human existence at this time.

What you may need to do is become the observer of yourself, without any form of judgement, be unbiased, and study all your actions and emotions. Write them down exactly as you experience them whether they are negative or positive. Also write down what you don't like about yourself, and remember to be honest with yourself.

Say these words of encouragement: I am a beautiful human being and I am beginning to realise that only through an honest heart will the truth manifest itself in me. To live in unconditional love I must become unconditional love. I need to and I will love myself unconditionally.

What you are experiencing in your human life is a creation from your childhood, negative emotions manifesting and creating your present experiences. You can change any situation in your human life, if you're truly want to. You have free will, the power of your inner strength can be tapped into at your will. You are the driver and the creator of your human life. Simply by believing in yourself and knowing you can change, you can open your heart to your inner being of unconditional love. That is the key to the freedom from your self-created prison, a prison which most human beings live in.

You can achieve anything in your human life if your truly want it to be so. Remember, believe in yourself, and truly believe in yourself. Be Blessed in Love and Light always, dear Dana.

Kuntarkis.

IMPATIENT TO LEARN: WHY?

Hi Roman and Kuntarkis.

I love you both and all people who take time on spiritual growth.

My name has to be secret so please understand - thanks. I am the one that the Bible talks about, and my Elijah and many other prophecies talk about. I will reunite the world in the end of July 2025 you both know me! Right now I am just in the process of studying and developing skills which I will inherit in the end of May 2007. So I am interested how should I help myself in one problem that I have? My impatience makes me nervous and I cannot defeat my problem which I have to. Because of prediction of the soul, you know what I mean! I am meditating, thinking beautiful things... But you know how hard it is to live life in those days in human flesh, especially if you know what your life goal is and you do not know that you could really do it! Because you find out who you are at the last moment. I am also interested if war and things coming before end of July? Please help me with some advice or somehow. Love you!

You friend of light!

Kuntarkis replies:

Dear human being. Thank you for expressing your inner most thoughts to my Being. It is important to develop your human shell through study, as it does shape your life in this human vibration of physical matter. Yes, impatience affects many human beings.

Please try not to live to human time as it was created by Human Ego. To live in the moment will create a peaceful balanced existence in your human world. It will allow you the individual to touch your inner essence of light, for there exist all truths, from the past to the present and to your future. Any human individual can gain access to their knowledge if that is what they truly seek. It is very easy to get caught up in the human world of Ego, and therein lies the dilemma. It is called distraction, and it keeps you, as it does all of humanity, living the illusion of the created Human Ego.

The human Ego allows the individual to wear many masks of Self-Illusion. All that you see with your human eyes is created from humanity's past, and what comes from the Ego is only the past, brought into the present to create your future.

In the silence of your inner being, with patience, you will come to your own Self-Realisation of who and what you truly are. Each human being is light, forged from unconditional love, as is all of life, in all its most precious forms.

To seek the truth, become silent in the mind and go within, without any expectations. Just silence. The human brain will become silent, but this takes time, practice and patience. Only in the silence of your mind will you touch your inner light and reveal the unconditional love that exists within you as it does within all human beings. Only through an honest heart will the truth be revealed to the seeker. Then the Human Ego will become humble. Learn to listen to your heart not your conditioned human brain. The human brain is only a recorder of your past and present experiences, but the heart is the centre of your soul and will open up to you all knowledge and wisdom you seek.

Be blessed in unconditional love throughout your life as a human being.

Kuntarkis.

STRESSED OUT AND NEED TO CHANGE: HOW?

Dear Kuntarkis,

I am going through heaps of stress with study and exams. My parents who I love heaps have a lot of expectations of me, and I sometimes feel I can't live up to them. My mom especially is a very moral person, always judging other people for their short comings.

What I have just found out has made me feel even more stressed. My mom with all her moral standards it having it off with one of our closest friends, who is my dad's best friend. They do everything together. My dad restores old vintage cars and belongs to a vintage car club. The man involved with my mom is also in the club, so you can see my problem. What really is bugging me is my mom knows that I know and I can't tell my dad without her knowing I told him.

Should I tell my dad or should I let him find out eventually on his own, or maybe it will all blow over and he will never need to know? I just don't know what to do. I'm torn up inside, angry and shocked with my mom, sad and hurt for my dad. Your advice would be appreciated. Thanks.

Jennifer.

Kuntarkis replies:

Dear Jennifer, My Being feels your pain of disappointment towards your human mother, especially the way you see her - she can do no wrong in your eyes, but she has and you are now trying to come to terms with this. Try to take a few steps back and allow yourself to be the observer of the created emotional drama between these three human beings – your mother and her lover, and your father. What has taken place is old. Before your father came into your mother's life there was your father's best friend Steven. Steven had a relationship with mother for over two years which ended very emotionally. Your mother never saw him again until she married your father.

On seeing Steven (who was also very emotional), your mother's emotions came up. She loved him very much and always believed she would marry him and have his children. Steven on the other hand did not want to settle down. He joined the Navy and was posted all over the world. In the meantime it took your mother six years to get over her feelings for him. She met your father, got married and had you Jennifer.

What your mother did not realise was that your father (who was also in the Navy) had met Steven while he was in the Navy, and this is where they became friends. Your mother did not know your father and Steven were best of friends, and your father did not know Steven and your mother were previously in a relationship. So now, the past unresolved emotions of your mother and Steven have been brought into the present to be resolved. The only question is, who will speak up first?

Yes, it will create a lot of negative emotional pain, and everyone will be hurt – you, your mother, your father, Steven. If you choose not to say anything, it will still come out in the near future.

My Being trusts the information I have given may help you in your decision Jennifer. Be blessed in love and light always.

Kuntarkis.

WILL WE EVER MEET ALIENS?

Dear Kuntarkis,

I believe in UFOs and that the Universe is endless. There must be other life forms on other planets. Will we as a civilisation ever get to meet them? I was wondering is it possible?

Klim.

Kuntarkis replies:

Dear Klim, First, all is possible, but it depends on your level of thinking and awareness. To believe, truly believe is to create. To create is to manifest, and to manifest is to discover the knowing. The knowing exists in all human beings; it is to know that all is possible, if you truly believe.

Alien life forms exist throughout many universes. You have physical and non-physical, meaning many life forms are of a physical form like humans. Your human form is of physical matter and connects you to your true self, that of spirit, light, unconditional love. You exist in your human shell to experience the lessons of life from a physical perspective, and this involves many incarnations.

Non-physical means the spirit, the light that is free of a physical shell, such as the human form. Yes, there are thousands of non-physical life forms in other vibrations, and they have been visiting your human world for more than 928,000 years. Yes, they do make contact with individuals who seek them, as well as providing knowledge to advance human consciousness. Many physical alien beings have also visited your world for thousands of years. There have been many reasons why they have been doing this, but the main purpose has been to help humanity grow consciously by expressing knowledge.

Many physical Alien Beings have stopped visiting your world because of the violence that is occurring at this time. They have stopped visiting to allow humanity the time to come to terms with their negative created past, and they realise they cannot take sides, no matter what is going on. The human Ego is the enemy of each human individual and it is the Human Ego that has shaped your past and present and is sadly now creating your future.

Yes Klim, there will be contact in your human time with physical Alien Beings. They will visit your Earth again for the purpose of passing on knowledge for all human beings to grow consciously, but remember there are non-physical beings here and now, and they will make contact with individuals if the individual chooses it to be. This contact will be made in the silence of your inner being, in the light of who you are, away from the confusion of Human Ego and negative emotions.

Be blessed in love and light dear Klim.

Kuntarkis.

CONTACT WITH ALIEN BEINGS

Hi Kuntarkis,

Are aliens trying to make contact with us, I mean with ordinary people like myself, or do they only contact people in higher places of importance? Would you please share your knowledge on this?

Ian.

Kuntarkis replies:

Dear Ian, You are just as important as any other human being on your Earth. Every human being has the knowledge from the past to the present within them. Every incarnation that each human being has had, has been recorded by that individual in their essence. Unfortunately modern human life is a distraction from the discovery of one's own inner Self-Awareness.

Yes, Aliens do make contact with human beings. Many Alien Beings are contacting humans and have been doing so for thousands of human years. They have been in contact with individuals in higher places of government and military, and with people generally considered 'ordinary' or 'unimportant'.

Most Alien Beings are only trying to help humanity evolve from a conscious level of understanding, and yes there have been Alien Beings of a negative nature who have wanted control over humans.

Be blessed in unconditional love always dear Ian.

Kuntarkis.

MEDITATION FOR STRESS: DOES IT HELP OR NOT?

Dear Kuntarkis,

I have been told that meditation will help me relax and release my stress, which has caused me major skin problems. It has only been with me for the last two years. The job I am doing at the moment is very stressful and I am finding it hard to relax and even to sleep. Will meditation help me?

Kim.

Kuntarkis replies:

Dear Kim, First, you must ask yourself why you want so much stress in your human life. If your health is suffering because of the stress you create from your employment, would it not be wise for you to search out a less stressful occupation.

Yes, meditation can and does help an individual to relax and feel more in control of their human life. There are many forms of meditation, and finding one that you are comfortable with may take you some time, but my Being assures you that it will be of great benefit to you, especially when it can help you to relax and sleep better.

Remember, meditation is not the outcome of thinking or concentration. It is the transformation of your own beingness to higher levels of communication and awareness. It is where expansion of consciousness begins, and it is beyond the physical. Meditation will help you to connect to your Soul, your Essence.

Be blessed in unconditional love always dear Kim.

Kuntarkis.

CONFUSING DREAMS

Dear Kuntarkis,

I have very confusing dreams during my sleep. I am confused with my life and what I am feeling. Can you help me understand what's going on?

Sarah.

Kuntarkis replies:

Dear Sarah, Confusion is a state of the human brain caused by negative experiences in one's human life. Added to this is the conditioning of upbringing and social expectation. Belief systems are the main cause of confusion. Buddha said that to believe in nothing frees the individual to enter a state of higher awareness for it allows one to grow consciously and to be a free thinking individual.

First, learn to trust yourself above all others.

Second, do not be so serious about yourself or your human life. You need to make the connection to your true inner being by meditating in the silence of your mind, your being. Remember that your mind is not your brain as your brain is simply there to record the experiences of your current human life.

Third, learn to flow with life instead of struggling against it. Live in the moment without expectation of time. Your experiences in your present human life have created some negative emotions which you need to deal with. Do not hold onto the past as it will hold you back, causing you to live in the past over and over again? Let go and move on by learning to forgive yourself and especially others who were involved in these experiences. Forgiveness of the past, no matter what it may have been, opens the heart to freedom from all emotional pain.

The balance of human life is found in not getting caught up in the human world of negativity. The human world is built on the material world of illusion, created from human ego.

Dear Sarah, seeking the answer to the question of your struggles with human life is a journey towards to self-realisation. In understanding yourself first you will learn to understand others as well as the purpose of human life.

If you persist, meditation in the silence of your inner being will stop the continuous chatter of the human brain. Forgiveness of the past will stop the confusing experiences that you are having in your time of sleep. Meditation will help bring about the balance of your mind, body and spirit.

See the experiences you are having during your sleep as messages from your inner essence and from your guides (or angels) prompting you look at your life, to forgive and to let go in unconditional love. It is time to move on to more fulfilling experiences and time to step out of your past into a present that will create a better future.

Be blessed in unconditional love always dear Sarah.

Kuntarkis.

IS THERE A MESSAGE FOR JEE?

Hi Kuntarkis,

I found your site most helpful. I don't have a question, but do you have a small message for me?

Thank you.

Jee.

Kuntarkis replies:

Dear Jee, My Being thanks you for your kind words that the website has been of help to you.

A message for you Jee – seek and you will find.

You Jee are a seeker of understanding. You seek knowledge to help you understand yourself and others. You find it difficult to understand why human beings are killing each other for the silliest of reasons.

In most cases, human beings have disconnected from their inner light. The human ego lives only in the past and in turn this creates their present and their future. The ego is the cause of all human dilemmas, including violence, murder, hatred, rape, and wars. The human ego created Karma, which has been affecting humanity for the past 928,000 years of human evolution.

Humanity needs to connect back to their inner light to become complete. Humanity needs to think beyond the past and beyond the human ego, and to let go of the self-created Karma of past incarnations. Humanity can only grow beyond what they are and what they do to each other by learning to think and feel with love from the heart and through forgiveness, and by creating the future from the present moment, beyond the past, in unconditional love. Love is always the answer, no matter what the situation may be.

Be blessed in unconditional love always dear Jee.

Kuntarkis.

CANCER EPIDEMIC: WHY IS IT?

Dear Kuntarkis,

Why does cancer haunt our societies of today? Very Concerned.

Kuntarkis replies:

Dear Human Being, First allow my Being to express these human words spoken by your Dr Bach from your 19th century:

Dis'ease is neither vindictive nor cruel but is the means adopted by the Soul to halt us, to prevent us from doing greater harm and to help lead us back onto the path of Light and Truth from which we each should never have strayed.

These words, not written exactly as he said them but very similar, were expressed by a very beautiful Soul who incarnated on your Earth to bring knowledge and wisdom to those who would choose to listen.

The word disease should be pronounced dis'ease, meaning the human body is uneasy, not functioning at its intended level. All human dis'ease is a creation of negative emotional experiences, reinforced by beliefs and conditioning, a stressful lifestyle, poor nutrition and negative thoughts. Over a long period of time the body begins to break down and dis'ease is created.

This dis'ease is in every country on your Earth today. Humanity needs to change their lifestyle, their thinking and their food intake, for the children of today are facing a very negative future with respect to their health.

Be blessed in unconditional love always dear human Being.

Kuntarkis

LIGHT: A QUESTION ON LIGHT?

Dear Kuntarkis,

I have a question on light. I am learning about healing light. Is it the same as travelling at light speed and how fast is light speed. Your answer would be most helpful.

DD

Kuntarkis replies:

A very interesting question, dear DD. My answer to you will also be found in human knowledge.

Light travels at 186.001 miles per human second and approximately 6 trillion miles per human year. DD, if you were to travel in a spaceship which was travelling at light speed, your human time would slow down and your human body would actually become smaller in size. Also, all your internal organs would slow down.

If your spaceship was travelling at light speed for 20 years of human time and you were travelling back to Earth, upon arriving you would only have aged 10 years, so your expectancy would have doubled.

Where my Being comes from is a non-physical vibration. We no longer need flesh bodies to live or survive. My world is 417,000 light years from your Earth and is called Nar'Kariss. Our beings are known throughout many universes as the Nar'Karones. We help those who seek knowledge. To travel from our vibration to yours takes a Nar'Karone a micro second of human time, space and distance does not exist in our vibration because we travel using thought projection to arrive at our destination.

On another level of consciousness all human beings have this knowledge. In your time of sleep your Astral Body travels vast distances and can cover thousands of miles in one night of human time and then be back in the human body within a moment of human time. Limitations are set by the individual through beliefs and fears. However, every human being can and does experience light travel in their time of sleep to some degree.

You have all heard the saying the knowledge is within each of you. This is the truth, but it only takes practice to believe in yourselves.

Be blessed in unconditional love always dear DD.

Kuntarkis.

APPRECIATION FROM A FELLOW LIGHT WORKER

Greetings from the Ancient One.

Hello Kuntarkis,

While seeking ways to Integrate Spirit in Cyberspace I came upon the Blossom of your Being which is your website. I enjoyed your Gateway of Golden Light. Sharing of the Self, Enlightens and Educates thereby giving one a Sense of Reverence. May you walk a Path of Wisdom into the arms of Sacred Mother Earth?

My name is Michael Teal. I am a Poet, Psychic and Spiritual Advisor in Hamilton on the Shores of Lake Ontario. I was pleased to peruse your pages for learning the Ways of others is a Gift for the Soul. Thank you for sharing your Intended Path and the Light within You. I wish you a Journey of Growing Spirit Immersed in Light and Love.

May yours be a Transcendent Vision Awakening Kindness and Filling you with Heartfelt Inspiration?

Yours in Intuition and Intellect

Michael Teal

the Ancient One

http://www.bardic.on.ca/ancient

Roman replies:

Dear Michael, Thank you for your kind words regarding our website. You are indeed a poet and we feel you are a being full of Light and Love. It is good to see people like yourself helping others to understand their lives and their purpose as a human being.

We believe knowledge should be shared with all who seek, with any human being who chooses to learn and evolve. It not only helps them but helps all of humanity.

May love always fill your heart and your very Being?

Love from our hearts to yours.

Roman & Ilona.

WHAT DOES THE EAGLE MEAN?

Dear Kuntarkis,

I was wondering what my spiritual name is? And when I meditate I always see an Eagle, He is always by my side. Why is he there, what does it mean & could you please tell me how many spiritual guides I have around me.

Love and Light

Mariette.

Kuntarkis replies:

Dear Mariette, because human beings on Earth originated from the planet called Nar'Kariss, even though there are three forms of DNA that has made up humanity as it is in this most precious moment, all human beings have a Spiritual Name that has been with them for over 928 thousand years of human time.

Your spiritual name is 'Nequiess' and it means in the Nar'Karone language 'The Path to Freedom'. You say that when you meditate you always see an eagle. The eagle, like most birds, represents freedom. You are wanting to step outside of the human world of confusion and to be like a bird flying free. You Mariette are seeking freedom.

In this moment of your current human life you have 11 spirit guides. They are there to help guide you through your human life to experience different lessons of learning and understanding. Your main spirit guide is of a female energy and her guidance is to help you balance out your past. Her name is Sophia, and yes, you and Sophia were connected in your past incarnation as a human being.

Be blessed in love always dear Mariette.

Kuntarkis.

UNUSAL EXPERIENCE OF MELTING FACES: WHY?

Greetings Kuntarkis.

Once again I thank you for your time, energy, love & insight. This question is not about my personal experience but that of a close friend. Recently, my friend expressed to me that she is experiencing a rather unusual occurrence when she looks at certain people. She has not made any notes, but I have advised her to.

When she looks at people sometimes half of their face is distorted & the other side perfectly normal. In her description she has compared it to a melting wax effect. These people are still living and seem to be living normal lives and it is not the same people in every occurrence so it does not appear to be happening every time she sees the person.

I have not read anything on this, yet I have seen it portrayed in "Hollywood" movies as something "spooky" which is why she is probably reluctant to research it herself out of fear. Your answers do not create fear and are filled with an abundance of love & compassion. I am so thankful for the opportunity to ask these types of questions. My friend has given me permission to ask this of you and I feel whatever you can share will put her mind at ease.

Thanks again Kuntarkis for your help.

Nat.

Kuntarkis replies:

Dear Nat, There are human beings (who have expressed their experiences to my Being) who have and are experiencing similar phenomena.

From what you, Nat, have described about your friend's experiences, she is seeing two sides to the human being. You have heard the saying on your Earth 'the good side and the bad side', 'the two sided coin'. Human beings wear many masks of deception, the masks of illusion where you only see what a human individual wants you to see about themselves.

Many human beings have a dark side to themselves that they do not want others to see. As a human being grows consciously and allows unconditional love to manifest within them, that unconditional love emanates also outwardly. That individual can see many things about others - good things as well as bad. Your friend should see this as a lesson in life, to see the fears that many human beings carry around throughout their incarnations. It will make her more aware.

Be blessed in love always.

Kuntarkis.

EXTRA-TERRESTRIAL EXPERIENCE: EXPLAIN?

Greeting to Kuntarkis,

I sincerely hope that this email finds you both in the best of health and spirit! I am so thankful to see that you guys are continuing your incredible work in raising the vibration and consciousness of humanity.

The reason why I am writing you guys this time is because as of lately, I've been coming across a lot of information regarding humanity's DNA. For the most part, the information that I've read is pretty consistent. Many channels are reporting that this is the blueprint to not only our physical lives but to our Over Soul or higher selves. Would you guys please contact Kuntarkis and ask him the following questions?

1- What does DNA mean from his ascended/spiritual perspective?

2- What is its purpose and what are the benefits of having a 12 strand reactivation?

3- If Extra-Terrestrial's manipulated our DNA, why?

Lastly, I feel that I may have been taken aboard an alien-craft in this life (perhaps multiple times) - as memories of being pulled up while asleep in bed, at a very fast rate of speed has never left my mind. Up until recently, I've thought this to be another astral experience but now I am really beginning to feel that it was far more. I also remember seeing a small light brown or beige craft slowly shifting form, next to or under a larger craft that I was pulled into; don't remember anything after that.

Would you please ask Kuntarkis if this was an actual event with Extra-Terrestrials or not?

Your attention to this email is sincerely appreciated.

Sincerely,

Tony.

Kuntarkis replies:

Dear Tony, My Being sends you greetings. In answer to your question on DNA, there is no ascended or spiritual perspective. DNA is a creation of man alone. It has no meaning beyond the third vibration of the physical realm.

The 12 strand reactivation is also a terminology of man's creation. A human man created the term about 69 human years ago.

Extra-Terrestrials did manipulate a species on your Earth but it was not human. It was a combination of ape and Extra-Terrestrial DNA to create a peaceful species, one which would not be aggressive toward Alien beings. It created a human being which is referred to as the Asian race on your Earth. This took place many thousands of human years ago.

All Asians on your Earth to this most precious moment are directly linked to the Extra-Terrestrials known as the Greys, with a combination of both Extra-Terrestrial and primate (ape) DNA.

Tony, you have not been taken on an Alien ship. Your Astral Experiences are being advanced by your willingness to advance yourself consciously. Your astral body is entering high vibrations. There will come a time in your human learning where you will consciously remember all that you experience.

Be blessed in unconditional love always.

Kuntarkis.

FINDING THE TRUE-SELF

Hello Kuntarkis,

I was wondering, do I have a spiritual name?? And if so, what is it??

Sorry to be bothering you.

Best Wishes,

Jessica.

Kuntarkis replies:

Dear Jess, when a human being learns to accept themselves as they are, and accept the unconditional love of their own soul, this unconditional love will emanate outwardly for all to see. They become the living truth of who they truly are - a facet of their own soul simply existing as a human being experiencing their own journey of self-realisation, and that they are indeed a part of all that is in all universes.

The above is your journey of self-realisation. Your spiritual name is 'Jarrabarear' and it means 'The wind that moves beyond what is present'.

Be blessed dear Jess in unconditional love always. Believe in who you are.

Kuntarkis.

CONTACTING YOUR SPIRIT GUIDE

Hello to you Kuntarkis,

It has been some time since I have contacted you.

I am wondering and looking for some specific signs that my guide is contacting me. I am aware that during my meditations is the best time to connect with my guide but that is very general. I usually start off by asking that my higher spirit open up and allow the vibration of my guide to enter. But what specific signs does my guide use to let me know that she is contacting me. I suppose I am asking about how I can channel my guide and other higher level energies. What actual steps, rituals or exercises can I do to channel my guides?

Thank you,

Callan.

Kuntarkis replies:

Dear Callan, First what is most important is to completely believe in yourself. Have no judgement, no expectations at all. In spirit world there is no time, no stress, and no expectations. To put it simply, they have all the time in the world!

When you meditate in the stillness of your mind, in your quiet place, without any interference, as you sit upright take note by listening to your breath on the intake and the exhale. Feel as if you are alone in your Universe. Feel the beat of your human heart and feel that you are sinking down deep within your inner being. Do this for five minutes of your human time.

Begin to concentrate on your guide's name by calling her essence by name - As'charre - over and over, many times, then ask her to sit with you. Trust yourself, for trust is the key to the opening of your heart, as the heart is the centre to the connection of your Soul.

Begin to communicate with her essences. Ask her questions. Truly learn to listen. It is not for her to make contact, it is for you as a human being to truly believe in spirit. That is truth, to believe in yourself is to believe in spirit.

Be blessed in unconditional love always, and remember, set aside a time each of your days to practice your connection to your spirit guide As'charre.

Kuntarkis.

COMMUNICATING WITH SPIRIT GUIDES

Dear Kuntarkis,

I would like to know what my spiritual name is, since I have never felt deeply connected with my earthly names.

I think I have a spiritual guide because I could feel her spirit with me but for some reason her identity is never revealed to me, although I tried to communicate with her, asked for her name and to reveal herself so that I know what she looks like, but I never got a response or manifestation. Please help me to make this connection. If there is a reason why she chooses to not reveal her identity, I also honour that wish.

Thank you and many blessings,

April.

Kuntarkis replies:

Dear April, Truth and trust are the most important lessons to learn from your human incarnation, meaning to discover your Inner Truth is to truly trust your own Being.

Your spiritual name is 'Carmissear'. You April have been evolving as a human being on this planet Earth for nearly one million years. As a Nar'Karone you have been evolving for three million years of human time. So April, you have been around for a very long time.

Yes, one of your closest spirit guides is of a female energy. Her most recent incarnation was in your human time of 1817. She was born in December 1817 and passed away in the human year of 1893. Her name was Mignonette and she was of French nationality.

Mignonette has not chosen to reveal herself. Her essence as spirit is always there for communication as well as for your human eyes to see. Please remember, spirit world vibrates at a much higher frequency while the human world vibrates at a much slower frequency. It is up to you as a human being to raise your energies to spirit world. It does take time and patience, and a true heart. The more unconditional love you feel in your heart the more it will help you to raise your energy levels in order to be able to accept higher vibrations.

Never give up. You will communicate with spirit if your desire is strong. Manifestation begins with you. To see is to create. To believe from your heart is to manifest. Time is irrelevant. The power source of manifestation is within you. Trust yourself and love who you are. April, you are indeed a beautiful human being on a journey of self-discovery.

Be blessed in love always.

Kuntarkis.

CHANGE FROM WITHIN

To Kuntarkis,

Thank you so much for your reply. I am humbled that you are speaking with me. I am so thankful that I am seen as a loving human being; I do worry, I agree. I guess I always just want to be a better person in some way, hopefully this is not the worst someone could want, or lesson for someone to understand, and surmount. Thank you so much for speaking with me. I have been meditating daily for 2 weeks, and already feel more centred, and calm towards tomorrow. I am not as preoccupied with having to solve, or do many things. I am just content in being. Mediation is amazing, thank you for the advice.

I was wondering, do you sense this change in me? Do you see me actually typing this to you now, or scan to find me in the energy? Can you see the last 3 husbands that have died in my life? Do you sense the disease in me? How does this work? Is this too invasive a question into the unknown mechanics of the Universe? I almost feel like you are already working with me in an abstract way. Is it possible to know my true spiritual name, and if there are others working with me?

Thank you, and I hope to hear from you soon. Feel free to find me in my meditation (if this is possible.)

I am looking into the organization you recommended.

Your loving brother here on Earth,

Richard.

Kuntarkis replies:

Dear Richard, My Being is glad for you that you have found a form of peace in your meditations. Meditation will allow a human being to discover their true self. It will help bring the balance of your connection to you as a Spirit Being living a human life. The balance of your human self and the spirit of who you are, the Soul, is one of the most important lessons for all humanity to learn and to come to that self-realisation of the knowing.

We the Nar'Karones are unbiased in how any form of life is evolving. What is more important is how you Richard sense any change within yourself. Because you have asked a direct question of my Being, the answer would be yes, there are changes.

In our existence to this present moment we think of any entity within our own energy by name and a connection is created. Everything in all universes is created from energy, and yes, there are many, many levels of energies.

Look at human life like this example. Every human being, meaning to be born into a physical vessel of flesh, has some degree of Karma that needs to be completed. That karma can be a positive or negative lesson. Karma is the creation of the human individual and is carried over from many past incarnations until the imbalance is brought into balance.

One of the most common problems that a human being has is their past. Not only the past from their present human life but also the past from their previous incarnations. Many human beings continue to live their old created habits from one lifetime to the next. This can and does stop the individual from growing consciously.

Dis'ease in a human body can only exist where fear exists. As the human individual Dr Bach said: Dis'ease is neither vindictive nor cruel. It is the means adopted by the Soul to halt you and prevent you from doing further harm, and to lead you back onto the path of Light and Truth from which you each should never have strayed.

That statement is the truth. Dis'ease is fear and fear is created from negative experiences, from the past to the present and it creates the future.

Your spiritual name is A'Pukree meaning 'one who climbs the highest mountain, one who is always seeking freedom'.

Yes there are other spirit guides who are helping you. Your main guide who has been with you throughout your present human life is Helen. Helen was your sister in a previous incarnation.

Feel free to call my Being by name in your meditations. If you feel an energy that has a cool feeling around your shoulders and head, you have felt my presence.

Be blessed in unconditional love always.

Kuntarkis.

IS MY CAREER PATH RIGHT FOR ME?

Hi Roman and Kuntarkis,

Thankyou for your guidance. I would really like to know if I am on the right career path. I still feel something is missing. My passion is singing and I dream of being able to make a good living from what I enjoy doing the most. I think fear of failure stops me from following my heart. Can you see this as part of my reality or am I born here to do something else? I would also like to know if the man I have been spending time with is good for me or can

you see me being with someone else? Apparently I was meant to meet my soul mate before the end of 2005.

Love and Light,

Gabrielle.

Kuntarkis replies:

Dear Gabrielle, to dream is a thought which is created from energy. If you truly believe you want to be a singer and make a living from it then you need to ask yourself if this is what you truly want. Fear cannot be a part of it.

Fear is a only human word created by man and this word 'fear' has been the cause of all pain, misery, failure, and disappointment throughout human history. So Gabrielle, do you truly want to be a singer? If you do, then cancel out the word 'fear' from your beliefs and conditioning and tell yourself in this moment "I am a singer, a very good singer. I am a beautiful human being and everyone wants to come and hear me sing."

Believe in yourself and believe in your talent and abilities. You will find out that many others will also believe in you. Your reality can be whatever you wish it to be in your current human incarnation. Do not listen to negative human beings. If you believe that you are a singer, known in this moment you are a singer and put the action of positive energy into your human life so your desires can be manifested into your reality.

The human male in your life can be very good for you if his energies are positive towards you and he will support visions for your future. Your soul mate is yet to come, but only you can make that happen. You will know when that moment arrives.

Be blessed in unconditional love always,

Kuntarkis.

HELLO FROM ROMANIA

Hello to Kuntarkis,

My name is Eduard Diaconu and I am from a town called Pitesti, in Romania. Sailing on the Internet these days, we have found a link to your website. Now, I must say that we were truly amazed by your vision over the human spirit, and by your efforts to make a difference. I am writing you in the name of a small group of students living here. We are some kind of a research and study group, trying to evolve our spirit, mind, and body, and to maintain a high state of awareness regarding the reality which surrounds us.

Sadly, here in Romania it is almost impossible to do such a thing, especially when you use methods which are generally considered as "unorthodox" (that's because our main path has an oriental source). Most of the people in our country have a pretty narrow vision regarding spirituality, and anything which they cannot understand, they classified it as some kind of "heresy" and never look at it again; they are refractory and rigid. Fortunately, there are also open-minded people. Their number is small and their struggle is big, but the fight for freedom will never cease. Anyway, after a long endeavour, we have succeeded to open a public library.

We had the chance to have on our side a town councillor, and with some help from him, we have officialised our group as a Non-Governmental Association. Then, to open this library was relatively easy. Though, we still have some minor problems in finding a proper location for it. Right now, the library is located in a pretty old building, but we hope that we will find a more proper location in a short time. Well, we have just started this "adventure" with the library (a year ago, nobody knew about us), and those small problems are almost inevitable. But what was really important was done. At the moment, our patrimony consists in approximately six hundred books and almost two hundred magazines, plus some video tapes and music on CD's and audio tapes. The subjects of all those are centred on oriental spiritual traditions and philosophy, but we also have books focused on western spiritual paths. And, even if the vast majority of our books are in English, there are days when we have more than 10 visitors. People are really interested, especially in eastern traditions. We also have a website. It's small and pretty unsophisticated, but, for now, it's all we can do regarding this issue. Here is the address: www.sundari.go.ro

Once again, we must say that we are very glad to come across your website. You are doing a great job. And so, if you don't mind to change a thought or two from time to time, please give us a sign.

Our very best wishes,

Eduard & friends.

Kuntarkis replies:

Dear Eduard and Friends, My Being wishes to express from my heart to your hearts that you are my Brothers and Sisters of Light. Even though your journey in your current human life can be harsh at times, all of you are doing a very important job – you are bringing knowledge to those who need it. All of you are Bearers of Light. Human's beings like yourselves are the new teachers of humanity. To believe is to create; to create is to manifest that reality within yourselves and humanity. We the Nar'Karones are very aware of human beings like yourselves, helping humanity in its own evolution.

You asked for a sign in your meditation. Form a circle and always place the White Light within yourselves and around the circle - this creates a form of protection from negative energies. Call my name three to four times slowly, Kuntarkis, then ask for my Being to stand in the centre of your circle. Project White Light to the centre of that circle - do it slowly so it builds up the energies. Then from your hearts ask a question and truly listen from your hearts. If all of you in that circle are true of heart and truly believe my Being is present, then it shall be manifested.

Be blessed in unconditional love always,

Kuntarkis.

CANCER AND FALLING PREGNANT

Hi Kuntarkis,

Thank you for continuing to write and inspire. I am 33 and dealing with my second round of breast cancer. I begin radiation this week. I was wondering if you can tell me if I will be healthy in the future and what I should be doing to keep myself well. Also, my husband and I have been trying to have a baby for the last 3 years without success. Can you tell me if I will ever be able to get pregnant? Can you offer me any suggestions that might help us with inviting a soul to join our life?

Thank you

Amy.

Kuntarkis replies:

Dear Amy, My Being sends healing light to you. My Being realises how hard it must be for you. Human dis'ease was created by the human ego over human 600,000 years ago. It has plagued humanity to this present moment and was create from negative emotions, reinforced by negative foods that human beings consume.

What is unfortunate is the breakdown of the human genes, especially over the last 150 years of human time. There is an emotion that haunts you Amy -your self-worth, especially how you feel about yourself. Please realise in this most precious moment you are a beautiful human being, a beautiful human woman, and you deserve to be healthy, and to also bear human children.

Before you can become pregnant you may need to do a little work on yourself. First believe in yourself. Believe you deserve to be healthy by doing some research on eating healthy and doing some regular amounts of exercise, Yoga would be a good start. Also when you feel negative towards yourself, stop in the moment and realise it is a personal choice to be negative or positive. You can change your thoughts in the moment and change them to a positive way of thinking. Doing affirmations is a very good beginning, how you express the words of your affirmation is very important. Always put your thoughts on your heart, even place your hands over your heart and feel your own love, then express your affirmation and feel it coming from within your very being.

You will become pregnant and have two human children, but first you need to work on yourself. It is very important for you to do this so you can have healthy happy children. Always believe in yourself - you are an individual, you have the power of change within you right now.

Be blessed in unconditional love always dear Amy.

Kuntarkis.

ATTRACTION FROM A COLLEAGUE

Hi Roman, and Kuntarkis,

The reason I am writing is because I would like to get Kuntarkis' insight regarding a person of whom I work with. This person and I have worked closely together for about 5 years. I feel that this person is very unhappy and wants to be free but does not know how. I also feel that this person is harbouring either, a profound attraction, admiration fascination or deep love for me (not sure which one) but he tries to hide these feelings by acting nonchalant towards me. I also feel that this person and I were connected in previous lifetimes because we get along so well. Am I right about these assessments? If I am incorrect, please tell me why am I picking up on these vibrations? Also, if I am correct, I would like to know if this person will ever come clean about their feelings to me. Please provide some clarity.

Regards,

Anthony.

Kuntarkis replies:

Dear Anthony, There are many, many human beings who want to be free from their present life, yet what most cannot accept is they alone hold to the key to their freedom.

The power of self, meaning the individual, can create or uncreate anything. But because of fear, created beliefs and human life circumstances from childhood into adulthood, many are held back from truly living a happy and being content in their present human life.

Anthony, it is quite obvious you have feelings for this human being you speak of. Since you have feelings for this human being, to be true to yourself would it not be wise to say something. In fact Anthony, you are using your natural awareness. You are picking up on these vibrations for a reason, so you may need to act in order to discover if you are correct or incorrect. Whatever the outcome, you are learning to trust yourself, are you not.

Yes, you have had other incarnations with this human being you speak of. The reason you are picking up on that awareness is to make you more aware of your surroundings, and that life is infinite and all of humanity are truly connected to each other and all other life forms, whatever their form may be.

Be blessed in unconditional love always.

Kuntarkis.

WHAT IS EARTH'S FUTURE?

Hi Kuntarkis,

Can you tell me where Earth is heading? I'm talking about the Mayan calendar, Prophecies, the Bible, Earth Changes, Bird Flu, a Ascension, Predictions is it all starting to happen in 2006, 2008, 2010 and / 2012 or even further on like 2020. I'm feeling a bit immobilized because of all the talk. I have friends who have had visions that speak of the horror and carnage. I know I shouldn't be this way, but it has made me think "why bother with planning for a future, and I find myself just sitting around waiting, and not being very goal driven or enthusiastic about starting new ventures etc., and what about the economic collapse etc.

Sometimes I think it's negativity they are feeding to people and putting into the world. Then I think about how it has been written about for so long, since the time of Jesus Christ. Will it really happen? Do you know when? What's my role? Why am I here?

Thanks

Fiona.

Kuntarkis replies:

First Fiona, please be silent in your human brain; be still and listen to your heart. Your heart has no fears, it only has love for you. Your human brain holds all your fears and it will only create confusion. Try not to listen to others so much but listen to your heart. Your heart is the connection to your Soul, your connection to who you truly are.

You asked why you are here. Most can create many reasons for why you are here, yet in all honesty, you, as all human beings, are here to learn the lesson of letting go of the past and to learn what unconditional love is. The lesson is simple, but because of human ego over the last 928,000 years of human evolution, much fear and confusion has been created in human beings from one incarnation to the next.

The human ego has, through fear, created so much violence and negative emotion which needs to be released and forgiven before the balance can be brought into the present. Everything that has been written from the human past is an idea of truth from another, and because human beings are fearful by nature, some individuals from the past can only write of negative situations which have been carried forward and taught in the present by fearful human individuals.

Fiona, learn to forgive. Learn to love who you are; a beautiful human being on a journey of Self-Realisation. Think in a positive way and create a positive energy within you and around you. Only the human individual can change human understanding, and only unconditional love can change the human created past of violence and ignorance. Create your life in a positive loving way and you will begin to see your surroundings from a different perspective. Do not allow what others say about predictions of what is to come to create a fear of change in you.

When you change yourself into a higher vibrating human being, then you will know the truth and you will not become depressed over what others are saying about the human future. You will realise that it is simply a creation of the human past brought into the present. Until the Human Ego is dissolved, this will not change. Change yourself and your thinking and your surroundings will change for the better. Every human being is so much more than their physical self, all of Humanity are Co- Creators in the vastness of the universe. Each of you as humans, are 99% pure energy, you are less than 1% physical matter, on an average each of you are made up of 80% water, your human body has over 4 Quad Trillion cells, each of those cells makes up every part of your human self, and each works in harmony with each other. Your human body is living consciousness and every human being has the ability to connect with their cells and communicate in order to heal any health issues that may arise.

One of the best ways of communicating with your Cellular Structure, is Meditation by stilling the Mind to halt the chatter of the human brain, if you believe and persist it will be manifested.

Be blessed in unconditional love always Fiona.

Kuntarkis.

A VERY PROFOUND DREAM

Dear Kuntarkis,

I recently had a very profound dream that has led me on a search for truth. In my dream I looked up and saw a spacecraft which at first didn't appear to be solid, but dimly outline. At once, it formed into a solid image. In the next moment, a man appeared and we began to talk. He told me he was my father and had been looking for me. Most of the conversation that took place, I could not remember, but in the end he wanted me to go with him. I was so excited, but torn because I did not want to leave my daughter behind. There was a woman with him that was firmly against bringing "her".

I feel this dream is a message for me. I would truly love some enlightenment of what this means.

Also, the name "Miccah" rings in my head, but I haven't made the connection of who this is (?) I have always yearned to learn my "true" name as well. If you feel this is something you could help me understand, I would greatly appreciate your help.

With Love,

Robin.

Kuntarkis replies:

Dear Robin, A large number of human beings have different experiences with Aliens. There are many different worlds beyond your Earth. In fact, there are thousands of dimensions, vibrations, and different levels of consciousness, just like human beings on Earth have many different levels of awareness and understanding.

One of the major problems that exists on your Earth is fear. Fear is a self-created cycle in each human being. Some can accept Aliens and truly believe in them while others are very fearful of them, due to their fear of the unknown.

What many human beings do not understand is that many have already given their permission to be taken into Alien Spacecraft's before incarnating in their present life, and because in many cases their experiences are negative, they then condition themselves and create a fear of these beings. To be taken away by Aliens Beings causes their self-created fears to come to the surface and even though the experience may not actually be negative, they will react with fear and create a negative experience from it.

However, many human beings who have been taken have also had very positive experiences which can and do help bring about a deeper understanding of their own purpose of human life.

The spacecraft you saw in your time of sleep was real - you were having an out of body experience (which every human being has when they go to sleep). The entity told you he was your father so that you would feel comfortable with him. He was not going to take you away from your daughter - he was only taking you into his craft to help you open up your inner consciousness and awareness and to show you that there is so much more to human existence than just the physical self.

That is the message for you Robin - to help you step beyond what is the known. The name Miccah is close. It is spelt a little different - 'Mirrichki' - that is the entity's name. If you wish his presence to be with you, go into the silence of your inner being and place the light of love and protection within and around you. Call his name to make contact with his energies. But remember, it is your choice alone. Nothing is ever done against your will.

Be blessed in unconditional love always dear Robin.

Kuntarkis.

I NEED HELP TO CURE MY ILLNESS?

We received these next two questions from people with terminal illnesses, and have put them up together as the answer below is relevant to both of them. Roman has answered these questions from his own experiences with lung cancer.

From Dieter in Denmark:

I have cancer, which they call Hodgkin son's Disease, and attacks the lymphoma system. I have already gone and had treatment like chemotherapy, radiation treatment and two transplantations. The doctors have made it quite clear to me that if any more cancer is shown after the treatment, there is no more they can do. Since then I have had more tests and they show more cancer is growing. A friend of mine said to me maybe I should look at doing or getting advice on alternative medicine. I was looking through the internet and came across your site and how Roman cured his lung cancer. Can you help me or share some of your knowledge on this? Thank you for receiving my question.

From Gur pal in Hong Kong:

A friend from Brisbane has told me about your self-healing capacities that you built for personal cure. I live in Hong Kong and work at present. I have Cirrhosis of Liver due to HEP C, which I unfortunately got by getting a blood transfusion. I am beginning to show signs of cancer of the liver and most of the liver is non-functional with an enlarged spleen. I don't eat meat, but once in while take seafood, eat vegetables, drink skimmed milk and take home-made yogurt daily, as this is the only source of protein I have. I cannot eat lentils due to gas and indigestion I get with them. I eat whole-wheat stuff and have to avoid acid-producing juices, such as orange and apple. I do meditate using prayer as my focus and imagery for focus and relaxation (at present I am not regular in my meditation but trying to get back into practice). My job and home life has been stressful but I am trying to get away from it all. Transplant of liver is suggested due to HEP C, as it has eaten away some of my liver. Of malignancy is the second reason. I guess that is all I know about myself. My friend said you might have some suggestions for me. Will be keen to hear from you.

ANSWER FROM ROMAN:

Dieter and Gur pal, I will share my own personal experience of healing my self-created lung cancer with both of you.

First I want to say this: Modern science/medicine has no comprehension that the body is a perfect healer when given half the chance. They think the body is like a car, and when something breaks down, you replace it or remove it. That is so far from the truth. All dis'ease originates from some unresolved emotion that is lurking in the depths of one's past, even if it doesn't seem on the surface to have been created that way. Unless you figure out what lies behind the dis'ease, it will keep coming back, no matter how many times you attempt to cut it out or drug it out, as we have seen many times over the last 50 years of medicine fighting dis'ease. That being said, does not mean medicine/science or drug therapy should be ignored. In fact it has its place just like alternative medicine. One should always seek professional help first and then make one's own conscious decision, that is called being personally 100% responsible and naturally it is your right as an individual.

Once a person can accept 100% that the body can heal itself completely, which goes against everything we have been conditioned to believe in, then and only then is there a possibility of a complete cure. The mind is an extremely powerful tool and must be enlisted if 100% success is to be obtained.

Curing a terminal illness is more than just changing your physical lifestyle and habits. You must also change your entire attitude, and open your mind completely to understanding that the body has the ability to heal itself without drastic medical intervention. In reality, science doesn't really fully understand how to cure such dis'ease or why some people survive and others don't. At the moment it is a "hit and miss" affair, and they hope the patient will survive. And yet, people like myself (and there are hundreds of thousands of them worldwide) have the answer because we are living proof of the experience that terminal illness can be eradicated without drastic measures, if one is willing to seek out the knowledge.

The main problem, Dieter and Gur pal, is if science can't prove it, people such as myself are labelled crackpots and airheads, or just plain lucky. If you are prepared to have a completely open mind and become 100% personally responsible, e-mail me again and I will explain exactly why you have created your dis'ease, and why from an emotional level the cancer has struck your lymphatic system Dieter, and you're liver Gur pal. Dieter and Gur pal, it is your choice alone to attempt this journey, and let me say at the outset it will take all your courage to trust in the divine healing power of your bodies.

Here is the cleansing diet I used. What I am about to write may sound too hard to do, but you see, I know it works, and you have to remember it is for your health's sake as well as your life. You have to ask yourself how important your life and health are to you…

1-Stop all intake of all animal products and by-products, including seafood because seafood is meat. That means eat nothing that comes from an animal - no milk, no butter, no cheese, no flesh.

2-Drink as much green tea as you like. Add grated or thinly sliced fresh ginger to it. Drink hot or cold. Very good cleanser for the body, especially the liver.

3-No drugs or chemicals, no junk food, no soft drinks, no smoking, no coffee or alcohol. Only green tea and herbal teas.

4-Drink a minimum of 8 full glasses (250ml each x 8 = 2 litres) of filtered water daily for cleansing and flushing out toxins from your body. More than 2 litres of water is better.

5-Drink freshly made fruit juices daily - 1 in the morning and 1 at lunchtime. Drink freshly made vegetable juices daily - 1 mid-afternoon and 1 at dinnertime, and if you feel like more than 1 glass at a time, it will not hurt you. Use celery, apple, beetroot, carrot, capsicum, ginger and potato. Remember, the quantities you use are at your discretion. Potato is a cancer eliminator. You may not like the thought of raw potato juice but it will be good for you. Ginger is a cleanser for the body and has been used for thousands of years in Asia. Drink as many glasses of fresh vegetable juices as you like, it will only do you good, but don't forget to make sure you still drink a minimum of 8 full glasses of water daily.

6-Have fresh fruit for breakfast daily like paw (papaya), kiwi fruit, bananas, mangoes, apples, strawberries. Just a little of each if you desire, or 2 or 3 different types at a time.

7-Eat a good fresh salad for lunch. Include lettuce, tomato, cucumber, capsicum, parsley, mushrooms and onion, and fresh herbs. Slice it all up, and make a dressing without oil by mixing apple cider vinegar or the juice of half a lemon, with a little pure unrefined sea salt, fresh black pepper, and some French mustard with some filtered water if it is too acidic for you. Mix thoroughly and toss your salad with it. Do not be afraid to eat too much salad - it will only do you good as it will help give you all the nutrients your body needs, but also will help cleanse your body of toxins. Cabbage green leaves in your fresh juices are highly recommended, and anything as green leaves or vegetables is very potent. All green leaves and vegetables have their own form of natural protein.

8-For dinner eat raw food. Chop up another salad by using fresh cabbage, grated beetroot, grated carrot, sliced cucumber, sliced mushroom and add some chopped spinach or silver beet, and include more fresh herbs. Use the same dressing as in item **7** above.

If given the right foods and the right thoughts, the human body is self-healing, because whatever we think we will become, and if we do not feed our body with good food, then over a period of time it will break down and dis'ease takes hold.

If you decide to go on the cleansing programme I have written here, be sure to do it for 3 months at least. If you follow it, and especially if you meditate on a regular basis and get rid of all the stress in your life, no matter what, and if you are 100% honest with yourself, you will begin the healing process in Divine Light.

As for protein, there is protein in all foods, even vegetables and fruit. In fact, too much protein feeds cancer cells, so cut out the concentrated proteins while on this cleanse.

I cured my lung cancer with the same programme and I looked at my life and my emotions. I learnt to love and care for my being, and I let go of all my stress and the limitations that I alone created. Whatever we each create in our lives (even if we don't believe we created it!) we can also uncreate, whatever it may be. The power is within each of us. If you could both have a complete break from your work life to help heal yourselves, it would also release the stress in your life. There is a lot I can say, but I will allow you to try what I have written out here for you.

Also, read up on the product called <u>spirulina</u>. It is a natural product and very high in iron. Iron is the building block for your Immune System - without it we would not survive in a healthy state. It also has many other vitamins and minerals essential to health. It is a complete food. I took it during my healing and have continued to use it ever since, which is a little over 16 years ago.

Please always remember, seek Professional help first and discuss it with your doctor or practitioner. In the end you are responsible for your life always. Just because I cured myself does not mean I can cure anyone else, in fact I can't I can only give you guidance from my own personal experience.

Be Blessed in the Light.

Roman (& Kuntarkis)

FEAR OF PERSONAL RESPONSIBILITY

Hello Kuntarkis,

This is my reflection. It's like standing on the edge of a precipice and trying to reach out to grasp something for dear life, but you find there's nothing there, no parachute. And you have to rely on yourself, but all you can see happening is yourself free falling, and no matter how hard you try, the Universe knows when you're not being quite genuine, and keeps grading you harshly and says "nope, do it again". Just a cold yard stick. Well I wish for the illogical. I wish for a compassionate God who will say everything will be okay, no matter what. I don't wish to rely on myself. I'm not big enough or strong enough. Okay, I'm done now.

Elizabeth.

Kuntarkis replies:

Love and Forgiveness of Self is the beginning of Self-Realisation. That you as a human being, are responsible 100% for what has been created in your own life, whether it be the past or the present, or the future, will govern the situations or relationships you bring into your human life to experience along the path of your own personal Evolution.

You ask for a compassionate God, as if you believe your God is judging you, there is no God placing judgment upon you. The only human being placing judgment on you is YOU.

If you, Elizabeth, are not getting the answers you want, then stop for a moment and ask yourself "who am I asking?" Is it your true self that is in perfect balance and also knows to be 100% responsible for all self-created events or limitations, and not to blame another, whoever they may be? Or are you asking your Ego, who can only give you an answer based on your past, whether it is positive or negative?

This is something you need to clarify for yourself, and stop blaming others for the self-created negative events in your human life. Know your true self, which is infinite and all knowledgeable, can give you all the answers you seek from life. Learn to trust in yourself and your life will have harmony and peace, and bring balance of mind, body and spirit as one. You do have the knowledge. Seek and ye shall find Elizabeth.

Be Blessed in the Light.

Kuntarkis.

HOW DO I FIND HAPPINESS?

Dear Kuntarkis,

Hi Kuntarkis, my question is, there are times when I feel a void within, like a restlessness which I can't explain, but which results in a feeling of unhappiness which is very frustrating. It's frustrating because you may do things to change your moods etc., and these are helpful but only temporary.

I can only conclude that doing things physically may distract me, but they don't fill the void. So how do we as human beings reach contentment? What must we do? There are those who say contentment is not anything to do with doing, but I think you Kuntarkis understand what I am trying to say here. I guess to put it more simply, how do we remain happy, or is it not as simple as that? Can you share some thoughts on this?

Papinda.

Kuntarkis replies:

Dear Papinda, first to the end of your question. Yes, it is as simple as that. But because human beings come from Ego, which is their fears and insecurities created by their beliefs and conditioning, the real problem lies with the Human Ego. Only when each human being comes to that understanding and decides to dissolve their Ego, which is simply the past, into the nothingness from which it first came, and see the falseness that has been created, only then can the truth of existence manifest itself. By doing this, fear, insecurity, judgement, greed, lust, cruelty, vindictiveness, domination, in fact all the traces of Ego will no longer be present, and respect and unconditional love will be almighty present on this Earth.

It is the responsibility of each human being to grow beyond their Ego. The Ego is very perverted in this third dimensional matter world and no one can do it for another. Only by becoming the living truth meaning yourself, you will then become the living example for others to grow in consciousness beyond the Ego world. What I will say Papinda, is when you do let go and dissolve your human Ego, you will fill the void you are experiencing, for it is your Soul crying out to you in love trying to show you how false your life truly is. You are a powerful being, caught up in your conditioned Ego world that really has no substance or truth.

The Ego world for every human being has been created from their past, from their parents, and their parents before them, and so on. Look within, and listen deeply. Your Soul is reaching out and asking that you love yourself. Know you can create in your life whatever your heart desires. It all begins with you Papinda.

Be Blessed in the Light of Creation.

Kuntarkis.

AFFIRMATION FOR SAMER

Dear Kuntarkis,

I have a request. Could you please give me an affirmation to help me grow strong and realise I am more than what I see each morning when I wake up and look in my mirror? I would be most grateful. Thanks.

Samar.

Kuntarkis replies:

Dear Samar, I truly believe in you. Since I am a stranger to you and express that I believe in you, there is no reason for you not to believe in yourself. I trust from my Being this collection of human words will help you.

Be Blessed in the Light of Creation's totality.

Affirmation for Samar

I am an Infinite Being of Light, filled with Love, Beauty, Strength and Compassion.

I express my Essence to all Life, as I know my Love is Endless, My Love is Timeless, my Love is Ageless.

I, who am connected to all of Life, share my Knowledge to all that choose to Listen, and gain their own Wisdom of Inner Truth.

I am a guide only and I express through Creation the Book of Life that is Limitless in all things.

I am that I am. I am Light in its purest form and I am Infinite. I expand my Inner and Outer Being in pure Bliss.

I am Love. I am Light. I am that I am, no more, no less.

Kuntarkis.

HOW DO I RECOGNISE NEGATIVE FORCES AROUND ME?

Hello Kuntarkis,

Recently, I asked for a healing to help me sever negative psychic ties and to develop unconditional love and forgiveness for those negative forces who tried to bring and hold me down. The last ten months had been a spiritual awakening AND a spiritual war at the same time. I was told that until I feel I can forgive the individuals involved (including my husband of 19years) through my soul, I will not lose my anger. I am working on seeing the whole traumatic experience as a strengthening tool or growth method. I was also told this is very difficult for me because I have a "very special light around me that is pure and it was attacked".

My question: How can I identify the negative psychic forces of this world and those of the higher one who are attached to me? I do not wish harm. I want to understand. I have been told of another "spiritual conflict "on the horizon in about 10 to 12 months. This one is not completely finished yet and the thought of another so soon has me concerned. Any light you could share in this area would be greatly appreciated. I have not only myself to take care of, but also two metaphysical children as well to protect until they become of age.

In Light, Susan.

Kuntarkis replies:

Dear Susan, it was very nice of you to write to me, and I trust what I am about to explain to you will be of some help for your journey of Conscious Growth.

First, self-healing is the greatest realisation for any being throughout all the Universes, and through unconditional love you will find the beginning of your awakening to your true self that is within you. And yes Susan, spiritual learning can sometimes feel like a war.

The art of forgiveness is to forgive yourself first, as all things, no matter what, are only lessons of life. When you can forgive others you will also be able to let them go on their own journey in life. As human beings you each bring people into your lives to learn certain lessons and when you each are ready, you then choose to go beyond that lesson of human life. Unfortunately, many humans cannot let go because of their own insecurities, which holds them back from evolving beyond that lesson.

Susan, there is no right nor wrong, nor good nor bad, only what each human being has been conditioned to believe. Everything is just an experience of life, not to be judged as negative or positive. A hard concept to accept, but that is the truth, and only the truth can set each human being free from all self-created limitation, which includes the human Ego. And I assure you Susan, the human Ego is at the centre of all negative beliefs in your third dimensional matter world.

Your Soul, Susan, is the essence of your totality and the Soul does not judge. The Soul is a pure state of being; unbiased, non-judgemental, it just is. The Soul loves each of you unconditionally, and places no rules or conditions upon you. The Soul is endless, ageless, timeless and eternal. The Soul allows you to learn the lessons of human life for as long as it may take. It is each human being's responsibility to learn their chosen lessons of life and to go beyond their present level of thinking.

Susan, you, as all human beings, are very special. The light that is within you and surrounds you is your essence, and very few human beings can see that light. Only when the mind and body is pure, and when one becomes and is the living truth will one see this light. All of life from the beginning was light and you each are a part of the light. No one is greater or smaller, the only difference is your consciousness and your level of understanding. Anyone who says that they are greater than another is speaking from their human Ego, and Ego exists only in belief systems created from the past, which comes from negativity.

The first thing I would suggest to you Susan is to stop and listen to no one, but to listen to what your heart is telling you. You have a great force within you which you can connect to by believing in yourself, through first forgiving yourself and loving yourself unconditionally. Stop and look at what you are thinking and expressing in your daily life, and remember that what you think, you become. It is your choice, your free will. When you are feeling negative, stop and look at why you feel this way and you will begin to realise that you have a choice to be negative or positive. Sadly, the upbringing from a child, which becomes your beliefs and conditions, plays a very important part in human life, and can hold human being back from conscious growth for their entire life.

You asked how you can identify the difference between the psychic forces, being either negative or positive. It is very simple Susan. Take a look at your life, but look with an open mind and an honest heart. If a human being has fears and insecurities they will draw to themselves negative energies which can be in the form of people or just negative situations in life. For example, what you as human beings would call soap operas that appear on your television sets. Most of them are all based on drama, which are all created from negative energies, and what you will find is that those who watch these programmes have much negativity in their lives, but they also enjoy the drama. Susan, sit and watch and look to see what I am expressing to you. You will see that even the actors who play those parts have the same form of character in life as they do in fiction, and they also love the drama, and have large Egos, causing them to create negativity around them and within their lives.

So if a human being is negative they will attract negative energies into their life and it goes on and on. Only the individual can choose to grow beyond the negative energy and stop attracting those forces into their life. No human being has to have conflict in their life if they choose not to. By looking at your life and how you feel and think, you will be able to grow beyond your present moment, and you, as all, will change the level of your thinking and your consciousness will grow.

Remember Susan, only you can complete or end a negative situation because you have the power to do so. By forgiving yourself you can then forgive others, and by loving yourself unconditionally you will begin to love others the same. You will no longer have conflicts in your life and any negative energy that comes into your vibration, you will see it for what it is, be it people or situations, and you will not react, but simply let it go in love.

Believe in yourself and you will set yourself free.

Be Blessed, dear Susan, in the Light.

Kuntarkis.

CONFUSED ABOUT MY LIFE

Hello Kuntarkis,

I'm feeling confused about my life at the moment and it's affecting my relationship as well. He is a beautiful person so supportive I can see a future together however at the same time I'm feeling unsure I seem to have lost my direction and focus. Can you offer some advice?

Monica.

Kuntarkis replies:

Dear Monica, It is always hard to see the light at the end of the tunnel when one's life

is full of confusion. Confusion is a collection of conflicting fears, beliefs and conditioning from one's human life, which in reality is only the past.

It is the past dear Monica that holds you in fear and doubt of yourself and of your present relationship. Those fears create uncertainty in every part of your human life.

You are a beautiful human being. You need to believe in yourself, in what you want from this human life of yours, and also in your present relationship. The past, whatever it may be, should not create your present or your future. Your direction must come from your heart, not your fears. At this present moment you are being directed by your fears which are governed by your past experiences of human life. See the past as just that - the past. Do not judge your past as good or bad, right or wrong, negative or positive, but just as experiences. See with your beautiful heart what it is that you, Monica, wish from life and then begin to go forward and to create it. Love your human man just for who he is and your journey in life will be less confusing.

Walk in love and may love always be with you Monica.

Be blessed in love and Light always.

Kuntarkis.

WHAT HAPPENED TO AMY WROE BECHTEL?

Hi Kuntarkis,

I have a question I would like answered specifically if you could... It doesn't concern me directly however it has been a local mystery for four years. A young woman named Amy Wroe Bechtel disappeared while running in the mountains near Lander, WY. She has never been found. Could you please tell me what happened to her, why and if she'll ever be found?

Thanks

Let.

NOTE: Before we look into any missing persons cases we request the following information:

It is important to send a description report with a photo of the missing person. The local police would have such a report. The reason we ask this is that some people's requests are hoaxes - they do it for kicks and waste our time and energy. I am sure you would understand how important it is for us to verify all such requests as genuine. You can e-mail a scanned report, or mail a photocopy to us to the following address.

Roman Harambura, P O Box 1053 Coolangatta, 4225 QLD

<u>**Kuntarkis replies:**</u>

Dear Leticia, Thank you for your response in providing information on Amy Wroe Bechtel. It

is always very sad when a human being goes missing, especially when another human being causes the person to go missing.

Looking into Amy's disappearance, it is sad for my being to inform you that her energy no longer exists in your physical plane, meaning her human body is no longer alive. What is most sad is that a male human being ended her life because of his own fears and fears of rejection from his childhood. He was rejected by his human mother and never felt the love of one human being who should have given him the support and love he needed as a child to grow

into adulthood.

Because of his fears of rejection that run deep within him he has become an unbalanced human being, and because he was rejected by Amy, he took it personally and became obsessed with her. He did however keep his distance so Amy would not find him out. This male human being has done this before with other women and has caused those great emotional stress and pain. He took out his anger on them with violence and rape, the only difference being he had not taken their human life. But he did with Amy because she knew her attacker. He waited for her in the bushes off the path where she would run for exercise. He attacked her from behind, hitting her on the back of the head and dragging her body off the main path in case another human being came by and saw what was happening.

As Amy was being dragged by her attacker she regained her consciousness and fought with him. It is a very sad situation when a human male loses control because of his past and takes it out on another human being. His lust for human sex and then killing that human life shows that there is no conscious growth in that male individual, only human Ego at its worst.

When my being comes into a human body, my being can see the full pictures of Amy's last moments of human life, feeling her fears and pain that she experienced with her attacker. Amy's remains are buried in the mountains of Lander Wyoming and South Pass. It would be very hard for any human being to find her remains, but they are there.

Her attacker lives in the area. He is at this moment in human time 29 years of age, 1.73 metres tall with dark brown hair that has some grey showing through. He has a thin face and pale skin with freckles on his face and body. His body is also thin. His eyes have dark rings around them which shows he does not drink much water. He becomes quite nervous when speaking to human females to the point that he may stutter when trying to express himself. He lives with his mother. His human father left when he was only two years of age.

From a human perspective, this human male should be brought to justice so he can be tried in your court of law and pay for the crime he has committed against another human being. But even if he is not found out in his present physical life, Creation will balance the imbalance he has caused and it will be brought into balance somewhere along his being's evolution in time to come.

If you Leticia have any further questions on Amy Wroe Bechtel, please feel free to ask my being. May love and happiness always be within your heart?

Be Blessed in the light of Creation's totality

Kuntarkis.

LOOKING FOR GOOD NEWS

Hi Kuntarkis,

Please send me good news from the heavens. All the talk of war and the end of the world has caused immense dread in me. Any good news?

Thanks.

Kuntarkis replies:

Dear Human Being, It is understandable that many of your kind are feeling down over the attack on American soil, and yes, it seems that humanity relishes negative events more so than positive events. Many would say humanity enjoys the excitement of anger more so than the love of the heart.

This is sad, but can be easily changed if all human beings would allow themselves to bathe in the liquid Light of Creation's totality and unconditional love. It is in unconditional love that lies the truth and the path to freedom and a blissful life on your planet Earth.

It is your media that believes the only good story is one full of drama. That is a complete untruth. It only sells their papers and boosts their ratings. Your species are in this moment of life going through negative fields of energy, so all of you are forced to look at yourselves and your created past. Yes, there will come a moment in time where all dramas will no longer exist, but it must start with the individual raising their own consciousness. The truth is within you and always has been. Look deep into your being - seek and ye shall find.

Be Blessed dear human being. Even though it may be hard to believe at this moment in time, unconditional love really is the answer.

Kuntarkis.

RECTAL CANCER: WHAT IS THE METAPHYSICAL TERM?

Dear Roman and Kuntarkis,

What emotions might be associated with rectal cancer? And do you believe chlorella powder to be as effective as spirulina? What about wheat grass? Are you still cancer free?

Caroline.

Roman replies:

Dear Caroline, from a metaphysical perspective, the emotions related to rectal cancer are deep resentment and anger that has been created over a long period of human time. It means not being able to let go of the past, but wanting to hold on, and not forgiving oneself or others. It is a self-destruction from within. One of the phrases I use and say, it's like rust eaten at metal. The same goes with cancer, it is eaten us away from within.

Chlorella powder is as effective as Spirulina, and Wheat Grass is also as good. I am still free of my created lung cancer, and I have more energy in my human body than before. I am now 63 years of age. I train in the art of Ch'ing, which is a combination of yoga, stretching, Tai-Chi, Kung Fu, isometrics and meditation. Meditation plays a very important part in any human dis'ease. My diet is vegetarian meaning I consume only foods of plant origin, no form of animal flesh, no eggs a little cheese (non-animal rennet). I find Tempeh, Tofu, lots of bean mixes, I have lots of fresh salads and fresh fruit, love my green tea.

Be blessed dear Caroline. Knowledge is freedom from all pain and fears. May the Light always shine within you and around you?

Roman.

NOSTRADAMUS' PREDICTIONS &
THE ATTACK ON AMERICA

Hi Kuntarkis,

I have just discovered your website while looking up info on Nostradamus. I am curious to why if Nostradamus has warned the world on numerous occasions in history of tragic things happening, why can't our world leaders take note and change the path. If Nostradamus has predicted that World War 3 will begin after as quoted "In the city of God there will be a great thunder. Two brothers torn apart by Chaos, while the fortress endures, the great leader will succumb, the third big war will begin when the big city is burning". Can this be changed or will Nostradamus' prediction be inevitable?

P.S. I have really enjoyed reading your information on Nar'Karones and info on us as humans. May I suggest you put together a message for the planet sending love and kindness asking the world to generate love and compassion to not only the victims in America but also to the people responsible for the attack on America. Maybe then this world could live in peace. If you could put something together and send it back to myself and maybe a few more people and request them to send it on to 5 people each (similar to a chain letter) we could generate enough loving energy to maybe change the future. I believe that our ancestors back on Nar'Kariss would feel this to be a positive thing.

Sending you Loving Kindness

Carlene (On the Sunshine Coast QLD).

Kuntarkis replies:

Dear Carlene, Yes, it is true that Nostradamus gave humanity a map of future events to come on this Earth, and yes, they have in reality all come true. The time factor can change in human time because of the levels of negativity created on Earth. The reason the human leaders do not take note or listen with an open mind and heart is because their Egos do not allow them.

The truth is before humanity and it is humanity's choice to take notice, for that is part of the learning process towards conscious growth. The knowledge is within every human being and every human being can obtain the truth of what has been and what is to come. At this point in human time it is the human Ego that is supreme. In truth, the leaders on your Earth have no wisdom, which is what is needed to gain an understanding of what Nostradamus was expressing, and to listen with the heart and not the human brain which has been conditioned by emotions from the past. The past must die before the real can come into existence so that each human being can open their hearts and Soul to the living essence of the Light that is dormant within all of humanity.

Peace is to come on Earth when all of humanity finds peace within themselves, and yes, events can change if human society changes their ways. You dear Carlene can create a difference on your Earth. The power and your inner voice is within. Bring it to the surface and express it on your paper and on your e-mails. You will see how you formulate words of wisdom which will give a deeper meaning and understanding to those who read them. I put the challenge to you Carlene to put together a message of Love and Compassion to share with all of your human kind. You have the power of expression - just believe in yourself and you will do it. I will send you my energies of love and you can then generate the energy that will express your most inner feelings. You will know when this will be so?

My being thanks you for viewing Roman and Ilona's website. It is human beings like yourself that can make a difference to your world. Thank you for your honesty in your remarks about the Nar'Karones. That truth is recorded in your living Essence of Light that is infinite.

May Love and Truth always be within your heart and be blessed in the Light of Creation's totality.

Kuntarkis.

HOW DO I ORGANISE AN S.O.S. COURSE?

Dear Roman,

How do I take a course on this? I am interested in organizing a group to do this, but I lack the information and am seeking your counsel.

Patt.

Roman reply:

Dear Patt, Thank you for viewing our website, and we trust you have found it of interest. To your question regarding the Guided Imagery course, it is a short course of 13 hours over six weeks. Because the course is so short, we would normally run it in our local area, which now would be in Adelaide, Australia. We have offered people an alternative option - interested people from interstate or overseas can benefit their growth and awareness as well that of their friends by organising a seminar or event of their choosing. You Patt can do this on your own or with a group if you are interested in organising something like this. If you are interested I can e-mail you further details.

First of all, we need to know where you live (do you live in Adelaide, or do you live in Australia - if so, which town and state), and how many people you believe you can organise. If you live overseas, you would have to organise a VERY large number of people to cover our costs, as we are non-profit. And of course, which course are you interested in organising, or do we assume you are interested in organising a guided imagery course?

Once we have that information we can plan the event and get back to you with specific details and requirements.

Kind regards,

Roman.

WILL MY BUSINESS WORK OUT?

Hello Kuntarkis,

Thankyou for your advice on my "CONFUSING" life situation. I have addressed it as my past and I look forward to my future. At the moment I am starting a new business adventure with a close friend and I feel it could really take off. Do you have any insight into what we are planning to do and invest in and if it will be successful or not?

Thanks again Monica.

Kuntarkis replies:

Dear Monica, Human life is full of events which are occurring each moment that passes. Some are considered negative and others positive because of the way humanity has been conditioned from one incarnation to the next. It seems the negative aspect is always more overwhelming in human events than the positive.

Negativity is only a learning tool and once mastered should be seen only as the past and an experience of human life. You Monica have a great strength within you and you can be a limitless being who can create and succeed in any venture you choose to take on. The power of your new venture is you - to see and create by using your imagination and then putting in the action. By truly believing in yourself first, you Monica will create what you want from your human life, even if it seems that your venture is not coming together as you would like it to.

Keep a positive mind always and know truly from your heart that you will and are succeeding in everything you do with your human life, for life is always moving forward. Never look back and always keep smiling.

Be Blessed dear Monica in Love and Light always.

Kuntarkis.

IS KUNTARKIS A US PLANT?!!!

To the one called Kuntarkis,

Why does Kuntarkis target the Muslim leaders as receptors of 'evil' or negative game playing from higher forces, yet ignores the criminality of the rape and pillaging of the USA? Is not the next generation of Bush regime responsible for the 'hatred' generated from the Middle East? How can the US be so bombarded, yet refuse inner contemplation of their past sins? Is Kuntarkis a US plant from their security / propaganda forces? GO FBI - CIA!

Laurie.

Kuntarkis replies:

Dear Laurie, My being wishes to thank you for taking the moments of your human time to express your words. Yes, my being can see your point of view. There is a great evil all over your planet Earth, as it has been in your past history and as it is today. On my home planet Nar'Kariss we the Nar'Karones do not see our expressions of words as negative or positive. To us what is important is the expression of truth. To judge what is right or wrong, good or bad, is in reality an untruth in itself, as all of life throughout all Universes are experiences not to be judged as right or wrong, good or bad.

You have 7 billion human beings on your Earth and it would be fair to say you then have 7 billion truths. Yet it is only the idea of what truth is because it comes from beliefs and conditions of your past human lives. Truth lies in the moment of each experience and then becomes the past. If each human being were to go within themselves and still the human brain of its chatter and confusion, they would touch the essence of their true being and would see all of your history' to the present moment, and you Laurie would see the real truth of human evolution.

If you would take the time to view other articles on this website, you would see Laurie that my being has written many words on many cultures and countries of your Earth, and my being is very aware of America's past. What is more important Laurie is not to see things as negative or positive, but as they truly are. Step beyond your beliefs and conditioning, as they are simply the human Ego, created from the past which is what holds each human being in the past with their fears and insecurities. To see the whole picture without judgement is to see the truth, and it is the truth and only the truth that can set all of humanity free from their self-created pain and misery. Even though it may sound negative to you Laurie, it is the truth. It's all in ones thinking.

Be Blessed in Love and Light always dear Laurie.

Kuntarkis.

WILL I SURVIVE?

To Kuntarkis,

After colorectal surgery at the age of 46 it was July1999. I removed myself from one hospital which said a permanent colostomy was absolutely my future! I got up and left. I went to Boston and I am in one piece. Thank GOD for that strength... I did the 6 month round of old style chemo in the hand once a week. I refused radiation to local spot. Fear of future problems. Hopefully God directed me there too. Now after cat scans of stomach, pelvic in Jan of 2001, spot on right lower lung showed up. Went for full lung scans - one more on right lung and one on mid left... Death sentence given by my doctor. He could not look me in eye...

80 percent return he says, maybe 20 something else. I would not let him scan everything again, realising he is looking for more return so he can give me chemo. Blood work was fine. So from Feb 6 till June 6 I agreed to do lungs again. NO more spots but all 3 a bit larger, approx. 1 to 2 cms. Since June 6 I have gone through much inner pain. I have a home I am trying to keep, and a son am trying to help to go off to a nice college, getting a start I did not have, and me feeling alone, scared, denial stark reality. I say knowing others have had to feel this I cannot tell if I will be lucky and strong, or it is the calm before the storm.

I pray and wish that I have worried for nothing and the scans just caused pain that is unnecessary. HOW MUCH CONTROL does anyone truly have.

Thankyou for listening and encouraging people...

Suzanne.

Kuntarkis replies:

Dear Suzanne, First, you are a very brave human being, and from an emotional perspective,

over your 46 years of human life, in your present incarnation you have suffered deeply. Emotion is a negative aspect of all human existence and it is always based in one's past, which in turn comes into the present and then creates one's future.

Emotions and stress go hand in hand with many human beings. Dis'ease is the end result which brings pain and misery. When human beings are born into this vibration of physical matter, there is no emotion. Emotion is only created from upbringing through beliefs and conditioning, and one of the main causes of dis'ease in the human body is the food that is consumed from childhood to adulthood. When you combine emotions and stress with poor nutrition the end result is human dis'ease.

You asked dear Suzanne how much control you as an individual truly have. The answer is, as much as you want to. You are truly the Creator of your life in every facet and you can change any situation in your life if you truly want to. First, believe in yourself. Take a moment in your human time and sit in front of a mirror. Look deeply into your eyes and see yourself as a beautiful human being who deserves to live life to the fullest.

Second, say the following words:

I love myself, my being, right now and forever more. I accept who I am in this most precious moment of my life, and I will learn to love myself unconditionally. I will change my life as I wish to. I will feed my body, my mind and my spirit with good fresh food and plenty of fresh clean water. I allow my human body to be healthy and wise so that I will live life in a joyous happy vibration of thoughts. I will smile and others will see who and what I truly am. All dis'ease will no longer haunt me.

Suzanne, thoughts are very powerful. They can create a life of negativity or one of positivity. Your thoughts are your creation. Remember what Jesus said from your past - what you think you will become - and that is the truth. You are a very kind human being Suzanne. It was nice to hear from you. Take care of yourself and your human son.

Be blessed in the Love and Light of Creation's totality always, and know you

are the power and the Light is within you.

Kuntarkis.

WHO ARE THE NEW CHILDREN?

Dear Kuntarkis,

I have heard and read about the New Children or Indigo Children as beings who came to earth to help us. Why did these children come and will everybody on earth become one when the earth changes.

Thankyou,

Elizabeth.

Kuntarkis replies:

Dear Elizabeth, The New Children you speak of are beings of Light who have not lived in a physical vibration of matter. They choose to incarnate into a physical body to experience and to learn of humanity. They bring a new vibration of energy, wisdom and knowledge, to help all humans to grow beyond what is presently being experienced by humanity, known on your Earth as the Human Ego. The human Ego is causing all the pain and negative emotions. The Ego must be recognised by each human being so that it can be dissolved back into the nothingness from which it was first created.

These beings of Light will experience all facets of human existence, and they will have human children to plant the seeds of change. Even though it will take many of your Earthly years, humanity will evolve out of the darkness that has surrounded your Earth for so long. Human consciousness will expand beyond the past, and all human beings will experience these changing vibrating energies of light. Peace will come to your Earth and human beings will no longer have fear of self, of others or of other nations. Unconditional love will replace the Ego and the Light will be felt in all living beings.

Yes, this is the purpose of Creation so that the balance of life can come into existence on your Earth.

Be blessed in love always dear Elizabeth.

Kuntarkis.

BEING GAY

Hello Spiritual Traveller,

I am writing you in response to a response that you had given to a questioner who had asked "Why Am I Gay?" The response that you had given made sense to me but I am not sure if I believe that the reason that you had given, applies to all who are gay. I will give you a brief explanation as to why I say this and why this issue have deeper meaning to me... All of my teens to mid-twenties was overshadowed with sadness, depression, anger, loneliness and suicidal thoughts because I realized early on that I was gay. I did not/ nor could not accept my homosexual nature (being black was indeed hard enough). It wasn't until about 8 years ago, that I made a judgment that would ultimately change my outlook on myself and life. I contacted a physic who without hesitation told me that I was fighting demons related to my sexuality... He also told me that I (my higher self) choose to be gay because in this life, I had to experience persecution. The reason for my (higher self!) wanting to experience persecution is because I had died in one of my previous lives (in mid-Atlantis) with a FEAR of persecution. Therefore, in order to perfect and grow spiritually, I had to overcome the fear by accepting who and what I am. This message resonated in me, it was a "light bulb moment"! From that day on, I began to slowly but surely accept myself and rebuild, as a result, I am happier and more at peace with who I am. This information was a catalyst to my thirst for MY TRUTH because each soul chooses his/her own vehicles for learning and growing spiritually... I haven't had a thought of suicide in years. I've become very caring, compassionate, loving, sensitive and most importantly I've become very spiritual. Many spiritual things have happened to me since... My reasoning for this great change in me is because I have connected to the authentic person that I had chosen to be. My question to you is this... Do you feel that my scenario a logical aspect or reasoning for homosexuality?

Kuntarkis replies:

Dear Spiritual Traveller, My Being thanks you for taking the moments in your human life to express your most inner thoughts. Every human being is on their own journey of self-discovery, and what is important to each human being is the discovery of one's own inner truth. Every human being on your Earth has the right and the free will to be who they choose to be, be it negative or positive. It all depends on their parent's genetics and their upbringing, their level of understanding and their level of thinking.

What may suit one human being may in turn not suit another. To let go of the past and all the traces of human Ego is to be set free from pain and misery. It allows the inner spirit to guide the human vessel beyond all fears that were created by the individual. With freedom comes Truth, Love, Compassion, Understanding and Wisdom, for that is the Essence of being Spiritual.

What my Being may feel about your reasoning for homosexuality is irrelevant. What is most important is what you believe about yourself and what you want to create in your life. My Being is not to judge but simply to express my thoughts to those who may need guidance.

Unconditional Love is the path and the journey for a higher conscious understanding which will allow the human individual to see beyond their boundaries of self-created limitations. Unconditional love will open up all knowledge of one's existence to all past incarnations. It reveals the natural process of all life. The human Ego allows only fear to be present from the past and to be carried into the future, for fear and the human Ego are the true enemy of humanity. It is wise to remember that the choice is always there for the individual to make.

Be Blessed dear Traveller on your journey of self-discovery in love and light.

Kuntarkis.

OUTER BODY EXPEREINCE

Hello Kuntarkis,

I am an African American male who accidentally came across your sight while researching data about the great pyramids. I am truly thankful for finding you, your incredible wisdom and insight! My reason for writing you is this... About 3 years ago, I was lying on my couch watching television. At some point, I had fallen off to sleep but I remember being completely conscious (in mind) of everything that was going on in the room. I believe that I was attempting to wake my body up but I was paralysed... I could not move my body nor open my eyes... My body felt very heavy and weak... I could feel my right spirit arm moving back and forth very, very slowly, as if it were trying to fit back in place... All throughout my body, I felt a fuzzy, tingly kind of vibration. Now I had experiences like these before but the thing that made this one different is that there was light emanating through my eyelids; the equivalent to looking towards the sun with my eyes closed (keep in mind that there was NO SUN light in the room at the time). After (what I believed to be) my spirit arms settled, I had regained control and activity over my body. By this time, my heart was beating fast and I was feeling a little dazed at what had just happened to me... I have not shared this experience with many people because most people that I know don't believe in outer body experiences nor reincarnation (I KNOW that I've been here many times before). I am 95% sure that this was actually my higher self at work but 5% (doubt) feels that this could have been an outside spirit or entity at work... Could you shed some insight as to what this experience could have been?

Thanks!

Anthony.

Kuntarkis replies:

Dear Anthony, What you experienced was a near separation of your Astral body from your physical vessel. It is a natural occurrence in all forms of life, but not many have memory of the event. If you were to practice by seeing your astral body separating from your physical vessel, you would open up a vibration to higher forms of knowledge and understanding. Every human in their time of sleep does separate from their human vessel, but again not many are aware of the experience, and if they do remember, they refer to them as dreams, which is far from the truth.

The light that you Anthony were seeing is the essence of life itself. All forms of life throughout all Universes are created from light itself. What you were experiencing and seeing was your true self beyond physical form, and that light is the healing light that all healers use. You are a natural healer and yes you have had thousands of incarnations before your present incarnation. What is most important for you Anthony is to believe in yourself and trust yourself in all things you do and experience? To heal yourself is to be able to heal others. Go forward and experience life itself.

Be Blessed in the light of Creation that you are a part of and which is a part of you.

Kuntarkis.

QUESTION ON REINCARNATION

Dear Kuntarkis,

I have read quite a few books on reincarnation and find the subject very challenging to my beliefs. You have said many times that only with an open mind will one grow beyond their present level of understanding. I must say you are right. My question is what happens to all the soldiers that died in the first and second world wars. I would appreciate a reply. Thankyou for helping me open a new doorway to my life.

Tina.

Kuntarkis replies:

Dear Tina, It is good to see you are learning about the process of human development and Reincarnation, and allowing yourself to have an open mind and honest heart. My Being feels you can and will step beyond your present beliefs. You Tina have truly begun your journey of self-realisation, for there is more to human existence than what humanity would like you to believe.

To your question on your First and Second World Wars of your 20th century and the soldiers that died in it. Many who died in the First World War on your Earth have since incarnated and fought in the Second World War. But many are still fighting the First World War because of where they are in the Astral Vibration, within the Fourth Dimension. From the moment of their physical death, they have been reliving those last moments of their life in the Astral Vibration, including reliving the negative emotions over and over again. Others have reincarnated and fought in wars once more. It all depends on their fears, beliefs and conditioning from their physical lives.

Many of the soldiers who died in your Second World War have also reincarnated and have been experiencing different aspects of life, but many are still caught up in the Astral Vibration, not knowing they are physically dead. This should be of major concern to humanity because a lack of knowledge and understanding causes much pain, confusion and misery. Every human being should be given the opportunity to understand the process of human life and human death; what actually happens to the Spirit when death occurs and the knowledge and awareness of entering the Astral Vibration. When a spirit enters the Astral Vibration upon death and knows they have a choice of not being caught up in that vibration, they can move on in their personal journey of existence by letting go of their human fears and human Ego. The whole process of human evolution would be less painful and confusing if human beings were educated on the purpose of life and death through Reincarnation.

My Being trusts this response will give you, dear Tina, a little more to think about. Yes, knowledge is the key to freedom. A lack of knowledge is the key to misunderstanding and ignorance of the human Ego.

Be Blessed dear Tina in Love and Light always. Keep seeking the truth and it will appear to you and manifest in your life.

Kuntarkis.

PROPHETIC DREAMS

Hello Kuntarkis,

I have a question that I feel needs an answer, mainly because of what is going on around this crazy world. I have had this terrible feeling inside of me for the last two years. I had a dream where this planet was on fire and I was told by my angel that it was because of misunderstandings of different nations, and that terrorism was the main cause, and how we couldn't solve our differences. My question is, where is Bin Laden hiding and is he connected to Saddam Hussein, and was the attack in Bali connected to Bin Laden or Hussein? Please give me an answer as I am a victim of September 11.

Very angry and sad.

Kuntarkis replies:

Dear Human Being, What you have asked is a reasonable question and yes, it does need a truthful answer. First allow my Being to feel your pain, your anger and your sadness. My Being sends to your heart a healing energy of Light for your loss.

The human called Bin Laden is in hiding in Baghdad. His purpose in hiding is to take away the attention of the media and governments so he can focus and plan his next terrorist attack. Bin Laden is connected to Saddam Hussein and has been following his orders for all attacks of terrorism on your world. The attack on the place called Bali was planned over the last 17 months of your Earth time and was instructed by Saddam Hussein through Bin Laden and terrorist connections in Bali. Any city or nation around your Earth is a target. The humans who create the pain and suffering have been highly conditioned into certain belief systems. You could say they are brainwashed from a young age. They know who to pick and who to train. They are in every city and country around your Earth.

Saddam Hussein is behind every terrorist act - at this time he is keeping a low profile. It is his plans for the future that all human beings need to be aware of. He sees himself as 'God' and uses the image of your past Hitler as his main driving force. He wants to become the master of your world, the supreme leader of humanity. Your world at this present moment is in great danger and it is terrorism that will be the downfall of all humanity if not brought under control.

It is the past of the human Ego brought into the present that can and will create your future, be it negative or positive. Every human being needs to open their heart to the truth so all can see the falseness that surrounds all human beings. It is past negative emotions that need to be forgiven, and unconditional love for all of life that needs to be expressed.

Be Blessed dear human Being in Love and Light always.

Kuntarkis.

FORGIVENESS YOU MAKE IT SOUND SO EASY

Dear Kuntarkis,

You speak a lot about forgiveness – to forgive others for what they have done. And you say the only way to grow beyond the present is to forgive the past and all the hurts. It sounds so easy, so why does my heart hold onto all my pain? I don't understand. I want to forgive but it is so difficult. Can you explain how to make it easier to forgive?

Joyless.

Kuntarkis replies:

Dear Human Being, True forgiveness does come from the heart centre, and yes all human beings can forgive and dissolve all pain and hurts into the nothingness from which they came. But you as an individual must take a moment to stop and ask yourself this question: do I truly want to forgive the past? Ask this question from your heart centre, and then listen in the stillness of your Being, not from your pain, anger or Ego.

The human Ego does not understand forgiveness. It only understand your past, your pain, your anger – the hurts that have been conditioned into you from the past which then come into your present. If forgiveness is not understood, then how can an individual forgive?

Forgiveness allows you to step into your future without emotional baggage. It allows you to step beyond the pain and anger. It breaks the chains which have helped keep you a prisoner unto yourself. When you are truly ready to let go of your pain, anger and past hurts, then and only then can you the individual truly forgive the past. Only then will you see your past as a memory of experiences, neither negative nor positive, simply as lessons of life.

One of the greatest lessons for all human beings is unconditional love for self and all of life. Unconditional love allows you to see the truth. It opens your heart and your understanding, and allows you to see with new eyes. It will allow you to be full of joy and happiness, where the human Ego only allows you what it understands – the past, be it pain, suffering, and negative emotions.

Look all around your world and see the conflict, suffering and confusion. Ask yourself, why? It is a lack of forgiveness, a lack of understanding, and a lack of unconditional love. For humanity to grow, the individual desperately needs to start looking at their ability to forgive, to understand and to love unconditionally. The power of forgiveness is within all human beings, as is unconditional love. But when will each of you choose to forgive and love unconditionally so that humanity as a whole can progress in consciousness?

Be Blessed dear human Being in Love always.

Kuntarkis.

<u>FEARS</u>

Dear Kuntarkis,

I would like to know where I'm at in my life, and what my purpose in this world is. I have a lot of fears and don't know why. All I want is to be happy. Can you please help me?

Thankyou.

<u>Kuntarkis replies:</u>

Dear Human Being, when a human being is confused about their life, it is very difficult to see beyond the present moment in life. Your beliefs and conditioning, and your experiences up to a point, will create confusion and it may not seem clear where your human life is heading.

Your fears are a creation of your childhood, encoded in your genetics from your human parents. Every emotion that your parents experienced is encoded in their genetics and in turn passed onto their children, be it negative or positive, and that alone can create your path in life.

One thing must be understood. You as the individual can change any circumstance in your life if you choose to, for you are the power in your life and the driver of your present and your future. Try and see fear as the past which can and does manifest itself into the present. Everything in life is energy and fear is simply another type of energy which can be released and dissolved if the individual is willing to let it go. Live only in the moment and then you will begin to create your future. Your future can be whatever you choose it to be. It is your past that holds you in fear and you can let the past be the past if you choose to. Believe in yourself and believe you deserve to be happy. Be positive in all things you do, no matter what, and you will find life will be balanced and happy.

Be Blessed in Love and Light always.

Kuntarkis.

PAST LIVES

Dear Kuntarkis,

I have a question about past lives - you were able to inform Marie, back in July 2003, about her experiences as a healer and where they came from. I am attempting to ask without anticipation, if you have any information about mine, and my group's past lives, and interactions. Have we always been a group? Are we a higher-density form of life manifesting as a group of humans?

We, myself included, possess a very strong drive to "save" or "change" the world, and we seem to be getting closer and closer daily to achieving that goal, of course through changing ourselves and our realities (And it WORKS!) I have an impression that I have had a recent past life that had a brief showing of a desert in the US, it "felt" like a memory from the 1960's - I think it was the Sonora desert. (I was born into this incarnation in 1978, in Canada, and have never been to any US Desert, so this memory is odd), and before that, I have the impression that I died during a mission towards the end of WW2. This is sort of odd to me, because I'm not sure if I would have been a soldier - at least, I will not be one now.

To rephrase my question in a more precise way, can you reveal some truths as to what came before me? How did I know enough to pick THIS incarnation, as it's a really, really good one - where did I learn this knowledge was it my last life? I am going through the process of remembering, and so it is difficult to know where these memories and impressions that I get, more and more frequently, are coming from. My psychic and healing gifts are at an all-time high, but only because of the Work I'm doing with the self. Have I always been into this work, and did I fail in my mission in my past life? Do I repeatedly put myself in "Casandra-Syndrome" type situations where I pointlessly try to blast truth to those who haven't asked, resulting in my choosing the Path of the Fool? This isn't the first time I've walked this path, is it?

Thank you for the service that you provide to humanity. May your knowledge of the universe be forever in balance?

Tovy.

Kuntarkis replies:

Dear Tovy, My Being expresses love and joy to you and all the ones you associate with in your current incarnation as a human being. First, my Being feels the need to express a truth about who you are and where you come from. Understand, all life forms are created from magnetic energy, which many call the Light of Totality.

All life forms come from a single atom which evolves into many atoms, creating different structures of life forms. No matter what it becomes, that atom in itself is evolving as living consciousness. There are many human beings who come from the planet or realm of Nar'Kariss. Many Nar'Karones choose to incarnate to experience human form to help the evolution of humanity.

Whether you Tovy choose to accept my expressions is your choice. The truth is, within you, your very essence, is a recording of all your past experiences. You are a Nar'Karone who has lived many human existences in order to help heal this most precious Mother Earth, as well as helping human beings who choose to learn and grow in awareness beyond their current level of understanding.

Your answer is yes, you do put yourself in situations in expressing your truth to some who do not wish to listen. Please understand, it is also a part of your growth. It will pass and those who choose to learn will come into your vibration of healing energies. What you are experiencing is emotions of your conditioning from a child into adulthood. Please be patient, as you will step beyond your present into a more aware state of consciousness.

You as an infinite Being of Light, before you chose to incarnate into your present human life, you chose all the circumstances that would be experienced in your present moments. Your knowledge is infinite, as it is within all human beings.

Tovy, as you evolve and become compassionate towards all forms of life, and as you begin to accept yourself for who you are in unconditional love from your inner being to your outer self, you will realise where you truly come from and all your past memories will be there for you to view at your wish.

Remember dear Tovy, become the living truth of who and what you express, and others will see you as your truth. They will be attracted to your energies of love and truth. One thing you may need to practice if you choose to – believe, truly believe in yourself and everything that you feel. Everything is for a reason.

Be Blessed in the Light of Creation's Totality, of which all life forms are a part of.

Kuntarkis.

(20) YEARS OF GRIEF OVER RAPE

Hi my name is Marcella.

I have experienced a lot of body pain in recent years and have been diagnosed with Post Traumatic Stress Disorder after a serial rapist attacked me over 20 years ago. I wish to no longer be effected mentally, physically or spiritually by this horrendous event - how can I release it forever and get on with living my life not just surviving. Thankyou love and light to you.

Marcella.

Kuntarkis replies:

Dear Marcella, Yes, you are being affected physically and mentally by a memory of your past experience. My Being is always saddened by what humans do to other humans. There is no justification for any human to cause harm or pain to another. Since your experience happened many of your Earth years ago, is it not time to forgive and let go in unconditional love? Please feel from your heart that forgiveness is the key in dissolving the pain of negative emotions. First you must have the willingness to forgive yourself, and to accept yourself in unconditional love.

When you can forgive yourself and love yourself unconditionally without any anger, hatred or judgement, and be completely unbiased towards yourself, then you will be able to forgive your attacker and the emotional pain he caused you. This does not mean that you will forget the experience. What it does mean is there will be no negative emotion attached, and you will not carry it into your next life as part of karma. In letting go of the past, dear Marcella, your human body will also let it go and will come into balance with the mind and the spirit. You will see it as an experience, neither negative nor positive. It will simply be the past.

Please, if you choose to, try this little exercise and allow your heart to be open. Feel your unconditional love, which is present in all of humanity and all life forms. Find a quiet place for yourself and either lay on the floor or sit in a comfortable chair. Close your eyes and breathe in and out. Feel your lungs expanding as you breathe in. Hold the breath for a moment and then exhale. Tell yourself to relax. Then, using your imagination, your natural abilities, put your attention onto your heart centre. Your heart will release unconditional love. Feel your heart opening up – see it, feel it, know it – as your heart opens you can see or feel a light that is pure in its essence.

This light of unconditional love begins to expand all the way down to your toes, and then all the way up to the top of your head. Give yourself some precious moments to experience this wonderment of light and love that you dear Marcella are a part of, as is all of humanity and all life forms. Feel this love and light beginning to expand all around your outer human body and allow yourself to experience your true self. You are an infinite being that is ageless, timeless, endless and eternal. Your human body is simply a vehicle for you to experience physical life. As you truly feel your own unconditional love, say "I who exist in this moment of my own reality truly forgive myself and love myself in unconditional love." Feel it, believe it, and truly believe it and the truth will manifest itself.

Now see your attacker in your mind's eye standing before you. Tell him you have been very angry for what he did to you and that he had no right to cause you so much pain. With an open heart tell him you completely forgive him in unconditional love and let him go, and that the karma between you both is now dissolved. Remember, this can only happen however if you truly forgive from your heart. Simply saying the words and then feeling angry towards him will not work! See your attacker fading into the distance and believe from your heart that this is happening. If you truly believe and are sincere in your forgiveness, it will be manifested into your reality. Again, breathe in deeply and exhale knowing from your heart that you no longer need to hold onto the pain from the past. The past is the past. The present is the present and holds the pure opportunities of a new day.

Do this exercise as many times as you need to? The truth is in believing in yourself and accepting that you deserve to be a happy, joyous and loving human being. When you believe in yourself you can manifest anything into your reality.

Be blessed in love always dear Marcella.

Kuntarkis.

WANTING TO BE OR BECOME SPIRITUAL

Dear Roman and Kuntarkis,

I stumbled on your site while surfing the net and as I say that, I wonder was it an accident. Anyway I am trying to become a more spiritual person but I just do not know where to start. I have been trying to meditate but I just cannot seem to last it out. I feel I should be doing something but I have no idea what. I see plenty of advertisements about how to reach your inner self but where does one start.

Brendan.

Kuntarkis replies:

Dear Brendan, Please first realise you are already a spiritual being. Your true essence is spirit. You as all human beings are on a journey of self-discovery. Everything you experience as a human being leads you one step closer to self-realisation. See yourself as infinite. You as all human beings are a conscious expression of Creation's totality, meaning you are a part of everything and everything is a part of you.

The chattering of the human brain must be still in order to gain the benefits of meditation. Meditation is not concentration nor is it thinking. Meditation is the stillness of the mind. It is a means of transformation to elevating your being and your mind to higher realms of communication, not only to your own inner knowledge which is infinite, but also to other worlds, realms and vibrations.

Brendan, allow yourself to experience all facets of life. Read more books on spirituality, go to some courses for developing your natural abilities, and persist in your meditations. Begin with only five minutes per session and as you become more comfortable, increase the sessions to 10 or 15 minutes. You may find a regular group meditation or meditation circle to be of benefit in these early stages of learning. There are many options and places to start. Take the first step and the following steps become easier.

Be blessed in love always.

Kuntarkis.

MY RELATIONSHIPS ARE GOING BAD

Hi Kuntarkis,

I've had many relationships that have all turned bad. Now I'm in a new one and I moved interstate to be with him. He's great but somehow I'm making it turn bad. I don't want to lose this one.

Paul.

Kuntarkis replies:

Dear Paul, It is your fear from your past that destroys your relationships. You have a fear of rejection and you deny yourself to be loved by you the individual. As a child you never felt accepted or good enough, and this emotion has been conditioned into your genetics. Because of this negative creation, the emotion has followed you throughout your human life.

You want to be loved so much by another, yet you do not allow yourself to be loved and accepted by yourself Paul. Your fear of rejection will always follow you throughout your human life unless you are willing to forgive yourself and let go of your past. Many human beings are haunted by their past experiences and hope by ignoring them that their emotions will simply go away.

But the fear will not go away until you face your fears – your fear of rejection and of not being accepted by others. Paul, you are a beautiful human being and you have within you an endless river of love to give to others.

First Paul, please give some love to yourself. Allow this love to manifest within your heart. Face your fears and see them for what they are. Fear has no power except the power you give it. Dissolve your fears and live in the present moment, and the past will be the past. You will live your life in balance with joy and harmony.

Be blessed in love always dear Paul.

Kuntarkis.

ASTRAL NIGHTMARE

Dear Kuntarkis,

I have a couple of questions that has been eluding me for a while now and I know that you are one who will provide the logical answers. About 2 months ago, in the early hours in the morning (still dark outside), I was in bed asleep and I felt that all too familiar vibrating pressure and sensation all throughout my body that usually produces some very vivid and power out of body experiences. In my mind, I tried to control the experience but instead, I felt the sensation of slowly falling downward while in a horizontal position... I had no control, everything appeared pitch black! As this was happening, it felt as if something or someone of a negative force was pulling me upward by my ankles. From there, I felt a sense of panic like never before while out of body... My heart began racing and I felt a mild, hot stinging sensation all throughout my physical body. I also remember seeing flashes of flame-like orange light. I didn't see any other being but I did see a flash of an angry image to my human likeness...

This was a terrifying and unforgettable experience... All I could do in my mind was repeatedly call Jesus by name and was gently placed back into my body. I still don't know nor understand what this experience was all about... I've meditated on it and asked my spirit guide's to show or tell me what this was but the answer has not been given (at least not that I am consciously aware of). Would you please tell me what this experience was all about and what I can do to avoid such a thing from happening again during an outer body experience? Also, could you please tell me what my spirit guide name is?

Your brother in light and spirit,

Anthony.

Kuntarkis replies:

Dear Anthony, Human beings always seem to want to control every situation and event in their lives so they can produce an outcome they feel comfortable with. What you were experiencing was an out of body experience. Your astral body was venturing out of your physical shell, and because your mind and body were aware of this experience, you were trying to control it.

As your astral body was pulling away from your physical body, and because you could not control the experience, your physical self-became fearful and created images that caused you fear, so your heart began to race. The orange light you saw at that moment was your aura. The angry image was your own self-image of fear, created by your human self which in turn pulled your astral body back into your physical body.

Anthony, do not try to control your next experience. Just go with the flow and you will experience many wonderful things which will help you in your own awareness and conscious growth. Fear has a way of creating many illusion that stop human beings from experiencing other existences and other worlds and vibrations.

The astral body can only venture out into the fourth vibration/dimension. Your light essence of spirit can and does venture into many vibrations far beyond the astral world. When your astral body is out of your human shell nothing can harm you except yourself, meaning what you create from your own fears which are based on your human experiences, such as from when you were a child, from your beliefs and conditioning, and so on. Remember, fear has no power, only what you the individual give it.

What is created by the individual can also be uncreated. Using the name Jesus repeatedly was a good sign of faith and trust, and the one called Jesus who was born in the year 4BC and died in the year 29AD is in reality living a human existence on your world today. He is a teacher of knowledge today as he was then,

Be Blessed dear Anthony in the love of the light always.

Kuntarkis.

IS THERE A CURE FOR DIABETES

Dear Kuntarkis,

Reading your story on illnesses in the August edition has opened my eyes and also my understanding. I believe we each create our own illnesses from our emotions and of course junk food. Both of my children suffer with diabetes. One is 7 the other 11, and it seems they will be on insulin for the rest of their lives.

Neither I nor my husband suffer from diabetes but my mother has since she was 19. How come I was lucky to miss out yet my children did not. Will there ever be a cure. I'm always hoping...

Cadie.

Kuntarkis replies:

Dear Cadie, The cure for diabetes is not in drugs or insulin created by humans because these are only 'Band-Aid' cures. They are naturally a very profitable business which prolongs the problem. To find or discover the solution to diabetes one must first discover why it has been created in the first place.

The answer lies in your production of processed foods. Nearly everything has sugar added to it. The human body cannot over a long time handle too much sugar consumption. Eventually the genetics begin to break down. When a human adult has a child those faulty genetics are passed on to the child and over a number of lifetimes, the continuous bad lifestyle habits and diet will create diabetes in younger children, many before they reach the age of 12, and some of your human children are now being born with the dis'ease.

Humanity needs to ask this question of themselves: why is it in the last 13 years of your Earth time has diabetes become such a threat to human society? Only in the last 17 years diabetes has increased by 29% and it is growing at an alarming rate.

You as a mother of human children should consider the following. The human consciousness exists in every cell that makes up the human body. The human body can cure any defect or dis'ease. It is a miracle within itself, for every cell has the knowledge to reproduce itself if it is given the opportunity and correct nutrition to do so. This means what you put into your human body, both food and thoughts) will govern how well the human body works.

Even if a human being has diabetes or any other dis'ease, to consume natural foods of your Mother Earth, to drink plenty of clean water, to avoid living within the pollution that plagues your cities, and by dealing with negative emotions and stress (stress being the greatest factor in creating all human dis'ease), you will give your cells the opportunity to recreate themselves correctly and reprogram your genetics so the healing process can begin naturally. That is a cure within itself.

Be Blessed dear Cadie in love and light always.

Kuntarkis.

KNOWLEDGE OF AURAURALITE/AULMAURACITE?

Greetings with Love and Light,

I commend you for your assistance with helping the Humans, Star seeds, Indigos, Crystalline and Crystalline/Octarines. So I say this now, Thank-you. I would like to ask you for assistance.

My question is not anything specific, nor is it to "make" me a believer. Believing is not a problem for me. I ask that in your spare "Time" so to say, that you observe me if you feel inclined, and please give me insight as to the growth of my being, physical mental and otherwise, offer suggestions. One specific question I have though is on the stone Aurauralite/Aulmauracite. What knowledge you have about the stone. I thank you for your time in reading this e-mail.

Love, Light, and laughter sent to you all, Thank you.

Quinton.

Kuntarkis replies:

Dear Quinton, to your specific questions on the stone Aurauralite/ Aulmauracite, ethically it would be best that my Being not express an opinion regarding the man-made stone. It would be best for you to obtain knowledge of it from the following website:

http://www.mistychouse.com/Aurauralite/Aurauralite-toc.htm. As an individual you can make up your own mind regarding what you believe or

disbelieve.

You asked of my Being to observe you and to offer suggestions regarding your spiritual growth. More to the point, to give you insight into your physical, mental growth and your awareness.

Spiritual knowledge comes to a human individual when that individual has personally taken responsibility for all of their self-created negative actions which have been created over their past and present incarnations. Through an honest loving heart of unconditional love for all life forms, no matter what they may be, love will be almighty present within that individual. Every negative action will create a negative reaction for that individual, just as positive actions create positive reactions. Every human being on your planet Earth has created negative actions, and the results of these actions have followed them throughout their lifetimes. The human Ego is the creator of all negative actions, and these actions are created from fear, anger, violence, vanity, domination, greed, lust, murder, wars, and rape and so on.

The purpose of human life is to come to that realisation and to learn to understand that negative actions hold back conscious growth within the human individual as well as for all of humanity. Only through forgiveness, honesty, truth and unconditional love can the individual break free from their own self-created prison of negativity. This may sound harsh, but it is the truth that sets the individual free from the human Ego and the self-created misery of the human individual.

Become humble in all that you do. Forgive yourself and all who have caused you pain from the past to your present. Have only love in your heart for yourself and all life forms. Do not eat of the dead, only of plants from Mother Earth. Think loving thoughts of your own being and project only loving thoughts to all others. Be willing to listen to others without judgement or opinions. This is in reality how a True Human Being lives when on the path of spiritual awareness. Such a human being has evolved themselves into a being who has understanding and compassion, one who has gained the wisdom of their inner being and is expressing that wisdom outwardly.

Be blessed dear Quinton in unconditional love always.

Kuntarkis.

TWIN SOULS

Hello Kuntarkis,

I am a twin, not identical (i.e. not from the same ovum as my brother). Through our lives we have noticed a connection like knowing when the other is in pain and such. Now that we are older and have begun to grow more spiritually we have noticed things more deeply.

In the past one of us has been experiencing a trauma, actually physically while the other was going through a mirror of the same but psychologically, then at a later time the role would reverse what my brother had experienced physically and I psychologically I would then go through a physical experience. These occurrences I can see from the time we were about 16 and have been increasing in intensity, we are now 27. This is a time in our lives I feel is very important, I feel it is the beginning of a new cycle.

My brother was born first, he was very small and did not breath on his own, the doctors were afraid that he would not live and so they called for a Chaplin to have us baptised. Ten minutes later I was born, I was bigger than my brother and immediately let out a big cry as I took my first breath when immediately my brother then kicked and with great effort took his first breath and began to cry.

We were very sick and small and were kept in hospital for a long time. My brother longer than me for he had asthma and other problems. All through our lives he has had a rougher time with his health and learning than me. But it seems in our spiritual development he is sometimes stronger than me. We have often wondered when recounting the story of our birth if he had in fact waited for me or if our souls were one and had to wait for both bodies before they could enter us.

My question is what are twin souls? And how do the souls of fraternal twins (like me and my brother, two eggs fertilised at the same time) differ from the souls of identical twins (One fertilised egg that divides to form two foetuses)?

We now know that we need each other so much for when we are close we don't struggle so much.

Thank you in love and light,

Sarah.

Kuntarkis replies:

Dear Sarah, My Being thanks you for writing. Yes, it seems both of you being born into a human vessel had suffered in your early years as human children. Even though it can be hard to accept your experiences, it is what you as spirit beings already chose before entering the human vibration of physical matter.

It is also what brought both of you closer to each other. You are right in saying you feel it is the beginning of a new cycle - for both of you. To your question, what are twin souls, some human beings call it Soul Mates, and others call it Twin Flames. In reality these terms have the same meaning.

Twin Souls are of the same energy. You are a spirit being, a form of living energy. A soul can split their energies by one, two, three, and four and so on. The main purpose of these energies incarnating from the same soul is to help each other grow in awareness and to experience different facets of human life. They can all be male, or all female, or male and female. They can be siblings, parents, friends, colleagues or lovers, and the bond between them can become very special - no matter what happens, this bond will not be broken.

Twin souls can be born together in the same family or can come into contact at a later time in human life. They can be born to other families, even in other countries, and still meet in their current life at some point. As a spirit, you choose the experiences and even the circumstances that will surround you throughout your human life.

There is in reality no difference between the souls of fraternal twins, like you and your brother, or the souls of identical twins. All it means is the energies of one soul have split to make two individuals. These circumstances are chosen by the spirit at that moment in human life. That is one reason why you can sometimes struggle in human life when both of you are separated, and when in most cases you are closer, life seems more simple and easier to handle with everything seeming to be in the right place. Would you not agree Sarah?

Many twin souls are born separate and to other families in other states or countries. It is very true that two human beings of the same soul can meet along the path of life and become husband and wife, or become extremely close friends. It can be a negative or positive experience, all depending on the individual, their human ego's beliefs and fears, and their conditioning. It is always up to the individual to grow in awareness and to expand their understanding, to accept new ideas and to help others grown beyond their negative self-created limitations.

Always remember in your heart dear Sarah, human life is like a dream - you can shape it any way you choose it to be - it is all in the level of one's thinking.

Be blessed in unconditional love always.

Kuntarkis.

WHAT DOES MY FUTURE HOLD?

Hi Kuntarkis,

My question is what will I be in the future? This puzzles me and haunts me. Any insight would be appreciated.

Kuntarkis replies:

Dear Human Being, You can be whatever you as a human individual chooses to be. You are the power of your own destiny. Just because you have been conditioned to think a certain way, act a certain way, does not mean you cannot go beyond what you are in this moment of your human life.

Your human parents are your guides. Now you are 22 years of age, you are a free thinking individual who can create anything you choose to. It is all in how you see yourself. Go beyond your present understanding, you're thinking. Step bravely beyond what or how you see yourself in your present moment of life. Be willing to accept new ideas by having an open mind and heart. Step forward and be willing to experience other facets of life. You are a very loving and beautiful human being who wishes to help others in their time of need.

Ask yourself "What do I truly want from my life?" Listen to your first answer and write it down. Then look at how you can begin to create that dream and make it reality. It does not matter what it is. Human life is all about experiences which will help you grow as an human individual in your awareness, to set you free from your past and to teach you how to live in the moment of life.

What my Being can share with you is that you have chosen in your present incarnation to help others find themselves. First you need to find yourself, then you can help others do the same. Listen to your heart for therein lies the truth and the answers to all your questions. Always ask your questions from your heart and you will be lead in your chosen direction. Trust yourself always.

Be blessed dear human being in unconditional love always.

Kuntarkis.

ELOHIM AND THE DUALITY OF HUMANITY

To Kuntarkis,

I am wondering if you, Kuntarkis and Roman would please post something about the true origin of mankind and how we've become to have a multidimensional life form. You see, I came across a website http://www.watchman.org/profile/raelianpro.htm on the net about this man named Rael (you may have heard of him) who speaks of meeting an Elohim from space some 31 years ago. He tells a story of how the Elohim told him that they are responsible for the creation of all living life on planet earth. He also teaches that the Elohim (galactic scientists) taught him that there is no such thing as a soul and spirit; that eternal life is only achieved through cloning.

He does teach one thing that Kuntarkis has been stating for a long time and that is that there is no God in the sense that so many humans believe to be. I have to be honest in saying that I do feel in my heart that there is some truth to what this man is saying but my experiences most certainly proves beyond a shadow of a doubt that we have some kind of consciousness beyond the human vehicle.

The teachings that Kuntarkis shares on your website is far the most compelling and truthful that I've come across. Therefore, any detail information about the true origin of mankind and spirit is greatly needed and appreciated at this time.

Thank you all so much for all that you do in the name of love and light.

Tony.

Kuntarkis replies:

Dear Tony, First, the human word Elohim means female and male - Elo is female, him is male. From a human understanding, the two elements are needed to create, such as creating a human child requires a male and female.

The word Elohim goes back to when the Bible was written by man and where the word Elohim represents the God, the creator of all that is. It is the individual's choice to believe or not believe in this, yet the truth of all that has been and all that will be is within the essence of who you are as a human being. All knowledge is within each human being.

What an individual believes and even teaches others is of their own making, whether it is negative or positive - it is up to that human individual alone. There are so many different truths upon your Earth, every human being believes they know the truth, yet all truth that comes from the outside of man (outside the individual rather than within) is only the idea of truth.

There are many who long to believe in something or someone because so many do not believe in themselves. They believe they are not worthy or capable of ever finding truth so they look to the outside, to someone else or others, in order to feel they belong.

A human body cannot exist without the energy of the spirit. Without the spirit the human body would perish or exist in a coma supported by medical equipment. Once a spirit decides to let go of the body, the energy cord which connects the spirit to the body will disconnect and the human body dies. This is the balance of life.

Be blessed in love always Tony, and please remember all is not what it seems on your Earth. There are those who are creating great confusion to all who seek knowledge and truth. Again, truth is within the individual, and the rest is the created illusion of fear.

Please note: In the story section, look up story number **44** called **Origin of Humanity**, it will explain in more depth how Humanity actually began.

Kuntarkis.

SEEING AND COMMUNICATING WITH SPIRIT

Hi Kuntarkis,

Thank you for the response to my previous question. I have another question.

How did you come to know the name of my spirit guide? This question does not come from scepticism just real joy and surprise. You see I have been asking for a long time what my guide's name is but I feel I never received an answer. What I did receive was a clear inner voice telling me that names are not of a concern or are not important in the spirit world. Names are given to make us who are living to feel comfortable. We as physical forms are constantly working in "boxes". We feel safer but we miss so much. Just because we cannot see outside of our personal box that we constructed with fear, doubts, anger etc., does not mean that there is nothing outside those walls. I feel that this is telling me to trust my gut feelings and begin to let go of the fear of not being able to physically see or hear for that matter, to actually allow myself to fully receive guidance. I am still interested in if you have made contact with my guide, if so how does she feel? What is she like? Did she live in a human body?

Also I did often feel touches on my leg or on my toes while sleeping at night. I may have felt them on my head as well, but when it started happening a lot I got scared and asked them to communicate in a different way. Of course it does not happen as often, strangely I miss the attention. I once woke up in the night and was still in a very heavy delta wave pattern of consciousness, this time is my most receptive time for psychic awareness, and I saw standing at the end of my bed two very faint figures. One was a woman I felt who was holding the hand of a little girl. The girl asked the woman if I could see them in a very curious playful voice. As I started to realize what was happening they faded away with each blink. I often get these visits.

Thank you for replying to my email and I hope I might be able to meet you or book a session someday with you Kuntarkis. I'd like it if you would keep corresponding with me. I am also interested in your thought on my questions. Of course I'm sure you have lots of emails to reply so I will be patient.

Blessings to you.

Callan.

Kuntarkis replies:

Dear Callan, Depending on the vibration in the world of spirit, there are many doorways to different levels of consciousness. In our own dimension we the Nar'Karones are no longer inhabited by the ego of dense matter flesh bodies. In your world you travel by your transportation vehicles such as cars, buses, trains, ships and airplanes whether they take you to another part of your city or to another country.

We travel by thought. We see our destination and we arrive at that point by thought alone. It is like opening a door to another realm. There are scientists on your planet who are working in the field of Space within Space, like bending Space, this is a real phenomenon. My Being has met with your guide As'charre in the astral vibration connected to your inner worlds. It is true that in spirit world names are not a concern for each being knows another by the light of their aura.

Your guide As'charre lived in your human year of 581AD in a small village called Pracknerr (forgive the spelling, but it has been phonetically spelt), just outside of Egypt. Her human parents were the leaders of the village. They had four children and you Callan were the youngest son. You were very close as a family and you and your sister As'charre were the best of friends. You always looked out for each other. Even though you were the youngest in your family during that lifetime, you were always very protective of As'charre.

In your present life As'charre has chosen to be your guide to protect you and guide you in what you seek from your human life. In the silence of your mind through meditation you will make contact and communicate with As'charre. Believe in yourself, never give up.

Be blessed in love always.

Kuntarkis.

WHY CAN'T EVOLVED BEINGS STOP HUMAN SELF-DESTRUCTION?

Hello Kuntarkis,

Since your kind have advanced in their understanding and evolved beyond the physical world of matter, as you put it, why can't you stop the wars and violence on our world? Is there an answer or are we as humans doomed to live in violence and fear forever?

Sick of it all.

Kuntarkis replies:

Dear Human Being, if all human beings felt what you are feeling then there would be no violence. Violence is humanity's past, brought into your present, and fear is the trigger which causes your history to constantly repeat itself. The repercussions of all negative actions from humanity's past must be brought into balance.

It is the lesson of all human beings to learn to let go of their negative creations and to learn to forgive without judgement. Each human being can only come to this realisation when they forgive themselves for their past negative action and thoughts. By forgiving yourself you learn to forgive others. It is the human ego of fear that creates so much negativity. It is the human ego that is your enemy. Dissolve the ego and you dissolve the enemy within.

If there was no Human Ego present in humanity, then your world would be free of wars, murder, rape, greed, lust, or violence. Misery and pain would not or could not exist on your Earth. Humanity would not be clouded by negative energies and the human race would turn toward developing the mind towards a deeper understanding of Love and Compassion for all life forms. There would be equality for all human beings. There would be respect for each other. No one would think of ever harming another human or any other life form. There would be no vanity or jealousy, or judgement upon another. Human beings would work in harmony with each other and with nature, rather than against each other and against nature. No companies would create poisons to harm you or your children, no pollution in your environment, no slaughtering of animals. You would eat of the plant kingdom, respect sentient beings and respect the Earth that give your life and sustains your human life.

Each human being needs to come to the their own realisation, that yes, it is the Human Ego that has created all the misery and pain you are now experiencing; it is the Human Ego that is the enemy and that it is responsible for the conflict that continues to repeat itself lifetime after lifetime, over thousands of generations, thousands of incarnations.

Think upon these words:

How many are willing to face their fears?
How many are willing to listen to their heart?
How many are truly willing to listen to us?

Be blessed in unconditional love always.

Kuntarkis.

BLUE STAR BEING

Dear Ilona and Roman,

It's a pleasure to see that you guys are shining brighter than ever - In my opinion, you guys are the best! The reason why I am writing this time is because I really need Kuntarkis' insight on yet another vision that I've had... I was recently reading a book titled "The Blue Star Trilogy - book 1" through Celestial. Blue Star is a being from another world whose wisdom and guidance for humanity is channelled through a lady by the name of Celestial. While reading the book, I saw a clear and precise vision of a Being (in my head) that was unlike anything I have ever seen. Let me describe Him - He had light-pinkish skin with a large heart-shaped head. He had facial features that looked almost identical to a lion or cat (no fur). His eyes were small, slanted, and wide-set, with a slit for Iris. I also remembered that he had short and straight, platinum white hair on the top of his head. I felt that this was an elder of his kind. My question to you is this, was this a figment of my imagination? If this was not my imagination, who is this being and why did he permit himself to be seen by me? Was this a vision of Blue Star himself? Is he trying to communicate?

I truly understand that I do have a world-view that most would consider bizarre or crazy but I see things as my experiences have afforded me. I've seen and experienced things that are simply out of this world! Would you please tell me why I am experiencing all these things that are so beyond the norm in our world?

Thank you for all that you do!

Anthony.

Kuntarkis replies:

Dear Anthony, Yes, you do have visions that are out of your human world of understanding. Is it is a blessing for you to open other doorways to other realms? They are not bizarre or crazy, it is just that not many human beings have your understanding, and there are many human beings who would love to have your kind of experiences, would they not.

The Being you speak of is not known to my Being. My Being has travelled in so many universes, yet there are other realms that my energies have not yet discovered. We the Nar'Karones have in your human time only existed without a flesh body for just over 700,000 years, so yes, there are other Realms and Universes that are beyond any form of measure, which are yet to be explored and discovered.

One thing you must always remember dear Anthony, imagination is the beginning of any form of manifestation. It was the beginning of Creation in all its forms of life, in all its universes. This Being you saw, you were meant to see and experience, and yes there will be more to come to you. Believe, always believe the impossible that is where all truth is almighty present.

Be blessed in unconditional love always.

Kuntarkis.

MIGRAINES, CONSTANT NOISE IN MY EAR'S AT NIGHT: WHY?

Greetings Kuntarkis,

Firstly I thank you for your last response, and for all the help and knowledge you freely give to all who ask. I have a few questions:

1. My father Graham is having migraines at the moment. He would like me to ask you what is the cause of his migraines and how can he find a cure?

2. I am hearing continuous thunderous type noises in my ears at night before I go to bed. I am aware this could be a guide. Is it? What is the exact purpose of this happening to me and how much longer will it go on for? It's actually happening to me now as I type. Is there something I can do to help the process? Is it related to the fact that I enjoy having healing hands placed a short distance from my ears? Is it a guide talking to me but the connection (phone line) is not right yet? Is this leading to me becoming Clairaudient?

My life purpose is about becoming a composer of music that I receive like a medium. Is what I'm hearing directly related to how I am going to receive the music that I will compose? I mean will the music come in a Clairaudient fashion or as ideas for composition? Or are these the same thing?

Blessings,

Romen.

<u>Kuntarkis replies:</u>

Dear Romen, Your human father, Graham, who suffers from migraines, may need to have his eyes checked, and as well he would also benefit from cleansing his blood and body through a detoxification diet. The pollution in his body is at a higher level than usual because when your father rides his bicycle, his lungs are taking in more air from the exertion than he would normally breathe in. Riding in traffic means more polluted air passes throughout his lungs and therefore into his blood stream where it is distributed throughout his human body.

Polluted oxygen passes to the brain via the blood and this is a primary cause of headaches and migraines. Many foods consumed by human beings are also full of toxins and chemicals which build up in the human body and create an overload on the kidneys and liver, and this in turn unbalances the human body both physically and on an energy level.

Toxins will eventually lead to the creation of human dis'ease, so it is important to cleanse the human body from toxins and pollutants. It would be good for your father to research some products that will help him eliminated the toxic build up in his body. There is one product that Roman uses. It is called Quick Cleanse and can be bought at a health food store.

Romen, the noises you hear which you call thunderous type noises, they can be created in many ways, from a human level or a spiritual level. From a human level it would be wise for you to have your hearing checked and tested to see if there is any physical degeneration occurring. On a spiritual level ringing in the ears can mean a spirit guide is working on you so communication can be established between you and spirit world.

How long it takes to open the doorway to spirit communication depends on you. There is no time factor that can be used as a gauge. To help the process it would be good for you to discipline yourself by putting aside some human time daily for meditation. An example would be spending 15 minutes each, at a time when you will not be distracted or disturbed. While it is not necessary to meditate at the same time every day, it will help you establish a pattern and to discipline yourself into making a commitment each day for this task.

Try meditating for 15 minutes each day to stop the chatter in your human brain so you can just be in the moment. Yes, it does take a strong will, but you may need to ask yourself Romen if the outcome, no matter how long it may take, will be worth it to you.

Yes, a guide is communicating with you, and yes, the "phone line" as you call it needs to be improved by you, so you are both vibrating at the same level of energy, meaning you are receiving information at the correct frequency so you can understand it.

Yes, by disciplining yourself and opening up to spirit communication you Romen will develop your clairaudient abilities.

Yes Romen, from a soul level you have already decided to become a composer of music, but as a human being on a journey of Self-Realisation you must first discover that only you can create it. By becoming a Co-Creator, the music you want to create will come from your willingness to discover the Creativeness that is already within you and all around you.

Be blessed in unconditional love always.

Kuntarkis.

SUPPORTING SOMEONE IN NEED

Hi Kuntarkis,

What's the best way to support someone when they're going through a weird phase when you can't see or speak to them?

I've managed to create a situation where I have no physical contact or communication which isn't a bad thing and kind of ironic given the situation! It's just that now I know he's feeling a little disillusioned and disappointed, and while I know that it's part of his learning and I have no responsibility over what happens. I want him to know that he can get through it and grow and he can be in control of his life.

If I never connect with him in human reality again, whether he does or doesn't care or ever think about me I don't think it matters anymore - I guess I want him to know how amazing he is and send some sort of message that may be beneficial at this time without making him attached to me. Now that I'm a little stronger I feel I can do it - kind of like an anonymous angel in his dreams or something - do you have any advice?

Thankyou so much.

Sita.

Kuntarkis replies:

Dear Sita, Love is the eternal link that binds all human beings to each other. The Human Being is connected to their Spirit, their Spirit is connected to their Soul, and their Soul is connected to the totality of Creation. Creation is a part of all things, as all of life in all its forms is a part of Creation.

For you to send love from your heart to your human friend is indeed a very special gift. Simply connect to your heart by placing your focus, your will, on your heart centre and feel or see a ball of white light at your heart centre.

Then in your mind's eye see your friend in his human form and project that ball of white light directly to his heart centre and say "I send you this ball of love and allow you to go on your own journey of life. Be well. Be balanced in love always." and see him going in his own direction.

If you place the right intention in what you are doing then it shall be done in love always.

Be blessed in unconditional love always dear Sita.

Kuntarkis.

I AM LOST AND HAVE NO DIRECTION

Dear Kuntarkis,

I have been given your address for myself to receive some spiritual guidance from you.

My name is Sarah. I am 29 and separated from my husband now for 8 months with my four children. I feel somewhat "lost" and unsure of how to behave and what actions to take in my life. I also feel unlucky in love and I truly want to be loved by a man - to have my soul-mate. I feel "down" a lot and feel like my cup is over-flowing. I was wondering at all if there are any words of help or guidance that you could possibly provide me with as I feel my life is so worthless and energy-draining.

I also believe that you can tell me what my spiritual name is and why it was chosen for me....

Looking forward to be hearing from you.

Sarah.

Kuntarkis replies:

Dear Sarah, Your human life is in no way worthless. You are a beautiful spirit as you are a beautiful human being. Remember Sarah, like attracts like. You need to go beyond your fears of the past and you need to love yourself unconditionally. Stop putting limitations on yourself. Stop putting yourself down.

You need to change your programming. When you feel negative about yourself and the human world, stop in that moment and say the following words (or similar):

"I will go beyond what I am feeling about myself. I will change my negative thoughts to positive thoughts. I do truly deserve the best life has to offer. I will change. I am changing. I have changed. I will see myself with new eyes. I do love myself unconditionally and I will attract a human male into my life now because I truly deserve to be happy, so I can share my happiness with my beautiful children. I will love in the moment and I will attract happiness, joy, love, wealth and good fortune into my life now and forever more. I will. I have. I am."

Sarah, each human being needs to become the observer of their own life. Step back and see your life for what it is. It may cause you some pain, but through forgiveness and facing your fears you will then create a world which will give you a positive outlook, not only for yourself, but for your human children too, so it gives them the opportunity to grow up with complete love in their hearts.

Be blessed in unconditional love always Sarah.

Kuntarkis.

LOST LOVE OF HER LIFE

Dear Kuntarkis,

I am in a sticky situation. I felt love with a friend of mine last year. I have never met anyone who makes me feel this way... We do have a problem - his ex-found out she was pregnant and told him when she was 9 weeks. He was in shock. He thought he should do the right thing and stick by her. The baby is born now he still tells me he thinks of me every day, as so do I of him. What to do. I feel he is the one. He makes me feel so comfortable.

I also have something else that is in the back of my mind. When I was 20 I was diagnosed with leukaemia and had to undergo treatment, chemo and bone marrow transplant. I wonder about kids down the track and life of a family... I am 29 now.

Thank you,

Rosalind.

Kuntarkis replies:

Dear Rosalind, My Being wishes to say thankyou for your question concerning the human male you would like to have a relationship with. Please try and understand, your present and future is in your hands. If you feel strongly towards him then would it not be wise to truly express to him how you feel? Ask him to tell you how he truly feels towards you. Depending on the outcome of both your answers, you and your friend need to make a decision which will help all who are involved.

If a decision is not made, it will only cause you, Rosalind, pain, and depending on his answer, pain to him as well. Does he love the human female he is with or is he with her simply because of the human child? These questions need an honest answer from all who are involved.

You choose in your current life as a human being to experience unconditional love, as well as a human family, meaning children with a loving human male. This will come about, but you Rosalind need to deal with your present feelings with the human male who is with another human female who has a child with him. This needs completion before you can move on.

You have come a long way Rosalind and you have experienced many emotions in your life. Yet all will come into balance. Believe in yourself, and believe in your heart - it will guide you on your path to joy, peace and happiness.

Be blessed in unconditional love always.

Kuntarkis.

TRUTH IN MY DREAM

Dear Kuntarkis,

I recently had a very profound dream that has led me on a search for truth. In my dream I looked up and saw a spacecraft which at first didn't appear to be solid, but dimly outline. At once, it formed into a solid image. In the next moment, a man appeared and we began to talk. He told me he was my father and had been looking for me. Most of the conversation that took place, I could not remember, but in the end he wanted me to go with him. I was so excited, but torn because I did not want to leave my daughter behind. There was a woman with him that was firmly against bringing "her". I feel this dream is a message for me. I would truly love some enlightenment of what this means. Also, the name "Miccah" rings in my head, but I haven't made the connection of who this is (?)

I have always yearned to learn my "true" name as well.

If you feel this is something you could help me understand, I would greatly appreciate your help.

With Love,

Robin.

Kuntarkis replies:

Dear Robin, A large number of human beings have different experiences with aliens. There are many different worlds beyond your Earth. In fact, there are thousands of dimensions, vibrations, and different levels of consciousness, just like human beings on Earth have many different levels of awareness and understanding.

One of the major problems that exists on your Earth is fear. Fear is a self-created cycle in each human being. Some can accept Aliens and truly believe in them while others are very fearful of them, due to their fear of the unknown.

What many human beings do not understand is that many have already given their permission to be taken into Alien Spacecraft's before incarnating in their present life, and because in many cases their experiences are negative, they then condition themselves and create fear of these beings. To be taken away by Aliens causes their self-created fears to come to the forefront and even though the experience may not actually be negative, they will react with fear and create a negative experience from it.

However, many human beings who have been taken have also had very positive experiences which can and do help bring about a deeper understanding of their own purpose of life.

The spacecraft you saw in your time of sleep was real - you were having an out of body experience (which every human being has when they go to sleep). The entity told you he was your father so that you would feel comfortable with him. He was not going to take you away from your daughter - he was only taking you into his craft to help you open up your inner consciousness and awareness and to show you that there is so much more to human existence than just the physical self.

That is the message for you Robin - to help you step beyond what is the known. The name Miccah is close. How it is spelt is a little different - 'Mirrichki' - that is the entity's name. If you wish his presence to be with you, go into the silence of your inner being and place the light of love and protection within and around you. Call his name to make contact with his energies. But remember, it is your choice alone. Nothing is ever done against your will.

Be blessed in unconditional love always dear Robin.

Kuntarkis.

I ALWAYS HAVE QUESTIONS FOR YOU

Greetings Kuntarkis,

As you may already know, I have been dealing with dis'ease -A.I.D.S. now for years, but now I know in my heart that I am allowing it to leave my body. I feel like I am truly on my path; maybe just the very beginning, maybe further. I don't know. I wanted to ask you about modern medicine. I have been strictly a vegetarian for a few years, then vegan, and now about 50% raw, and feeling amazing. My body seems to be beginning to thrive, and I am not sure if it because of my meditation and diet and state of mind, or also reacting to the drugs. I have such a desire to stop the drugs now, so I won't be clouded spiritually, but I do not know if I am physically ready. I truly don't feel like I am going to die because of this dis'ease anymore. I just feel it. I am sure you can tell me this. What about the medicine for me?

Oh, I am also excited about taking courses in homeopathies here by my house. I was wondering what you thought about this for me. I am not going to live in fear by being apprehensive to be around sick people. I am truly excited. I am not meant to sit in front of a computer my entire life. I know I have more to offer.

I want you to know that your words always resonate to my core, and that I have been loving myself so much more. I truly don't seem to have stress. I always have a sense of calm.

Thank you for speaking with my brother Josh, he is a beautiful person and has always been so dear to me, as you can see. We have been the closest two brothers can be. I am also perusing the Holosync you suggested, and need to go on to the next level, but I am out of work. Do I still need this, or has it opened me up enough to meditate without it? One more thing, is my vibration rising? Sorry for so many questions.

Last thing, I promise: may I ask why I still have allergies?

Love and light,

Richard.

Kuntarkis replies:

Dear Richard, It is good to see you have been creating many positive changes in your human life. It is complete truth. By becoming a vegetarian or vegan you see life from a very different perspective, and yes, the grey cloud will dissipate.

Many, so many human beings are clouded in their thinking and their understanding, they allow stress to control their human life. In many it leads to depression. Refined foods and packaged, processed foods are not healthy for the human body. Animal products, which are consumed by humans, do lead to some form of degenerative human dis'ease and even physical death.

Human habits like smoking, drugs, alcohol, junk food and poor hygiene prevents a human being from growing consciously. It keeps them in a negative space and becomes their excuses. It is called a fear of change, but it is still their choice, their free will.

For you Richard it is good to do the courses on homeopathy. It will open new avenues for you and even give you new opportunities, and yes, you do have a lot more to offer to yourself and others.

My Being feels at this time in your human life that you do not need to go to the next level with Holosync. Just keep using what you have now and allow some time for it to do its work and settle the conscious growth and expansion within your Being. This could easily be up to one year of your human time. It is important to resist the temptation of manipulation by advertising hype (I believe you understand the meaning of this statement). You will know within yourself when it is time to continue with the program, if indeed you need to continue with it. You may find it was simply a starting point to get you on your way and now you can take it from here. Keep it up – it will help you open new doors in your life. Also keep meditating in the stillness of your mind.

Yes, your energies are vibrating at a higher frequency.

Be blessed in unconditional love always Richard.

Kuntarkis.

IF I CANNOT SEE IT OR TOUCH IT TO ME IT IS NOT REAL: WHY?

Dear Kuntarkis,

I find it very hard to believe in something I cannot see or feel. In a way I do believe in you because of the knowledge you write about, but how can I learn to believe in what I cannot see or feel?

Peter.

Kuntarkis replies:

Dear Peter, Never hope, it only leads to hopelessness because hope is a negative state of thought. However, to have Faith and Trust is a positive state of thought. Start by believing in yourself. You are very special as all human beings are, so do not dwell on negative thoughts by saying "I cannot see, I cannot feel". Every time you do this you are reconfirming your own negative truth and beliefs, the outcome of which can only be "I cannot see or feel".

Change your words to "I can see, I can feel", and learn to truly believe in what you are saying. Learn to have faith in yourself. Only by believing can you then manifest that reality into your human life.

Be blessed in unconditional love always Peter.

Kuntarkis.

INFIDELITY, MY HUSBAND

Dear Kuntarkis,

I am very confused in my relationship concerning my husband. I found out six months ago he was sleeping with one of my best friends, and has been for the past twelve months. I don't know what to do. Can you give me some spiritual guidance please? I am lost. I really love him from my heart.

Candy.

Kuntarkis replies:

Dear Candy, The pain you are feeling is natural when trust is betrayed between two human beings who made a commitment together. It is not the commitment before your human god, but it is the commitment that comes from the heart that is most precious. Love, Truth, Honesty and Communication is everything, in any relationship.

The human world is full of Ego, never truly realising that emotion has been controlling human individual's right throughout human history. It is the cause of all wars that have plagued humanity and is still plaguing human beings to this very moment.

My Being cannot give you the answers that you seek; my Being can only give you the guidance through knowledge. You Candy must make your own choices and decisions. You need to ask yourself from an honest heart, why has your human partner sought companionship from another. If you seek truth then you need to confront him openly, but not in anger, from your heart. Then you can make your decision in how you will handle your situation. You may also need to confront your best friend, and find out why she also willing to betray your trust.

Always remember, human beings are on your planet Earth to learn many lessons. The self-created Human Ego is the negative side of humanity, and emotion is a part of ego, whereas feelings are a part of your human heart, the centre of love itself. If you allow yourself to understand your present situation from the heart it will help you make your decisions in what you need to do.

Truth leads to Forgiveness of self and others, deceit leads to only pain and misery. Truth will always set you free from pain or misery, especially when it comes from your Heart Centre of Unconditional Love.

Be blessed in love always Candy.

Kuntarkis.

ABDUCTIONS BY ALIENS

Hello Kuntarkis,

Do Aliens still visit our planet, and do they still take people from Earth onto their spacecraft's? An answer would be most helpful. Thank you.

Steven.

Kuntarkis replies:

Dear Steve, Yes, there are different Aliens from different worlds who have been coming to your Earth for thousands of years. Most come just to observe human beings, yet there are others who are in physical form who come to your Earth for scientific reasons.

Many thousands of human beings have been taken into what you refer to as spacecraft's, for many different reasons. Some for scientific purposes, some for experiments, and some to pass on specific knowledge for use in future situations in the evolution of humanity. My Being must express to you Steven, believe in yourself, especially your meditations. Never give up on yourself. It will all come together as you progress through your human life.

Be blessed in love always.

Kuntarkis.

FEAR FOR A SAFE WORLD

Dear Kuntarkis,

I am so concerned about what is happening around the world, there is so much unrest, so much violence between countries and people, will it ever end? Will peace come to the people of Earth? Is there a solution to what is happening? I am very concerned.

Iris.

Kuntarkis replies:

Dear Iris, There is a lot of good occurring on your Planet Earth. What is important is for human individuals not to dwell on the negative expressions of others, but to see what is happening. Do not place judgement on the negative actions which others are creating. If individuals allow themselves to be affected by the creations of negative energies from others, they then become infected by that negative creation.

This in turn does not help humanity grow consciously. Instead it keeps humanity locked in the past, and the past, if not dissolved, creates the future. So it is very important for human beings like yourself to see what is happening around your world, but to remain unbiased. Do not allow it to make you feel negative. Become a beacon of Light, and express unconditional love from your inner being to whoever is creating those negative actions upon your Planet Earth. You can do it Iris, remember, every thought either negative or positive can become reality. Thought is living energy it is unbiased.

Be blessed unconditional love always.

Kuntarkis.

REACHING MY CROSSROAD IN LIFE

Dear Kuntarkis,

I have reached a crossroad in my life and I truly am not sure which path to take. I have worked on my spirituality for many years but always feel I am just not there yet. I basically don't know what my calling is. I continue to seek knowledge, never really settling into one belief. Sometimes, I feel that I should do energy work or energy healing. Other times, I have completely lost faith. I have become very cynical. I think partly because of the death of my father 6 months ago, I have just decided why bother. I have so wanted my father to give me some sign. Anyway, thank you so much for letting me speak my piece.

Sincerely,

Amelia.

Kuntarkis replies:

Dear Amelia, Searching for knowledge is an important part of life as human beings, especially for your own conscious awareness, yet to search outwardly for knowledge or truth can become confusing to any human individual, especially if it is someone else's truth or belief system.

Maybe you, Amelia, at times in your human life have lost faith because the truth or knowledge you are seeking outwardly does not feel good from your own heart, and at times you become cynical toward others and even yourself. This is understandable. The truth on the outside in a world of confusion only creates more confusion because that truth may only be an idea of truth itself.

To discover truth one must put aside all that they believe truth to be, especially if that truth comes from others. You Amelia, are truth itself. To become the living truth of totality you need to discover that truth from within your inner being and make that connection to your own Soul. Once you make that connection, the knowledge of truth will be manifested through you. You will then know your true meaning in life. Again, go within the silence of your inner self, and be patient with yourself. Meditation in the stillness of your mind can be the greatest opening to the wonderment of self-discovery. The true meaning of silence is the key to fulfilment, to the Knowing of who you are in this vastness of Infinite Consciousness.

Believe in who you are, for you are a Divine Spark of Living Consciousness.

Be blessed in unconditional love always Amelia.

Kuntarkis.

THIRD WORLD WAR: WHEN IS IT?

Dear Kuntarkis,

Is it true there will be a third world war, and will Australia survive?

Kerr.

Kuntarkis replies:

Dear Kerr, The answer you are seeking, dear human being, cannot be given as an indication to whether or not there will be a human third world war.

More to the point of truth, humanity is the creation of their own future. If humanity creates negative actions, then there are countries around your world who will react to those negative actions, and in turn create more negative reactions. That is why there have been well over 157,000 wars on your Planet Earth since human beings have lived on Earth.

The only reason wars have plagued humanity for so long is negative emotions that have been carried throughout human history.

If humanity continues to proceed on the same path, then yes, there will be a Third World War. But if human beings can go beyond the Human Ego of negative emotions, and let go of the past, live in the moment, and learn to love all forms of life unconditionally, then there will no longer be a need for wars. Unconditional love and the Willingness to Forgive is the key to Freedom from a negative past.

Be blessed in unconditional love always Kerr.

Kuntarkis.

WHAT WILL HAPPEN TO US IN THE 5TH DIMENSION?

Hello Kuntarkis.

There is a lot of literature out there regarding our imminent (Earth and its inhabitants) ascension to the 5th dimension. Personally, I don't doubt this for I feel physically that there is something wonderful that is going to happen. However, if we ascend to the fifth dimension, what will happen to our jobs, our university degree, our friend, families, and our society? What awaits us in the fifth dimension?

Jun.

Kuntarkis replies:

Yes Jun, there is a lot of literature about Ascension into the 5th Dimension. Most of it is based on truth, but also some of it is fantasy, which is unfortunate because it will hold back individual's from conscious growth. It will be quite a while, from the human time frame, before all human beings elevate their Consciousness into the 5th dimension. Each human being must become responsible for their Ego and all their created negative situations in their human life. My Being must say this is already happening on your planet Earth. Just look around you and see all the violence that is occurring around your world. The past from each individual is coming forward and revealing itself in a negative way. This must happen before conscious growth can be raised. And yes, you are right Jun, there is something happening that is wonderful for all of life on this planet Earth. There are many different levels of conscious energies coming within this 3rd dimensional matter world, which will help on a grand scale over the next 1,000 years of human time.

Your concerns in the Ascension to a non-physical matter world is understandable at this moment in time because of the level of your thinking. Please do not take offence to my statement, but it is only the beliefs and conditioning of your human life, which is also in your genetics, that makes you feel concerned about perhaps not having the physical things you now have which identify your human life, those being your job, your degrees, your friends, your family and your constructed societies. Let me put it another way. Ask yourself from an honest heart and an open mind, why do you believe what you believe today? You see Jun, everything that a human being creates is done by thought, and then created physically into the matter vibration, where there are limitations. But when one lets go of their beliefs and conditions of life, and grows consciously beyond the 3rd dimension matter world into the 4th dimension, and then into the 5th dimension, all things are created by thought and manifested in that vibration. It is like saying, if you can imagine a cup in your mind, you then create it directly without having to go through the process of physically creating it as you would in the 3rd dimension.

Your whole level of thinking and doing will change, and all will be created from another level of understanding. There will be no negative energies at all. You will not lose your friends or family because we are all family; we all come from the same place. There is no anger or hatred or violence, only respect for all life that exists throughout the Universes. The Earth is a school room for all the human beings who live upon it; it is a place for learning to deal with fears and insecurities that have been created over hundreds of thousands of your Earth years.

So Jun, the responsibility is upon each human being to grow beyond their self-created world of Ego and Self-Created limitation. It is a simple step to take, yet many thousands of human years can or will pass, but in truth time is only illusion, is it not?

May the Light of totality be blessed upon you always?

Kuntarkis.

WHY AM I GAY?

Hello Kuntarkis,

My name is Roger and I live in Australia. I am a homosexual and have been all my life. At 34 years of age, I am completely lost and I don't understand why I am the way I am. My Father and my two brothers, and my Grandfather are all straight, yet I am not. Please if you could give me some insight and especially the truth as to why I am attracted to men.

Roger.

Kuntarkis replies:

Roger, I will give you the plain truth and nothing but the truth, because only in truth can one's conscious growth be ever present. There are two reasons why you are what you are.

The first is the hardest for any human to accept. It is in your food, and more to the point, in the animals that you consume. For the last 57 years of your human time, synthetic hormones and antibiotics have been fed to your animals that you have all been consuming. Your genetic information in the human genes are changing on a grand scale, which has become a real concern with the evolution of your species.

Ask first yourself this question from your heart - why is this so? Over the last 30 years homosexuality has increased in men by 39% and in women by 27%. This means 1 in 5 men and 1 in 7 women are homosexual, and it is on the increase. Your homosexual species is becoming prevalent in younger and younger humans.

Again, ask yourself, why is this so? Because when you were conceived, and then when you were developing in your Mother's womb, every emotion and every feeling your parents had, whether negative or positive, became a part of you. Also, with all the foods they both consumed (remembering the animals consumed have been fed synthetic hormones and antibiotics, which in turn will affect the quality of your parent's reproductive cells), became a part of you through your genetics. The imbalance in your parent's hormones at conception, and then your Mother's hormones while you were developing, from what she was consuming, were creating the effect within your developing human body, and this resulted in confusion with your genetic information. That is, whether you were to be a male or a female.

You Roger, as all homosexual human men, may have the appearance of a male on the outside, but within you are feeling feminine. Your whole physical being is not completely male or female. This is where the real problem lies.

The second reason is your thoughts. What you think, negative or positive, you will become, because it is anchored in the beliefs and conditioning you have acquired from your experiences throughout your life. The longer you think a certain way, the harder it is to change those thoughts, beliefs and conditioning. Your thoughts help create the human individual, and your emotions from your life experiences will shape your life in every way. Let's say a human male who is homosexual and decides to be with a human female and has some human children, there is a big possibility that one of the human children will be homosexual, because of genetic transfer. Genetics are encoded with Cellular Memory and if a human child has certain experiences in their human life, it can and does activate cells which can be a big influence on that human child.

I could talk to you, Roger, with so much more depth on your question, but I must allow you to choose whether or not you want to continue this discussion. What I will say is this: unless the dis'ease is changed in each human, and the emotions that are attached to it resolved by taking personal responsibility for what has been created, the imbalance within your human species will separate your society in your time to come. We, in our own kind went through this dilemma and suffered with the same dis'ease, which on your planet is called AIDS. To understand how nature works is to understand why AIDS is affecting your homosexual species so much.

Nature sees it as an imbalance, and nature is a part of Creation's totality. The balance must be brought back into existence so your human species can evolve, and what is to come will bring the balance of mind, body and spirit. Change your thoughts and you're conditioning, and conscious growth will expand your vision and your reality.

Be Blessed in the Light Roger.

Kuntarkis.

DO FAIRIES HAVE WINGS?

Dear Kuntarkis,

I have a question. I am 11 years old and live in a beautiful place that is full of forests. My question is, do Fairies have wings like Angels, and are they tiny or like grown-ups?

Allie.

Kuntarkis replies:

Dearest Allie, you are indeed very lucky to live amongst nature, and yes Fairies do exist. They are tiny, and they are a part of the Elemental World that helps keep your planet in balance.

Fairies do not have wings in reality. That idea was created by the humans long ago who wrote about Fairies on your paper. The myth has continued ever since.

Allie, I know you see them, and all their beautiful colours. Don't ever lose that because you are very special, and you will write books one day yourself about your Fairy friends. Keep your heart open and keep that beautiful smile. They love you very much.

Be Blessed with the Light.

Kuntarkis.

WAS HITLER REALLY ASSASSINATED OR MURDERED?

Hi Kuntarkis,

I have asked my grand-daughter to send you my question as I am 87 and my hands are not what they used to be. I was born in Germany in 1913 and went through both world wars before coming to Australia in 1951 with my 2 daughters. My husband was killed in Germany because he worked with the underground against Germany. My question is, was Adolf Hitler shot in the head along with his wife, as they say in history books? I am asking you this because I read some of the works on your website. Thankyou.

Helen.

Kuntarkis replies:

Dear Helen, bless you, for you are indeed a very brave and beautiful human being. You have experienced much pain in the past and I can understand why you are asking your question.

First, the Germans were quite advanced in their science, which allowed Hitler to have a double, someone who looked just like him, especially since 9 attempts were made on his life, and one was nearly successful. That is why he had a double made of himself through plastic surgery 6 months before the Second World War ended. Hitler himself had surgery on his face to change his appearance. He already knew the war was lost and made plans for his escape which were already under way, as were the escapes of hundreds of Nazis, many move to America, especially some of the scientist.

What was interesting about Hitler was that everything was already arranged. His assassination along with his wife's was carried out. Even his wife did not know his double existed. Hitler allowed his double and his wife to be shot. His 2 children were adopted by a Nazi couple who were given entry into the United States. The children were well looked after, and have since grown up and had families of their own. Hitler escaped Germany with his mistress and lived out his days in a small town in Switzerland. They did not have any children as she could not bear them. The mistress died 26 years later from cancer, and Hitler died 17 years ago from bowel cancer. They were both cremated, no one in that town new of their past.

Please Helen, allow yourself to understand from your loving heart that everything in Creation is for a reason, and it is forgiveness that sets the soul free from all pain, sorrow and limitations. You Helen have a story to tell. Maybe you should allow your young grand-daughter to tell it for you. It would be a great healing for you and for the many others who would read your book of knowledge.

May you Helen be blessed in the Light always?

Kuntarkis.

SCARED OF GHOST

Hello Kuntarkis,

I have a problem with my fear of ghosts. Let me tell you my story. I am 28 years old and live in Yorkshire. 2 years ago my father died of a heart attack which they tell me was stress related. We did not have much of a relationship, as he was always away on business trips, and I grew up in a boarding school. You see, he was well off so he could afford it and also my Mother died when I was 11. My Stepmother didn't like me and always caused ill feeling between me and my Dad, which is why I was put into a boarding school in the first place. I hardly ever saw my father, so we were stranger to each other. The last 7 months I have been dreaming of him nearly every night and what's really freaky is on several occasions he has appeared to me in my home. Sometimes I would be in the kitchen making a meal, and would suddenly get this cold chill run right through me. I would look up and there he was smiling at me. I think he was trying to talk to me but nothing came out of his mouth, and his hands were stretched out as if he wanted to embrace me. Naturally I began screaming! I have told other people but they don't believe me. On 2 occasions I was looking in the mirror and he suddenly appeared with the same smile. I am scared because I don't know what to do. Can you help me understand what is happening to me? I am desperate.

Genevieve.

Kuntarkis replies:

Dear Genevieve, first, thank you for your courage in writing to my Being. I do understand how you must feel, especially since you have not been given the understanding of what has been presenting itself to you. First, be assured your Father is not wanting to hurt you or scare you. He has obtained the knowledge in spirit world, which some call the Astral Plane or the 4th dimension, to come to you because there is some unfinished business between you and him.

I say this from my heart, my soul - he is so sorry that he never spent the time with you over all those human years. Only now does he truly understand the pain he put upon you. You see Genevieve, he admits he did not know any better because of his own upbringing. As a child he was never given the love and attention he wanted so much. He also grew up alone, so he was conditioned to be like that. His greatest fear was rejection and unknowingly he did the same to you.

The reason he left you everything was to show you he truly loved you so much, and now he has come to you in spirit to ask for your forgiveness. And yes, he does want to embrace you. Please try and understand that nothing dies, only transforms into another form of energy. When he next comes to you, which I know he will, look into his eyes deeply and see his love for you. Find it in your heart to forgive him as it will be a healing for both of you. I have been asked to say that your father's first name is Edward and yes, you were and are always his little princess.

Be blessed in the Light dear Soul.

Kuntarkis.

HOW DO I TRUST THE MAN I LOVE?

Hi Kuntarkis,

I have been reading your website. Your information is mind boggling, and even though I am finding it hard to understand sometimes, I feel that it makes a lot of sense. You will probably find my question petty, but I need to ask you. I am 19 and madly in love with this man. He is 27 and every time he holds me I just crumble into his arms. When I look in the mirror at myself, sometimes I wonder why he is with me when he can have anyone he wants. Other women always play up to him. I have asked him about other women, if he has been with them, and he tells me no, that it's only business (he photographs models for magazines and he is in demand). Should I trust him or is it just me feeling insecure? How do I trust him? Please help me.

Fran.

Kuntarkis replies:

Dear Fran, allow me to express that trust is one of the most important parts of any relationship. From what you have said, you do not believe in yourself, nor do you trust your own feelings of truth. When you look into a mirror you should see that you are a beautiful, strong human being, and if you believe in yourself and that you deserve to have this man and his love in your life, then you truly do know the truth.

The most important thing you can do is trust yourself, love yourself be completely honest in all things, because then you will only have love in your heart. By believing in yourself you will be able to believe in others. It all starts with you, the individual. When love is present in your heart and your love is pure, you will bring into your life the same pure love. But if you have fear in your heart, then the only love that can come into your life is fear of love.

You deserve to have an honest, loving trusting relationship, so Fran, let your fears dissolve into the nothingness from which they first came, and believe in yourself as a beautiful human woman who deserves the best in life. Be still for a moment and ask yourself this question from the heart: can I trust the man in my life now? Listen to your first answer, for it always the truth and it is always from the heart. But only trust the first answer, for the rest that follow are from your fears, which are a part of human Ego, which is the falseness.

Be Blessed in the Truth and the Light Fran.

Kuntarkis.

CURIOUS FOR WHAT THE FUTURE HOLDS?

Dear Kuntarkis

Usually I am pretty patient when it comes to just about everything. But not with my future at the moment. I can feel something pulling at me, a new job, children, moving????... What is it? Whatever it is, it is taking me a long time for things to come to fruition. Do you have any ideas on what it might be? Could you please tell me what my immediate future holds? Something is telling me that whatever it is, is going to be big. Could it be pregnancy, career move, studying for career move, moving????? All of the above??

Thankyou for your guidance.

Stephanie.

Kuntarkis replies:

Dear Stephanie, It does sound like you are anxious to discover what your human life holds for the future. What is more important Stephanie is what is going on in your human life in this moment. Everything that you are in this moment of life comes from your past and all your experiences from the past, and how you think in this moment of life will create your future. Don't wait to look for it to come to you. You see Stephanie, you are the creator of your present and your future. What you are thinking today will become your tomorrow.

That is how all of life is, throughout all Universes - what you think you most certainly will become, be it negative or positive thoughts. All thoughts are your creation in your present moment, and they will become your future. Even in my vibration on Nar'Kariss we create through thoughts and manifest all that we require. Humanity creates by physical means, but in reality it is the same in principal, just different vibrations of energy, or as some would say, different levels of consciousness.

Stephanie, you can create anything you choose in life, but first look at who you are now and by using your imagination, see what you truly need from your human life, and then create it by physical action. If you truly believe in yourself, and are willing to be fully responsible as a human being, then you will find that all you desire will manifest into your human life. Learn to trust and love yourself with unconditional love and opportunity's will come to you to create your future and what you most desire.

If you seek pregnancy or a career, or wish to increase your knowledge by studying towards a career move, then you are already beginning to create your future. Ask yourself "What does Stephanie truly want from her human life?" Listen to your inner self and the answer will be there for you. When you seek from within yourself, the truth will manifest, but when you seek from others, it is only their truth. Which would you prefer? You Stephanie are a beautiful human being - always come from the heart, for the heart is your truth, while the rest is only Human Ego.

Be Blessed in Love and Light.

Kuntarkis.

WHAT HAPPENED?

Hello,

I thought I'd take you up on the offer of a question answered. I hope it is not too frivolous, but, it does weigh on my mind. If you could give me any insights, I would appreciate it. I was dating a man named Sharif and we were getting along pretty well and we broke up in June. His idea. I never understood what happened and how he feels or felt about the whole thing. Any insights?

Thanks, Let.

Kuntarkis replies:

Dear Lett, It is always hard and confusing when a relationship between two human beings

comes to an end, especially when one believes all is well and suddenly the relationship is no more, and no explanation is given. You are left confused and wondering what did you do wrong.

First dear Lett, don't blame yourself or be hard on yourself. You are not to blame so don't feel guilty. You have a beautiful heart and a loving nature, and not too far in your human future a man will come into your life. This man you called Sharif will only be a memory of your past. All of human life is just lessons of experiences, so don't get caught up on the negative aspect of what happened. See it as a lesson of life, forgive him as he has his own lessons to learn, and move on, for the future of your life will be most joyous.

Human beings on this most precious Earth incarnate life after life to learn and experience many facets of Human life, to gain knowledge and wisdom, and most of all to learn to be neither negative nor positive about life. The greatest lesson for all of humanity is to experience unconditional love from one's own being to another, and for all of life. Always see yourself as a special human being who has a lot to offer, and truly believe in yourself.

Be Blessed in Love and Light.

Kuntarkis.

AT CROSSROADS IN MY LIFE

Dear Kuntarkis,

I am at a crossroad in my life at the moment and unsure what to do next. I thought several months ago that I had found what I wanted to do with my working life but my passion has slowly diminished and now I feel as though I couldn't be bothered. I cannot understand why I can get so passionate and so much enjoyment out of something for a brief period and then one day I wake up and it's gone. I am at a loss.

Jennie

Kuntarkis replies:

Dear Jennie, First, allow my being to express that you are a kind and beautiful human being who truly comes from the heart. You must not be so hard on yourself. Please believe in yourself, that you do have the strength and the sight to see what you want from your human life.

But first thing, your passion for new adventures is your sight. See what you want and then create it from your strength, and yes, my being sees how you lose interest and then the inevitable comes, and it is lost in the maze of confusion you have within you.

Jennie, all of human life on this most precious planet has some amount of negative emotion that each human being must deal with before the real can come into the present moment. To take the negative emotion throughout human life prevents one from going beyond who they are and growing consciously in one's own awareness.

In this life your lesson is to forgive the past, for whatever reason that may be. Look back in your mind and still your brain. Look with your heart and the truth of what is holding you back will be revealed to you. By forgiving, you will allow the healing process to begin to dissolve your past negative emotions, and in turn this will allow you, dear Jennie, to love who you are unconditionally with no rules or past negative emotions. Your passion for life and what you choose to do with your life will come into your reality, and as you awaken each of your mornings, you will feel alive and energised about yourself and where your life is taking you, throughout all of your human life.

You Jennie will see with new eyes, and the colours of life that surround you will be brighter. You are a creative being - don't allow you're negative past emotions to be your ruler in your present moment, as they will become your future as well. You dear human being deserve much more than that. Believe and see and you will create. Use your most powerful gift - your imagination.

Be Blessed dear Jennie and May the Light of Creation's totality always be within and around you.

Kuntarkis.

PARKINSON'S DISEASE

Dear Kuntarkis,

I have a question about Parkinson's disease. Being 39 years of age I am concerned about ending up like my father. He is 67 and suffers badly with Parkinson's. It is hard for me to write to someone like you. It's not a part of my beliefs, as I am a great believer in God. But it seems there is nothing that can be done with my father. My wife encouraged me to write to you. Will I end up like my father? Yes or no? I am scared for myself and for my children.

Noel.

Kuntarkis replies:

Dear Noel, It is quite understandable that you are concerned about your human father, and yourself and your beautiful children. What I am about to express will take a lot of soul searching. I am sure you will agree that truth is most important. You Noel will always find truth within your very being. All you have to do is step beyond your human beliefs and conditioning.

All of human existence is passed on from one generation to another, and so on. Let us for a moment look at the example of a rose bush. If the rose bush is unable to obtain the necessary nutrients from the soil, it will be unable to grow strong from its encoded genetics. It would never truly be a healthy plant and many parasites would prey upon it, knowing it is weak and vulnerable. If other plants were propagated from the sick rose bush, in most cases genetic breakdown would occur over several generations of propagation, and the subsequent plants would be even less healthy than the parent bush. This is a simple example Noel, but it illustrates the importance of feeding your human body correctly and adequately, whether you are a rose bush or a human being.

Now let us look at a healthy adult male and female human being about 18 years of age. Place them on a diet of junk food, sugary soft drinks, alcohol and tobacco (including marijuana), or harder drugs, for about 8 of your Earthly years, and then have them mate to create offspring. Once the female is pregnant they continue their poor lifestyle and diet, which in reality is a very common and accepted way of life on your Earth. Their human bodies have been slowly breaking down. The cause is diet and lifestyle habits - the drugs of various types (both legal and illegal), refined sugars and salts, artificial food additives such as colourings, preservatives and flavours, toxic chemicals, and a lack of pure water. There are many more hidden by products in human food that many of your people would be horrified were they to discover the truth. It is all kept very quiet Noel, and you need to stop and ask yourself "Why?"

Your human bodies are your temples, and should be respected as such. When the human body is misused and abused it will naturally begin genetic breakdown. As human beings, you need to feed your bodies with healthy, fresh vegetables and fruits, and drink plenty of clean water to filter and flush out toxins through your waste and your sweat. All of human dis'ease is created in a two-step process. **Step one:** Negative Emotions which create Stress and Illness. **Step Two:** What you feed your Human Body. This is called **Cause** and **Effect.**

Parkinson's dis'ease is a name for when the human brain begins to die, which eventually shows by its effects on the rest of the human body. The bigger picture is genetic breakdown which is then passed on slowly through the generations of children that follow. Unhealthy parents create unhealthy children, and unless those children become aware of the importance of improving their health, then their children will be slightly unhealthier, and so on, genetic break down continues from generation to generation.

Look around you Noel, your family, your friends, your country, your world. Never in human history has there been so much dis'ease on your Earth as there is today. Look at the children on your Earth who are being born more frequently with rare or terminal dis'ease than ever before. Stop and ask yourself "Why?" The answer is simple, but your scientists are unable to see it, or more to the point they may not want to see it.

Noel, Parkinson's Dis'ease is the dying of certain brain cells, caused by the body not being fed the correct foods to produce the required chemicals to repair the dead cells and to maintain healthy function. Look at your diet Noel. Eat plenty of fresh vegetables and fruits, nuts and soya (such as tofu), drink at least two litres of clean water each day, and most importantly, give up your alcohol and tobacco, as these are the two main destroyers of brain cells. Learn to love yourself as you would your wife and children, and be sure to give them the same good foods so that they may grow healthy and strong, and that they may be aware of the real necessities of life so that their children will be healthy and strong, and so on.

Be Blessed Noel in Love for all. Walk in Light.

Kuntarkis.

SEARCHING FOR ATLANTIS: WHERE IS IT?

Hi Kuntarkis,

I am very interested in the Atlanteans civilisation. I have read many books on the subject and found them all uplifting, but I have also found some of them conflicting in their information. Can you please tell me if Atlantis really did exist and where it existed? Are we all descendants of the Atlanteans? If you could shed some light on the subject, I would be most grateful. Thank you.

Paul.

Kuntarkis replies:

Dear Paul, The answer to your question is yes, Atlantis was real. Highly evolved beings came to your Earth to bring balance, wisdom and technology to help humanity grow in consciousness. They respected all of life throughout all of the Universes. They came from a planet called <u>Nar'Kariss</u> **which is 417,000 light years from your Planet Earth.**

Paul, as you become more aware of the knowledge that exists within you, take what feels right for you to help your truth unfold. And yes, you lived as a human being in the time of Atlantis. Atlantis existed in the middle of what you now call the Bermuda Triangle. Even to this moment there is an energy imbalance in that area, which is why your human ships and aircraft have been disappearing in that region over the last 35,000 years of your Earth time. This will continue to occur until the energy is brought back into balance. Your Earth will then be aligned in harmony with nature. Paul, Roman present a number of seminars, one of which is about <u>Atlantis, Aliens and the Bermuda Triangle</u>. You may be interested to read their information about it on this website. Also in this book you will find information on Atlantis and the Bermuda Tringle.

Be Blessed in Love and Light throughout your existences always.

Kuntarkis.

UNSEEN FORCES

Dear Kuntarkis,

My name is Shari. I'm 29 and have been a student of Raja Yoga meditation for over 8 years. I have always found it to be very enjoyable. I like to feel in control of my life and I am always interested in anything esoteric or alternative to mainstream belief. I have read many books on self-healing, reincarnation, karma, and aliens, and I must say that since I have been reading the information on this website, I feel I have expanded my understanding even further, especially about other worlds, and more to the point, the unseen forces that you speak about. I truly believe they exist and can see how they are able to control weak minds.

This is a concern to me. I feel I need to grow stronger in my own awareness, and I believe our world is so confused about everything, that people have become weak in their minds and their bodies. It is true, isn't it, that when we become weak, the unseen forces can control and manipulate us into doing things we normally wouldn't do? My question is, can these unseen forces control beings like yourself Kuntarkis, or is it just us poor emotionally retarded humans who fall prey to them? Also, is meditation a guaranteed way of blocking them from controlling our thoughts? What do you think?

Shari.

Kuntarkis replies:

Dear Shari, It is always an honour for my being to hear from such a human being as yourself. It shows you are very open minded and that you are indeed an individual. You care about yourself and others, and this shows you are a conscious being who is evolving beyond your human beliefs and conditioning. Your thirst for knowledge is in itself an expansion of your inner essence wanting to know the truth, and you do know it is the truth that separates one who lives in human Ego from one who live in consciousness. Dear Shari, always seek your answers and truth from within your being, and know in your heart that knowledge is freedom, whereas the human Ego will always be your prison.

You Shari are a strong minded human being and you listen to your heart. Do not concern yourself, for you will not fall prey to the unseen forces. We the Nar'Karones exist beyond their energy vibration, for they could not exist in our vibration of Light - they would dissolve into the nothingness and return to the Light. I can assure you Shari, this is not what they want. They enjoy their games and their ability to control other worlds. That is why it is so important for human beings to grow beyond their human Ego and become conscious of their surrounding worlds. If human beings became consciously aware, they would indeed see the truth about the unseen forces and their power over humanity.

Shari, you ask about meditation being a guaranteed way of blocking these unseen forces. Yes, meditation is useful for this, but only if the person is true to themselves, and is beyond human Ego. A human being who has fears and insecurities will still be influenced by the unseen forces, regardless of whether or not they meditate. You see, fears and insecurities are present wherever negative emotions exist, for they are like a beacon, and the unseen forces home in on the negative energy.

A human being must deal with their negative emotions and become fully responsible for every action they take in their life. They must learn to love themselves unconditionally, and to still their mind in meditation to allow the process of connecting with their inner divine Light. It is through this process of self-realisation that you Shari will find the key to open yourself to the wonderment that is your Spirit. Then all the truth of knowledge will be seen before your eyes.

Walk in the Light Shari for the Light is within you and protects you. Be Blessed dear Shari in Love and Light always.

Kuntarkis.

BEST WISHES FROM KYM

To Kuntarkis,

I've just read your channelled writings and I found them to be truly beautiful pieces of communication. I wanted to wish you well in your quest and ask that you be blessed in your future with channelled communication.

Kym.

Kuntarkis replies:

Dear Kym, My Being has been asked to thank you for your kind remarks concerning Roman and Ilona's website. It is good to see that human beings like yourself are progressing in your understanding and your awareness of life itself. We the Nar'Karones have a single purpose and that is to express knowledge which is infinite in all dimensions. We realise that all of life in all Universes have the right to be individuals and to grow in consciousness.

We make contact with those who are willing to listen. In opening their hearts to the unconditional love that exists in all forms of life, we can share wisdom and understanding so all may grow into balanced human beings who care for each other, because in reality, all human beings on this most precious Earth are indeed brothers and sisters. You are all of each other, it is only the human Ego of the past that holds humanity in conflict and confusion. Fear is your enemy. Love is your truth and the path to complete freedom.

Be Blessed dear Kym in your present incarnation and May Love follow you always.

Thank you.

Kuntarkis.

I FIND THIS HARD TO BELIEVE: COME ON?

To the one called Kuntarkis,

Ok, I will admit this. I am feeling a little silly even writing this... the concept of alien beings, other dimensions, spiritual energy, healing, those things all make sense to me and I do believe in them. But the idea that a being of light is being channelled through a human body and that this being can answer questions we may have... I must say it is hard to swallow but obviously intriguing or I wouldn't be writing this.

1- I am 26, male and just now getting into massage therapy.....included in this was a brief introduction to reiki healing. I was fascinated by it. Working with peoples bodies and healing them. I feel I am on to something right for me. My mother told me I have healing hands and for the longest time I have drowned out my spiritual side for the fear of having to be religious. I'm opening up to a new consciousness for myself now. One that tells me to do what I want to do and believe in it, to be kind to other people and do well for myself and others. Am I on the right track? Of course I know that my new state of mind is the right track, but what about massage? Will I do massage or possibly become a healer? I felt and saw things when I did reiki but the lessons were short lived. Please give me input.

2- I went through a long period of depression anxiety and terrible emotions. I thought I had found my soul mate and my fears and obsessiveness ruined it for me and ruined my life. I am finally "out of the woods" so to speak and relearning to be care free and to forgive myself in what happened to me? Why did I have to go through all that? Will my soul mate Sarah and I ever get together again and if so, can I do it without a mental break down, or is it not meant to be for us?

3- What are your thoughts on hell? Would god really make souls suffer eternally? Why would a teacher of love torture people and souls for not believing in others ideas of god and the church?

4- My grandmother has been ill. I feel I can hear her calling out to receive healing. I haven't been attuned yet. Will this happen and will I help her?

5- Are you really a being from another world or just a very enlightened human soul?

6- I have always felt different than others. I have always felt I was on another level than some. Is this true?

Please help. I'm young, sometimes lost and have so many new emotions and thoughts coming at me that I can't sort it all out. I really want to find my way through this awkward change in my life.

Thank you so much.

Guy.

Kuntarkis replies:

Dear Guy, My Being thanks you for taking the moments in your human life to express your thoughts. My Being understands your hesitation and concerns. My Being is simply here in your human vibration to express knowledge to those who wish to listen and advance their consciousness. All that my Being expresses has only one purpose, and that is to help humanity step beyond the negative human Ego that has been controlling all humans on this most precious Earth for so long.

You Guy have begun your own journey of Self-Discovery, and you are being led by your spirit guides. It is you who has chosen to listen to your inner self, that part of you which is your true essence of Light, which exists in all of life in all universes. Every human being is a healer, but not many become aware of this fact. Your Mother was telling you the truth that you have healing hands, but you must believe in yourself and your inner essence, that you, as all of life, are connected to every other being and form of life throughout all universes.

Massage of the human body is a natural healing method, and yes, if you decide, you will use massage as part of your healing methods.

Depression is a state of the human brain created from beliefs and conditioning of the past, based on experiences of negative emotions, and manifested physically. It is fear that creates situations in a human being, and yes it was your fear that helped destroy your relationship. But always remember Guy everything in life is simply a lesson for your own growth. You are the creator and the driver. What you experienced in that situation will make you a stronger human being.

The Earth you exist upon is a classroom for learning. That is why human beings live many incarnations in a physical vibration of matter - in order to understand themselves and all of life; to let go of the human Ego and to evolve beyond the physical realm; to gain a higher understanding of other vibrations, other forms of life, and other universes.

If you Guy are meant to be with the one called Sarah, then as you both grow in your own space and time, you both will attract each other into each other's vibrations again. It will be your choice as much as Sarah's choice. Love yourself unconditionally and send light of love from your heart to hers. Have no expectations.

You ask my Being about thoughts of Hell. Hell only exists in fear which has been created by man alone. Each human being creates their own hell on Earth from their own fears of negative emotions created over many lifetimes. The word 'Hell' was created to control and dominate the masses. Man alone created the concept of the God of your times, and yes, as you put it, a God of unconditional love would not allow or place judgement upon its children or cause suffering. As it is upon your Earth today, it is man alone who has caused all pain and suffering upon humanity, created from fear alone.

You asked about your ill Grandmother and if you can heal her. First you are a healer now. The Light of Creation is within and around you as it is in all of life. To believe is to create, and to believe is to heal. My Being will express a simple affirmation you can say so you may believe in yourself:

I am of my own Self-Divinity. It is Creation within and around that does the healing, as it is within the healer and the one being healed. I am Light, I am that I am, I am Divinity.

Send her love and light from your heart. See the light emanating from you to her and believe you are doing this. It is important also for your

Grandmother to accept the Light, for each are responsible for the healing process.

My name is Jecuss Kuntarkis. The name Jecuss was given to my Being in the human year 4BC. When my Being incarnated into a human body, the human parents I had at that time gave me the name of Jecuss, from Hebrew meaning 'bright star'. Kuntarkis has been my name for over a million of your Earthly years. In our vibration time has no meaning. I simply am who I am - one who travels to other realms and expresses knowledge to help the evolution of different species.

Yes, you Guy are different, yet the same as all of humanity. What you are feeling is different. All of humanity comes originally from a planet called Nar'Kariss. Most human beings are caught up in their own world of confused thoughts. Some awaken quicker than others. You are one of those looking for truth in your confusion. The truth is within you. It always has been and always will be there for you. When you feel ready, go within the silence of your mind. Be persistent and never give up the search for the truth. If you seek truth, truth will then seek you out and open your awareness and understanding to all things in life and its meanings. You must believe in yourself, and love and forgive yourself in unconditional love, for unconditional love is the key to freedom and will break the chains of the human Ego.

Now to your question regarding the 'Moth man' by John Keel. Only when a human being opens their heart will the truth manifest itself. There are thousands and thousands of universes and within those universes there are many different vibrations and dimensions. Within all of them there are many different forms of life, in all shapes and forms.

The physical form is one of the hardest to live and experience, because of pain, negative emotions, and human Ego which exists in all forms of physical flesh vibration. Physical matter vibrates at a much lower frequency than other forms that exist in higher vibrating energies. Life in other realms and dimensions have been visiting your third vibration for many of your Earthly years. That is why throughout your human history there have been strange stories and sightings of different creatures, 'flying saucers' and other phenomena. The ones you call the "Moth man" can exist in a physical vibration as well as higher vibrations. They do not come to harm, but to help and to warn humanity of what is to come in your human future. It is the human Ego that creates the fear, confusion and misunderstanding of these beings.

The "Pessuties", which they are known as to other civilisations, did not realise the fear that humanity has and misjudged their timing in contacting human life. The "Pessuties" have left this vibration but will return again in your future around 2047 to try making contact again.

You may find previous articles on this website of interest, particularly August 2001 "The Unseen Forces: Who actually controls humanity" and October 2001 "The Unseen Forces and their role in the attack on America".

Be Blessed in the Light of Creation and May Love and Light fill your being. Believe in yourself Guy.

Kuntarkis.

Reply from Guy...

Thank you so much. If you and your being are ever in the San Francisco bay area, I would love the opportunity to sit and talk. Your answers feel true to me, even though I think I knew these things deep inside myself. It brought tears to my eyes to know I have made contact.

Thank you.

Guy.

CAN CAT'S REALLY HEAL?

Greetings Kuntarkis,

I have a question about cats, and their purpose. I know about cats' healing power delivered through vibrational frequencies known as purring, but is there a special lost secret about cats, their healing and spiritual abilities and their "purpose"? (IE: Why were they domesticated, and who discovered that they could be?)

This question also ties in with the lost knowledge of an "unspoken" or non-verbal communication practiced by the ancient peoples. At the moment, the "Kogi Tribe" and a lost Maya tribe in South America are the only two living tribes that still speak this language. They also consider the rest of us "dead" due to having lost this awareness outside the Self.

Can you tell me anything about those who passed on their knowledge of vibration/sound/frequency and the Golden Ratio (1:1.618) to the Egyptians? Is there a relationship between the Non-Verbal Kogi Heart language and the purring of cats? And is there a way that I can learn this language once again, and help to re-teach it to others?

Kuntarkis, the Spiritual Giant within me is ready to burst forth and flood this world with Love for each being. Until a teacher vibrates to me in this realm, I only have you and your wisdom for the answers I seek.

Peace and Good Fortune to you, Roman & Kuntarkis.

Tovy.

Kuntarkis replies:

Dear Tovy, Thank you for writing to my Being again. First your question on the human pet called cats. Every species that exists on your planet Earth has a natural healing ability, mainly because everything is created from living magnetic energies that are present in all of life. There is no special lost secret concerning cats. Cats were all created from the larger species - Tigers, Lions, Pumas, Jaguars, and so on. The Egyptians caged many species and mated them over and over again until they created the perfect pet for the Emperors and Queens. It was a Queen nearly 5,000 of your Earthly years ago who suggested to her Emperor that they should use the cat as a created God on Earth. All other cats were classed as inferior and the people were allowed to have them, which is why they became so popular.

Man today has created many more different species of cat. Tovy, everything in all universes evolves in their own space and time. Take your planet Earth. When each species evolves beyond the present understanding and are willing to let go of the old, the level of consciousness will expand to higher forms of awareness, and all animals that consume the flesh of another to exist, will no longer be present on your planet Earth. All will eat of the plants. There are no carnivores beyond the third dimension of physical matter. The awareness of self and living consciousness is the path to all infinite knowledge that exists from the past to the present and to the future.

There is a language within all human beings, known to you as Sanskrit. It is the language of the Nar'Karones, and it is a universal language. Yes, you can bring forth the knowledge if you choose to in the silences of your mind.

Be Blessed in Love and Light always. Believe in who you are.

Kuntarkis.

IS IT TRUE LOVE?

Dear Sir,

I have met on the internet 1½ years ago a Russian girl and we have since written to each other almost every day. I was recently in Russia to visit her for the first time and all the feelings I had about her from our correspondence were the same in reality. She is an intelligent, sensitive and sweet girl and despite the fact that she has very little money, I was not allowed to pay for almost anything while I was there (3½ weeks). The problem is that I am not in any way rich and cannot afford to support her in Europe (where I live) and I am also unsure if she would want to come as she has a ten year old daughter from her marriage. I love and miss her very much and I know that she feels the same. Her Chinese astrological sign is a red horse, and we have used that as a nickname for a long time. While I was in Moscow, where I stopped for two days en route I stayed in a hotel. I was beginning to doubt the sanity of travelling half way across the world to meet someone I had only exchanged e-mails and photos with and decided in my mind, that if the trip turned out to be a failure I would forget all about looking for spiritual love. In the hotel there were paintings outside each room. I decided to take a photo of some I had noticed and liked on the way into my room. I did this and then for the first time looked at the picture outside my room... it was a picture of a red horse. Although I have heard of synchronicity I am very sceptical and the experience both reassured and frightened me at the same time.

My question to you is, are we destined to be together and if so how can I make it possible? If possible I would like it if you can give me some detail that shows your answer is genuine. I have a naturally sceptical mind, but I love this girl and I am desperate!

Mike.

Kuntarkis replies:

Dear Mike, My Being has been told that many human beings have been seeking human relationships on or through the internet. It seems many have been successful and many have failed. Yet it is no different to meeting someone at a party or while doing your shopping. On your Planet Earth there is a human partner for every human being, and these partnerships do come into union by attraction of energies. Depending on the level of understanding and awareness, each human being attracts the same energy into their life. All human life has one purpose - to grow in consciousness by letting go of past beliefs and negative emotions.

Every human being is the Creator of their own existence and experiences. You can create into your human life any circumstance you choose. The human female you speak of can come completely into your vibration if you truly wish it to be so. If you Mike are true of heart and the human female is also true of heart, and your love for each other is unconditional, then all will come into balance. One of the great gifts for all of life is thoughts. Thoughts are living energies and if the power of thought is projected into physical actions, then those thoughts will be most certainly created.

To seek for Spiritual Love is to seek from your heart. That is where all unconditional love is created. When a human being can truly unconditionally love themselves as an infinite being of light, then that being will attract into their human life a being of similar nature and energies, and when this happens, life will be bliss. Believe in yourself and believe from your heart, not your human brain of confusion.

Be Blessed in Love always and trust all your decisions.

Kuntarkis.

IS MY HUSBAND CHEATING ON ME?

Hello Kuntarkis,

My husband and I were having serious problems (arguments) since this spring, mostly about finances (we work together which exacerbates things). We have been married 8 years, and have two small children, aged 5 & 3, and the 3 year old has serious developmental disabilities, leading to lots of additional stress, strain, expenses. In June, he was abroad for two weeks promoting a project we had worked on, then almost immediately had to go to Chicago for one week, for a showing of our project.

Upon returning from Phoenix, my husband started acting as he had never before in 8 years of marriage - a constant, cold hate, almost, as opposed to being angry in an arguing way. I was hurt, and also confused, most of all, because it was relentless and had no seeming cause.

In late July, as I am preparing laundry and getting ready to spray it with prewash, I find a folded up piece of paper (folded over and over into a smallish square). It was an email, sent to my husband, on a Hotmail account that certainly I had never known of (I subsequently learned that the opened Hotmail account two days after returning from Chicago, 6/27. It was from a woman named Ellen, and it said "Dear George, Sorry we keep missing each other. So it's o.k. for me to email here? I have a friend here until later this morning. She lives in the suburbs and spent the night...so I'm fixing breakfast and clearly not working very hard. I have a ton of work to do too, but hope to have more time later this afternoon to write or chat. Hope all is well...thanks for the beautiful email. EZ"

So, I ask my hubby what this is all about. Actually, I asked him who Ellen is. First, he went into a monologue about how I never do the laundry, then he storms out of the house. Subsequent to that, his story is that he was hoping to become a new client of this woman's and to obtain a book advance. Obviously, his story is that this was a platonic friend, and that I am crazy.

Please, I need feedback. I just don't know what to think! What do you all think about the content of her email? I NEED INSIGHT!! I have such a feeling in the pit of my stomach, and I'm being eaten up by suspicion and mistrust. This hurts me badly, Irrespective of what happened between the two of them, I feel betrayed, in the deepest sense: the lack of honesty, and what that means for our marriage. That he can look me in the face and lie. But at the same time, I am ripped apart by doubt - whether the final version I got from him is basically it, or whether the two of them were lovers. Whether I can trust my husband or not - that is fundamental. My instinct goes back and forth.

Shannon.

Kuntarkis replies:

Dear Shannon, My Being thanks you for taking the precious moments in your human life to express your concerns about your human husband. My Being can give your insight into your problem, but you must understand my purpose for being here in this human vibration – it is certainly not to place judgement on another.

It is true to say your human husband, to use your own words, "is and has been acting a little strange". Stress created about your finances can cause a lot of confusion on both sides. Even though a human being makes a commitment to another such as marriage, can and does end in a negative emotional situation. In your present world, 68% of relationships have negative emotional creations and most of those involve some sort of an affair in deceit. It seems human beings get bored very easily and seem to think 'the grass is greener on the other side of the fence'. Yet the truth of it is that it does not take long for the grass to go brown.

It is all to do with the human Ego, created from negative experiences from one's human life. You Shannon already know the truth. It always comes from your heart. A suggestion – confront your husband. Ask him if he has been having an affair. When you ask him, look into his eyes and observe his reaction to your question. When you listen from your heart you will know the answer. Then it is your choice how you as an individual will handle this situation. But remember, getting angry will not solve the problem, it will only enhance it.

Be Blessed in Love throughout your human life and know that all experiences in your human life are simply lessons of learning and understanding and forgiving.

Kuntarkis.

WANT TO KNOW ABOUT PAST LIVES?

Hello Kuntarkis,

I wanted to know if there is anything intuitive you could tell me about my past lives. I have always felt that there was something more to all of this, my life, this world everything. But I also am now feel a very strong connection to my past. I am wondering what I may have or have done that makes me feel the way I do now, kind of unsettled, unfinished.

I also was wondering if you know of my sister. Her name was Rhonda and she has to be one of the most beautiful souls I have ever known. She was very sick on this Earth and I always found it ironic that a soul so good could have a body so sick. Is there anything more you can tell me? I really don't want to be pushy Kuntarkis. I know you have limited time and can only answer so many questions, but my sister is a part of my life I don't think I have managed to close. We were so close spiritually and emotionally, I just want to know if she is okay and if she would have any messages for me.

Thank you Kuntarkis. I have questioned in my head the truth behind all of this but now I am believing that somehow by contacting you that we are all part of something that most people won't even open their minds to. I wish they would. Thanks again.

Also, I am curious as to how you are channelled. Are you always present with Roman or does he have to meditate to find you?

Guy.

Kuntarkis replies:

Dear Guy, It is good to see you are allowing your own Being to step beyond and seek answers that would normally be never asked. One of the biggest barriers to personal growth is beliefs and conditioning. Fear prevents the individual from seeking the truth. The Light is present within all human beings, as it is within all of life.

To your curiosity on how the human Roman channels my Being. First, he calls my name in his thoughts and my Being is then present. My Being can be light years away from your planet Earth, but since time has no barriers in non-physical form vibrations, it would be less than a micro of a second in human time. My Being does also step down through vibrations and steps into his human form. He steps out and can choose to observe or go on his own journey of learning. I can use his form, his human body as naturally as Roman would, so in reality we are two beings using one human vessel.

To your question on your past lives. Guy, it would take thousands of pieces of paper to explain all your past incarnations. Every life and every experience you have had is recorded in your Cellular Essence, and you can bring this forth if you choose to. It will take time, and it would be of benefit to you. But it must also be said, even though the past can help you understand yourself, it is the moment that will teach you all about yourself. One thing my Being must express to you Guy, you have been a human man of the cloth many, many times (a priest). You have always believed in the truth, even in this lifetime of yours.

To your human sister you call Rhonda, her vibration of energies does not exist within the Astral World of departed spirits. It then must be said her spirit has let go of her pain and has passed through the gateway of Light to be reborn in a human body. My Being feels you had and still do have a deep love for your human sister, even though there were negative emotions. Yet that is part of learning and understanding. Always let go of the past and forgive the past - forgiveness is the first step towards healing and wisdom.

One thing must be said and understood. Every human being is an individual and the individual choses all their lessons in life. Even though it may seem unfair, there is always a reason, in all that concern the individual, it is free will, and it is not a law for law does not exist in Creation. It is simply the balance of life.

Guy, you have opened the door to something wonderful. Keep seeking the truth from within and all answers will be there for you. The power is in you as in all of life. Be Blessed in Love and Light and trust yourself and all your decisions. It all comes from within.

Kuntarkis.

WHAT DOES 'JECUSS' MEAN?

To Jecuss Kuntarkis,

Forgive me if I am being a little personal towards you, but I was wondering about your first name. Jecuss, is that Hebrew? Would you mind explaining it to me because I am curious?

Ella.

Kuntarkis replies:

Dear Ella, My Being has been asked about my name Jecuss before, which I have been told by Roman was explained on an old issue on the website but has since been removed.

The name Jecuss means Bright Star and was given to my Being in your human year 4BC. My Being chose to incarnate into a human vessel to not only experience human life but also to express teachings of knowledge to humanity. My human parents were very special to my Being and they gave me the love, understanding and courage to face human life and what was to be.

So, from that incarnation I have kept the name Jecuss close to my inner Being, if you dear Ella wish further information on your question, please feel free to ask my Being.

Be blessed in the love of Creation always, and May the Light shine through you always. Believe in yourself.

Kuntarkis.

WILL TERRORISM EVER END?

Dear Kuntarkis,

Will the terror of terrorism ever come to an end, or are we as a civilisation to suffer with it for eternity. I am scared and fearful for my family and my friends.

Katrina.

Kuntarkis replies:

Dear Katrina, Fear for yourself, your family and friends, your nation and your world is a concern that is affecting every human being on your Earth. Terrorism has been a part of humanity for a long time in human terms. What has happened is sad and unjust to the innocent, mainly because it is the public who are being affected by terrorism.

We the Nar'Karones had similar situations on our home planet of Nar'Kariss a very long time ago when we were still in flesh body form. What we began to realise was that we were losing the battle for change. Too many innocent Nar'Karones were losing their lives to the ones who did not want the changes. They wanted the Wars, Violence and lusted after the power of Greed and Domination to control what they believed was the weak. A decision was made and War was declared on all those who opposed the changes for higher learning.

The Nar'Karones were opposed to any sort of violence, yet we could not allow the innocent to be slaughtered, and especially we could not allow the suffering of our children. We brought every Nar'Karone into the service for all Nar'Karones. Anyone caught from the opposing side for causing violence was imprisoned and held without any further notice. There were no trials that went on and on like on your Earth. The guilty paid the price for their violence. They were given the opportunity to change, but many would not.

You see Katrina, it is in the thinking created by negative emotions that results in violence and imbalance. Some just love to cause pain to others and bring violence. It justifies their existence and beliefs, and in most cases these people will never change. They are driven by fear, anger and hatred.

In every civilisation, every individual must make the decision for change, whatever it may be. Each must strive for the same purpose, the balance of mind, body and spirit to bring peace and harmony to all who seek it. The bad seed must be removed or change can never be. It is like cancer eating away other cells. Eventually there is nothing left.

It will take many of your Earth years to completely dissolve terrorism in your societies. But the responsibility is not only with your governments, it is also with you the individual. Become more aware of your surroundings and become a part of dissolving the terrorism.

Be blessed in love always.

Kuntarkis.

WILL MY RELATIONSHIP WORK OUT?

Hello Kuntarkis,

I have been reading some of your writings on relationships, negative emotions and changing for the better. My question is: I am in a relationship with a man who only sees black and white. He doesn't believe in anything if it is not physical or material, yet he thinks I am weird and strange because I believe in fairies and spirits, even aliens. Will my relationship ever find some sort of balance or am I wasting my time? Could you please give me any guidance on my problem?

Simone.

Kuntarkis replies:

Dear Simone, when one partner decides to grow in another direction that is their choice, and yes, it is of benefit to learn and advance your understanding and consciousness to a higher level of awareness so you may grow together. But if the other chooses not to grow in that way, it is their free will. It is important Simone for any human being to want to grow consciously and in their awareness. The more you grow the more you will begin to let go of the old things in your human life, whatever they may be.

Each human being attracts a similar energy to themselves, meaning attracting a similar thinking partner or friends, for certain lessons. If one outgrows the old, then in most cases there will be a separation of those energies. It is a natural occurrence in all of life.

It is alright to have different views on life and other topics. The Nar'Karones believe and know that unconditional love for another being is far more important. If you Simone love your partner in the purest form of unconditional love, then all else is unimportant. The highest form of awareness and conscious growth is unconditional love, is it not Simone? Give this some thought and see how you feel.

Be Blessed in Love and Light always.

Kuntarkis.

ANYONE CAN BE A HEALER

Dear Kuntarkis,

Is healing for everyone, or only the chosen few? Can anyone do healing on themselves as well as anybody else? Could you give some explanation, as I am concerned by what others have told me?

Heather.

Kuntarkis replies:

Dear Heather, Yes, healing energies are for everyone. All life forms on your Earth, be it human, animal, mineral or plant, can use healing energies which are infinite.

To learn to heal is simple for any human being. Believing in the healing energy is the first step. To gain a little knowledge of how to heal others and yourself is the second step. We the Nar'Karones always taught our young children the healing method of our society. It became a part of our existence. Healing energies are all around you, your planet and your universe.

My Being will express a simply step to take and practice if you would like to try. **First**: Believe in yourself no matter what others say to you. You Heather are an infinite being of light in human form. **Second**: Find a quiet place like a room where you will not be disturbed by anyone physical. **Third**: Sit quietly in your own space or lay down. What is most important is to be comfortable with yourself.

Take several deep breaths in and out slowly. Feel the air filling your lungs and moving throughout your inner body. Relax, and as you breathe, put your awareness on your heart centre. Feel like there is a white light of energy emanating from your heart centre. Believe it is increasing in size and becoming a ball of white light.

As you see the ball of white light, see the light emanating throughout your inner body – your lungs, stomach, blood, liver, kidneys, in every part of your inner body, moving through your veins, and then out through the pores of your skin, so it is all around you outside of your physical body.

As you Heather become more comfortable with your practice of healing yourself, you can begin to send healing light to whoever you wish. Believing in yourself is the first step to healing.

Be blessed in the healing light of Creation always.

Kuntarkis.

DRINKING URINE FOR HEALTH REASONS: NEGATIVE OR POSITIVE?

For Kuntarkis,

You might find this question a little unusual. I would appreciate your input. There is a practice by some people who first thing in the morning drink their own urine. I have read about it and have been told it is very good to do for the mineral contents. I believe in looking after myself. Is there any truth or benefit in doing this, and is it safe? Many thanks.

Stefan.

Kuntarkis replies:

Dear Stefan, My Being thanks you for having the courage to ask your unusual question. To understand how your human vessel operates and its functions is very important in maintaining your health as a human being.

Considering the amount of pollutants that are in your airways and all the harmful chemicals used in your foods today, your liver and kidneys are always working overtime. 78% of human beings do not drink enough pure water to flush out the harmful toxins that accumulate within the human body, and many toxins are stored in fat cells and muscle tissue.

When a human being lays down to sleep many functions closedown while others are put into action to clean out the harmful toxins. These toxins are then eliminated through the urine, making it dark yellow and cloudy. To drink this urine would most certainly not be good for your health, and by doing so you would be placing the concentrated toxins, your human body had worked so hard to remove, back into your stomach and therefore to run back into your organs. This is not a wise idea, but it is your choice.

In reality Stefan you would be wiser to drink more pure or filtered water and the benefits you will gain will be far greater for your health.

Be Blessed in Love and Light always.

Kuntarkis.

DESPERATE TO SEE SPIRIT

Dear Kuntarkis,

I have spent nearly 30 years trying to see spirit and even aliens. No matter how hard I try it has been fruitless. I have been to many circles for discussions and meditation and they all promise I will see if I allow it. Nothing has happened. I am a believer. How can I see them? Can you help me in any way?

Desperate to see.

Kuntarkis replies:

Dear Human Being, wanting to see so desperately can also be a negative. It is like human couples wanting desperately to have a human child and when they finally give up and let go the struggle, they conceive and are blessed with the human child they have been desiring for so long.

To believe, to truly believe, can be a far greater power in itself. My Being feels your frustration, yet expectation can be a test, a great learning for any human being.

You see my friend, some human beings can see spirit, some can smell spirit, some can sense spirit, and you my friend can sense spirit. They are there all around you like they are around all human beings. They are always trying and are willing to communicate with those who can allow themselves to stop the human chatter of the human brain long enough to pick up their frequency.

Spirit can see human beings most of the time because they vibrate at a much higher frequency than human beings. Just listen in the stillness of your being. Try this and keep trying – never give up. My Being cannot tell you when you will see spirit, but you can in the quiet stillness of your being, in your own space and energies where there are no confusing energies of fear from others.

My Being will come to your Being when your mind is still and when there is no chatter from your human brain. If you wish you will know if my Being is before you.

Be Blessed dear human Being in Love always.

Kuntarkis.

ENERGY BLOCKAGES

To Kuntarkis,

I am so thankful for this opportunity to receive such high knowledge. I would like to thank you for offering this unique service and is there some way of returning the energy?

I have been on the spiritual path for my entire life and it has been a process of intense learning and discovery. I am at a stagnant point now. I know my spirit is evolving more rapidly every day but I have some difficulty in separating my brain from my consciousness.

I would like any information you can provide regarding the specific blockage of energy in my solar plexus, the current relationship I am in (whether I am avoiding certain lessons) and the purpose of my life at this moment.

I understand this is a lot of information but I would like simply to ask, offer any reciprocity I can, and receive that which is meant for me. Thank you so much.

Blessed be,

Eve.

Kuntarkis replies:

Dear Eve, My Being thanks you for your kind words. It is true that you Eve have taken a path towards learning and understanding your spiritual essence in your current incarnation.

You say you are at a stagnant point in your human life. It is called 'time out'. You may need to segregate your energies and allow yourself some personal space for the things you enjoy doing. Please do not be so hard on yourself. Take on a new challenge. Look deep into yourself and ask yourself what would make you feel whole and complete. Listen in the stillness of your mind, for only there will you truly know yourself, only there will you separate your human brain of chatter from your mind of unfettered consciousness.

The blockage of energy in your solar plexus is a build-up of negative experiences from your past, from your childhood and into adulthood. Eve, there are negative experiences from your past that you are holding on to. Because of this you are creating your present and even your future. This is why you are feeling a little lost in your direction in life. This is also creating the unhappiness you are feeling in your current relationship.

Finding love in yourself is the greatest healer of all the pain human beings create from their negative experiences. Love is forgiveness without words, without expectations, without judgement. Unconditional love is the path to completion and to achieving balance of mind and body.

What you are avoiding Eve is the self. It is only your fear, and yet fear is simply another form of energy. It has no power over you, only the power you give it. All human beings have the power to control their destiny and create a bright, positive future. You Eve do have the courage and strength to overcome any obstacle in your human life. My Being believes in you. Now you need to believe in yourself, your dreams, and your human needs.

Trust yourself. Face your fears and love yourself unconditionally. You will find the courage and strength to know yourself and your path in life. You chose in this lifetime to heal yourself so you could help others to heal themselves.

Be blessed in unconditional love always.

Kuntarkis.

TRYING TO CONTACT FRIEND

Hello Kuntarkis,

I have been trying to contact a friend. He passed May 2, 2004. I was able to contact my mother who passed Dec.14, 2003. I have her voice on tape. She promised that she would come back and tell me that she was alright. I was very happy about this. But I am finding it very frustrating not to be able to contact my friend, Kurt. He was only 42 when he passed. He promised to be my psychic buddy. It is very disheartening to me. Can you advise me?

With Love and Light,

Rebecca.

Kuntarkis replies:

Dear Rebecca, My Being sends you love in the form of friendship, for your loss. To lose two who were close to you is a hard experience for any human being. Maybe you are trying a little too hard to contact your friend Kurt.

Even though he expressed to you that he will be your 'psychic buddy', please remember that every human individual has their own journey in life.

Being in the spirit world can have many effects on a spirit first entering that vibration. It all depends on how that individual lived their human life. In many situations they recreate exactly the same circumstances in spirit world as they had in their physical world prior to passing over. So if they passed over in fear, pain, or violence, or in a hospital for example, then often that is what is recreated.

The other reason you may not be able to contact Kurt could be because you are emotional about the situation. Your energies vibrate at a different frequency to the spirit world. Spirit world vibrates at a much higher frequency, so in order to contact spirits you must still the chatter of the human brain and calm the emotions to enable you to vibrate at the same level, and this can only be done through meditation in the stillness of the mind.

Meditate in your heart from your love centre. Drink plenty of water and eat more raw foods like fruit and vegetables to cleanse and balance your human body. This will make meditation and raising your energies much easier. Keep trying - you will achieve your goal.

Be blessed always in love.

Kuntarkis.

BLACK MAGIC AGAINST ME: Why?

Dear Kuntarkis,

I need your opinion on a problem I've been facing. I'm being affected by black magic against me for a long time. It finally reached a peak and put a halt to all positive activities in my life at the end of last year.

1. Is this due to Karma I owe?
2. When will my life get back to normal?

Your answers and guidance can help me get back to a normal life again. Thanks for taking the time to assist me.

Colin.

Kuntarkis replies:

Dear Colin, Always remember within the centre of your heart is your truth. Your most inner feelings, your love centre, it is the power source of all human beings. The human heart can be one of pure love in all its actions through an individual's life, or it can be so cold in its hate that it turns to stone where no love can be seen or felt. It all depends on the individual's way of life and their thinking.

If you, Colin, come from love, no black magic can ever be a threat to you or placed upon you. When you feel this negative energy of black magic being sent to you, stop in the moment of your human life, close your eyes and put your thoughts on a ball of pure white light. Feel or see this ball of white light coming from your heart centre and allow this light to expand throughout your inner being, expanding outwardly all around your physical body. Believe this is happening and it will be so.

As the white light is all around you, say these words from your heart:

I, Colin, believe in myself and I know I am an infinite being - endless, timeless, ageless, and eternal. I am living in the moment of life and I am always protected by the light of Creation. I send all negative energies back to the sender(s) as they are not mine. I do not accept them. From this moment on I will only draw positive energies into my human life and grow from these experiences. I truly love who I am and I send my love that is infinite, to all I come into contact with, for this action alone will enhance and enrich my life as a human being. This I say and this I will do.

Remember Colin, what you think about yourself you will become, so love yourself in unconditional love. Love is the gateway to self-realisation and freedom from self-created limitations always.

Be blessed in love and believe in yourself - then your energies will be positive and then others will believe in you.

Kuntarkis.

MY SPIRITUAL NAME: WHAT IS IT?

Hi Kuntarkis,

I am contacting you hoping you can help me. I am wondering what my spiritual name is and if my life will ever be my own? Looking forward to your reply.

Best wishes,

Bernice.

Kuntarkis replies:

Dear Bernice, The power of truth is always within you, but you Bernice have to believe that you are an individual, and that you have the right of free will to live your human life as you choose it to be.

Because human beings grow up in a family circle (with particularly strong influences from their human parents) many become highly conditioned in certain beliefs from both negative and positive experiences, which then influence and shape their human lives from their childhood into adulthood.

One of the main problems within human society is the expectations placed upon a human individual. These expectations can and do create many negative emotions for the individual. Fear is one of the most prevalent negative emotions that plagues human beings on your Planet Earth.

One thing you Bernice need to ask yourself - do you truly deserve to live your life as an individual, and do you have the right of free will to be your own person, to experience your life as you choose it to be?

If the answer is '**No**' then you will always live in the shadow of others. But if your answer is '**Yes**' then you need to make a conscious decision and be brave enough to begin your journey of discovering your own path in your human life, instead of walking a path chosen or dictated by others.

In the end, you Bernice can only truly change your human life. The power of this decision is yours alone. It is all in your thinking. Change your thinking and you will begin to change your life.

In answer to your question regarding your spiritual name, the name is 'Varsenna' and it means 'the sun's energy'. This name has been with you always throughout all your incarnations. In your meditations see the sun at the bottom of your spinal cord in the shape of a glowing ball. Draw your strength and courage from the sun - it will help you in all your human decisions. Always remember - to believe is to create.

Be blessed in love always.

Kuntarkis.

WHO IS ESCHER?

Hello my name is Callan.

I live in Queensland. I've been involved in metaphysics for many years. I astral project often. I also believe I have connected with my spirit guide but I have never completely channelled my guide. I had an impression of a name when meditating a long time ago. It was Escher. Does this mean anything to you? Do you know of any entity named Escher? Also I was wondering if you offer guided channelling workshops or if you teach people to channel. Please email back.

Regards,

Callan.

Kuntarkis replies:

Dear Callan, My Being thanks you for sharing your expression of words. Your question on the human name Escher does not have any known meaning that I have been able to discover. The main guide in your human life at the present moment is called As'charre, and she has chosen to be with you throughout your present incarnation.

As your main guide she can and will help you in your search for spiritual knowledge. The best way to connect with her energies is through your quiet time of meditation. As'charre is the one who touches the top of your human head which gives you the tingles you have been experiencing.

You do have a strong ability to achieve anything you want from your human life Callan. Remember, thoughts are very powerful so please be careful what you think and express for they will become reality. Go forward Callan and always believe in yourself. You are truly a spiritual teacher.

Be blessed in love always dear Callan.

Kuntarkis.

<u>GROWING CONSCIOUSLY</u>

Hello Kuntarkis,

I have a few questions for you. Please assist me in trying to consciously grow as much as possible while I am in this present incarnation?

How may I best practice freeing my spirit/astral self from my body, to learn and explore? I would much like to return to the beautiful, peaceful places where I have visited deceased friends and relatives in my past "travels", which I relayed to you last summer. The love, beauty and freedom of those planes are too overpowering a memory to let go of, and I would wish to return and develop as often as I could.

Why do I feel so attached to my son - I often feel that my purpose in life was almost solely to guide him. Sometimes I weep with joy simply thinking of him. Why was I taken "inside" the womb while sleeping and shown him as a developing foetus (whereupon I kissed his head and afterward eagerly awaited his birth)? Am I on the right track or neglecting something else due to my focus on him?

Are there any items regarding my previous incarnations that may assist me in understanding, or overcoming an obstacle, in my present incarnation? I would particularly like to lose weight and become healthier so as to be with my son on Earth as long as possible, or permitted. But I would also enjoy a greater conscious understanding of who, what, or where I've been before.

With peace & love.

DG.

Kuntarkis replies:

Dear DG, The purpose of the experiences you have had concerning astral travel and meeting deceased friends and relatives was to show you that there is no such thing as death. Only the human body passes away and decays back into the Earth from which it was created. To experience conscious astral travel and have full memory of these events, a human being must be willing to set aside some time for self-discipline and self-development.

Meditate on a regular basis (once or twice a day), and be willing to look at yourself by examining your emotions and the way you think and feel. Negative emotions such as anger, resentment, jealousy, hatred and judgement are only some examples of emotions that human beings carry with them throughout their human life. These negative emotions prevent conscious growth in many ways. Learning to live in the moment of life without stress or depression is also a very important factor.

Food is another very important factor in conscious development. Always remember, what you put into your human body you will become - foods which have a negative effect on the human body will cause you to be negative in attitude and emotion. Such foods hinder personal growth and physical well-being. Eat only natural unrefined foods grown from the Earth, not highly processed foods.

Thoughts are very powerful. What you think about yourself and others is very important because what you think you will become. Everything is energy and energy can be created into both negative and positive forms, so how an individual projects their thoughts is up them.

The attachment you feel towards your son is because you and your son are of the same energies. Yes, you are to help guide him in his life as a human being, so yes it is very important for you to have a happy balanced life for yourself so he has the opportunity of developing also a positive existence for his present and future. Many human mothers experience being inside the womb while sleeping, but do not remember it. This experience is to help create a strong bond with the human child to be.

One of your main obstacles to overcome is self-doubt and self-pity, but to also love yourself unconditionally - to love yourself as you are without any form of judgement and to believe in yourself. Eat good food and drink plenty of water, do some regular exercise, and most of all love who you are always.

Be blessed in love always dear DG.

Kuntarkis.

WHY AM I EXPERIENCING HEADACHES?

Dear Kuntarkis,

Firstly, thank you for accepting questions and being so generous with your time and energy.

I have recently begun journeying in my spirit world after a long hiatus. Simultaneously I have noticed an increase in headaches. Could my journeying be causing the headaches? If so, what might I do to avoid this?

Lisa.

Kuntarkis replies:

Dear Lisa, When a human being makes a conscious choice to undertake their personal journey of self-realisation, in discovering who and what they truly are, there is an expansion of conscious growth. Your level of thinking and your level of awareness changes. So it would be a natural occurrence for your physical human body to also go through changes.

What is most important for you as a conscious human being is to be fully aware of your emotions and your feelings so you can balance your human life accordingly. Your human headaches are a reaction to your energy levels changing. And yes, your journey is causing, or rather more to the point, adding to your headaches.

To help you in avoiding the pressure your journey is creating, be aware of what type of foods you are consuming. Your human body is going through some changes, especially on a physical level as well as an energy level. Your consciousness is expanding beyond what your human brain currently understands.

Drink at least two litres of filtered water per day, consume more natural foods, like nuts, fresh fruits, fresh vegetables, and eat more legumes, meaning all kinds of beans.

It may also be of great benefit for you Lisa to cleanse your body and your blood. A good health food shop will be able to advise you on what products to use.

Be blessed in unconditional love always.

Kuntarkis.

WILL MY BUSINESS BE SUCCESSFUL?

Dear Kuntarkis,

I would like to know if my new business (Counselling & Reiki and English tutoring to children up to grade 7) will become fruitful. It has been approximately 5 weeks since my partner and I began this new venture.

Kind regards

Maria.

Kuntarkis replies:

Dear Maria, Your question seeks hope and a prediction of the intangible. Hope as a human word is in reality a negative. Hope can only lead to hopelessness. However, my Being believes in you Maria, and my Being truly believes you and your partner will succeed in your new venture, and it will be fruitful.

My question to you Maria is this: Do you and your partner believe in yourselves? If your answer is yes, then it cannot fail, would you not agree?

Never look to the future – look to the moment and know in your heart that your new venture is completely successful. See it in your mind's eye and see it overflowing. Send out positive energy to everyone and believe and see them coming to you and your partner. See them wanting your services and even handing over the exchange of energies, meaning your human money.

Remember this, what you think you become. What you believe about yourself, be it negative or positive, is reflected back to you from others, so it is important to always come from your heart, be ethical and compassionate. Others will then feel and see this about you and they will come to you and your partner over and over again. They will trust you and that is very important in any kind of business or relationship, but especially where their personal well-being or their children are concerned.

Be blessed in unconditional love always Maria.

Kuntarkis.

CURIOUS ABOUT MY PAST LIVES

Hi Roman,

Have I been a scientist before? If I have could you give me any names that I would know? If not could you give me some idea of what I was working on in the past that might link with what I'm doing now? It's not urgent or terribly important that I know but it would be cool!

Thankyou very much!

Sita.

Kuntarkis replies:

Dear Sita, Yes, you were a human scientist in your human year of 1491 in the land of Scotland. Your name was Ivan McLaren and you worked on inventions that helped farmers. You were called by your people a dreamer - your thoughts always took you away from your human reality. You dreamed of creating something wonderful and you used to study birds. You believed that humans could also fly, but with a little help. Throughout your human life you spent all of your spare time trying to invent and build a flying machine that would allow a human being to fly like a bird.

Yes, you most certainly are a dreamer, even in this current incarnation of yours, and yes, you have a great imagination which can help you greatly in this present life. Never stop believing in yourself; never give up Sita. Always believe in your visions, for they can and will be manifested into your human reality, if that is what you truly wish. Be inspired by YOU.

Be blessed in unconditional love always.

Kuntarkis.

COULD WE BE TWIN SOULS?

Hi Kuntarkis,

My friend Bennie and I are supposed to be twin souls. Is it true that I may be feeling his pains and depression about us?

Thank you.

Carlene.

Kuntarkis replies:

Dear Carlene, to believe from your heart is to know the truth. If you truly believe that Bennie is your Soul Mate, or as others put it, you're Twin Soul, then that is your truth. My Being can say this - you and your human friend are of the same energy source, so yes, you are Twin Souls.

To feel another, or their pain or their joys, means there is a strong connection to each other, not only as Human Beings, but as Spirit Beings as well.

When you feel their pain or depression that is a time when you need to be strong and send only unconditional love to that human person. See them wrapped in a ball or blanket of white light. If you truly believe in the love of the light then it will be manifested.

Trust yourself Carlene.

Be blessed in unconditional love always.

Kuntarkis.

SPIRITUAL SELF-SACRIFICE

Dear Kuntarkis,

I don't know if you are able to offer assistance but here goes.

I am a single woman in my mid-30s. I have never been married nor have any children (personal choice). For the last 15 years as opposed to being involved in relationships etc., I have devoted most of my time to spiritual work.

I am now wondering whether the self-sacrifice has been worth it. I feel stagnant in my spiritual progress, particularly because I have discovered so much yet have not had anyone special in my life to share these experiences and insights with. Also I would dearly love to be in a loving relationship, but I am a bit concerned that I might not be able to handle such a relationship because I have basically been on my own for a long time.

Am I destined to work my path alone (in the physical sense) or will I be given the opportunity to experience true love?

Thank you

Frances.

Kuntarkis replies:

Dear Frances, My Being wishes to say thankyou for sharing your feelings. Not many human beings truly share what they are feeling. In our civilisation we the Nar'Karones have for so long shared exactly what we as individuals have felt throughout our existence. By sharing our feelings we have learnt to trust not only others but especially ourselves. Yes, you have chosen a path of inner learning, and yes, you chose to devote a part of your present human incarnation to gain a greater understanding of spiritual knowledge.

There are so many human beings who walk upon your Mother Earth, lost in a maze of complete confusion, and many, so many, walk barren spiritually throughout their human life, unaware of who or what they truly are, caught up in the beliefs and conditioning of their human ego of self-created illusion. This is the true sadness of human life.

Yes dear Frances, it is your moment to open up your heart. Ask your Soul - is it time for you to meet your Soul mate and experience a balance of your human life. You are meant to have a loving relationship. Remember, the past is now the past. Send out your loving energies in order to attract similar energies into your vibration.

Remember, you are only alone if that is what you truly believe, but you are truly never alone.

Be blessed in unconditional love always.

Kuntarkis.

MEDITATION TO EFFECT CHANGE: YES OR NO?

To Kuntarkis,

I wanted to let you know that I joined the Centerpointe Program per your advice after thoroughly researching and educating myself on what they are accomplishing, and I am having changes occur already. Am I right?

I have been using this technology (through meditation) for about 6 weeks, and do feel different. I am calmer towards my life journey, and where it is going without knowing, and this is okay. I feel more in control, and in the moment. I also feel more centred; as if I look out through both eyes more, kind of down the bridge of my nose, instead of to the side (if this makes sense).

I think I may be seeing energy auras after my meditation, is this so? I also almost feel like when I look at my reflection after meditating, I see more of the physical aspect that is not the true me, it is a strange sensation. It also seems the worries of the world, and the journeys of others have seemed to wash away. I am not preoccupied with violence, or terrorism, or anything really, just happy to be. I am also feeling MUCH better health-wise, and I know that lowering my stress, and tapping into my higher consciousness must play a part. I feel like I have found the one missing piece: meditation, and everything will now fall into place.

Kuntarkis I want to thank you for your loving guidance and wisdom. I am always here to receive it, and open for any quantum assistance. I AM READY.

The truth you spoke about "not loving myself enough" resonated to the core of my being, and instantly affected me. I know that I have always been selfless in being there for others, but never really allowed myself to just be me. I now don't care if I don't change the world, or am a signed musician, or renown, because that is not what is important. What is important to me now is to live in accordance with love for EVERYTHING - including myself, and to continue to develop spiritually. I hope you sense these changes within me, and can feel my deepest love radiating for you, and for everyone.

One question: I am wondering if during meditation I should try and contact you, or Helen directly, or just quiet my mind and wait.

P.S. Thank-you so much Roman for affording me this incredible opportunity to connect with Kuntarkis.

Forever your brother of light and love,

Richard A'Pukree.

Kuntarkis replies:

Dear Richard, One of the most powerful tools a human being can use in meditation is there imagination. Put your thoughts to the centre of your brow (to your Third Eye) and use your imagination by believing, truly believing that you as a single entity will manifest that reality into your human existence.

That is how to create your reality in your physical world of matter. Seeing the human aura is simply shifting your consciousness to the left or right. It is going beyond what you believe to be truth. Truth is infinite. It is called the **'Knowing'. To believe is to create and to create is to manifest. When you manifest it becomes your reality, does it not?**

Yes Richard, it would be of great benefit to you to develop your spirituality. If you choose to make contact with my Being by meditating in the stillness of your mind, my Being will become aware of this. However, it must be remembered that it takes discipline to raise one's vibration to higher planes of communication.

My Being is aware of your growth and it is good to see. Take care and always believe in yourself from the outer to the inner you my friend always.

Be blessed in unconditional love always.

Kuntarkis.

SPIRIT GUIDES AND PETS

Good day to you Kuntarkis.

I have a couple of questions I'd like to ask, one that's really been pressing on my mind lately. The first one is about Spiritual Names. I've read about them on numerous occasions through your answers, and I was wondering what mine was. Also I'm wondering how many guides are with me at the moment. I know of one, who's made her presence felt. My second question, and I know this may seem very strange, is regarding my dog. I've been worried about him lately. A few weeks ago, he had a major operation to remove a cancerous growth from his chest. He came through alright, but since then he's not been eating properly. We'd give him his tea, and he'd probably take about one or two mouthfuls, but that would be about it. I was wondering if there's something else going on, something that we've missed. Do animals have spirit guides, and if so is he being watched over and taken care of?

Thank you for your time.

Katherine.

Kuntarkis replies:

Dear Katherine, Every human being that is currently experiencing a human existence is in reality a being from a planet called Nar'Kariss, and the people from that planet are called Nar'Karones. Every Nar'Karone was given a spiritual name at their birth. Their name, no matter where they exist in this moment, is a part of who they are. The Nar'Karones were once physical beings in flesh bodies, like humans, but they evolved themselves out of the realm of physical matter, the third dimension, and now exist in the fifth dimension as beings of pure consciousness no longer limited by or bound to flesh bodies.

Your spiritual name is 'Gretimoki' and means 'to work with the elements'. At this present moment in your human life you have four spirit guides. Your main guide is of a feminine energy and her last life on your planet was in the human year of 1801. You were twin sisters in that time.

To your question on animals and whether or not animals have spirits guides. Animals do have a form of spirit guides but are not as evolved as spirits guides like humans have. The human being is a Thinking Being which has a living consciousness. Whereas animals are a part of the energy just as the plants, birds and fish of your world. Animals do not become guides to humans. Once an animal has passed over, its energies join back to the source and are transformed into another form of life or existence that forms the fabric of your physical third dimension. But all animals are evolving at their own pace just like the human being.

Regarding your dog, he is suffering the psychological effects of the operation – he found the experience traumatic. Give your dog love and make his life a happy one. You are a natural healer Katherine – it may be good for you to give your dog a healing by projecting love and light to him and seeing him recovering and returning to his happy self.

Be blessed in unconditional love always. Believe in yourself.

Kuntarkis.

SEARCHING FOR THE TRUTH

Hello Kuntarkis,

I have been studying philosophy for the past 15 years and I was given your web address by a friend. On searching through your information I have come to an understanding which I will say took a lot of searching in myself. I have also been quite deeply involved in a religious faith, as you would call a belief system. I would like to say Kuntarkis that you have opened my eyes to many other possibilities in my search for the truth. I have many questions to ask of you, and if I am permitted I will ask these over several months. First I would like to ask you, what is a true human being? Would you answer this for me? Thank you Kuntarkis, I await your reply and yes, please put this up on the website. My name is Dominic.

Kuntarkis replies:

Dear Dominic, there were and are many true Human Beings on your planet which you call Earth. I will choose one as an example. First let me say there are two types of humans on this Planet Earth, one is the Human Being and the other is the Human Animal. What separates the two is Consciousness. The true Human Being is one who elevates themselves beyond Human Ego, and in all things they do, they come from the heart. They are the living truth of what they express and do in life, never harming any other form of life, seeing all things as equal in the higher form of Evolution. They are selfless and do not force their knowledge onto others, but they allow all human individuals to choose their own path in life. They help only those who ask or wish to be helped. They emanate Unconditional Love to all and place no judgement on others. They are unbiased in all things. They know who they are and what they are, and where they are going, and they experience each moment in life as a learning, neither negative nor positive.

When you walk into their presence you feel the love projecting from them. They only eat of the plants of your Mother Earth, never consuming any form of animal. This keep's their Consciousness connected to Creation's Totality. It is in this level of Consciousness where they live Is complete bliss.

The example I wish to give is of the one called Jesus. He truly was, and is, a True Human Being. To the Essene's he said "If you eat of the dead, you in turn become the living dead." What he was saying was that when you eat of animals, the flesh stays in your bowels anything from 20 to 80 hours of your time and ferments, and the toxins of this fermenting pass through the walls of your bowels into your blood which poisons your human body. This is a major cause of the increasing incidences of bowel cancer on your planet.

On the other hand there is the human animal. It lives on instinct and cunning. Its fears and insecurities are based on the beliefs and conditioning of its life. The human animal is a carnivore - one who consumes the dead. It wears many masks of life, one for each occasion. It is judgemental, vindictive, domineering, and holds a great deal of hatred and anger. These are some of the traces of Human Ego, and this is what prevent the human animal from raising not only its level of thinking, but also prevents its conscious growth.

There is so much more that can be said Dominic, but let it be said, only when each human lets go of their self-created limitations, which are based on their beliefs and conditions, and includes all of their fears and insecurities, will the real human come into being. That is, only when each human lets go of their Ego will the truth come into existence. Each human must see the falseness in order to allow the truth to manifest within and around them. Knowledge is the greatest wealth and unconditional love is ultimate freedom.

Yes Dominic, the truth will set each human being free from all their self-created limitations.

Be blessed in the Light Dominic.

Kuntarkis.

PRESIDENT KENNEDY

Hi Kuntarkis,

Are all your people on your planet as open as you are? Since you seem to be able to open up the past and see the truth, is it true that our former President Kennedy was murdered by the Government? And yes, I would like to know the truth. Awaiting your reply.

Hayley

Kuntarkis replies:

Yes Hayley, the truth is more important than life itself. It not only brings peace of mind, but it allows you to live life without judgement. You learn that truth itself sets you free from the Ego world of materialism, allowing the unconditional love within to expand, and your awareness of self-realisation comes into being. The one you call your past President Kennedy is still a touchy subject with many trying to cover up the truth. Yes, he was eliminated because he did not think as others in power at the time did. But you see Hayley, the truth always comes to the surface, however long it takes. That is the balance of Creation – all will be revealed in time.

Be blessed in the Light.

Kuntarkis.

MISSING DEPARTED HUSBAND

Hello Kuntarkis.

I would like to say 4 years ago the father of my children was killed in a car accident and nobody ever got to say good-bye. I think about him every day and really have not come to self-closure of this whole life changing tragedy. Do you have any way to tap into his spiritual senses and see if he is okay and if he knows we love him and miss him more every day? Please respond.

Christi

Kuntarkis replies:

Dear Christi, thank you for writing to my Being. Your trust is very much appreciated. I must say dear Christi, the pain and the loss of your dear husband and loving father of your children is always very hard to accept. Such a loss is especially difficult when you and your children could not even have the opportunity to have said goodbye from your loving hearts. I feel your pain because I am a part of you, as we each are a part of each other. When we open our heart to the infinite love that exists within us, we can come to a realisation, that yes, we truly are a part of each other.

You ask my Being if I can tap into his spirit self. That is an easy process and you also can do this, as it is very simple. First, sit in a quiet room or you can lie down, and then place your hands over your heart. Take three deep breaths to centre and calm yourself, and then using your inner knowing, or some would call it your higher self, or even your imagination. See a bright light in your heart centre and allow that light to expand right throughout your human body. Then see that light expanding all around your body so that you are completely encircled within the light. Now visualise your husband standing before you. Send some light from your heart centre to him so he is standing in the light, and tell him you miss him and you love him very much. It is most important to do this from an honest heart, as you can express this light and your love far better if you can feel it, sense it or see it. You you will experience your truth.

At this point you can ask any questions of him that you wish. If you would like to try and do this simple exercise with your children, it may also help them to cope and understand better what has happened to their loving father. I would also like to say that the more you do this exercise the better it will be, so do it as many times as you like or feel the need to.

Christi, if you believe in spirit guides or angels, I would like to express to you that all human beings, living in a physical body on this third dimensional world have them. And yes, they do help guide all human beings during their physical lives, and then also when you pass over into spirit world. To answer your question, your husband is fine and is learning to understand his present situation. Missing him is understandable, as humans must go through a grieving period to grow from what has happened.

You are a strong and beautiful human being, and even though your husband will always be in your heart, your life is already changing and many more experiences will come to you as you grow in your own truth. If you wish to ask anything more, please feel free to do so.

Be blessed in the Light Christi, and your human children.

Kuntarkis.

HOW DID MY FATHER DIE?

Mr Kuntarkis,

Could you please answer my question? I am 14 years old and I live with my mother and brother. Two years ago my father died. He was a policeman and died in the line of duty. That is what we were told, and ever since then I have been having a dream. It is the same one, over and over. It is about my Dad. I wake up crying, and I feel lost because something is telling me there was more to his death. Can you shed any more light on this please? I'm sorry, but I don't want to give my name.

Kuntarkis replies:

Even though you do not give your name, I know who you are and I am saddened for you for your loss. Your father chose to be an officer of the law because he wanted to help people, especially the weak. He is a wonderful Soul. It is a sad situation on your planet when one takes the life of another, for life is precious. Your father's life was taken out of fear. You see, when one is taking the poisons of drugs, the human loses control of their senses, and fear takes over. They are working on instinct, not from a balanced mind. The only peace I can give you is your father is with you and he has no pain. He loves you very much, and each time you hold the little doll you loved so much as a child, remember him as he gave it to you. The dreams will end very soon. Remember always that your father called you his little angel.

Be blessed in the Light little angel.

Kuntarkis.

RUSSIAN SUBMARINE TRAGEDY

Hello Kuntarkis,

My name is Steven, I live in Colorado. I don't believe in wars, but I did feel very sad for those Russian sailors who perished in their underwater coffin. They must have been very frightened, knowing they were going to die, and just waiting for the end. Was there anything more the Russian government could have done, or was there more to it?

Steven

Kuntarkis replies:

Yes Steven, you are right. There are no winners or losers in Man-Made Wars. All wars or conflicts are based on the fears and insecurities that are within each human individual. It is like saying that there is no enemy on the outside, for the enemy is within each human being. And if each human being worked to dissolve their Ego, which is where fears and insecurities come from, then your species would have no wars, and peace and harmony would be almighty present. But you see Steven, there are many on your planet Earth who enjoy the conflicts of life – it gives their existence meaning and power which they believe in. What was sad was the Russian government would rather let their sailors die than ask for help from other nations. And yes, there was more behind the tragedy, but it would be best for all concerned not to say any more, as it may cause more conflict.

Be blessed in the Light.

Kuntarkis.

IS THE FUTURE WRITTEN?

Dear Kuntarkis,

I have always wondered about the future. It seems to be on my mind always, and some of my friends think I'm just wasting my life away. Is it true that our future is written or can we make our own future?

Curious Joe

Kuntarkis replies:

Well Curious Joe, you are a dreamer, always using your imagination. That is goods as long as you put some action into it. I will explain it this way – many of your species live in the past and bring that past into their present, which in turn creates their future. If it is a negative past, it will not only create a negative moment in the present, but also a negative future. On the other hand, one who dreams in the future and puts no action into it, but always says "one day I will do that", will also never achieve their dreams because they are not putting the action, or energy, into the present moment. Instead they are dreaming of a future that is always out of reach.

Joe, time was created by humanity, and have you noticed how your time is getting faster? Time as you know it is only in the third dimensional matter world. It does not exist in realms outside of a physical matter body. If each human being could live in the moment and dissolve their emotional conflicts, your world would be at peace with all of life. The secret of all life is one word – IMAGINATION. Whatever you imagine you can create. It is up to each of you, for the power is within you, as you all have it. Act on your imagination!

Be blessed in the Light Curious Joe.

Kuntarkis.

CRYSTAL POWER

Hi Kuntarkis,

I have been involved in spirituality for about 3 years. Before that I was a devoted Christian, but they could not give me the answers I was seeking, so I joined a Spiritual Church and it's great. My question is, can crystals give me power in developing my psychic abilities?

Judy

Kuntarkis replies:

Dearest Judy, the gift of life is making your own choices and experiencing other facets of human life. Good for you Judy – keep seeking and you will find what you are looking for.

To your question about crystals. Crystals do not give you the power, as you Judy are the power. You are connected to all things and all things are connected to you. Knowing this is one of the greatest Self-Realisations a human being can have. Yes, the Crystals will enhance your natural abilities. Crystals are a form of communication device. Just like your tape recorders, they can hold information for you and you can retrieve that information out of the Crystal either as pictures or words – it is your choice. If you want to record a message into your personal Crystal hold it to your heart, place a white light all around you and then express your message into your Crystal. When you have finished say these words I am now complete in my expressions and all that I have expressed is now recorded on my Personal Crystal.

When you wish to listen to your message or messages from your personal Crystal, again hold you're Crystal to your heart see yourself in a bubble of Light, then say I wish to listen to my message and listen from your heart. The power in knowing it can work is you as the human individual to believe in yourself. So remember dear Judy, you are the power and the Crystals enhance your power. They are a Gift from Mother Earth to Humanity.

Be blessed in Love and Light.

Kuntarkis.

LOOKING FOR THE ANSWERS

Dear Kuntarkis,

I am always on the internet and looking for solutions to help heal my life. I seem to be running out of options. I just can't seem to get my life on track. Can you offer any advice for me? I'm always looking.

P.P.

Kuntarkis replies:

Dear P.P., Interesting how human nature seems to look in the wrong places for solutions, especially when they are personal. You have been looking for so long, maybe it is time you should be looking within yourself and discover the wonderment of knowledge that you dear P.P. have within you. All answers can come from within if you trust yourself. The power and strength of that decision is yours for the asking. Remember, ask from the heart and you shall receive.

Be Blessed dear P.P., for you can find the solution if you just trust yourself.

Kuntarkis.

WEDDING STRESS

For Kuntarkis,

Hi, my name is Tony and I have a question to ask of you. I'm getting married in November this year and my future wife's parents want the wedding in their church. They are very persistent about it. Then of course, my parents would like to have the wedding in their church. I personally don't care which church and nor does my future wife. We have discussed it, but have not made a decision. Being unbiased, what do you think?

Tony.

Kuntarkis replies:

Dear Tony, Well it seems you two have a decision to make. There are a few answers, but choosing the right one to keep everyone happy will test your patience. You could marry in your parent's church which would make them very happy, but your future wife's parents unhappy, and this could cause problems for you later on. Or you could marry in your future wife's parent's church which will make them happy, but your parents unhappy. So after all that, who are you trying to please? Or is it a case of just keeping the peace? You both could go one step further and please both sets of parents by having two weddings, but then which wedding and at whose church will come first?

The more you try to please everyone, the more complicated it becomes, and the more stressful it becomes. You and your human lady must ask this most important question: What is it that you **both want?**

Sit and ponder a while on that question and see what both of you come up with. You as individuals have the right to choose the circumstances concerning the ceremony which will express your commitment and love to each other. If you both make a decision which may make your respective parents unhappy, you will have to discuss it with them and try to come to an agreement that will please all parties. But remember that this is '**Your**' special day, and ultimately you and your bride must do what will please both of you. Your parents have had their wedding days. Now it is your turn.

Blessings to both of you, and may love always fill your hearts and your children to come. All is bright, and you both are meant to be together.

Kuntarkis.

FEAR FOR MY LIFE

Dear Kuntarkis,

I cannot give my name because it will not only put my life in jeopardy, but I feel also my parents could become involved, or even harmed. I will explain. My emotions have been running high for the last three years. I was on my way home and missed the turn-off to my part of town. I ended up in a part of town that is not the best place to be. Driving around and scared to ask anyone, I stopped to look at my street directory when I heard something like gun shots. A moment later a car came speeding down the street towards me and then stopped in front of my car. I can tell you I was frozen. It seemed like forever - I couldn't move, and then the car sped off.

As soon as it was out of sight I drove off and somehow found my way onto the right road and managed to drive home. I didn't tell my parents. The next day at work I was reading the paper and I noticed two people had been shot where I had stopped my car. I have sold my car and bought another car just in case the shooters come looking for me. Should I worry or not?

Concerned person.

Kuntarkis replies:

Dear Human Being, Some would say that as a human citizen you have the responsibility to go to your police and tell them what you have seen, as the families of those killed are looking for answers to the senseless death of their loved ones. Others would say don't get involved as it has been three of your Earthly years since the incident and no-one will remember, so just let it be because it isn't your problem.

First to put you at ease. The two who committed the crime are not looking for you. They didn't even know you were in the car. The only reason they stopped was to make a decision about what to do next. You have allowed yourself to live in fear for the last three years, and that alone would cause you immeasurable stress. Please understand that you are not in any danger. The only decision you have to make is what is the right thing to do? Do you go to the police and tell your story and reveal yourself as a witness after the fact, or just let it pass away as a lesson in life. That decision can only come from you, and you alone.

As for the two human beings who committed the crime, even though they may not be caught, justice will be served in some form or other. No one can create imbalance and get away with it, for nature will bring it into balance somehow, somewhere. That is a part of Creation - balance is justice. So you must ask yourself what you will choose and the choice is yours dear Human Being. Whatever you decide, once you have made your decision, allow it to be.

Be Blessed in Love and light always.

Kuntarkis.

ARTICLE ON CRYSTAL SKULLS: REAL OR FALSE?

Hello Kuntarkis,

Could you please answer this question? I was reading an article on the crystal skulls and I was wondering how much truth is in the story. If you know of them, can you communicate the so-called knowledge that is recorded in the skulls? From what I have read, it seems no one can physically tap into the knowledge, and would the knowledge benefit humankind?

Ben.

Kuntarkis replies:

Dear Ben, It is good to see that you are seeking a deeper understanding, for knowledge is freedom. So Ben, be curious and keep reading. You have an interesting life ahead of you.

To your question on the **Crystal Skulls**. They are the **Parumhy**. The name means '**Infinite Knowledge - the Existence of Five**', the five referring to the five **Elements of Creation: Fire, Water, Air, Earth, and Spirit**. It is said that whoever obtains all five of the skulls, and who is able to learn how to obtain the Infinite Knowledge within them, they will have the ability to transcend throughout all Universes and be limitless in all things.

A human being would have to be pure of heart and beyond Human Ego, and be filled with unconditional love for all of life, to be able to obtain this knowledge. There will come a time in human history where all '**Five Parumhy**' will be brought together for the higher good of humanity. The beings who created them will return to your Earthly vibration and help humanity understand the purpose of Life. The knowledge will be given to humanity. And in turn will help you grow consciously and with unconditional love. Human Ego will be no more, for it will dissolve into the nothingness from which it first came.

Ben, the knowledge of the '**Parumhy**' will help humanity in a way that is beyond their present understanding, as at this moment the knowledge of humans is 'old knowledge'. And yes, my being can communicate with '**Parumhy**'.

Never stop seeking Ben. Always be curious and never accept an answer at face value. Seek deeper to find the truth and the truth will find you. Be blessed always dear Ben, in the Light.

Kuntarkis.

HAS THE PAST CAUGHT UP WITH ME?

Kuntarkis,

It took a lot of courage for me to write to someone like you. Don't misunderstand me. I am a believer in other forms of life. For anyone to believe that we are the only ones in the Universe would surely be very ignorant or very stupid.

I am 38 and very happily married to a wonderful man for the last 7 years. We have two beautiful children. When I was 14 I was molested by my father and uncle for about two years. My mother knew what was going on but was too afraid to do anything about it. I escaped the misery of my life and ended up a prostitute on the streets of Hong Kong. When I was 26 I had saved enough money to come to Australia.

I was very lucky for the first time in my life, and ended up living here. I did study in Accounting, got a good job and after a few years I met my husband. I never told my husband about my past - I was too ashamed. My whole life changed for the better. I felt I had dealt with my past. The problem is my parents are now coming here for a holiday, and now my past is causing me a great deal of stress. My husband invited them to stay in our home. I feel I can't allow this because of how my father and uncle violated me. I feel my husband will not understand why I feel this way and I am afraid to tell him of my past because he may feel disgusted with me. I'm afraid my world will fall apart, that all the good that I have had will now come to an end.

I feel very alone and scared. If I tell him he may leave me. I don't want to lose him or my children. What should I do? What would you do? Kuntarkis, it feels strange writing to you, as I feel I have known you for a long time. Can you offer me any advice?

Cori

Kuntarkis replies:

Dear Cori, Yes, you do have a lot of courage, and you have a most beautiful heart filled with love and compassion. Cori, you have experienced a hard human life and the lessons of your life have shaped the person you are today.

Don't allow the demons of your past into your present moment. See the past as only a memory, experiences that are neither positive nor negative. What your human father and uncle did to you was not right by human standards. In the eyes of human law, they should be brought to justice because they took away your innocence, and took advantage of the trust you had in them, the trust that a human daughter believes she will be loved and protected by her human father.

I understand your pain and emotions, and how you do not want your father in your home, especially with your two daughters. Cori, you have a decision to make. Do you allow your father into your home, say nothing, shut your eyes and trust all will be well? Or do you open up your heart of pain to the man who loves you with all his heart and would walk on fire to prove his love and devotion to you?

It is the truth always that sets each human being free from their pain, especially when they come from their heart. Cori, you believe in truth. Trust yourself and whatever decision you make. It will be for the better. Trust in your husband's heart, love and understanding. He is not blind, and he sees and feels with a good heart. All will be well Cori. You have had a long and hard journey and in this most precious moment of your life is your greatest reward.

Be Blessed in Love always, dear Cori.

Kuntarkis.

MY DAUGHTER IS ON DRUGS

Dear Kuntarkis,

I have always wanted to believe that there are other forms of life on other planets, and because I am in the business of the internet, I came across your website. I have a daughter who is 16 and I believe she has been on drugs for the past 2 years. I know it is a social thing in our society today among the young, and I have tried not to react, but I feel her whole character has changed. She lies, steals, and hangs around other drug users who seem to have a very strong influence on her. When we talk it always ends up in a screaming match. She has been caught for shoplifting 4 times, and if caught again she may end up in a detention centre.

Being a single parent I feel helpless. A friend of mine told me about a place where you commit your child and they help them dry out and also support them emotionally to help them feel good about themselves. As a parent I would love to be able to solve this problem, but I feel as if my daughter sees me as the enemy. Can you see a clear light at the end of the tunnel?

Desperate mother - Hazel.

Kuntarkis replies:

Dear Hazel, Yes, I can see the Light at the end of the tunnel, and it will be bright for you and your human daughter. It will take some human time. Your daughter sees you as the enemy because she feels responsible for the break-up of your marriage with her father. It began so long ago for her. When she was very young she heard you and your husband exchanging heated words, especially as your husband did not want to have children. His career was his goal in life which is his right to choose. But when he expressed how he felt about your child Tracey, she did not understand, and she created her own belief that her father did not want her and has never loved her.

Your daughter's pain is deep and the negative emotion has been with her for a long time. The more you try to help her, the more she pulls away. Your friend has offered you some very positive advice about the drug rehabilitation centre. They will help her and you will have your daughter back. She will see the Light and come to a better understanding of herself. She will also see you with new eyes. Tracey loves you very much, but she is unable to see past, her pain at this time. Given time and help, this will change.

Trust your decisions for they are your strength. Be Blessed dear Hazel in Love and Light always.

Kuntarkis.

ILLNESS & PERSONAL GROWTH

Dear Kuntarkis,

Thank you for having a web site, as it was no accident that I found the site, as I have been looking for others, who maybe going through the same spiritual growth as myself. I found your site, it has confirmed a lot of what I have been going through myself, since I have opened up myself. I understand through letting go of my fixed ideas, and through the guidance that I have also received. I understand that our illnesses and sicknesses, is through resisting our own pathways in our lives, and have tried to teach this on several fronts, including how to love yourself. What I am asking of you, if you could tell me whether this is through blockages of the past, as I have found that it always comes to an end, without really going anywhere. And the other question that I am asking, is about physical depression that I am experiencing in my life at this present time. If it is possible I would like some more understanding of this lesson, as I have not been able to fully understand how to heal this side of myself as yet.

Your loving Spiritual brother Alan.

Kuntarkis replies:

Dear Alan, It is good to see and hear human beings like yourself truly want to grow beyond the present human Ego that exists in this vibration of physical matter. You are a beautiful spirit existing in a human vessel.

Alan, all pain exists from the human past of beliefs and conditionings of an individual's life, created solely for learning and understanding. But it is unfortunate that many human beings carry their past incarnations into their present life, which because of fear, created their present and their future.

When the past hurts and negative emotions are not looked at and not understood, those negative emotions prevent an individual from growing consciously. Unconditional love from the centre of your Beingness is the only way to release oneself from the past. If you Alan feel pain from your past, it means you have not fully forgiven yourself and others. The past is holding you back from truly stepping beyond the grip of human Ego.

Humanity created the negative human Ego to learn from and to understand the lessons of human life.

It is the human Ego that now controls humanity and keeps humanity in fear. All the material possessions one gains from a human life cannot solve emotional issues or bring life into harmony and balance. While material possessions are a need, they are also a distraction from the truth. You dear Alan, as all of humanity are connected to the Light of Creation that is present in all of life in all Universes. Your feelings of depression are your human Ego's control over you, based on your conditioning and beliefs. But there is a way to dissolve all your pain back into the nothingness from which it was first created.

First meditate in the stillness of your Being, your Essence, no matter how long in human time it takes. Allow yourself to be true to yourself. Totally accept yourself as you are in this moment of your life. Feel your heart to be full of love and kindness for yourself and all of life. Feel this unconditional love emanate within you and all around you. Have this love present every moment of your existence. See any negative emotions as the past which need to be remembered as the past, for it is only a memory a lesson of life neither negative nor positive, without judgement. Place the Light of Love into all things you do and around you always – believe in Love and Love will believe in you.

Please feel free to express to my Being whenever the need arises. Alan, be Blessed in Love and Light always.

Kuntarkis.

INNER TURMOIL: WHY?

Hello to Kuntarkis,

My own angels aren't as verbal as you, so I'm writing to ask about them. Often times I struggle to not second-guess my divinations when I ask higher beings for advice. Most of the time, I am told that I already know the answer too many of my questions. This being the case, I am trying to find the right questions to ask them. My question to you: I have been spiritually and emotionally tempered by being a child of a divorced family. I can handle high degrees of stress, and I am a natural healer. I feel with every ounce of my being, pain that others suffer. My parents remarried, and are both happy. How is it that I am still filled with turmoil inside, and cannot find inner balance even though my personal life is in harmony? The stress has caused me stomach troubles which is exactly where the tempering of my emotions is rooted.

Am I shedding negative karma all the while building good karma? I haven't truly cried in 8 years. People tend to look towards me with respect and an open ear when it comes to spiritual dialogues, but sometimes I feel fake, because I am still burning inside. How can I transform that negative energy into a positive, outgoing force?

Tovy.

Kuntarkis replies:

Dear Tovy, My Being thanks you for taking the precious moments in your human life to express your thoughts. Angels and spirit guides are quite verbal in their own expressions, but are rarely heard by the human ear, mainly because of the difference in energy frequencies, being due to the vibration they exist within. Angels and spirit guides are always talking to human beings. That's why it is important for human beings to still their minds of the physical distractions of human life so you can tune into these energies of higher vibrations of sound.

When you ask a question Tovy, your guides are communicating to you directly. It is because of the difference between energy vibrations that the connection is not clear. Meditation through the stillness of one's mind can and will lead you to becoming a more open channel for this communication.

The reason for your temptations is that an emotion was conditioned into you as a child and genetically imprinted from your parents. Many human beings will deny this statement yet it is the truth that human parents do pass on all their emotions to their children, be they negative or positive. Stress is a negative emotions that will lead to sickness and dis'ease. There is no positive to being able to 'handle' stress because stress is the major cause of dis'ease and death in your Earthly societies.

To feel another's pain is being compassionate and caring, as long as you do not take on the negative emotions of that pain, for it will be bad for your own human health. You are a natural healer Tovy, but always remember, there are many levels of energies for healing. If you feel turmoil inside of yourself it means you have not completely forgiven yourself or even others. To be a healer of the Light you must become the Light in all things in your human life. Balance of mind, body and spirit is the path to self-discovery of your true essence.

Yes, you are shedding negative energies (Being Negative Karma) from your human life, and through an understanding of your own Unconditional Love you will be building positive energies (Positive Karma) for this incarnation and future incarnations.

Your stress is causing you to have stomach problems. It is a build-up of too much acid in your human body which represents your past emotions. As a child you were very hurt about your parents' divorce. The emotion has carried through to your present moment in life. Forgiveness from your heart in Unconditional Love is freedom from all negative emotions. Every negative emotions can be transformed into a positive energy. It will take a little work on your side, but my Being believes in you. You Tovy must believe in yourself and you will succeed. Just remember Stress Creates Acid in your human body which is a Negative, and Stress is Created by the human individual.

Be Blessed in Love and Light throughout your human life always.

Kuntarkis.

FEAR FOR MY SON'S SAFETY

Dear Kuntarkis,

I am facing one of the hardest situations of my life which is causing me much heartache and stress. I am trying as best as I can to protect my son, as he is in danger of being hurt physically and emotionally and also in danger of being abducted by his biological father, whose family has a history of child abduction.

I love my son more than anything and every day I am worried about his future, if he is exposed to his father who I know would hurt my son out of spite against me. I would not be able to continue living if I lose my son and constantly worry about his safety and well-being. Could you please tell me if my son will grow up to be a good person or if this experience will affect him negatively? I believe that my son is an old soul and that he has come here to teach us something. My son is my whole life, could you please shed some light on the outcome of my situation. Thankyou very much for any help.

Kerry.

Kuntarkis replies:

Dear Kerry, My Being feels your pain and yes it would create a lot of stress in your human life and also your human son's life, causing emotional pain to him as he grows into adulthood. The scares from a negative upbringing can influence his future. When a human parent or human child is living in a stressful situation it does create a lot of confusion, and it does not allow one to think clearly.

What is important for you is to make a decision. If you are concerned for your son's well-being and future regarding his biological father doing him harm, then speak with your human law enforcement if you have not done so already. Explain your situation and your fears of what may happen. Another alternative is to move far away and start a new life. Many human beings have been in similar situations and moved to other places so they can live in peace and provide a positive environment for their human children.

If any human being lives in a negative situation, it can and does create a negative lifestyle, and it does affect a human being emotionally, physically and mentally, especially children who are easily influenced and conditioned by their surroundings and their human parents. Such a life will affect their present and their future. Human children need a loving balanced upbringing so they can pass those experiences on to their children. You Kerry do have the strength and the courage to see through all your decisions. Believe in yourself and you will always make the right decision for yourself and your human child.

Be Blessed in Love and Light always.

Kuntarkis.

UNUSUAL BONE GROWTH

Hi Kuntarkis,

My friend suggested that I ask for your advice. I have bone growing on the top right hand side of my head. Actually, it is very close to the very top/centre of my head. It is not a cyst. At times it gives me headaches and sometimes it swells up. I have had an operation to remove the scar tissue that surrounded it. Could you please tell me what it is that I need to understand about myself?

Regards Jo.

Kuntarkis replies:

Dear Jo, Thank you for writing to my Being and your question concerning metaphysical reasons for an unusual bone growth on the top of your head. First I would like to reassure you the growth is not connected to any past emotions that you need to look at. The bone growth that is growing on the top of your head is because there is incorrect genetic information being sent to this section of your head, and yes, it can cause pressure, resulting in headaches. The swelling is fluid being sent there to protect and cushion the tissue, which is a natural protective reaction from your body.

There are two options for you Jo to look at. Your first option is to keep seeking medical attention and observation. Your medical professionals may advise removal of this growth or they may suggest some form of medication to help ease the pressure and reduce your headaches. It is always good advice to get a second opinion from a Medical Professional.

Your second option would be to use the power of your Inner Being through meditation to focus on connecting with the Light and seeing yourself restructuring the growth and stopping it from continuing to grow. By meditating in the stillness of your mind and connecting with your inner self you will also connect with your physical self and mental self. This will take a lot of self-discipline and self-trust. You can open the door to all parts of your human self through the power of your inner Being. Remember your human body is a healing tool and any malfunctions can be rectified provided the right thoughts and the right food are put into the human body. Believe in yourself and love yourself in unconditional love, and the Light will be there for you to help you heal your vessel. But it is the unwavering belief in your own ability to do this that will ultimately enable you to succeed.

Be Blessed dear Jo in Love and Light always.

Kuntarkis.

MENINGICOCCYL FEAR

Dear Kuntarkis,

My concerns are about our safety in our homes, our neighbourhoods and our cities. Whenever I watch the television I seem to hear about someone dying of some painful disease. This disease called meningococcal scares the hell out of me and I'm concerned for my children. I don't believe in drugs but I fear for my children who are very young. Where does this new disease come from?

Thank you. Roslyn.

Kuntarkis replies:

Dear Roslyn, Yes, my Being can understand your concern for your human children. The dis'ease you speak of is a mutation created by some very unethical scientists on your Earth. It was developed for the purposes of Germ Warfare, naturally this would be denied by Governments or even the Military and was to be used to destroy human soldiers as quickly as possible. It has not been fully developed but your scientists are working on the bacteria so that it kills within a matter of hours after release into air or water.

Many of the nations on your Earth have been developing these deadly germs for war. One of the biggest problems that no matter how much your scientists may try to contain the bacteria, all bacteria mutates and evolves into other strains. This means bacteria can become one hundred times more potent and therefore more deadly to the human body and to all of life that exists on your planet.

What should be of the greatest concern is the ever growing weakness overall of the human immune system in most human beings. This is due to several reasons. The first is genetic breakdown - unhealthy parents passing on weak genetic information creating and therefore producing unhealthy children. The second, which influences the first, is poor nutrition. Food consumed by the majority of humans today does not rebuild the immune system or the body as a whole, but reduces the immune system and breaks down the human body genetics. The third is stress, meaning all the negativity humans express to each other and all the stress experienced in day to day life and reinforced by poor diet. The fourth is toxicity - from drugs (including so-called medications and pain killers), alcohol, and pollution in air, food and water.

Unless humanity takes responsibility for its creations, your world and everything that lives upon it yourselves included, will be eventually Self-Destroyed. You may not see it because the deterioration is gradual, but there will come a time when humanity will reach the point of no return. Changes must take place now. The people of Earth must demand their leaders care for the Earth and for all that live upon the Earth. The people must also recognise their role and responsibility in caring for the Earth and for themselves. Change can come about if it is truly desired and if it is understood how important and crucial these changes are.

Be Blessed in Love and Light always dear Roslyn.

Kuntarkis.

TIME & DARKNESS

Dear Kuntarkis,

I read your article on your home planet called Nar'Kariss. I have always believed that other life forms exist. It's fascinating to read books and see Alien movies. One of the things that I am curious about is, there is no time or darkness in your dimension. How do your people survive without sleep or even time? Also, I've started a meditation course and I am really enjoying it.

Jinn.

Kuntarkis replies:

Dear Jinn, My Being feels your joy on your journey. If you persist by doing meditation it will open the doors to your inner knowledge of self-awareness. Always trust in yourself and what you experience in your quiet time. Have no expectation, only listen to your inner voice, for that is where true learning for human beings begins.

On my planet Nar'Kariss we need no darkness for sleep time because the Nar'Karones do not have physical bodies to repair or rest. A human needs their sleep for resting, rejuvenating and repairing their human body, as well as for learning on another level of consciousness. Time as it is on your Earth cannot exist in a vibration of the fifth dimension. As humans evolve through many physical incarnations they require a body for each incarnation. The Nar'Karones have no need for time as we do not have physical bodies or anything of physical matter in our vibration. We live in the moment, but we do continue to evolve our consciousness by transforming our energies. All it means is we are in a different level of consciousness.

Be Blessed in Love and Light always dear Jinn.

Kuntarkis.

SMOKING SUPPRESSING EMOTIONS

Hello Kuntarkis,

You have a very interesting way of expressing words. You touched my heart and it made me cry, which I have needed to do for a long time. I have a problem and no matter what I do I can't seem to stop. I have been smoking for 29 years and find I am smoking more as each year goes by. At 45 my health is not really good. Even walking I can't seem to breathe correctly. What do you think?

Maria.

Kuntarkis replies:

Dear Maria, Yes, you have suppressed your emotions for a long period of time. You also know why you began your habit. You came from a broken home and your father had his own negative emotions that he grew up with. He and your mother both smoked. There was no love in your family for you or your two sisters. Both your parents had a very hard and cruel childhood, and they made your childhood the same as theirs.

Yes, you are a product of your parents past – their negative experiences are encoded in your human genetics. At the age of 16 you ran away from home and connected with the same energies and emotions that came from your parents. Your experiences brought in human males who represented your human father in your relationships, and this caused you a lot of pain. So much pain to the point that you would not have any children so they would not suffer the same as you have.

Maria, you are a very loving and beautiful human being. Yes, it is time to let go of your past even though it is hard to forgive your parents. But forgiveness is part of the healing process, and even though it is hard to forgive yourself, it is also a part of the healing process. You have decided not to have any more human males in your life, and that is your choice. But again you are punishing yourself, not believing that you deserve to be happy.

You do deserve to be happy. You do deserve to be loved by your own being and by other human beings. You also deserve to be healthy. So is it not the moment to say "No more will I punish myself. Enough is enough."

Say to yourself "I do deserve to be loved and to have a fulfilling relationship if I choose it to be so. I Maria forgive my father and mother, I let go of the pain in forgiveness and unconditional love. I also forgive myself. I love myself unconditionally. In this moment I realise I no longer need my habit of smoking. I let it go in love and I know I am at peace with myself." Say it as many times as you wish.

Be Blessed in Love always Maria.

Kuntarkis.

PROPHECY OF DEATH

To Kuntarkis,

Could you please give me an answer to this question: I feel I am going to die before I am 40? Is this true?

Julien.

Kuntarkis replies:

Dear Julien, No, you are not going to pass over at 40 years of age. The human being who told you this was being irresponsible. Julien, allow yourself to believe in yourself, your own natural abilities. Every human being knows when they will pass over into spirit world. This knowledge is within you, as it is in all human beings.

You Julien are your future. You create it according to your knowledge and thinking. How you see yourself, you become. So see yourself larger than life and you will not be disappointed. One of the greatest lessons in human life is to feel Joy and to live Joy, to be happy is a state of your mind, believe it and it will become your life.

Be Blessed in Love always.

Kuntarkis.

BOYFRIEND STOLE FROM ME: Why?

Dear Kuntarkis,

I have been reading some of your messages about karmic pay back from another life. It makes sense to me, because my ex- boyfriend did the dirty on me. I felt there was something wrong, but didn't listen to my inner self. What he did was to steal some of my valuables and my money. I did report it to the police but they didn't give me much hope in getting any of it back. Should I let it go or what should I do? I still feel betrayed.

Megan.

Kuntarkis replies:

Dear Megan, Yes, sometimes the lessons of human life can be cruel. Your ex-boyfriend Peter did betray your trust. When you allowed him to move in with you, you felt you could trust him. It can be dangerous trusting another human being without knowing more about them. You only knew him for six weeks and allowed him to move in. Within three weeks of moving in he stole from you and then disappeared. It was a little irresponsible of you, don't you agree?

When a human being avoids telling you anything about their past, and uses negative emotions to avoid the subject, then listen to your heart for the truth. Your ex-boyfriend is very fearful. He has never faced his responsibilities in life. He is a story teller and uses it to gain sympathy, affection, and to get his own way. Peter is a manipulator who would do anything to manipulate another to his advantage. That is how he gets through his human life, creating more and more Karma for himself. Please do not feel bad about this situation. He will not come into your human life again.

Your thoughts are correct. He has done this to other human females and sadly he will continue to do it. It is all he understands. Forgive him Megan and allow your human heart to be full of unconditional love. Send this love to him in your mind's eye and say "I forgive you Peter and I let you go in Love". If you Megan can do this from an honest heart, your lesson from your past incarnation will be complete. So never see the past in anger, only in a balanced mind. Move on with your learning in your life.

Be Blessed Megan in Unconditional Love. May the Light of Creation shine within you always.

Kuntarkis.

SEXUAL LEARNING

Kuntarkis,

I have been told by others in certain groups of teachings that sexual intercourse is important to my spiritual learning. Could you please tell me if this is correct? I thank you in advance.

Lutz.

Kuntarkis replies:

Dear Lutz, My Being cannot tell you if sexual intercourse for spiritual advancement is right or wrong. In reality there is no right or wrong only human beliefs and conditioning. It is humanity that places labels on what is right or wrong, good or bad, positive or negative.

If a human being comes from Ego, then yes, from a human conditioning right and wrong does exist. But if a human being comes from a heart full of unconditional love, then that human being would not do or be involved in wrong, bad or negative situations. Only a heart full of fear would create such negative aspects in one's human life.

Every human being learns at their own pace. As they advance their thinking their learning changes. All teachings upon your Earth are there for a reason. As you learn and progress Lutz, you will know when to move on to another lesson in your human advancement, but it is important to know when to let go and move on. That is why you must trust yourself in all that you do. Listen to your heart, not your human ego.

One thing must be made clear. Sexual intercourse was created for the procreation of your species, just as in your animal kingdom. Sexual intercourse simply to have sex is not love. Love comes from the heart centre. Love is the purest form of universal energy that all life was created from. The human Ego created lust and greed for it owns selfish purpose. Seek the heart and truth will always be with you.

Be Blessed in Love always Lutz.

Kuntarkis.

DREAMS OF A BETTER LIFE

Greetings Kuntarkis,

My homeland is Africa. I come from a small village and a poor family. I have had good luck and moved to America the land of opportunity. I am going to school and learning to become a builder. I would like to settle in America and marry and have many children. I would like to become rich by building many homes. I believe I can do this as I would like to give my children a much better life than I had in my village. My question is will I do this? Is my dream too big or can I do this?

Mbundu.

Kuntarkis replies:

Dear Mbundu, You have a dream, a vision of self-empowerment. You have taken many steps to complete your quest. Your first step was to see yourself in America. This you have created. Your second step was your education to learn to become a builder of homes, and this you are creating. Your third vision is to build your own home and to build other homes. Your fourth vision is to settle in America, marry a human female and have human children so they have better opportunities in their human lives.

You have already created your map of life to be rich and successful, and you have the power, strength and courage to achieve all of these goals, so you must succeed. Is not your answer "yes" to all of the above questions?

Be Blessed in Love always Mbundu.

Kuntarkis.

PAINFUL FEET: WHY?

Dear Kuntarkis,

For the last six years I have not been able to wear any type of shoes, only thongs or slide-on. I have inherited gout in both of my feet. At 37 I noticed every time I put my shoes on and walked for a while, my feet would become very painful and sore. I have been to doctors and was put on drugs which made me sick, so I stopped taking them. I have been to a naturopath and it has helped a little but the problem is still there. Is there anything you can tell me that might help me get rid of this gout?

Thanks,

Bill.

Kuntarkis replies:

Dear Bill, The human body is a miracle of nature's creation. Every cell in your human body has its own form of consciousness and there are well over four quadrillion cells that make up the human body. The body can repair any illness if given the right nutrition. It is true you inherited your father's genetics which passed the predisposition for gout to you. However, it is lifestyle which caused the predisposition for the illness to manifest itself physically.

Your father drank very little water and consumed too much red meat. He drank too much alcohol and smoked too many cigarettes. At the age of 62 he also had gout and could no longer work. Sadly, he was a very angry man with a need to dominate. He became very impatient when things were not done his way. Does this send a message to you Bill?

You are 43 years of age and you are suffering your father's pain. Your consumption of foods are close to your father's, and yes you have some anger to release from your childhood. Through your father's genetics and your upbringing you have carried your father's guilt onto yourself. These emotions need attention. First, learn to love yourself from the heart. Second, learn to forgive yourself then forgive your father for the pain he placed upon you as a child.

When you feel comfortable with yourself, look at your diet. If you are truly serious about healing your gout then change your diet. Eat fresh fruits and vegetables, drink two to three litres of pure water each day. Give up coffee, alcohol, drugs or cigarettes, and the eating of any kind of meat, and instead eat tofu, beans, brown rice, and lentils. There is more good natural protein in legumes than there is in animal flesh. Make sure that 70% of your food intake is raw in a 7 day cycle and the other 30% can be cooked.

Only by cleaning out the poisons and toxins from your tissues can you begin to rebalance your body and allow the natural healing process to occur. You can do this Bill. Your health and mobility depends on it. Just remember it is the acid that is created from animal flesh that causes many different illness in humans.

Be Blessed in Love always.

Kuntarkis.

FIGHTING DARK FORCES

Hello Roman,

Hello and greetings to you. I have a question for Kuntarkis. For the last 10 years I have been fighting the dark forces. I am very spiritual and have been seeking God for many years now. I live in India and have a sister who has been attacking me with black magic. She is evil and has been trying to destroy me for a very long time now. It has been my spirituality and intuition and my strong faith in God that has kept me sane. I would like to understand more about why this is happening to me.

What is the lesson I am to learn here, and have I harmed my sister in other lifetimes that she hates me so much. Because in this lifetime I see nothing that could have caused such hate in her. Help me understand please. Thanks.

Naomi.

Kuntarkis replies:

Dear Naomi, Yes, it can be difficult in human families where one human child feels cheated, that their parents have given more love and attention to one child more so than another. This is the case in your situation. Love and hate are of the same energy. It is the human individual that creates love into love, hate into hate. It all depends on the individual and their experience through their human life as a child into adulthood.

It is not your fault what your human sister is feeling. It is her own creation of her past incarnations, brought into her present human life. She alone is responsible for her created actions. If she continues on her present path she will only experience a human life of her own self-created misery of hate. What your sister expresses is only expressed back in the same form of negative energies.

You Naomi have a beautiful loving heart. From your present learning in human form, your purpose in this life is to be a beacon of light that is unconditional love. In some of your past incarnations you were a teacher of love and truth. Always allow love to be the centre of your being, and remember, what an individual thinks they will become; what an individual does to another, be it negative or positive, they will always have it expressed back upon themselves.

Walk your path in the light and the light will illuminate your way.

Be blessed in love always.

Kuntarkis.

OUT OF BODY EXPERIENCE (O.B.E)

Dear Kuntarkis,

I saw a being during an out of body experience and I am wondering if you could please tell me what he/she was and what was he/she trying to tell me. I will describe him/her as best I can. As I was hovering in my bedroom above my body and marvelling at the beautiful light emanating from my hands, I looked up and saw a being with a yellowish or whitish thick albino skin (not sure if I was seeing this in my room or through the window or another dimension). His entire head was shaped just like the head of the sphinx in Egypt. He had close-set black, large oval eyes (almost hollow looking). He/she also had a prominent brow-line. There was no facial nor hair on the head. He/she had a much chiselled face that almost looked like a human skeleton but broader. He/she also had thick humanoid lips and small teeth with a gap between them.

There appeared to be two smaller beings on his left and right side but I didn't see their features as I was focusing more on him because I was truly taken not by only this presence but also by the vibration that I was feeling from this sight. This being was speaking to me but I could not hear his/her voice. Would you also please tell me what he/she was saying and should I be concerned about his/her presence? If so, what should I do to protect myself during future out of body experiences?

Your help in making sense of this matter is so much appreciated.

Kuntarkis replies:

Dear Human Being, Your experience is rare - most human beings do not have the pleasure of such knowing. From what you have described and expressed, the entity and energy is one from the Tevashekar Species. These beings do not have physical bodies like humans. They have vast knowledge and understanding of many worlds and have existed for over 491 million years in human terms.

The other two entities you mention are smaller facets of the same Being. They are equivalent to the children of that being, just as human beings have children who are in fact facets of their parents. The Tevashekar split their energies to create new beings and these new beings become individuals, but they are still connected to the main energy from which they were created. Again, much like human beings procreating physically, these beings procreate as pure energy.

The one who spoke to you without words, but through the mind, has expressed knowledge which will come out in you as you become more aware of your own existence. Listen to your inner being for all the answers. There is more about you than you realise at this moment in your life. These beings are no threat to you. Believe in the Light for therein lies the truth of all things.

Be blessed in love always.

Kuntarkis.

SPIRITUAL NAME

Dear Kuntarkis,

For some time now I have been trying to tune into my spiritual name and its symbol. Can you please give me some assistance with this quest? I feel it is important for me to realize this as it will help me with this lifetime journey.

I have also been told that my 'work' will start in a year or two as a very powerful healer/teacher. Can you please give me more insight into this wonderful work for community? I know this is true for it is in my heart.' I'm at the brink of something very big that has to do with the new dimension that earth has slipped into.

Many blessings to you

Deborah.

Kuntarkis replies:

Dear Deborah, Your spiritual name (that has been with you for many of your past and present incarnations) is Nelateer. It is an ancient name from the past civilisation of the Mesopotamians, who existed on your planet over 22,000 years ago of your human time.

One of their most worshipped gods was called Sasahar who gave all names to those who held positions of importance in that society. The name Nelateer means "those who choose a path in healing others".

One thing must always be remembered - when one chooses a path in serving others, whatever the reasons may be, it is important to heal thyself first before healing others. Look at your own life, that is, your health, your thoughts and emotions towards yourself and others. It is important to be balanced in mind, body and spirit, and to love yourself completely unconditionally. As the light of love shines within and around you your consciousness will bring and attract higher energies for healing.

Deborah, believe you are what you are in this moment of human life, not in two years' time, for time is only a creation of man alone. It does not exist in reality. To believe you are in the moment is to know you exist. Yes, the truth is within your heart centre - it is called the Knowing.

The New Dimension that you speak of, which you believe Earth has slipped into, will give all of humanity an opportunity of coming to terms with the self-created human Ego. Humanity cannot advance forward in consciousness until the self-created negative past of each human individual has been confronted and resolved.

The past actions of all human individuals are responsible for the negative creations that are being experienced on your planet at this very moment. Only through total understanding and forgiveness through unconditional love can humanity advance consciously beyond the negative past and present.

The answers of truth are within every individual. Seek your truth from your own being for therein lies the knowing of all that you seek.

Be blessed in love always dear Deborah.

Kuntarkis.

Deborah's reply:

Many, many blessings to you Roman and Kuntarkis. Thank you so much for this insight! My spirit is soaring. This name feels so right and comforting to me. Was there a symbol with the name?

And thanks for the wonderful advice, yes I agree fully. I have always been too critical of myself, which can translate into criticism of others. I have been working on surrendering to the light and love. I have made progress, but still need to do my 'homework'. I ask teachings from my guides and angels at all times.

Sounds like humanity is going to be on a rocky but enlightening road for a while. It will be something to behold!! Again I shower you with love and light.

Deborah.

IS MY DAUGHTER WITH ME?

For Kuntarkis,

I read your story on being fit in mind and body last month. Thank you for answering a question which I have had on what has been a deep rooted problem for many years of my life. It made so much sense to me.

I love your honesty – it warms my heart. I wish most people (like our governments) were like you as the world would be a far better place.

I have one question. I lost my daughter 11 years ago to leukaemia. She was 17. Is it true that I feel her presence around me sometimes? When I dream of her, am I really with her, or is it just my missing her terribly.

Thankyou.

Lilly.

Kuntarkis replies:

Dear Lilly, My Being is honoured that my expressions have helped you answer some questions. Yes you have carried the pain of blame, that in some way you were responsible for your daughter's illness and passing over to the spirit vibration. Please be assured you are not responsible, even though it is a painful experience for human beings to go through. It is a part of the life cycle of living and dying when you exist in physical form.

Death is misunderstood in Western society, mainly because it is hardly spoken of. In many of your Eastern cultures the understanding of death is taught as part of life, and an acceptance of it is taught from childhood, so death to these cultures is accepted as part of the cycle of life. Most of your Western societies have a fear of death, do not talk about it openly and therefore never come to terms with it when faced with the death of someone.

Lilly, to your question. Yes, you are feeling her presence. Your beautiful daughter Tess has been with you since her passing over, and yes you are with her in your time of sleep. What Tess is expressing to you concerning her human death is true. Tess does not blame you in any way for having leukaemia. She loves you with all her heart and always will. Lilly, you gave her so much love while she was on your Earth and she is so grateful for the precious moments you both experienced together as mother and daughter.

The hardest lesson for you Lilly is to now let go of Tess so she can move on with her journey in consciousness, and so you can also move on with your human life. From her heart Tess knows you will always love her and she will always live in your heart. It is time for you to experience more joy in your human life and joy it will be.

Be blessed dear Lilly in love always.

Kuntarkis.

WHAT IS SPIRIT WORLD?

To Kuntarkis,

Is spirit world a beautiful place to live, or is it just another fantasy made up by people? Just wondering if there is any truth to it.

Confused.

Kuntarkis replies:

Dear Human Being, at your tender human age of 13, life can be very confusing. It is good to listen to others expressing their own truth in what they believe does or does not exist. That is also how all human beings learn different lessons and truths of life.

There are many, many different truths which can and do help human beings gain different and deeper understandings. Everything has truth to some degree but your heart is the centre of all knowledge and truth. Ask from your heart any question and truly listen, the first answer is always your truth.

Spirit world is like your human world. There are many different levels of spirit world just like there are many different levels of your human world, the only difference being that you need a physical body to live in your human world where you breathe air, and need to eat, drink, exercise and rest your human body.

In spirit world a physical body does not exist. Both worlds have their purpose. In both worlds you live an existence where you learn, love and experience joy, pain, sadness and happiness. All these experiences are a part of the process of human life. The spirit world is much like the physical human world – it is a place to learn and grow.

Be blessed in love always.

Kuntarkis.

WHEN IS LEARNING COMPLETE?

Dear Kuntarkis,

How will I know when I have learnt all my lessons and have no more to learn?

Will.

Kuntarkis replies:

Dear Will, You have asked a very interesting question.

You will know when your heart is full of unconditional love for your own being and for all other life forms that exist in all Universes. You will express Joy, Love and Happiness in all that you undertake in your human life. Your thoughts will not express any form of judgement but will only express love to others and you will be honoured to share your Wisdom, Understanding and Knowledge to all who seek it.

However, it must be remembered that no one, regardless of where they exist or how evolved their consciousness may be, never stops learning. We may become teachers but we are always students first. As you learn and grow in consciousness the lessons of life change. Always be willing to accept change, for change brings growth.

Conscious growth has many levels of learning. Only by changing your level of thinking, and therefore your thoughts, can you begin the process of self-realisation. Will, only you as an individual can decide if you have no more to learn – you are the power within your existence.

Be blessed in love always.

Kuntarkis.

I NEED MOTIVATION

Dear Kuntarkis,

I wish to find the faith and strength in myself to move forward and do what's best for my life. I have a lot of free time and it would be great to spend that time on practicing meditation and manifestation, but I expect (by looking at my past) that the instant gratification is so low that I may only last 1 or 2 days -or not even begin in the first place. Do I have a psychological block? If so what is it; what belief do I need to change and how best do I do that? Lack of Motivation was an issue I had strongly at University which led to not completing the final year. I fear that my experience at University may also hinder my belief in myself -towards getting things done.

I have spent a lot of money trying to become 'motivated', and I am aware that I may be chasing the wrong 'idea'. However, I believe in you Kuntarkis, I am sure that you are able to understand me and where I'm coming from instantly.

Blessings,

Romen.

Kuntarkis replies:

Dear Romen, Human fear is a creation of the self from one's past. Fear is created from negative experiences and begins even before you are born into your human body.

Every human emotion that your mother experienced during pregnancy is genetically recorded in her cellular matter as well as in yours. Your human father's sperm also has recorded emotions and experiences from his human life that are passed onto you. All of these emotions, negative and positive, are genetically transferred to you while your body is being formed.

As you grow from childhood into adulthood these encoded emotions can be and are activated by situations and experiences in your human life. Most of humanity are not aware of this occurring, but it would be correct to say that most human beings are clones of one or both of their parents, living out their human life through those emotions, rarely discovering or knowing their own individuality.

To be free of negative emotions is to be free of the limiting beliefs and conditioning from one's past. Only by living in the present moment will the individual begin to understand the true meaning of 'just being' in the moment of life itself.

Romen, you say you lack motivation. Yes, there is some truth in your statement. But more to the point, you do not believe in yourself. You have a fear of success, and that is where your psychological block lies. What does fear of success mean? It could mean that you feel you are an unworthy being, or that you are unworthy of achieving success; or it could mean that if you achieve your goals, then what will you do next? For many, the cycle of 'failure' is a way of life, and to change this cycle would mean changing the way one sees themselves.

You do not need to change any belief about yourself to overcome this fear, but rather you need to unconditionally love yourself. Romen, you do not need to physically prove yourself to anyone, not even to you.

The purpose of human life is not about how much a human being can create in the form of material wealth. Humans have been incarnating on your Earth for almost 1 million years and have had thousands of different life experiences. Romen, you have had over 86,000 human incarnations on Earth.

It is true that you have been chasing what you refer to as 'wrong ideas', or as some would say 'going around in circles' while trying to find the truth in the world of humanity outside of yourself. This is akin to finding a needle in a haystack, and while there is nothing wrong in searching for truth in this way, it will take you far longer to discover the truth you seek.

My Being has but one purpose – to pass on knowledge to all human beings so each human being can gain the awareness of self. You Romen, as all human beings, have the knowledge of Creation already within you, but it is your human journey of self-discovery that will connect you with this knowledge.

You are first a spirit, and your spirit is connected to your Soul. Your Soul is the totality of all that is – your Soul is infinite in its knowledge from the past, to the present and even the future.

If you persist, in the silence of your mind you will discover your true self. Through that discovery you will find the motivation you seek. You will also find the faith, courage and strength to do anything you choose to do. However, you must remember that the past is the past. But in the moment, in the stillness of your inner being you will find the meaning of true meditation because meditation is not about thinking or concentrating, it is a transformation of the mind to higher places of communication. You will not only communicate with spirit world but you will also connect to your Soul.

Be blessed Romen in unconditional love always.

Kuntarkis.

WHAT IS MY PURPOSE?

Hello Kuntarkis,

Do you know what my purpose in this life is? I feel that I will soon see spiritual beings, is this correct? When I see colours around people, what does it mean?

Thank you.

Fiona.

Kuntarkis replies:

Dear Fiona, for my Being to tell you what the purpose of your human life is, would mean taking on your personal responsibility. It would be best if your question was answered as follows:

The whole purpose of human life is to learn the lessons of what each human being has chosen to learn prior to incarnation. Lessons can come in many forms and appear under many circumstances. One of the biggest lessons for every human being is to let go of the past and to learn to live and accept the moment.

The past is a creation of the human Ego, created from Fear. Yes, fear comes in many forms. But fear has no power, only the power each human being chooses to give it. And yes, it does depend on the negative and positive emotions a human being experiences throughout their life. Fiona, to believe in yourself, to truly believe is to advance your Conscious Growth.

To see colours around human beings is to see the aura. The aura of a human being tells everything about them, from their past to their present. It can be negative or positive depending on that individual's life experiences. It should also be noted that to have the ability of seeing these colours means also having the wisdom and compassion not to judge what you see. Should a human being with these abilities become judgemental or egotistical about the personal knowledge they are viewing about other human beings through seeing their aura. This ability will be shut off by their higher self so they do no harm to themselves or others.

Be blessed in unconditional love always.

Kuntarkis.

ABOUT THE PLANET NAR'KARISS

Dear Kuntarkis,

I thank you for the information, but I would like to know when the planet Nar'Kariss existed. That is what type of civilisation they are. The name of Angels and higher souls connected to me.

Magnus.

Kuntarkis replies:

Dear Magnus, We the Nar'Karones exist to this present moment, but we no longer exist as physical beings, we exist as living consciousness connected to each other. We think and create or manifest on a single level of consciousness, communicating by thought. Thought creates form and sound on different frequencies.

Our world, Nar'Kariss is 417,000 light years from your home planet Earth. We transformed to light bodies from physical bodies many thousands of human years ago. Our civilization has existed for millions of human years. We have been in your Earth vibration for the last 928 thousand years of your human existence. You are our brothers and sisters. 87,000 of you were placed here on Earth to evolve in your own space and time and we have been observing your growth for that period. There is so much more I could explain to you, but it would take many pages of writing. There will be a book coming in your time and it will be called: **The Book of Knowledge-I am Alien.** It will be a combination of many Stories of Expressions and Questions and Answers from human beings all around your Planet Earth.

Magnus you asked who as higher souls, are connected to you. As you are aware every human being has spirit guides connected to them and these guides are in communication with you all the time, as they are with all human beings. Spirit guides are there simply to help keep you on track so each human being comes to their own self-realisation that they are an infinite spirit on a journey of self-discovery of reconnecting with the Soul.

When a human being learns to have complete trust in themselves and truly believe in their own spiritual awareness, they step beyond the human ego's self-created illusion of fear, the fear which has haunted human beings for their entire evolution. In stepping beyond the fear one can allow their heart to open and experience the awareness of unconditional love.

Magnus, the path to inner truth is no longer the unknown, for this path is the knowing of all that is and it is attainable by all who seek it.

Be blessed in unconditional love always.

Kuntarkis.

QUESTIONS ABOUT LIFE

Dear Kuntarkis,

I was honoured to be put in contact with your site by a friend. I have a few questions about my life, and I was hoping you could help answer. I feel like part of the reason for me to be here is too wrap up old karma, and gain mastery over conditions that have hindered me in the past. I finally feel like I have the tools necessary to learn about unconditional love, the cause of past actions and the ability to gain mastery in this life by the loving grace of God.

It is still an everyday challenge but it is becoming easier as long as I stay committed to myself and the balancing of past energy and actions. I guess my questions are - what is the specific purpose for my spirit's journey on Earth? Who are my guides and how do I stay connected to my purpose and mission?

Finally I have an intense desire to lead a humanitarian or spiritual organization, is this a part of my mission and do you see this happening for me?

I am honoured to ask these questions of you, and if you could answer them or shed light upon my soul path would be appreciated.

In love and service,

Randy.

Kuntarkis replies:

Dear Randy, It is an honourable commitment of the human self to want to help human beings in need, for whatever reason it may be. If you Randy want to lead a humanitarian or spiritual organization then from a human perspective you will need to put the action into your desire so there can be a created and manifested outcome.

Every human being that is present on your human world is there to resolve some form of Karmic debt from the past to the present. Karma was created because of the evolution of the human ego, and it is the human ego that is responsible for all the wars and violence perpetrated upon humanity throughout human history.

Yes, you are as you put it, wrapping up past Karma. The tools to human mastery lie in connecting to your Soul. To connect to your Soul is to take recognition that you are the Soul. Connecting is done through the silence of your human brain, to halt the constant chatter, to allow your mind to connect to higher vibrations and in that nothingness you will connect to your Soul. The most common way to connect is through meditation. Meditation teaches the individual to silence the mind and stop the chatter of the human brain, and this will allow you to hear your inner voice.

Meditation, if persisted with, will help you stay connected to your desired purpose, your intended mission. If you truly believe in yourself and take the moments to persist in your quest, you will create and manifest your desires into reality.

Your specific purpose in your current incarnation is to resolve your Self-Created Karma, and also to learn to love yourself, your being in unconditional love. By doing this you will help guide others in experiencing the same reality.

You have spirit guides from past life connections as well as two spirits guides from other vibrations. One of your other lessons in this human life is to trust and believe in what you feel. Try and not come from the human brain, for it will only give you past recorded memory. Try to come from your heart, for the heart always gives you the truth of the knowing.

Be blessed always in unconditional love

Kuntarkis.

SEARCHING FOR THE MEANING OF LIFE

Hello Roman and Kuntarkis,

I sent an email last night to you Roman and felt the need to send another one. I have spent the day perusing your web site and I must admit I am fascinated and intrigued by what your site has to say. I am a very sceptical person by nature and have spent the best part of my adult life searching and seeking "something". Religion turns me off and makes me want to run the other way. There is something in what you have to say that "resonates and stirs" something within me to want to know more, I don't often feel that. I would like to ask Kuntarkis a question or 2 please.

May you always feel blessed in life?

Suzanne.

Dear Kuntarkis,

I am searching for more meaning in my life and have always felt "different" from others and that I was perhaps here by mistake, as this life has been to date mostly full of pain and suffering and one of isolation through being misunderstood by others. I am very sensitive by nature and believe myself to be a good person though my life experiences have caused another part of me to see life and the world through less innocent eyes. I do not want to waste this lifetime caught up in anger, bitterness and resentment and have worked very hard in overcoming a lot of things so far. I feel like the world is happening and I am out of step with it, and the best way to describe this feeling is like I have been "forgotten." Which leads me to feel that I am here by mistake or that I reincarnated at the wrong time and because I have known much sorrow I believe that in a previous incarnation I must have really been an awful person to have brought such negative karma to this life. Any help and advice from you would be greatly appreciated and could you let me know if I have spirit guides with me and if I have a spiritual name.

Thank you so much for your time and I send you peace and love.

Suzanne.

Kuntarkis replies:

Dear Suzanne, One of the first things for you as a human being to acknowledge and accept is that you are a beautiful human being and a beautiful spirit who is simply on a journey of self-discovery and letting go.

Yes, you Suzanne in this lifetime chose as a human being to pay back past Karmic debt in one lifetime. What is unfortunate is that a human being tends to focus only on the negative aspects of their negative experiences and constantly holds onto those negative emotions, which in turn continue to create their present and influence their future.

By sitting in the stillness of your mind, your Being, you will help bring yourself into balance and allow yourself to see the whole picture without emotion, rather than distorted fragments through subjective eyes. Emotions, as opposed to Feelings, are the negative side of humanity and hold the human individual in their past and their pain, preventing the individual from seeing the truth that exists within, the truth that is the connection to the Soul and the inner voice.

There is no truth on the outside, only an idea of someone else's truth, a truth that is the creation of another individual. What exists on the outside is the truth of the past, always being brought into the present and creating the future. This is the work of the fearful Human Ego, for the Human Ego can only create from what it knows, it's past.

Remember Suzanne, you incarnated into this lifetime because you chose to of your own free will. You will overcome all your obstacles in this lifetime as a human being. Learn to reconnect to your Soul and your journey in your current incarnation will result in great joy. You will know who you truly are, a spirit of divine unconditional love, and you will share this knowing with all who choose to listen to the inner wisdom and knowledge you will share.

See your human life as an opportunity to grow beyond your present understanding. What you are feeling about your life is only what the Human Ego is capable of understanding. The human Ego is the enemy which holds the individual back from conscious awareness and growth.

Yes, you have nine spirit guides with you at different moments in your life. One of these guides is with you always. Her name is Lyuba and yes, she was connected to you in a past incarnation. Your spiritual name is 'Mishaya' and means 'Sun and Moon'.

Only by stepping beyond the emotion of one's life can a human being see the light within themselves.

Be blessed in unconditional love always dear Suzanne.

Kuntarkis.

I WANT TO MEET MY SOUL MATE

Dear Kuntarkis,

I have grown into my maturity through many painful relationships. Before I depart this earthly existence, I wish so much to experience a beautiful relationship with a true love for the first time in my life.

My questions to you Kuntarkis: Is there any indication in my karmic blueprint that I will meet my soul mate in this life, and if so, at what point in my life will this union take place?

I am so very grateful for your insight and help.

April.

Kuntarkis replies:

Dear April, Human life is an illusion created by the mind and manifested by the Soul. Yet, since the mind creates through thoughts, it opens up many possibilities to the human creative side of the imagination. In reality you April, are a very powerful entity, as all human beings are. If you truly believe in yourself and your abilities, through your thoughts you can create and manifest anything into your human life if you truly want to. Spend the moments pondering on what my Being has expressed to you.

Yes, you can have your Soul-Mate in your life if you truly want this to manifest. There is no time factor involved as you alone choose the moment for this to be your creation, and yes every human being deserves unconditional love in their human life.

To achieve this one needs to dissolve all their negative emotions by facing themselves and allowing themselves to experience unconditional love. One of the lessons of human life is to open up their connection to their Soul, this will allow a human being to experience unconditional love of themselves and to know the true meaning of love for all of life in all its forms.

Be blessed in unconditional love always.

Kuntarkis.

WILL WE GET BACK TOGETHER?

Hello Kuntarkis,

My ex-boyfriend wants to be friends and to make sure that everything will work out between him and me. I'm fine with that. He still wants to be with me, he just told me that he needs more time to get things straightened out. Which I'm okay with I just want to know if him and me will ever get back together? Everybody else is saying that we will because of what he tells them and how he acts around me. He is my world, he is everything to me. I love him so much that I hope that we do get back together. He told me before we broke up that I'm the only one that really cares about him. I still do. I still love him and I miss him. All I want is to talk to him alone with interruptions from anyone or anything. How can I talk to him without all those things? I need help, please help me with this.

Ashley.

Kuntarkis replies:

Dear Ashley, Perhaps it is time you took your human head out of the sandpit you have been living in. Look around you and see that your problem is only a grain of sand in the greater scheme of human life. The human world you live in is in pain and confusion. There is more violence on your planet now than the sum of what has been created over humanity's entire existence.

Is it not more important for you Ashley, to grow up and become a little more responsible for your own actions in your human life, rather than giving away your power by having everyone feeling sorry for you because you have nothing else to talk about except your past human boyfriend?

Life is about growing not complaining. Stop and think with reason. If you let go of your past, meaning your past boyfriend, will your life suddenly come to an end? No - it will not. You will move on to the next experience of human your life. Let go of your past, your fears and move one. You may surprise yourself Ashley.

Be blessed in unconditional love always.

Kuntarkis.

NAME OF MY GUIDE PLEASE?

Dear Kuntarkis,

I am happy for your answer. You did not mention the name of beings connected with me so that I may focus on them while doing meditation. Now I know my spiritual name what use will it be to me existing in this present world. I need to know and how to be spiritually aware.

Magnus.

Kuntarkis replies:

Dear Magnus, You ask of my Being for further information on your guides' names so you can meditate on their names. I will respond to your request with the following example:

The one known as Jesus once had a follower who asked many questions and Jesus expressed many answers, but the follower would not try to learn his own lessons of life. Jesus looked at him with love in his heart and said "For that answer, seek and ye shall find".

My Being has expressed many answers but sometimes my Being also realises that certain human beings need to learn to have faith and trust in themselves. Magnus, to truly discover your own inner truth is to discover the compete Bliss of the Knowing.

Allow my Being to express this to you: Meditate on your spiritual name with discipline, even if it takes many meditations. If you truly desire to know your guides names then you will persist and you will never give up. In this you will find true conscious growth and become fully aware of the knowing.

Be blessed in unconditional love always.

Kuntarkis.

WHO HAS AN AURA?

I was wondering who actually has an aura and what is it please.

Amie.

Kuntarkis replies:

Dear Amie, Every living entity, no matter what form it may take, has an Aura field within and around itself, including plants, animals and insects. The aura is an electromagnetic field of energy surrounding the physical form and emanates outwardly from the etheric body. It is a form of radiation formed by the seven major colours of the universe, on your Earth called the rainbow.

Be blessed in unconditional love always.

Kuntarkis.

CROP CIRCLES ARE THEY REAL OR FALSE?

Dear Kuntarkis,

Are the crop circles for real or were they made by people?

Jessie.

Kuntarkis replies:

Dear Jessie, Yes, the creations that you Jessie refer to are created by a race of beings called the **Nar'Karones.** They have watched over humanity for nearly one million of your Earthly years. Crop circles are a form of communication to help human beings realise they are not alone. If you study the Crop Circles and do some research on your internet, you will gather information that will relate to the formations or designs of the Crop Circles. They are placed on your Earth to make a connection with humanity and it won't be too long in your human future, when the creators of the Crop Circles will make a connection for communication with humanity.

Be blessed in unconditional love always.

Kuntarkis.

SUCCESS IN MY LIFE: WHEN?

Hello Kuntarkis,

I would like to know will I ever achieve my dreams, and how old will I be?

Thank you in advance.

Witley.

Kuntarkis replies:

Dear Witley, Many ask the same question of my Being. If you truly believe in yourself and in who you are, then the answer will always be yes, you will reach your visions your dreams. The age is not important if you live in the moment and put the action into your visions now. You will create it in your future. At this moment you are 16. It will be in your early 30's and you will be very pleased and happy. Never lose your dreams or your visions, for you are the power in your human life. You create everything, every thought you as a human individual have can become your reality. Never stop believing in yourself, use your Imagination.

Be blessed unconditional love always.

Kuntarkis.

FATHER HOME SAFE FROM WAR

Dear Kuntarkis,

My Dad is involved in the war in Baghdad. Will he come home safely? Can you tell me this please?

Chris.

Kuntarkis replies:

Dear Chris, Life is a never ending circle always changing, letting go, and living new experiences. Yes, your human Father will return to you in safety.

Be blessed in unconditional love always.

Kuntarkis.

QUEEN OF SHEBA

Dear Kuntarkis,

I saw a program on television about the Queen of Sheba. Was she only a legend or a real person?

Becky.

Kuntarkis replies:

Dear Becky, The one you call, '**The Queen of Sheba**' was in reality a living spirit experiencing a human life. Born upon your Earth around **1015 B.C.** which is in your Earthly time. There are many different stories that are correct in your history, some are close to the truth, and some are simply fantasy. But yes, '**The Queen of Sheba**' was indeed a living truth. She was a seeker of wisdom and truth, which allowed her to gain the knowledge that she deserved so much.

Be blessed in unconditional love always,

Kuntarkis.

TREASURE HUNTER

Hello Kuntarkis,

I am very interested in finding out if there is any truth about hidden treasures from the past, like pirate's treasure, hidden gold in America, and lost treasures from the 2nd World War. Do some of these treasures still exist?

Robert.

Kuntarkis replies:

Dear Robert, You are a seeker of wealth materially, but still a seeker. Yes to all of the above. There is great physical wealth still hidden in your caves, in your Earth, and in your oceans from the past. Many treasures will be discovered by humans in your future and many will not.

Be blessed in unconditional wealth always.

Kuntarkis.

PERSONAL SOUL FOOD AFFIRMATION'S

Affirmations are a wonderful tool for Personal Growth, Self-Improvement, Self-Empowerment, and Goal Setting. We use affirmations all the time, but the secret is, knowing how to use them in a Positive way. For example, if you say to yourself over and over, "I can't do this, I'm not good enough" you create a negative belief about yourself, you are literally saying I am not worthy of success, I am not worthy of being loved, so on and so on.

As we grow into adult hood we have ingrained that negative trace about ourselves, it's like saying, like attracts like, being negative or positive, the choice is always ours alone. Yet that is not to say we cannot change, we can, by changing our thinking towards ourselves, that's why affirmations are so powerful. We can change our thinking by the power of our will to become positive expressions in each of our lives, by changing our negative thoughts about ourselves and others into positive ones. That's where affirmations can help put all of us onto the road to freedom from our own self-created way of thinking.

Affirmations are used in many ways, from athletes, entertainer's preparing themselves mentally for competition or performance, to the humble prayers people use daily. Positive affirmations is used to overwrite the negative beliefs we have adopted, and they can be anything from a few simple words to a more elaborate offering.

Affirmations are designed to help build self-esteem and self-confidence, reminding us that we each are something far greater and more powerful than the trivialities which hold us back in everyday life. Used once a day, or several times a day for greater effect, affirmations when practiced with sincerity, will help you feel a difference inside, as well you will begin to feel good about yourself.

Note: chose the ones that make you feel good.

Soul food Affirmation's: Grieving (1)

I will allow myself to grieve for it's a natural process of human life.

The pain that I am feeling must be, so I may learn and understand that I have chosen this experience.

The experience of grieving is for my higher good, and enables me to grow beyond this emotion with an understanding that it is my choice alone how long I grieve.

The sooner I let go and forgive the sooner I can move on with my life and be a better human being, one who has grown stronger and more aware of the natural process of human life.

This I say. This I experience. This is my choice.

I am love. I am my soul. I am that I am.

I am infinite.

Author: Kuntarkis.

Soul Food Affirmation: Changing Beliefs (2)

I, (your name), can admit to myself that I have been living to a truth filled with belief systems, and yes, this has limited me and inhibited me in expressing myself in what I truly believe life to be.

From this moment on I will try with all my being to consciously make my connection to my Soul.

By doing this I am taking personnel responsibility in all that I do and say. I will also listen to my inner self, my Soul, for that is being a true individual. That is inner truth.

This I say and this I am doing.

I am my Soul. I am that I am.

Author: Kuntarkis.

Soul Food Affirmation: Creating my Future (3)

I wish to be a creative being. I see myself as a creative being. I am in actual fact a creative being and I have been creating all that I am from the past to the present.

I am creating my future from the present moment.

I have in this most precious moment one of the strongest realisations.

I am in fact a creative being, for every moment that is what I am doing.

I'm being creative.

I say unto myself, from this moment on I intend to create my life exactly how I wish it to be, because I am truly the power source of all that I am.

I am my Soul. I am that I am.

Author: Kuntarkis.

Soul Food Affirmation: Deserve Good Fortune (4)

Ask yourself the question, and be true to yourself in your answer, because truth sets you free, whereas lies imprisons you in a world of illusion and fear, and fear is the self-created word of ego. Now, ask yourself this question:

Do I (your name), deserve to have a life that is full of joy, happiness, peace, unconditional love and good fortune in my present human life?

(State your answer, yes or no)

If yes, then I make this conscious choice in this moment to face myself, my ego, from my own self-created illusion, and I will begin the process of changing how I think and feel about myself, because if I do this, I know I will begin to see others in a different light.

The negative aspect of human life was simply to learn the lessons and then to let go and move on, to let the past be the past, not to be relived over and over again, for that is simply fear.

Fear is created by beliefs' and conditioning.

You, dear sisters and brothers, were never meant to stay in the land of the fear.

Again, it simply lessons of life, once experienced you understand, and then move on. That is conscious evolution that is unconditional love that is finding freedom.

Be blessed in love always.

Author: Kuntarkis.

Soul Food Affirmation: Imagination (5)

To believe in imagination is the first step to awareness and conscious growth. If you the human individual practice any form of meditation you are using your imagination, and through imagination you can manifest any reality that you can envisage. This is using the power of thought.

As I sit and ponder I allow images to be created in my mind, for my mind is my whole being. I will, through my thoughts, create images of how I want my life to be, and I will practice this daily, even for a few moments.

I truly believe in myself that I am much more than just this human body. I am living consciousness, expressing through a physical self. Yet I am so much more. It's my journey to discover the unknown essence of who I am.

I am that I am, infinite in all that is. I am light.

Author: Kuntarkis.

Soul Food Affirmation: How I see
myself is how I see others (6)

Is this my truth or simply my own created illusion from my negative past, which has become my present, and sadly my future?

I will stop in this moment and look at myself without any judgement, and if I see the illusion of my own self-created ego, I will, from this moment on, begin the process of changing my thinking towards myself and others.

I will begin to tell myself that I am worthy of love, and through that statement I will allow the process of love to flow through myself, every moment of my life. I will love who I am in the essence of love itself.

I am that I am. I am Light.

<u>Author:</u> Kuntarkis.

<u>Soul Food Affirmation: Joy of Love (7)</u>

To bring Joy to your heart is to bring the Joy of who you are to others, because you emit the Joy of Love from your very Being.

You are the Joy, Love the Knowledge: It is all around you and within you always, as is the Joy of Christmas. It all begins with you, does it not?

Admit this: what I feel, I become: What I think, will be manifested into my life.

Only you can receive Joy, Happiness, Love and Wealth. It is all in your thinking.

The power of imagination is the power of self-manifestation, which always becomes one's reality.

The choice is always yours alone, be it negative or positive,

For Free Will is a Gift.

<u>Author:</u> Kuntarkis.

Soul Food Affirmation: Shift in Consciousness (8)

I want to change my Reality and become a more positive
human being.

I know by changing my reality, I am changing my thoughts,
and by changing my thoughts, I am creating a shift in my own
consciousness.

I will expand my own awareness in everything that I do and
create, and thereby become a more positive human being.

I will create my own reality, which will not only enhance my
future, but also help others in a more positive manner. This I
say, and this I will do. I am that I am.

I am Light.

Author: Kuntarkis.

Soul Food Affirmation: Channel of Light (9)

From this moment on I will become a channel for knowledge.

I will share this knowledge with all who choose to listen. I will
be a channel of unconditional love, and I will be a Light for
all to see.

In this most precious moment I make a pledge to my higher
self, that I will let go of all that is no longer needed and
replace it with understanding, compassion, truth, love and the
will to continue my path in my human life.

I am a Channel of Light:

A Channel of Healing, of Knowledge, of Unconditional Love.

I am Light. I am that I am.

Author: Kuntarkis.

Soul Food Affirmation: Hope is a Negative (10)

To believe in something you cannot see is more powerful in reality than to believe in something you already can see or believe.

It is like saying "I hope one day I will go there". Hope is a negative, for to hope in reality leads to hopelessness.

But to have faith or trust is to truly believe in yourself or others. That is truly being positive. It is all in the word, is it not?

Author: Kuntarkis.

Soul Food Affirmation: Mother Earth (11)

As I walk upon this most precious Earth I call home I will allow myself to feel the presence of Mother Earth herself.

I will in my quiet time send unconditional love to the Earth. To all life forms, to spirit world,

And especially I will send White Light to all disincarnate spirits, to help them in their transition from the physical to the spirit plane.

I will guide them not only to go through the Light, But also to help them understand that they no longer need to hold on to the pain that they created while in physical form.

I will help to teach and guide them that unconditional love is forgiveness.

This is what I will do.

I am the Light, the spark of Creation.

What is within Creation is also within my Being.

I am Light, I am that I am.

Author: Kuntarkis.

Soul Food Affirmation: Healthy in Mind and Body (12)

I am a positive person. I am full of Love and life.

I am full of vitality. I am always healthy in mind and body.

I love and accept myself. I am a beautiful person, and have a beautiful heart.

I can do anything I choose to do. I am strong, I have a strong will.

Today I will accomplish all my tasks.

I love myself and I love my body. I will focus on the positive side of life.

As I wake from my sleep I realise I have two choices: create a negative day or a positive day. I choose on this day to be completely positive in all that I do.

I see with new eyes all that surrounds me including the opportunity for change. I will create more positive outcomes in my life today, NOW.

I choose to be healthy in mind and body, now and in every moment to come.

I love who I am, NOW.

<u>Author:</u> Kuntarkis.

<u>Soul Food Affirmation: I am Immortal (13)</u>

To know that I am Light is a truth within itself.

To know that light is infinite is to have a self-realisation that I am also infinite.

To be infinite is to realise that I am immortal in the scheme of all that is.

I am Light. I am that I am... I am a being on a journey of self-discovery.

That is what I am. I am that I am: Light itself.

<u>Author:</u> Kuntarkis.

<u>Soul Food Affirmation: Who I Truly Am (14)</u>

To reach out to my Soul is to reach out to who I truly am. That connection to my Soul will change my level of understanding forever.

I will not be ignorant anymore. By knowing my Soul I will allow myself to know the Light of all that is within me, within Creation, with totality.

I will walk through life and allow my light, my all, to guide my footsteps in my human life.

I know the Light. I know my Soul. This is my freedom. This is my knowing the Light.

Author: Kuntarkis.

Soul Food Affirmation: Let go of the past (15)

From this moment on I will learn to forgive and let go of the past; I will see it simply as a memory.

I will begin in this moment – the NOW – to create my future from a more loving and understanding heart.

I will, yes, I WILL live moment to moment, and I will open my human eyes to what surrounds me and be more aware of my surroundings.

I know by living my truth from a loving heart, I will become the Living Truth.

I love Mother Earth. I love Spirit. I love my Soul. I am living in the Now.

I am that I am, the Living Truth.

Author: Kuntarkis.

Soul Food Affirmation: Born into Physical life (16)

From the moment I was born into this physical life,

I have understood that I am special, that I am worthy of creating great things in my life as a human being.

I realise that I have the potential to accomplish anything I put my mind to.

I will from this moment on allow myself to grow consciously and become aware of any opportunities that come into my life.

This includes having or attracting someone into my life, and

Having a loving, caring, balanced relationship with that person.

I deserve the best from life, and to this I will commit my energies to bring it into my present and have it fully manifested into my reality.

Author: Kuntarkis.

Soul Food Affirmation: More than Physical self (17)

I have come to realise that I am far more than just this physical self.

I know at this present moment I am living a physical existence in this third dimensional world.

Yet to my present understanding I am far more than this physical self of dense matter. I am a Spirit which is endless, timeless, ageless and infinite.

Even though my Spirit is a part of my physical self, my Spirit can never perish. My Spirit is a facet of my Soul.

I have also begun to realise that I can, though the power of my will and thoughts, project my Spirit outside of my physical self, and be fully conscious of this event.

Through my mind's eye I will manifest this into my reality with full awareness, and I will enter into the vibration of Spirit World where I will learn, observe and bring back knowledge into my physical world to help my being understand that there are many levels of consciousness.

I will practice this each day of my life and be fully conscious of all of my experiences and actions, and I will use this knowledge for the higher good of all life forms.

This I say and this I will do, now.

I am, I have, and I will project my Spirit right now.

Author: Kuntarkis.

Soul Food Affirmation: Self-Created Fears (18)

From this moment on I will not allow my self-created fears to rule my life.

I have come to my own self-realisation that I can make any changes required in my life if I choose to, at any given moment.

I choose this moment and I will begin with something small. I allow myself to recognise that I have beautiful eyes, and when I look at my eyes in the mirror I know I am looking into my Soul.

I am my Soul and I know my Soul helped to create this beautiful human being that I am in this moment. I will, through my beautiful eyes, see the beauty in everything that I look upon.

This is my first step to ultimate freedom from self-imposed limitations. This is my truth, my truth alone. I am that I am.

Author: Kuntarkis.

Soul Food Affirmation: Change my thinking: (19)

I, the individual, in this most precious moment of my life, will change my thinking and my understanding towards myself, and I will change how I see myself in this present incarnation that I am experiencing.

Even though I am experiencing many negative creations in my human life, I will from this moment on not judge my life, or anyone else's.

I will learn to calm my emotions and to see opportunities for me to learn from. One thing I am completely positive about is the knowing that I am an infinite spark of living consciousness on my own journey of Self-Realisation.

I will seek love in all I do and experience, for it is Unconditional Love that will open the door to the self and give me the Freedom and Peace I am seeking.

Author: Kuntarkis.

Soul Food Affirmation: I will Seek Truth from within: (20)

I have come to realise how important truth is to me. I have decided that from this moment on I will seek truth from within my own inner Being.

I know there are Seven Billion truths on this planet, but I also know they are each individual's idea of truth. I know every human being has their own idea of truth and that is okay with me. I will be open to their truth without any form of judgement or criticism.

I will open my mind and my heart, and in the silence of my Being, I will ask my Soul to guide my being to truth itself.

I am that I am. I am the Living Truth.

Author: Kuntarkis.

Soul Food Affirmation: I am searching (21)

I am searching,

Yet I ask my Being "what am I searching for?"

For truth, for knowledge, for peace, for

Harmony, for joy, for unconditional love.

Do I search outwardly or inwardly?

To search outwardly is to search from a Physical understanding, but to search inwardly is to search from a Spirit understanding.

Both are just as good, but one will take a lot longer.

"Which one will I begin with? Does it matter?"

No, it does not matter. Both will lead you to the same truth, but you alone are the one who must make that choice.

"So which one will I choose?"

The balance of all of life is when it comes into union, the union of Spirit and flesh as one.

Author: Kuntarkis.

Soul Food Affirmation: Spiritually and Emotionally (22)

I will persist in advancing myself Physically, Spiritually and Emotionally to become a better Human Being, and to advance myself Consciously so my future Incarnations will lead to new lessons in Human Life rather than repeating the same lessons over and over again.

This I say and this I will do.

Author: Kuntarkis.

Soul Food Affirmation: Go Beyond your Present (23)

To change your life, first begin by changing your thinking. Go beyond your present way of seeing yourself and the world you have created around yourself.

The past is the past. Do not allow the past to keep creating your future. You are responsible for your life and all the actions you have taken in your life, be it negative or positive, for you alone have created your present life as a human being. It all begins with you. So what are you going to do?

Will you change to a higher understanding and grow consciously? Or will you keep blaming others for how you turned out?

You are the power of your own destiny.

Author: Kuntarkis.

Soul Food Affirmation: Stand before myself (24)

As I (your name) stand before myself, looking into a mirror of self-reflection, I know all that I am and have been is a creation of my past. All that I am to this moment in my life is a creation of my childhood into adulthood.

My fears of my past are my creation of cause and effect, be it negative or positive. I now realise that all lessons and experiences, whether negative or positive, are not to be judged by myself or others. They are simply lessons of my human life. As I sit in my quiet place of peace I allow all my thoughts to be present, not to see them as good or bad, simply as thoughts of expression. I realise what I think of myself I will eventually become, so from this moment on I will not place judgement on myself or others. I will allow the natural process of my life to create my present and my future, and be completely unbiased to the negative and positive aspects of my life and others. I will allow life to just be in the moment.

I love my being as I love my Soul. I am that I am.

Author: Kuntarkis.

Soul Food Affirmation: The moment of truth (25)

The moment of truth can only be manifested when I, the human individual, make a conscious decision to step beyond my past and be willing to face myself.

When I am willing to dissolve my own created ego, only then can the truth be manifested, only then can unconditional love be a part of all that I do.

I am Love.

I am Light.

I Am that I Am.

Author: Kuntarkis.

Soul Food Affirmation: Collection of thoughts: (26)

This is a collection of thoughts to help you make a closer connection to your Soul'.

I am the Soul,

I am the Light,

I am Love,

I am Will,

I am the moment of life.

Yes, I the individual have come to my own understanding that I am an infinite spark of living consciousness.

I truly am timeless,

I am ageless,

I am endless,

I am eternal.

To connect to my Soul I need to become aware that I alone must make this personal journey to go within my Being, to become true to myself and take full responsibility for who and what I am.

I must ask my Soul to guide all my human affairs because by allowing,

The Light of my Soul to shine through my human self,

I will bring balance to all that I do, to all that I am.

I am the Soul.

I am that I am.

Author: Kuntarkis.

Soul Food Affirmation: Open my heart (27)

I (your name), in this most precious moment of my life, open my heart and allow my unconditional love to flow throughout my inner being and outer self.

I no longer hold onto my pain of the past. I release all my pain and I see it dissolve in my light.

I truly believe that I am a spirit being living a physical human life, simply here to learn and experience.

I will live only in the moment and I will give myself more moments to understand my own feelings, and I will walk through life with an open heart and mind. This I say as my truth and this I will do.

I am that I am - Light itself.

<u>Author: Kuntarkis.</u>

<u>Soul Food Affirmation: Allow myself the freedom (28)</u>

I sit in the stillness of my mind and allow myself the freedom to become whoever I choose to become and to experience whatever I choose to experience in this present life that I alone have chosen.

I allow myself to create and be responsible for all my self-created circumstances from the past to the present.

I am a beautiful human being in this most precious moment of my own created existence.

I love and respect who and what I am.

I am a Spirit being who is infinite in all things.

I am that I am, now and forever more.

I am Love.

<u>Author: Kuntarkis.</u>

Soul Food Affirmation: Who am I? (29)

Who am I?

I am an infinite, timeless, ageless, eternal Being of Light on a journey of self-realisation.

What am I?

I am a spark of living consciousness, a spirit who is connected to all of Creations totality. I have always been and always will be almighty present in the moment of all that is. In this most precious moment of my existence I am experiencing the life of a physical human being in order to learn and understand the lessons I have chosen, be they negative or positive. Everything is my choice. This I truly understand.

Where am I going?

Wherever the flow of energy takes me, depending on my awareness and understanding of who I truly am. I will step beyond my own self-created limitations, my boundaries which I alone have created from my own fears. I am first a spirit being who can create harmony, joy, love and balance in my life as a human being. I have the courage and strength to become whatever I choose to be.

Yes, I truly am infinite. I am that I am.

Author: Kuntarkis.

Soul Food Affirmation: Love yourself unconditionally (30)

To love yourself unconditionally is to love others unconditionally.

To believe in yourself is to believe in others.

To forgive yourself is have the understanding and wisdom to forgive others.

To have an open mind allows you to listen to others without prejudice and judgement.

To step beyond the fears of your past is to live a life without limitations or boundaries.

To heal yourself is to gain knowledge, wisdom, understanding and compassion to help heal others.

To step beyond self-created ignorance is to step into complete bliss.

To meditate in the stillness of your mind, your inner being, is to enter the inner chamber of your infinite wisdom.

To dissolve the human ego is to set yourself free from all the fears and insecurities that have been created from your past through negative experiences from one life time to the next.

To have love in your heart for all forms of life, no matter what form they may be, is to be a true human being: one who is full of compassion and love, one who has infinite knowledge of all Universes, one who has the understanding and knowing of the true purpose of life.

Author: Kuntarkis.

Soul Food Affirmation: I choose now (31)

I choose now, in this moment of life, to step into the Light of Creation.

I am a part of Creation's totality as I am a part of all life forms throughout all Universes.

All life forms throughout all Universes are a part of my Being of Light.

We are all brothers and sisters on a journey of self-discovery to the realisation that we are all infinite beings of living consciousness.

My Being expanding in consciousness is an awakening for all other universal life forms.

I am and I choose to be a beacon of light for all to see, to grow from and to expand beyond the physical flesh of matter into pure consciousness with the full awareness of my Being in the moment of life.

Author: Kuntarkis.

Soul Food Affirmation: Expressed by Kuntarkis (32)

The following small affirmation was expressed by Kuntarkis when he was in human form. He was speaking to a group of people and the following question was asked:

How will we know the truth? Will it come to us in form (another human being? Words (spoken or read) or symbol (physical manifestation in nature)?

Kuntarkis replied:

Each of you shall know the truth, only when you know yourself.

Kuntarkis Explains:

Dear Human Beings of Earth, the truth is almighty present within all human beings. It always has been and always will be.

Remember, the human ego is your enemy. It keeps the individual locked away in their thinking, a mental prison created by humanity alone.

The Truth can only come through self-realisation when conscious awareness is present, not human ego.

Unconditional love from the heart is the opening to your inner truth.

To know thy self is to find completeness and bliss.

Author: Kuntarkis.

Soul Food Affirmation: To make me complete (33)

Spirit of Light, I ask that you come into my Being; to make me complete, that I may become aware of your presence and of my own Light that is of Creation's totality.

I ask Spirit of Light to protect my essence, my spirit, my all, from all the darkness that has and is surrounding this most precious Mother Earth.

I ask Spirit of Light to help me cleanse my Being of all self-created negative thoughts and actions. That they be dissolved back into the nothingness from which they were first created.

I realise by cleansing my being of all negativity I will begin to see life with new eyes, that truth will also become a part of my life.

For I choose Light and now I am light itself.

Thank you Spirit of Light forever more.

I am that I am.

Author: Kuntarkis.

Soul Food Affirmation: I am the power in my human life (34)

I am the power in my human life.

I am the master of all my creations in my human life.

I create all my thoughts, be they negative or positive, and they create every circumstance or action.

To admit this to myself, my own Being, makes me realise that I can create a life of negative actions which will create only pain and misery for myself and others.

OR

I can choose to create positive actions in all that I do in my human life.

Positive actions will not only benefit my own Being but also others.

By doing this for my own growth and learning I will create a more balanced positive energy which will create peace and harmony within me and all around me.

This I choose to do in this most precious moment.

Author: Kuntarkis.

Soul Food Affirmation: I will love you forever (35)

I (your name) will pledge to my inner and outer being that I will love you forever. I will, yes I will. And I will search and discover who I truly am in this infinite universe that I am a part of.

I know I have walked upon this most precious Earth many, many lifetimes and I have experienced many lessons of life.

I promise to unlock the secrets of my past that are encoded in all my cells, to truly discover my truth. I will truly become one with all things as all things will become one with me.

I feel my strength within me to step beyond what I am and I feel my love expanding into infinite space. Oh how I truly am connected to all of Creation's totality – the light. The light is completeness and bliss.

Author: Kuntarkis.

Soul Food Affirmation: Move onto new experiences (36)

Is it not true that change is all about letting go of the past, to move onto the new experience? Then I choose to change, to let go, to forgive myself and anyone who has caused me pain.

I also choose to be more responsible for my actions in my life. I will stop and think before I do, and if I feel it could cause harm to another, I will not proceed in that action.

I will also be careful with my thoughts towards myself and others. I will recognise when I am placing judgement upon myself, and especially others.

I can admit to myself that I do need change in my life, so I will change how I feel about myself and I will allow myself to grow to be a better, happier person.

And I will learn to love myself, truly love myself.

<u>Author:</u> Kuntarkis.

<u>Soul Food Affirmation: I see all the Pain and Misery (37)</u>

I walk through life and see all the pain and misery that we humans create from one lifetime to the next. Each of us have the power of Light within us and around us to stop the suffering that creates such pain for all our Sisters and Brothers.

I know we are all connected to each other and that we are all created from the same Light of Creation. It is only our Ego from our created past that continually creates our pain in the present and the future.

I, the individual, choose this moment not to be part of the Ego's past.

I let go of all my pains and suffering by expressing only Light to all my Sisters and Brothers, no matter who they are or what they have done.

I forgive myself and all my Sisters and Brothers, and now choose to express from the Light within my heart, now and forever more.

I am Light. I am Love. I am Infinite.

<u>Author</u>: Kuntarkis.

<u>Soul Food Affirmation: I am Infinite (38)</u>

I am an infinite Being of Light, living and experiencing a human existence. I have begun to become aware of my connections to this planet called Mother Earth. I realise my flesh body is made from the clay of Mother Earth, the Spirit within me is a spark of the spirit from Mother Earth, and the elements of Fire, Water, Earth, Air and Spirit that make up my Being are within all of life.

I sit in the stillness of my mind and my thoughts go out to Mother Earth so I can connect with the essence of Mother Earth. I ask for healing and forgiveness for all the pain humanity has placed upon and within Mother Earth. As I am healed in the loving energies of Mother Earth I project back the same energies of love and healing to help bring the balance of Peace, Harmony and Forgiveness upon Mother Earth. For without Mother Earth we as human beings could not exist and experience life's wonders.

I am blessed in the love of our most precious Mother Earth.

<u>Author: Kuntarkis.</u>

Soul Food Affirmation: On Nar'Kariss (39)

My Being was asked to provide an affirmation that was used on "Nar'Kariss".

I would like to share it with you... When you express the following words please feel them from your heart centre- the effect will be overwhelming. Please enjoy.

The Light is my strength. Creation is my truth. Love is my essence and ultimate path to freedom, self-realisation and the wonderment of my own Beingness.

In the knowing that I am a part of everything and everything is a part of me, I give of myself to the Universal Mind of Creation's totality freely, for the good of all life.

For Creation and I are one, therefore the self, which is ego that stands in the way, must be dissolved before the real can come into being, through unconditional love alone.

I am Light, I am Love.   I am infinite and eternal. I Am that I Am.

Author: Kuntarkis.

Soul Food Affirmation: What keeps me blind from seeking? (40)

I want to know who I am. I want to know what I am. I want to know why I am.

Or is my answer beyond myself? Is it my human confusion keeping me from the truth?

Is it the pain that I alone have created through my life in human form that keeps me blind from ever seeking beyond my present understanding? Or is it my beliefs and my conditioning that allows me to live a life of confusion and illusion?

Then how do I break the chains of my self-created prison, surrounding me every moment of my life?

To have the courage to step beyond who you have become is the beginning of your transformation; the transformation from your life as Ego to Living Consciousness'.

Remember, you are a spirit living a physical human life and that inner knowledge is freedom. When the mind is free, the spirit soars.

Author: Kuntarkis.

Soul Food Affirmation: Coming to Self-Realisation (41)

I have come to the realisation that I walk through life with no awareness only beliefs, conditioning and fears. I have now had a conscious realisation that my fears have created my past and present.

I have consciously decided I will not allow my fears to create my future. I am stepping out of my dark place of safety and stepping into my light. I realise, only in the light of Unconditional Love can I break free from my fears of the past and present.

I will step into my future from the present moment with Unconditional Love for myself and all of Creation's life forms.

I am that I am. I am Light, now and forever more.

<u>Author</u>: Kuntarkis.

<u>Soul Food Affirmation: I stand on the edge of time (42)</u>

I stand on the edge of time. As I begin my journey through this human life that I have chosen. I accept the knowing that I alone have created every experience and circumstance that has shaped my life up to this most precious moment.

I have and I will take Personal Responsibility for all of my actions, be they negative or positive. I admit my Self-Created faults that have caused my pain, and I admit that I have also imposed this pain upon others.

From this moment on I will no longer place judgement upon myself, nor upon others. Through forgiveness and letting go of all my pain and suffering, which I accept that I have created, I will no longer blame others for my fears and pain.

I will replace my pain with Unconditional Love for my personal growth and understanding, and I will fill my heart, my Soul, my very being with the Light of Creation. I will emanate this Light to all who come into my life's journey.

I admit now in this most precious moment that I love myself as I would love all forms of life. For the first time in my life my eyes are truly opened. I see with new eyes the beauty in all life, for I am on my journey of Self-Expression.

I am love. I am an infinite being of Creation's totality.

I am that I am. I am Light.

Author: Kuntarkis.

Soul Food Affirmation: Communicator of Knowledge (43)

I can and I will allow the energy from my being to flow throughout my essence so I can become a Communicator of Knowledge.

I will sit in my quiet time, without thoughts and without emotions, and I will allow my Spirit to write through my Being the knowledge that is infinite.

It will flow through my Being on paper so that whoever wishes to read and be inspired, can also become a Communicator of Knowledge for the higher good of all.

I will choose to be a Light Worker in the totality of Creation, of which I am a part of, as is all of life.

I am that I am.

Author: Kuntarkis.

Soul Food Affirmation: I am questioning my beliefs (44)

I believe I can choose to believe in anything I want to believe in, yet I am beginning to question my beliefs in what and who I am. There is a feeling deep within me, and I am beginning to question my truth.

I have decided to step beyond my beliefs and conditioning of my life, and I now seek a deeper more clear understanding from within myself.

I need to find out who or what is driving my life in its present direction. I will do this for myself and my own advancement to my consciousness. I simply am one who seeks the truth and the meaning of my existence.

Who am I?

Seek and ye shall find.

<u>Author: Kuntarkis.</u>

<u>Soul Food Affirmation: I am happy (45)</u>

I am a happy, loving human being. I have happy thoughts in myself and I express happy thoughts to my friends and family, and to whoever I meet.

I believe happiness creates the balance of my life and I deserve to be a happy loving human being.

So each morning when I awake I will express only happy thoughts and throughout my life, my happy thoughts will be an expression of my true self.

I love my happy thoughts as I truly love my own Beingness and life itself.

I am happy.

<u>Author: Kuntarkis.</u>

Soul Food Affirmation: To pause and think (46)

There is a moment in everyone's life when one needs to
Pause, to Stop and Think:

Who am I truly? Am I this solid mass of physical self, living
day to day, and existing in the confusion that surrounds me?
Or is this all a dream, created from my past, through my
beliefs and conditioning?

Am I living my past over and over again, only seeing my
life through confusion? Or am I living a past of genetically
encoded information, passed onto me from my parents.

When I pause, stop and think I see so many similarities
between myself and my parents. Sometimes when I look into
a mirror, my fears are present. I still have not discovered my
Individuality.

In this moment I make a promise to myself – I will spend
many more moments seeking from within myself my Identity,
my Truth, my Path in life. When I have children I will make
it my Quest to Enlighten them, to help them discover their
true self and their individuality. This I say and this I will do
for the good of all concerned.

Author: Kuntarkis.

Soul Food Affirmation: I walk upon this precious Earth (47)

I walk upon this precious Earth that has been created by
Creation, and which I am part of.

For the first time in my human life I realise that Love is
the most important lesson for all of Humanity to learn and

experience. All other lessons in life have no purpose if Love, being Unconditional, is not a part of those experiences.

I need to be true to myself. From this moment on I will love who and what I am with all my Being. I will allow love to emanate within me and all around me. I will express this Infinite Love to all from my Truth and I will share my Knowledge and Understanding with whoever chooses to listen.

Unconditional Love is the key to Forgiveness and the path to emotional freedom, for wherever Love exists, Truth will be present.

The human Ego is of a negative energy and cannot exist where there is Love.

I am love. I am light. I am reborn in Love and Light.

I simply am an Infinite Spirit. I am that I am.

<u>Author:</u> Kuntarkis.

<u>Soul Food Affirmation: Spirits of Light (48)</u>

I (your name) call upon the Spirits of Light to help me become aware of my own Self-Created surroundings, to give me insight into what I have attracted into my life.

For the first time in my life I am fully aware that I need to make changes for my growth, by letting go of all things that no longer have a meaning in my life, and not allow any more negative distractions to keep me from reaching my goal in life.

Even though it may cause pain to me and to others, I do realise it will be a step towards my Conscious Growth, Awareness and Understanding.

I now step into the Light and heal my past to create my present and my future.

I am that I am. I am Light.

<u>Author:</u> Kuntarkis.

<u>Soul Food Affirmation: Love within my Heart (49)</u>

I release in this moment of my human life the Unconditional Love within my heart.

I allow this Unconditional Love to emanate within my being and around my outer self.

It helps heal my pain and fears so I may let go of my past, and so that I may come to my own Self-Realisation that I am truly a being of Unlimited Light.

I can heal and share this light of Love with all who come into my presence, for we are all beings of Infinite Light, and Unconditional Love is our Birth-Right.

I walk in the Light now and forever more. I am that I am.

<u>Author:</u> Kuntarkis.

<u>Soul Food Affirmation: I sit quietly in the Light (50)</u>

I sit quietly in the light of Creation and allow my Mind, my Being, to be still.

I allow myself the Moments for Communication not only for my own inner Being, but also for my Brothers and Sisters who live in other Realms and Dimensions.

I ask and I send my request for Communication, to exchange Knowledge and Wisdom for the good of my Being, for humanity and all of life.

I wait and I sit in the Stillness of my Mind, my Being, always in the Light of Creation's totality, now and forever more.

Author: Kuntarkis.

Soul Food Affirmation: Every moment of my human life (51)

Every moment of my human life, I confirm to myself, my being, that I am, I will, I have stepped beyond my fears, my beliefs and my conditioning.

I will go forward in the knowing of my true self.

I alone have the Power, Strength and Courage to transform my being into a human being who will no longer be bound by the Self-Created Limitations of the Human Ego.

I choose Light. I am Light – infinite in the scheme of all life.

I give of myself to Creations totality for the higher good of all life.

Author: Kuntarkis.

Soul Food Affirmation: I raise my awareness (52)

In this most precious moment of my life, I raise my awareness to many levels of consciousness, for my Being is expressing and experiencing many different dimensions at the same time.

I allow my life in this moment to be in total bliss.

My mind, my all, is free from all distractions of Human Ego.

In the Stillness of my Mind I allow and bring forth the Knowledge of the Knowing, from the Past to the Present, and into the Future, so I can share my all for the good of all life.

I am truly blessed now and forever more.

<u>Author:</u> Kuntarkis.

<u>Soul Food Affirmation: Truth is what I seek (53)</u>

Truth and only the truth is what I seek.

I have finally come to the understanding that my search for the truth has always been outside of myself, from the words of others.

In accepting the words of others I have given away my Power and Personal Responsibility. I have come to a Self-Realisation that I am an Infinite being of light, a part of all life.

I keep an open mind to all things and I am always willing to listen to others. But I realise that I have the Knowledge of the Universe within my very being, my Essence, my Soul.

I pledge unto myself a simple truth. I will go within my being: I will listen and learn to understand my human self. I will grow as a living being of Light and expand my Awareness.

I will seek the Knowledge of Truth from the past to the present moment, and in turn will create my future in total balance. I also commit myself to helping others discover their truth, which is within them as it is within all of life.

I will ask three questions:

1. Who am I'? I am that I am. No more. No less.

2. What am I? I am a Spirit being living and experiencing a human existence.

3. Where am I going? Through the grace of Creation, wherever my being takes me.

Author: Kuntarkis.

Soul Food Affirmation: The dark clouds of my mind (54)

As I walk in the dark clouds of my mind, I recognise the negative emotions that have surrounded me throughout my life. I see how they have shaped the level of my understanding and thinking, and how I feel about myself and those around me.

I have decided in this moment of my existence to look at all my negative emotions one by one.

I will choose through my free will to forgive all those who have caused my being and my life pain, from the past to the present moment.

I choose to forgive myself in Unconditional Love, and I choose to be kinder to myself and those around me.

I will be more careful in my thoughts, to not project negative energies to myself or anyone else. Instead, I will project a deeper understanding, beyond Human Ego.

I will project pure Unconditional Love without judgement.

I will allow this healing process of my human life to give my being Wisdom and an understanding heart so that I may grow in Consciousness for the good of all life in all Universes.

I accept who and what I am, now and forever more. My self-realisation is in the knowing that I am an Infinite Spirit being living a human physical life in this most precious moment.

Love is ...I Am that I Am.

Author: Kuntarkis.

Soul Food Affirmation: Present in this moment (55)

I, who am almighty present in this moment of my Self-Created reality, choose to step and grow beyond my present level of thinking and understanding.

I will allow my being to progress to a Higher Vibration in pure Consciousness so that I can enhance my Natural Psychic Abilities in order to manifest for the higher good of all life.

Through my understanding of Creation, I will Channel Light in pure Unconditional Love. I will allow my Human Ego to dissolve into the nothingness from which it first was created. I will allow it to become the past, only to be seen as a memory of my life's experiences.

I am that I am- Ageless, Timeless, and Endless, beyond Third Dimensional Thinking.

I stand in the Light. I am the Light now and forever more.

Author: Kuntarkis.

Soul Food Affirmation: I sit and Ponder (56)

I sit and ponder with thoughts of this most precious Earth that I live upon. As I sit, I feel it is the moment to help heal the Earth and all of Humanity by giving and sending my Endless river of Love and Light to all, without any form of judgement.

I forgive all who cause pain to others, from the past to the present moment. I realise those who cause pain to others have so much pain within themselves, that is this pain which drives them to be Blind and Foolish.

So I ask of Creation to fill all those in pain with Love and Light, to ease their pain and to help them come to a better understanding that all of life is most precious.

Live in Love and the Light will shine forever and ever. So be it.

Author: Kuntarkis.

Soul Food Affirmation: In the stillness of my being (57)

In the stillness of my being I sit and ponder on my physical life, and I have come to Self-Realisation that I am Truly Responsible for all I have experienced and Created in my life.

I, in this most Precious Moment of my life, allow myself to see the Truth, and only the Truth, with new eyes and an open heart, without any form of judgement.

As I bathe in liquid Light of Creations totality, I allow myself to Love and accept my physical form as it is, in this most Precious Moment of life.

I am aware that I can change anything about myself, or my form, if I choose to.

I admit to myself that I am a Spark of living Consciousness, that I am connected to all of life and all of life is connected to me.

I will go forward in life, moment by moment, knowing that my past is only a memory of experiences, neither negative nor positive.

I will become a living example of Living Consciousness and share my truth with others who seek a Deeper Understanding to the meaning of life itself.

Author: Kuntarkis.

Soul Food Affirmation: Guidance in my life (58)

I allow myself just to be in this most beautiful moment of my existence.

I choose to still my Mind, my Being, to listen to my most Precious Inner Voice, and ask for Guidance in my life of Earthly matters.

I have made a Conscious decision to become Fully Responsible for my life and my actions.

As I sit in silence I allow the chatter of my Human Ego to express itself and then to become still and allow my Inner Voice to express to me what I need to hear.

I will each day of my life see the beauty in all of life, and I will learn to express my true self to others, and love myself and others in Unconditional Love always from my heart.

<u>Author</u>: Kuntarkis.

<u>Soul Food Affirmation: Stop all the chatter in my human brain (59)</u>

I (your name), in the silence of my Being, stop all chatter in my human brain. Though the power call Creation, that I am a part of, I bring forth my Light of protection.

I become Fully Conscious and aware of any negative energy within my being and around me. My Light is strong and fully present in my vibration, and this Light protects me, my being, and every moment of my reality.

I walk in this human life without Fears and without Ego, and I express my Unconditional Love and Knowledge to all who choose to listen.

I am that I am, infinite in the scheme of life, here, now and forever more.

<u>Author</u>: Kuntarkis.

Soul Food Affirmation: The higher good of all life (60)

I, who believe in my existence in this most Precious Moment of life, give of myself to Creation's Totality, for the higher good of all life throughout all Universes.

I allow my being to be an open Channel of Light so that I may express from my heart Unconditional Love, Truth and only the Truth, and give of myself Infinite Knowledge for all who choose to listen from their hearts.

Author: Kuntarkis.

Soul Food Affirmation: Become the living example (61)

For I will become the Living Example for others to Grow Consciously so that all may have the opportunity to become the Living Essence of the Light of Totality, and I so become it.

I walk in the Light, I am the Light and the Light is within me and around me, throughout my existence, I am infinite, I am that I am, and I open my whole being to all of life and bathe in the Liquid Light of Infinite Wisdom.

I am in perfect balance in Mind, Body Spirit and Soul. Now.

Author: Kuntarkis.

Soul Food Affirmation: (62) Creations Centre for Infinite Knowledge

In the eye of Creation I am almighty present in the now, my moment of life. I bring into my Awareness my Self-Realisation that I am an infinite being of Unlimited Knowledge. Even though I live in a flesh body and I know I am limited in this Third Dimensional Vibration, I draw upon the Light of Creation's Totality to expand my vision and raise my Consciousness beyond my present level of thinking.

I am willing to change, and see with new eyes, the truth that it is I who has created and set my own limitations. But I know I can break the chains that have been holding me back, and I dissolve my past negative thoughts and emotions into the nothingness from which I first created them – from my own fears.

I walk in the Light of Creations infinite knowledge. I unconditionally love my own being and devote myself to the higher good of all life. I am that I am- a Spark of Consciousness in Creation's totality.

Author: Kuntarkis.

Soul Food Affirmation: I stand before myself (63)

I stand before myself – Silent in my Mind – and express from my heart, my very being that I have been living in my belief systems of life long enough.

I now choose to break the chains that have surrounded me all of my life, and I am truly willing to Grow in Consciousness beyond what I have been.

I am willing to open my Mind and my Heart to a greater understanding of all life.

I am seeing life from this moment as a journey of my own Self-Realisation and a discovery of who I truly am.

I am a being of Light, and I love who and what I am, now and forever more.

I am that I am – infinite, always connected to everything, and everything connected to me.

I express my Knowledge and Wisdom to all who choose to listen.

Author: Kuntarkis.

Soul Food Affirmation: I accept I am a Spirit (64)

I, who am most precious, step beyond my present understanding of life.

I am willing to grow beyond the Self-Created beliefs and conditions of my existence.

I accept I am a Spirit Entity, housed in a flesh body; it is my right as a living conscious being to raise my Consciousness so I will become a living example for others to see and to grow from.

I am a part of all things in existence, I still my mind of all the Ego's chatter and I touch my Inner Divinity.

I am Light and I walk in the Light.

Author: Kuntarkis.

Soul Food Affirmation: I live in this Human Life (65)

I am a Conscious Living being, experiencing a human existence.

It is not important how long I live in this Human Life, but HOW I live it.

I recognise my Truth that comes from within, and I see the Illusion that surrounds me. I make a Conscious Decision to cut myself free from the Ego in my Self-Created world.

I now become aware of my True Self, which is Spirit.

I free myself from all Limitations, bring forth my Inner Creativeness, and learn to Love and accept myself, my being, in Unconditional Love.

I share my gained wisdom with all that choose to listen and learn of the Truth of Creation.

I am that I am.

<u>Author:</u> Kuntarkis.

<u>Soul Food Affirmation: I am a Divine Being (66)</u>

I am a Divine Being, a Spark of Consciousness, and a Spirit living in a human body.

I am a very important Spark of Light, for without me the Universe would not be complete.

I feed my body good food and I feed my mind good thoughts.

I love myself unconditionally and share my Love and my Light with the Earth and all of those who live upon it and within it.

I have the Power to Create whatever I need from life and I share my wealth with others.

I am always open to new ideas for my own growth, and by becoming the living example of Truth, others can learn and grow in Consciousness.

I know. Who I am. What I am. Where I am going.

I walk in the Light, I am the Light, I am a part of all Life and all of Life is a part of my being.

Author: Kuntarkis.

Soul Food Affirmation: I love you Creation (67)

I love you Creation, for I am you, and You- being Totality – are within everything.

I am a Spark of Consciousness from Your Totality. I invoke pure Consciousness into my Heart centre now, and I allow my Inner Being and Outer Self to be saturated in Your Light, for this Endless, Infinite river of Love and Light fills my whole essence.

I now send this endless river of Love and Light to Mother Earth, and all of Life upon her and within her, for healing and balance of Mind, Body and Spirit, bringing all things into union.

I am Strong, I am healthy and full of vitality, I Am that I Am.

Author: Kuntarkis.

Soul Food Affirmation: For the higher good of all life (68)

I am an Infinite Being, living and experiencing my existence in Human form.

But I know I am Spirit, which is Eternal, and I expand my Consciousness and my Awareness for the higher good of all Life.

I walk and express in the Light. I Am Light. I Am that I Am.

Author: Kuntarkis.

Soul Food Affirmation: Life is Reality (69)

The moment in Life is reality.

All else is Illusion, created by the Human Ego for distraction.

I am Light, I am Love, and I am that I am.

Author: Kuntarkis.

Soul Food Affirmation: I invoke the Light (70)

I invoke the Light of Divine Love and Healing, which is almighty present within me, as it is within all things.

I heal my Body, my Mind, my all, and I allow the Light of Love to expand from my Inner Being outwardly around my aura.

I send this Divine Love and Healing, which is Endless, Timeless, Ageless, Infinite and Eternal, to all who live upon and within this planet called Mother Earth and help bring balance of Mind, Body and Spirit to all life that exists in Creation's totality.

I am that I am. I am Light, I am Love. I am Spark of Consciousness of Creation.

Author: Kuntarkis.

Soul Food Affirmation: I am in perfect balance (71)

I am in perfect balance in Mind, Body, Spirit and Soul.

As I invoke the essence of Light and Healing into my being now, I listen to what my body is telling me and I put in good foods and thoughts to keep it in perfect balance and harmony, every moment of my life.

I am Light. I am Light. I am Light.

I am my Soul.

Author: Kuntarkis.

Soul Food Affirmation: Creation and I are one (72)

Creation and I are one,

Therefore the self (Ego) that stands in the way must be dissolved before the real comes into being, through Unconditional Love alone.

Author: Budda.

Soul Food Affirmation: I am the Light and the Force within (73)

I am the Light and the Force within.

What I am is Spirit, which is Infinite, Which is Eternal and Immortal.

I have Strength and Courage to accomplish anything I set my mind to.

This is my moment in life, and each moment to come I pull to myself the Wealth of Creation Totality, Happiness, Joy, Love, and an overflowing abundance of all good things in life.

All knowledge is formed from, All Knowing, All Powerful Infinite Energy of Creation's Totality which I am, and always will be a part of.

And that Infinite Energy is mine to use, here and now.

And I am One with Creation Totality.

So I am – so it is.

Author: Kuntarkis.

Soul Food Affirmation: The Light is my Strength (74)

The Light is my Strength.

Creation is my Truth.

Love is my essence and Ultimate Freedom to Self-Realisation, in the knowing that I am a part of everything and everything is a part of me.

I walk in the Light, I am the Light,

A facet, a particle of Creation's Totality, for Creation and I are one.

Therefore the Self which is Ego must be dissolved before the real can come into being, through Unconditional Love alone.

Author: Kuntarkis.

Soul Food Affirmation: I am a Limitless being (75)

I am a limitless being on a journey of Self-Discovery.

For I know I am so much more than my physical self, as I am far beyond my own physical essence.

For Energy is Everything, and Everything is Energy.

I am Weightless, I am Timeless, I am Endless I am Ageless.

That is what I am

I am Light, I am Light, I am Light

I am my Soul.

Author: Kuntarkis.

Soul Food Affirmation: Infinite Riches (76)

I have in this moment, chosen to look at my life and to see the things I no longer need.

From this moment on, I will let go of my Resistance, I will no longer hold onto the past, for the past is the past, simply a memory.

I will attract Infinite Riches into my life now.

I will change all my negative thoughts in this moment to positive thoughts.

Every moment that I have a negative thought I will stop in that moment and say out loud, no more will allow these negative thoughts to affect my life.

I will change my conditioning and my beliefs, I will learn to Love who I am in this moment.

My resistance is a Creation from my past conditioning and beliefs, which Created all my Fears in my life to this very moment.

I let them go "Now", and return them back into the nothingness from which they were first Created, in pure Love always.

I am Love.

Author: Kuntarkis.

Soul Food Affirmation: My Universe (77)

In the heart of my Universe, I am a Co- Creator of my Beingness,

I have come to my own Self-Realisation that I alone created.

My life, my form, for my life is my Responsibility,

Every action and every thought was my own Creation.

Knowing this Truth has indeed set me free, from my own Self-Imposed pain, I choose now, to let go and move on to new experiences in my life.

To the Universal mind, I say, thank you and bring it on.

Author: Kuntarkis.

Soul Food Affirmation: In the name of Creation (78)

In the name of Creation, I call on the Spirits of Light,

To stand guard at the doorway of my Soul, my very being.

Protect me from the Forces of Darkness and Deception.

Guide me on my true path of Love, Light and Truth.

I commit myself to the Light and Love of Creation Totality.

From this moment on and forever more.

I am Light- I am Love.

Author: Kuntarkis.

Soul Food Affirmation: I would give unto you (79)

I would give unto you all the Love, the Knowledge the Wisdom.

For I would not have you ignorant to your own Spiritual Evolution.

For the way is simple, but you must possess the qualities.

To balance the Mind, the Body and the Spirit.

So your development becomes.

The Simplicity of life.

I am that I am, no more no less.

Author: Kuntarkis.

<u>Soul Food Affirmation; I am Divinity (80)</u>

I am Divinity,

I am Divinity,

I am Divinity,

I am all there is, and all that will ever be.

I am Divinity,

I am Infinite Consciousness, connected to everything, and everything is connected to my being.

I am Divinity,

I am Weightless, I am Timeless, I am Ageless, I am Endless.

That is what I am.

I am Divinity,

I am Divinity,

I am Divinity.

<u>Author:</u> Kuntarkis.

CONCLUSION

After reading this book, some of you will feel excitement, some of you will be amazed by the knowledge you have acquired. While others will be left unsure of what to think. Whatever we as human beings are searching for in our own life, whether it be emotional happiness and stability, love, self-awareness, knowledge, truth, peace, balance or some form of Spiritual understanding to our connection with not just our physical self, but our connection to the Universe our maker.

We will never find it unless we as human individuals find the balance of life of all, within ourselves first. There is so much knowledge in this book, and yes it can take a lifetime to digest it, to come to our own self-realisation that in truth we as human beings are indeed not alone. We as individuals need to come back to the self to understand how we each have become the person we are today and what continues to reinforce the things that make us who we are.

As human beings, we need to raise our own Consciousness, to learn the lessons of understanding Emotion and then to let go and move on to becoming a feeling person, full of Love, full of Compassion, full of Wisdom, so we as people can past this understanding onto the next generation, no longer bound to the ignorance's of the Human Ego. If we as a species, do not come back to the source, that is Creation, we will continue to search endlessly and follow the same ignorance we as humans created in the past and continue to create it in the present and into our own future.

The knowledge that Kuntarkis has shared with us, is the knowledge of wisdom, which if put into practice by the human individual will begin a process of raising the vibration of humanity. Beings like Kuntarkis are always willing to share knowledge, it is up to each of us to open our hearts and our minds, so we can elevate our awareness, our Consciousness to higher planes of communication.

As the writer of this book, I say unto the reader, once you have finished reading this book of knowledge, put it aside, and allow yourself time to think about what you have read. Every so often if you get the feeling to reread a story on a certain subject, or some of the questions and answers that is you're Awareness your Consciousness prompting you the human individual to seek more knowledge, more understanding.

That also goes with Affirmations, as you are aware there are (80) of them, the more you express an Affirmation on a regular basis, with the right intention, things begin to happen in a more positive way, your life begin to change for the better. We as human beings can no longer follow the path we have all created, we are all in some way responsible to some degree. If we were truly honest to ourselves, and looked at what it happening all around our world, we as human beings should feel discussed, change must begin with us first, if we want to change the world we must become the change first.

So if you the reader enjoyed my first book called **Entrapment,** and since you read this book called, **The Book of Knowledge-I am Alien, you probably through your own understanding; your awareness, came to the conclusion that I the writer/author of this book, and Kuntarkis the expresser of knowledge are in fact the same entity, the same being, we are one. But that understanding of truth must be yours alone,** so I trust you enjoy my next book called, **The Long Journey Home,** which will be available towards the end of 2015. To all the human beings that live on this most Precious Earth we all call home, may Love always be present within your hearts, as my Love for all human beings is with each of you always. **Be blessed in Unconditional Love, may your journey be fruitful and safe.**

EVOLUTION THROUGH CONSCIOUSNESS PRESENTS ONE DAY SEMINARS

ATLANTIS, ALIENS & THE BERMUDA TRIANGLE

A technologically advanced society, the Atlanteans civilisation existed for approximately 720,000 years on the island of Atlantis. They were predominantly vegetarian for most of this time, and were a peaceful and non-violent race. The Atlanteans respected all living things, and believed themselves to be connected to all the other forms of life that they shared their existence with. As such, they were very environmentally aware, understanding the importance of not disrupting the delicate balance of the Earth's ecosystem. These highly evolved beings enhanced and amplified the sun's energy through the humble quartz crystal. They used this energy for lighting their glorious cities, for scientific and technological advancement, and also for enhancing their telepathic communication, and to aid them in levitation.

DREAMS: REALITY OR FANTASY?

Conservative mainstream beliefs tell us that dreams are the figments of overactive imaginations, or that they are powerful projections of inner desires and emotions from our subconscious mind. This seminar will take you out of the conservative and into the creative as we explain why we dream and how dreams are actual experiences. We can learn a great deal through our dreams, and often when we cannot find a solution to our dilemmas during our waking hours, we will find clarification and resolution during our time of sleep. Dreams cannot be interpreted in a generalised way because our dreams are very individual and unique expressions of ourselves. During this seminar personal messages will be given that may help participants understand why they are having certain experiences during their sleep.

LOVE: FINDING & LIVING LOVE

Love is perhaps the most sought after prize by every human being
that lives, and yet it evades most people for their entire lives. For
centuries we have expressed our feelings about the joys and treachery
of love through literature, music, theatre, painting, sculpture and
dance. But as a race of beings we are no closer to understanding and
knowing what love is, and where to find it, than our ancient ancestors
were centuries ago. Love is not an unobtainable prize at the end of a
gruelling competition filled with hardship and sorrow. Love is a state
of being that can be achieved by everyone, and can be taught to those
who do not understand. Love begins with acceptance of self... it exists
within each of us. By learning to love and accept ourselves we learn
to truly love others also. Finding and living love is a journey of self-
discovery, and is obtained by changing the way we think and feel about
ourselves. In so doing, we open the door to a well of love just waiting
to be shared.

HEALING: UNDERSTANDING HUMAN DISEASE

Dis'ease is our body's way of telling us we are mismanaging our
physical selves; it is not a consequence of poor genetic engineering,
but a consequence of mismanagement over several generations. Roman
himself has had terminal lung cancer, which he was expected not to
survive beyond eight months after diagnosis. That was 26 years ago,
and there is not a single trace of cancer in his body. From his own
experiences, you will learn how the illness we create can be uncreated
with a few changes in lifestyle and habits. Even the common ailments
of our affluent Western society can be eradicated without conventional
medical treatments. The key lies in understanding how and why we
create dis'ease.

MEDIUMSHIP: USING YOUR NATURAL PSYCHIC ABILITIES

Probably the most famous psychic and visionary ever to be known
to humanity was Nostradamus. Displaying his psychic abilities by
the age of ten, by the time he was in his late twenties Nostradamus
began documenting his predictions. In all, his predictions spanned
ten centuries - up to the year 2500. With his visions of aeroplanes,

submarines, atom bombs, and spaceships, it is difficult to ignore some of Nostradamus' amazing prophecies for a man of his time. We all have psychic abilities that can help us in our daily lives; they simply need some practise! If you would like to learn how to use your natural psychic abilities, then this seminar is for you. Roman is a skilled and practised medium with over 30 years' experience. He will share with you the knowledge he has obtained in developing his psychic senses over his lifetime.

REINCARNATION & KARMA

Reincarnation, or the belief that we have lived lives before, is an age-old concept that has shown too much proof to be simply an old wives tale. Hundreds of documented cases show people remembering visions of a past life that they could not possibly have read about in books. So why did reincarnation come about? The great teacher Buddha taught his disciples about the law of Karma through the Wheel of Life. Karma is the law of Cause and Effect (this same teaching is also found in Christianity - "What ye sow, so shall ye reap"), and the Wheel of Life defines reincarnation. To many people, Reincarnation and Karma are a part of human life. We choose to live life after life to repay debts, to learn lessons, or to merely complete what we did not complete in our previous life. In this seminar you will learn how Reincarnation and the law of Karma can affect your present day life.

THE ELEMENT WORLD

Do you remember how, when you were a child, you used to read stories about fairies and goblins, or perhaps someone used to tell you stories about the little people that lived in the bottom of the garden? Maybe you had an imaginary friend that no-one else could see, or perhaps when you closed your eyes you could be with your special friends. Guess what? They were real...

The Element World is the invisible world that exists hidden amongst our hectic societies. They serve a very important purpose, for they help to balance the Earth, and to re-establish stability where human interference has caused chaos and severe damage to our planet. Without their unseen efforts, our planet and our entire existence would become obsolete. The Element Kingdom is fighting an uphill battle to make human beings more aware of their actions upon the Earth's delicate eco-system. In this seminar you will learn about the beautiful beings who are desperately trying to re-educate us and save our home, and also how you can help them through your awareness of the environment and your actions.

WE ARE MADE OF STAR DUST

<u>WHO ARE WE?</u> We are living Consciousness embodied in what we believe is a physical vehicle.

<u>WHAT ARE WE?</u> We are living energy. In actual fact we are 99.9% pure energy, and only a minuscule amount of matter.

WHERE DO WE COME FROM? We come from the elements and matter that formed the Earth upon which we evolved. Everything that chemically makes up our planet is found within us. And where did it come from? From the gaseous clouds of dust particles that incubated and gave birth to our solar system within the womb of our own galaxy. We are literally made of star dust.

<u>WHERE ARE WE GOING?</u> We are moving towards a higher level of Consciousness and thinking which will eventuate in peace and harmony. Wars and conflict will be abolished when each of us takes Personal Responsibility for our own level of understanding. In accepting all things without fear and aggression we will take our rightful place alongside all highly evolved beings within the universe.

EVOLUTION THROUGH CONSCIOUSNESS PRESENTS SHORTS COURSES

THERE IS LIFE AFTER MEAT (24 hours over 8 weeks)

Our society is so used to eating meat at every meal that people find it hard to comprehend how simple, nutritious and economical vegetarian cuisine really is, not to mention that it is better for your health. Vegetarianism promotes a stronger immune system, helping to prevent the serious illnesses and diseases that are the hallmark of the average Western diet. People eat meat at every meal because they are used to it; it is simply habit. Gradually converting to a vegetarian diet from one of meat, you'll find in a short period of time that you won't really miss flesh. Rather, you will begin to appreciate the subtle flavours of the vegetables, fruits and legumes that you have been ignoring all these years!

All recipes demonstrated are original and easy to prepare, and you will find to your surprise that vegetarian/vegan cookery is easier and cleaner to prepare than meat cookery. So no more excuses! Do it for your health's sake.

GUIDED IMAGERY (13 hours over 6 weeks)

The mind is a powerful tool that can be used to enhance the quality of our daily lives, and can even help us to create all the health, wealth and happiness we desire. This course uses simple meditation techniques that require as little as 5 minutes practise each day; all you need to do is make the time for yourself to take those 5 minutes out of your 24 hour day. Meditation and guided imagery has assisted many people recovering from illness, as well as helping people increase their relaxation levels after a hectic day at work, or after exercise. Guided imagery will also help those wanting to increase their creativity and imagination. In fact, meditation and guided imagery can be used and experienced by everyone; young or old, ill or disabled, unemployed or corporate high-flier. Those working through personal trauma and depression will especially find meditation helpful in accelerating healing process.

SIMPLICITY OF SPIRITUALITY

(15 hours over 6 weeks)

Have you ever gone to a talk or course on Spirituality and come away more confused than you were to start with? There are a great number of facets to this fascinating subject, and all too often they can be covered vaguely, or made to sound far more complicated than they really are. At the end of the day, it may well leave you wondering in which direction to turn to decipher the information you have received.

In this course we ask you to open your heart and mind, and to put aside for a moment what you understand Spirituality to be. Listen, ask questions, and help guide yourself to your own understanding of Spirituality through the infinite being that exists within you. Spirituality is simple; it is a way of life. Not a belief system, not a religion, not a condition. It is the means through which you can contact your Divinity and experience the truth and love that lies within you.

CREATING YOUR REALITY THROUGH SELF REALISATION (12 hours over 6 weeks)

We are all born with the same potential, and apart from our physical features, only our life's experiences separate us as human beings. Within us all there is an unlimited potential to create whatever we desire. But in order to create our desired reality we need to create inner harmony first. Finding a deeper understanding within ourselves will help us overcome personal fears and anxieties, and will assist in raising our Self-Worth and Self-Esteem. Creating your reality begins with looking at the attitudes, conditioning and belief systems that we have acquired throughout our lives, and to then dissolve any of those mental hurdles that may be hindering us from progressing both physically and emotionally. Knowing that each of us create our own reality enables us to take Personal Responsibility for who we are. By understanding our inner self we learn to trust in ourselves, and to know beyond a doubt that we can achieve or obtain whatever we desire. We learn to understand that we can make miracles happen when our hearts and minds are in the right place.

CH'ING - BREATH IN LIFE: PHASE 1 (24 hours over 8 weeks) (Beginner Course)

Note: This course can be presented as a weekend seminar.

The philosophy of Ch'ing was passed on to Roman by his teacher, who himself was taught the ancient arts of philosophy and martial arts discipline by the keepers of the knowledge of the ancient Chinese masters. Over the years, Roman has developed his own understanding of Chi - the power of breath - and how it can be used by all people, regardless of their physical condition, in everyday life for improved health, mental clarity and physical fitness. *Ch'ing - Breath in Life* will help you flow with life, not struggle against it.

This course is an introduction to relaxation, stress management and body management that is derived from the ancient Chinese philosophy of Ch'ing. Meaning *mind-body-spirit as one*, the course is formulated around Tai Chi, stretching, isometrics, deep breathing and meditative relaxation techniques. Developed by Roman through his many years of the study and practice of martial arts and meditation, *Ch'ing - Breath in Life* is suitable for all ages and all fitness levels. This course includes original exercises developed by Roman.

CH'ING - BREATH IN LIFE: PHASE 2 (24 hours over 8 weeks) (Advanced Course)

Note: This course can be presented as a weekend seminar

This course follows on directly from *Phase 1*, and provides a maintenance programme, as well as extending the exercise repertoire. Providing additional exercises, relaxation and stress management techniques, *Phase 2* completes your health and relaxation routine. *Phase 2* is only available to those who have completed *Phase 1*.

EVOLUTION THROUGH CONSCIOUSNESS PRESENTS WEEKEND SEMINARS (OVER 2 DAYS)

BALANCING THE MIND, BODY & SPIRIT

Balance in life does not come from just being rational, or from being a health and fitness fanatic, nor from immersing yourself in spiritual study. It comes from a balance of all three. In order to find balance, the Mind, Body and Spirit must all work in harmony to create that balance. Even if one of these is out of alignment, there can be no balance. Our stressful modern lifestyles are largely responsible for this misalignment which most people are oblivious to, and other than feeling occasionally a little disgruntled with their existence, on the whole, most of us have no idea that we are out of balance until we consciously make an effort to understand the importance and necessity of balancing the Mind, Body and Spirit.

This seminar examines the three principles of life that can help us create the balance we have been lacking. Once that balance is found and understood, you will wonder at how you could ever have said that your life was fulfilling and satisfying.

SIMPLICITY OF LIFE

The purpose of this seminar is to show people how they have stopped thinking the little things in life that are important. And yet it is those little things, like enjoying a picnic with your family, or walking in a rainforest, even working in your garden on a sunny afternoon, the simple things in life, that can give us the most pleasure.

Happiness does not come from owning an expensive house and car; it does not come from enormous amounts of money. Happiness comes from the simple things in life; from understanding that you make your life what it is, not from what you possess or how large your bank balance is!

CREATING YOUR REALITY THROUGH SELF REALISATION

Condensed from a 6 week course into a weekend seminar, please refer to notes under, Short Courses. A work book/ manual is supplied in this seminar.

THE POWER OF SELF

Who Am I? I Am that I Am.

What Am I? I Am Spirit.

Where Am I Going? Wherever my Being takes me.

To know and accept that you are the power in your life that makes everything happen is to understand the Power of Self. It is the difference between believing in destiny and living to it, or accepting that destiny can be altered by free will. Power of Self in reality is a total recognition of one's own Personal Responsibility. It is the knowing that you are a spiritual being born with the free will to make choices and decisions in your life for your highest good. The Power of Self is never abused; a person who understands their true power will not go out of their way to vindictively or spitefully harm another - that is only a fearful Ego at work. Peace and tranquillity within the self comes from knowing that you have the power to change or create anything in your life.

Discover your true identity by examining the "I Am" principle. The "I Am" principle helps us relate to understanding that we are all important in the scheme of the Universe. We are all sparks of Universal Consciousness, sparks of Creation. Learn about

thought and energy, about how expression of that energy, whether it be negative or positive can create. Learn about the Kundalini & the Inner Knowing that lies within us all, and how important it is to understand the power of Kundalini energy before activating it. Activating the Kundalini helps us to safely raise our consciousness. It also opens us up to the Inner Knowing of our higher self, or soul, giving us the privilege of spiritual vision into the many and vast realms of the Universe.

SIMPLICITY OF SPIRITUALITY

Condensed from an 8 week course into a weekend seminar, please refer to notes under *SHORT COURSES*.

WINDOWS THROUGH TIME

Time is endless. In fact, time does not really exist, except in our third dimensional world where we human beings have created it to live by. Look at time as a form of energy. When you tap into that energy at any given point, you can create a "WINDOW" through which to look, be it into the past, the present or the future.

A book is very similar to a window in time. We open it to read and study its content in order to gain a deeper understanding of a subject, or to simply expand our knowledge. You can look through the windows of time in much the same way, and gain far deeper insights and facts than any book could ever give you. Why? Because when you step through a window in time, you can actually be there and experience that moment without ever having to leave your home, or your century. Look at it as bending Space, there is Space within Space, Dimensions within Dimensions, and Universes within Universes.

Learn about the great civilisations of eras past, including Atlantis, and find out what caused them to eventually decay and die out. It is fair to say that we seem to be continuing to repeat history. Yet from the great civilisations of the past we can draw parallels to our own civilisation that can enable us see where we are faltering, in order to change the course of human history from one that keeps repeating itself, to one that is progressing beyond our current level of consciousness. Learn about Reincarnation & Karma and what Buddha first referred to as the Wheel of Life, and find out why we have to learn to get off the Wheel of Life in order to bring us back to the realisation that we are spirit before we are physical.

A SPIRITUAL JOURNEY INTO THE PAST, PRESENT & BEYOND

A Spiritual Journey into the Past, Present & Beyond is a seminar whose aim is to show that each of us are timeless, Spiritual Beings, not limited or bound by the physical world we exist within. Through an understanding of Channelling and its many forms and purposes, we can tap into a limitless resource from which we can gain all knowledge; we can tap into the Universe that exists around us and within us. Through Channelling we can raise our own Consciousness, and through the expression of the knowledge and wisdom we gain, we can help advance the Consciousness of all humanity.

This seminar includes an introduction to Channelling and how one can develop and hone their natural Channelling abilities, as well as how those skills can be utilised in everyday life to empower our existence, such as discovering the real truth behind significant events that have occurred, and what choices the future may hold. It also examines Extra Terrestrial contact with humanity, and how Channelling can open us to the knowledge and wisdom these beings offer us if we are willing to open our minds to their existence.

THE CELESTIAL CONNECTION

Each of us, whether we wish to admit it or not, are Celestial beings - we are indeed Spirit, pure energy, creation in its living essence, and as such we are connected to the many other Celestial beings that fill our universe. Although we come from the same collective Universal Consciousness, in the third Dimension we have cut ourselves off from that level of understanding and Conscious Awareness, and replaced it with "FEAR", suspicion and limiting beliefs. Yet in reality, our third dimensional lives are only a small part of our entire existence.

We are in actual fact vast beings beyond our own imaginations. Feeling the struggles and anxieties of living an average, everyday life within a highly conditioned society, we have lost sight, from a very young age, of our truly Celestial origins.

This seminar examines the five Metaphysical Elements of Fire, Water, Air, Earth and Spirit. In particular this weekend seminar looks at Extra-Terrestrials, Walk-Ins, Time Travellers, and travelling within parallel worlds. A must to experience and not to miss.

SPIRITUAL DEVELOPMENT, MEDITATION AND DISCUSSION GROUP

WEEKLY TOPICS

1. Imagination (why and how to use it)
2. Thoughts and Energy (It's all in your thinking)
3. Past, Present, Future (Where do you live?)
4. Beliefs and Conditioning (Enemy or Blessing)
5. The Art of Meditation (The Purpose and Why)
6. Understanding the Self – Love vs Unconditional Love, Forgiveness of Self and Others
7. Healing: Self and Others/Human Dis-ease
8. The Human Aura and Life Force
9. Emotions and Feelings
10. Reincarnation and Karma (Cause and Effect)
11. Life and Death (The Purpose of Life)
12. Spirit World/Astral world/Fourth Dimension
13. Dreams: Reality or Fantasy
14. The Human Ego (Negative or Positive)
15. The Five Elements of all Life
16. Grief and letting go (Why)
17. Self Realisation (Who and What you are)
18. The Earth (a Living Spirit) and the Element World
19. Evolution through Consciousness
20. Spiritual Growth (The Power is within You)
21. What is Creation/Formless substance
22. Personal Responsibility/Genetics
23. Who am I/What am I/Where am I going
24. Personal Affirmations (The benefits and why)
25. The Human Brain and the Mind
26. Knowledge and Awareness (Freedom)
27. Uncreating the Created (Human Dis-ease)
28. Relationships – Self and Others
29. Your Passion in Life/Self Expression

30. A Fit Body = A Fit Mind (Your greatest wealth)
31. Balance: Mind/Body/Spirit (How to achieve it)
32. Where does all of life come from – living energy
33. Your Soul (What is it and where is it)
34. Meduimship – your natural psychic abilities
35. Dimensions and vibrations explained
36. Remember, just because you can't see it does not mean it doesn't exist
37. What you think you become, what you eat you become
38. UFOs – Alien Beings explained
39. Atlantis and the Bermuda Triangle
40. Automatic Writing
41. Terrorism of the Human Ego
42. Negative entities feeding on humanity
43. Living your Truth and knowing the Light
44. Comas and Death: Where does the Spirit go
45. Crop Circles (True or False)
46. The Kundalini Energy (Purpose and Why)
47. Origin of Humanity
48. A journey of Self Realisation and Bliss

EVOLUTION THROUGH CONSCIOUSNESS PRESENTS SEMINARS/WORKSHOPS/ SHORT COURSES/LECTURES

Please note: Only a small amount of Participant's Comments have been listed here from different Seminars Roman has presented over the last thirty years. Also in most cases their surname has not been used, as requested by the individual for privacy.

PARTICIPANT'S COMMENTS

THERE IS LIFE AFTER MEAT (One day Seminar)

The meals were: Wonderful and easy to prepare.

The notes supplied and the discussions were: Enlightening and interesting, knowledgeable and helpful.

The presentation was: Comprehensive.

Overall comments: I enjoyed all the meals prepared.

Debbie.

The meals were: Tasty, super nutritious, healthy and fabulous to eat.

The notes supplied and the discussions were: Very helpful and comprehensive and informative. It has made me think twice and look at labels before I buy.

<u>The presentation was:</u> Well thought out and well organised. I enjoyed watching the meals being made. That was very helpful knowing veganism is still nutritious.

<u>Overall comments:</u> I liked the idea of knowing what foods had what vitamins and minerals, and knowing things that were beneficial and not beneficial. Helped me work out a balanced diet.

Paula.

<u>The meals were:</u> Loved the meals! I didn't feel bloated or heavy, which sounds awful, but it's an issue I have had to deal with before.

<u>The notes supplied and the discussions were:</u> All discussions/notes were very insightful and helpful. I have already implemented a lot of the suggestions re vitamins and supplements. I appreciated the additional suggestions on meals given by Roman.

<u>The presentation was:</u> Excellent! Very thorough. Questions answered well. A wealth of knowledge.

<u>Overall comments:</u> This course expanded my horizons, helped me grow, and is more than vegan cooking, it's a lifestyle course!! Excellent! You give freely of yourselves, and that's appreciated!! You're both angels.

Papinda.

<u>The meals were:</u> Colourful, delicious and very well planned and presented. Give yourselves a pat on the back!

<u>The notes supplied and the discussions were:</u> Very thorough, given a lot of information, and was well structured. Easy to read and understand. It helped me to take responsibility and to understand what I am putting into my body.

<u>The presentation was:</u> Excellent! Ilona, you are very good at what you do. Don't lose that.

<u>Overall comments:</u> I thank you both very much. I am so glad I had this opportunity to learn about the food I am eating, and about myself at the same time. You have done a marvellous job, you should be proud off yourself. Thank you again for this opportunity. I will have to put this into practice.

Kelly.

<u>The meals were:</u> Full of wonderful features, colour and tastes. I will enjoy making each of the meals and I am encouraged to create my own.

<u>The notes supplied and the discussions were:</u> Fantastic. So much to learn about.

<u>The presentation was:</u> Very enjoyable. Couldn't have done it a better way. You presented every lesson wonderfully.

<u>Overall comments:</u> I feel your work is always of the highest degree. I love your work and both of you. I feel you are both so very special, and through your work it shows.

Michelle.

SIMPLICITY OF SPIRITUALITY
(Weekend two days or eight weeks)

Surprisingly simple. The course helped me find a lot of hidden truths about myself, to relax about life, and the biggest lesson - to love! I have nothing but praise for this course. Thanks Roman and Ilona. Roman teaches spirituality in a way which makes it interesting and exciting. So many people talk about spirituality as spooky, witchcraft, and weird. I became frightened and reserved about spirituality before I did this course. I now find it a challenge and a true part of life.

Tracey A (Promotions Officer)

Very interesting. I particularly enjoyed the guided meditations and the healing. I also liked the way you encouraged questions and participation from the group. I thought you were both very open and genuine people who gave a lot of yourselves. It was good the way you demystified the whole process, and empowered us all to do our own growing spiritually. This course has definitely helped me find my own spirituality and given me the means to develop this. Many thanks to you both.

Margaret C (Psychologist)

What I liked from the start was what you have kept saying throughout - that is, what both of you are telling us is already within us. Exactly the simplicity. It was the button pushing. That's what you both do - and that's all it is. Push the right buttons and allow the person to go from there. Exactly as it should be.

Victoria P (Law student)

Coming from a strong religious belief system, I was looking for something to help me grow spiritually - but certainly not to exchange one set of rules for another, no matter how different. I've found what I was looking for; the power is within me.

Margaret D (Laboratory assistant)

Thank you both for providing a large screen through which we have seen the clarity of our inner senses and the strength and love of those always with us.

Owen S (Boat builder)

Thought provoking. A major source of knowledge and understanding on my path of learning and love. I sincerely thank you both.

Suzanne P (Lawyer)

We have both been launched into a fascinating new world. We look forward now to the future.

John & Kathleen B (Print business owners)

I think it's a knowing we all have, but may have forgotten. You have a way of helping people remember, and believe, the truth and reality that comes from within. Thank you.

Catherine L (Single mother)

The best course I've ever attended. Given without expectation or prejudice. Thank you for giving your experience and time. It is much appreciated. Looking forward to hearing from you again.

Brigitte O (Plant Nursery manager)

The course allowed me to experience many things previously unknown, and allowed me to think and understand who I am. Thank you.

Emma T (Civil engineer)

I would recommend your course to many people, as it gave me a better understanding of myself and the feelings I have, but never expressed. I experienced a great deal of release of emotions. Thank you, love you both.

Cynthia H (Public servant)

I have found it extremely uplifting and mind expanding. Some areas I just couldn't quite come to terms with. I wish the course could go on forever, but I realise this can't be so. But thank you for a most uplifting experience.

Jan L (Pensioner)

In a way, you are not really teaching us anything, just reminding us. Thank you. It was great.

Jason S (Brewery employee)

Roman and Ilona, I thank you both for teaching me so much. It has really taught me to be a much more understanding person. I like myself a lot more, and now I find I have more patience with other people.

Bev L (Mother)

Stimulating subjects for opening one's mind. A starting point to frustration or perhaps fulfilment. Thanks.

Vaughan M (Bookshop owner)

Fabulous, very positive and supportive. I was very happy that both of you and the course "happened" at this time. Thank you and I wish you success and fulfilment.

Kathy H (Musician)

I came to further my knowledge, which I did. I enjoyed the course. I will think about what I've learnt. Everything happens for a reason.

Amy T (Book Importer)

I've thoroughly enjoyed coming each week. I've learnt a lot and as you say "had a lot of buttons pushed". I'm a happier, more balanced person for having attended and I love myself now - thanks to being in your presence. I had no expectations about what the course would be like, so I have enjoyed hearing all of what you have said and know a lot of it is my truth. I'm glad we met.

Elaine H (Executive Secretary)

It's been great. I am very sorry that it ended, but it goes on. Many thanks for all of the learning.

Michael K (Scientist)

Wonderful! Has really opened my eyes. There's a lot I don't understand yet but it's given me things to think about and learn from for years to come. Thanks for everything.

Karen V (Nutritionist/Dietician)

I'm very sorry the course is over. Please can we have another? I feel I have learnt a lot and it has been great to be taught (even an honour) by you two and your guides. My grateful thanks.

Veronica C (Shift Worker)

Since starting the course I have been writing a letter to you. Each time I start to write I answer a question for myself, or other questions have come while I was writing. Each question I have asked I found the answer in a variety of ways myself. I know I have never asked a question in class but all have been answered. I have really enjoyed the course and will continue to learn from it.

Carol D (Occupation unknown)

It has changed my life. I now know that everything I want is obtainable to me. Thank you.

Craig C (Sales Representative)

Very informative, opened up a lot of areas and questions within me, and I feel in the course of time I will be able to go within and find the answers. I would like to thank both of you for sharing your experiences and knowledge to help guide others like myself.

Elaine M (Actress)

Good. Some buttons pushed. Reinforced some of my own ideas, and created some more possibilities...

Jeff O (Occupation unknown)

As I was totally ready to hear and learn about spirituality, I found the course enlightening, well presented and a perfect grounding for my future personal development. The course showed me what I may have never discovered, helped me find many truths within myself, and see the wonderful side of life as myself.

Candace W (Occupation unknown)

Very interesting. Have enjoyed the different topics that were covered. Has changed my views on a lot of things even though I didn't agree with everything. I think Roman and Ilona are beautiful people who I think are very genuine.

Josie B (Homemaker)

Thank you for your presence - I have changed my direction in life and feel extremely

Grateful for your guidance.

Rex C (Businessman)

I enjoyed the course very much and was given lots of things to think about. No buttons were pushed really as I like to keep an open mind and found most of your information very believable. I have always believed life is a continual learning experience and I look forward to learning much more. I do hope I can get in touch with my inner self.

Valerie D (Occupation unknown)

It was a great course; everything which was spoken about really made me stop and think and look at my life. Thanks for sharing and pushing the buttons.

Kerri H (Single mother)

CREATING YOUR REALITY THROUGH SELF REALISATION

I enjoyed the aspect of honestly looking at oneself, accepting oneself and loving oneself. It's great. I have really appreciated today, and look forward to exploring my inner self/feelings more deeply.

Cheryl H (Aged Carer)

I enjoyed the simplicity of the day. The day reinforced some things I'd heard before, but wasn't ready to do anything about, and it introduced me to some new concepts. Self-Love is so difficult for me, but I feel more able to tackle it now.

Wendy H (Promotions Consultant)

I liked the opportunity to face my fear and rid myself of it. Also enjoyed the meditations and learning how to use the information presented among the residents (of the nursing home). Great. Enlightening.

Carol N (Aged Carer)

I liked everything about the day. Very balanced presentation, a relaxed atmosphere, excellent.

Eugenia P (New Age course presenter)

It was very relaxing and it made sense. Pushed some buttons - thanks Roman! I really enjoyed both you and Ilona's company, and the food! I think I need to see you for some more button pushing... Thanks once again. Much love.

Genevieve P (Sales Representative)

I enjoyed the extraordinary quality of the lectures. A truly wonderful day surrounded by good vibrations. Roman is an exceptionally gifted speaker.

Peter S (Occupation unknown)

I liked everything, especially the meditations. Thanks again for a wonderful course. You have pressed a few more buttons! I have grown so much over the last year. Your love and understanding is great.

Alison S (Sales Assistant)

Loved the relaxed atmosphere and the honesty. Very informative day.

William C (Occupation unknown)

I overcame the butterflies in my stomach - "expectation" - and enjoyed the rest of the day, especially seeing others learning. It was a wonderfully enlightening day, and not as tiring as I thought it would be.

Amanda T (University Graduate)

Informative, interesting, sometimes mind blowing! I enjoyed the day, although I had some problems accepting some aspects. Because of your truth (explanation) I was able to understand why (I had difficulty).

Muriel B (Aged Carer)

Loved everything about the day. I have learnt so much. You are both very interesting people to listen to, and very warm. I could not have had a better 8 hour seminar.

Donna D (Nurse)

Very well presented. Enjoyed the raising up of thoughts long hidden.

Roger A (Public Servant)

I found it thoroughly enjoyable and enlightening. Confirming many of the truths I have always known. You left me with a lot to think about and practice.

Hazel T (Occupation unknown)

Lovely food. Genuine presentation of the course. Good value. Just great, simple. Seems to cover anything and everything on life. Thank you.

Ross C (Occupation unknown)

Liked the unassuming way you conduct yourself in sharing all this wonderful knowledge and love. Great. Enlightening, warming, stimulating.

June O (Health shop owner)

I enjoyed the direct approach of the subject. Very satisfied. Well done.

Edith M (Pensioner)

Overall, I liked the positive attitude towards life and living. The day has given me a lot to think about. I know what I should (be doing) and think I know what I want to do. It is now to have the strength to do it.

Pam M (Occupation unknown)

Great. Thank you for taking me a little further along my spiritual path.

Julie R (Occupational Therapist)

Very informative and enlightening. I am only sorry I can't attend the classes because of work commitments.

Des R (Shift worker)

I had a lovely day and would like to attend more of the same.

Janet J (Massage therapist)

The atmosphere was very calming, the people just beautiful, and the information fantastic. Excellent.

Vicki E (Musician)

I enjoyed the day very much and feel very good about myself. The information given will be very useful to me in future.

Barbara L (Pensioner)

It was all lovely and totally unexpected. I thought it was just going to be a motivational seminar similar to others I have done. I thoroughly enjoyed this day and wish you well. Thank you for sharing your truths.

Pat M (Aged Carer)

The day confirmed a lot of information for me that I had already received. I send you Ilona and Roman my love, and thank you.

Helen P (Aged Carer)

I enjoyed the honesty and new ideas for us all. You are beautiful people to be with. Thank you.

Paula C (Occupation unknown)

It was very informative, giving a different insight to our life and those around us. Very good.

Susan R (Occupation unknown)

I particularly liked the exploration of one's self.

Jan R (Life Line Counsellor)

Everything was dealt with extremely well, I found the day extremely interesting and informative.

June H (Occupation unknown)

I liked hearing someone who thinks and believes as I do. It was a very comfortable day.

Joan C (Occupation unknown)

You were open to the process. As Roman stated, he did not want to be confined to a strict agenda. I would have liked more discussion, however I realise this is determined by the members in the group. Thank you for sharing your truth with me.

Lisa B (Occupation unknown)

OTHER SEMINARS

Very informative and presented at all attendee's levels. Interesting enough to make you want to learn more.

Peter G

Everything was really great. Very reassuring to know that I am on the right track. Its staying "in touch" I have difficulty with. The course gave me some answers.

Denise H

It was good knowing that there are others who feel there is a spirit world, and being able to listen to your experiences. I have been given a direction to take now.

Wendy J

I liked the frankness and the openness to understanding, and I liked the way of looking at life to better improve and help yourself as a person. Very enjoyable, relaxing day. It lived up to my expectations and opened me up to a new light that may help me through my difficulties, whether they be great or small.

Tina L

Everyone was able to face their truth and find some, if not all of their answers. Thank you Roman and Ilona for today. I believe everyone gained from the day, even those who were a bit sceptical. Enjoyed your company.

Bob N

I liked the feeling of being in a group of people willing to explore new concepts. The aura readings were very interesting.

Heather N

It showed me the truth of my ways. I will never again be judgemental. An excellent seminar. I have learnt a lot today about myself.

Pam T

I enjoyed the variety of topics covered, the presentation and the relaxed and friendly manner overall. It was a very enjoyable day.

Anne C

I liked the fact that we are all being directed to find answers ourselves from within. Great day, everyone was in tune, it was relaxed and informative.

Margaret D

It was very informative and clarified a lot of things for me.

Glenda H

I enjoyed the explanation of different subjects available and the freedom of "talk-back". This seminar has left me wanting to know more.

Ann L

Liked the simplicity of the knowledge that you gave. Very enlightening and applicable for my future growing.

Cheryl M

A good refresher of many truths I have gathered over the years. I found the course was high-level, covering a lot of ground.

John M

Informal and friendly. I know now I need to listen to my inner and have the courage to act on the information.

Coral R

I thoroughly enjoyed Roman's presentation. The energy was very loving. I especially liked that what we do all comes from within. I liked your experiences and ideas put across, and that it was left to our free will.

Bev R

I liked the quiet, clear explanation, the continuity and that you were able to pick up the threads after many interruptions. Very informative. I would like to experience more seminars.

Rita R

Basically I was put back in touch regarding diet, time for myself and meditation. Very pleasant enjoyable day.

Cecile S

Interesting content, relaxed style. Thoroughly valuable and interesting information, but it left me wanting to understand more.

Rosalind W

I was able to establish within myself my ability to begin to love and achieve my desires. I am extremely happy that I have been allowed the opportunity to receive knowledge through both of you - knowledge which I have suppressed within me.

Diane A

I believe that this has gotten me ready to start to get over my problems and to deal with them. I thought that it was great. I kept pushing away dealing with my mum and didn't have a good cry, but now it's got me thinking.

Danielle B

I liked learning what past lives all are about for me now. What they are for - to show me something and teach me all about life. I enjoyed Roman's honesty and sharing. I do feel each of us are very connected in some way.

Judy C

The atmosphere was very light and loving. During the past lives readings you could really feel love for the person.

Belinda M

Very interesting, and learnt a lot. This is my first seminar. I really didn't want it to stop, there is so much to learn. I believe, but my husband does not. Today was my first step to attend with him knowing? Thank you.

Alison S

I liked the past life readings and the wide coverage of the topics. Great. Maybe we should have asked more questions to make it more interactive.

Jason S

I liked the way you both presented yourselves and the comfortable energies that were around. I wanted you to keep going on and on.

Michelle S

I liked being told the truth - it makes me realise I won't heal until I cry. I have to change my life to feel good about myself. I thoroughly enjoyed today knowing we have guides looking after us. I certainly want to find out who they are. Thank you very much for your time.

Christine W

My questions were answered before I asked them. Some very unusual ideas which provoked much soul searching.

Esther W

Very relaxed atmosphere, I liked everything. I found the experience very helpful. The seminar was extremely well presented. Roman is a truly gifted speaker and presenter, the knowledge just seemed to flow from his lips. What amazed me about him he had an answer for everything.

Tina M

EVOLUTION THROUGH CONSCIOUSNESS PRESENTS: ROMAN HARAMBURA MOTIVATIONAL MENTOR/LIFE COACH/ AUTHOR/WRITER

Ask yourself the following questions:

1- Do you feel unmotivated?
2- Do you find it hard to get up in the morning?
3- Do you always feel you are making excuses for not completing a project or reaching your goals?
4- Do you have low self-esteem or self-worth?
5- Do you believe in yourself?
6- Do you lack self-discipline?
7- Do you find it hard to make decisions in your life?
8- Are you stuck in a job that makes you feel like you just want to scream?
9- Do you have a "FEAR of SUCCESS" or you may feel like you don't deserve to be for filled in life?
10- Do you want to change?
11- Stop-Think for a moment, then ask yourself this question: If I had a choice to do anything with my life, what would my true "Passion" be? I bet you had to "Think" about that question, what is really sad, we as people are not given the knowledge in how to use our greatest Gift, and it's called: "IMAGINATION", it like saying whatever we can imagine we can create.

If you have answered "YES" to any of the above questions, than maybe you need a Motivational Mentor/Life Coach.

Call: Roman Harambura for a Free chat. Mobile- 0439 686 736 or Email: kuntarkis@gmail.com (web address: www.evolutiontc.com Note: Taking on new clients "Now", only eight (8) spots available. This call can change your life.

ROMAN HARAMBURA
INSPIRATIONAL SPEAKER,
METAPHYSICAL CONSULTANT,

PO BOX 1053 Coolangatta, QLD 4225
Web:www.evolutiontc.com Email: kuntarkis@gmail.com
Mobile: 0439686736

PRESENTED BY ROMAN HARAMBURA
Spontaneous Speaker - Inspirational Speaker
Author/Writer

BUSINESS	Knowledge
Sales	Wholesale & Retail
Marketing	Public Speaking
Service	Conferences
Communication	Exhibitions
Motivation	Displays
Trainer	Colours
Product Demonstrations	Stress Management
Team Builder	Emotions & Feelings
Problem Solver	Energy
Ethics	Personal Empowerment
Goals	

PERSONAL, SPIRITUAL & PHYSICAL AWARENESS

Environmental & Social Awareness

World Events

Free Will: Leader & Follower

Philosophy

Spirituality

Dreams & Reality

Human Ego

Meditation-Creative Visualisation

The Human Self

Mind, Body & Spirit & Soul

Yoga

Ch'ing - Breath in Life

The Human Beginning

Human Genetics

Carnivore's vs Vegetarians

Human Disease & Why

Light & Darkness - Why

Who put us here & why?

Where do we come from?

How long have we been here?

The Truth about Evolution

Creation - God or Gods

U.F.O.'s & Alien Civilisations

Government Conspiracies

Good vs Evil

Human Love & Unconditional Love

Mother Earth - Living Organism

Lost Civilisations

Why Wars? The Truth.

The Human Brain & the Mind

The One Universal Language:

Sanskrit

Past - Present – Future

BOOKS AVAILABLE

Entrapment by: Roman Harambura & Ilona Schultz

Book of Knowledge-I am Alien by: Roman Harambura

PERSONAL ENDORSEMENTS FOR ENTRAPMENT THE BOOK

I've personally known Roman and Ilona for over 23 years and have come to understand the knowledge that Roman teaches to be extraordinary. He has a very unique way of expressing topics that very few others have barley touch upon; Together with Ilona's skills and expertise and her understanding of Romans personal work, this Book Entrapment has been created. Entrapment expressed from the heart in love, explains in depth, the very one thing many dare to talk about -The Truth, the True Meaning of 'The Human Ego'. Covering a vast number of topics, simplified, yet intense and straight to the point, Entrapment is very fulfilling, nourishing and provides food for thought'.

When you finish reading this book, you will come to the understanding that here within lays the Secret – 'Unleashed from your Comprehension' of the contents of this Book- OR

Rather – Personal Tool; to find your own inner Freedom.

Love to All,

Michelle

Director: Meisha Face & Body Artistry and Entertainment.

The Book Entrapment is beautiful in its simplicity and clarity of writing. Having read a number of spiritual, life enhancement, soul journey and self-development books I am impressed that this book is an easy read but heavy with meaning and intent. It is written with love giving the reader an insight into the meaning of life and relationships that would be difficult not to understand. It is about standing in your own truth and not a truth that ego has created. It is about understanding the importance of loving oneself before we can truly love others and have others love us unconditionally. Sadly fear plays a big part in today's world and this book expresses in terminology everyone can grasp, just how easy it is to get hung up on fear and ego instead of taking total responsibility for self and learning to stand in one's truth.

Sharyn. (Queensland)

In the Seminars I felt inspired. Inspired beyond my wildest ideas of life's possibilities. I felt empowered and permitted to imagine. I felt invited to know my heart until all of life is rhythm and rhyme.

And what a book!

Entrapment explains and guides us along life's only real concern. Empowering us to really be. Showing us how to love our life and live our truth. And in turn, allows an introduction to a man whose knowledge and experience gives life to some of our wildest

Ideas of life's possibilities'. Roman is truly an Inspirational speaker and presenter, knowledge flows from him like water flows down river, it never ends.

Michael, (Adelaide.)

"The first book by the authors Roman Harambura and Ilona Schultz, called Entrapment, takes the reader on a journey through 5 very important aspects of life; Ego, Fear, Love, Responsibility and Truth. Each one defined by knowledge and understanding by both individuals, using language and words in a simple yet profound manner, speaking directly to the individual who chose to take on the journey. The choice, then, is indeed ours, showing how far we have come, how much we have learnt, and still how far we have to go. To understand the ego, those fears that keep us back, will take us on the path of reality, our truth, and though it may be a bit scary at times, it is well worth it in the end.

The talks and seminars held over the years give the audience a lot to take away. In fact, one must leave behind any judgment and preconceptions about what they are about to experience, and come in with an open mind and open heart, and even if you don't agree on all things expressed, it will surely open your eyes to new ways of seeing the world around you.

If nothing else, the knowledge and understanding gained will teach one thing; do not fear the impossibility of life, for in the universe, everything is possible'.

Katherine'. (Australia)

Roman is a true inspirational speaker. The way Roman expresses himself in his seminars, leaves you feeling alive, and gives you a new purpose to life. Roman provides you with the understanding on how to live in this world, and to see people and yourself for who they are without judgement. I have attended many of Roman's seminars, and have always experienced absolute recognition of my inner self through Roman's teachings. He is a true inspiration.

I was very excited to find out that Roman had published his first book, Entrapment. All I can say is that it was worth the wait. Entrapment is clear and easy to understand, and I would recommend this to anyone who is looking to improve their life and themselves. Entrapment wakes you up to who you can truly be.

I found that my work life, personal life and relationship are in perfect balance, and that I don't bring in negative situations into my life, which I truly believe this is due to Roman's teaching. I would highly recommend Roman and his work to anyone who is seeking a deeper understanding of themselves. You have nothing to lose, only to gain his wisdom to discover yours.

Kelly (South Australia)

Administration Manager.

Entrapment is one of the most challenging and confronting books I've read. Entrapment will take you on a personal journey of self-understanding. It will bring to light everything in your life that holds you back from finding inner happiness and success. It will challenge your belief system; cause you to confront your fears, emotions and the personal baggage we all carry around. Entrapment then gives you the necessary information and knowledge you will need to make changes in your life. It will set you on a path to finding that place of peace, freedom and happiness. No matter what your circumstances are this is a must read.

Coralie Chernysh. (Gold Coast)

Certificate iii Com. Services Dipl. Social Welfare.

Many people are searching for answers, and over the years I have read many Self-help books. I have still not found the right answers until I read Entrapment it has given me the guidance I have needed. What fascinates me about Roman is how he just seems to express knowledge from within himself. I have been to some of his seminars in the past, when people ask him questions he seems to already have the answers, everything just seems to flow from him. I can't wait for his second book.

Adam (Cabinet Maker/Forman) Queensland.

I have attended many of the Seminars and Workshops over the years and they have helped develop my life and have given me a deeper understanding and enhanced my own capabilities that I utilised each day. Through the teachings of Roman's Knowledge, the Expression of his Deep Love and Openness of his Heart towards his work and towards Humanity's Growth - I highly recommend attending and actually hosting a Seminar through 'Evolution through Consciousness'. You never know', you may just find the answers you've been searching for to guide you too your higher understanding of your own true potential.

Michelle (Gold Coast)

Director: Meisha Face & Body Artistry and Entertainment

As an investigative journalist and mother there are many days when it seems there is not enough time to complete the tasks in hand. We are all living increasingly busy lives and forget or refuse to take precious time out for ourselves. To be efficient in our work and patient at home we each need to regain the essential arts of relaxation and contemplation. I myself have only known Roman for a short period of time, in his book launch for Entrapment and hearing his presentation at S.T.A.R.S, I felt it would be of great benefit for your future health and the wellbeing of your loved ones, who would also benefit greatly by the easy read step-by-step lessons laid out in Entrapment.

Nerida Marshall, Creative Director for S.T.A.R.S. (Screen Theatre and writers Studios), Gold Coast, Australia.

Lightning Source UK Ltd.
Milton Keynes UK
UKOW05f0132220517
301710UK00001B/100/P